UNEMPLOYMENT INSURANCE

IN THE

UNITED STATES

Analysis

of

Policy Issues

Christopher J. O'Leary

and

Stephen A. Wandner

Editors

1997

W.E. Upjohn Institute for Employment Research
Kalamazoo, Michigan

Library of Congress Cataloging-in-Publication Data

Unemployment insurance in the United States : analysis of policy
  issues / Christopher J. O'Leary, Stephen A. Wandner, editors.
     p. cm.
  Includes bibliographical references and index.
  ISBN 0-88099-174-7 (cloth : alk. paper). — ISBN 0-88099-173-9
(pbk. : alk. paper)
    1. Insurance, Unemployment—United States. 2. Insurance,
Unemployment—United States—History. 3. Insurance, Unemployment—
Government policy—United States—History. I. O'Leary,
Christopher J. II. Wandner, Stephen A.
  HD7096.U5U633   1997
  368.4'4'00973—dc21   97-40086
                                            CIP

The facts presented in this study and the observations and viewpoints expressed are the sole responsibility of the authors. They do not necessarily represent positions of the W.E. Upjohn Institute for Employment Research.

Cover design by J. R. Underhill.
Index prepared by Shirley Kessel.
Printed in the United States of America.

For Grace and Marleigh

Foreword

Unemployment Insurance in the American Economy was published in 1966. Written by William Haber and Merrill Murray, this book remained the definitive work on the unemployment insurance system for the next twenty-five years. By the 1960s, the Upjohn Institute had already staked out unemployment insurance as one of its primary fields of emphasis. Merrill Murray was part-time on the staff of the Upjohn Institute, and Harold Taylor, then Director of the Institute, encouraged the authors to pursue the book. The Institute funded the effort and assisted with the publication of the book.

In 1980, Saul Blaustein discussed with Wilbur Cohen, a key figure in the development of the federal-state UI system in the United States, the concept of a new book that would update and expand upon the 1966 work. Merrill Murray had passed away, but William Haber, nearing age 90, agreed to help. The Institute enthusiastically agreed to support the effort, as it had the original.

During the 1980s both Cohen and Haber passed away. Meanwhile, the scope of the new project had grown considerably from the original concept. Blaustein, now working alone, decided to split the work into two parts, with the first part covering the fifty-year history of the system from its inception in 1936 to 1990. This work, entitled *Unemployment Insurance in the United States: The First Half Century*, was published by the Institute in 1993.

Chapters of the Haber and Murray book were divided into five parts. The Blaustein book essentially followed the format of the first two parts, paralleling and expanding the discussions on the nature of the unemployment problem, the objectives of unemployment insurance, and how unemployment insurance developed abroad and in the United States. After a discussion of unemployment insurance provisions in the Social Security Act of 1935 and the beginnings of the system, Blaustein devoted almost two hundred pages to the evolution and growth of the system over the next fifty years, while the original work covered the growth of UI in only thirty-five pages of text. This difference reflects both the need to cover an additional twenty-five to thirty years of experience and the incorporation of new material on the older period. The emphasis of the Blaustein book remained historical. Blaustein discussed how the system and coverage expanded through the 1960s, were put under financial strain by the recession of the 1970s, and evolved new approaches to financing. A brief discussion in Haber and Murray on state legislation became a major chapter in Blaustein, in which state laws and experiences were compared—with emphasis on events in three years, 1948, 1971 and 1990.

This current volume, *Unemployment Insurance in the United States: Analysis of Policy Issues*, was intended to encompass and expand on the topics covered in Part III of the Haber and Murray book, "Issues in Unemployment

Insurance." Blaustein produced early drafts of some of the chapters of this book, and Murray Rubin, then a private consultant but for many years a senior policy analyst in the Department of Labor, was commissioned to complete the work. Rubin produced initial drafts of a few chapters, but sadly, passed away before completion. Chris O'Leary, senior economist on the Institute staff and specialist on unemployment insurance, took over the production of this volume.

In 1995, with joint funding from the Upjohn Institute and the U.S. Department of Labor, a conference was held to help celebrate the fiftieth anniversary of the Institute and to provide a forum for presentation of papers commissioned by the Institute and slated to become chapters in the policy issue volume.

The issues of coverage, eligibility, adequacy of benefits, duration of benefits (including extended benefits), labor market attachment, benefit financing, fraud and abuse, and federal-state relations, are all covered in this volume, as they were in the original work. These are still the broad categories of issues facing federal and state legislative bodies concerning unemployment insurance. Many specific concerns regarding UI have changed in response to changing circumstances and attitudes. For example, Paul Decker's chapter, "Work Incentives and Disincentives," summarizes what is known about the issue of whether UI payments discourage job search and provides insight into the even more recent concern with getting UI beneficiaries back to work more quickly. The recessions of the 1970s and 1980s greatly strained the financial integrity of the UI Trust Fund and gave rise to questions of trust fund adequacy. What was done about this problem is discussed in Mike Miller, Robert Pavosevich and Wayne Vroman's chapter on "Trends in Unemployment Insurance Benefit Financing." The current congressional interest in devolution is reflected in an excellent discussion provided by Tom West and Jerry Hildebrand in their chapter, "Federal-State Relations." Overall, this book should become an essential reference for anyone interested in the state of knowledge about the policy issues facing the UI system.

O'Leary was joined in this effort by Steve Wandner, who is a visiting senior research associate at the Urban Institute on leave from the U.S. Department of Labor. Together they guided this work to completion, including commissioning papers, writing chapters, organizing the conference, editing the papers, and generally preparing the manuscript for publication. O'Leary and Wandner did an outstanding job in bringing this major work to fruition.

Robert G. Spiegelman
Executive Director Emeritus
W.E. Upjohn Institute for Employment Research
December 1996

Preface

This book attempts to present an accessible survey of what is known about how the federal-state system of unemployment insurance (UI) works in the United States and to offer ideas for further improvement of the system. To faithfully accomplish such a challenging project required the dedicated effort of many experts on the UI program.

The chapters for this book were originally written for and presented at a conference held in June 1995 at Kalamazoo, Michigan. The conference was jointly sponsored by the U.S. Department of Labor and the W.E. Upjohn Institute for Employment Research. It was a main event in the celebration of the Institute's fiftieth anniversary.

At the conference, after each chapter was presented by the author, extensive oral and written comments were provided by a primary discussant who suggested ways to improve the content and exposition. Other conference participants also offered comments on each chapter. Following the conference, almost all chapters were extensively rewritten, based on input from discussants, conference attendees, and the editors.

The introductory and concluding chapters were written by the editors. Strong contributions from the talented researchers who wrote the other chapters made this task a pleasure. The chapters are structured so as to naturally form a comprehensive book on UI policy, yet at the same time remain independent self-contained tracts on each topic. While this dual aim resulted in a small degree of overlap, we felt that the value of the book as a reference will benefit significantly. For example, rather than listing all references together at the back of the book, we place chapter-specific references at the end of each separate chapter, thereby providing brief topic bibliographies.

Having completed our attempt at this substantial project, we now hold our predecessors—William Haber, Merrill Murray, and Saul Blaustein—in even greater esteem. We are indebted to them and also to Wilbur Cohen and Murray Rubin for laying the foundation for the present volume. We also thank the chapter authors, without whom this project would have been impossible. Brief biographical sketches for them are provided in the section "about the authors," which appears near the back of the book. We also thank the conference chapter discussants, who are recognized individually in the notes to each chapter. Many other friends of the Upjohn Institute and experts on UI who attended the conference also contributed valuable and constructive guidance for the project. These included the scholars who served as session chairs for the conference: Bob Spiegelman, Gary Burtless, Bob LaLonde, Carl Davidson, Frank Brechling, Susan Houseman, and David Fretwell.

We offer special thanks to Janet Norwood for delivering the keynote address at the conference in June of 1995. At that time Dr. Norwood was serving as chair of the Advisory Council on Unemployment Compensation. Prior to that she had a long tenure as commissioner of the U.S. Bureau of Labor Statistics. From her unique perspective, she offered comments which both sharpened the focus of the conference and helped to celebrate the fiftieth anniversary of the Upjohn Institute.

For special assistance with chapters 1, 5, 15, and the performance measurement section of chapter 13, the editors would like to thank Dr. Burman Skrable of the UI Service in the U.S. Department of Labor, who also contributed chapter 10 to the book. Others in the UI Service whom we would like to thank are Norman Harvey, who originally developed the historical analysis of UI performance measures presented in chapter 13, Tom Stengle, who provided graphics and tables for chapters 13 and 15, Diana Runner, who provided tabulations of UI state law data for chapter 15, John Palumbi, who provided special data tabulations and analysis that appear in several different chapters, Kurt Schlauch and Wayne Gordon, who provided information on the UI experiments and worker profiling, and Virginia Chupp, Jerry Hildebrand, Diana Runner, Jon Messenger, and John Palumbi, who reviewed the text of several chapters.

We also acknowledge the special contributions of Saul Blaustein and Murray Rubin, who worked on an earlier attempt at this book. While chapters 5 and 6 both contain new material, Murray Rubin is listed as a co-author for each chapter because much of his earlier work was incorporated. Similarly, Saul Blaustein's work was incorporated into chapter 1, for which he is listed as co-author. We also benefited from the on-going input and encouragement received from Saul Blaustein throughout the course of this project.

Finally, we thank the W.E. Upjohn Institute for Employment Research for supporting our effort in many ways. At the Institute, clerical assistance and help in organizing the UI conference were provided by Claire Black, Ellen Maloney, and Phyllis Molhoek; final copy editing was organized by Judy Gentry; and management support was provided by Randall Eberts, Allan Hunt, and Robert Spiegelman. In particular we thank Bob Spiegelman for helping to initiate this project at a time when completion seemed a distant hope.

As editors of this volume, we are responsible for any errors and for policy judgements. We and the chapter authors have been free to express our own opinions. As a result, the text reflects the opinions of the authors and editors. It does not necessarily represent the positions of the W.E. Upjohn Institute for Employment Research, the United States Department of Labor, or other organizations with which chapter authors are affiliated.

Christopher J. O'Leary
Stephen A. Wandner

CONTENTS

UNEMPLOYMENT INSURANCE

IN THE

UNITED STATES

Analysis

of

Policy Issues

CHAPTER 1

Policy Issues
An Overview

Saul J. Blaustein
W.E. Upjohn Institute for Employment Research, retired
Christopher J. O'Leary
W.E. Upjohn Institute for Employment Research
Stephen A. Wandner
Urban Institute and UI Service, U.S. Department of Labor

The federal-state program of unemployment insurance (UI) is well established among economic institutions in the United States. It has an undeniable influence throughout the economy, affecting personal incomes, employer taxes, federal-state relations, and interstate competition for industrial production and employment.

The UI program serves a variety of functions that help frame employment relations between Americans. Over the nearly sixty years since the program's inception, these functions have come to be accepted and relied upon by both workers and employers.

UI partially replaces lost income for individual workers who are involuntarily unemployed, and, in the aggregate, it helps to maintain purchasing power during economic downturns. It reduces the dispersal of skilled workers when employers impose temporary layoffs and helps prevent the breakdown of general labor standards during such periods. Some features unique to the UI system in the United States are designed to encourage employers to stabilize employment levels.

During the twentieth century, the existence of a reliable system of unemployment compensation has become a hallmark of a developed, modern industrial economy. Rapidly growing middle-income countries, from central Europe and sub-Saharan Africa to southeastern Asia, are experiencing urbanization of their peoples and are seeking systems for insuring incomes. There is a recognition that workers in an industrial economy are separated from the subsistence guaranteed by the land in an agrarian society. When designing a safety net for workers, these emerging nations are faced with two broadly differing strategies concerning UI.[1]

The UI approach popular in Europe emphasizes income replacement without much attention to return to work or to stabilizing employment. The American UI system presents a distinct alternative, which is custom designed to operate in a competitive market economy. The system in the United States emphasizes individual responsibility, while the European system views unemployment compensation as a social obligation.

At the core of most contentious issues in the federal-state UI system in the United States is the struggle between social generosity and individual responsibility. These competing interests must be weighed to determine matters such as the scope of coverage, the requirements for benefit eligibility, the appropriate level and duration of benefits, and the distribution of the financing burden.

Social attitudes about the unemployed as workers and income providers shape the public view of unemployment. Perceptions about employers as business operators and job providers influence how the public sees employer responsibilities for workers. Also critical to resolving UI issues are public attitudes regarding the proper role of government in dealing with the problem of unemployment.

The diverse issues generated by conflicting public opinions are difficult to sort out neatly. Yet, this chapter attempts to make a brief exposition of some of these attitudes and of the broader and more fundamental controversies they engender so as to help illuminate the later discussions of specific program issues. In the next section, the genesis of the UI program and the controversies surrounding it are examined. This analysis begins with a brief review of the historical context of UI and is followed by a discussion of public attitudes toward unemployment and about UI. The third section of this chapter, which considers UI in the larger context of economic security, includes a discussion of the distinctions between UI and welfare programs, UI as part of the whole social safety net, and the role of UI in the overall economy. Conflicting and shifting viewpoints about the causes of unemployment and the character of the unemployed then lead to an overview of the basic controversy concerning the UI program's effects on the incentive to work. Fifth, the subjective element of an individual's unemployment is considered as the basis for questions about fairness and efficiency in administration and about possible fraud and abuse of the system. The sixth section discusses the controversy arising from employers and workers pressed to advance their particular economic interests in regard to issues of UI taxation and benefit levels. The conflict inherent in the federal-state relationship on which the UI system is built is subsequently reviewed as a source of dispute in the program. The chapter concludes with reflection on whether and how knowledge about the working of UI is used to improve the system.

Genesis of the Program and Controversy

Historical Context of Controversy

The federal government's adoption of a major, active role in social planning during the Great Depression provoked widespread public controversy because that move departed from the traditional *laissez-faire* approach of government. Prior to the 1930s, unemployment was not regarded as much more than a temporary and occasional problem, an inevitable seasonal or cyclical malady of industrial society. Once business and employment recovered, public concern about unemployment faded. Workers who experienced much unemployment were often seen as responsible for their own predicament. They were viewed as either not industrious enough to hold steady jobs or fundamentally flawed in their character. In cases where job and wage loss produced temporary family deprivation, local privately funded welfare agencies were regarded as the appropriate sources of assistance. In some areas, public unemployment relief was provided by local government.[2]

Public UI proposals were advanced in a number of states before 1930, but these initiatives were not broadly accepted given prevailing attitudes. The thought of federal government intervention to deal with unemployment was an even more remote idea and viewed as probably unconstitutional. Most employers did not see provision for the unemployed as a responsibility of business. The few who did thought that unemployment benefit plans should be provided by employers on a private, voluntary basis.

The reality of mass unemployment during the depression of the 1930s made clear that personal deficiency was not the only cause of the problem. As joblessness reached into the homes of executives, white-collar workers, and skilled mechanics—people who heretofore had been untouched by unemployment—the realization grew that the industrious and efficient worker as well as the marginal, unstable, lazy worker could be affected. Moreover, the problem was not of brief duration; unemployment persisted. Personal economic hardship among the jobless became widespread. Efforts to ease these difficulties overwhelmed private welfare resources and local government relief. Resistance to large-scale government assistance for the unemployed could not long withstand the pressures exerted by the massive needs of so many over so many years.

Old attitudes began to give way, though not willingly or universally. The exposure of millions of workers and their families to the indignity of applying for and accepting relief shifted opinions sufficiently to broaden the support for unemployment benefits provided on an orderly, prefunded, social insurance basis. Employer organizations continued to resist the coming of UI, but with the continuation of the depression, it could no longer be denied.

The federal-state unemployment compensation program was authorized as part of the Social Security Act enacted August 14, 1935. As a result of *tax offset* inducements contained in the companion Federal Unemployment Tax Act, by July 1937, in all states plus Alaska, Hawaii, and the District of Columbia, legislation had been passed to create UI programs. "The constitutionality of the state and federal laws was challenged in several states as soon as [UI] taxes became payable on employment after January 1, 1936. The U.S. Supreme Court upheld the constitutionality of the New York law in November 1936, and that of the Social Security Act and the Alabama Unemployment Compensation Act in May 1937" (Rosbrow 1986, p. 7). In writing the majority opinion, Justice Benjamin Cardozo asserted that it was not a lack of compassion for the unemployed, but rather a reluctance to competitively disadvantage native industries that discouraged states from independently establishing UI systems before 1935.

While the depression altered general attitudes enough to make the federal-state UI system possible, the opposing points of view did not disappear. Today, UI is widely accepted as a permanent public program. Millions of Americans, however, still find it difficult to accommodate themselves philosophically to the idea that unemployed workers should be allowed to receive benefits as a matter of right even if they do not appear to need them. Unemployment is recognized as a continuing problem, although it is more acute during dips in the business cycle than at other times. Most unemployment is viewed as the consequence of impersonal economic forces, but during nonrecession periods, the belief that unemployment is the fault of the worker usually resurfaces. Thus, this classical view of unemployment lives on within the populace and forms a significant basis for continued controversy about many UI aspects and for resistance to the program's expansion and improvement.

In the 1980s and particularly in the 1990s, this perspective on unemployment has been partially offset by a growing public awareness of the impact of permanent worker dislocation, which results from increasingly competitive markets at home and abroad and from the impacts of rapid technological change. The widespread potential for worker dislocation has caused the public to be more concerned about unemployment, even in nonrecessionary times.[3]

Public Attitudes toward Unemployment in a Market Economy

As noted, the general view prior to the 1930s was that unemployment was primarily the result of the individual's own deficiency. The experience of the Great Depression shook this position, but its hold on the public mind has remained a strong force, making difficult nearly every effort to extend and improve the UI program.

One expression of this view appeared in the *Wall Street Journal* in 1914:

> Let any man ask himself how often has he seen really industrious workmen out of employment for any length of time, except by their own choice in a labor dispute? The man who wants work can get it, and can soon establish a character that will get him better work (*Wall Street Journal*, March 5, 1914).

In her classic 1930 analysis of case studies of unemployed persons, Clinch Calkins summed up the earlier attitudes as follows:

> There are several widely held ideas about unemployment. . . . One of them is that unemployment comes only in hard times. . . . A second presumption is that under unemployment only those who have been too thriftless to save suffer. And still a third, the most pervasive of all, is that if a man really wants to find work, he can find it (Calkins 1930, pp. 20-21).

A quarter of a century after the federal-state UI system had been established, a sample survey of urban Ohio households gave evidence that a large proportion of Americans still held to the idea that those who truly want work can always find a job. When asked "whose fault is it when people become unemployed?" 37 percent of employees, 38 percent of the self-employed, and 58 percent of employers interviewed put the blame on the unemployed themselves (Ohio State University Research Foundation 1963). Among employees, those in professional occupations were most likely to respond this way (48 percent). Professionals were also least likely to experience unemployment. Among unskilled workers, the proportion blaming workers for their own unemployment was much less (23 percent). The higher respondents' educational attainment, the more likely they were to blame a jobless worker for being unemployed and, as noted by the survey report:

> The people with the greater amounts of formal education, presumably the most informed people, are those who most likely have been exposed to the ideas of economics, including the widely-held notion of involuntary unemployment. Yet this seems to make little difference regarding their beliefs about the reasons for unemployment. It must be, therefore, that this attitude is the manifestation of a more-or-less deeply held belief that is not susceptible to alteration or modification merely through exposure to the thinking and opinions of those generally regarded as "experts" (Ohio State University Research Foundation 1963, p. 33).

Adams (1971, p. 22) reviewed a 1965 Gallup Poll conducted for the *Washington Post* in which 75 percent of a national sample responded yes when asked, "Do you think many people collect unemployment benefits even though they could find work?" (*Washington Post*, September 16, 1965). Respondents were more likely to answer in the affirmative if they had higher incomes and more education.

Since the 1960s, there have not been any surveys specifically measuring the extent of public belief that unemployment is the fault of the individual. Views expressed on occasion in the news media or by business and political leaders give evidence that this attitude still holds to a significant and influential degree. These opinions may be heard as complaints that positions go unfilled while jobless workers crowd the UI rolls.[4]

Recognition that the unemployed may not always match the requirements of the vacant jobs, or that their location may be wrong, or that employers seeking workers may not always be willing to offer reasonable wages sometimes tempers such a blanket indictment. Citing case studies of unemployed white collar workers, a March 1993 cover story in *Fortune* magazine said that "while the economy is growing steadily again, more than nine million Americans remain jobless, victims of changes they cannot control" (Erdman 1993, pp. 40-49).

Regardless of who is to blame for unemployment, the American public regards it as a serious national problem. When asked in 1994 by Princeton Survey Research Associates for *Newsweek* magazine, "How concerned are you about the effects of unemployment and a lack of good-paying jobs?" 92 percent of the national sample of 742 adults said that they were either somewhat or very concerned.

In a series of national surveys conducted between 1988 and 1995 by the Hart and Teeter Research Companies for NBC News and the *Wall Street Journal*, registered voters were asked, "Which of the following list of economic issues facing the country do you feel is the most important right now: inflation, unemployment, interest rates, the Federal budget deficit, Federal taxes, or the U.S. trade deficit?"[5] The survey was conducted more than a dozen times, at approximately six-month intervals. Unemployment and the federal budget deficit always topped the list of most important economic issues. In June 1988, unemployment was picked by 28 percent, while 34 percent said the deficit; by January 1992, as unemployment had risen, 53 percent said unemployment, while 16 percent said the deficit; and by January 1995, as unemployment fell, the responses were nearly identical to those in June 1988. Public sentiment expressed in these survey results clearly reflects the competing pressures on UI policy makers. Notably, survey respondents indicated the third most pressing economic issue to be federal taxes.

Public Attitudes toward Unemployment Insurance

Many Americans have viewed UI not as a social insurance program but more like welfare and other public assistance programs. As such, these individuals consider UI as running counter to such historic values as individual and local self-reliance and a free market economy. Writing in the mid-1950s, the historian Max Lerner noted in his study *America As Civilization* that the process of social reform and increased assumption by the state of responsibility for certain needs of the people had been going on since the start of the century, and that the process was opposed throughout by various interest groups, in part by invoking those historic values. These public programs developed with great difficulty, much reluctance, and almost grudgingly. Lerner wrote that Americans

> have responded piecemeal and in irregular fashion to the need for workmen's compensation, unemployment benefits, old-age insurance, subsidized low-cost housing (etc.) . . . what has emerged in each area of welfare is the acceptance of the principle of responsibility but with the least challenge to private enterprise, the least burden on the tax structure, and the greatest reliance on the voluntary principle. The broad formula has been for the government to set a floor below which security and welfare cannot fall, to use government funds for the more claimant forms of social insurance but to let the others go, to give the states the widest possible discretion, to steer away from centralized authority and administration...to put the burden of expanding the programs upon continued popular pressures (Lerner 1957, p. 131).

In this passage, Lerner identified the heart of much of the basic UI controversy. The program was designed to minimize any disruption to the private free market system. Political pressures work toward keeping it contained. Employers have sought to keep their responsibility for financing unemployment compensation narrow and limited. Through its experience-rated UI tax structure, the program seeks to allocate responsibility for benefit charges among those businesses giving rise to those charges; this tax structure thereby also gives employers an incentive to avoid layoffs and to stabilize employment.[6] Experience rating also results in constant pressure from employers to keep compensation levels at a low level of protection, so that benefit charges and UI taxes can be held to a minimum.

From the beginning, the states have enjoyed wide discretion in setting specific benefit and tax provisions of their UI laws. Furthermore, there has been resistance to any attempts to set federal minimum standards or to any strengthening of federal authority in the program. Expansion of the program has usually occurred only when organized labor has been strong enough, or when unemployment has been widespread enough, to bring sufficient pressure on the state legislatures or on Congress to act.

Despite resistance, government entitlement programs have multiplied and expanded over the years. UI evolved into a broader program than at first deemed appropriate or affordable when it was initiated during the Great Depression. The system now covers nearly all wage and salary workers and provides much longer periods of protection than it did originally.

Adams (1971) provided a comprehensive review of American sentiments in *Public Attitudes Toward Unemployment Insurance*. In summarizing evidence of declining American support for UI from the 1930s through the 1960s, as preserved in the archives of the Social Security Administration by the Roper Center, Adams wrote the following:

> The Social Security Act programs were deeply rooted in the Great Depression experience. The effects of that experience on public attitudes have diminished as time has passed and memories have dimmed. . . . Those people who were 10 years old or over in 1930 and therefore may be presumed to have personal memories of the Great Depression years constituted 50 percent of the population over 19 years of age in 1965 . . . 38 percent by 1970 . . . and 22 percent by 1980. . . . The impact of the Great Depression on attitudes toward the unemployed and unemployment insurance will be transmitted indirectly, if at all, to succeeding generations, and this fact may be expected to have substantial influence on the program in the future (Adams 1971, pp. 17-18).

By the 1980s, for many Americans, the expansion of social programs and government regulation of economic activity had gone too far. This reaction lent support to attempts at limiting the scope of some programs, to reducing their size, and to restoring the vigor of free market principles throughout the economy.[7] In the mid-1990s, the exigencies of persistent federal budget deficits further curtailed government largess and involvement.

These trends have affected the UI program as well, influencing the movement toward more restricted eligibility, more punitive disqualifications among beneficiaries, and more limited levels and duration of benefits.[8] Nonetheless, nationwide surveys of public sentiment indicate broad-based support for the present system of income security for workers. When asked in 1987 by an ABC News/*Washington Post* survey if spending on UI should be increased, decreased, or kept about the same, 86 percent of a national sample of 1,505 adults said that spending should be increased or kept the same. When the National Opinion Research Center asked the same question in 1990, 75 percent of 1,217 adult respondents in a national survey said that spending on UI should be increased or kept the same. In January 1995, when the *Los Angeles Times* asked a national sample of 1,353 adults, "Do you think government should cut back spending on unemployment insurance programs?" only 30 percent answered yes.

In the 1990s, the reality of increased worker dislocation, greater public awareness of this issue, and the need to provide early, systematic reemployment assistance resulted in a policy response that began directing the UI system more toward reemployment. The 1993 Worker Profiling and Re-employment Services (WPRS) system mandates nationwide an additional UI eligibility requirement of early active reemployment efforts for beneficiaries who are identified as most likely to exhaust their entitlement. The emphasis on reemployment—and economic development—further resulted in legislation allowing states the option of using UI trust fund money to help "profiled" beneficiaries become self employed; the enabling legislation was included in the North American Free Trade Agreement (NAFTA), which was signed into law by President Clinton in November 1993. The UI program has also adopted an ongoing, *active* approach toward the prevention of unemployment; this strategy is based on state "work sharing" programs. Work sharing schemes have been included in the UI provisions of 18 states since 1978, when California enacted the first work sharing program in the U.S.[9]

The ebb and flow of prevalent views about the role of government in the economy and society will no doubt continue indefinitely, influenced largely by how economic conditions affect public attitudes generally. That ebb and flow will ensure the continuation of controversy surrounding UI as it reflects the tensions between social equity and economic efficiency.

Unemployment Insurance and Economic Security

The Welfare-Insurance Dichotomy

The widespread hardship endured in the 1930s made large public relief programs politically acceptable. At that time, the typical worker struggled alone to sustain a family, which tended to be larger than is the average family late in the twentieth century. Multiple-earner households were comparatively rare in the 1930s. Loss of work by the breadwinner put families into a crisis situation very quickly. The depression spread penury like a plague among families that heretofore had escaped serious unemployment. Needy individuals and families who accepted relief suffered social indignity and loss of self-respect. Consequently, the concept of unemployment benefits provided on an insurance basis had considerable appeal.[10]

The idea that contributions to a reserve fund, based on earnings, could provide workers surety against the risk of total wage loss from unemployment came to be regarded as far superior to reliance on charity or on relief, which required a painful public admission of poverty. Rights to UI benefits were earned through working; the question of demonstrated individual need was irrelevant. The insurance concept became and remains important to workers.

UI is *social insurance*, not private insurance. The major differences between the two are summarized in table 1.1. Indeed, many of the features of UI that make it social insurance also mean that its existence would be impossible under private arrangements. Without government mandate, nothing like UI as we know it would be available: because of a type of *market failure*, private markets would not provide what society requires as generalized insurance against unemployment for workers.[11]

Table 1.1 Major Differences between Social and Private Insurance

Social insurance	Private insurance
1. Compulsory	Voluntary
2. Minimum floor of income protection	Larger amounts available, depending on individual desires and ability to pay
3. Emphasis on social adequacy (welfare element)	Emphasis on individual equity (insurance element)
4. Benefits prescribed by law that can be changed (statutory right)	Benefits established by legal contract (contractual right)
5. Government monopoly	Competition
6. Costs difficult to predict	Costs more readily predictable
7. Full funding not needed because of compulsory contributions from new entrants and because program is assumed to last indefinitely	Must operate on fully funded basis without reliance on new entrants' contributions
8. No underwriting	Individual or group underwriting
9. Widespread differences of opinion regarding objectives and results	Opinions generally more uniform regarding objectives and results
10. Investments generally in obligations of federal government	Investments mainly in private channels
11. Taxing power readily available to combat erosion by inflation	Greater vulnerability to inflation

SOURCE: Rejda (1984, p. 40).

The UI program aims to provide protection against a risk so widespread that it is social in scope. Without some organized system of relief against unemployment, massive problems of social dependency could result. UI benefits provide a minimum floor of protection that prevents individuals from becoming a social burden and that collectively helps to minimize fluctuations in aggregate consumer spending. This *public good* would not be available without government-mandated participation in the system. If the UI program were voluntary, it would collapse very quickly. Workers with a low risk of job separation would realize that they could save money on premium payments by breaking away and forming their own low-risk pool. This would eventually result in those with a high risk of unemployment facing premiums so large that they would go uninsured, leaving them with public or private social assistance as their only means of income security.[12]

Social insurance embodies both the incentive aspects found in private insurance contracts and the eligibility features required by considerations of social adequacy. Private insurance contracts provide payment for losses due to occurrence of the insured risk, with the compensation amount dependent on premiums paid. Social insurance bases amounts of payments on some estimation of presumed need, so that compensation is not always directly related to contributions, and eligibility is not always based on the ability to avoid the risk. UI places a ceiling on how far benefits can go in compensating for wage loss, thereby reducing the fraction of earnings replaced for higher-wage earners. Some state weekly benefit formulas weight the benefit-wage replacement ratio to favor low-wage earners. Some states provide allowances for dependents. These provisions reflect the social welfare intent of the program to concentrate benefits more on those who are presumed to need them more. Although its insurance character is well established and supported, the extent to which the program should reflect welfare objectives has been a source of some controversy.

There is a handful of features that objectively distinguish UI from welfare. When characterizing social insurance, Rejda stated five clear distinctions from social welfare, which apply to UI and can be summarized as follows.

1. UI benefit levels are predictable since they are based on explicit formulae that apply to applicants uniformly, while in relief programs the benefit is dependent on the degree of need demonstrated.
2. Financing is done out of specifically earmarked taxes, while public assistance is paid from general revenues.
3. All those covered by UI are participants in the program, with only a fraction ever drawing benefits, while only those who apply for and receive benefits are participants in social welfare programs.
4. No stigma attaches to the receipt of a UI payment, "which provides compensation for wage loss as a matter of right with dignity and dispatch."[13]

5. The UI program presumes need due to the economic loss resulting from unemployment, while general relief requires demonstration of need, often including the shedding of personal assets.

The last of the preceding differences probably has contributed most to the UI controversy. The welfare aspects of UI have been drawn into question because of the changing perception of the economic position of American workers and their families. The circumstances of the average worker today are far different from those of the average worker more than a half century ago. By and large, the public in the 1990s is less likely to regard unemployment with the same sense of urgency or to see the unemployed so generally in such desperate straits as was the case in the 1930s. Need is not so widely presumed to be as universal or as evenly felt among various segments of the unemployed.

In the Great Depression, the real extent of the unemployment problem was not precisely known. Estimates hovered in the range of 15 to 25 percent of the labor force being out of work (Levitan, Mangum and Marshall 1981). Reliable national income accounting and labor force estimation practices were undeveloped.[14] Since that time, information about the operation of the economy has steadily improved, and, for better or worse, has guided national economic policy. The result of this evolution, together with other institutional reforms in the social, legal, banking, and trade sectors, has been that none of the ten economic recessions since 1946 has even approached the widespread collapse of economic activity suffered in the 1930s (Moore 1980; U.S. Department of Commerce 1995).

This relatively stable labor market has greatly reduced the personal fear of unemployment. For the large majority of Americans, the Great Depression is an item in history rather than a personal memory. Most have never known serious unemployment or felt its consequences close at hand. Many do not identify with the unemployed. On the other hand, increasing worker dislocation over the past twenty years has spread the potential for permanent job loss, bringing the uncertainty of employment to white-collar workers, where it previously belonged primarily to blue-collar workers.

Workers today also enjoy a much improved standard of living. The multiple-earner household is more the rule than the exception, giving many families a broader income base and less vulnerability to the effects of job loss by one family member. Unemployment for any lengthy period can still produce heavy financial strains, even disaster, as many households have built their higher living standards on a base of substantial indebtedness as well as on increased income.

There has been some pressure for better protection under the program for the unemployed who clearly are in need. Some UI critics see the program largely as protection for the middle-class worker: many of the poor, low-wage, or marginal workers who are unemployed are either excluded or receive very inadequate benefits. It has been suggested that, to broaden access to the program, eligibility requirements be relaxed so that marginally attached workers may qualify for some UI benefits. Sharply increased minimum weekly benefit amounts could be justified on the ground that existing low minimums inadequately support even a subsistence standard of living. Others argue that benefit levels are sufficient, but that benefit durations are inadequate. Many industrialized nations supplement UI benefits with *unemployment assistance,* which provides means tested income support for people who have recently exhausted UI benefits. Unemployment assistance usually is available for up to a year, with the idea that it will prevent slippage into long-term dependence on social assistance by prolonging the period of hope for reemployment.[15]

The atmosphere of controversy surrounding specific UI issues has been intensified due to the conflict between calls for expanded welfare content in the UI program and calls for closer adherence to strict insurance principles in the face of a growing perception of general worker affluence and of a narrowed presumption of need. However, by a large margin, the public as of 1980 still regarded the payment of unemployment benefits as earned insurance rights rather than as welfare assistance. A national survey conducted in 1980 by the Survey Research Center of the University of Michigan found that almost twice as many American families characterized unemployment compensation as "earned insurance" than thought it was "part of our welfare system" (59 percent to 32 percent). "Households in which one or more members were unemployed at some time during the two years prior to the surveys more frequently viewed unemployment compensation as earned insurance, especially if the unemployed household member actually received unemployment compensation (78 percent) . . . [compared with] 56 percent of the households who had no unemployment experience during the prior two years" (Curtin, Gordon and Ponza 1981, p. 41).

Defenders of the program's insurance principle emphasize that UI is not intended as a measure to overcome existing poverty but rather to prevent descent into poverty. Although workers today are generally better off than their counterparts of earlier times, they still face the real risk of job loss with severe consequences. Relatively few wage or salaried workers could long withstand a total loss of their earnings before their achieved standards of living were damaged badly. Even in multiple-earner families, where the loss of one income may be partially cushioned by the remaining incomes of other household members, the loss may be severely felt because of high customary expenditure and consumer debt levels.

The lack of adequate welfare support for needy, involuntarily unemployed persons who can and want to work and who fall outside the scope of UI is a problem that the system cannot effectively resolve in its present form. Helping the poor unemployed to overcome their poverty through employment is a policy no one can oppose. Preventing workers from slippage toward poverty because of prolonged temporary job and wage loss is a more manageable task.

The values of the insurance approach go beyond that of using presumed need instead of the individual needs test. Insuring against wage loss due to involuntary unemployment makes at least as much sense as insuring a home against fire damage or a car against theft, regardless of the personal ability to absorb the financial loss. Wage loss is only partially insured, with limits applicable as to amounts and length of time. Employer payments into public funds for unemployment benefits are part of the cost of labor compensation, which includes wages and other fringe benefits. Workers earn UI rights through their employment and indirectly pay part of the premium by accepting wages that are somewhat lower than they would be in the absence of UI (Anderson and Meyer 1995). Regardless of personal financial circumstances, if their employment terminates involuntarily, workers have the right to unemployment benefits until they either find other employment or exhaust their entitlement. Unemployment benefits are not a charge on society as a whole, financed out of general government revenues, as is the case with welfare. Within the context of these UI characteristics, presumed need remains valid regardless of individual variations in need. Loss of income can be damaging to the unemployed worker's household finances if not limited to some reasonable degree.

Unlike private insurance payments, unemployment benefits reflect certain overtones of welfare since some of the limits satisfy social policy goals rather than purely actuarial considerations. Hence, UI is *social* insurance. The implicit presumption of need also has socially oriented limits. The controversy in applying limits focuses on the weekly amount and on the duration of payments.

The Role of Unemployment Insurance in the Overall Economy

One of the main reasons UI is compulsory public social insurance as opposed to private insurance is because it is the only way to achieve nearly universal coverage in the population. In performing the central income replacement function, with nearly all workers covered, the system works to arrest declining income of the unemployed, reduce the potential increase in welfare dependency, and slow the decline in aggregate spending when the economy moves into a recession. The direct cost of UI is paid by employers through payroll taxes. It has been argued that these costs affect the economy by influencing business location decisions.

In the aggregate, UI benefits constitute a nonnegligible portion of total spending in the economy. As summarized in table 1.2, between 1938 and 1995 UI benefits usually hovered in a range between one-quarter and three-quarters of 1 percent of gross domestic product (GDP). The annual figures in the table also make it clear that UI contributes a larger share of total spending in recession years than in expansion years and that the boost in spending is appreciable and rapid. For example, during the 1957-1958 recession, UI benefit payments rose from 0.39 percent to 0.77 percent of GDP, and, during the 1974-1975 recession, payments rose from 0.41 percent to 0.74 percent of GDP. Burtless (1991, p. 38) has argued that "changes in the system over the past decade have eroded the value of unemployment insurance both as income protection for the unemployed and as an automatic stabilizer." It is easy to see in table 1.2 that the spike in benefits as a percentage of GDP was much smaller in the 1990-1991 recession than in many previous postwar recessions.[16] This partly reflects the tighter eligibility conditions and diminished real benefit levels imposed by many of the states in response to financial crises in the early 1980s.

Table 1.2 UI Benefit Payments as Percentage of U.S. GDP, 1938-1995

Year	UI benefits (thousands)	UI as percentage of GDP
1938	393,783	0.46
1939	429,298	0.47
1940	518,700	0.52
1941	344,324	0.28
1942	344,083	0.22
1943	79,644	0.04
1944	62,384	0.03
1945	445,867	0.21
1946	1,094,845	0.52
1947	775,142	0.33
1948	789,931	0.30
1949	1,735,991	0.67
1950	1,373,113	0.48
1951	840,411	0.25
1952	998,238	0.29
1953	962,219	0.26
1954	2,026,868	0.55
1955	1,350,264	0.33
1956	1,380,728	0.32
1957	1,733,876	0.39
1958	3,512,732	0.77
1959	2,279,018	0.46
1960	2,726,849	0.53
1961	3,422,558	0.64
1962	2,675,565	0.47
1963	2,775,222	0.46
1964	2,521,575	0.39
1965	2,166,011	0.31
1966	1,771,292	0.23
1967	2,092,364	0.26

Year	UI benefits (thousands)	UI as percentage of GDP
1968	2,029,957	0.23
1969	2,125,809	0.22
1970	3,847,312	0.38
1971	5,935,925	0.45
1972	4,520,809	0.37
1973	4,090,573	0.30
1974	6,107,448	0.41
1975	11,986,137	0.74
1976	9,305,600	0.51
1977	8,666,091	0.42
1978	7,998,880	0.35
1979	9,241,720	0.36
1980	14,191,178	0.51
1981	13,879,278	0.44
1982	21,100,164	0.65
1983	18,510,200	0.52
1984	13,231,491	0.33
1985	14,682,332	0.35
1986	15,950,231	0.36
1987	14,190,743	0.30
1988	13,240,757	0.26
1989	14,205,321	0.26
1990	17,975,980	0.31
1991	25,478,724	0.43
1992	25,066,162	0.40
1993	21,758,380	0.34
1994	20,979,858	0.30
1995	21,278,429	0.29

SOURCE: U.S. Department of Labor (1996); U.S. Department of Commerce (various issues).

When we look at the dollars of UI benefits as a share of GDP, we see only the direct first-order effect of UI on aggregate spending. It should be recognized that spending of UI benefits becomes money income to others who again spend a part of it, and so on. The cumulative effect of all the spending is called the multiplier. For the nation as a whole, Oaxaca and Taylor (1983, p. 6) estimated that "for each dollar of UI benefit payments in 1975 . . . disposable income was increased by $1.02." Percentage effects estimated by Oaxaca and Taylor (1986) of UI benefit payments on local economies were even larger, at 3.18 percent of real disposable income in Phoenix and 2.16 percent in Tucson for 1976.[17]

UI is also considered to have an impact on the economy because of the payroll tax charged to employers to finance the system. While Anderson and Meyer (1995) estimate that this cost is partly shared by workers who contribute to the system by accepting lower wages, it has been argued widely that UI taxes are one of the factors figuring into business decisions about where to locate or to expand operations. This thesis was put forward more generally in terms of all area-specific tax levies by Due:

> On the basis of all available studies, it is obvious that relatively high business tax levels do not have the disastrous effects claimed for them. . . . However, without doubt, in some instances the tax element plays the deciding role in determining the optimum location, since other factors balance (Due 1961, p. 171).

Interstate variation in business taxes was examined by Wheaton (1983), who suggested that these differences may affect business location decisions within small geographic areas such as at interstate borders. Among individual categories of taxes that vary across states, Wheaton (1983, p. 85) estimated that property taxes constitute 42 percent of tax payments; UI taxes are tied for second with state corporate income taxes, each of which receives 18 percent of total state tax payments made by business. In a survey article, Newman and Sullivan (1988, p. 232) conclude that "the most recent studies, employing more detailed data sets and more refined econometric techniques, have generated results which cast some doubt on the received conclusion that tax effects are generally negligible." While the role of UI as a built-in economic stabilizer is widely acknowledged as significant and useful, interstate differences in the employer cost of the program remain an area of constant controversy.

Unemployment Insurance as Part of the Social Safety Net

The social safety net in the United States is an intertwined web of public and private programs that naturally divide into two main categories. One group of programs is for labor force members with a reasonable history of job attachment; eligibility for these programs is usually independent of individual or household income levels. The other group provides benefits without regard to attachment to the labor force and generally requires a low-income test. UI may be viewed as a keystone in the arch supporting that portion of the U.S. social safety net designed for workers attached to the labor force.

In testimony before the Subcommittee on Department Operations, Nutrition and Foreign Agriculture, Committee on Agriculture of the U.S. House of Representatives, Jane L. Ross, Director for Income Security Issues of the U.S. General Accounting Office, provided an overview of means-tested programs:

> In fiscal year 1992, the federal government provided about $208 billion in six areas of need for low-income people. When state dollars are included, the total amount of spending reached $290 billion.
>
> The welfare system comprises about 80 programs, representing about 15 percent of total federal outlays in fiscal year 1992. Included in the system are AFDC, Medicaid, SSI, and Food Stamp programs. These four means-tested programs accounted for 20 percent of the $700 billion spent in fiscal year 1993 on the 10 largest entitlement and mandatory spending programs.[18] The system's nearly 80 programs target low-income individuals and families to meet two broad objectives: (1) to provide basic support and health care for those who are often unable to support themselves—the aged, blind, disabled, and children—and (2) to provide transitional assistance to able-bodied adults and their families while promoting self-sufficiency. table 1 [1.3] highlights the federal spending levels in some of the largest programs in each area (Ross 1995, p. 2).

Table 1.3 Selected Means-Tested Programs in Six Functional Areas (Dollars in Billions)

Functional area/program	FY 1992 estimated expenditures
Income support	
Aid to Families with Dependent Children	$13.6
Supplemental Security Income	18.7
Earned Income Tax Credit (EITC)	9.6
Medical care	
Medicaid	67.8
Medical Care for Certain Veterans	7.8
Food and nutrition	
Food Stamps	23.5
School Lunch	3.9
Special Supplemental Food Program for Women, Infants and Children (WIC)	2.6
School Breakfast	.8
Housing	
Section 8 Housing Assistance	12.3
Low-Rent Public Housing	5.0
Education and training	
Stafford Loans and Pell Grants	11.1
Job Training Partnership Act (JTPA)	3.9
Head Start	2.2
Job Opportunities and Basic Skills (JOBS) Training Program	.6
Other services	
Social Services Block Grant (SSBG)	2.8
Child Care and Development Block Grant (CCDBG)	.8
Child Care—AFDC, Transitional, and At-Risk	.8
Community Services Block Grant (CSBG)	.4

SOURCE: Ross (1995, p. 3).

Many industrialized nations bridge the gap between UI and welfare with a program of *unemployment assistance,* which is a means-tested benefit for people who have recently exhausted UI benefits. In the United States, while the duration of UI benefit payments may be extended depending on the condition of the economy, there is no standard benefit program to help individual UI benefit exhaustees in the absence of a widespread recession.

Apart from UI, the main body of public programs for people with labor market attachment or aspirations consists of retraining programs. In testimony before the U.S. Senate Committee on Labor and Human Resources, Clarence C. Crawford, Associate Director of the U.S. General Accounting Office for Education and Employment Issues, stated that

> . . . legislation enacted in the last Congress identified at least 163 programs administered by 15 different agencies that provide about $20 billion in employment training assistance for adults and out-of-school youths..."employment training programs" refers to programs or funding streams that (1) help the unemployed find jobs, (2) create job opportunities, and (3) enhance the skills of participants to increase their employability (Crawford 1995, p. 1).

This list includes everything from the Food Stamp Employment and Training program administered by the U.S. Department of Agriculture to improve the ability of food stamp recipients to gain employment, increase earnings, and reduce their dependency on public assistance, to the All-Volunteer Force Educational Assistance program administered by the U.S. Department of Veterans Affairs, which aims to assist in developing a more highly educated and productive workforce by helping service-persons readjust to civilian life through educational benefits. The complexity of eligibility conditions and benefits available from the 163 different federal employment and training programs has spurred efforts to establish a unified "one-stop-shopping" training system.

The reemployment system most closely linked to the UI system is the state-operated Employment Service (ES). While there have been calls for a new institution to act as a reemployment clearing house, the ES has been touted by some as the natural point of entry for one-stop shopping. The ES is an existing agency with a statutory funding stream authorized by the Wagner-Peyser Act, and it has strong state relationships with existing offices in 1,700 locations.

The widespread ES presence has also raised the issue of whether a newly proposed one-stop reemployment services delivery system needs another physical institution. Simultaneously, there is recognition of the prospect that the new institution could be a *virtual one-stop-shopping* place for reemployment services, operating in cyberspace as an electronic network among existing physical locations. Eligibility for various programs and options available to an individual could be determined through the electronic information network. Under virtual one-stop shopping, the system would be most encompassing if any existing agency could serve as a port of entry, so that there would be one-stop shopping with multiple points of entry.

The ES link with the UI system was forged through cooperation in enforcing the work test for UI benefit eligibility. Further links have been provided since 1982, as the ES has been involved in referring beneficiaries who exhaust UI entitlement to retraining programs administered under the Job Training Partnership Act (JTPA). The most recent reemployment initiative in UI, the Worker Profiling and Reemployment Services (WPRS) system, has relied heavily on the ES to provide early intervention reemployment services to UI claimants identified as being most likely to exhaust benefits.

Historically, there has been a general reluctance to fund active labor market programs other than the ES from the Unemployment Trust Fund. Congress and the executive branch have faced strong opposition from the employer community regarding possible funding of retraining and other reemployment services from the Unemployment Trust Fund. Employers believe that active labor market programs should be paid for out of general revenue and question their responsibility for training the potential workforce of competitors. Since the Unemployment Trust Fund frequently contains a large reserve for recessionary periods, it has often become the target for alternative uses when reserves increase during periods of low unemployment.[19]

With increased concern about maintaining employment and returning unemployed workers to productive jobs, the UI program has taken a more active role in reemployment policy. UI funds are being used to pay for two types of active employment efforts: work sharing, which is a form of partial UI benefits, and self-employment allowances, which are UI benefits received while starting a new business. On the other hand, there is no movement to allow the Unemployment Trust Fund to pay for retraining or reemployment services such as job search assistance. Under the WPRS initiative, the UI program conducts profiling, but the provision of reemployment services, such as testing, counseling, job clubs, and job search workshops, cannot be funded by the UI system. These services must be provided by the ES or the JTPA program. Together, these active labor market efforts are linking UI with initiatives that strengthen the social safety net and help labor force members from slipping toward public support.

Incentives for Job Search and Employment

Along with the view that the unemployed generally could find work if they wanted to is a related belief that the payment of unemployment benefits diminishes the recipient's incentive to work or to seek work. The disincentive argument has been made against UI since the earliest days of its consideration. It is part of the philosophy that social programs weaken the work ethic, sap self-discipline, and create a growing dependence on transfer payments that "have imposed a rising burden of taxation on working families which has provoked a spirit of anger and frustration with American democratic institutions" (Gilder 1981, p. 137). This threat of moral decline and malingering has been the prime argument by opponents to broadening the UI system.

During the 1970s, when many states constrained weekly benefit amounts and the duration of benefits they provided, even as unemployment levels were rising, the disincentive case was pressed more forcefully. Higher unemployment rates were alleged to be due, at least in part, to generous UI benefits. These charges relied on a body of research that empirically tested for evidence of the effects of unemployment benefits on the level and duration of joblessness. Researchers attempted to measure how changes in various parameters of the program, like the weekly benefit amount, the wage replacement rate, and the entitled duration of benefits, influenced the duration of insured unemployment. No two studies were exactly comparable. They differed with respect to the types of data used, the specifications of the hypotheses to be tested, the definitions of the variables, the behavioral assumptions adopted, and the kinds of analytical approaches applied.[20]

Despite their noncomparabilities and varying results, the studies did supply evidence in support of the effects hypothesized. For example, after reviewing the methodology and findings of a dozen studies of the effects of UI on the duration of unemployment, Hamermesh concluded that

> the best estimate—if one chooses a simple figure—is that a 10-percentage point increase in the gross replacement rate leads to an increase in the duration of insured unemployment of about half a week when labor markets are tight. This is not an exact figure, but it does appear that there is some effect, certainly above zero and probably less than one week (Hamermesh 1977, p. 37).

The findings of these studies suggest that increased UI liberality reduces the incentive to return to work. Research about the size and significance of the work disincentive has continued. Some analysts have advanced the countervailing thesis that, by allowing recipients to search more extensively for suitable work, improved benefits enhance the efficiency of the labor market. Thus, a rise in unemployment duration could prove beneficial to the economy as well as to the recipient in the longer run. Attempts to measure the favorable job search effects of UI have been few and have not been regarded as satisfactory (Welch 1977). Overall, findings from research done in this period provided some support for stricter benefit eligibility rules and less generous payment levels so as to minimize work disincentives.

It was argued that the narrow gap between the net after-tax wage workers might earn on a job and the weekly UI benefit amount was an important element contributing to the disincentive effect of unemployment benefits. Feldstein (1974) focused on this factor and showed how taxes withheld from wages could severely limit the monetary advantage of working over drawing benefits. His analyses helped to support the case for taxing unemployment benefits as income, a policy adopted beginning in 1979 for recipients in households with incomes above specified levels, and applied universally regardless of income levels beginning in 1986. A study by Solon (1985), examining the experience in Georgia during the first year the new tax policy took effect, provided some evidence that benefit recipients at income levels subject to the tax had a significantly shorter duration of unemployment, on average, than recipients at similar income levels the year before the tax applied. Recipients at lower income levels showed no reduction in average duration levels over these two years.

The work disincentive argument, fortified by the research findings, was used by those who wished to curtail the liberality of the UI program. The taxation of benefits was a direct outcome of this movement. As Vroman (1990) documents, the benefit funding crises experienced by many states following the back-to-back recessions of 1980 and 1982 exerted further pressure on the states to restrict benefits and to tighten eligibility rules.

More recent studies of UI work disincentive effects have used different or refined research methodologies.[21] Katz and Meyer (1990) produced some of the biggest disincentive effect estimates yet. They found that a 10 percentage point rise in the UI wage replacement rate increased the average duration of insured unemployment by 1.5 weeks. Davidson and Woodbury (1996) have found estimates closer to results from studies done in the 1970s. Using an equilibrium search and matching model calibrated with data from several UI field experiments conducted in the 1980s, they found that a "10 percentage point increase in the UI wage replacement rate can be expected to increase the unemployment duration of UI claimants by between 0.3 and 1.1 weeks" (Davidson and Woodbury 1996, p. 25).

Among both researchers and policy makers, there has recently been great interest in positive reemployment incentives for UI beneficiaries. While stricter eligibility rules with respect to job search requirements may be considered something of a stick, the spur to reemployment efforts is viewed more as a carrot. Positive reemployment incentives have appeared as a natural alternative to further costly administrative monitoring of compliance with work search requirements. The Office of the Chief Economist of the U.S. Department of Labor summarized research findings from a variety of experiments testing new reemployment incentives for UI beneficiaries.[22] Field experiments involving randomized trials of various positive reemployment incentives for UI beneficiaries have been conducted in the states of Illinois, Massachusetts, New Jersey, Pennsylvania, and Washington. These incentives have included cash bonuses, self-employment allowances, referral to retraining, and individually tailored job search assistance. The experiments have led the way to federal legislation permitting states to offer self-employment allowances and requiring referral to job search assistance for some UI recipients.

The compulsory initiative to come out of the research on positive reemployment incentives for UI claimants, the Worker Profiling and Re-employment Services system, was required by legislation enacted in 1993. This system has given a new, positive role to the cooperative agreement between UI and reemployment service providers—the public employment service and the JTPA system. Previously, the only link between the two organizations was that, in most states, the employment service helped to enforce the UI work test, largely through registration with the employment services as well as with some placement efforts. For claimants identified as being most likely to exhaust UI benefits, participation in reemployment activities is an additional eligibility requirement for continued benefit receipt.

Fraud and Abuse

To qualify for UI benefits, in addition to being involuntarily separated from work, the individual must want employment, be able to work, be available and prepared to take a suitable job, and make appropriate efforts to regain employment. These conditions are imposed in an attempt to affirm that unemployment is an insurable risk, that is, to reduce the *moral hazard* in UI, the risk of compensating malingering rather than genuine unemployment. An individual's unemployment following a job separation can be, to a greater or lesser degree, a function of how much he or she truly wants to work. The worker files for UI benefits for each week claimed as a week of unemployment. It is administratively very difficult to monitor whether the worker is earnest about actually becoming reemployed. This is a classic example of the *principal-agent* problem, which is familiar in private insurance markets. Unless the claimant admits a lack of interest in working, there is no objective way of assessing the genuine desire for work, short of being able to offer a suitable job opportunity. The UI system seeks evidence in other ways, mainly on the basis of the individual's pattern of behavior or circumstances, which might indicate a weak interest in

working. This largely subjective approach is a difficult one to administer. It is a process open to a wide range of judgment; it is fraught with
suspicion and uncertainty and is frequently contentious.

Historically, certain kinds of UI claimants have tended to arouse
more suspicion about their reemployment intentions than others. These
include spouses of fully employed workers, students and other teenag-
ers living with their parents, workers between seasonal jobs, and pensioners. Since involuntary unemployment is difficult to prove in so
many situations, one school of thought holds that the provisions of UI
law should be strict enough to ensure that benefits go to only those who
are unquestionably and demonstrably involuntarily unemployed. The
other school of thought holds that the unemployed worker should be
given the benefit of the doubt and that the law should be liberal in testing the readiness of the worker to find employment. This philosophical
difference partly explains the variation in eligibility rules across
states.[23] It also helps to explain the variation in the severity of the disqualifications imposed. For example, the first school of thought would
apply blanket disqualifications to all persons who quit their jobs to
relocate geographically with a moving spouse. Those holding to the
second school of thought would permit the payment of benefits to such
workers if they demonstrated that they were available and able to work
in the area of their new residence. In fact, there has been a gradual
tightening of eligibility conditions for a wide variety of causes, and
there has been a similar tightening of disqualifications from receiving
benefits from a fixed time period to the entire duration of the spell. This
has been a fight that benefit rights advocates have gradually but
steadily lost in the states.[24]

The subjective character of unemployment is an important factor
contributing to the differential treatment of claimants across jurisdictions. Apart from variations in statutory provisions that reflect opposing schools of thought, there are differences among the states in
administrative policies and procedures as they are applied in determining the validity of claims. The potential for abuse in this troublesome
area, both by the claimant and of the rights of the claimant, constitutes
another source of controversy for the program.

The perception of the extent to which beneficiaries abuse the UI program affects attitudes toward many of its provisions. Periodically, the
system has been subject to attacks in the news media, which attempt to

prove, or at least to imply strongly, that benefits are being paid to large numbers of "loafers, quitters, schemers and cheaters."[25] The instances of abuse described run the gamut of situations involving violations of specific provisions in many of the state laws. Examples cited often include students, pregnant women, women who have quit their jobs to fulfill marital obligations, seasonal workers, and vacationers, all of whom, in the opinion of the critic, are not very interested in taking work and therefore abuse the system by drawing benefits. Disqualification provisions for voluntary quitting or discharge for misconduct are attacked as being too lenient and leading to abuse of the system. The cases are not always situations in which outright fraud is perpetrated but include ones in which the worker is alleged to have taken advantage of some provision or interpretation of the law in a manner that constitutes an abuse. The criticism is directed at the offending provision as one allowing the payment of benefits when it should not. These cases generally are not run-of-the-mill examples but are unusual ones that, in most instances, have been the subject of review by appeals tribunals, even by the courts, and in which benefits have been awarded. Such cases are usually on the borderline; otherwise, they would not have reached the appeal stage. The U.S. Department of Labor has often found that the facts cited by the critics are taken out of context and fail to include the extenuating circumstances that led to the final award of benefits (U.S. Department of Labor 1960). Occasionally, a presumably fraudulent case is identified in the media with information not previously available to the administrative agency. Given this information, the agency would not pay the benefits.[26] The media criticisms often select particular cases because they support an attack on the legal provisions that permit the payment of benefits in such instances.

Given the criticisms of the mid-1970s and the mounting pressures exerted by the financial strains most state programs experienced, it is not surprising that the trend turned strongly in the direction of stiffer eligibility rules, more severe disqualifications, and tighter administration. The first move was a broadened and strengthened application of work search rules. Many states increased requirements for claimants to furnish specific evidence of their job search, usually by indicating the names of a minimum number of employers contacted each week.

In response to concern about the potential for fraud and abuse in the UI system, Burgess and Kingston (1980) undertook a six-city study of the accuracy of benefit payments for the National Commission on Unemployment Compensation. They estimated that 50 percent of benefit overpayments identified by intensive study, ex post, were due to either the "failure of claimants to conduct active job searches or by claimants' unavailability for work" (Burgess and Kingston 1980, p. 508). These findings led to more comprehensive research to develop and test a method to intensively audit a random sample of claims paid. Such a study was conducted in five states between April 1981 and March 1982. The results from this more involved investigation indicated that about 14 percent of all benefits paid in these states during the period were in excess of the entitled amount. Furthermore, the principal reason for the overpayments, accounting for nearly half to four-fifths of the total amounts overpaid in each of the states, was inadequate work search—failure to meet the work search requirement which was not detected when the claim was filed and processed for payment.

Beginning in calendar year 1988 as the Benefits Quality Control Program, the random sample audit procedure was introduced as a standard operation throughout the nation. It has produced estimates of error rates similar to those found in the pilot studies. In calendar year 1993, for all states reporting, the estimated error rate was 8.8 percent of a total of $21.05 billion in benefit payments.[27] This error rate is in line with rates of the last few years, but lower than estimated in the first few years that benefit payment accuracy was checked by random audit.

The trend among the states toward stiffer enforcement of the work test was reversed following nationwide implementation of the Benefits Quality Control Program. It may be the case that the relaxed stringency of the work test is due to an effort on the part of the states to lower their error rates, and to perform better on the quality control random audit, since failure of the work test remains a prime reason for payment errors.

Debate continues over whether an active weekly work search requirement applied generally to claimants contributes much to speedier reemployment in many cases. Reasonable and useful job search may call for different approaches, depending on a claimant's occupation and experience, on the recruiting and hiring practices of potential employers, and on the current condition of the labor market. Many states provide for certain exemptions or departures from their active search requirements to reflect these practical realities. This approach makes for even more complexity but attempts, at least, to minimize fruitless efforts by claimants and annoyances to employers that serve only to satisfy a bureaucratic rule but do not lead to reemployment. Is the evidence of substantial overpayments of benefits an indication of widespread abuse? Of a lack of interest in work? Would stricter enforcement of the work search requirements eliminate many benefit payments, or would it induce claimants to make more effort to meet the requirements even if it served no other purpose?

Up until recently, the work test was generally a mechanical process: if individuals indicated that they were able and available for work, and if they listed three separate employer job search contacts or, in some states, simply indicated that they searched for work, usually nothing else was done by the state agency. Some states claim to check the validity of listed work searches contacts; this is unlikely.

The decline in the UI work test is mostly in the elimination of the certification of having searched for work with a given number of employers in the previous week and naming those employers on the continued claims form. These changes may partially reflect an effort to reduce reported error rates under the Benefits Quality Control Program.

A field experiment conducted in Tacoma, Washington, investigated whether the traditional work test of requiring three employer contacts reduced UI benefit duration and payments relative to no work test or to significantly more intensive work search requirements. Based on this experiment, Johnson and Klepinger (1994) estimated that, if UI checks continue with self-certification for continued receipt and no reporting requirement, benefit duration will increase by 3.3 weeks relative to the traditional work test. In addition, they found that significantly more aggressive work search assistance is likely to shorten benefit duration by about half a week as compared to the customary three contacts work test. The evidence from Washington resulted in the U.S. Department of Labor funding an additional alternative work search experiment in Maryland.[28]

There is no doubt that there are cases in which claimants take advantage of provisions in state laws that permit some latitude in interpretation. Recent trends have lowered that latitude and, thus, have reduced opportunities for abuse. The tightening of eligibility rules and stiffened enforcement have also eliminated some claims that were previously regarded as valid and free of any questions. To the extent that the public sees UI abuse as a serious problem, the program will be controversial in those areas suspected of vulnerability to such practices.

In evaluating the overpayments issue, Kingston, Burgess, and St. Louis (1983), who pioneered the random audit procedure, noted certain "features of the unemployment insurance program which contributed significantly to the problem." Prominent among these were the complexity of the program's eligibility provisions and policies, the limitations in administrative resources that made it unlikely that agency staff could monitor claimant compliance with the rules effectively and equitably, and the weaknesses in the program's incentives for detecting and restraining improper payments.[29] Reflecting more broadly on ways to reduce problems of fraud and abuse, Burgess and Kingston identified six desirable features of a UI system:

> (1) appropriate economic incentives for all system participants, including strong incentives for claimant self-compliance; (2) to the extent possible, simple rather than complex system features and eligibility criteria; (3) to the extent possible, little emphasis on intensive administrative scrutiny of claimant behavior and motives in the routine operational system, with emphasis instead placed on self-compliance with relatively objective and easily measurable criteria; (4) minimizing the administrative discretion that makes selective application and enforcement of eligibility criteria possible; (5) horizontal equity for system participants; and (6) incentives for both administrative efficiency and smaller administrative bureaucracies (Burgess and Kingston 1987, pp. 258-259).

Conflicting Employer and Labor Views of the System

Long before the establishment of the federal-state UI system in the United States, both employers and labor opposed it as a compulsory public program, although for different reasons. Labor's reservations were founded in suspicions developed following many years of consistent hostility by government authorities toward worker efforts to organize and to press demands for better wages and working conditions. The principal union leadership stood against any governmental involvement in labor-management relations and preferred to deal directly with management to resolve mutual problems. It was not until 1932 that the position of organized labor shifted to support for UI.

Employer opposition was also rooted in history as well as in classical economic theory. Starting with the decline of feudalism and continuing through the industrial revolution to the dominance of modern corporate enterprise, the tradition of employer responsibility for the personal welfare of employees weakened to the vanishing point. Individual employers could and did sympathize with individual workers who suffered the hardships of unemployment, but this was usually separated from any economic responsibility.[30] Applying classical economic theory, unemployment was viewed as the result of a temporary imperfection, an imbalance in the market that was readily corrected as wages adjusted to levels at which the demand for labor would absorb the excess supply. Tampering with the operation of this mechanism, such as by government intervention, was thought to endanger the corrective process and to possibly delay or prevent the restoration of equilibrium at full employment. In this context, UI was regarded as interference in the market adjustment.

The massive and prolonged unemployment of the depression damaged the credibility of classical economic theory. The theory held that, in the long run, prices would adjust so that markets would clear, meaning that unemployment would vanish. In response to this line of thinking, John Maynard Keynes, who advocated government management of aggregate spending in the economy and who changed the way economists view severe economic recessions, wrote that "in the long run we're all dead" (Heilbroner 1953, p. 251).

Although the momentum for UI began to build, employers generally held to their opposition. Since the proposed plans placed most or all of the UI financial burden on employers, their opposition focused on the taxes to be levied on them. The UI taxes were viewed as a further impediment to business, at a time when most were struggling to stay afloat, and as a competitive disadvantage in interstate commerce (Ewing 1933, p. 13). Moreover, the tax reversed historic trends by compelling employers to assume some responsibility for the welfare of their employees, representing another step back from free enterprise. Opposition on these grounds was expressed by Noel Sargent of the National Association of Manufacturers before a select committee of the United States Senate in 1931: "Penalization of employers because of unemployment resulting from conditions over which the employer has little control is both ethically and economically unjustified" (U.S. Senate 1931).

The injection of experience rating into the UI system made the program more acceptable to employers. It was reasoned that, by allocating benefit costs to those businesses giving rise to compensated unemployment, experience rating helped to keep UI consistent with the free market system. The costs of the goods and services produced by insured workers thus would also reflect the costs of benefits paid to them if they experienced involuntary unemployment. Because of market competition, employers, seeking to minimize costs, are motivated to avoid or minimize unemployment of their workers. In this way, it is argued, experience rating serves the twin goals of appropriate economic cost allocation and employment stability. Furthermore, the tax offset scheme introduced by the Federal Unemployment Tax Act of 1935 allayed most fears about competitive disadvantage across states.

These theoretical concerns were prevalent before 1935, when the Social Security Act required states to establish UI systems. After the system was up and running, there was an added practical concern by employers about experience rating. As noted earlier, UI costs at the outset were on the whole less than they were expected to be and well under the standard tax rates levied by the states. The only way allowed under the system to reduce tax rates was through experience rating. As experience rating spread and tax rates declined, many employers became increasingly sensitive to benefit costs and to charges against their accounts.

The concept took hold among employers that they should pay only the cost of benefits related to their own layoffs of workers. This view is a major reason for general employer advocacy of many restrictions on benefit payments to workers whose unemployment is not attributable to their employers. Labor has opposed experience rating, claiming that it leads employers to be restrictive about their employees' benefit rights and to challenge claims unjustifiably so as to keep down charges and tax rates.

Labor and management have been natural antagonists with respect to UI. Employers generally resist any expansion or liberalization that would add to costs. Labor's interest is to press for generous levels of benefit support during unemployment, for as long a period as necessary, with relatively few restrictions on eligibility. The confrontation of these diametrically opposed interests assures conflict on nearly every aspect of the program.

Since specific UI elements are defined by law, the conflict usually centers on the legislative process, mostly at the state level. The detailed provisions of state law are of prime importance to employers, individually and collectively, given their sensitivity to cost. Few sophisticated employers feel that they can stress or even discuss candidly their concern over costs. Much of their discussion and debate deals with less tangible matters such as "insurance principles," "equities," "abuses," and "work disincentives," arguments that play useful roles in legislative maneuvering. On the other side, labor's efforts stress the hardships endured by the unemployed and the inadequacy of UI benefits to alleviate deprivation and suffering. Not all employer and labor representatives hold unreservedly to these positions. Many come to a responsible conclusion with a balanced resolution of the conflict. At times, the two sides may bring an agreed upon bill before the state legislature, the result of concessions and compromises. This approach does not always serve the public's best interest, however, if employers agree to a benefit increase in return for labor's agreement not to oppose a tax reduction, with the solvency of the fund weakened in the process.

Throughout much of the program's history, employer influence at the state level in many parts of the country has been greater than that of labor in shaping UI provisions. Where union strength has been more concentrated, as in heavily industrialized states, the results have been more balanced. Labor, however, has felt that its views have received a better response at the federal level than in the states, at least until 1980. Labor has favored more federal UI control, such as through the imposition of minimum benefit standards, and even complete federalization of the program, arguing that unemployed workers have been treated inadequately and inequitably under widely disparate state laws. Employers oppose increased federal control of the program, usually on the basis of political philosophy, arguing the dangers and inefficiencies of operation or dominance by a remote, cumbersome central government.

Beginning in the late 1970s and continuing into the 1990s, the federal government has increased the number of federal compliance rules that affect the discretionary authority of states over their own UI laws. However, these changes have not usually been supportive of organized labor's goals for the program. Union membership in the United States has declined dramatically in the past half century, falling from 35.5 percent of the work force in 1945 to 15.8 percent in 1995 (*1995 World Almanac and Book of Facts*, p. 154). The influence of organized labor has in advocating its UI objectives has accordingly diminished. The financial difficulties encountered by many of the states in the 1970s, 1980s, and 1990s have pushed UI taxes higher despite the usual employer resistance. It seems fair to say, however, that some of the past extremes of the employer-labor UI controversy have eased somewhat. Responsible leadership on both sides is usually able to reach some reasonable accommodation to protect the system's basic integrity. Moreover, the narrower employer and labor concerns are giving way more often to broader public considerations.

Federal-State Relationships and Conflicts

The decision at the outset to establish UI as a federal-state system did not end striving for a wholly federal system after the program began. Champions of the federal approach, some of whom held important staff positions at the Social Security Board, pressed their case strongly during World War II, when the state employment services were nationalized. As noted earlier, the Board itself recommended that UI also be converted to a uniform federal program. The Truman administration opposed the return of the employment service to the states after a period of wartime federalization. State officials successfully organized themselves to help defeat attempts to eliminate or to reduce their role in the employment service at that time. As a result of these early experiences and later because of a states' rights philosophy, state employment security administrators generally looked upon nearly all subsequent federal legislative proposals to broaden UI as efforts to assert greater federal control over the system, even well after any active hope for federalization had been abandoned. Opposition to these proposals frequently was ideological and did not address their intrinsic merits.

Throughout much of the first four decades of the UI program, employer groups allied themselves with state administrators in opposing liberal federal proposals, which labor tended to support. Not all state officials lined up in the same way during this period, but the majority of them did. On the whole, this combined opposition succeeded in blocking, slowing, or limiting changes in the system through federal laws. For example, federal minimum benefit standards have been proposed repeatedly, often with broad support, as a means of overcoming the persistent failure of the majority of states to provide adequate benefit levels under their own provisions. On a few occasions, one or more of the proposed standards came close to passage, but in the end, none was ever adopted. Preference for retention of state control of these matters was a major factor in the outcome, even in cases of acknowledged program inadequacies.

The federal role in the UI system, nevertheless, did expand as the result of two major developments beginning in the 1970s. One was the permanent provision of extended benefits for the long-term unemployed during periods of high unemployment, as mandated by the permanent federal-state shared program adopted by Congress in 1970. The other development was the widespread insolvency of state UI funds during the 1970s and 1980s, which called into play the provisions of the federal loan fund. Repeated use of federal-state shared extended benefits plus wholly federal supplemental extensions during the 1970s and 1980s gradually increased the number of federal rules applicable to benefit entitlement provisions, which heretofore had been exclusively state concerns. Although the federal rules applied only to the extended and supplemental benefits, they could not help but influence regular state benefits as well.

The financial problems of the period produced even more pervasive federal influence over state programs. Blaustein (1993, chapter 9) describes how the evolution of federal loan and repayment provisions structured incentives and penalties that have induced states in debt to restrict benefit eligibility and benefit levels and to increase tax levies in order to overcome insolvency. During the 1980s, a number of federal requirements were also enacted that had some direct impact on state benefit provisions; in effect, these amounted to federal benefit standards. In these cases, however, the requirements operated to make states pay less rather than more in benefits. It is ironic that such federal provisions circumscribing state control should have been put through by a Reagan administration that was publicly committed to reducing the power and role of the federal government and to strengthening the role of the states in the interest of a "new federalism." The basic purpose of these provisions, however, was to lower the costs of the UI program, and this could be done expeditiously only by amending federal law with respect to the federal, rather than state, UI programs.

There has been an uneasy balance of power between the states and the federal government over the administration of the UI program. Federal law specifies broad administrative standards to which the states must conform. States are free to structure and operate their UI programs within these broad constraints. Over time, federal constraints have declined. Highly detailed budgeting in the 1950s and 1960s—when the purchase of individual capital equipment items had to be approved by the U.S. Department of Labor—changed to broader categorical grants in the 1970s. Finally, the states were given "bottom line" authority between grant categories beginning in 1986. Despite this gradual relaxation of administrative rules, over the years, this entire area has been a source of friction between the two partners in the system. In the mid-1980s, the Reagan administration moved to alter that arrangement by proposing "devolution." The federal government would surrender many of its responsibilities for and power over state program administration. It would also reduce the federal unemployment tax by an amount equivalent to that portion going to support state program administration. States would then be left free to determine how they preferred to administer their own programs and how to finance the costs involved. Despite years of federal-state controversy, as of 1997, the system for financing state administration remains unchanged. Many states have claimed that a fair share of administrative financing dollars has not been returned to them because of federal efforts to reduce the persistent annual federal budget deficits. Meanwhile, in the face of rapid improvements in information processing capabilities, there has been no agreement on what constitutes efficient administration of UI.

The nature of the federal-state system is such that some conflict between the two partners is inevitable. Given the federal structure of our governmental arrangements, it would appear that the particular UI approach chosen offered a means of serving urgent national economic needs while preserving the state and local fabric that comprises the web of our society. The balance is a delicate one, never perfect, and often in flux. Some critics of the federal-state approach to UI see the problem of unemployment as increasingly countrywide, requiring a national remedy. Others see the problem as varied as the nation's geography and believe the solution cannot lie in application of broad uniform standards; they favor more state control and experimentation, out of which would emerge better solutions. Still others feel that the existing system provides the framework for debate yielding the best balance of federal and state ideas.[31]

Despite conflicts between the states and the federal government, the federal-state relationship in the UI system has retained support in the 1990s. While there is an active movement to return training programs and even the public employment service to the states in the form of block grants, the federal-state UI system looks quite secure. The advantages of a highly decentralized UI system with a measure of federal oversight are appealing from both policy and political perspectives at a time when the twin missions of the UI program—providing individual income assistance and macroeconomic stabilization—continue to have wide public backing. Although the balance of responsibilities in the federal-state UI system is apt to fluctuate, the basic structure of the system is likely to remain intact for the foreseeable future. The same cannot be said for other employment and training initiatives. Part of the explanation for this difference may be the strength of the federal-state nature of the UI program.

Judgment as a Source of Disagreement

Even if there were no conflicts of interest in UI, many issues would be difficult to settle to everyone's satisfaction. Rarely are there matters for which the facts available are completely adequate to answer all the questions involved. Research and data analyses can go far to narrow the areas of uncertainty and dispute that surround specific issues. Yet the research results are not always altogether clear-cut and unqualified. The data and their analyses are not always directly or perfectly relevant to the issue at hand, and the conclusions inferred are not entirely unequivocal. As has been noted with regard to the work disincentive studies of the 1970s, for example, researchers can differ in their methods and in the types of data used, with varying results. These studies have supplied an idea of the direction and general magnitude of some disincentive effects, but the question remains unresolved as to whether the effects measured are significant enough to warrant specific policy action. The research even makes possible estimates of the consequences of such action through simulation techniques, but here, too, there are limitations because not all the factors that can influence events have been accounted for, or because some factors may change and turn out to be more critical than expected, leading to unanticipated results.

What remains, therefore, is the need to evaluate the implications of the information provided and finally to exercise judgment about the policy action proposed. In making such judgments, people will differ because no one is free from predilections or biases or, stated more positively, because individuals hold disparate values. For example, where to set the weekly UI benefit amount is an issue that involves value judgments. Given that a prime objective of the program is to alleviate hardship during unemployment, the weekly amount should be adequate to satisfy that end. But what is adequate? How is hardship to be measured? Benefit adequacy research has examined various measures of expenditures of the unemployed as the levels to be sustained by the benefit received. What should be included among those expenditures is debatable. Furthermore, for a given definition of expenditures, what proportion of beneficiaries should receive a benefit adequate to sustain them—50 percent? 67 percent? 90 percent? How should the concern about the effects of higher benefit amounts on recipient work incentives be weighed in considering a level to set? How should the effects on costs and taxes be taken into account?

In short, a number of subjective judgments are called into play in deciding weekly benefit amount policy and almost every UI provision. For nearly every feature of the program, multiple choices exist concerning what the policy should be. Each provision adopted by a legislative body usually represents a choice among alternatives, based on the judgment of the majority of the legislators and often achieved through compromise and trade-offs. Controversy need not be a bad or destructive fate for UI as long as reasonable adversaries maintain mutual respect for their differing judgments. Many objective observers would likely agree that the results can improve and strengthen the program, as they have over the life of UI in the United States.

NOTES

1. See Wandner, Robinson, and Manheimer (1984) for a discussion of UI schemes in developing countries.

2. See the discussion in Breul (1965).

3. Brechling and Laurence (1995) provide an extensive analysis of how experience-rated UI tax systems might deal with the problem of financing permanent as opposed to temporary layoffs.

4. One of the most prominent of these expressions came from President Reagan at a press conference in January 1982, when, in response to a question about the gravity of the current unemployment problem, he noted having recently counted many pages of help-wanted advertisements in the newspaper, implying that there were plenty of jobs available (*New York Times*, January 20, 1982, p. A-30). A later "explanation" of his comment acknowledged that some of the jobs listed called for skills that many of the unemployed did not have.

5. The surveys involved random samples of between 1,000 and 1,500 each time the question was asked. Results of the surveys were provided by the Roper Center at the University of Connecticut.

6. In chapter 8, evidence on the extent to which the experience-rated UI tax system acts to stabilize employment is reviewed.

7. Opposition to government transfer payments may be part of the reason that Blank and Card (1991) found that only about 70 percent of those eligible for UI benefits actually draw them.

8. In February 1995, an attack on UI came from very high in the federal government. Within weeks of being seated as Speaker of the U.S. House of Representatives, Newt Gingrich said, "if you're not at work, why are we paying you...[unemployment insurance] is not a vacation fund." He cited UI as an example of a government program that discourages job creation by encouraging out-of-work people to sit and collect money instead of learning new skills (Rice 1995).

9. Similar linkages between unemployment compensation and active employment measures have been forged in other Organization for Economic Co-operation and Development (OECD) countries. See Brodsky (1994, pp. 58-59).

10. An excellent overview of the history and philosophy of the insurance concept is given in Malisoff (1961).

11. A similar argument about social security is made by Cohen and Beedon (1994).

12. While the weekly UI benefit is limited because of social adequacy considerations, private supplementary unemployment insurance is available. Workers may purchase—in a fashion similar to credit life and disability insurance on loans—unemployment insurance that guarantees periodic consumer loan payments during unemployment up to a certain duration. This option may represent a significant supplement in a consumer society where virtually everything from homes and cars to groceries and air travel may be purchased on credit.

13. Blaustein (1993, p. 47), from a statement of UI objectives issued by the U.S. Department of Labor, Bureau of Employment Security, in 1955.

14. In the United States prior to the 1930s, the only reliable employment data came from the decennial census. The census relied on the *gainful worker* concept, which excluded unemployment since most of the unemployed held a job at one time or another during the interview year (Levitan, Mangum, and Marshall 1981, p. 77).

15. Blaustein (1981) proposed a type of unemployment assistance as part of a suggested three-tier system of job and income security for workers.

16. Note that the benefits listed in table 1.2 do not include payments for extended or third-tier programs.

17. A further stabilizing influence may be exerted by the UI benefit financing mechanisms. While UI benefit payments increase during recessions, tax payments by employers for those benefits occur gradually over a period ranging between 4 and 24 calendar quarters later. The full benefit repayment burden is not placed on employers during recessionary times.

18. The $700 billion figure for 1993 includes the largest entitlement program, social security old age pensions, which does not means test payments.

19. Striner (1972), who advocated using the Unemployment Trust Fund for training, provides an early comparative review of active labor programs and financing in Europe and the United States. A more recent review is provided by Schmid, Reissert, and Bruche (1992).

20. See papers in the symposium edited by Arnold Katz (1977).

21. Atkinson and Micklewright (1991) provide an excellent survey of the literature.

22. See section 5 of U.S. Department of Labor, Office of the Chief Economist (1995).

23. Part of the present variation in eligibility rules across states has resulted from changes over time in response to the realities of the differing industrial mix of employment and unemployment and the impact of these on benefit payments and UI tax levies.

24. The trends in statutes can be followed in the various revisions to U.S. Department of Labor, *Comparison of State Unemployment Insurance Laws*.

25. Examples are Gilmore (1960, 1964); and "Another Ripoff?" *Sixty Minutes*, April 25, 1976.

26. A claimant for unemployment benefits interviewed on the CBS *Sixty Minutes* program of April 1976, who admitted that he did not seek or want work, a fact he concealed from the state agency when he filed his claim, was disqualified from drawing benefits the morning after the program was shown.

27. See U.S. Department of Labor (1994).

28. Results from the Maryland experiment are to be available in late mid-1997.

29. See Kingston, Burgess, and St. Louis (1983).

30. Nelson (1969, p. 47) states that "at least twenty-three company unemployment-insurance funds, covering approximately 60,000 workers, were in operation at one time or another between 1916 and 1934. There were never more than sixteen plans in effect at one time, and this peak was reached only in 1931."

31. This is the view advanced by Rubin (1983) at the conclusion of his book.

References

Adams, Leonard P. 1971. *Public Attitudes Toward Unemployment Insurance.* Kalamazoo, MI: W.E. Upjohn Institute.

Anderson, Patricia M., and Bruce D. Meyer. 1995. "The Incidence of the Unemployment Insurance Payroll Tax." In *Advisory Council on Unemployment Compensation: Background Papers*, Vol. 2 Washington, DC: ACUC, July.

"Another Ripoff?" 1976. *Sixty Minutes*, CBS Television News, April 25.

Atkinson, Anthony B., and John Micklewright. 1991. "Unemployment Compensation and Labor Market Transitions: A Critical Review," *Journal of Economic Literature* 29: 1679-1727.

Blank, Rebecca, and David Card. 1991. "Recent Trends in Insured and Uninsured Unemployment: Is there an Explanation?" *Quarterly Journal of Economics* 106 (November): 1157-1189.

Blaustein, Saul J. 1981. *Job and Income Security of Unemployed Workers.* Kalamazoo, MI: W.E. Upjohn Institute.

_____. 1993. *Unemployment Insurance in the United States: The First Half Century.* Kalamazoo, MI: W.E. Upjohn Institute.

Brechling, Frank, and Louise Laurence. 1995. *Permanent Job Loss and the U.S. System of Financing Unemployment Insurance.* Kalamazoo, MI: W.E. Upjohn Institute.

Breul, Frank R. 1965. "Early History of Aid to the Unemployed in the United States." In *In Aid of the Unemployed*, Joseph M. Becker, ed. Baltimore: Johns Hopkins University Press.

Brodsky, Melvin M. 1994. "Labor Market Flexibility: A Changing International Perspective," *Monthly Labor Review* 117, 11 (November): 53-60.

Burgess, Paul L., and Jerry L. Kingston. 1980. "Estimating Overpayments and Improper Payments." In *Unemployment Compensation: Studies and Research,* Vol. 2. Washington, DC: National Commission on Unemployment Compensation.

_____. 1987. *An Incentives Approach to Improving the Unemployment Compensation System.* Kalamazoo, MI: W. E. Upjohn Institute.

Burtless, Gary. 1991. "The Tattered Safety Net: Jobless Pay in the United States," *Brookings Review* 9, 2 (Spring): 38-41.

Calkins, Clinch. 1930. *Some Folks Won't Work.* New York: Harcourt, Brace.

Cohen, Lee M., and Laurel E. Beedon. 1994. "Social Security Principles and the Range of Paygo Options for Long-term OASDI Solvency." Paper prepared for the Gerontological Society of America meetings, Atlanta, November 20, 1994.

Crawford, Clarence C. 1995. "Multiple Employment Training Programs: Major Overhaul Needed to Reduce Costs, Streamline the Bureaucracy, and Improve Results." Testimony before the Committee on Labor and Human Resources, U.S. Senate.

Curtin, Richard T., Christopher J. Gordon, and Michael Ponza. 1981. "Coping With Unemployment Among American Households" *Economic Outlook* (April).

Davidson, Carl, and Stephen A. Woodbury. 1996. "Unemployment Insurance and Unemployment: Implications of the Reemployment Bonus Experiments." In *Advisory Council on Unemployment Compensation: Background Papers,* Vol. 3. Washington, DC: ACUC, January.

Due, John F. 1961. "Studies of State-Local Tax Influences on Location of Industry," *National Tax Journal* 14, 2 (June): 163-173.

Erdman, Andrew. 1993. "The New Unemployed," *Fortune*, March 8, 1993: 40-49.

Ewing, John B. 1933. *Job Insurance*. Norman, OK: University of Oklahoma Press.

Feldstein, Martin. 1974. "Unemployment Compensation: Adverse Incentives and Distributional Anomalies," *National Tax Journal* (June): 231-244.

Gilder, George. 1981. *Wealth and Poverty*. New York: Basic Books.

Gilmore, Kenneth O. 1960. "The Scandal of Unemployment Compensation," *Reader's Digest* (April): 37-43.

_____. 1964. "The Scandal in Unemployment Insurance," *Atlantic Monthly* (February): 84-86

Haber, William, and Wilbur J. Cohen. 1960. *Social Security: Programs, Problems, and Policies*. Homewood, IL: Richard D. Irwin.

Haber, William, and Merrill G. Murray. 1966. *Unemployment Insurance in the American Economy: An Historical Review and Analysis*. Homewood, IL: Richard D. Irwin.

Hamermesh, Daniel S. 1977. *Jobless Pay and the Economy*. Baltimore: Johns Hopkins University Press.

Heilbroner, Robert L. 1953. *The Worldly Philosophers*. New York: Simon and Schuster.

Johnson, Terry R., and Daniel H. Klepinger. 1994. "Experimental Evidence on Unemployment Insurance Work-Search Policies," *Journal of Human Resources* 29, 3 (Summer): 695-717.

Katz, Arnold, ed. 1977. "The Economics of Unemployment Insurance: A Symposium," *Industrial and Labor Relations Review* 30, 4 (July): 431-525.

Katz, Lawrence F., and Bruce D. Meyer. 1990. "The Impact of the Potential Duration of Unemployment Benefits on the Duration of Unemployment," *Journal of Public Economics* 41 (February): 45-72.

Kingston, Jerry L., Paul L. Burgess, and Robert D. St. Louis. 1983. "The Unemployment Insurance Random Audit Program: Some Results and Implications." Report prepared for the U.S. Department of Labor, Employment and Training Administration, Unemployment Insurance Service, November.

Lerner, Max. 1957. *America as a Civilization*. New York: Simon and Schuster.

Levitan, Sar, Garth Mangum, and Ray Marshall. 1981. *Human Resources and Labor Markets*. New York: Harper and Row.

Malisoff, Harry. 1961. *The Insurance Character of Unemployment Insurance*. Kalamazoo, MI: W.E. Upjohn Institute.

Moore, Geoffrey H. 1980. *Business Cycles, Inflation, and Forecasting*. Cambridge, MA: National Bureau of Economic Research.

National Commission on Unemployment Compensation. 1980. *Unemployment Compensation: Final Report*. Washington, DC: NCUC.

Nelson, Daniel. 1969. *Unemployment Insurance: The American Experience, 1915-1935*. Madison: University of Wisconsin Press.

Newman, Robert J., and Dennis H. Sullivan. 1988. "Econometric Analysis of Business Tax Impacts on Industrial Location: What Do We Know, and How Do We Know It?" *Journal of Urban Economics* 23: 215-34.

1995 World Almanac and Book of Facts. 1994. Mahwah, NJ: Funk and Wagnalls.

Oaxaca, Ronald L., and Carol Taylor. 1983. "The Effects of Aggregate Unemployment Insurance Benefits in the U.S. on the Operation of a Local Economy." Unemployment Insurance Occasional Paper 83-3, U.S. Department of Labor, Employment and Training Administration.

_____. 1986. "Simulating the Impacts of Economic Programs on Urban Areas: The Case of Unemployment Insurance Benefits," *Journal of Urban Economics* 19: 23-46.

Ohio State University Research Foundation. 1963. "Use of and Attitude Toward the Ohio Bureau of Unemployment Compensation: A Research Report." Project 1472, Columbus.

Rejda, George E. 1984. *Social Insurance and Economic Security*, 2nd ed. Englewood Cliffs, NJ: Prentice-Hall.

Rice, Marc. 1995. "Gingrich Tells Class Unemployment Insurance Reform Needed," *Associated Press*, February 25.

Rosbrow, James M. 1986. "Fifty Years of Unemployment Insurance—A Legislative History: 1935-1985." Unemployment Insurance Occasional Paper 86-5, U.S. Department of Labor, Employment and Training Administration.

Ross, Jane L. 1995. "Means-Tested Programs: An Overview, Problems, and Issues." Testimony before the Subcommittee on Department Operations,

Nutrition and Foreign Agriculture, Committee on Agriculture of the U.S. House of Representatives.

Rubin, Murray. 1983. *Federal-State Relations in Unemployment Insurance: A Balance of Power.* Kalamazoo, MI: W. E. Upjohn Institute.

Schmid, Gunther, Bernd Reissert, and Gert Bruche. 1992. *Unemployment Insurance and Active Labor Market Policy: An International Comparison of Financing Systems.* Detroit: Wayne State University Press.

Solon, Gary. 1985. "Work Incentive Effects of Taxing Unemployment Benefits," *Econometrica* 53 (March): 295-306.

Striner, Herbert E. 1972. *Continuing Education as a National Capital Investment.* Kalamazoo: W. E. Upjohn Institute.

U.S. Department of Commerce. Various issues. *Survey of Current Business* .

U.S. Department of Labor. 1960. "Analysis of Reader's Digest Article: The Scandal of Unemployment Insurance." In *Social Security: Programs, Problems, and Policies*, William Haber and Wilbur J. Cohen, eds. Homewood, IL: Richard D. Irwin.

_____. 1994. "Unemployment Insurance Quality ˙Control 1993 Annual Report." Employment and Training Administration, Unemployment Insurance Service, July.

_____. 1995. "Comparison of State Unemployment Insurance Laws." Employment and Training Administration, Unemployment Insurance Service.

_____. 1996. *Unemployment Insurance Financial Data,* ET Handbook No. 394, Employment and Training Administration.

U.S. Department of Labor. Office of the Chief Economist. 1995. *What's Working (and what's not): A Summary of Research on the Economic Impacts of Employment and Training Programs.* Washington DC: U.S. Department of Labor, January.

U.S. Senate. 1931. "Unemployment Insurance: Hearings before a Select Committee on Unemployment Insurance." 72nd Congress, 1st session, pursuant to Senate Resolution 483, 71st Congress.

Vroman, Wayne. 1990. *Unemployment Insurance Trust Fund Adequacy in the 1990s.* Kalamazoo, MI: W.E. Upjohn Institute.

Wandner, Stephen A., John Robinson, and Helen Manheimer. 1984. "Unemployment Insurance Schemes in Developing Countries." Unemployment Insurance Occasional Paper 84-2, U.S. Department of Labor, Employment and Training Administration.

Welch, Finis. 1977. "What Have We Learned from Empirical Studies of Unemployment Insurance." In *The Economics of Unemployment Insurance: A Symposium*, Arnold Katz, ed., *Industrial and Labor Relations Review* 30, 4 (July).

Wheaton, William C. 1983. "Interstate Differences in the Level of Business Taxation," *National Tax Journal 36*, 1 (March): 83-94.

CHAPTER 2

Coverage and Recipiency
Trends and Effects

Laurie J. Bassi
American Society for Training and Development
Daniel P. McMurrer
Urban Institute

Two key measures of the responsiveness of the unemployment insurance (UI) system to the needs of the labor force are the percentage of the labor force that is covered under the UI program and the percentage of the unemployed who actually receive UI benefits. Although these two indicators are inextricably linked, they have consistently moved in different directions since the inception of the UI system (figure 2.1).

With regard to coverage, the percentage of the labor force that is covered under the system has been rising over time, generally as a result of changes in federal law. By this measure, the system appears to have become responsive to the needs of an increasing portion of the labor force. Simultaneously, however, the percentage of the unemployed who actually receive UI benefits has been in decline since data first became available in 1947. In part, this long-term decrease can be attributed to broad external trends, including those in the demographic and industrial composition of the labor force. In addition, there is some evidence that changes in federal and state UI laws have made it more difficult to qualify for benefits. Regardless of its exact causes, the decline in recipiency suggests that the UI system has become less responsive to the needs of workers. Thus, the two trends in system responsiveness appear to have partially canceled out one another.

52

Figure 2.1 Percentage of Workers Who Are Covered and Percentage of Unemployed Workers Who Receive UI Benefits, 1950-1993

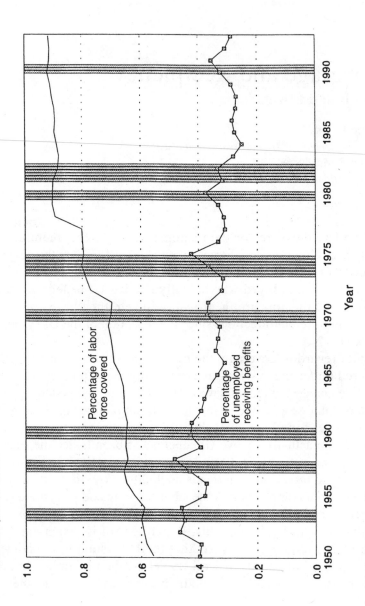

SOURCE: U.S. Department of Labor.
NOTE: Shaded regions represent recessions from peak to trough.

The percentage of the labor force that is covered under the UI system is defined as the percentage of jobs in which an employer pays UI taxes on a portion of a worker's wages. An employer who is required to pay UI taxes must pay taxes for all employees. Thus, whether or not a worker is covered under the UI system is fully dependent on the particular status of the worker's employer(s).

Over time, federal coverage requirements have been extended so that the vast majority of employers are required to pay UI taxes, resulting in coverage for the vast majority of employees. If a worker who is covered becomes involuntarily unemployed, that worker can receive UI benefits if all state monetary and nonmonetary eligibility requirements are met. Coverage may thus be considered a precondition for eligibility, as workers who are not covered cannot be eligible to receive benefits, even if they meet all eligibility requirements.

Eligibility among those unemployed workers who are covered under state UI systems is based on a combination of factors. *Monetary* eligibility requirements are designed to ensure that those who receive UI benefits had a substantial attachment to the labor force prior to their unemployment. Only covered wages are considered in making a determination of monetary eligibility. Thus, if an individual has two jobs, and only one of the jobs is covered under UI, then only the wages from the covered job are considered in determining eligibility (and in determining benefit levels).

Nonmonetary requirements are designed generally to ensure that a UI recipient (1) is involuntarily unemployed (i.e., was laid off from work) or voluntarily left work for good cause, (2) is available for work, and (3) is actively seeking work. The first of these conditions (along with monetary eligibility requirements) determines whether an unemployed worker initially qualifies for benefits. The second and third of these conditions must be satisfied on a continuing basis throughout an unemployment spell. If they are not satisfied in any given week, the worker is ineligible to receive benefits for that week. In this chapter, eligibility is discussed primarily in regard to its effects on recipiency among the unemployed.

The receipt of UI benefits by an unemployed worker (the percentage of unemployed workers who receive benefits is often referred to as the "recipiency" rate) requires that the worker be covered under the UI system, make a claim for benefits, and be found to have met all eligibility requirements. Thus, an individual's receipt of benefits is a function of a combination of three general factors: coverage provisions, an individual's decision to apply for benefits, and state eligibility standards. Similarly, the percentage of all unemployed individuals who actually receive benefits is a function of these factors.

Coverage

Original Coverage Provisions

At the inception of the UI system in 1935, federal law required only employers in industry or commerce to be subject to UI taxes, and then only if they employed eight or more workers during at least 20 weeks of the year. Among the effects of the initial federal provisions were the exclusion from coverage of workers in small firms, workers in agriculture and the public sector, and seasonal workers.[1]

Blaustein suggests that the decision to limit initial coverage was primarily a practical one, in that it would allow the administrative burden to be lessened in the first years of the program, while still ensuring that a significant percentage of workers would be covered. He suggests that there was always an expectation that coverage would be extended— ultimately to all workers who could be subject to involuntary unemployment (Blaustein 1985). Others, however, have provided different reasons for some of the coverage exclusions; in particular, they argue that the decision to exclude agricultural labor from coverage was rooted in discrimination and racism (see Norton and Linder 1996).

Expansion of Coverage

Federal law has been amended on a number of occasions to extend coverage to various groups that were excluded under the original law. It should be noted that most expansions of coverage were preceded by significant opposition and by dire predictions of the harmful effects that would result. Rarely have these objections had substantial merit (Blaustein 1985).

Coverage was first expanded in 1954, when federal law was changed to extend coverage to all commercial or industrial employers with four or more workers. In 1970, the law was amended again, requiring employers to pay UI taxes if they employ one or more workers during at least 20 weeks of the year or at a payroll of at least $1,500 in any calendar quarter.

The 1970 UI amendments also extended coverage to employees of nonprofit organizations who employ four or more workers.[2] Through a combination of the 1970 and 1976 UI amendments, coverage was further extended to all employees of state and local governments.[3] In addition, the 1976 amendments included new coverage for some agricultural workers. Employers with ten or more agricultural workers in at least 20 weeks of the year or with a payroll of at least $20,000 in any calendar quarter were required to pay UI taxes.[4]

A number of other smaller extensions in coverage have occurred since the creation of the UI program. Federal civilian employees were included in the system in 1954, when a separate program was created to cover them. Former members of the military were added under various pieces of legislation in the 1950s, with a separate program also created for them.[5] Puerto Rico entered the system as a "state" in 1960, and the Virgin Islands were included under the 1976 amendments.

Overall, as a result of the extensions of coverage since the beginning of the program, UI coverage today is nearly universal. It extends to more than 90 percent of all civilian employment in the United States, and almost all wage and salaried employees are covered. Only four significant coverage exceptions remain.

Remaining Exclusions from Coverage and Effects

First, agricultural workers who are employed on farms that are defined as "small" are not covered in many states. Second, workers who are classified as "self-employed" are also excluded from coverage. Ambiguities in this definition, however, have caused certain workers— who should be covered under some other coverage requirement—to be excluded from coverage because they are classified as self-employed independent contractors. Third, household workers of employers who pay wages less than $1,000 per quarter are excluded from coverage, and, fourth, employees of religious organizations are excluded. Each of these four categories will be discussed briefly.

Agricultural Workers

A large percentage of agricultural workers remain uncovered by the UI system as a result of the "small farm" exclusion, which exempts small farm employers from coverage requirements. This is the most significant remaining gap in the coverage of wage or salaried workers. The exemption of small farm employers from paying UI taxes can affect even those migrant workers who do a significant amount of their work on large farms. Because their wages from small farm work are uncovered, it is possible that the inclusion of only their large farm wages (i.e., the covered wages) in determining monetary eligibility may result in the workers' failing to meet monetary requirements, even if their *total* wages would have made them eligible. Reasons cited for the small farm exclusion include the poor economic position of small farmers, as well as practical problems related to difficulties in covering workers who, by the nature of their work, are likely to have many different employers or who include a relatively large percentage of undocumented aliens.[6]

The problems associated with agricultural coverage have been exacerbated by the inclusion of a special Federal Unemployment Tax Act (FUTA) rule allowing agricultural workers who are supplied by a farm labor contractor (or "crew leader") to be considered as employees of the crew leader under certain circumstances. The practical effect of this rule in many cases has been to assign UI reporting and taxpaying responsibilities to crew leaders, among whom worker advocates report widespread noncompliance. Thus, even among those agricultural workers who should be covered under existing requirements, the crew leader provision frequently creates problems for workers who attempt to secure those benefits. Further exacerbating the extent of these problems, the use of crew leaders has increased significantly in recent years (Martin 1994).

Blaustein (1985, p. 22) notes that "the trend in the organization of agricultural activity has continued in the direction of consolidation of farms and large-scale commercial enterprises. This process both calls for and makes possible investment in more productive methods and equipment that raises output with less labor or with more efficient use of labor. As farming increasingly resembles other business activities, the grounds for exclusion of farm employers from coverage grow narrower and weaker."

It should also be noted that eight states have expanded their agricultural coverage provisions beyond the federal requirements of the 1976 UI amendments. A large percentage of the nation's farm workers reside in these eight states, which include the major farm labor states of California, Florida, and Texas. California covers agricultural workers on the same basis as workers in all other industries, resulting in almost universal coverage of farm workers in that state. In California, agriculture is a negative reserve industry, meaning that unemployed workers in agriculture receive more in benefits than agricultural employers contribute to the system. Between 1983 and 1992, agricultural employers paid an average of $114 million in UI taxes, while unemployed agricultural workers received an average of $259 million in benefits (Martin 1994).

Because a relatively large percentage of workers on small farms are already covered under state law, the cost of a federal extension of coverage to agricultural workers on the same basis as other workers would be relatively small. Rough approximations suggest that additional benefit costs could be between 1 and 2 percent of current total UI benefits paid.[7]

Self-Employed Workers

Generally, considerations related to moral hazard are cited as the primary explanation for the continuing exclusion of the self-employed from UI coverage in most states. In particular, coverage is considered to be infeasible because of difficulties in determining whether unemployment is involuntary, in identifying what income has been lost, and in determining whether or not a self-employed worker is employed or unemployed in a given week (U.S. Department of Labor 1995). Each of these concerns reflects the moral hazard inherent in any effort to provide insurance against unemployment to workers who control whether or not they are employed in any given week and who also control the documentation of this unemployment. Haber and Murray (1966, p. 147) suggest that these difficulties make it "obvious" that the self-employed cannot be covered in the UI program.

Indeed, only one state—California—allows self-employed workers to apply for any sort of self-coverage under the UI program. Under this provision, self-employed workers who become unemployed can receive UI benefits on a fully reimbursable basis, meaning that they must pay back all benefits received, dollar for dollar, after returning to employment status. Program administrators report that the use of the program is extremely limited.[8] Thus, California, in effect, confronted the moral hazard problem by ensuring that workers cannot profit by manipulating the system. It is likely that a strict program such as California's is the only means through which coverage could be extended to self-employed workers without significant moral hazard.

While the exclusion of truly self-employed workers from coverage may appear to be reasonable—assuming the occurrence of the various administrative difficulties that could develop as a result of their coverage—there are a number of troubling issues that result from the exclusion of such workers. Most significantly, the actual classification of workers as self-employed has created numerous problems. There are incentives for employers to attempt to categorize workers as self-employed independent contractors.

Indeed, a phenomenon has developed, relating to the emergence of new groups of workers who are incorrectly excluded from UI coverage by virtue of their classification as independent contractors. It should be recognized that this phenomenon has been driven primarily by forces external to UI; however, the development has had a direct impact on the UI system, both by excluding workers who should be covered and by denying the system revenues from UI taxes that should have been paid but were not.

For federal tax purposes (including those of FUTA), employment classification is based on a set of twenty common law factors. These factors are determined by the Internal Revenue Service (IRS) and are designed to determine "control" in a work relationship, which is critical in differentiating between those who are employees and those who are truly self-employed. For state tax purposes, many states use a broader definition of employee than the federal common law test.

Under this system of classification, a significant number of workers are misclassified under the IRS system as independent contractors, which has important implications for the UI system. Estimates suggest that over 4 million workers are misclassified annually, and this is projected to increase to 5 million workers in the next ten years (Coopers and Lybrand 1994). In 1984, the IRS estimated that one of seven employers misclassified workers as independent contractors (IRS 1989). Misclassification of workers appears to be more pronounced in certain industries, including construction and finance, insurance, and real estate. Firms with fewer than 100 workers were also more likely to misclassify employees as independent contractors.

Some of this misclassification is certainly unintentional and may result from the ambiguous system of defining employment relationships. Other misclassifications, however, are certainly intentional, as employers can avoid payment of payroll taxes (employers avoid social security taxes in addition to state and federal UI taxes), as well as some employee benefits and other costs associated with compliance with the law. Employers who misclassify employees are able to cut costs and to gain a competitive edge over other firms that comply with classification laws. As a result, workers who should be included in the UI system are unable to draw benefits if they should become involuntarily unemployed.

Household Workers

Household workers of employers who pay less than $1,000 per quarter in wages are not covered under the UI program. Opposition to the coverage of these workers centers on administrative obstacles. In particular, difficulties in enforcing tax collection and wage reporting requirements have been cited as arguments against the extension of coverage (e.g., Haber and Murray 1966; Blaustein 1993). Recent publicity has highlighted similar problems in enforcing social security tax provisions for household workers. Administrative difficulties in enforcing the work search requirement for unemployed household workers have also been cited as an obstacle to providing full coverage to household workers. The existing coverage of workers in households that pay more than $1,000 per quarter, however, appears to nullify this concern. More generally, the experience of some states that have provided broader coverage for household workers for decades suggests that administrative obstacles to coverage can be overcome (Blaustein 1985).

Employees of Religious Organizations

Workers who are employed by religious organizations are excluded from coverage. In general, it appears that this exclusion reflects both the desire to maintain the general tax exemption for religious organizations as well as concern about the constitutional mandate to separate church and state.

Coverage Policy Issues

Overall, the extension of UI coverage to the vast majority of wage and salaried workers represents a significant success for the UI program. Nevertheless, as Blaustein notes, "the coverage issue in unemployment insurance has dwindled to minor proportions overall. Perhaps because that is so, it is difficult to overcome the tendency toward indifference and neglect about closing the gaps further. For those who are excluded, coverage is important. To provide more complete coverage does not appear to face any obstacles more serious than apathy. It should be done" (Blaustein 1985, p. 30).

While most workers who face a risk of involuntary unemployment are covered under the UI system, those workers who remain uncovered are found disproportionately at the low end of the wage distribution and often work in jobs for which there is a significant risk of unemployment. Many are workers who have a substantial attachment to the labor force and are workers for whom UI benefits would represent a critical component of income support when unemployed. As a result, the arguments for continued exclusion of these workers from the system should be seriously examined.

Justifications for the continued exclusion of agricultural and household workers, in particular, revolve primarily around practical considerations and cost and do not rest on more philosophical grounds. In light of the program's history of demonstrating that many expected administrative burdens related to coverage could actually be managed quite effectively, strict scrutiny should be given to the validity of practical arguments against the coverage of excluded groups.

For all groups of excluded wage and salaried workers, financial considerations—such as concerns about the additional benefit costs from including currently uncovered workers—should be weighed against the significant benefits that would accrue by covering those workers. In addition, efforts should be made to minimize the effects on the UI system that result from the ambiguous external system for classifying employees. Finally, additional attention should be paid to the system of optional, reimbursable UI coverage offered to self-employed individuals in California, in order to determine the feasibility of extending coverage on a similarly limited basis to self-employed individuals.

Recipiency

Measurement

Two statistics have primarily been used to measure recipiency. The first is the ratio of the Insured Unemployment Rate (IUR) to the Total Unemployment Rate (TUR),[9] and the second is the ratio of UI claimants (IU) to the total number of unemployed (TU).[10] The two ratios are highly correlated (figure 2.2). The IUR/TUR is more difficult to interpret than the IU/TU because of various mathematical complications related to the definitions of the populations being counted. Nevertheless, the IUR/TUR ratio is widely reported, and the IUR itself is of particular importance because it represents the primary trigger for the federal-state Extended Benefits (EB) program. Both ratios are based on a measure of the number of UI claimants, collected by state on a weekly basis.

The total number of claimants, however, includes some individuals who do not receive UI benefits but are counted among the insured unemployed for any given week. Three primary groups of individuals fall into this category: (1) individuals who are on a one-week waiting period before the beginning of their benefit spell; (2) claimants who are ultimately denied benefits for nonmonetary reasons; and (3) claimants who are disqualified from collecting benefits in a given week for reasons that include the requirement that recipients be able and available for work and that claimants who are working not exceed a given level of income in a week. The inclusion of these groups has tended to inflate the measure of UI recipiency by 10 to 15 percent per year (figure 2.3). Thus, a third, less frequently used, measure of recipiency is the number of actual weeks compensated, which excludes claimants who do not receive benefits in any given week, as a percentage of total unemployment.

62

Figure 2.2 Recipiency Rates for Regular State UI Programs, 1950-1993

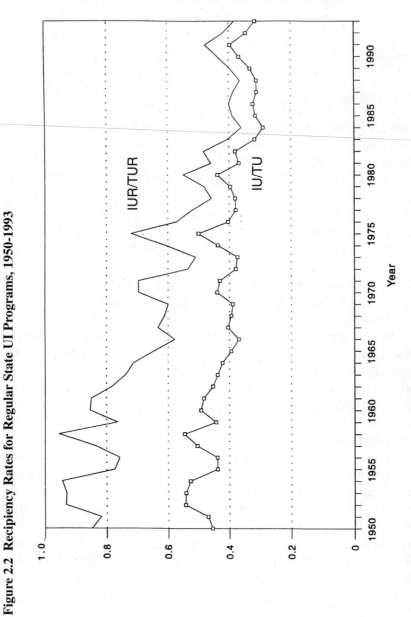

SOURCE: Council on Economic Advisors (1994) and U.S. Department of Labor.

Figure 2.3 Ratios of UI Weeks Claimed and UI Weeks Compensated to Total Employment, 1950-1993

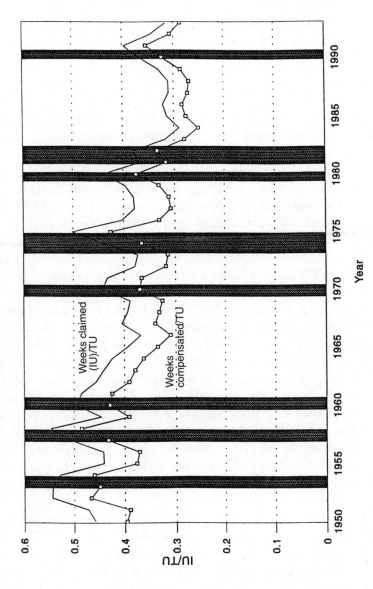

SOURCE: Council of Economic Advisors (1994) and U.S. Department of Labor.
NOTE: Shaded regions represent recessions from peak to trough.

All three measures are correlated with one another, and because of their varied use, all are cited at some point in this chapter when considering research regarding recipiency. The IU/TU measure is encountered most frequently in the research literature; thus, it is this measure to which reference is most frequently made in the discussion contained in this chapter.

Trends in Recipiency

Using any of the three measures discussed above, the percentage of unemployed workers who receive UI benefits under regular state programs has exhibited two significant trends: (1) a long-term trend, in which the national recipiency percentage has declined slowly and consistently since the 1940s; and (2) a more recent trend, in which the recipiency percentage dipped dramatically between 1980 and 1984 and has remained near that low rate throughout the 1980s and early 1990s.

Recipiency measures vary considerably across states, with 1993 ratios of claimants to total unemployed ranging from a low of 15 percent in South Dakota to a high of 64 percent in Alaska (see table 2.1). Over time, most state rankings (relative to other states) on recipiency have fluctuated significantly. That is, most states have had relatively higher recipiency rates in some years and relatively lower rates in other years. (It is likely that much of this fluctuation is a result of variations over time in state economic conditions.) Among those states that have especially high or especially low recipiency rates, however, there is less variation in their rankings relative to other states. For example, since annual state recipiency data first became available in 1976, neither of the two states with the lowest average rank—Virginia and Texas—has ever ranked higher than 43rd among the fifty states. Similarly, neither of the two states with the highest average rank—Alaska and Rhode Island—has ever ranked lower than 7th among the fifty states.

In the long term, the IU/TU ratio has declined by approximately 40 percent since 1947, the first year for which data are available. The ratio has consistently displayed (1) an overall downward trend and (2) some cyclical variation during periods of recession, as job losers—who are more likely to be eligible for benefits—represent a higher percentage of the unemployed during these periods, when layoffs tend to increase.

Figure 2.4 illustrates the relationship between the IU/TU and the unemployment rate over time. The overall downward trend suggests that the UI program has served an ever-decreasing percentage of the unemployed.

Table 2.1 Ratio of Claimants to Total Unemployed, by State, 1993

State	IU/TU	State	IU/TU
Alaska	63.6	Florida	30.1
Hawaii	53.1	North Dakota	30.0
Vermont	53.1	Michigan	29.8
District of Columbia	45.3	Missouri	29.4
Connecticut	45.0	Colorado	28.5
Washington	44.4	Wyoming	28.5
Oregon	43.3	Arizona	28.3
Idaho	40.5	Mississippi	27.7
Pennsylvania	39.9	Kentucky	27.5
Wisconsin	39.8	Maryland	27.5
Rhode Island	39.7	North Carolina	27.2
Montana	38.9	Utah	27.0
New Jersey	38.7	Maine	26.2
Arkansas	37.6	South Carolina	25.4
Massachusetts	36.5	Ohio	24.9
Iowa	36.4	West Virginia	23.5
Nebraska	35.8	Alabama	22.5
California	34.6	Louisiana	21.8
New York	34.5	Texas	21.4
Tennessee	33.7	Georgia	21.3
Puerto Rico	33.0	Oklahoma	21.1
Delaware	32.1	New Mexico	20.7
Nevada	32.0	Indiana	20.6
Illinois	31.8	New Hampshire	20.3
Kansas	31.8	Virginia	17.0
Minnesota	31.6	South Dakota	15.3

SOURCE: U.S. Department of Labor.
NOTE: Data for the Virgin Islands are not available.

66

Figure 2.4 Recipiency Rate for Regular State UI Programs and Total Unemployment Rate, 1950-1993

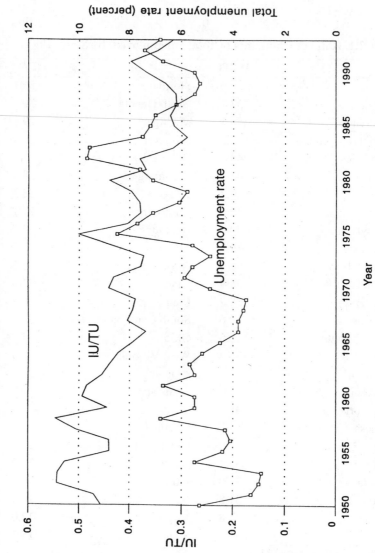

SOURCE: Council of Economic Advisors (1994) and U.S. Department of Labor.

The long-term decline in UI recipiency was combined with a pronounced drop in both measures of recipiency during the early 1980s. By 1984, the number of UI claimants as a percentage of total unemployment had dropped to 28.5 percent, the lowest recorded percentage since data were first collected in 1947. The ratio increased slightly after 1984 but has remained lower than its historical average.

The period since 1980 is also the first one during which recipiency measures did not increase significantly as the unemployment rate peaked.[11] This represents a fundamental shift away from the dynamic trends that had marked the UI program since its inception.[12] Burtless and Saks (1984) also find a fundamental shift in dynamics, in that the extremely strong statistical relationship that had existed between insured unemployment and the number of job losers unemployed for less than 26 weeks deteriorated significantly in the early 1980s.

Research on Trends in Recipiency

The long-term and recent declines likely were caused by a combination of factors that tend to have similar effects upon the UI system. To date, the long-term trend has generated relatively little research interest. The research that does exist, such as that by Burtless and Saks (1984), suggests that the long-term decline is partially a result of broad shifts in the demographics of the labor market, coupled with industrial shifts. To the extent that the percentage of the unemployed receiving UI benefits has decreased over the long-term, the UI program has become unresponsive to the needs of a growing portion of the unemployed population.

A number of researchers have worked to identify the causes of the recent decline in national UI recipiency. The federal government began to support research efforts on this and related issues in the early 1980s, and lingering questions about the primary causes of the decline have fueled continuing research efforts since that time. In addition, two sets of supplemental questions to the Current Population Survey were funded that address the reasons why unemployed individuals do not receive benefits.

Causes of Long-Term Decline in Recipiency

Research suggests that the long-term decline in UI recipiency is primarily a result of broad changes in the demographics of the labor force and in industrial composition. In addition, it is likely that evolution in state policies has also contributed to the secular decline in the recipiency rate (see chapter 15 of this volume, as well as Blaustein 1993).

Burtless and Saks (1984) suggest that a primary cause of the decline in the IU/TU ratio before 1980 was the changing demographic composition of the jobless. Throughout the 1960s and 1970s, as many women and young workers from the baby boom generation entered the labor force, they also became a higher percentage of the unemployed. As a result, men of prime working age, who are the most likely to receive UI benefits, declined considerably as a percentage of the unemployed. Burtless and Saks find that such demographic changes explain a large percentage of the decline in the IU/TU ratio before 1980.

While the demographic changes described by Burtless and Saks declined in their impact after 1980, other demographic changes have continued or even accelerated in the 1980s and 1990s. Perhaps the most significant change is the continuing rise in the number of two-earner families. It is likely that the increase in two-earner households has reduced the need of some workers to apply for UI benefits upon becoming unemployed. Thus, it is possible that various broad demographic changes have continued to have a negative impact upon UI recipiency. Factors that affect current receipt of benefits are discussed in a later section.

The shift of workers from manufacturing and other industries with high UI recipiency rates was also identified by Burtless and Saks as a primary cause of the long-term decrease in recipiency, although they report that it is quite difficult to estimate with precision the magnitude of this effect. As will be discussed, the downtrend in manufacturing also has been identified as a significant cause of the recipiency decline during the 1980s.

Causes of the Recent Decline in Recipiency

Considerable inconsistency exists in the research examining the decline in UI recipiency that occurred in the early 1980s. The variability of the results is an indication of the difficulty that researchers have had in quantifying the impacts of various agents. Four primary factors have emerged as the most common explanations of the short-term decline in recipiency: (1) federal and state policy changes, (2) population shifts to states with traditionally low UI claims rates, (3) the decline in the unionized percentage of the work force, and (4) the decline in the manufacturing sector of the economy. It is likely that a combination of some or all of these elements contributed significantly to the short-term decline.

During the 1980s, several changes in federal and state law appear to have contributed to the reduction in the percentage of the unemployed who received unemployment benefits. Overall, the U.S. General Accounting Office (GAO 1993) finds that policies designed to improve the solvency of state trust funds had the effect of reducing UI recipiency among unemployed individuals. Most significantly, numerous state laws were changed to restrict eligibility and to reduce benefit levels. In part, these state laws were in response to federal policies that provided incentives to states to adopt more restrictive legislation for regular state unemployment programs. A number of federal laws, most notably the decision to tax UI benefits, also directly reduced the value of unemployment benefit levels.

Federal Policy Changes. During the 1980s, a number of significant changes were made in federal law governing state UI trust funds. Beginning in 1982, states were required to repay federal loans to their trust funds with interest (previously, the loans had been interest-free, and there was some uncertainty whether repayment would be required at all), and states with loans were induced to adopt other specific measures to ensure solvency. Overall, these changes provided incentives to states to avoid the need for future loans by reducing the scope of state benefit programs. In addition, states were given other direct incentives, linked to federal EB funds, to tighten UI eligibility requirements and to reduce UI benefits. Taken as a whole, these federal policy changes were reflected to some extent in state policy changes.

Federal laws also were changed in ways that directly and indirectly affected the recipiency rate. In 1979, UI benefits were partially taxed for the first time, and in 1986, all unemployment benefits became subject to taxation. This change reduced the effective value of applying for benefits and would therefore be expected to decrease the number of people who choose to apply for benefits. States also were required to reduce or eliminate UI payments to unemployed workers receiving pensions or social security payments. Corson and Nicholson (1988) find that, overall, between 11 percent and 23 percent of the total decline can be directly attributed to various federal policy changes. Specifically, between 11 and 16 percent is due to partial taxation of benefits and up to 7 percent to less generous EB programs.

State Policy Changes. During the 1980s, many states adopted tighter monetary eligibility standards or stricter disqualification provisions for their regular UI programs. GAO (1993) reports that forty-four states tightened their standards in one or both of these regards between 1981 and 1987. Further, the increase in a state's minimum earnings requirements was nearly five times greater among the twenty states with the lowest levels of trust funds than among all of the remaining states. States have also tightened other aspects of eligibility, as they increasingly disqualify individuals for misconduct or for refusal of suitable work. It is likely that many of these state changes came about in response to the federal incentives to tighten eligibility, although it is impossible to determine the precise impact that changes in federal legislation alone had on the policy decisions of states.

Some research has found that these and other changes in state policy account for a significant percentage of the decline in recipiency. Corson and Nicholson (1988) find that 21 to 54 percent of the decline in recipiency between 1980 and 1986 is attributable to state policy changes. Specifically, the decline is due to the following: 9 to 11 percent to increases in denial rates for disqualifying income, 3 to 11 percent to increases in the minimum earnings required to qualify for UI, 2 to 11 percent to increases in the denial rate for misconduct, up to 13 percent to changes in voluntary separation standards, 5 percent to reductions in maximum duration of benefits, and 2 to 4 percent to changes in wage replacement rates.[13] In addition, they find that the IU/TU ratio would have increased between 1 percent and 13 percent as a result of reductions in work test denials, thereby partially canceling the effects of the other factors. Burtless and Saks (1984) also conclude that state legislative and administrative changes are the primary cause of the decline in recipiency, but they do not present estimates of the magnitude of the effects of these changes.

Baldwin and McHugh (1992) suggest that state policy changes account for 54 percent of the decline in recipiency rates between 1979 and 1990.[14] They suggest that the decline can be attributed to the following: 21 percent to increases in the minimum earnings required to qualify for UI, 16 percent to increases in the earnings required to qualify for the maximum benefit, 8 percent to increases in the number of states with disqualification periods for job quitters, 7 percent to increases in the number of states with disqualification periods for refusal of suitable work, and 1 percent to increases in the number of states with right-to-work laws.[15] An updated work, however, found sharp reductions in the apparent effects of state policy changes (Baldwin 1993).

Blank and Card (1991) find little evidence that state policy changes had any impact on recipiency. They do find that individual eligibility for UI benefits appeared to decrease slightly as a result of tighter state eligibility standards, although these effects were offset by increasing wage levels. They suggest, however, that application rates among the eligible appeared to fall in the early 1980s, accounting for some of the decline in recipiency.

Population Shifts. An increasing share of U.S. unemployment is located in southern and mountain states, where the IU/TU ratio consistently has been lower than the national average. Thus, as the percentage of national unemployment located in these states increases, the national IU/TU ratio would be expected to fall accordingly. This is a long-term demographic trend, occurring throughout the last three decades and continuing into the present. Blank and Card (1991) find that these regional shifts in population accounted for approximately 50 percent of the decline in the national IU/TU ratio between 1977 and 1987. Vroman (1991) suggests that these shifts may have accounted for 25 percent of that decline, and Corson and Nicholson (1988) attribute 16 percent of the change to geographic population shifts.

Decline in Unionization. The proportion of workers who are members of unions has fallen significantly since the 1950s. Between 1979 and 1988, the unionization percentage declined from 23.8 percent of the labor force to 18.8 percent (Curme et al. 1990 and Kokkelenberg and Sockell 1985). Because unions have traditionally represented a powerful source of information regarding available benefits for unemployed workers, it is possible that the decrease in union membership exacerbated any existing information problem among the unemployed. In addition, unions have often facilitated the filing of members' UI claims by helping to guide them through the UI system. Finally, the members of many unions are only eligible for supplemental unemployment benefits paid by their union if they apply for regular UI.

Blank and Card (1991) attribute 25 percent of the decline in recipiency to the decrease in unionization. Baldwin and McHugh (1992) assign 29 percent of the reduction in recipiency to the decline in unionization. Vroman (1991) also points to the potential importance of the unions' information role by noting that the most important reason for nonapplication for UI benefits by unemployed individuals is their belief that they are ineligible for UI. If individuals' understanding of eligibility is incorrect, then eligible workers may not be applying because they believe they are ineligible.[16]

Decline in Manufacturing. As noted, Burtless and Saks (1984) suggest that industrial shifts contributed to the long-term decrease in recipiency. This trend continued in the 1980s, as manufacturing as a percentage of total employment fell by 22 percent between 1979 and 1990. This factor has also been identified as a significant cause of the short-term decline. Corson and Nicholson (1988) find that between 4 percent and 18 percent of the decrease in the UI claims ratio can be attributed to the decline in the manufacturing sector, while Baldwin and McHugh (1992) attribute 16 percent of the total decline in the IU/TU ratio to this factor. In addition, Corson and Nicholson (1988) observe that an unemployed worker previously employed in manufacturing is 25 percent more likely to collect UI than a similar worker from another industry. It should be noted that analyses by Corson and Rangarajan (1994), and Baldwin (1993) both unexpectedly find that a decrease in manufacturing employment actually leads to an increase in the IUR.[17]

Overall, the decline in manufacturing is closely linked to the decline in unionization, because unions traditionally have been composed disproportionately of workers in the manufacturing sector. Thus, the effects of these factors may be difficult to separate.

Who Receives UI Today: Analysis from the SIPP[18]

In an analysis of the characteristics of all unemployed individuals who were not receiving benefits, the Congressional Research Service (1990) found that such individuals were typically young, did not head families, and were not the primary source of income within their families. Generally, they had lower-than-average incomes both before and after their unemployment spell. As expected, the study also found that, as attachment to the labor market decreases, the likelihood of receiving UI benefits also falls. Even among those individuals who had been employed full-time for an entire year before the beginning of their unemployment spell, only 42 percent received benefits.

An additional analysis of the attributes of the unemployed who do receive UI benefits at some point during their unemployment spell is reported in table 2.2. These figures are based on an analysis of the Survey of Income and Program Participation (SIPP) and cover unemployment spells that occurred between 1989 and 1991.[19]

It should be recalled that there are a number of reasons that unemployed individuals may not receive UI benefits. These factors fall into five general categories. First, the job may not be covered under the UI system. (This is most likely to affect agricultural workers on small farms or self-employed individuals.) Second, the person may not satisfy the monetary eligibility requirements for the program. Third, the individual may not satisfy the nonmonetary eligibility requirements. Fourth, some unemployed workers may satisfy both sets of eligibility requirements and choose not to apply for benefits. Finally, some jobless persons who satisfy eligibility requirements may not realize that they are eligible for benefits.

Effects of Demographic and Economic Factors on Recipiency

The results in table 2.2 provide some evidence that demographic and economic factors have been responsible for at least part of the decline in recipiency, generally supporting conclusions reached by a number of earlier researchers.[20] Specifically, the SIPP analysis found that if individuals earn relatively high wages, work in the manufacturing sector, work full time for the entire year, are a member of a union, live in the Northeast, or are job losers (rather than job leavers) they will be more likely to receive UI benefits when unemployed.[21]

Table 2.2 Percentage of Unemployed Workers Who Receive UI Benefits, by Gender and Race

Worker characteristic	Total	Women		Men	
		White	Black	White	Black
Overall	27	21	18	34	25
Wage rate					
Less than $5.00	12	12	20	9	24
$5.00 to $7.49	31	31	40	28	38
$7.50 to $10.00	50	48	56	53	40
More than $10.00	63	39	na	70	67
Poverty status prior to unemployment					
In poverty	16	12	12	22	17
Not in poverty	30	23	25	36	27
Occupation/industry					
Blue-collar, manufacturing	56	50	65	58	55
Blue-collar, nonmanufacturing	41	36	45	42	33
White-collar, manufacturing	56	50	30	62	na
White-collar, nonmanufacturing	25	22	na	32	38
Service	15	16	13	14	11
Hours of work					
Full-time, full-year	51	44	60	54	51

Part-time, full-year	27	24	37	30	27
Full-time, part-year	33	27	32	37	41
Part-time, part-year	10	11	8	10	4
Union status					
Member	61	42	48	68	57
Nonmember	29	25	25	33	30
Metropolitan status					
Metropolitan area	26	21	15	33	26
Nonmetropolitan area	29	21	26	37	21
Region of the country					
Northeast	38	30	28	45	44
South	21	18	19	26	18
Midwest	26	18	9	35	21
West	28	20	7	35	29
Reason for unemployment					
Job loser	44	40	41	49	35
Job leaver	8	6	11	10	19

SOURCE: Bassi and Chasanov (1996) analysis using the SIPP research file. The total sample size used varied by worker characteristic: 5,283 for the wage rate data; 8,619 for the poverty status data; 6,260 for the occupation/industry data; 6,287 for the hours of work data; 6,504 for the union status data; 8,221 for the metropolitan status data; 8,619 for region of the country data; and 4,167 for the reason for unemployment.

NOTE: "na" indicates that an estimate cannot be provided due to small sample sizes. Due to missing data, less than half of the sample was used for the following demographic groupings: wage rate, occupation/industry, hours of work, union status, and reason for unemployment.

Thus, as the percentage of the workforce that is in possession of these attributes has decreased, the percentage of the unemployed workforce that receives UI benefits has declined. Further, since many of these attributes are more likely to describe men than women, they also help to explain why unemployed men are more likely to receive UI benefits than are unemployed women. For similar reasons, whites are more likely to receive benefits than are blacks.

General Effects of State Monetary Eligibility Standards

Table 2.3 summarizes the results from simulations of monetary eligibility among SIPP participants.[22] Overall, 56 percent of the unemployed satisfy their state monetary eligibility requirements; this ranges from a little more than one-third of black females to approximately two-thirds of unemployed white males. As expected, monetary eligibility rises with wages and with attachment to the labor force.

The majority of the unemployed who do not meet their state monetary eligibility requirements are either new entrants to the labor force, reentrants to the labor force, or individuals with sporadic labor force attachment.[23] Of the unemployed who do not meet their state monetary eligibility requirements, 64 percent do not satisfy the requirement of their state that they have earnings in at least two of the four quarters in the base period.[24] Of the monetarily ineligible individuals who do fulfill the two-quarter requirement, 23 percent fail to meet the base-period earnings standard. The remaining 13 percent (who meet the other two requirements) fail to meet the high-quarter earnings requirement (table 2.4).

In all likelihood, any liberalization of states UI eligibility rules would not affect the majority of the unemployed who do not currently meet the two-quarter earnings requirement (since UI was never intended to provide assistance to new entrants and reentrants to the labor force). It is likely, however, that at least some of the unemployed who meet the two-quarter earnings requirement but fail to satisfy the base period or high quarter earnings requirements would be affected by changes in state earnings standards.

Combining the results of tables 2.3 and 2.4 indicates that the group of those who have worked for at least two quarters but still fail to meet their state monetary eligibility requirements includes 18 percent of all unemployed white women, 13 percent of all unemployed black

Table 2.3 Percentage of Unemployed Workers Who Meet the UI Monetary Eligibility Requirements in Their State, by Gender and Race

		Women		Men	
Worker characteristic	Total	White	Black	White	Black
Overall	56	54	35	64	47
Wage rate					
Less than $5.00	56	58	54	54	57
$5.00 to $7.49	76	78	72	74	81
$7.50 to $10.00	92	91	95	93	90
More than $10.00	93	91	na	94	95
Occupation/industry					
Blue-collar, manufacturing	83	81	88	85	75
Blue-collar, nonmanufacturing	75	72	na	75	76
White-collar, manufacturing	84	82	86	86	na
White-collar, nonmanufacturing	70	70	na	78	66
Service	55	57	47	58	45
Hours of work					
Full-time, full-year	93	95	96	92	92
Part-time, full-year	88	91	89	86	84
Full-time, part-year	67	67	58	67	70
Part-time, part-year	42	45	37	42	32

(continued)

Table 2.3 (continued)

Worker characteristic	Total	Women		Men	
		White	Black	White	Black
Metropolitan status					
Metropolitan area	57	55	36	64	49
Nonmetropolitan area	55	53	34	63	41

SOURCE: Bassi and Chasanov (1996) analysis using the SIPP research file. The total sample size used varied by worker characteristic: 5,283 for the wage rate data; 6,287 for the hours of work data; 6,260 for the occupation/industry data; and 8,221 for the metropolitan status data.

NOTE: "na" indicates that an estimate cannot be provided due to small sample sizes. Due to missing data, less than half of the overall sample was used for the demographic groupings above.

Table 2.4 UI Monetary Eligibility Requirements the Unemployed Fail to Meet, by Gender and Race (in percentages)

Fail to meet	Total	Women		Men	
		White	Black	White	Black
Two-quarter earnings requirement	64	60	80	58	79
Base-period earnings requirement	23	27	10	26	13
High-quarter earnings requirement	13	13	10	16	9

SOURCE: Bassi and Chasanov (1996) analysis using the SIPP research file.
NOTE: The total sample size of unemployed who were monetarily ineligible for benefits was 3,786: 2,506 failed to meet the two-quarter requirement; of the remaining individuals who met that requirement, 867 failed to meet the base-period requirement; and of the remaining individuals who met those two requirements, 413 failed to meet the high-quarter requirement or similar requirements. Totals may not sum to 100 due to rounding.

women, 15 percent of all unemployed white men, and 11 percent of all unemployed black men. Additional tabulations (not included in this chapter) indicate that, in comparison with other unemployed persons, the individuals in this category earn extremely low wages and have very high poverty rates prior to the onset of unemployment.

Determinants of Receipt among the Monetarily Eligible

It should be recalled that, in addition to monetary requirements, unemployed individuals must satisfy a variety of nonmonetary requirements in order to qualify for and maintain ongoing eligibility for UI benefits. No currently available data base enables distinctions to be made among the unemployed who satisfy these nonmonetary requirements and those who do not. The SIPP does provide information on one important related factor: whether an unemployed individual lost the previous job or quit the job. The vast majority of those who quit their jobs are ultimately ineligible for UI benefits. Tabulations from the SIPP indicate that, among the unemployed who meet monetary eligibility requirements, 58 percent of those who lost their jobs receive UI benefits, while only 14 percent of those who quit receive benefits.

Some of those who have lost their jobs and who do not receive UI benefits may have been fired for cause and, therefore, may be ineligible for UI. Others may fail to meet some other aspect of continuing nonmonetary eligibility. Some may not be aware that they are eligible for benefits. Still others may choose not to apply for benefits for some reason—perhaps they expect to be unemployed for only a short period of time, or perhaps they have adequate income from other sources (e.g., a working spouse) and do not go to the trouble of applying for benefits.

Recipiency Policy Issues

The decline in recipiency has raised considerable concern because it affects the two primary functions of the UI system. First, it reduces the capacity of the system to provide adequate insurance to workers who face the risk of involuntary unemployment. Fewer workers receiving benefits reduces the insurance value of the system. Second, the system's capacity to stabilize the macroeconomy through the automatic countercyclical injection of funds into the economy is compromised. This is affected by recipiency in two ways. First, as the percentage of unemployed workers who receive benefits decreases, fewer benefits are paid during recessions. Second, the IUR is the primary mechanism through which the EB program is activated during recessions. Because recipiency is reflected in this measure, the decline in recipiency has reduced the likelihood that extended benefits will trigger on during a recession, thereby reducing its capacity to stabilize the economy during downturns.

Thus, the very effectiveness of the system is, in part, a direct function of the percentage of the unemployed whom it serves. It appears that the recipiency decline is a result of a combination of factors. To the extent that the decline resulted from personal decisions by unemployed individuals not to apply for benefits, there is somewhat less cause for concern: the program has still met the first goal for those people, but they have elected not to take advantage of it. In that case, only the second goal is endangered. However, to the extent that the decline has resulted either from policy changes directly or from public policies that have not been adjusted to address relevant external developments (e.g., demographic and economic changes, declines in unionization) there is indeed cause for concern, for the program's capacity to achieve both goals will have been compromised.

The discussion in this chapter suggests that the second scenario is supported by much of the research literature. There are a number of steps that can be taken that may help to reverse this trend and to increase the number of recipients among involuntarily unemployed individuals with a substantial attachment to the labor force. Perhaps most important among these is to encourage states to determine monetary eligibility by using hours of work—rather than earnings—as a measure of attachment to the labor force. Doing so would end the current situation, in which low-wage workers must work more hours than high-wage workers in order to qualify for UI. This change could affect the eligibility of up to 15 percent of all unemployed workers. These are primarily low-wage workers who meet the requirement of having earnings in two quarters but do not have a sufficient level of earnings to meet either the base-period or high-quarter earnings requirements.

This potential increase in eligibility resulting from a change to an hours-of-work requirement would be partially offset by a decrease in the number of high-wage workers with low labor force attachment who are eligible. Alternatively, states could simply set their earnings requirements low enough to ensure that minimum wage workers with a substantial labor force attachment are able to qualify (this would not affect high-wage workers with low labor force attachment). In 1995, the Advisory Council on Unemployment Compensation recommended changes in state standards that would allow all workers with at least 800 hours of work in a base period to meet state monetary eligibility requirements.[25]

There are also a number of steps that could be taken to decrease the rate of nonfiling by unemployed individuals. Improving the information that unemployed workers have about the eligibility requirements of the program could enhance filing, and might offset the portion of the decline in recipiency that has been caused by the slippage in unionization. Changes in certain federal policy incentives, including a reduction in the taxation of UI benefits, could also have the effect of decreasing nonfiling.

The above changes could have a positive effect on the recipiency rate by directly affecting UI policies. At the same time, however, it is possible that these changes could be offset by more fundamental, structural elements of the system, which also may explain some of the decline in UI recipiency. For example, because states finance the vast majority of UI benefits through a tax on employers, any interstate competition to attract businesses could serve to reduce UI tax rates (as well as any other corporate taxes that are set by the states) to a level lower than would prevail in the absence of competition. Because it is clear that, in the long run, the relationship between solvency and benefits is a direct one, then decreases in taxes would necessitate decreases on the benefit side as well, all else being equal.

Although a number of studies have found that UI taxes do not play a significant role in business location decisions, all that is required for competition to develop is a *perception* by some states that UI taxes do affect such decisions. There is evidence that this perception does exist in many states. One recent study found that almost half of all states cite low UI tax rates in their economic development literature as a positive reason to relocate to that state. The study also found empirical evidence that states do compete in setting UI tax rates, and that this competition has had the effect of reducing average tax rates (Bassi and McMurrer 1996). This finding supports economic analysis suggesting that interstate economic competition would result in "inefficiently low levels of UI benefits [being] provided" (Hoyt 1996, MM-10). Thus, if interstate competition were present in the UI system, it would likely result in an ongoing decline in the relevance of the system, potentially undermining other direct policy efforts to increase the percentage of the involuntarily unemployed who receive benefits.

Conclusions

All else being equal, the extensions of UI coverage to new groups of workers should have raised the percentage of unemployed workers who receive UI benefits. However, as coverage has expanded since 1954, the percentage of the unemployed that actually receives benefits has declined. The simultaneous occurrence of these trends in coverage and recipiency represents cause for concern. It suggests that the overall UI system, *even as it directly changes by covering a larger percentage of workers*, has not been adjusted to respond to the evolving realities of the work force.

The combined effect of the two trends also suggests that one form of equity within the system has been eroded, as employer taxes that are paid on the wages of an *increasing* percentage of the labor force have gone to finance benefits for a *decreasing* share of the unemployed population. Stated somewhat differently, costs of the system are currently spread across a larger number of employers, while the percentage of workers who actually receive benefits has decreased. This effect increases to the extent that employers can pass UI payroll taxes on to workers in the form of lower wages, and the effect is greater in states that have low taxable wage bases, where low-wage workers necessarily pay a disproportionate share of the taxes that are passed on by employers.[26] Overall, it is clear that the real benefits accruing from the increase in the percentage of the labor force covered under the system have been rendered significantly less important as they have been offset by a substantial decline in the capacity of the UI system to be a presence in the lives of involuntarily unemployed individuals.

Editors' Note. As this book goes to press, recent research on some issues addressed in this chapter has become available. On the issue of interstate competition in UI tax policy, Wayne Vroman finds no persuasive evidence that such competition has occurred. Similarly, Vroman finds no evidence that states have implemented policies intended to shift costs of income maintenance from the UI program to welfare programs. (See Wayne Vroman (forthcoming), "An Analysis of Interstate Competition in the Unemployment Insurance Program," UI Occasional Paper, Unemployment Insurance Service, Employment and Training Administration, Washington: U.S. Department of Labor, and Wayne Vroman (1997), "Unemployment Insurance, Welfare and Federal-State Interrelations: Final Report," UI Occasional Paper 97-2, Unemployment Insurance Service, Employment and Training Administration, Washington: U.S. Department of Labor.)

NOTES

Much of the research in this chapter is based on analyses that the authors have conducted as staff members of the Advisory Council on Unemployment Compensation. Additional information in some areas can be found in the three annual reports of the Advisory Council. The views expressed in this chapter are those of the authors and do not necessarily represent those of the members or the staff of the Advisory Council on Unemployment Compensation.

1. Many states, however, chose to employ more liberal coverage standards from the beginning, particularly on requirements regarding the size of firm. The existence of more liberal coverage standards in various states has continued throughout the history of the program.

2. This provision did not apply to employees of churches or other religious organizations. Nonprofit employers were offered the choice of either reimbursing the state for only those benefits chargeable to them or paying the state UI tax in the same manner as other covered employers. Nonprofit employers were also offered the option of forming a group to pool their benefit liabilities through a common reserve fund. All nonprofit organizations remained exempt from the federal unemployment tax.

3. The reimbursement option was made available to all state and local government employers, and such employers remained exempt from the federal unemployment tax.

4. Estimates suggested that at least 50 percent of agricultural workers would be included as a result of this change.

5. Costs for both groups are financed entirely by the federal government out of general revenues.

6. See testimony from various agricultural groups at Advisory Council on Unemployment Compensation hearing, New York City, September 8-9, 1994.

7. This figure represents the estimate of the additional cost of extending agricultural coverage to all farm workers in those states that have not yet extended coverage. It was derived by extrapolating the experience and negative agricultural balances in the State of California.

8. There has been no evaluation of the effect of this programs, and there are no statistics available on the extent to which it has been used.

9. The IUR is defined as the number of regular UI benefit claimants divided by the average number of people in UI-covered employment over four of the last six completed calendar quarters. The TUR is defined as the number of all active unemployed job seekers divided by the total civilian labor force.

10. The specific measure of recipiency used by researchers in examining this question has varied. Corson and Nicholson (1988) examined both ratios but focused upon the IU/TU, which they call the UI claims ratio. Blank and Card (1991) also examined this measure, which they call the fraction of insured unemployment. Vroman (1991) focused upon the IU/TU ratio as well. Baldwin and McHugh (1992) examine IU/TU, but they include EB recipients in addition to regular state UI recipients.

11. It is likely that part of this change in dynamics can be attributed to the unusual back-to-back recessions during the 1980-1983 period. Some recipients who exhausted benefits during the first recession were likely to have been ineligible for benefits during the second recession, thereby limiting the increase in recipiency during the second recession.

12. The IUR/TUR and IU/TU ratios can be statistically predicted quite accurately for the years *up to 1980* by knowing only two variables: (1) the year (a reflection of the long-term decline of the system) and (2) the unemployment rate (because of the tendency for the ratio to increase significantly during periods of high unemployment). Since1980, however, the recipiency ratios no longer consistently demonstrate the same statistical relationship to these two variables.

13. Any apparent discrepancy in totals is due to rounding error.

14. Baldwin and McHugh's findings (1992) have been reformulated in the text in order to facilitate greater comparability between these results and those of other studies. In particular, Baldwin and McHugh report that state policy changes account for 97.4 percent (rather than 54 percent) of the total net change in the IU/TU ratio. Overall, they find three primary factors that decreased the IU/TU ratio, along with other factors that partially offset the decrease. Thus, when only the three factors that decrease the ratio are combined, they are larger than the net decline. As a result, each of the factors independently appears to be a large percentage of the net decrease. In order to determine the relative impact of each factor, the percentage of the overall negative impact upon the IU/TU ratio that is attributable to each of those factors must be calculated. These calculations indicate that state policy changes account for 54 percent of the decline in IU/TU, decreased unionization for 29 percent, and decreases in the manufacturing sector for 16 percent. The remaining 1 percent is attributable to the lagged unemployment level.

15. Any apparent discrepancy in totals is due to rounding error.

16. A recent supplement to the Current Population Survey (CPS) will allow this question to be answered more definitively, but the results will not be available for some time.

17. Corson and Rangarajan (1994) emphasize that this result is unexpected and suggest that it should be viewed with caution.

18. The analysis reported in this section draws heavily on work by Bassi and Chasanov (1996). While data limitations make it impossible to distinguish among many of these reasons for nonreceipt of UI benefits among the unemployed, the Survey of Income and Program Participation (SIPP) is arguably the best available information for these purposes. Using the CPS, Blank and Card estimate that between 1977 and 1987, only 43 percent of the unemployed met their state's eligibility requirements. Their estimate is, however, very rough because the absence of retrospective earnings data in the CPS introduces error into the eligibility simulations (which require quarterly earnings data for 18 months prior to unemployment). Two special CPS supplements (1989-90 and 1993) do, however, include information on why unemployed individuals do not receive UI benefits. Consequently, the CPS can be used to analyze somewhat different issues than can be analyzed with the SIPP. Vroman (1991) is an example of this approach. The SIPP is preferable for two main reasons: (1) it contains longitudinal, quarterly earnings data, which are necessary for simulating UI monetary eligibility, and (2) the most recently available cohorts of the SIPP include information on whether individuals quit or lost their jobs. Individual monetary eligibility can be estimated for each individual in the SIPP by applying simulation models of UI eligibility to the SIPP data.

19. In interpreting this table and those that follow, it should be noted that some variables in the SIPP (e.g., hourly wage rate and union status) are frequently missing. Consequently, only a subset of the SIPP sample is available for cross-tabulating UI receipt by these variables. As a result, the disaggregated UI receipt rates may be substantially different from the overall receipt rate.

Further, the levels of UI receipt reported in the SIPP (like most other relevant data bases that are not based on administrative data) tend to be several percentage points below the officially reported levels. There are several possible explanations for this discrepancy. First, the officially reported statistics include individuals who have filed for benefits, although some of these individuals are not actually receiving benefits. Second, it is likely that receipt of benefits is frequently underreported by respondents to the SIPP (and other major surveys). Third, the officially reported statistics on UI receipt implicitly weight unemployment spells by their duration, whereas the data in table 2.2 are based on spells of unemployment and do not make any durational adjustment. Since individuals experiencing short spells of unemployment are less likely to apply for UI, this conceptual difference in the two measurements undoubtedly accounts for some portion of the discrepancy.

20. See, for example, Baldwin and McHugh (1992), Blank and Card (1991), Burtless and Saks (1984), and Broman (1991).

21. Individuals who had no earnings during the base period (i.e., new entrants or reentrants to the labor force) were excluded from the analysis.

22. These estimates understate monetary eligibility to the extent that individuals have underreported their income in the IPP. According to the simulations, approximately 3 percent of the unemployed who are calculated to be ineligible for UI report that they do, in fact, receive UI benefits. Thus, either the simulations are incorrect because of underreported income, or these individuals are receiving UI benefits in error. Undoubtedly, some additional individuals who are simulated to be ineligible do, in fact, meet the monetary eligibility rules in their states but do not receive benefits.

An additional source of error results from using the state in which an individual resides as the basis for the simulations. To be accurate, the simulations should be based on the state in which an individual works (although this information is not available in the SIPP). Unlike underreporting of income, however, this latter source of mismeasurement is unlikely to cause any systematic bias in these estimates of eligibility.

23. A small percentage of these individuals may have a long-term continuous labor force attachment but may fail to meet the two-quarter earnings requirements because of two or more spells of unemployment within a short period of time.

24. It should be noted that not all states use all three of the general monetary requirements discussed in this paragraph. The individuals who are reported as being ineligible by each of the requirements are only those whose state has such a provision in its law. Thus, individuals who worked only one quarter, but whose states do *not* require earnings in at least two quarters, are *not* included in the groups of workers who are identified as having been disqualified for failing to meet that requirement.

25. The Advisory Council on Unemployment Compensation made other recommendations related to nonmonetary eligibility, including the elimination of exclusions of seasonal workers from UI eligibility in some states, and the elimination of requirements in some states that workers seek full-time employment.

26. For evidence on the extent to which employer UI taxes are shifted to workers, see, for example, Anderson and Meyer (1994).

References

Advisory Council on Unemployment Compensation. 1994. "Report and Recommendations."ACUC, February.

———. 1995. "Unemployment Insurance in the United States: Benefits, Financing, Coverage." ACUC, February.

Anderson, Patricia, and Bruce Meyer. 1994. "The Incidence of the Unemployment Insurance Payroll Tax." Paper prepared for Advisory Council on Unemployment Compensation, Washington, DC.

Baldwin, Marc. 1993. "Benefit Recipiency Rates Under the Federal/State Unemployment Insurance Program: Explaining and Reversing Decline." Doctoral dissertation, Massachusetts Institute of Technology.

Baldwin, Marc, and Richard McHugh. 1992. "Unprepared for Recession: the Erosion of State Unemployment Insurance Coverage Fostered by Public Policy in the 1980s." Economic Policy Institute Briefing Paper.

Bassi, Laurie J., and Amy B. Chasanov. 1996. "Low-Wage Workers and the Unemployment Insurance System." In *The American Woman, 1996-97*, Cynthia Costello and Barbara Kivimac Krimgold, eds. New York: W.W. Norton.

Bassi, Laurie J., and Daniel P. McMurrer. 1996. "Unemployment Insurance in a Federal System: A Race to the Bottom?" Unpublished paper.

Blank, Rebecca M., and David E. Card. 1991. "Recent Trends in Insured and Uninsured Unemployment: Is There an Explanation?" *Quarterly Journal of Economics* 106:1157-1189.

Blaustein, Saul. 1985. "Coverage: The Narrowed Issue." Unpublished paper.

———. 1993. *Unemployment Insurance in the United States.* Kalamazoo, MI: W.E. Upjohn Institute.

Burtless, Gary and Daniel Saks. 1984. "The Decline in Insured Unemployment During the 1980s." Report submitted to the U.S. Department of Labor.

Congressional Research Service. 1990. "The Uncompensated Unemployed: An Analysis of Unemployed Workers Who Do Not Receive Unemployment Compensation." 90-565 EPW, Congressional Research Service.

Coopers and Lybrand. 1994. "Projection of the Loss in Federal Tax Revenues Due to Misclassification of Workers." Paper prepared for the Coalition for Fair Worker Classification, Washington, DC.

Corson, Walter, and Walter Nicholson. 1988. "An Examination of Declining UI Claims During the 1980s." Unemployment Insurance Occasional Paper 88-3, U.S. Department of Labor, Employment and Training Administration.

Corson, Walter, and Anu Rangarajan. 1994. "Extended UI Benefit Triggers." Unemployment Insurance Occasional Paper 94-2, U.S. Department of Labor, Employment and Training Administration.

Council of Economic Advisors. 1994. *Economic Report of the President.* Washington, DC: Government Printing Office.

Craig, Steven G., and Michael G. Palumbo. 1994. "Policy Interaction in the State Government Provision of Unemployment Insurance and Low-Income Assistance." Paper prepared for Advisory Council on Unemployment Compensation, Washington, DC.

Curme, Michael A., et al. 1990. "Union Membership and Contract Coverage in the United States, 1983-1988," *Industrial and Labor Relations Review* 44 (October): 5-34.

Haber, William, and Merrill G. Murray. 1966. *Unemployment Insurance in the American Economy.* Homewood, IL: Richard D. Irwin.

Hoyt, William. 1996. "Interstate Competition in the Unemployment Insurance Program." In *Advisory Council on Unemployment Compensation: Background Papers,* Vol. 4. Washington, DC: ACUC.

Internal Revenue Service (IRS). Compliance Measurement Group. Research Division. 1989. "Employer Survey: Report on Findings, Strategic Initiative on Withholding Noncompliance." U.S. Department of Treasury.

Kokkelenberg, Edward C., and Donna R. Sockell. 1985. "Union Membership in the United States, 1973-1981," *Industrial and Labor Relations Review* 38 (July): 497-542.

Martin, Phillip L. 1994. "The H-2A Program: Trends, Issues, and Options." Paper prepared for Advisory Council on Unemployment Compensation, Washington, DC.

Norton, Larry, and Marc Linder. 1996. "An End to Race-Based Discrimination Against Farm Workers Under Federal Unemployment Insurance." *Unemployment Compensation: Continuity and Change Symposium, University of Michigan Journal of Law Reform* 29: 177-216.

U.S. Department of Labor. 1995. "Comparison of State Unemployment Insurance Laws." Prepared by Employment and Training Administration, Unemployment Insurance Service.

U.S. General Accounting Office. 1993. "Unemployment Insurance: Program's Ability to Meet Objectives Jeopardized." Report #HRD-93-107, U.S. General Accounting Office.

Vroman, Wayne. 1991. "The Decline in Unemployment Insurance Claims Activity in the 1980s." Unemployment Insurance Occasional Paper 91-2, U.S. Department of Labor, Employment and Training Administration.

Weaver, R. Kent. 1995. "Rethinking Federal and State Roles in Unemployment Insurance." Draft paper prepared for Advisory Council on Unemployment Compensation, Washington, DC.

CHAPTER 3

Initial Eligibility for Unemployment Compensation

Walter Nicholson
Amherst College
Mathematica Policy Research

States impose initial eligibility requirements to define which workers who lose jobs in covered employment may actually begin to draw regular unemployment insurance (UI) benefits.[1] These requirements serve two general purposes: (1) to insure that the worker has had sufficient employment experience to qualify for UI benefits (so called "monetary" provisions), and (2) to test whether the worker is not responsible for his or her job loss ("nonmonetary" provisions). Implicit in these objectives is the philosophy that UI benefits are intended as wage loss insurance against the risk of involuntary unemployment. Other causes of unemployment are not compensated through the UI system in the United States, although they often are in other countries.

This discussion of eligibility provisions begins with a description of the general concerns that have motivated policy developments. Then a brief survey of existing state laws is provided. Because state provisions regarding initial eligibility are quite varied, the research on the effects of these differences is also surveyed. Finally, there is a brief outline of some of the remaining unanswered questions about initial eligibility provisions and a description of how further research might inform the development of UI policy.

Some Conceptual Issues

Monetary eligibility provisions are employed by the states to ensure that workers have a sufficient employment history to qualify for UI benefit receipt. Frequently such provisions are justified as arising from the need to assure workers' "attachment to the labor force" (Haber and Murray 1966; U.S. Department of Labor 1994). Strictly speaking, however, existing monetary requirements do not do that: state requirements are not concerned with the UI recipient's current labor market status, but rather with his or her employment history. Of course, it may be true that, in many cases, employment history is a reasonably good predictor of current labor force status, especially in making the distinction between those workers who are unemployed and those who are not in the labor force. However, there are important circumstances where history is not a good proxy for current labor force status. For example, retirees may have significant employment histories but may have no intention of taking a new job, even if one is readily available. Alternatively, new entrants to the labor force may be actively seeking work but have no employment history with which to establish an entitlement to benefits. The distinction between current labor force status and employment history has at times led to considerable controversy over UI regulations, such as those related to the treatment of pension income.[2]

A somewhat different rationale for monetary eligibility provisions derives from the notion of an "earned right" to UI benefits as insurance. Under this conception, a worker's employment history creates an increasing right to benefits should a layoff occur. Provisions that tie UI entitlements to earnings history tend to reflect this insurance-like view of eligibility provisions. The fact that eligibility also depends on the conditions of the worker's separation from employment and on his or her continuing availability for work might be regarded as similar to other types of insurance provisions that seek to reduce the moral hazard associated with insurance coverage.

Measuring employment history to assess monetary eligibility poses a variety of conceptual problems, and the states have taken a wide variety of approaches to this matter. Some of the major issues include the following: (1) the length of time over which the employment history is to be measured; (2) whether "employment" is to be measured by weeks, hours, earnings, or by some combination of these variables; (3) whether the specific time pattern of employment matters, or whether individuals with identical totals (such as total weeks worked, or total earnings during the "base" period) are to be treated identically; and (4) whether some types of employment (for example, seasonal or informal employment) are to be excluded from the history for purposes of eligibility calculations. Decisions made about each of these issues will obviously affect the eligibility of specific types of workers for benefits. In addition, such seemingly inconsequential definitional questions may also build adverse incentives into the affected labor markets. For example, there has been a long-standing concern that UI coverage of seasonal employment may effectively provide a subsidy to such jobs (Murray 1972). More recently, concern about displaced workers has raised the issue of using relatively long labor market histories as a way of targeting benefits to those for whom unemployment entails a significant loss of job-specific human capital.[3] Adoption of such special provisions might reduce the risks associated with long-term employment, creating a variety of unpredictable labor market effects. Even decisions on more mundane matters, such as whether employment is to be measured by earnings or weeks, can create adverse incentive effects: an earnings-based criterion would favor short-term, highly paid jobs whereas a weeks-based criterion would favor part-time employment. Often states attempt to mitigate these effects by coupling their basic eligibility provisions with subsidiary requirements that seek to soften such incentives.

Nonmonetary provisions that relate to initial eligibility for UI are concerned solely with the claimant's job separation. Other nonmonetary provisions that focus on continuing eligibility (such as the claimant's continuing attachment to the labor force while collecting UI) are discussed separately in chapter 4. With regard to separation, the primary concerns of UI legislation have been to address the issue of "fault." The notion that UI benefits are intended for workers who lose their jobs through "no fault of their own" is deeply ingrained in the philosophy of the system,[4] and virtually all policy interest has been in applying the concept of "no fault." Before examining such operational issues, it may be useful to ask why the determination of fault has been of such concern. After all, other forms of social insurance, such as workers' compensation or Aid to Families with Dependent Children (AFDC), pay only modest attention to the question. Part of the explanation may lie in the nature of the moral hazard being addressed. With workers' compensation or AFDC, there may be less concern that clients become eligible through their own conscious actions (although the vast literature on disincentive effects associated with these programs suggests otherwise). In the case of UI, voluntary job separations are common, so it is possible that availability of UI may have a major impact on workers' choices.

A more important explanation for the focus by legislators on fault, however, may be that UI is financed through an experience-rated system of employer taxes. Under such a system, many employers (that is, those who are not at a state minimum or maximum tax rate and therefore are "effectively experience rated") have a direct interest is assuring that they are not charged for benefit payments for which they are "not responsible." Only by so doing can they assure that their premium payments accurately reflect the labor market risks that their operations actually entail. Employers may therefore be quite active in pressing for the adoption of various fault provisions into UI statutes.

Determination of fault in the job separation process has tended to focus on three types of issues: (1) voluntary separations; (2) discharges, especially for employee misconduct; and (3) involvement in labor disputes. Complex eligibility criteria have been developed for each of these topics, often with little coordination among the states. These varying provisions have probably had some differential impact on the types of job separations that actually occur.

Before reviewing the relatively slim amount of empirical literature on the possible size of the labor market impacts of differing UI provisions, a summary of actual state laws that pertain to initial eligibility will be provided. Since this treatment must be brief, the interested reader is directed to the invaluable "Comparison of State Unemployment Insurance Laws," which is updated periodically by the U.S. Department of Labor.[5]

State Requirements for Monetary Eligibility

All states utilize a one year "base period" for measuring employment history.[6] The definition of this period varies from state to state, however. In some cases the period consists of the 52-week period immediately prior to layoff, whereas in others there may be a substantial lag between the end of the base period and the layoff date (or, more properly, the date at which the worker first files for benefits). All states require that an individual must have earned a specified amount of wages or must have worked for a specified number of weeks during the base period to qualify for benefits.

Recently, a few states have experimented with "alternative" base periods for workers who fail to meet their usual eligibility standards.[7] The purpose of using such an alternative is to allow the states to focus on more recent earnings history so that workers with irregular employment patterns are more likely to be eligible. In his review of these provisions, Vroman (1995a) finds that they do indeed increase eligibility for low-wage, part-time, and intermittent workers. Adoption of the provisions tends to raise the number of UI recipients by 6-8 percent and to increase annual benefit payments by 4-6 percent.

The states have adopted a wide variety of formulas for defining monetary eligibility.[8] A brief summary of these requirements is provided in table 3.1. Four types of qualifying requirements are currently used: (1) multiple of high quarter wages (twenty-four states), (2) multiple of weekly benefit amount (fourteen states), (3) a flat earnings requirement (six states), and (4) weeks or hours of work requirements (seven states). Many states also use alternative qualifying requirements for those workers who do not meet the primary requirements. A brief description of each of the primary requirements indicates how they operate in practice.

- **Multiple of High-Quarter Wages**. Workers are required to earn a certain dollar amount in the highest quarter of their base period. To qualify for benefits, they must then have total base-period earnings that are a multiple of this amount. Typically states require a multiple of 1.5 times high-quarter earnings, that is, one-third of total base-period earnings must be outside the high quarter.

Table 3.1 Monetary Eligibility Requirements in 1994

State	Formula	Earnings for minimum weekly benefit	Earnings for maximum potential benefit	Distribution requirement[a]	Seasonal restriction
Alabama	1.5 HQ[b]	$1,032	$12,869	2Q	-
Alaska	Flat	1,000	22,250	2Q	-
Arizona	1.5 HQ[c]	1,500	14,429	2Q	-
Arkansas	27 wba[d]	1,215	19,812	2Q	X[e]
California	1.25 HQ[c]	1,125	11,958	-	-
Colorado	40 wba	1,000	27,144	-	X
Connecticut	40 wba	600	12,680	2Q	-
Delaware	36 wba[c]	966	12,190	-	X
District of Columbia	1.5 HQ	1,950	17,420	2Q	-
Florida	20 weeks	400	26,000	2Q	-
Georgia	1.5 HQ	1,350	19,238	2Q	-
Hawaii	26 wba	130	8,762	2Q	-
Idaho	1.25 HQ	1,430	19,858	2Q	-
Illinois	Flat	1,600	12,285	$440	-
Indiana	1.25 HQ	2,500	15,786	$1,500	X
Iowa	1.25 HQ	1,090	16,458	2Q	-
Kansas	30 wba	1,860	19,500	2Q	-
Kentucky	1.5 HQ	1,500	19,283	$750	-
Louisiana	1.5 HQ	1,200	17,428	2Q	-
Maine	Flat	2,287	15,444	2Q	X
Maryland	1.5 HQ	900	8,028	2Q	-
Massachusetts	30 wba	2,400	27,083	-	X
Michigan	20 weeks	1,340	19,810	2Q	-
Minnesota	1.25 HQ	1,250	23,790	2Q	X
Mississippi	40 wba	1,200	12,870	2Q	X
Missouri	1.5 HQ[c]	1,500	13,650	2Q	-
Montana	1.5 HQ	5,400	21,700	2Q	-
Nebraska	Flat	1,200	12,009	2Q-$400	-
Nevada	1.5 HQ[c]	600	17,940	2Q	-
New Hampshire	Flat	2,800	24,500	2Q-$1,200	-
New Jersey	20 weeks	2,460	20,242	2Q	-

State	Formula	Earnings for minimum weekly benefit	Earnings for maximum potential benefit	Distribution requirement[a]	Seasonal restriction
New Mexico	1.25 HQ	1,285	8,537	2Q	-
New York	20 weeks	1,600	11,980	2Q	-
North Carolina	1.5 HQ	2.324	21,996	2Q	X
North Dakota	1.5 HQ	2,795	19,302	2Q	-
Ohio	20 weeks	1,702	12,376	2Q	X
Oklahoma	1.5 HQ	4,160	15,405	2Q	-
Oregon	18 weeks	1,000	22,720	2Q	-
Pennsylvania	40 wba[c]	1,320	13,080	.2 wages	X
Puerto Rico	40 wba[c]	280	5,320	2Q	-
Rhode Island	1.5 HQ[c]	1,780	22,389	2Q	-
South Carolina	1.5 HQ	900	15,834	2Q	-
South Dakota	--	1,288	13,104	20 wba	X
Tennessee	40 wba	1,560	19,240	6 wba-$900	-
Texas	37 wba	1,480	23,589	2Q	-
Utah	1.5 HQ	1,900	23,881	2Q	-
Vermont	--	1,628	9,405	-	-
Virginia	50 wba	3,250	20,800	2Q	-
Virgin Islands	1.5 HQ[c]	1,287	16,458	2Q	-
Washington	680 hours	1,825	30,600	-	-
West Virginia	Flat	2,200	26,500	2Q	X
Wisconsin	30 wba	1,380	15,795	8 wba	X
Wyoming	1.4 HQ	1,650	18,333	2Q	-

SOURCE: U.S. Department of Labor (1994).

a. 2Q means earnings required in two quarters in the base period. Other figures refer to earnings required outside the high quarter.

b. HQ means high-quarter earnings.

c. Significant alternative qualification requirements in addition to that listed.

d. wba means weekly benefit amount.

e. X indicates that a state has such restrictions.

- **Multiple of Weekly Benefit Amount**. States first compute the weekly benefit amount for which the worker would be eligible—typically, a fraction (1/26 is common) of high-quarter earnings—and specify a multiple of this amount as the base-period earnings required for eligibility. Because all states have minimum weekly benefit amounts, this minimum level determines the minimum total earnings in the base period required for eligibility.
- **Flat Amount**. States require a certain dollar amount of total earnings in the base period. Often, flat earnings requirements are also accompanied by quarterly distribution requirements that prevent qualification solely on the basis of a single short-term job.
- **Weeks or Hours of Work**. This requirement stipulates a minimum number of weeks (hours) of work at a specified minimum weekly (hourly) wage over the entire base period.

The operation of these formulas in practice is more complex than these summary descriptions imply. A state's detailed requirements are probably only fully understood by individuals actually involved in the claims-taking process. In its *Summary of State Unemployment Insurance Laws*, however, the U.S. Department of Labor does compute a minimum base-period earnings requirement that permits some degree of cross-state comparison. These figures are shown in the second column of table 3.1. Overall, there is a considerable degree of variation in required base period earnings among the states. Requirements range from a low of $280 in base period earnings in Puerto Rico to a high of $5,400 in Montana. Some authors have made use of this variation to estimate the effects that different monetary eligibility requirements have on patterns of UI collection. Because of the complexity of the actual formulas, such estimates should be viewed with caution.

The third column in table 3.1 reports the minimum base-period earnings required for receipt of a state's maximum weekly benefit amount. Again, there is substantial variation in these figures, primarily because maximum weekly benefit amounts also differ significantly across the states (see chapter 5). As these figures show, obtaining a complete picture of the overall generosity of a state UI program necessitates understanding the interaction between monetary eligibility requirements and methods of computing weekly benefit amounts.

The final two columns of table 3.1 indicate a few of the special requirements that the states have implemented in order to bar certain types of employment from resulting in UI eligibility. Practically all of the states have distribution requirements that prevent eligibility based on employment in only a single quarter. The stringency of these provisions varies in relatively complex ways among the states. Although most states do not make a distinction between seasonal and other employment in determining UI eligibility, fourteen have adopted special provisions intended to restrict the eligibility of seasonal workers.[9] These states have developed a variety of different ways of defining "seasonal employment." Some use an explicit designation of certain industries as being seasonal. For example, processing of perishable food is defined as seasonal in Delaware, tourism is defined as seasonal in Minnesota, and special eligibility requirements apply to cigar workers in Florida. Other states have sought to establish a more universal definition of seasonality, often based on the length of regularly recurring periods of employment and unemployment. In principle, wage credits earned by workers in seasonal industries can typically be used to establish UI eligibility only for unemployment experienced during periods in which these workers were usually employed in their seasonal jobs. General UI eligibility requirements can only be met using wage credits earned in nonseasonal work. The degree to which such restrictions are enforced is uncertain.

State Nonmonetary Initial Eligibility Requirements

State UI laws incorporate a wide variety of nonmonetary requirements that affect initial eligibility. Most of these relate to the conditions of the employee's separation from his or her employment. Describing variations in state practices is made difficult, not only by the large number of issues that are addressed in state laws, but also by varying administrative procedures that have a significant impact on how such statutes operate in practice. The first part of this section focuses on principal variations in the laws themselves. Later, administrative procedures that are used in the determination of nonmonetary eligibility are briefly discussed.

Table 3.2 summarizes state laws as they relate to three of the primary provisions affecting nonmonetary eligibility: (1) voluntary leav-

Table 3.2 Nonmonetary Initial Eligibility Provisions in 1994

State	Voluntary leaving			Misconduct		Labor dispute	
	Good cause restricted[a]	Inclusions[b]	Period[c]	Period[c]	Gross[e]	Period[e]	Excluded[f]
Alabama	X	2	D + 10 wba	3-7	R	P	-
Alaska	-	-	5 + 3 wba	5	A	S	C,L
Arizona	X	-	D + 5 wba	D + 5 wba	-	O	C,L
Arkansas	X	1	D + 30 days	7	-	O	K
California	-	2	D + 5 wba	D + 5 wba	-	P	K
Colorado	X	2	10	10	A	O	K
Connecticut	X	2	D + 10 wba	D + 10 wba	-	O	K
Delaware	X	1	D + 4 wba	D + 4 wba	-	S	K
District of Columbia	X	-	D + 10 wba	D + 10 wba	-	P	K
Florida	X	2	D + 17 wba	D + 17 wba	A	O	K
Georgia	X	-	D + 10 wba	D + 10 wba	R	S	K
Hawaii	-	-	D + 5 wba	D + 5 wba	-	S	-
Idaho	X	-	D + 16 wba	D + 16 wba	-	O	-
Illinois	X	3	D + 4 wba	D + 4 wba	R	S	K
Indiana	X	4	D + 8 wba	D + 8 wba	R	O	-
Iowa	X	1	D + 10 wba	D + 10 wba	R	S	-
Kansas	X	4	D + 3 wba	D + 3 wba	A,R	S	-
Kentucky	X	-	D + 10 wba	D + 10 wba	-	P	K
Louisiana	X	-	D + 10 wba	D + 10 wba	R	P	-
Maine	X	2	D + 4 wba	D + 4 wba	A	S	C,L

Maryland	X	1	D + 10 wba	5-10	A	S	K
Massachusetts	X	4	D + 8 wba	D + 8 wba	-	S	-
Michigan	X	1	D + 7 wba	D + 7 wba	A,R	0	K
Minnesota	X	4	D + 8 wba	D + 8 wba	A,R	P	C,L,K
Mississippi	X	-	D + 8 wba	D + 8 wba	-	S	K
Missouri	S	2	D + 10 wba	4-16	A,R	S	-
Montana	X	-	D + 6 wba	D + 8 wba	A	0	L
Nebraska	-	-	7-10	7-10	R	S	-
Nevada	-	-	D + 10 wba	D + 15 wba	R	P	-
New Hampshire	X	1	D + 5 wba	D + 5 wba	A,R	S	C,L
New Jersey	X	-	D + 6 wba	5	A,R	S	-
New Mexico	X	-	D + 5 wba	D + 5 wba	-	0	-
New York	-	-	D + 5 wba	D + 5 wba	A	0	-
North Carolina	X	1	D + 10 wba	D + 10 wba	-	0	-
North Dakota	X	2	D + 8 wba	D + 10 wba	-	0	-
Ohio	-	1	D + 6 wks	D + 6 wks	R	0	K
Oklahoma	X	-	D + 10 wba	D + 10 wba	-	S	K
Oregon	-	-	D + 4 wba	D + 4 wba	R	P	C,0
Pennsylvania	-	-	D + 6 wba	D + 6 wba	-	S	K
Puerto Rico	-	-	D + 10 wba	D + 10 wba	-	S	-
Rhode Island	-	2	D + 4 wks	D + 4 wks	-	0	K
South Carolina	-	-	D + 8 wba	5-26	A,R	P	-
South Dakota	X	2	D + 6 wba	D + 6 wba	-	0	K

(continued)

Table 3.2 (continued)

State	Voluntary leaving			Misconduct		Labor dispute	
	Good cause restricted[a]	Inclusions[b]	Period[c]	Period[c]	Gross[e]	Period[e]	Excluded[f]
Tennessee	X	2	D + 10 wba	D + 10 wba	-	P	K
Texas	X	2	D + 6 wba	D + 6 wba	-	S	K
Utah	-	-	D + 6 wba	D + 6 wba	A	S	L,K
Vermont	X	1	D + 6 wba	6-12	A	S	K
Virginia	-	-	D + 30 days	D + 30 days	-	0	-
Virgin Islands	-	-	D + 4 wba	D + 4 wba	-	P	K
Washington	X	2	D + 5 wba	D + 5 wba	R	0	-
West Virginia	X	2	D + 30 days	6	A	S	C,K
Wisconsin	X	4	D + 4 wba	7 + 14 wba	-	P	K
Wyoming	X	1	D + 12 wba	D + 9 val	-	S	-

SOURCE: U.S. Department of Labor (1994).

a. X indicates that good cause is restricted to work-related causes or those attributable to employer.

b. Good cause specifically includes sexual harassment, compulsory reitrement, to accept other work, claimant's illiness, or to join armed forces (number indicates the number of these specific inclusions in state law).

c. D means disqualification for duration of unemployment. Other periods are in weeks. Figure after + is earnings or employment required following end of spell to reestablish eligibility. wba refers to multiples of weekly benefit amount.

d. Additional restrictions for gross misconduct: A means additional duration or requalification restrictions; R means restrictions on wage credits from prior employer.

e. S represents occurrence during work stoppage; P represents occurence while dispute is in active progress; 0 represents other.

f. Dispute excluded if employer fails to conform to contract (C), prevailing labor law (L), or engaged in a lockout (K).

ing, (2) discharge for misconduct, and (3) involvement in a labor dispute.[10] All states permit workers who have voluntarily quit their jobs for "good cause" to collect benefits if they meet other eligibility provisions. Definitions of good cause differ substantially among the states, however. Table 3.2 shows that most states restrict the "good cause" exemption to reasons for leaving that are directly related to the employment situation.[11] States that do not impose such a limitation sometimes permit the good cause exclusion to apply to "good personal reasons" as well. Several states also specify by statute certain reasons for voluntary leaving that are *per se* considered to be "good cause." These are quite varied, but a few of the specified reasons for leaving a job are common enough to be summarized in "Comparison of State Unemployment Insurance Laws." Those specifically listed include the following: (1) sexual harassment, (2) compulsory retirement, (3) leaving to accept other work, (4) illness, and (5) joining the armed forces.[12] Table 3.2 reports the number of these specific exclusions contained in each state's laws. Of course, the precise definition that applies to each of these conditions also varies considerably across the states, and the specifics change frequently as a result of annual legislative initiatives and legal determinations (many of these changes are summarized annually in the *Monthly Labor Review*). Providing a simple overall summary of whether a state has a stringent or relatively lax voluntary leaving policy is, therefore, a difficult task.

Most states (forty-five in total) disqualify a worker who has voluntarily left his or her prior employment without good cause for the duration of the unemployment spell. In order to regain eligibility, individuals must then earn a minimum specified amount, usually phrased as a multiple of the weekly UI benefit. Once this subsequent earnings requirement is met, however, claims for benefits can be made based on base period earnings from the previous employment (i.e., the job that was voluntarily left), although often such benefits are not directly charged to the employer.[13] Eight states use a disqualification period of a fixed duration. These states also usually require some minimum employment before reinstating the claimant's eligibility.

Disqualifications for discharges due to misconduct are in many ways similar to voluntary leaving disqualifications. State specifications of "good cause" restrictions are often framed in identical ways, and periods of disqualification are in many cases the same (see table 3.2).

The primary unique aspects of misconduct provisions relate to states' willingness to specify degrees of misconduct together with accompanying differential disqualifications. Ordinarily, discharge for inability to perform on the job is not considered misconduct. Even negligence in performing the job may not be sufficient cause for a misconduct disqualification if the negligence was unintentional and had relatively minor consequences. Repeated negligence on the job or willful violation of company rules will result in a misconduct disqualification in most states, however. Many states also include additional penalties for especially "gross" misconduct, that is, misconduct involving illegal activity or serious safety violations. Table 3.2 indicates those states that either impose additional disqualifying restrictions for gross misconduct (denoted by A in the table) or place restrictions on the wage credits earned on a job from which the employee was discharged for such conduct (R).

All states have provisions in their UI laws that disqualify workers involved in a labor dispute. However, only a few states define "labor disputes" explicitly. A key issue is the distinction between strikes and lockouts. As table 3.2 shows, twenty-seven states exclude lockouts from disqualification, but that exclusion decision has proven to be quite controversial. It is often difficult to determine whether a particular work stoppage is a strike or a lockout, and employers may lawfully lock out workers when a union engages in "whipsaw strikes" (that is, strikes against a changing set of targets of the firms in an industry). Labor disputes that can be shown to have resulted from a firm's violation of labor law or from a firm's failure to conform to an existing contract are also often excluded from disqualification (see table 3.2 for a summary).

Only one state, New York, specifies a fixed period of disqualification for participation in a labor dispute (7 weeks). Hence, in that state it is quite possible for strikers to collect UI benefits after a period of time. In fact, however, most strikes in New York are of relatively short duration, and few striking workers actually collect benefits. Indeed, Hutchens, Lipsky, and Stern (1989) argue that the New York law is relatively stringent because it does not require a "work stoppage" for UI disqualification. In many other states (those denoted by an (S) in the table), labor dispute disqualifications come into play only when operations have been severely curtailed at the struck establishment. In these states, in situations in which operations at the struck firm continue at close to normal levels, there may be no disqualification, and strikers may collect benefits.

Defining which workers are actually participating in a labor dispute has also proven to be controversial. States have tried to develop ways of identifying "innocent bystanders," so that their unemployment can be differentiated from that of active participants in the dispute. For example, workers who fail to cross a picket line are usually defined to be participants as are workers who help to finance a dispute other than by their regular union dues. On the other hand, workers who are temporarily laid off at locations remote from a labor dispute (because of, for example, parts shortages) are usually eligible for benefits, especially if they can be shown not to be "directly interested" in the outcome of the dispute.

The administrative procedures through which benefits may be denied for failing to meet nonmonetary eligibility criteria are complex and may affect which claimants actually receive benefits. Such procedures can be categorized into four general stages as summarized here. (For a further discussion, see Chasanov and Cubanski 1995.)

- **Fact Finding.** Information is collected from both the claimant and the employer to determine the facts of the job separation.
- **Adjudication.** UI administrators examine the facts of a case and collect whatever additional information may be necessary to determine whether the separation meets the criteria specified in state laws.
- **Determination.** An initial decision regarding eligibility is reached by the UI staff. Most cases, for which there is no disagreement between the claimant and his or her employer, do not reach the stage in which a formal "determination" is made. Nationally, about 20 percent of new and additional claims for regular state UI benefits experience determinations, although this percentage does vary significantly among the states. Somewhat more than half of all separation determinations result in a denial of benefits.
- **Appeal.** Adverse determinations can be appealed by either the claimant or by the employer. Most lower authority appeal decisions can also be further appealed to a higher level. In recent years rates of appeal of separation determinations have risen signifi-

cantly, especially for issues involving misconduct. Currently more than 20 percent of misconduct determinations are appealed.

Implementing these procedures is relatively costly to the states. For example, Vroman (1995b) estimates that issues surrounding nonmonetary determinations and appeals on separation issues account for about 15 percent of total UI administrative costs. A detailed look at the procedures also shows that the states differ significantly in how they approach the various stages. Corson, Hershey, and Kerachsky (1986) examine six representative states and find few commonalities. The processes by which decisions are reached and the quality of information on which those decisions are based appear to be influenced both by general attitudes of state policy makers and by pressure to meet federal performance standards. State procedures and their resulting outcomes may also have been influenced by an increasing willingness of the parties to challenge initial findings of UI eligibility. Most importantly, a number of observers have suggested that experience rating of firms prompts an increasing willingness to contest claims. As shown in the next section, however, the research evidence on this is ambiguous.

Ultimately, about 10 percent of all new and additional UI claims are denied over separation issues through the determination process. That figure says little about the total impact of nonmonetary eligibility provisions, however, since the overall level of claims activity may also be affected by state laws and by the ways in which these laws are enforced. What limited information there is on such overall effects is summarized in the concluding part of the next section.

Research Findings

In comparison to the voluminous research on the job search effects of UI benefits and potential durations, there has been comparatively little quantitative research on the effects of UI eligibility provisions. Given the complexity of the provisions and the variety of behavioral effects they may engender, this is not surprising. Still, this seems a very promising area for future research. Hence, the goals of this brief survey are to provide an overall indication of the direction that existing research has taken and to highlight some of the principal unanswered questions that remain.

Monetary Eligibility

Two different approaches have characterized research on the effects of monetary eligibility provisions. Econometric analysis has primarily used aggregate data to examine whether differing state eligibility provisions have detectable effects on labor market outcomes. A common method has been to use simplified versions of state monetary eligibility laws, together with average wage data, to calculate the number of weeks the average worker would have to be employed in order to achieve eligibility. For example, Nicholson (1981) followed this procedure in a study of state exhaustion rates. He found that each additional week of average earnings required for UI eligibility was associated with a reduction of between 1.1 and 2.3 percentage points in the state exhaustion rate (although the results were not always statistically significant). A possible interpretation of this finding is that more stringent monetary eligibility provisions do indeed achieve the goal of eliminating from UI eligibility some of those workers with weak labor force attachments. Using a similar approach in examining reasons for declining UI claims during the 1980s, Corson and Nicholson (1988) found that more stringent monetary qualifying requirements had a significantly negative effect on UI claims. They show that changes made by the states during the late 1970s increased the weeks employed required by UI eligibility by 0.2 weeks, on average. This greater stringency may have accounted for between 3 and 10 percent of the significant decline in UI claims during the 1980s.[14]

Aggregate studies of the effects of monetary eligibility provisions have paid relatively little attention to the distribution requirements in state laws.[15] One hypothetical simulation of earnings patterns prepared by the Advisory Council on Unemployment Compensation (1995) suggests that these requirements can be quite important in determining which types of low-wage workers qualify for UI. In general, the requirements were found to be more likely to disqualify part-time, full-year workers than to disqualify full-time, part-year workers (although these workers may be affected by state seasonal restrictions). Hence, such requirements may significantly affect part-time workers' ability to qualify for UI, but there appears to be no quantitative estimate of the size of this effect.

The use of micro-level data to examine monetary eligibility requirements is severely limited by many states' failure to retain data on ineligible claims. Several early studies that were used by states in developing their eligibility requirements are reviewed by Haber and Murray (1966, pp. 256-264). They conclude that few part-time workers could meet the then existing UI qualifying requirements. The authors go on to recommend that "a requirement of 20 weeks of substantial earnings is about right" (p. 264), but the criteria being used to make that judgment are not clearly stated. In any case, the 20 week standard has become embedded in a variety of UI policy initiatives. For example, changes made to the extended benefits (EB) program in the early 1980s instituted a 20 weeks of work requirement (or its equivalent for states with other types of qualifying requirements) for EB eligibility. The intention of the change was to adopt a more uniform requirement across the states and to focus EB eligibility on those workers with a significant employment history. A simulation study of the effect of this change (Corson and Nicholson 1985) found that its impact was relatively minor—reducing national EB first payments by approximately 5 percent. Emergency EB programs instituted since 1980 have contained similar uniform qualifying wage requirements that have also disqualified relatively few recipients.[16] For more generous states, however, the impact was much larger. In Wisconsin, for example, the authors calculated that EB caseloads were reduced by over 24 percent relative to the then existing 15 week standard in that state. Although various suggestions have been made about using more stringent base-period employment standards, together with longer base periods, for EB eligibility, none of these has been enacted into law.

Several recent studies have examined the effects of changing monetary eligibility requirements for UI in Canada. Because the Canadian system is quite similar to that in the United States, findings from these studies may offer insights on experiences in this country.[17] Some of the most intriguing evidence is associated with the Canadian Variable Entrance Requirement (VER), which tailors monetary eligibility standards to provincial unemployment conditions. As a result of changes to the VER undertaken in 1990, Canada now requires between 10 and 20 weeks of base-period employment as regional unemployment rates decline from 15 to 6 percent. The regional variation thereby imparted into monetary eligibility standards and the unusual circumstances surrounding implementation of the new requirements have provided the source for a variety of empirical investigations. For example, Christofides and McKenna (1996) find that a significant number of jobs terminate once they have reached the standards specified under the VER. These effects seem to have been the largest in those provinces where average job durations were the shortest. Similarly, Green and Riddell (1993a) examine a "natural experiment" in which, because of a delay in enacting the 1990 legislative changes, several regions had their eligibility standards temporarily raised from 10 to 14 weeks. This change had a detectable effect on the labor markets of those regions. Specifically, employment durations lengthened a bit (primarily because layoffs were delayed), and the measured unemployment rate during this period fell by as much as 0.4 percentage points.

Overall, the Canadian results suggest that monetary eligibility rules may have their most important labor market impacts by changing the characteristics of some, relatively marginal, jobs. That is, the rules provide incentives for both employers and employees to adopt employment patterns that maximize UI entitlements. The size of such effects in the context of the total labor market in Canada is unknown, however. In the United States, experience rating of UI taxes may work to mitigate the size of such effects. Again, however, there appear to be no quantitative estimates of such impacts.

Of the specific employment exclusions contained in state monetary eligibility statutes, those related to seasonal employment have received the most attention. Studies have focused both on simple measurement of the number of seasonal workers who collect UI and on the potential labor market consequences arising from the subsidization of such employment. The important early survey by Murray (1972) provided the impetus for much of this research. In that survey Murray reviews many of the studies that the states used in developing their regulations with regard to seasonal industries. Those studies tended to find that repeat use of UI was centered in seasonal industries—especially construction. Murray does not explicitly evaluate the allocational significance of this finding. Rather, he adopts the position that such receipt of UI is appropriate so long as workers continue to meet availability for work requirements (see chapter 4) during their off-seasons.

More recent concerns about the potential allocational effects of UI coverage of seasonal work have focused primarily on the impact of incomplete experience rating. Findings from large, nationwide data bases tend to confirm that more complete experience rating dampens seasonal fluctuations in labor demand, especially in construction and in durables manufacturing (Card and Levine 1994) and in retail trade (Anderson 1993). Generally, these studies do not take state seasonal exclusions explicitly into account, however, so that their implications for policy with respect to initial or continuing eligibility are not clear.

That eligibility provisions can have a major impact on a seasonal industry is perhaps best illustrated by the case of the Newfoundland fisheries. Extension of unemployment benefits (with relatively weak eligibility provisions) to the fisheries in 1957 had the effect of significantly expanding that industry (Ferris and Plourde 1982). Indeed the Newfoundland Royal Commission on Employment and Unemployment concluded that UI eligibility had created "pressure...to qualify as many people as possible for UI" and that this had become "the main form of income security in Newfoundland" (cited in Green and Riddell 1993a). Whether such dramatic results characterize isolated pockets in the more integrated labor markets of the United States is not known.

Nonmonetary Eligibility

Perhaps because of the complexities inherent in characterizing state nonmonetary eligibility provisions, research on the effects of such requirements is of modest proportions. A procedure followed by some researchers is to use nonmonetary disqualification rates as explanatory variables in regressions on outcomes such as UI claims. For example, Corson and Nicholson (1988) find that rising separation denial rates in the late 1970s may have accounted for between 2.4 and 24 percent of the decline in UI claims during the 1980s.[18] However, the use of denial rates in this way does not provide any direct means of inferring what the effects of changes in actual UI laws or administrative practices might be. Hence, the policy conclusions that might be drawn from such correlations are frequently ambiguous.

The most extensive study of the relationship between actual state practices and observed denial rates is by Corson, Hershey, and Kerachsky (1986). These authors use a pooled cross section, time series analysis for 51 UI jurisdictions over the period from 1964 to 1981. Although they do find a few statistically significant relationships, overall they encounter difficulties in differentiating between the explicit exclusionary effects of more stringent separation regulations (which, *ceteris paribus,* should increase denial rates) and the behavioral effects of such regulations on workers' willingness to claim UI benefits in the first place. For example, they find that states that deny benefits for the duration of the unemployment spell for voluntary leaving have *lower* denial rates than those with less stringent regulations, possibly because these provisions deter claims. On the other hand, they find that states that restrict good cause exemptions to employment related situations (a more stringent regulation) have higher denial rates. Hence, the authors' statistical analyses (and their detailed case studies of individual states) suggest caution in interpreting the meaning of observed UI denial rates and their possible correlations with other UI outcomes.

Similar ambiguities in the interpretation of data on administrative actions in the UI system characterize the recent paper by Vroman (1995b). In this paper, the author identifies two major trends in the aggregate data. First, although nonmonetary determinations have declined somewhat from their peak levels in the 1970s, appeals volume increased throughout the 1965-1993 period. Within these general trends, both determinations and appeals connected with employee misconduct have grown in relative importance, whereas actions involving voluntary quits have diminished. However, major differences among the states continue to exist in all of these measures, and reasons for such differences remain largely unexplained.

In the final sections of his paper, Vroman uses pooled data from fifty UI jurisdictions over the 1988-1993 period to examine UI appeals, especially those that are employer-initiated. His general goal is to determine whether possible increasing employer activism in contesting claims (sometimes with the use of UI service bureaus)[19] has had any measurable effect. Ultimately, however, the author is not able to measure such impacts accurately because of the overall complexity of the UI administrative structure and because his only measure of employer incentives, the Experience Rating Index (ERI[20]), has many shortcomings. Still, by providing a thorough and careful examination of this underused data set, Vroman sets forth a useful basis for future research into UI administration of nonmonetary eligibility determination.

With regard to the treatment of labor disputes, Hutchens, Lipsky, and Stern (1989) provide a detailed statistical analysis of the effect of state disqualification provisions on strike activity. As in other studies, they utilize a pooled cross section, time series analysis over the period from 1960 to 1974 and demonstrate that UI provisions have a clearly detectable effect on strike frequency (although no unambiguous impact on strike durations). Specifically, they find greater strike frequencies tending to occur in states that permit strikers to receive benefits if operations of their employers continue or in states that permit benefits to innocent bystanders; these results are especially found in states with generous UI programs.

Hutchens, Lipsky, and Stern also provide a detailed analysis of the 1981 strike by air traffic controllers, illustrating some of the complex ways in which the labor dispute provisions in UI laws interact with laws regulating misconduct disqualifications. Because the strike was technically illegal, most states took the position that their provisions regarding misconduct took precedence over labor dispute issues. In these cases, most controllers could collect UI only after a disqualification period. A few states (most notably Michigan) took the position that the strike was not sufficient in itself to warrant a misconduct disqualification and that normal labor dispute provisions in state law should take precedence. In these cases, the controllers were usually awarded benefits. This wide variety of outcomes, experienced by workers who were all in essentially the same position, highlights the increased fairness that might be achieved by moving toward more uniform nonmonetary eligibility provisions on a national basis.

Conclusion

This review of state provisions for initial eligibility for UI suggests four broad areas in which future research might aid in the formulation of policy.

- the usefulness of variable monetary eligibility requirements
- how monetary eligibility provisions affect the ability of workers in "nonstandard" employment situations to collect benefits

- relationships between seasonal exclusions and incomplete experience rating
- the desirability of moving toward more uniform nonmonetary eligibility requirements

Variable Eligibility Requirements

The minimum earnings required for UI eligibility are relatively modest in most states.[21] Although greater earnings are often stipulated if the worker is to qualify for maximum benefits or durations, these extra requirements are also quite modest in many cases. As discussed earlier in this chapter, little is known about the effects of these requirements or about their ability to target UI benefits to recipients in the most efficient ways. Policy makers have similarly made few attempts to explore the utility of tailoring monetary eligibility standards to meet specific policy goals. Two such adaptations are used frequently in other countries and might be more seriously considered for the United States: (1) varying eligibility standards in response to labor market conditions, and (2) tying the potential duration of benefits more closely to work history.

Basing eligibility standards on labor market conditions might achieve two goals. It would make the UI system even more responsive to the business cycle by increasing payments to those recession victims who have been laid off after only a short time on the job. This increased sensitivity might improve the economic stabilization properties of the regular UI system and (perhaps) mitigate some of the need for the adoption of emergency extensions during recessions. Reducing eligibility standards during periods of declining labor demand would also provide increased protection to newly hired workers when they most need it. This would, therefore, represent a way of providing greater insurance protection during periods of higher layoff risk in much the same way that extending UI potential durations provides increased protection against the lengthening unemployment spells experienced during recessions. Similarly, because of the strong procyclical behavior of quits, such a policy change might mitigate the need to monitor and adjudicate voluntary leaving issues.

There are several ways in which state UI systems could tighten the connection between potential durations and work history. Most obviously, states could adopt increasingly stringent base-period employment requirements if workers are to be eligible for maximum potential durations. This would further strengthen the notion of an "earned right" to more generous UI benefits. To the extent that prior employment tenure is correlated with workers' losses of job-specific human capital, such an approach would also be consistent with providing greater benefits to those who have suffered the greatest losses.

Any explicit use of employment history to target special re-employment assistance to displaced workers would probably require the use of a longer base period, however. That purpose is already served to some extent in the Trade Adjustment Assistance program by requiring certification of trade impact. Currently, such certification enables workers who can demonstrate that imports contributed to their unemployment to receive an additional 26 weeks of UI benefits following exhaustion, providing they agree to enter an appropriate training program. This has the effect of focusing benefits on workers with significant employment histories (Corson et al. 1993). Devising administrative methods for collecting longer base period employment information might provide a similar way of focusing longer UI potential durations on more general categories of displaced workers, especially those suffering major economic hardships.[22] Administrative costs associated with moving to longer base periods in the context of current UI data systems could be quite high, however.

Monetary Eligibility and Nonstandard Employment

Existing provisions for monetary eligibility are implicitly based on a "standard" model of employment in which a single employer certifies that the worker has had sufficient employment during the base period specified in state law. The employer usually must also certify that the worker meets nonmonetary eligibility provisions—most importantly, that he or she has been involuntarily laid off. As employment situations become increasingly diverse, this model may no longer be appropriate in many circumstances, including (1) regular, part-time employment; (2) temporary employment; and (3) self-employment or independent contractor status.

Current monetary eligibility standards tend to discriminate against those whose employment is part-time, especially for low-wage workers

(Advisory Council on Unemployment Compensation 1995). This approach may possibly have been acceptable in earlier times, when part-time work tended to be associated with weak labor market attachment. However, the rapid growth in flexible working arrangements has made such an assumption increasingly untenable. Deciding whether it is desirable to expand UI coverage to workers whose employment is primarily part-time involves a number of important trade-offs.

Although much early research tended to treat growth in part-time work arrangements as a labor supply phenomenon, more recent research focuses on the demand side of the market. Assuming that part-time and full-time workers are nearly perfect substitutes, an increasing use of part-time workers may be explained by a decline in their relative costs—especially because the hiring of such workers may involve lower levels of "quasi-fixed" costs (Oi 1962; Ehrenberg and Smith 1991). Whether the exclusion of low-wage, part-time workers from UI eligibility has contributed to this trend is not known. Given prevailing levels of UI taxation, such an effect does not seem implausible, however. Hence, relaxation of monetary eligibility requirements to increase the eligibility of part-time workers (this would primarily necessitate the relaxation of the requirements that most earnings occur in the high quarter) could have the effect of slowing the growth in such arrangements.

Reducing restrictions on part-time workers' access to UI might also pose administrative difficulties in assessing both initial and continuing eligibility. Certainly existing voluntary leaving statutes would have to be modified to develop clear standards about when a separation had actually occurred. In addition, continuing eligibility provisions would have to be adapted to meet the circumstances of individuals looking for part-time work. Making such changes does not seem to pose insurmountable problems, however, if the goal of providing increased protection to part-time workers were judged to be an important expansion of the safety net that UI provides.

The challenge in providing adequate UI coverage to workers in temporary employment centers on how job separations are to be defined. In this regard, the situation is similar to seasonal employment in that workers maintain some attachment to their jobs. In the seasonal case, it appears likely that UI coverage of gaps in employment will provide a clear subsidy to temporary jobs. From workers' perspectives, however, there may be somewhat more certainty associated with return to work at a seasonal job than with the assurance that a new temporary job will materialize. Hence, availability for work may be more difficult to appraise. Although anecdotal evidence suggests that regular, temporary employment may be on the increase, there is currently little data with which to estimate its relative importance or simulate possible effects of alternative UI eligibility criteria. For workers associated with temporary employment agencies or who work on a temporary basis for a single employer, it may be possible to devise eligibility standards based on past patterns of regular employment, but no state has as yet made any major moves in that direction.

As described in chapter 2, the most significant issue involving UI eligibility for ostensibly self-employed workers involves the potential misclassification of employees as independent contractors. Because firms can significantly reduce their liabilities for both taxes and fringe benefits through such a classification, it seems likely that it has been adopted for many workers in types of situations that meet IRS standards for "employment." Whether UI coverage is extended to such workers depends on future initiatives by the U.S. Internal Revenue Service.

For workers whose jobs are truly of a self-employed character, extension of UI coverage poses a number of thorny issues. Again, most of these focus on matters of nonmonetary qualification. Because the adversarial conflict between employer and employee cannot be relied upon in this situation to provide unbiased information about the nature of the job separation, some other mechanism must be found. California has experimented with interview-oriented procedures, but their implementation remains controversial—especially with regard to how the self-employed should have UI tax liabilities assessed.

Seasonal Exclusions

The statistical research reviewed in the previous section confirms that availability of unemployment benefits may significantly increase the seasonal sensitivity of employment, especially in the presence of incomplete experience rating. The majority of this research has paid relatively little attention either to the explicit seasonal exclusions in state laws or to the probably more important implicit seasonal exclusions created by the distribution criteria in state monetary eligibility standards. Hence, we have a very incomplete picture of how unemployment compensation and seasonal employment are related. A more comprehensive examination would require both an appraisal of how UI availability affects the level of employment in seasonal industries and how such availability affects seasonal wage premia. In the absence of a relatively full modeling of the total labor market impact of UI, it is difficult to determine whether the correct policy response to potential subsidies to seasonal industries is the adoption of more complete experience rating or appropriate modifications to explicit and implicit seasonal exclusions by states.

Uniformity in Nonmonetary Eligibility Requirements

The significant interstate variation in nonmonetary eligibility requirements surveyed earlier in this chapter raises the issue of whether potential gains in simplicity, efficiency, and fairness might be achieved by moving toward more uniform national standards. Some very preliminary moves in that direction have been made with regard to continuing eligibility conditions that apply to extended benefits (see Corson and Nicholson 1985). Very little has been done about regular UI, perhaps because of constitutional difficulties in implementing national standards, but existing differences may pose inequities for claimants who can find identical circumstances treated very differently (as illustrated by the air traffic controller case). More generally, differences in state nonmonetary eligibility provisions may have allocative significance both in terms of how local labor markets operate (the evidence from Green and Riddell (1993a), on local Canadian labor markets is quite convincing on this point) and in terms of the overall location of economic activity among the states. For example, it would be surprising if the significant effects of UI on strike activity found by Hutchens, Lipsky, and Stern (1989) had no impact on the willingness of some firms to locate in a state. Given the difficulties in characterizing state laws and procedures, however, relatively little is currently known about the likely size of such effects.

NOTES

I would like to thank Patricia Anderson, Walter Corson, Alec Levenson, Karen Needels, Chris O'Leary, and especially Craig Riddell, who offered a number of suggestions about ways in which this chapter could be improved. Participants in the conference "Unemployment Insurance in the United States," sponsored by the W. E. Upjohn Institute and the U.S. Department of Labor, also offered many thoughtful insights on this topic.

1. Eligibility requirements for the regular UI program also apply to programs for military personnel (UCX) and for federal employees (UCFE). They are also relevant to programs that require regular UI collection prior to participation, including regular extended benefits (EB), emergency extended benefits (FSB, FSC, and EUC), and trade adjustment assistance (TAA) benefits.

2. For a discussion of the evolution of pension offset legislation in UI laws, see chapter 12.

3. No state currently uses more than one year of labor market history in determining UI eligibility, although such provisions are relatively common in other countries (Congressional Research Service 1992).

4. The history of the notion of "fault" as it relates to job separations in both private and public UI systems is discussed in Blaustein (1993).

5. An annual summary of changes in state laws also appears in the *Monthly Labor Review.*

6. In some cases, mainly involving disabilities, the base period may be extended.

7. The six states that include an alternative base period in their eligibility provisions are Maine, Massachusetts, Ohio, Rhode Island, Vermont, and Washington.

8. Throughout this discussion, the fifty-three primary UI jurisdictions (fifty states, the District of Columbia, Puerto Rico, and the Virgin Islands) will be referred to as "states."

9. Other special exclusions in UI initial eligibility laws include students hired by their educational institutions, school employees during the summer months, and professional athletes during the off-season. Most states also disqualify self-employed earnings from conferring UI eligibility, although a few (for example, California) have experimented with limited inclusions of such earnings.

10. Other disqualification provisions relate to fraudulent misrepresentation and to the receipt of certain kinds of income, such as severance pay, workers' compensation, and pensions. These provisions will not be explicitly examined here.

11. Although "good cause" is defined in relationship to the employment situation, there is usually no necessary finding of employer "fault." In some states, good cause also includes situations where family obligations lead the employee to leave his or her job. These obligations can include leaving to marry, leaving to move with a spouse, and leaving to perform domestic obligations. In many cases, these inclusions relate only to initial eligibility, and standard provisions for continuing eligibility still apply. The situation of workers who leave employment because of pregnancy is quite complex, involving issues both of initial and continuing eligibility. For a discussion see Brown (1995).

12. These exemptions must also be understood in the context of the continuing eligibility provisions of states. For example, a worker who leaves to accept other employment would be eligible only if that new job did not work out and he or she is then found to be able and available for work.

13. A few states also reduce UI entitlements either by an amount equal to the number of weeks of disqualification or by a fixed percentage.

14. A simple regression using cross section data for 1993 suggests that similar results hold across the states. In this regression, each additional week of employment required for UI eligibility was estimated to be associated with a reduction of approximately 2 percent in the ratio of insured to total unemployment.

15. The Nicholson (1981) study of exhaustion rates does report that states with no distributional requirements in their monetary eligibility provisions have significantly lower exhaustion rates. A possible explanation is that such states make it easier for seasonal workers to qualify for benefits, and that those workers typically do not exhaust their UI entitlements.

16. For example, Corson, Grossman, and Nicholson (1986) find that approximately 4 percent of regular UI recipients were made ineligible for the Federal Supplemental Compensation (FSC) program by the adoption of such requirements.

17. Monetary eligibility in Canada is based on weeks of employment. A "week of employment" is defined as any week in which the individual works at least 15 hours for pay or in which he or she earns 20 percent of the maximum insured earnings. Voluntary quits also incur disqualifications in Canada. Unlike the United States, however, in some cases new entrants and reentrants are eligible for UI in Canada. Also, in Canada, UI taxes are not experience rated. For a summary of various issues related to the Canadian system, see Green et al. (1994) and Green and Riddell (1993b).

18.The wide range in estimated effects stems primarily from complications in interpreting the impacts of *falling* voluntary separation denial rates during this period. The authors see this trend as arising from increasingly clear and stringent voluntary leaving provisions being adopted by the states, although they admit to some ambiguity on the point. A simple cross section regression using recent data from the states shows a negative correlation between misconduct denial rates and UI claims, but no significant effect for voluntary leaving denials.

19. These service bureaus contract with firms to handle their UI-related activities. Frequently, such services are also provided by accounting companies that handle firms' other payroll needs as well. Because providers of such services may encounter substantial economies of scale in addressing technical issues related to UI eligibility, it is possible that they may have been effective in contesting claims in order to reduce their clients' UI tax liabilities. Although employers' use of these services has expanded rapidly in recent years (and utilization rates are concentrated geographically), there are no quantitative estimates of their overall impact on the UI claims process.

20. The ERI is defined as the ratio of fully charged UI benefits to total UI benefits paid. This measure varies both from state to state and over the business cycle for a variety of reasons, many of which are unrelated to the effective degree of experience rating for the typical firm.

21. Generalizing from the wide variety of state requirements is difficult: it does appear that most state minima fall well short of requirements in other countries, although many other countries also offer unemployment assistance to those with little or no employment history. For a summary, see Congressional Research Services (1990).

22. For an analysis, see Congressional Budget Office (1990).

References

Advisory Council on Unemployment Compensation. 1994. "Report and Recommendations." ACUC, February.
_____. 1995. "Unemployment Insurance in the United States: Benefits,
Financing, Coverage." ACUC, February.
_____. 1996. "Defining Federal and State Roles in Unemployment Insur-
ance." ACUC, January.
Anderson, Patricia M. 1993. "Linear Adjustment Costs and Seasonal Labor
Demand: Evidence From Retail Trade Firms," *Quarterly Journal of Eco-
nomics* 108, 4: 1015-1042.
Anderson, Patricia M., and Bruce D. Meyer. 1993. "Unemployment Insurance
in the United States: Layoff Incentives and Cross Subsidies," *Journal of
Labor Economics* 11, 1, part 2: S70-S95.
Atkinson, Anthony B., and John Micklewright. 1991. "Unemployment Com-
pensation and Labor market Transitions: A Critical Review," *Journal of
Economic Literature* 19 (December): 1679-1727.
Blaustein, Saul J. 1993. *Unemployment Insurance in the United States: The
First Half Century.* Kalamazoo, MI: W.E. Upjohn Institute.
Brown, Mark R. 1995. "Pregnancy and Unemployment: Problems and Solu-
tions," Unemployment Compensation: Continuity and Change Symposium,
University of Michigan Journal of Law Reform 29: 13-20.
Card, David, and Philip Levine. 1994. "Unemployment Insurance Taxes and
the Cyclical and Seasonal Properties of Unemployment," *Journal of Public
Economics* 53, 1: 1-29.
Chasanov, Amy B., and Eileen Cubanski. 1995. "Understanding Denials and
Appeals in the United States." *Advisory Council on Unemployment Com-
pensation: Background Papers,* Vol. 4. Washington, DC: ACUC, January.
Christofides, L.N., and C.J. McKenna. 1996. "Unemployment Insurance and
Job Duration in Canada," *Journal of Labor Economics* 14, 2: 286-312.
Congressional Budget Office. 1990. *Family Incomes of Unemployment Insur-
ance Recipients and the Implications for Extending Benefits.* Washington,
DC: CBO.
Congressional Research Service. 1990. "The Uncompensated Unemployed:
An Analysis of Unemployed Workers Who Do Not Receive Unemploy-
ment Compensation." 90-565 EPW.
_____. 1992. "Unemployment Compensation in the Group of Seven Nations:
An International Comparison." 92-622 EPW.
Corson, Walter, Paul Decker, Phillip Gleason, and Walter Nicholson. 1993.
International Trade and Worker Dislocation: Evaluation of the Trade

Adjustment Assistance Program. Princeton, NJ: Mathematica Policy Research.

Corson, Walter, Jean Grossman, and Walter Nicholson. 1986. "An Evaluation of the Federal Supplemental Compensation Program." Unemployment Insurance Occasional Paper 86-3, U.S. Department of Labor, Employment and Training Administration.

Corson, Walter, Alan Hershey, and Stuart Kerachsky. 1986. *Nonmonetary Eligibility in State Unemployment Insurance Programs: Law and Practice.* Kalamazoo, MI: W.E. Upjohn Institute.

Corson, Walter, and Walter Nicholson. 1985. "An Analysis of the 1981-82 Changes in the Extended Benefits Program." Unemployment Insurance Occasional Paper 85-1, U.S. Department of Labor, Employment and Training Administration.

_____. 1988. "Declining UI Claims During the 1980s: Causes and Policy Implications." Paper presented to the Tenth Annual Research Conference, Association for Public Policy Analysis and Management.

Ehrenberg, Ronald G., and Robert S. Smith. 1991. *Modern Labor Economics: Theory and Public Policy,* 4th Ed. New York: Harper Collins.

Feldstein, Martin. 1978. "The Effect of Unemployment Insurance on Temporary Layoff Unemployment," *American Economic Review* 68 (September): 834-846.

Ferris, J.S., and C.G. Lourde. 1982. "Labour Mobility, Seasonal Unemployment Insurance and the Newfoundland Inshore Fisher," *Canadian Journal of Economics* 15, 3: 421-441.

Green, Christopher, Fred Lazar, Miles Corak, and Dominique M. Gross. 1994. *Unemployment Insurance: How to Make It Work.* Toronto: C.D. Howe Institute.

Green, David A., and W. Craig Riddell. 1993a. "Qualifying for Unemployment Insurance: An Empirical Analysis." Department of Economics Working Paper, University of British Columbia.

_____. 1993b. "The Economic Effects of Unemployment Insurance in Canada: An Empirical Analysis of UI Disentitlement," *Journal of Labor Economics* 11, 1, Part 2: S96-S147.

Haber, William, and Merrill G. Murray. 1966. *Unemployment Insurance in the American Economy.* Homewood, IL: Richard D. Irwin.

Hutchens, Robert, David Lipsky, and Robert Stern. 1989. *Strikers and Subsidies: The Influence of Government Transfer Programs on Strike Activity.* Kalamazoo, MI: W.E. Upjohn Institute.

Munts, Raymond, and Ephraim Asher. 1980. "Cross Subsidies Among Industries from 1969 to 1978." In *Unemployment Insurance: Studies and*

Research 2. Washington, DC: National Commission on Unemployment Compensation.

Murray, Merrill G. 1972. *The Treatment of Seasonal Unemployment under Unemployment Insurance.* Kalamazoo, MI: W.E. Upjohn Institute.

Nicholson, Walter. 1981. "A Statistical Model of Exhaustion of Unemployment Insurance Benefits and Some Implications for Policy," *Journal of Human Resources* 16, 1: 117-128.

Oi, Walter. 1962. "Labor As a Quasi-Fixed Factor," *Journal of Political Economy* 70 (December): 538-555.

Rejda, George R., and David I. Rosenbaum. 1990. "Unemployment Insurance and Full Cost Experience Rating: The Impact on Seasonal Hiring," *Journal of Risk and Insurance* 57, 3 (September): 519-529.

Topel, Robert. 1990. "Financing Unemployment Insurance: History, Incentives, and Reform." In *Unemployment Insurance: The Second Half Century,* W. Lee Hansen and James F. Byers, eds. Madison: University of Wisconsin Press.

U.S. Department of Labor. 1994. "Comparison of State Unemployment Insurance Laws." Employment and Training Administration, Unemployment Insurance Service.

Vroman, Wayne. 1995a. "The Alternative Base Period in Unemployment Insurance: Final Report." Unemployment Insurance Occasional Paper 95-3, U.S. Department of Labor, Employment and Training Administration.

_____. 1995b. "Disputes Over Unemployment Insurance Claims: A Preliminary Analysis." In *Advisory Council on Unemployment Compensation: Background Papers*, Vol. 4. Washington, DC: ACUC.

CHAPTER 4

Continuing Eligibility
Current Labor Market Attachment

Patricia M. Anderson
Dartmouth College

While one of the objectives of unemployment insurance (UI) is to reduce the financial hardship of job loss, it was not originally designed to be simply a welfare program for the indigent: it was to be an earned right for workers who become unemployed.[1] Thus, the program requires not only that recipients demonstrate past labor market attachment but that they maintain that attachment. The exact requirements for continuing eligibility for UI differ across state programs but share certain common characteristics. Thus, in all states, claimants must demonstrate that they are able and available for work, and, in most states, they are required to undertake an active search for a new job. All states also impose a disqualification for refusal to accept an offer of suitable work, although the severity of the penalty varies. Additionally, states differ in their definitions of suitable and of able and available, as well as in deciding what constitutes an active search.

The variation in state approaches to the issue of continuing eligibility is testament to the fact that there is no one way that is clearly optimal. However, the costs and benefits of the different choices made are often evident, as are the considerations that are likely to affect these costs and benefits. The next section begins to explore the various state approaches to continuing eligibility, starting with the able and available for work requirement. This discussion is followed by an analysis of active search requirements, and the section concludes by looking at the varying definitions of suitable work. The subsequent section looks at state practices in disqualifications, beginning with the types of disqualifications imposed by the states and the trends in state laws regarding this issue. Some background on the determination and appeals process is also provided. In the last two sections, the determinants of differences across states in continuing eligibility practices and in denial and appeal rates are explored, and some conclusions and directions for further research are provided.

Work Search Issues

Able and Available for Work

A basic requirement for continuing eligibility for UI benefits is that the claimant be "able and available" for work. Such a stipulation may at first seem to be a straightforward application of the notion that UI is only for workers with a current labor market attachment. However, there are several areas of controversy. This fact is illustrated by the variation across states and over time in the definitions of able and available for work. While the line between ability and availability may appear somewhat fuzzy, the question of whether a claimant is *able* to work is essentially one concerning the physical or mental condition of the worker. Since the claimant must have recently been able to work in order to obtain monetary eligibility for UI, this issue often boils down to the treatment of temporary health conditions. As seen in table 4.1, eleven states have a special provision that claimants "are not ineligible if unavailable because of illness or disability occurring after filing a claim and registering for work if no offer of work that would have been suitable at time of registration is refused after beginning of such disability" (U.S. Department of Labor 1994a). Within this group, Massachusetts and Alaska limit the period of time for which this waiver is in effect, to three and six weeks, respectively. Also, North Dakota limits the waiver to illnesses not covered by workers' compensation.

There has been very little change in state laws regarding ability to work since the issue was reviewed by Haber and Murray (1966), who noted that in January of 1965 there were nine states with temporary illness provisions. It is interesting that there has been almost no increase in this number over the past 30 years, even though at that time the

Table 4.1 1994 State Provisions on Ability and Availability for Work

State	Special disability provision	Able and available for			Special student provision
		Any work	Suitable work	Usual work	
Alabama	No	No	No	Yes	No
Alaska	Yes	No	Yes	No	Yes
Arizona	No	Yes	No	No	No
Arkansas	No	No	Yes	No	No
California	No	Yes	No	No	Yes
Colorado	No	No	Yes	No	No
Connecticut	No	Yes	No	No	Yes
Delaware	Yes	Yes	No	No	No
District of Columbia	No	Yes	No	No	No
Florida	No	Yes	No	No	No
Georgia	No	Yes	No	No	No
Hawaii	Yes	Yes	No	No	No
Idaho	Yes	No	Yes	No	Yes
Illinois	No	Yes	No	No	Yes
Indiana	No	Yes	No	No	No
Iowa	No	Yes	No	No	Yes
Kansas	No	No	No	Yes	Yes
Kentucky	No	No	Yes	No	No
Louisiana	No	Yes	No	No	Yes
Maine	No	No	No	Yes	No
Maryland	Yes	Yes	No	No	No
Massachusetts	Yes	No	No	Yes	No
Michigan	No	No	No	Yes	No
Minnesota	No	Yes	No	No	Yes
Mississippi	No	Yes	No	No	No
Missouri	No	Yes	No	No	No
Montana	Yes	Yes	No	No	Yes
Nebraska	No	Yes	No	No	Yes
Nevada	Yes	Yes	No	No	No
New Hampshire	No	No	Yes	No	No

(continued)

Table 4.1 (continued)

| State | Special disability provision | Able and available for | | | Special student provision |
		Any work	Suitable work	Usual work	
New Jersey	No	Yes	No	No	Yes
New Mexico	No	Yes	No	No	Yes
New York	No	No	No	Yes	No
North Carolina	No	Yes	No	No	Yes
North Dakota	Yes	No	Yes	No	Yes
Ohio	No	No	Yes	No	Yes
Oklahoma	No	Yes	No	No	Yes
Oregon	No	No	Yes	No	No
Pennsylvania	No	No	Yes	No	No
Rhode Island	No	Yes	No	No	No
South Carolina	No	No	No	Yes	No
South Dakota	No	Yes	No	No	No
Tennessee	Yes	Yes	No	No	No
Texas	No	Yes	No	No	No
Utah	No	Yes	No	No	No
Vermont	Yes	Yes	No	No	No
Virginia	No	Yes	No	No	No
Washington	No	No	No	Yes	Yes
West Virginia	No	No	No	Yes	No
Wisconsin	No	Yes	No	No	No
Wyoming	No	Yes	No	No	No

authors commented that "the continued payment of unemployment compensation during a temporary illness, particularly when no suitable job is available, is on the side of realism and meets a real need" (pp. 266-267). It would appear, though, that the majority of states have determined that this need is not best met by the UI system. The fact that the system is experience rated may explain this outcome, providing an argument for instead providing a separately funded disability insurance program.[2] As was discussed by Haber and Murray, while the fact that the system is experience rated does not actually mean that employers will pay only for unemployment for which they are directly responsible, this general feeling remains among employers.[3] Thus, periods of nonwork due to illness or disability may be seen to be outside the purview of an experience-rated UI system. Even without experience rating, if the system is meant only to provide insurance against unemployment, then other causes of non-work would fall outside the scope of the system.

The treatment of availability for work is somewhat more varied than that of ability. As seen in table 4.1, while all states require some sort of availability, certain states qualify that requirement to mean available for suitable work, while others require only availability for work in the claimant's usual occupation. Clearly, availability for usual work is less strict than availability for suitable work, while both are more liberal than requiring availability for any work. In practice, though, availability is often determined either in the affirmative based on job search activity or in the negative by job refusal. Thus, further exploration of the implications of different approaches to defining the type of work for which a claimant is available will be postponed until after the consideration of refusal of suitable work.

One of the most discussed availability issues in the Haber and Murray study is almost a nonissue today—that of the availability of women. In 1960, the labor force participation rate for all women was 37.7 percent, and for married women it was just 31.9 percent. The concern at that time was that women were not truly unemployed, but rather were occupied with household duties and thus were not available for work. By 1992, though, participation rates had risen to 57.9 and 59.4 percent, respectively (Ehrenberg and Smith 1994). Thus, the assumption that women in general, and married women in particular, are only marginally attached to the labor market has become much less valid.

Also 37 states had special provisions for pregnant women in 1960, with several states disqualifying pregnant women for the duration of their unemployment. Others imposed disqualifications ranging from four weeks to four months before childbirth and up to three months following delivery (Haber and Murray 1966). Again, the understanding was that new mothers were busy with household duties and were not available for work. Similarly, pregnant women were simply assumed to be unable to work, no matter what the actual health status of the woman was or the type of job. Today, federal standards prohibit such wholesale disqualifications (Blaustein 1993). As noted by Haber and Murray, pregnancy is probably best treated simply as an ability-to-work issue, which will differ across specific women and jobs. As was the case when considering temporary disability, it then becomes a question of the proper role of the UI system, in which it may be reasonable to consider a separate system of maternity benefits.[4]

One current availability issue to which states take slightly different approaches revolves around geographic location. In some states, claimants are deemed unavailable for work any time that they are outside of a certain geographic area. For example, Illinois considers claimants to be unavailable if they move to an area where the opportunities are substantially less favorable than in the original locality. Oregon and Virginia both consider claimants to be unavailable if they leave their normal labor market for the major portion of the week, unless they can show that a bona fide work search was under way in the labor market in which their time was spent. Alabama, Michigan, Ohio, and South Carolina require that the claimant be available in the locality in which the base-period wages were earned, or in a locality where similar work is available or normally performed. Arizona simply requires that the claimant live in Arizona or in any other state or foreign country with which it has a reciprocal arrangement. A requirement that a claimant look for work where the jobs are seems reasonable, and many states implicitly impose similar requirements under the rubric of the active search requirement. However, strict geographic stipulations that are tied to the past employment situation may be counterproductive if conditions have changed. In such cases, the state law may prove to be an impediment to mobility and may thus lead to inefficiencies.

Perhaps one of the most interesting issues raised in considering availability requirements is the treatment of students or of other individuals undergoing training. Based on a simple test of availability, many, if not most, individuals in school or training would be considered ineligible for benefits. In 1960, only a handful of states had provisions under which individuals in approved training programs could be considered available. By January of 1966, however, 22 states had such provisions, stimulated at least in part by debates surrounding the Area Redevelopment Act and the Manpower Development and Training Act ([MDTA] Haber and Murray 1966). Today, in order to receive the normal tax credit under the Federal Unemployment Tax Act (FUTA), states must not deny benefits to otherwise eligible individuals attending an approved training course. Thus, all state laws contain such provisions, although states may use any standard to approve training courses. In most cases approved training includes only vocational or basic education, so that most regularly enrolled students remain unavailable (U.S. Department of Labor 1994a).

As was the case with temporary disability insurance or maternity benefits, one could argue that training allowances are best handled outside the UI system. In fact, the MDTA program did provide for such allowances. Additionally, Haber and Murray indicate that, based on experience rating concerns that have been discussed, some employers opposed the new training provisions enacted at that time. A possible key to understanding the difference in the treatment of the issues of training and disability may lie in recognizing the different long-term implications of each. Clearly, looser availability requirements result in more current benefit payments by the state. However, in the case of training programs, it is possible that the investment in human capital could result in more stable employment in the future, leading to benefit savings in the long run. Additionally, earnings increases due to this investment may raise state UI tax receipts, although this benefit will be limited due to the low UI taxable wage base.[5]

Several experiments have been undertaken that attempt to measure the impact of training programs on UI outcomes.[6] For example, in Texas, New Jersey, and Buffalo, New York, short-term (either on-the-job or classroom) training was offered to dislocated workers. None of these three demonstrations found a significant impact of short-term training on earnings or employment (U.S. Department of Labor 1994b). However, the Texas study looked only at the first year following training, while in Buffalo only the first six months were considered, so any possible long-term impacts would not be detected in these studies. Only the New Jersey experiment had a long-term follow-up, although in that case the evidence on the likelihood of long-run benefits (Anderson, Corson, and Decker 1991) was mixed.[7] While the earnings and UI experience of the Job Search Assistance (JSA)-plus-training group in New Jersey were not significantly different from the experience of JSA-only group in the four years following the experiment, only a small fraction of the JSA-plus-training group took up the offer of training. Although conclusions based only on those receiving training are likely to be contaminated by selection issues, there is evidence that UI receipt in the years following the initial claim was slightly lower for the training recipients, while earnings were to some extent higher.

Programs not targeted specifically at dislocated workers have shown somewhat more positive effects on earnings (U.S. Department of Labor 1994b). For example, experiments undertaken at the San Jose Center for Employment and Training (CET) found that training resulted in earnings gains averaging more than $1,000 per year. Similarly, evaluation of the Job Training Partnership Act (JTPA) indicated that adults had earnings gains in the second year after completing training that averaged around $850. In both cases, the training programs were determined to have been cost effective from a societal viewpoint. Thus, while the evidence is somewhat mixed overall, there does exist some support for the idea of long-run savings to the UI system from encouraging training receipt.

Considerations of such possible long-run benefits of training cannot be the whole story behind the favorable treatment of training programs by the UI system, however, since such benefits are likely to accrue from many types of human capital investment. In fact, there is mounting evidence on the growing importance of general education to labor market outcomes.[8] As stated previously, though, most states make no exception for regularly enrolled students. In fact, as seen in table 4. 1, many states have special provisions showing that students are ineligible while attending school, with seven states explicitly continuing that ineligibility during school vacation periods, when the claimant is arguably available for work. Many of the states do qualify the blanket ineligibility of students, however. For example, Kansas and North Carolina do not disqualify those in full-time work concurrent with their school attendance. Similarly, Minnesota, Nebraska, and North Dakota allow receipt for students if the major portion of their base-period earnings came from services performed while in school. Other states' exceptions are somewhat more restrictive. Thus, Ohio indicates that individuals who become unemployed while attending school and whose base-period wages were at least partially earned while attending school will meet the requirement if they are available for suitable employment on any shift. Oklahoma will not disqualify students if they offer to quit school, adjust class hours, or change shifts in order to secure employment.

Job Search Activity

As noted earlier, one indication of availability for work is the act of searching for work. All states require registration at a local employment office as evidence of job search. Most states additionally require that claimants undertake an "active search" for work. States differ in how this requirement is imposed, but typically claimants must provide evidence of employer contacts each week.[9] Additionally, after some period of unemployment, an eligibility review meeting with UI staff is often required. As noted by Haber and Murray, one possible drawback to such active search requirements is that they may "result in a great deal of wasted effort that is a nuisance to employers and demoralizing to the worker" (pp. 268-269). Nonetheless, the number of states with an active search requirement has increased from thirty in 1966 to forty in 1994. Several states (Michigan, Delaware, Maryland, New Jersey, and Virginia), do allow for flexibility in reaction to changing economic conditions. Similarly, the provision is not mandatory in several other states (Oklahoma, Vermont, Washington, and Wisconsin).

While one intention of work search requirements, like other continuing eligibility requirements, is to prevent the UI system from becoming a welfare program, an obvious side benefit may be to assist in the reemployment of unemployed workers. The question then arises as to what sort of requirements can best meet these dual goals. Several experiments have been carried out assessing the impact of different approaches to work search. As noted by Meyer (1995), since most of these experiments offered additional job finding services, as well as imposed additional job reporting requirements, it is difficult to untan-

gle whether it was the extra services or the tightened eligibility requirements that led to the observed outcomes. In general, the more intensive
treatments were found to have resulted in reduced UI receipt and
increased earnings that outweighed the increased administrative
costs.[10]

Only the Washington Alternative Work Search Experiment also
evaluated the effect of lowering the work search requirements. The
results from this demonstration indicate that abandoning an active
search policy would increase UI outlays by $265 per claimant, making
it unlikely that any savings from reduced monitoring costs would be
large enough to offset this amount. In fact, the administrative cost of
the most intensive reemployment services tested in Washington was
estimated to be only $14.50, while that treatment reduced UI payments
by $70 per claimant (Johnson and Klepinger 1994).

A second recent area of research concerns self-employment. For a
displaced worker, it is conceivable that the most productive reemployment option is self-employment. However, individuals in the process of
starting up their own business would not meet the requirements of
being available and searching for work. Thus, the search requirements
of the UI system may actually serve as an impediment to productive
employment in this case. Recently, demonstration projects were undertaken in Washington and Massachusetts to determine the impact of
allowing for at least some claimants continuing access to the UI system
while they are starting up their own business.[11] In both cases, treatment
group members were more likely to become self-employed. Additionally, the length of unemployment spells was reduced. However, only a
small number of claimants actually became self-employed, implying
that the overall effects on unemployment were negligible.

Based on the encouraging results of demonstrations such as these,
federal legislation was enacted in 1993 to allow for self-employment
assistance programs conditional on the provision of increased reemployment services. Under the North American Free Trade Agreement
Implementation Act, states are permitted to establish self-employment
assistance programs that allow selected claimants who are engaged in
establishing a business to continue to receive periodic unemployment
payments (Runner 1994).

Additionally, Public Law (P.L.) 103-152 was enacted in November
of 1993 and requires states to establish and implement a Worker Profil-

ing and Reemployment Services System. This law defines such a system as one that

> (A) identifies which claimants will be likely to exhaust regular compensation and will need job search assistance services to make a successful transition to new employment;
>
> (B) refers claimants identified pursuant to subparagraph (A) to reemployment services, such as job search assistance services, available under any State or Federal law;
>
> (C) collects follow-up information relating to the services received by such claimants and the employment outcomes for such claimants subsequent to receiving such services and utilizes such information in making identifications pursuant to subparagraph (A); and
>
> (D) meets such other requirements as the Secretary of Labor determines are appropriate.

The law adds a

> requirement that, as a condition of eligibility for regular compensation for any week, any claimant who has been referred to reemployment services pursuant to the profiling system under subsection (j)(1)(B) participate in such services or in similar services unless the State agency charged with the administration of the State law determines -
>
> (A) such claimant has completed such services; or
>
> (B) there is justifiable cause for such claimant's failure to participate in such services (U.S. Department of Labor 1994b, p. 18).

Thus, the law tightens continuing eligibility standards for claimants identified as likely to exhaust benefits by requiring them to participate in enhanced reemployment services.

These new programs are arguably the most significant changes to continuing eligibility requirements in quite some time. Unfortunately, it is too soon to evaluate their impacts. It will be interesting to study the effect of the laws, not only on claimants' unemployment durations and reemployment outcomes, but also on eligibility determinations. One would expect that P.L. 103-152 would increase disqualifications, as claimants who would otherwise have been eligible can now be disqualified due to a failure to participate in the new services. At the same time, the availability of self-employment assistance would reduce disqualifications. Clearly, following up on the impact of these programs will be of much interest in the future.

The discussion so far has focused only on the search activity of a permanently displaced worker, but an important source of wasteful search may be that undertaken by those who are awaiting recall.[12] Thus, several states make exceptions for these claimants. For example, Delaware, Michigan, Ohio, Arkansas, and Missouri each specify that a claimant is deemed available and actively searching if the employer notifies the agency that the layoff is temporary. The proper treatment of those who expect recall, but are not given an explicit recall date is perhaps less clear. On the one hand, a large fraction of those who expect recall are actually recalled.[13] However, recent studies have found that those whose expectations are incorrect have longer unemployment spells (Katz and Meyer 1990 and Anderson 1992, for example). In many ways, then, the treatment of those expecting recall may really be considered as part of the broader question of whether search requirements should be revised during the length of the claimant's spell. Since, in practice, most states incorporate such changes under the scope of defining what constitutes suitable work, it will be discussed in this context.

Refusal of Suitable Work

All states provide for disqualification due to a refusal of suitable work. The states differ, however, in their approaches to defining what is suitable and in the penalties imposed for a refusal. Because of concern for labor standards, FUTA requires all states to provide that

> compensation shall not be denied in such State to any otherwise eligible individual for refusing to accept new work under any of the following conditions:
>
> (A) If the position offered is vacant due directly to a strike, lockout, or other labor dispute;
>
> (B) if the wages, hours, or other conditions of the work offered are substantially less favorable to the individual than those prevailing for similar work in the locality;
>
> (C) if as a condition of being employed the individual would be required to join a company union or to resign from or refrain from

joining any bona fide labor organization (U.S. Department of Labor 1994a, pp. 4-9).

Beyond this, states are free to use any criteria to define the suitability of a job, with most states using such things as the degree of risk to the claimant's health, safety and morals; the physical fitness and prior training, experience, and earnings; the length of unemployment, and prospects for securing local work in a customary occupation; and the distance of the available work from the claimant's residence (U.S. Department of Labor 1994a).[14]

As was mentioned when discussing the role of recall, it is possible that unrealistic expectations can result in delays in reemployment. However, the problem is not restricted to recall expectations, but may also apply more generally to the case of a worker who is not well informed about the wage offer distribution. Several states explicitly incorporate this type of thinking into their statutes, broadening the definition of suitable work as the spell continues. Many states adjust the definition of suitability based on earnings, although the minimum wage supersedes any other lower bound. For example, after 25 weeks of benefits have been received in any year, Florida declares suitable any job that pays at least 120 percent of the individual's weekly benefit amount. North Dakota specifies that, after 18 weeks, any job paying wages equal to the weekly benefit amount will be considered suitable. Iowa lowers the amount of gross weekly wages required for a job to be considered suitable in a stepwise fashion. Thus, in the first 5 weeks it must be at least 100 percent of the individual's high-quarter weekly wage, but, in weeks 6 to 12, just 75 percent, followed by 70 percent in weeks 13 to 18 and then 65 percent after that.

Thus, if misinformation about the job market led the individual's reservation wage to be set too high, requirements such as these that quickly revise reservation wages downward may not result in earnings losses due to inefficient job matches. Additionally, there will be the clear short-term gains to the UI system from decreased benefit payments, due either to earlier job acceptance or to more disqualifications. However, to the extent that the individual's reservation wage was set appropriately, such requirements may lead to earnings losses and thus result in long-term costs. Evidence on the role of UI-induced changes in unemployment on reemployment earnings is somewhat mixed. Early studies, such as those by Ehrenberg and Oaxaca (1976), Burgess and Kingston (1976), Classen (1977), and Holen (1977), found generally positive effects of UI benefits on both duration and reemployment earnings. Such results would indicate that the subsidy to search provided by UI allowed claimants to obtain better jobs, and by extension would imply that there could be losses from earlier returns to work. However, recent evidence from several bonus experiments indicates that the shorter spells induced by the bonus did not come at the expense of lower earnings (Meyer 1995), tempering this conclusion.

The prediction of long-term losses from less search is also dependent upon the proposition that on-the-job search is significantly less efficient than search while not employed. The relative inefficiency of on-the-job search is a basic tenet of theoretical models of search unemployment, but the empirical evidence is mixed. For example, Gottschalk and Maloney (1985) note that about half of all job changers are never unemployed, implying that their job search was on the job rather than off. Additionally, Blau and Robins (1990) find that the offer rate per employer contact is higher for employed searchers than for unemployed searchers. These findings would then indicate that on-the-job search may be just as efficient if not more so than unemployed search. By contrast, though, Holzer (1987) finds evidence that at least among the young, unemployed search is more effective. Also, individuals do quit into unemployment (about 37 percent of voluntary separations according to Gottschalk and Maloney), which would indicate that there are advantages to unemployed search for these individuals. Thus, the issue remains unsettled.

Beyond making a decision on the definition of suitable work, states must determine what constitutes an offer and a refusal. For example, if a claimant walks past a store with a "Help Wanted" sign in the window, has a job been offered and refused? As noted by Haber and Murray, "it is generally agreed that it must be clear to the claimant that he is being asked to take a job, that the conditions of the job are specified, and that definite acceptance or rejection of the offer is required" (p. 291). Questionable situations may arise, however. For example, an offer may not be made because the employer finds the person to be unsuitable. Depending on the cause of this nonoffer, it may still be reasonable to disqualify the worker. If individuals deliberately sabotage their reemployment chances because they do not want to have to take the job, it is essentially equivalent to refusing an offer. Questionable situations such as these are typically considered on a case-by-case basis, so that in some instances it may be determined that an offer has in fact been refused, while in others it may be determined that a definite offer was not made.

Overall, the considerations that will affect the costs and benefits of different approaches to the definitions of suitable work and of an offer and a refusal are clear. However, given that the actual size of the relative costs and benefits remains undetermined, it is not surprising that the states have chosen to take many different approaches. No matter the definitions used, all states impose some type of disqualification once a determination has been made that an offer of suitable work was refused. Note that this is in contrast to the approach taken to ineligibility due to inability or unavailability for work. In those cases, payments are withheld for weeks in which the claimant is unable to work or is unavailable, but will be resumed when the condition changes. Refusal of suitable work instead leads to denial of benefits for a specific time period following the refusal, with determination of this time period differing across states. The next section will examine state approaches to disqualifications more closely.

Disqualification Practices

Types of Disqualifications

There are three main approaches taken by the states in imposing disqualifications for refusal of suitable work: disqualifying applicants for a fixed number of weeks, for a variable number of weeks, or for the duration of unemployment.[15] As seen in table 4.2, the majority of states (thirty-nine) disqualify claimants for the duration of unemployment, while only eight states impose a variable week disqualification, and just six states impose a disqualification of a fixed number of weeks.[16] The decision to impose a durational disqualification (as it is called), rather than a fixed or variable week disqualification, reflects a basic difference in assumptions about the source of unemployment. In limiting the length of the disqualification, a state is implicitly assuming that

Table 4.2 1994 State Provisions on Refusal of Suitable Work

State	Benefits postponed for		
	Fixed number of weeks	Variable number of weeks	Duration of unemployment
Alabama	No	1 - 10	No
Alaska	5	No	No
Arizona	No	No	Yes
Arkansas	7	No	No
California	No	1 - 9	No
Colorado	20	No	No
Connecticut	No	No	Yes
Delaware	No	No	Yes
District of Columbia	No	No	Yes
Florida	No	1 - 5	Yes
Georgia	No	No	Yes
Hawaii	No	No	Yes
Idaho	No	No	Yes
Illinois	No	No	Yes
Indiana	No	No	Yes
Iowa	No	No	Yes
Kansas	No	No	Yes
Kentucky	No	No	Yes
Louisiana	No	No	Yes
Maine	No	No	Yes
Maryland	No	5 - 10	No
Massachusetts	7	No	No
Michigan	6	No	No
Minnesota	No	No	Yes
Mississippi	No	1 - 12	No
Missouri	No	No	Yes
Montana	No	No	Yes
Nebraska	No	7 - 10	No
Nevada	No	No	Yes
New Hampshire	No	No	Yes

State	Fixed number of weeks	Variable number of weeks	Duration of unemployment
New Jersey	3	No	No
New Mexico	No	No	Yes
New York	No	No	Yes
North Carolina	No	5+	Yes
North Dakota	No	No	Yes
Ohio	No	No	Yes
Oklahoma	No	No	Yes
Oregon	No	No	Yes
Pennsylvania	No	No	Yes
Rhode Island	No	No	Yes
South Carolina	No	No	Yes
South Dakota	No	No	Yes
Tennessee	No	No	Yes
Texas	No	No	Yes
Utah	No	No	Yes
Vermont	No	No	Yes
Virginia	No	No	Yes
Washington	No	No	Yes
West Virginia	No	4+	No
Wisconsin	No	No	Yes
Wyoming	No	No	Yes

Benefits postponed for

after some period of time, general economic conditions are more responsible for the claimant's continued unemployment than is his or her earlier refusal of work. Additionally, this approach recognizes the fact that, in practice, the distinction between suitable and unsuitable work may be a fine one. This recognition is especially relevant to the case of variable week disqualifications, as it is possible to impose lower penalties in situations that seem particularly unclear. Recall, for example, the earlier discussion of difficulties that may arise in determining whether or not an offer has been made and refused.

By contrast, the assumption behind the use of durational disqualifications is that, had the claimants not refused the job, they would now be employed, and thus continued unemployment of any length should be considered voluntary and beyond the scope of the UI system. Most of the states imposing a durational disqualification also specify that a claimant must work a given amount of time or earn a certain amount before requalifying for benefits. In theory, then, the disqualification may last beyond the duration of unemployment and thus takes on a punitive characteristic. For example, consider a worker who at some point after being disqualified for a refusal accepts a new job. If the individual is then laid off from the new job prior to working long enough or earning enough to requalify, this new spell of unemployment will be uncompensated for as long as it lasts. In practice, however, the requirements for requalification are relatively low in most states, and thus the actual number of claimants affected in this way by such provisions is likely to be small. Perhaps more clearly punitive in nature is the practice of reducing benefits in conjunction with a disqualification. The reduction amount varies but is often set equal to the weekly benefit amount multiplied by the number of weeks of disqualification. Thus, in terms of future eligibility, it is as if the claimant collected benefits during the disqualification period.

As was the case with disability provision, the actual trends in state laws since 1966 have generally conflicted with the spirit of the discussion by Haber and Murray. At that time, they stated that "we would recommend against disqualification for the duration of unemployment in cases of refusal of suitable work" (p. 304). Despite such recommendations, the number of states using durational disqualifications along with requalifying requirements has grown substantially. In 1966, there were twenty-three states that disqualified a claimant for the duration of unemployment after a refusal of suitable work, while today that number has risen to thirty-nine. The tally of states reducing the number of weeks of benefits for which a worker is subsequently eligible has actually declined slightly, though, from 15 to 13. However, this is a fairly small change considering the strong statement by Haber and Murray: "Reduction or cancellation of benefit rights is punitive in character and has no proper place in an insurance program" (p. 305).

The Determination and Appeals Process

Given the severity of and possibly long-term consequences of disqualification, it is important to provide for an appeals process. In fact, federal law requires that there be an "opportunity for a fair hearing before an impartial tribunal, for all individuals whose claims for unemployment compensation are denied" (U.S. Department of Labor 1994a). All states allow not only individuals whose claims are denied, but also employers who have an interest, to appeal decisions on claims. Most states also provide for two appeal stages before cases can be taken to the state courts, with the decision of the first-stage appeals body being final in the absence of an appeal. Some states do allow for reconsideration of a decision within the appeal period, however. States are approximately evenly split between those that have a special board of review, board of appeals, or appeals board, and those where an existing commission or agency head handles appeals. In the former case, the members generally represent labor and employers, and, in some cases, the public. In the latter case, the appeals board is often the independent commission that administers the UI system in the state. Finally, all states also provide for judicial review by the courts, with the time limit generally ranging from 10 to 50 days.

Prior to the appeals stage, an initial determination was obviously made. The actual process of making a determination on whether an infraction has taken place is a multistep one. First, the state must identify that a situation exists requiring further investigation. The state then collects information on the circumstances from the claimant and from any other interested parties. This fact-finding procedure is followed by a formal hearing, during which the evidence is weighed and rules are interpreted as to how they apply to the case at hand. While these same basic steps are followed in all states, Corson, Hershey, and Kerachsky

(1986) find that there is significant variation across states in carrying out these procedures. The result is a wide variance in the number of determinations made in each state, and, ultimately, in the number of denials.

Given this variation, for some states the appeals process may be a key component of the system. Reliance on appeals may be especially common if the laws regarding continuing eligibility are exceptionally unclear or are administered in an inconsistent manner. Based on a survey of UI directors in each state carried out by the Interstate Conference of Employment Security Agencies (ICESA), the Advisory Council on Unemployment Compensation (ACUC) indicates that such problems are particularly likely in the case of refusal of suitable work. For example, while 42 states will consider a claimant to still be eligible if the refusal of suitable work is for "good cause," the survey reveals that the definition of good cause is generally determined on a case-by-case basis. Additionally, a follow-up survey of five states designed to assess the internal consistency of such determinations within a state found that three of the five states provided inconsistent responses to the question of refusal of suitable work. The ACUC goes on to note that "the general lack of published information regarding state nonmonetary eligibility conditions is likely to cause misunderstandings regarding nonmonetary eligibility. Such misunderstandings harm both claimants and employers, and also may place strains on resources of the UI system by causing additional appeals" (ACUC 1995).

In fact, total appeals have increased over threefold in the past twenty-five years or so, reaching 1.2 million in 1994 (ACUC 1996).[17] This growth took place both at the lower authority and higher authority level, but higher authority appeals have remained a fairly constant proportion of lower authority appeals over time. By contrast, the number of lower authority appeals has risen, not just in levels, but as a fraction both of initial claims and of total denials. A majority of appeals are filed over separation issues: nonseparation issues such as those discussed in this chapter made up just 33 percent of all appeals in 1994. On the other hand, nonseparation appeals as a percentage of nonseparation denials have doubled since 1971, increasing from 8 percent to 16 percent. Looking at the type of nonseparation issue, appeals related to both able and available for work and refusal of suitable work have fallen over this time period, while all other nonseparation appeals have increased.

Claimants continue to file appeals at a higher rate than do employers, but total employer appeals have increased in recent years. The rate of claimant appeals in 1994 was about the same as in 1983.[18] By contrast, the employer appeal rate doubled in that period. At the same time, the success rate of employers has been falling, both at the lower authority and higher authority level. It would seem, then, that employers have become more likely to appeal any given claim. Such behavior would be rational if either the costs of appealing had fallen or if the benefits of doing so had risen. One possible contributor to lower costs of appeal is the increased availability of third-party administrators, or so-called UI service bureaus. At the national level, these include such firms as the Frank Gates Service Company and the Frick Company. Similar services may also be provided by local associations. For example, the Employers Group (formerly the Merchants and Manufacturers Association and Federated Employers) provides human resources management to "nearly 5000 California private and public sector employers of every size and business classification" and lays claim to being "the nation's leading non-profit human resources management association."[19]

As is typical of UI service bureaus, the Employers Group offers to provide a multifaceted cost control program that covers six major activities: counseling, training, claims handling, auditing, analysis and reporting. Among other things, such UI service bureaus will take the lead in protesting claims and will provide representation at appeals hearings. These services are likely not only to reduce the cost of appeals (the service is generally covered as part of the overall agreement with the company) but may also increase the benefits if skilled representation raises the probability of a successful appeal. Studies of the appeals process provide somewhat mixed evidence on this proposition. Using 1994 data on appeals in Wisconsin, Ashenfelter and Levine (1995) find that retaining representation has no effect on the employer's success rate, although claimants who obtain representation are more likely to win. Kritzer (1995) comes to a similar conclusion, also with data from Wisconsin, but he notes that the most effective representation stems from expert knowledge of the UI system. Thus, service bureaus may be more successful than the average representative. It is important to realize, however, that there are significant differences across states in the total appeals rate, and thus the Wisconsin experience may not be typical. While less up to date, evidence in Rubin (1980), using over 11,000 appeals cases in twenty-four states from April of 1979, is supportive of these findings. Rubin concludes that, although claimants are more likely to win an appeal if represented, employers, on average, are actually less likely to win if represented. Each of these studies finds no significant overall benefit to employers of being represented, but the ACUC (1996) does find a positive effect for both employers and claimants.[20] While the evidence is weak for the positive benefits of representation, it still remains true that the costs of appeal are reduced via service bureaus, so we cannot dismiss the possibility that their increased use has affected the appeals procedure.

In sum, a recognition that there may be no "best" approach may well be the key factor in understanding why there appear to be so many differences across states in their approaches to the issue of continuing eligibility. For example, states face a precarious balancing act in setting policies on disqualifications for refusal of suitable work. A job that is clearly suitable for one individual may be just as clearly unsuitable for another individual. Thus, while there may generally be an advantage to explicit eligibility laws that are consistently applied, there is the real risk of losing the flexibility to deal with claimants as individuals, with the resultant determinations possibly being suboptimal. Consequently, we observe different practices and different outcomes across states. Possible determinants of this variation are considered in the next section.

Determinants of State Practices and Outcomes

Differences in State Continuing Eligibility Rules

While the costs and benefits of the various state strategies are fairly evident, it remains difficult to fully discern the causes of the differences in legislation across states. Some possible candidates include the political climate of the state, the level of experience rating, and the health of the state trust funds. It is hard to quantify such considerations, but some basic indicators of these state attributes are available. In an attempt to evaluate whether these types of factors seem promising as explanations of state differences in approaches to continuing UI eligibility, I estimated some very simple empirical models. Specifically, probit models were estimated on the probability of not having special disability laws, the probability of requiring availability for suitable, usual, or any work; the probability of having special student restrictions; and the probability of having variable, fixed, or durational disqualifications for refusal of suitable work.

The state characteristics used as explanatory variables are the average fraction of the state legislature that was Democratic over the 1980s, the fraction of that time period during which the governor was a Democrat, the average experience rating index (ERI) over the 1988-1992 period, and the state reserve ratio multiple (RRM) at both the peak (1989) and trough (1992) of the business cycle.[21] The political variables are meant to capture the inherent "liberalness" of the state and should be negatively related to stricter legislation. By contrast, the ERI should be positively related to stricter measures, since greater experience rating should increase employer opposition. The use of averages over past years is meant to be a proxy for long-run values of these attributes. The role of the RRM measures is slightly less clear, since stricter states are likely to see their reserves fall less quickly in a downturn, while states with generally lower reserves should be less likely to have more generous laws. It may be most appropriate, then, to think of the RRM at the peak as reflecting the adequacy of the state's reserves more generally, conditional on the RRM at the trough. Thus, the two measures are entered separately, rather than using an average, with the coefficient on the 1989 measure (the peak) generally being the one of most interest.

Table 4.3 presents the results of this exercise, along with a summary of the expected signs of the coefficients. For each of the models, a positive coefficient indicates that this state characteristic implies more severe provisions. Given the simplicity of this exploratory analysis, it is perhaps not surprising that the explanatory value of the models is generally low. Many of the coefficients are of the expected sign, although the majority of coefficients are not significantly different from zero.[22] Taking each of the basic state characteristics in turn, we see that having a Democratic governor is generally negatively related

Table 4.3 Exploring the Determinants of State UI Provisions

	Predicted sign of coefficient	No special disability provision (1)	Type of able and available (2)	Has special student provision (3)	Active search required (4)	Type of disqualification (5)
Democratic governor	(−)	−0.889	0.787	−0.487	−0.352	−0.285
		(0.823)	(0.670)	(0.701)	(0.792)	(0.809)
Democratic legislature	(−)	2.044	−0.480	−0.555	1.520	−3.003**
		(1.536)	(1.093)	(1.237)	(1.528)	(1.397)
Experience rating index	(+)	0.0122	−0.017	−0.008	0.023	0.010
		(0.030)	(0.024)	(0.024)	(0.031)	(0.029)
Reserve ratio multiple (1989)	(−)	−1.842	−0.809	−1.874*	−3.287**	−0.061
		(1.237)	(0.914)	(1.064)	(1.404)	(1.059)
Reserve ratio multiple (1992)	(+)	1.408	−0.092	1.345*	2.555**	0.348
		(0.934)	(0.670)	(0.758)	(1.018)	(0.822)
Number of observations		43	47	47	47	45
Pseudo R^2		0.112	0.119	0.077	0.216	0.141

NOTES: Positive coefficients imply increased severity of state provisions. Models (1), (3), and (4) are probit models on the presence of the named provision. Models (2) and (5) are ordered probits on the type of named provision. Standard errors are in parentheses. See the text for a complete description of explanatory variables. All models exclude Alaska, the District of Columbia, Hawaii, and Nebraska. Model (1) also excludes those states with separate disability programs. Model (5) also excludes states with combination provisions.
*Indicates significance at the 90% level, **at the 95% level.

to stricter state provisions, as expected. The one exception is that a Democratic governor is not negatively related to increasingly strict designations of the type of work for which an applicant must be able and available. Results are slightly more mixed for the impact of a Democratic legislature. There is a significantly negative effect on the probability of having stricter disqualification provisions for refusal of suitable work. The expected negative sign is also found for having a special student disqualification provision and for having increasingly strict designations of the type of work for which an applicant must be able and available, although these are not significantly different from zero. While still insignificant, the estimated impact of a Democratic legislature on the probability of not having a disability provision and on having an active search requirement is unexpectedly positive. Estimates of the effect of the state experience rating index are always insignificant, and the signs are also mixed. Only the peak reserve ratio multiple (1989) provides the predicted estimated effect for all five models. However, only the probability of having an active search requirement is significantly reduced. A corresponding, significantly positive effect on active search is estimated for the reserve ratio multiple at the trough (1992). While this exercise is suggestive of the types of state attributes that may be important, the overall results are disappointing and leave many questions unanswered.

Differences in Disqualification Rates

Not only do states take different approaches to setting the requirements for continuing eligibility for UI benefits, but there are significant differences across states in the determination of eligibility. Table 4.4 presents denial rates for able and available for work issues and for refusal of suitable work, by state, for 1982 and 1991.[23] In each case the rate is presented as the number of denials per 1,000 claimant contacts. The table also provides the mean and median denial rate for each year, as well as the standard deviation of the mean. Looking first at denials for able and available issues, the mean and median in 1982 are 5.4 and 4.9, respectively, but rates range from just 0.6 in Tennessee to 21.9 in South Dakota. In 1991, the mean and median are 5.9 and 4.3, respectively, and the range is similar to that of 1982, although now Utah registers the highest rate of 21.4, while Tennessee remains the lowest, at

**Table 4.4 State Disqualification Rates per 1,000 Claimant Contacts, 1982
and 1991**

State	Able and available		Refusal of suitable work	
	1982	1991	1982	1991
Alabama	3.6	3.4	0.1	0.2
Alaska	5.3	10.0	0.3	0.3
Arizona	10.2	11.5	0.3	0.3
Arkansas	5.7	7.0	0.3	0.3
California	6.4	8.3	0.2	0.2
Colorado	7.4	3.6	0.3	0.1
Connecticut	4.6	3.1	0.4	0.1
Delaware	1.9	4.9	0.2	0.2
District of Columbia	1.1	1.9	0.0	0.0
Florida	9.0	5.2	0.3	0.2
Georgia	5.2	4.8	0.1	0.2
Hawaii	6.1	9.1	0.4	0.5
Idaho	5.3	7.5	0.3	0.4
Illinois	4.5	2.8	0.2	0.2
Indiana	1.6	2.8	0.2	0.3
Iowa	6.8	3.3	0.2	0.2
Kansas	14.5	15.1	0.3	0.4
Kentucky	3.8	2.9	0.1	0.1
Louisiana	3.2	4.2	0.2	0.1
Maine	7.0	4.8	0.5	0.6
Maryland	2.3	5.0	0.3	0.2
Massachusetts	2.2	1.1	0.1	0.0
Michigan	4.0	2.5	0.2	0.2
Minnesota	6.9	3.6	0.2	0.2
Mississippi	2.8	5.1	0.2	0.6
Missouri	9.5	18.2	0.3	0.3
Montana	6.0	2.6	0.2	0.0
Nebraska	15.3	17.9	0.3	0.2
Nevada	6.0	4.3	0.4	0.4
New Hampshire	5.0	4.9	0.3	0.2
New Jersey	6.9	3.8	0.2	0.2

State	Able and available		Refusal of suitable work	
	1982	1991	1982	1991
New Mexico	2.8	5.0	0.1	0.2
New York	7.8	2.5	0.3	0.2
North Carolina	1.8	4.2	0.2	0.2
North Dakota	3.1	11.6	0.3	0.3
Ohio	4.7	1.9	0.1	0.1
Oklahoma	1.9	1.4	0.4	1.3
Oregon	4.9	5.5	0.3	0.3
Pennsylvania	2.2	2.2	0.1	0.1
Rhode Island	4.3	2.1	0.3	0.1
South Carolina	3.0	3.6	0.1	0.1
South Dakota	21.9	16.5	0.7	0.5
Tennessee	0.6	0.5	0.1	0.2
Texas	7.6	4.7	0.2	0.2
Utah	7.7	21.4	0.2	0.3
Vermont	1.8	1.8	0.2	0.3
Virginia	7.1	9.7	0.5	0.8
Washington	4.6	3.3	0.0	0.3
West Virginia	2.5	2.0	0.1	0.2
Wisconsin	1.4	4.9	0.2	0.4
Wyoming	5.8	8.7	0.0	0.4
Mean, Median	5.4, 4.9	5.9, 4.3	0.2, 0.2	0.3, 0.2
Standard Deviation	(3.9)	(4.8)	(0.1)	(0.2)

0.5. Overall, the variation across states in 1991 is slightly larger than in 1982.

A similar pattern is seen for the denial rate for refusal of suitable work, although the levels are much lower. In this case, the mean is 0.2 and 0.3 in 1982 and 1991 respectively, with a median of 0.2 in both years. Rates in 1982 range from negligible in the District of Columbia, Washington, and Wyoming to 0.7 in South Dakota. Similarly, in 1991, rates are negligible in the District of Columbia, Massachusetts, and Montana, but reach 1.3 in Oklahoma. As was the case earlier, the variation across states is slightly larger in 1991 than in 1982. There is, however, a strong correlation between denial rates in the two years within states. For example, as shown in table 4.5, the correlation between denial rates for able and available for work over the two years is 0.6927 and is significantly different from zero. Note that a correlation of 1 would imply that the two rates were identical, while a correlation of 0 would imply that there was no relationship across the two years. Looking at disqualifications for refusal of suitable work, there is a significant correlation of 0.5148 between the two years. There is also a correlation between the two different types of disqualifications within each year. This correlation is strongest in 1982, where it is 0.5699 and statistically significant. The correlation falls to 0.2190 in 1991 and is not significant at conventional levels.

Table 4.5 Correlations of State Denial Rates

	Able and available 1982	Able and available 1991	Refusal of suitable work 1982	Refusal of suitable work 1991
Able and available 1982	1.00	0.6927 (0.0000)	0.5699 (0.0000)	N.A.
Able and available 1991	--	1.00	N.A.	0.2190 (0.1225)
Refusal of suitable work 1982	--	--	1.00	0.5148 (0.000)
Refusal of suitable work 1991	--	--	--	1.00

NOTES: Probability of obtaining the estimated correlation if the true correlation was zero is given in parentheses. All correlations are calaculated based on the state denial rates shown in table 4.4.

These strong within-state correlations, combined with the large differences across states raise the question of what the key determinants of denial rates are. This topic is explored in some detail by Corson, Hershey, and Kerachsky (1986). They divide the factors likely to affect denial rates into five categories: (1) the characteristics of state laws, (2) the thoroughness of the administrative process in UI determinations, (3) the generosity of UI benefits, (4) the state of the economy, and (5) the general philosophy of the state towards UI claimants. Using quarterly data on denial rates by state from 1964 through 1981, they then estimate separate models for denials for able and available and for refusal of suitable work issues. In both models, state laws, other UI characteristics and external economic factors are used as explanatory variables.

Results from this exercise are generally disappointing, with only a few significant effects and some coefficients of the unexpected sign. For example, only the wage replacement ratio, insured unemployment rate, percentage insured unemployed in construction, percentage insured unemployed in manufacturing, and percentage men were significant in both cases, and, for refusal of suitable work, the presence of durational disqualifications was also significant. In all cases, each of these variables was estimated to have a negative effect on the denial rate. The negative effects of the composition of the insured unemployed were as expected, since these groups are more likely to be on temporary layoff and thus may be exempt from many of the requirements. The negative effect of the overall insured unemployment rate is supportive of the idea that in a weak economy there are fewer job offers to refuse. Its role in affecting denials for able and available issues is less clear. It may be that claims examiners are simply less likely to deny benefits when times are bad. Alternatively, active search requirements are often weakened during downturns, and able and available determinations are strongly influenced by findings on active search. Somewhat more puzzling is the role of the benefit replacement rate. The authors theorize that the replacement rate should enter positively, since more generous benefits should induce more marginally eligible people to make claims, and thus the negative effect can be considered surprising.

A similar model is estimated in ACUC (1996) on overall denials for nonseparation issues for states from 1978 to 1990, with correspondingly disappointing results. Only lower reserve ratios, lower unemployment rates, lower unionization rates, and unexpectedly shorter duration of UI benefits were significantly related to higher nonseparation denial rates. Thus, many significant across-state differences remain. Interestingly, some apparent regional patterns to the differences were found. For example, many of the states in the West have denial rates above what would be predicted from the model, while several states in the Southeast have denial rates below that predicted from the model. The study notes that similar behaviors by contiguous states may be interpreted either as cooperation or as competition among these states.

Corson, Hershey, and Kerachsky (1986) follow up their regression research with an in-depth process analysis carried out in six states. While the state-level regression models provide fairly unsatisfactory results, several conclusions emerge from this work. First, the authors find that a key factor is the rate at which states detect issues (referred to as making a determination), rather than the rate at which such determinations are denied. They then note that these determination rates "seem to reflect three general factors that vary from state to state: (1) the scope of work-search requirements and the methods used to monitor compliance; (2) the purposefulness and frequency with which claimants are questioned about ongoing eligibility issues; and (3) the consistency with which ongoing claims are reviewed." Additionally, they note that the organization of fact-finding and adjudication is likely to affect denial rates, with there being three main variable factors across states. These factors are identified as "the extent to which they insisted on conducting all fact-finding within the context of a recognized determination process," the "extent to which states relied on in-person interviews," and the extent to which the same staff person carried out both the fact-finding work and the adjudication.

While such conclusions are undoubtedly valid, they do not answer the more fundamental question of why there are such differences in these factors across states. As before, consideration of the costs and benefits of the approaches is likely to be informative. Many of the types of issues that should be considered have already been discussed in related contexts. For example, determination and denial rates are likely to be higher/lower if there are more/fewer requirements for continuing eligibility. Thus, the earlier analyses of special disability provisions, special student provisions, and of the definition of suitable work are applicable for ascertaining the likely costs and benefits of higher and lower denial rates. Few details are available on the administrative costs of the different approaches, although the work search experiments that were discussed provide some information. It is certainly likely, however, that the marginal cost of ferreting out every last ineligible claimant would vastly exceed the cost of maintaining such persons on the UI rolls. There may also be additional benefits from stricter enforcement in the form of deterrent effects. That is, unemployed individuals may not even apply if they think they will be denied UI benefits, although this form of deterrence is likely to be much more important for initial eligibility determinations than for continuing eligibility issues. However, Corson and Nicholson (1988) do find some significant effects of continuing eligibility variables on the ratio of the insured unemployment rate to the total unemployment rate. Similarly, Blank and Card (1991) find that the disqualification rate has a significantly negative effect on the take-up rate, as measured by the ratio of insured unemployment to initially eligible unemployment. It is likely, though, that the mechanism of the effect is through increased denials rather than via reduced applications for benefits.

Across-state differences in the rate of appeals of nonseparation issues have not been studied, but consideration of the results of analyses of total appeals may still be useful. The variation in appeals rates across states is large. ACUC (1996) notes that appeals as a percentage of denials as of 1994 range from highs of 73 percent and 56 percent in the District of Columbia and New Mexico, respectively, to lows of 4 percent and 5 percent in Nebraska and Idaho, respectively. As has generally been the case in this section, the results from attempts to explain such cross-state differences are somewhat disappointing. ACUC reports the results from regressions on appeals by employers and appeals by claimants, as well as on success rates by those groups, using state data for 1978 to 1990. While several variables are associated with higher appeals rates, the across-state differences remain significant. Again, there appears to be some geographic clustering, with a group of Midwestern states and a group of Southwestern states each exhibiting higher claimant appeals rates than would be expected. There is no sign of such geographic clustering in employer appeals rates. Similarly, several variables are associated with higher success rates, but the overall model fit very poorly. In this case, there was no apparent geographic clustering.

Conclusions

All states impose some sort of continuing eligibility requirements on UI recipients. While the specifics of the state laws vary, the basic requirements can be simply summarized. Claimants must demonstrate that they are able and available for work and generally must provide evidence of an active search for work. Benefits will be denied in any week that a claimant is unable to meet these requirements. Additionally, claimants may not turn down an offer of suitable work. Such a refusal will lead to a disqualification from benefits for not only that week, but for a specified number of weeks following the refusal. In many states, this disqualification is for the remainder of the unemployment spell. Exact procedures for denying benefits also vary by state, but, again, share common characteristics. Indications that continuing eligibility requirements are possibly not being met are investigated, and, following this fact-finding process, a formal hearing takes place. The determination may then be appealed, with most states providing two levels of appeals. If the appeals process has been exhausted, the determination may be brought to civil court for judicial review.

The absence of standardization across states appears to reflect the reality that there is no single approach that is clearly dominant in all aspects. Rather, there are costs and benefits attendant to the different approaches, and these costs and benefits are likely to vary across states. Another consideration is that the costs and benefits of the various approaches may fall on different segments of the population. It is well known that the political process can generally not be relied upon to provide the socially optimal result, even with the assumption of "one man, one vote" and truthful revelation of preferences. Given the even more likely scenario of differential political influence of the interested groups, the probability of not all of the states implementing the optimal legislation rises dramatically. Thus, a significant source of variation across states may well be differences in the political process.

Empirical analyses that attempt to pin down sources of variation in state laws, and in denials and appeals for continuing eligibility issues have generally provided disappointing results. Descriptive, yet in-depth, analyses of specific states have tended to be more successful at pointing to major causes of differences across states. These two observations are not inconsistent, since the descriptive analyses tend to pin-point factors that are difficult to quantify and thus have been excluded from the simpler empirical exercises. Overall, a deeper understanding of the issues that must be considered when deciding among the different approaches is likely to provide the most useful information on the variance across states. Consequently, the main focus of this chapter has been on discussing these issues and on discussing the most recent evidence relating to the likely costs and benefits of the choices made by the states.

While legislative change has generally been fairly slow, recent years have seen a marked acceleration in the adoption of new legislation on continuing eligibility. First, we have seen some states adopt a self-employment alternative to the work-search requirement. Second, all states have now begun to implement a profiling system. As part of this profiling system, some workers will be required to participate in reemployment services in order to maintain eligibility for benefits. Each of these changes was influenced by the results of random assignment experiments estimating the costs and benefits of different approaches. Careful testing of proposed legislation of this type is to be commended and encouraged. Additionally, study of the results of the actual implementation of these programs should be a high priority in the future.

NOTES

I thank Phil Levine, Chris O'Leary, and Henry Felder for their comments on earlier drafts of this chapter.

1. See Blaustein (1993) for a complete discussion of the evolution of the UI system in the United States.

2. The question of whether such insurance should be privately purchased or publicly provided is beyond the scope of this chapter. Note that an additional five states (California, Hawaii, New Jersey, New York, Rhode Island and Puerto Rico) run a separate disability insurance program that provides benefits for workers unable to work due to nonwork-related disability.

3. Pages 285 to 288 discuss this issue in detail. For the most part the points raised remain valid today.

4. As before, the question of whether these should be privately purchased or publicly provided is beyond the scope of this chapter.

5. The federal taxable wage base is currently just $7,500, although states can and do set higher levels. Chapter 8 of this volume discusses this issue in more detail.

6. Meyer (1995) reviews the UI experiments in general, although training issues are not discussed in depth.

7. See the full report for more details on the design and implementation of the experiment.

8. Levy and Murnane (1992) review the evidence for increasing earnings differentials among college-educated and noncollege-educated workers. Additionally, estimates of the return to education rise anywhere from 13 to 19 percent in studies using instrumental variables techniques to adjust for measurement error. For example, see Card (1993) and Butcher and Case (1994).

9. States differ in the mechanics of certifying continuing eligibility. Often, a claimant must send in a postcard on a regular basis. This practice can have interesting repercussions. For example, in Illinois—and many other states—the claimant must file every two weeks. As a result, analysis of the Illinois bonus experiment revealed that the hazard spikes every two weeks. See, for example, Meyer (1988) and Levine (1991).

10. See Meyer (1995) for more details on the design and outcomes of each of the experiments, which took place in Charleston, South Carolina and in New Jersey, Washington, Nevada, and Wisconsin.

11. Detailed discussions of the genesis of these demonstrations can be found in Wandner (1992), and a summary of the results is in Benus, Wood, and Grover (1994).

12. One should note, though, that requiring even claimants expecting recall to search may provide some benefits: individuals may enter into a more productive and/or more stable job match than the one to which they expect to be recalled.

13. According to a study by Katz and Meyer (1990), this fraction is almost 72 percent.

14. See U.S. Department of Labor (1994a) for more specific information regarding the stipulations made by different states.

15. For the case of variable week disqualifications, the exact number of weeks is set at the time the determination is made.

16. Florida and North Carolina have aspects of both variable and durational disqualifications and thus are each counted twice.

17. All of the statistics on appeals presented in this section are from ACUC (1996).

18. Note that this discussion refers to both nonseparation and separation issues, since the two were not reported individually. However, the majority of employer appeals concern separation issues. Also, for claimant appeals of nonseparation issues, the state is often the secondary party to the dispute, rather than the employer.

19. All quotes from the Employers Group are taken from their Web page at http://www.hron-line.org/info/info.htm.

20. This study uses the same basic data as the other studies from Wisconsin, but the source of the difference is difficult to pinpoint. It does appear that a lower percentage of the appeals from this study are coded as having representation, and that the total number of appeals is slightly higher.

21. Anne Case and Tim Besley provided me with the political variables (see Besley and Case 1994), while the ERI and reserve ratio multiples were obtained from Vroman (1994, tables 5 and 3), respectively. Since Nebraska has an atypical state legislative structure, it is excluded from the analysis.

22. A rule of thumb for determining statistical significance is that the reported coefficient be at least twice as large as the reported standard error.

23. I would like to thank Walter Corson for providing me with the rates for 1991. The 1982 rates are from table 2.1 in Corson, Hershey, and Kerachsky (1986).

References

Advisory Council on Unemployment Compensation. 1995. "Unemployment Insurance in the United States: Benefits, Financing, Coverage." ACUC, February.

_____. 1996. "Defining Federal and State Roles in Unemployment Insurance." ACUC, January.

Anderson, Patricia M. 1992. "Time-varying Effects of Recall Expectation, a Reemployment Bonus, and Job Counseling on Unemployment Durations," *Journal of Labor Economics* 10, 1: 99-115.

Anderson, Patricia, Walter Corson, and Paul Decker. 1991. "The New Jersey Unemployment Insurance Reemployment Demonstration Project Follow-up Report." Unemployment Insurance Occasional Paper 91-1, U.S. Department of Labor, Employment and Training Administration.

Ashenfelter, Orley, and Phillip B. Levine. 1995. "Unemployment Insurance Appeals in the State of Wisconsin: Who Fights and Who Wins?" Mimeo, Wellesley College.

Benus, Jacob, Michelle L. Wood, and Neelima Grover. 1994. "Self-Employment as a Reemployment Option: Demonstration Results and National Legislation." Unemployment Insurance Occasional Paper 94-3, U.S. Department of Labor, Employment and Training Administration.

Besley, Timothy, and Anne Case. 1994. "Unnatural Experiments? Estimating the Incidence of Endogenous Policies." NBER Working Paper No. 4956, National Bureau of Economic Research.

Blank, Rebecca M., and David E. Card. 1991. "Recent Trends in Insured and Uninsured Unemployment: Is There an Explanation?" *Quarterly Journal of Economics* 106, 4: 1157-1190.

Blau, David M., And Philip K. Robins. 1990. "Job Search Outcomes for the Employed and Unemployed," *Journal of Political Economy* 98, 3: 637-655.

Blaustein, Saul J. 1993. *Unemployment Insurance in the United States: The First Half Century*. Kalamazoo, MI: W.E. Upjohn Institute.

Burgess, Paul L., and Jerry L. Kingston. 1976. "The Impact of Unemployment Insurance Benefits on Reemployment Success," *Industrial and Labor Relations Review* 30, 1: 25-31.

Butcher, Kristin F., and Anne Case. 1994. "The Effect of Sibling Sex Composition on Women's Education and Earnings," *Quarterly Journal of Economics* 109, 3: 531-564.

Card, David. 1993. "Using Geographic Variation in College Proximity to Estimate the Return to Schooling." NBER Working Paper No. 4483, National Bureau of Economic Research.

Classen, Kathleen P. 1977. "The Effect of Unemployment Insurance on the Duration of Unemployment and Subsequent Earnings," *Industrial and Labor Relations Review* 30, 4: 438-444.

Corson, Walter, Alan Hershey, and Stuart Kerachsky. 1986. *Nonmonetary Eligibility in State Unemployment Insurance Programs: Law and Practice.* Kalamazoo, MI: W.E. Upjohn Institute.

Corson, Walter, and Walter Nicholson. 1988. "An Examination of Declining UI Claims During the 1980's." Unemployment Insurance Occasional Paper 88-3, U.S. Department of Labor, Employment and Training Administration.

Ehrenberg, Ronald G., and Ronald L. Oaxaca. 1976. "Unemployment Insurance, Duration of Unemployment, and Subsequent Wage Gain," *American Economic Review* 66, 5: 754-766.

Ehrenberg, Ronald G., and Robert S. Smith. 1994. *Modern Labor Economics: Theory and Public Policy.* New York: HarperCollins.

Gottschalk, Peter, and Tim Maloney. 1985. "Involuntary Terminations, Unemployment, and Job Matching: A Test of Job Search Theory," *Journal of Labor Economics* 2: 109-123.

Haber, William, and Merrill G. Murray. 1966. *Unemployment Insurance in the American Economy: An Historical Review and Analysis.* Homewood, IL: Richard D. Irwin.

Holen, Arlene. 1977. "Effects of Unemployment Insurance Entitlement on Duration and Job Search Outcome," *Industrial and Labor Relations Review* 30, 4: 445-450.

Holzer, Harry J. 1987. "Job Search by Employed and Unemployed Youth," *Industrial and Labor Relations Review* 40, 4: 601-611.

Johnson, Terry R., and Daniel H. Klepinger. 1994. "Evaluation of the Impacts of the Washington Alternative Work Search Experiment," *Journal of Human Resources* 29, 3: 695-717.

Katz, Lawrence F., and Bruce D. Meyer. 1990. "Unemployment Insurance, Recall Expectations, and Unemployment Outcomes," *Quarterly Journal of Economics* 105, 4: 973-1002.

Kritzer, Herbert M. 1995. "The First Thing We Do, Let's Kill All the Lawyers (or at Least Replace Them All?): Lawyers and Nonlawyers as Advocates." Mimeo, University of Wisconsin.

Levine, Philip B. 1991. "Testing Search Theory with Reemployment Bonus Experiments: Cross-Validation of Results from New Jersey and Illinois." Working Paper, Wellesley College.

Levy, Frank, and Richard J. Murnane. 1992. "U.S. Earnings Levels and Earnings Inequality: A Review of Recent Trends and Proposed Explanations," *Journal of Economic Literature* 30, 3: 1333-1381.

Meyer, Bruce D. 1988. "Implications of the Illinois Reemployment Bonus Experiments for Theories of Unemployment and Policy Design." NBER Working Paper No. 2783, National Bureau of Economic Research

_____. 1995. "Lessons from the U.S. Unemployment Insurance Experiments," *Journal of Economic Literature* 33, 1: 91-131.

Rubin, Murray. 1980. "The Appeals System. "In *Unemployment Compensation: Studies and Research,* Vol. 3, Washington, DC: National Commission on Unemployment Compensation.

Runner, Diana. 1994. "Changes in Unemployment Insurance Legislation in 1993," *Monthly Labor Review* 117, 1: 65-71.

_____. 1995. "Changes in Unemployment Insurance Legislation in 1994," *Monthly Labor Review* 118, 1: 60-64.

U.S. Department of Labor. 1994a. "Comparison of State Unemployment Insurance Laws." Employment and Training Administration, Unemployment Insurance Service.

_____. 1994b. "The Worker Profiling and Reemployment Services System: Legislation, Implementation Process and Research Findings." Unemployment Insurance Occasional Paper 94-4, Employment and Training Administration.

Vroman, Wayne,. 1994. "Some Issues in Financing Unemployment Insurance." Mimeo.

Wandner, Stephen A. ed. 1992. "Self Employment Programs for Unemployed Workers." Unemployment Insurance Occasional Paper 92-2, U.S. Department of Labor, Employment and Training Administration.

CHAPTER 5

Adequacy of the Weekly Benefit Amount

Christopher J. O'Leary
W.E. Upjohn Institute for Employment Research
Murray A. Rubin
Consultant

Overview

The unemployment insurance (UI) system was established to alleviate the distress and hardship caused by involuntary unemployment. Through weekly benefit payments to eligible claimants, the system helps maintain living standards during active job search. The adequacy of the weekly benefit amount in performing the income maintenance function can be gauged by the percentage of lost income that benefits replace. More directly, adequacy depends on how the weekly benefit contributes to maintaining usual levels of household expenditure.

When the federal-state UI system was established in the depths of the Great Depression, benefit levels were set at amounts widely regarded as adequate in terms of income replacement. Due to rapidly rising wage levels, by the end of World War II, UI benefit levels came to be viewed as inadequate. Since that time there has been continuing controversy over what the level of benefits should be and how the system should operate to provide these benefits.

Criticisms—that benefits are either inadequate or excessive—regularly surface during legislative considerations of benefit changes at both federal and state levels. Advocates of more generous benefits as well as proponents of benefit cutbacks can usually find support for their cause from research studies conducted over the years. During the 1950s and 1970s, benefit adequacy studies indicated that benefit ceilings were too low to allow many unemployed workers, particularly those with dependents, to meet basic expenses. On the other hand, studies of claimant job search behavior done over the past twenty years have focused on how the mere availability of unemployment benefits tends to cause substantial numbers of claimants to delay their return to work. Much of the history of the program, at both federal and state levels, reflects efforts to resolve in one way or another the inherent conflict in the UI program's main objective of providing adequate income replacement.

Over the years, a widely held view has formed that the weekly benefit amount should be high enough to sustain a worker and family without their having to resort to public welfare assistance, but that benefits should not be so high as to undermine the incentive to return to work. There has been little agreement on the specifics of how this principle should be implemented. For example, there is concurrence that the benefit should be wage related, but states differ widely in how they measure past wages, the amount of wages to be replaced by the benefits, and the highest amount of benefits that should be payable. There is disagreement also on such issues as to whether the benefit should represent a higher percentage of the wages of lower-paid workers and whether benefits should be increased for claimants who have dependents. These issues are the subject of this chapter.

The Right to Unemployment Benefits

The UI system was designed to be completely separate from depression-era relief programs, with eligibility determined by labor force attachment and benefit levels based on prior earnings experience. No stigma is related to the receipt of UI, which provides "compensation for wage loss as a matter of right, with dignity and dispatch . . . during periods of involuntary unemployment due to lack of work" (Blaustein 1993, p. 47).

UI presumes need due to the economic loss resulting from unemployment, while general relief programs require demonstration of need often to include the shedding of personal assets. The idea of basing benefits on demonstrated need was rejected at the outset so as to preserve the dignity of workers who find themselves in financial distress due to involuntary job loss, and to maintain the insurance nature of the program.

It may be that UI would generate less controversy if the objectives of the benefit amount were to relieve instead of to prevent poverty; if benefits were payable only to those unemployed who were clearly in need; and if the benefit amount were based on a calculated minimum budget somewhat above the poverty level for specific family sizes. On the other hand, one of the strengths of the UI system, which has generated widespread support, is the potential availability of benefits to virtually all workers who face the risk of layoff.

Federal law has been regularly interpreted as prohibiting states from establishing an income or means test as a condition for benefits.[1] Numerous state proposals to base benefits on factors other than unemployment and claimants' past work and wage experience have been successfully challenged as violative of the federal prohibition against using unemployment funds for purposes other than to pay "compensation," defined in federal law as cash payments (solely) with respect to unemployment (Dahm and Fineshriber 1980, pp. 84-87).

For example, proposals to require a longer waiting period for claimants with base-period earnings in excess of a specified amount have been rejected as introducing an element of need even though no means test was involved. A similar reaction awaited a variety of other proposals to introduce elements other than work experience as a basis for benefits: to establish stiffer qualifying requirements for claimants with working spouses; to reduce the severity of disqualifications for claimants with dependents; to increase benefits for individuals who are their family's principal support; to establish a schedule of lower benefits payable to higher-wage claimants.

A change from a program of wage-related benefits, payable as a matter of right without a means or income test, to a needs-based program would sacrifice a principle that is still vital to many. It would also alter a basic UI objective—from preventing poverty to alleviating poverty.

Wage-Related Benefits

Ideally, unemployment benefits should be sufficient to provide for a worker and family during a period of temporary unemployment without requiring drastic cuts in their standard of living. Since income and living standards vary widely among workers, an identical benefit amount for everyone would be too high in relation to some claimants' living standards and wholly inadequate for others. Nor is it a practical alternative simply to key each worker's benefit directly to the level of those expenditures that constitute the individual's living standard.

Ordinarily, living standards are established by income levels, which depend in most cases on earnings from employment. Therefore, a benefit amount directly related to wages will usually be related also to living standards. Moreover, a wage-related benefit reinforces the concept that UI is an earned right, based on contributions required by law to be paid by the worker's employer as "insurance premiums" against the risk of unemployment. A wage-related benefit will not improve a low standard of living caused by low income. The benefits merely support whatever standard of living was established by the claimant's wages. The benefits will also not support a sumptuous living standard created by a high income. Since UI is a *social insurance* program with the fundamental social aim of preventing widespread poverty, UI maximum benefit rates are imposed in all states to conserve funds so as to spread resources as widely as is practical.

There has never been much controversy in the United States over tying benefits to prior earnings. This practice is at odds with the eighty-year British custom of paying a *flat rate* benefit to all eligible claimants. This distinction is particularly surprising since so much else was borrowed from the British system. A flat rate for all has certain advantages. It can be keyed to an objectively established subsistence level— or accommodate any other objective desired; it is relatively simple to administer, easily adjustable, predictable, and easy to understand. It requires no means test, and it ensures an income floor for all unemployed who qualify.

The United States, and most other countries with UI systems, chose a different route. In every state in the nation, the amount of the weekly unemployment benefit is related to the unemployed worker's former wage. A uniform flat benefit for all recipients, regardless of the level at which it was set, was never considered feasible for the United States. This was partly because wage-related benefit precedents had been established, particularly in Wisconsin, but also because substantial regional, interstate, and area wage variations precluded the establishment of a flat sum that would be adequate, by any measure, for even a majority of beneficiaries. The flat benefit is also inappropriate where wage levels vary greatly within the same locality.

Replacing One-Half of Lost Wages

Since the beginning of the federal-state UI program in the United States, there has been general acceptance of the idea that the weekly benefit should replace one-half of the worker's lost weekly wages. There is little historical evidence concerning the 50 percent concept, but it appears that the idea initially became established primarily through the influence of the first UI law in Wisconsin.[2] Preliminary versions of the Wisconsin statute called for a flat-rate benefit, but, in the early 1930s, the idea of a wage-related benefit evolved. The only antecedent offering guidance about the rate of wage replacement was the workers' compensation program, wherein two-thirds of former earnings were usually replaced. While this seemed reasonable for workers who had lost the physical capacity to work, it was viewed as excessive for those required to be able and available for work. Furthermore, it was feared that two-thirds wage replacement would substantially diminish the incentive to actively seek work. One-half wage replacement was chosen as the natural alternative; the ratio was also selected because it was easy to understand and administer.[3] The Committee on Economic Security (1935) and the Social Security Board (1936) both recommended that benefits replace one-half of full-time weekly earnings. By 1938, all states had benefit rules that applied this principle.

The ratio suggested by the Social Security Board (1938) for consideration by the states was 50 percent of the unemployed worker's *full-time* weekly earnings. Reports on full-time wages were difficult to obtain from employers, particularly for workers with variable work and pay patterns. For this and other reasons, states increasingly began to approximate weekly wages on the basis of quarterly wage data. A few states have implemented an annual wage formula, which makes the weekly benefit a percentage of annual wages and thus departs entirely from a weekly wage-based benefit.

Most states now set the weekly benefit as a fraction of the claimant's earnings in the high quarter or two highest quarters of the base period in which the claimant earned the most. Most high-quarter formulas apply the 50 percent wage replacement concept by establishing the weekly benefit amount as half of 1/13 of the earnings of that quarter (or 1/26 of the high-quarter wages) on the assumption that the high quarter reflects full-time employment for all 13 weeks of the quarter.

While the principle of replacing 50 percent of lost wages has been widely accepted, many states now approximate a slightly different replacement rate. Currently, several states provide a basic weekly benefit amount equal to over 54 percent (1/24 or more of high-quarter wages), and a few states provide under 50 percent—not counting the states using the annual wage formula.

Some benefit formulas are weighted in favor of lower-paid workers. These workers' weekly benefits represent a higher percentage of their normal wages than do benefits payable to higher-wage workers. This is based on the idea that lower-paid workers generally spend a greater proportion of their income for necessaries than do others. Other states pay allowances for claimants' dependents, thereby also deviating from the 50 percent rule. The ceiling all states put on the weekly benefit amount is another exception to the 50 percent rule.

One-Half for Four-Fifths

The percentage of the beneficiary population eligible for one-half wage replacement depends on the level of the benefit maximum. In his January 1954 Economic Report to Congress, President Eisenhower recommended

> that the states raise the dollar maximums so that the payments to the *great majority* of the beneficiaries may equal at least half their regular earnings (Haber and Murray 1966, p. 180).

Soon thereafter, the goal was stated more clearly by the Federal Advisory Council on Employment Security which recommended that the maximum should be from 60 percent to 67 percent of the statewide average weekly wage. This was based on an estimate by Professor Richard Lester of Princeton University that the maximums in the original state laws would have been the equivalent of from three-fifths to two-thirds of average weekly wages in manufacturing in 1939. In that year, only 25.8 percent of claimants received the maximum benefit amount, indicating that the great majority of beneficiaries received 50 percent wage replacement.

The Kennedy and Johnson administrations recommended a benefit standard in their legislative proposals for UI, including a maximum weekly benefit equal to at least two-thirds of the statewide average weekly wage in covered employment. The same two-thirds recommendation was included in the Nixon administration's 1973 UI proposals, on the grounds that this would meet the goal of providing "at least four-fifths of the Nation's insured workforce half-pay or better when unemployed" (Becker 1980, p. 4).

Evidence on Wage Replacement Standards

From the earliest days of UI in the United States, there has been a presumption that if half of lost wages were replaced there would be the right balance between compensation for lost income and the incentive for return to work. This section begins with a review of the fraction of lost wages that has actually been replaced by the UI system on average over the years. This is followed by a review of constructive studies of benefit adequacy that have been done to estimate the appropriate level of wage replacement. The research is divided into five groups: household expenditure studies that estimate the spending habits of families at risk of unemployment, optimal UI studies that mathematically model ideal UI systems, consumption smoothing studies that examine the degree to which household spending patterns change due to unemployment, compensating wage differentials studies that analyze how wages differ depending on the risk of unemployment, and finally studies of what full unemployment compensation would be based on the economic theory of choice by the consumer-worker.

Aggregate Wage Replacement Ratios

While most states have benefit formulas intended to replace approximately one-half of lost wages, the maximum on payments guarantees that many high-wage workers will receive less than half their average lost earnings, and the minimum means that some low-wage workers may receive more than half their average earnings. The data in table 5.1 summarize the national historical experience on benefit adequacy using a very aggregate measure—the average wage replacement ratio (WRR). The national average WRR is defined by

$$WRR = \frac{\sum_{i=1}^{n} WBA_i / n}{\sum_{j=1}^{m} WE_j / m}$$

where WBA_i = the weekly benefit amount received by the ith UI recipient, n = the number of UI recipients, WE_j = the weekly earnings of the jth covered worker, and m = the number of workers covered by UI.

In the first few years of UI, earnings of covered workers were quite low, the WRR was quite high, and there was little controversy about the adequacy of the weekly benefit amount. Leading up to U.S. involvement in World War II, average weekly wages of UI covered workers gradually rose, causing the WRR to fall. This continued until 1945 when the WRR spiked up to reach 0.416 when first UI payments jumped from only half a million the previous year to over 2.8 million. In 1945, as the first postwar transition layoffs occurred among the average base-period earnings of claimants was dramatically higher for displaced workers with recent histories of high wages and long hours. Following this, as figure 5.1 shows, the WRR trended downward through the early 1950s. Since that time, the WRR has ranged between 32 and 37 percent, being approximately 36 percent in recent years.

**Table 5.1 Average UI Weekly Benefit Amount (WBA) in Dollars
and Wage Replacement Ratio (WRR) in the United States,
1938-1995**

Year	WBA	WRR	Year	WBA	WRR
1938	10.94	0.431	1967	41.25	0.347
1939	10.66	0.408	1968	43.43	0.343
1940	10.56	0.391	1969	46.17	0.344
1941	11.06	0.366	1970	50.31	0.357
1942	12.66	0.353	1971	54.35	0.365
1943	13.84	0.336	1972	55.82	0.361
1944	15.90	0.359	1973	59.00	0.361
1945	18.77	0.416	1974	64.25	0.365
1946	18.50	0.396	1975	70.23	0.371
1947	17.38	0.346	1976	75.16	0.371
1948	19.03	0.341	1977	78.71	0.364
1949	20.48	0.360	1978	83.67	0.364
1950	20.76	0.344	1979	89.68	0.361
1951	21.09	0.322	1980	98.95	0.364
1952	22.79	0.330	1981	106.61	0.359
1953	23.58	0.323	1982	119.34	0.371
1954	24.93	0.335	1983	123.59	0.368
1955	25.04	0.321	1984	123.47	0.353
1956	27.02	0.333	1985	128.23	0.351
1957	28.17	0.335	1986	135.72	0.357
1958	30.54	0.353	1987	139.74	0.352
1959	30.41	0.334	1988	144.91	0.348
1960	32.87	0.352	1989	151.76	0.355
1961	33.80	0.354	1990	161.56	0.361
1962	34.56	0.349	1991	169.88	0.364
1963	35.28	0.346	1992	173.64	0.354
1964	35.96	0.338	1993	179.69	0.369
1965	37.19	0.338	1994	181.53	0.361
1966	39.76	0.347	1995	187.30	0.363

SOURCE: U.S. Department of Labor (1992). Figures for 1993 and 1994 averaged from the four quarterly issues of *UI Data Summary,* U.S. Department of Labor.

Figure 5.1 also shows a general upward trend in the WRR since about 1950. Controlling for the changing occupational mix of UI claimants, Hight (1980) arrived at lower bound estimates of a 0.10 to 0.29 percent increase in the WRR per year over the 1950-1977 period. He concluded that there have been some real gains in adequacy over these years. Table 5.2 lists the WRR for each state in 1994. While the national WRR was 36.05 percent in 1995, WRRs across the states ranged from a low of 26.1 percent in California to a high of 52.8 percent in Hawaii. A total of fifteen states had WRRs greater than 40 percent in 1995.

Presumably, the WRR is used as a rough gauge of benefit adequacy because the data needed to compute it are readily available. It is the main measure of benefit adequacy regularly reported by the U.S. Department of Labor.[4] However, the WRR as computed by the preceding formula is a bit misleading. The denominator in the WRR considers wages for the entire population of covered workers, while the numerator considers only payments to beneficiaries. Properly, we should examine benefit payments relative to lost earnings of beneficiaries.

Vroman (1980), who provided a comprehensive review of possible wage replacement rate computations, called the series presented in figure 5.1 and tables 5.1 and 5.2 a "gross narrow wage replacement ratio." Vroman (1980, p. 170) also cited criticism that the measure underestimates the "true" replacement ratio because "unemployed workers receive lower wages than the average worker covered by the program." Using unpublished micro data on the actual pre-unemployment earnings of beneficiaries from Illinois, Michigan, Pennsylvania, Texas, Washington, and Wisconsin for various periods during the 1980s, the Advisory Council on Unemployment Compensation (1995, p. 138) estimated that the gross narrow wage replacement ratio understates the actual replacement rates by 25 to 30 percentage points.

The dramatic difference in wage replacement ratio estimates computed by the rather misleading gross narrow WRR formula and those produced using micro data on actual benefits and prior earnings convinced the Advisory Council on Unemployment Compensation (1995, p. 21) to recommend the following:

> The U.S. Department of Labor should calculate and report the actual replacement rate for individuals who receive Unemploy-

Figure 5.1 Aggregate Average Wage Replacement Ratio (WRR) in the United States, 1938-1995

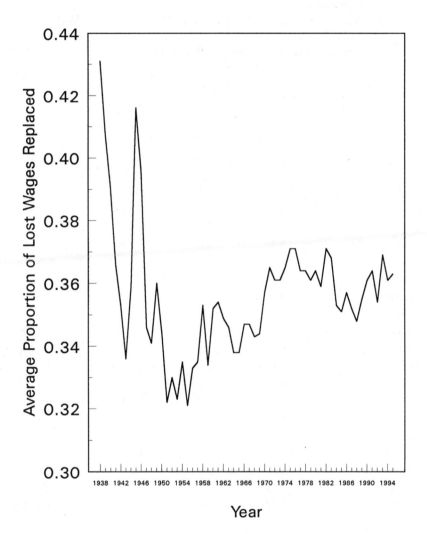

Table 5.2 State Wage Replacement Ratio (WRR), 1995
    State Maximum Weekly Benefit Amount (MaxWBA) in dollars,
     January 1996
    Max WBA as a Fraction of State Average Weekly Wage
     (AWW), 1996
    and Any Statutory Rule for MaxWBA as a Percentage of AWW

State	WRR	MaxWBA	MaxWBA/ AWW	Statutory rule (%)
Alabama	0.303	180	0.393	
Alaska	0.279	212	0.342	
Arizona	0.310	185	0.386	
Arkansas	0.410	264	0.645	66 2/3
California	0.261	230	0.392	
Colorado	0.393	272	0.528	55
Connecticut	0.318	350	0.519	60
Delaware	0.350	300	0.537	
District of Columbia	0.316	359	0.490	50
Florida	0.366	250	0.532	
Georgia	0.323	205	0.409	
Hawaii	0.528	347	0.678	70
Idaho	0.404	248	0.573	60
Illinois	0.361	251	0.436	49.5
Indiana	0.366	217	0.445	
Iowa	0.445	224	0.513	53
Kansas	0.435	260	0.578	60
Kentucky	0.374	238	0.532	55
Louisiana	0.267	181	0.398	66 2/3
Maine	0.380	202	0.463	52
Maryland	0.342	250	0.460	
Massachusetts	0.395	347	0.560	57.5
Michigan	0.377	293	0.500	58
Minnesota	0.436	303	0.579	60-66 2/3
Mississippi	0.336	180	0.451	
Missouri	0.312	175	0.358	
Montana	0.415	228	0.594	60
Nebraska	0.368	184	0.432	
Nevada	0.374	237	0.467	50

State	WRR	MaxWBA	MaxWBA/ AWW	Statutory rule (%)
New Hampshire	0.291	216	0.426	
New Jersey	0.382	362	0.547	56 2/3
New Mexico	0.358	212	0.496	50
New York	0.310	300	0.448	
North Carolina	0.407	297	0.638	66 2/3
North Dakota	0.429	243	0.628	60
Ohio	0.384	253	0.493	
Oklahoma	0.405	247	0.580	50-60
Oregon	0.374	301	0.612	64
Pennsylvania	0.412	352	0.661	66 2/3
Puerto Rico	0.312	133	0.452	50
Rhode Island	0.449	324	0.644	67
South Carolina	0.364	213	0.480	66 2/3
South Dakota	0.387	180	0.480	50
Tennessee	0.316	200	0.421	
Texas	0.365	252	0.492	
Utah	0.430	263	0.590	60
Vermont	0.369	212	0.472	
Virginia	0.338	208	0.414	
Virgin Islands	0.365	214	0.480	50
Washington	0.392	350	0.671	70
West Virginia	0.387	290	0.652	66 2/3
Wisconsin	0.414	274	0.570	
Wyoming	0.425	233	0.552	55

SOURCE: U.S. Department of Labor (1995a and 1995b).

ment Insurance. This replacement rate should be calculated by dividing the weekly benefits paid to individuals by the average weekly earnings paid to those individuals prior to unemployment (1995, p. 21).[5]

Vroman (1980, pp. 170-172) reported that some researchers using micro data have arrived at very high net WRR figures. Feldstein (1974), who was concerned with the adverse incentive effects of UI, estimated that the net wage replacement ratio is often more than 70 percent. Munts and Garfinkel (1974) found replacement rates in Ohio in 1971-1972 to range from 0.38 to 0.89 for several distinct types of family units. Corson et al. (1977) determined the average ratio of benefits to lost wages in 1977 to be 0.66.

However, when broader measures of macro wage replacement that consider uncovered workers and noncompensated weeks are computed, replacement rates are much lower. For example, Gramlich (1974) found that during the 1970-1971 recession, UI replaced only 6 to 8 percent of lost earnings for families headed by men, and 14 to 18 percent for families headed by women. While the gross narrow WRR for 1971 was 0.363, Edgell and Wandner (1974) estimated the macro replacement rate for UI in the U.S. economy to be as low as 20 percent.

The wage replacement ratio estimates produced in the 1970s also varied because of differential treatment of taxes in the computations. This was a very important issue prior to the 1986 federal income tax changes that placed income received as unemployment compensation benefits in the same tax category as income from labor earnings.

Household Expenditure Studies

The adequacy of a wage-related benefit is difficult to measure. The unemployment benefit does not guarantee anyone an adequate minimum standard of living: it provides partial wage replacement. The unemployed low-wage worker whose income was insufficient to maintain any but the barest living standard can count on only a minimum benefit (if he or she manages to qualify at all) providing an even leaner existence. For the unemployed wage earner whose income is high but whose family responsibilities are heavy, the maximum weekly benefit amount may often cover only a small portion of expenses. However, the same benefit amount may adequately cover not only necessities but also many incidentals for a single wage earner with a paid-off mortgage and few financial obligations.

In the early 1950s, when most claimants were unable to receive a 50 percent wage replacement because of low maximums, the pressure to raise maximums was often resisted by allegations that many claimants did receive a benefit equal to about half their take-home pay. No firm evidence was available to indicate how claimants were actually managing on their benefits while unemployed. As a result, the U.S. Department of Labor financed a series of UI benefit adequacy studies.

The results of these studies have been summarized by Becker (1961), Lester (1962), and Haber and Murray (1966). Becker (1980), while discussing the principles that should underlie any proposal for a federal benefit standard, reviewed the evidence from research in Tampa, Florida (1956), Anderson, South Carolina (1957), Albany, New York (1957), Portland, Oregon (1958), St. Louis, Missouri (1958), and Utica, New York (1958). These six similar studies were based on retrospective data on the income and expenditures of respondents during the period just prior to the survey date. Expenditures were divided into deferrable and nondeferrable categories. Spending on food, clothing, medical care, and housing constituted the nondeferrable group. Information was gathered on four household types. After examining these studies, Becker concluded that

> [n]one of the states came close to the proposed goal of paying 80 percent of the beneficiaries half or more of their gross wage . . . [and i]t is one of the weaknesses of the system that claimants without dependents' are treated much better than claimants with dependents (1980, p. 26).

He suggested that benefit adequacy could be generally improved if benefit maximums were raised and programs for dependents' allowances were expanded.

Becker (1961) found that benefits amounted to two-thirds or more of the income of unemployed single beneficiaries, more than 50 percent of family income for families with one wage earner, and about 40 percent for families with two wage earners. The 1950s studies demonstrated the usefulness of the one-half wage norm for assessing benefit adequacy. On average, benefits that were half or more of the wage were sufficient to cover nondeferrable expenses for all claimant household types (Becker 1980, p. 13).

The deferrable/nondeferrable distinction used in the 1950s studies was expanded by Blaustein and Mackin (1977). They added expenditures made on a regular basis to repay outstanding debt to outlays for food, clothing, medical care, and housing, and labeled this total as "recurring" expenses. Using this concept as a basis for evaluating UI benefit adequacy, they found that over two-thirds of the beneficiary households in South Carolina had adequate income in 1977. Nonetheless, they recommended increasing benefit maximums to improve adequacy.

Burgess, Kingston, and Walters (1978a, 1978b), who conducted a detailed benefit adequacy study in Arizona, expanded the Blaustein-Mackin definition of recurring expenses to include expenditures on transportation, insurance, regular services, and regular support payments. They labeled this concept "necessary and obligated" expenses and used it to assess benefit adequacy for seven recipient household types.

Burgess, Kingston, and Walters showed a wide disparity in how closely benefits came to meeting the ten groups of necessary and obligated expenses for different categories of beneficiaries. As in the previous studies, the two most important factors, in addition to the weekly benefit amount, in determining the economic condition of the family during unemployment were the number of members to be supported and the number who were contributing to the support. Benefits were most adequate for recipients who had no other household members and who lived with relatives: 44 percent received a benefit equal to 100 percent or more of their share of the ten categories of necessary and obligated expenses. The next most adequate category consisted of husband and wife units in which both members worked. For 23.4 percent, the benefit amount represented 100 percent or more of expenses.

Benefits were least adequate in situations where the recipient was the only earner in a household with three or more persons. For only 2.3 percent did the weekly benefit amount cover 100 percent or more of their expenses. For a majority of this category (56.1 percent), the benefit was half or less of the expenditures.

The low maximum weekly benefit amount was the principal reason for the disparity in the benefit-expense ratios among the different categories of Arizona beneficiaries studied. Sole wage earners, in households with two or more members including a spouse, generally had the highest wages and, consequently, were most often cut off by the maximum. For those individuals, the weekly benefit amount—usually the $85 maximum—was less adequate than for any other category of beneficiary.

The expenditure studies essentially consider benefit adequacy in terms of the extent to which gross wages or take-home pay are replaced for claimants at different income levels. A 1988 Congressional Research Service benefit adequacy study established three hypothetical claimants (each married with two children) at three preunemployment wage levels: low wage (102 percent of the 1986 poverty threshold for a four-person family); average wage (state 1986 average weekly wage for workers in covered employment); high wage (four times the 1986 poverty threshold for a four-person family). Benefits were calculated according to each state's provisions as of January 1, 1988. States were ranked from that with the highest replacement rate to the lowest (Congressional Research Service 1988, pp. 210-248).

Optimal Unemployment Insurance

Baily (1978) and Flemming (1978) originated theoretical, optimal UI models. The models are similar in that both attempt to solve for characteristics of the UI system that would maximize the expected lifetime utility of a representative worker. The UI program choice parameters for this problem are the wage replacement rate and the potential duration of benefits. Both Baily and Flemming assume an infinite potential duration of benefits, and each determines that optimal replacement rates are in the range of those provided by the states. Baily finds that

> [if the] degree of relative risk aversion by workers [is] unity, and if workers do not prolong their duration of unemployment very much as a result of UI payments [i.e., if the elasticity of a spell of unemployment with respect to a change in the benefit amount is about 0.15] then if the benefit-wage ratio is 50% it is about right (1978, p. 393).

The elasticity of unemployment with respect to the benefit amount assumed by Baily (1978) is in line with estimates summarized in chap-

ter 7. Flemming qualifies his statements with capital market considerations concluding that, under perfect capital markets, a replacement
rate of 50 percent is too high, and "[i]f there is no lending or borrowing
the optimal rates rise to about 75 percent (1978, p. 403)."

Davidson and Woodbury examine optimal UI with "an equilibrium
search and matching model calibrated using data from the reemployment bonus experiments and secondary sources" (1996, p. BB-4). As
did Baily and Flemming, they find that, if potential UI duration were
infinite, replacement rates should optimally be 50 percent. However,
Davidson and Woodbury also estimate that, if potential duration is limited to the standard 26 weeks, then the UI system should optimally
replace all of lost earnings.

Consumption Smoothing

An indirect way of assessing the adequacy of existing UI benefit
replacement is to investigate how workers' customary consumption
patterns change when they become unemployed. That is, would consumption decline appreciably during periods of unemployment in the
absence of UI benefits? Alternatively, is personal saving the real foundation for consumption smoothing, with UI simply acting to reduce the
dissaving that would naturally occur during periods of unemployment?

Grossman (1973), using data from the six state studies of UI benefit
adequacy done in the 1950s under the sponsorship of the U.S. Department of Labor, addressed the expenditure response to unemployment
for different categories of household members. Applying an allocation
of time model of consumer-worker behavior, he predicted that, in an
effort to maintain real income, people who become unemployed would
increase consumption of goods that involve relatively more home-
based production activity. Grossman found that the unemployed do
substitute leisure for market goods in an attempt to maintain customary
consumption levels, but that the response to unemployment of *secondary market workers* is much greater than for the primary earner in a
household.[6] He suggested that, as the labor force changes to include a
greater share of secondary workers, the transitory component of aggregate consumer expenditure would increase.

Hamermesh also studied how UI affects the pattern of consumption.
He concluded that UI benefits only partly help to smooth consumption

during periods of lost earnings due to unemployment, and that as much as half of the benefits received are spent as if "individuals were fully able to borrow or had sufficient savings to meet transitory losses of income without any disruption in their consumption spending." From this he argues that a "large part of UI benefits does little to stabilize the economy, because people consume them as if they were fully expected" (1982, pp. 110-111).

More recently, Gruber estimated that, in the absence of UI, average consumption expenditure by unemployed persons would fall by 22 percent (1994, p. 30). This is more than three times the decline estimated in the presence of UI. He suggested that the observed levels of wage replacement are appropriate only at fairly high rates of relative risk aversion.[7] Gruber also finds that UI helps to smooth consumption during the period of job loss but that it has no permanent effect.

Burgess, Kingston, and Walters (1978b) showed that Arizona recipients unemployed for 13 weeks reduced their spending on necessary and obligated expenses by at least 20 percent from pre-unemployment levels. Spending patterns were governed by the availability of other income as well as benefits: sources included savings, borrowing, sales of assets, and income from working members of the family. The amount of retrenchment was determined also by such intangible factors as claimants' prior anticipations of layoffs and expectations of reemployment.

For the 1950s studies, Becker (1961) found that, in states experiencing periods of prosperity, beneficiaries maintained their expenditures at almost normal levels. The cut in spending was much greater in states having recessions. Given these variables, perhaps all that can be concluded is that without UI, retrenchment would have come earlier and been more drastic—particularly for those families without much other income.

In an extension of the consumption smoothing studies, Hamermesh and Slesnick (1995) approached the question of UI benefit adequacy from the perspective of applied welfare theory and estimated household equivalence scales. Using quarterly household panel data for 1980-1993 from the Consumer Expenditure Survey published by the U.S. Bureau of Labor Statistics, they investigated the question: How well do UI benefits insure consumption streams against spells of unemployment? Their essential finding was that current levels of benefits adequately compensate households that receive UI benefits. However, they tempered their conclusion by noting that UI benefit recipiency is not universal among unemployed American workers.

While replacing lost income is the prime aim of UI, an explicit corollary goal of the system is to stabilize aggregate spending by maintaining purchasing power during economic down turns. Blaustein reviewed the aggregate adequacy of benefit payments in performing the countercyclical function of stabilizing aggregate spending in the economy (1993, pp. 59-60). Citing research summarized by Hamermesh (1977, pp. 62-64) and the econometric studies by Oaxaca and Taylor (1986), he concludes that UI has a small but significant influence in maintaining purchasing power so that "economic stabilization can legitimately be considered as one of the objectives of unemployment insurance." This is consistent with studies of consumption smoothing based on household survey data.

Compensating Wage Differentials

If labor markets are efficient, wages will adjust to compensate workers in jobs with a relatively high risk of unemployment. Efficient labor markets take into account the fact that UI provides direct compensation to beneficiaries involuntarily out of work. As a result, wage differentials across UI-covered jobs with varying layoff risks are smaller than they would be in the absence of UI.

Using data from the first nine waves of the Panel Study of Income Dynamics, corresponding to calendar years 1967-1975, Abowd and Ashenfelter (1981) estimated that compensating wage differentials range from about 1 percent in industries where workers experience little anticipated unemployment to over 14 percent in industries with substantial anticipated unemployment and unemployment risk. By one method they also estimate that the implicit price of UI, in terms of wage reductions, is about equal to the expected UI benefits. Abowd and Ashenfelter performed their computations based on sample average UI wage replacement rates by industry.

Anderson (1994), who has studied compensating wage differentials in a model of optimal UI, used replacement rates simulated for each individual from the statutory provisions of the states. He asserts that UI benefit levels prior to the 1970s were inadequate, but that past deficiencies have been corrected. Based on empirical analysis of data from the 1986 Current Population Survey, Anderson concludes that the prospect of UI induces workers "to accept a somewhat *lower* wage in industries that involve higher unemployment risk" (1994, p. 653). He also says that actual "UI benefits approximate the level that would exist if an efficient UI market were available...and that...the average wage offset for UI benefits is approximately equal to the cost of their provision."

The studies of compensating wage differentials find that markets do adjust wages to account for the risk of unemployment and for the presence of UI. The research also suggests that if the UI market were fully private, given wage rates currently prevailing in the economy, agents would voluntarily choose the level of income protection afforded by the present federal-state system of UI.

Consumer Choice Theory and Unemployment Compensation

Consumer expenditure surveys of the type done in the 1950s and 1970s, while extremely valuable, have proven to be quite expensive. Becker noted that for the benefit adequacy studies done in the 1950s, "[t]he time spent per interview averaged about three hours, with a range from one to fourteen hours, exclusive of the time spent in re-interviews of the more difficult cases" (1961, p. 23). The high cost of gathering data has resulted in small sample sizes, but a more fundamental problem exists with the traditional approach. These studies presume that the analyst may determine which categories of expenditure are "necessary" or which items a household may need most.

The problems of sample size and expenditure category selection have been addressed by using readily available large data sets and an agnostic approach to measuring unemployment compensation based on the economic theory of consumer-worker behavior. The methodology relies on a natural, theoretical approach to estimating the upper limit on unemployment compensation: solve for the lump sum payment, which, when given to unemployed individuals, makes them indifferent between their current lot and their pre-unemployment one. This lump sum payment might be termed "full unemployment compensation." It should be noted that this full compensation will be less than lost earnings, because there is a positive economic value to leisure.

The labor-leisure choice model of economic consumer theory can be used to examine compensation required for a worker who experiences involuntary unemployment. The ideas embodied in this approach may be understood by referring to the indifference curve analysis of figure 5.2. An unconstrained individual, with preferences as represented by the map of indifference curves labeled U^1 and U^0 in the figure, would reach an unconstrained optimum equilibrium on U^0 at point E enjoying L^0 units of leisure and Y^0 unites of income to purchase goods in the market. With T representing total hours available for leisure, L, and hours of work H, if market opportunities allow sales of fewer than the desired hours of labor services, say $\underline{H} = T - L^1$, a lower level of utility is reached on the indifference curve U^1 where L^1 units of leisure and Y^1 units of income are consumed. While there is a hardship experienced as a result of the associated earnings loss ($Y^0 - Y^1$), the utility loss is partly compensated by an increase in leisure, and the income required to fully compensate the constrained individual ($\underline{Y} - Y^1$) is less than the earnings loss.

Figure 5.2 An Indifference Curve Analysis of Full Unemployment Compensation

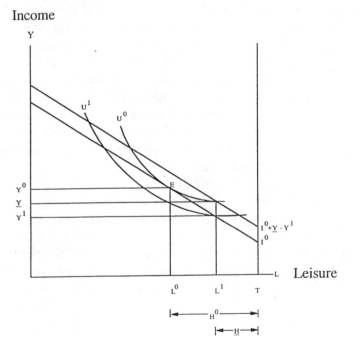

Alternatively, full compensation for hours of work at $\underline{H}$ which is less than the desired hours H^0 can be represented by the crosshatched area in figure 5.3. The compensated labor supply curve is constructed around the equilibrium (H^0, w^0) so that utility is constant. It is more wage elastic than the ordinary money income constant labor supply curve. The consumer-worker is indifferent between working H^0 at the wage rate w^0 and working $\underline{H}$ at w^0 if given the lump sum income represented by the crosshatched area in figure 5.3.[8]

Kingston et al. (1981) investigated the possibility of evaluating benefit adequacy on the basis of readily available survey (Continuous Wage and Benefit History (CWBH) and claims data. The authors concluded, however, "that information on income and household composition must be supplemented with actual or estimated data on household expenditure patterns to predict individual benefit adequacy values with a reasonable degree of accuracy" (Kingston et al. 1981, p. 43). Other writers have presented results that suggest a greater potential for applied theoretical methods to yield reasonable estimates of adequate UI compensation.

Figure 5.3 A Triangle Approximation to Full Unemployment Compensation

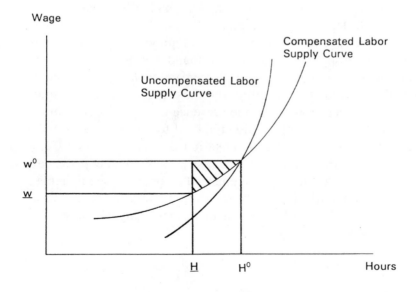

Ashenfelter (1980), in the context of a household model where unemployment is treated as a rationing constraint, estimated an approximation to a quantity that he refers to as the "lump-sum compensation required to restore the unemployed [rationed] worker's family to the welfare level of the fully employed family" (p. 552).[9] Hurd (1980) examined the cost of unemployment to the unemployed using an approximation similar to that of Ashenfelter, to study the experience of respondents to the 1967 Survey of Economic Opportunity. He estimated the required lump sum compensation to unemployed individuals by evaluating the area under this locus between the actual (constrained) and fully employed levels of labor supply.[10]

O'Leary (1990) estimated the lump sum compensation required to restore a single unemployed person with no dependents to the welfare level of a fully employed worker using both approximation and direct closed form solution methods. He also compared these results to the compensation forthcoming under various state UI programs. O'Leary (1996) then expanded the application of directly computing estimates of full compensation from closed form solutions, applying the method to six different types of household members working in the labor market, with and without dependents.

Empirical results based on theoretical models of consumer-worker behavior presented by Ashenfelter, Hurd, and O'Leary all suggest that the current UI practice of replacing one-half of lost wages tends to overcompensate for short spells of unemployment and undercompensate for long spells. O'Leary (1996) found that the presence of dependents affects full compensation to men and women in opposite ways. For the specification yielding the most plausible set of empirical results, O'Leary found that the presence of dependents significantly increases the full compensation required for unemployed women but slightly decreases the compensation due men.[11] Since UI is not intended to fully compensate the loss an individual experiences as a result of being unemployed, a financial inducement should remain for returning to work. Full compensation estimates suggest an upper bound on the share of lost income that benefits might replace.

Policy Issues

While there is a broad consensus on both the 50 percent wage replacement criterion and the concept of tying benefit amounts to previous wages, there remains controversy over how to accomplish these aims in practice. In addition to these matters, this section discusses practical aspects of allowances for dependents.

Benefit Formula

As summarized in table 5.3, four different kinds of basic weekly benefit amount formulas are used. Various applications of these four types result in a great variety of wage replacement rates (U.S. Department of Labor 1995a, table 304). Blaustein (1980), who studied thirteen states, showed that for claimants with 26 weeks of work at the U.S average weekly wage (then $233.30), the weekly benefit amount would range from 28 percent to 53 percent of wages across the states. At the extremes, claimants with identical wage and base-period employment experience could draw a weekly benefit almost twice as large in one state as in another. The actual weekly amounts for these claimants ranged from $65 to $123.

Table 5.3 Distribution of States by Weekly Benefit Amount Formula Type for the Years 1948, 1971, 1990, and 1995

Type of formula	Number of states by year			
	1948	1971	1990	1995
High-quarter wages	41	37	28	29
Multi-quarter wages			14	13
Average weekly wage	2	10	6	6
Annual wages	8	5	5	5
Total number of programs	51	52	53	53

SOURCE: Blaustein (1993, p. 293) and U.S. Department of Labor (1995a, pp. 3-35 to 3-38).

The major reason for the great diversity is that the states alone determine the weekly benefit amounts. State autonomy over basic program elements is a fundamental principle of the American UI system. The diversity itself has sometimes been an issue. Extreme differences across states in treatment of similar claimants provide support for those who urge greater uniformity through minimum federal benefit standards.

The four general types of formulas used by the states to compute benefits are as listed in table 5.3: high-quarter wage, multi-quarter wage, average weekly wage, and annual wage. Brief discussions of each type follow.

High-Quarter Formula

In more than half of the 53 UI programs in the United States, the weekly benefit amount is computed as a percentage of the claimant's wages in the calendar quarter of his or her base period in which earnings were the highest. In the majority of these "high-quarter states," weekly benefits are computed as 1/26 of high-quarter wages, on the assumption that the high-quarter wage represents income for full employment for all 13 weeks of the quarter. However, many claimants do not have 13 weeks of steady employment, even in their highest earning quarter. For them, the 1/26 fraction produces less than a 50 percent wage replacement. Accordingly, some states provide a fraction larger than 1/26 of high-quarter earnings. A 1/20 fraction would provide a 50 percent wage replacement for a claimant who had only 10 weeks of work in the high quarter and a 65 percent wage replacement for one who worked all 13 weeks. A 1/24 fraction represents a 50 percent wage replacement for an individual who missed one week, 46 percent for one who missed two, and 54 percent for a claimant with 13 full weeks of employment in the high quarter.

Some states specify more than one fraction (e.g., 1/20-1/25) for computing benefits. These "weighted" formulas provide benefits representing a greater percentage of pay to relatively low-wage claimants than to high-wage claimants. They thus offer wage-related benefits, but the benefit-wage ratios vary according to income. For this reason, these formulas have been opposed by some as introducing an element of need into the program. Others contest the premise that since low-wage workers spend a larger percentage of their income on essentials, their benefits should replace a higher share of their income. In this case, the argument is that many low-wage workers are members of high-income families.

Another problem of the high-quarter formula is that there may be a substantial gap between the time the claimant's earnings are measured for benefit purposes and the time they were actually earned. This is due more to the definition of the base period than to any inherent defect in the high-quarter formula. For example, most states define the base period as the first four of the last five completed calendar quarters immediately preceding the filing of a new claim. This is to allow a quarter interval for obtaining and recording wage data.

Accordingly, the base period for a claim filed April 1 would be the previous calendar year. The "lag period" would be three months. However, if the claim were filed March 31, for example, the first four of the last five completed calendar quarters would be the four quarters ending September 30 of the previous year. There would thus be a gap between the base period and the claim of almost six months. If the high quarter were the first quarter of the base period, high-quarter wages could be almost 15 months old. For this reason, some high-quarter states have narrowed the gap by defining the base period as the most recent four quarters under certain conditions.[12]

Multi-Quarter Formula

While some states with a high-quarter benefit formula have boosted the fraction applied to earnings somewhat above 1/26 to compensate for possible unemployment during the high quarter, the quarter with the highest earnings in the year certainly has either the least unemployment or the most overtime earnings and perhaps both. In recent years, several states have switched from computing benefits as a percentage of the claimant's high-quarter earnings to setting the weekly benefit amount as a percentage of the average quarterly income in more than one quarter, usually in the two highest income quarters in the base year. Washington State in 1977 was the first to use a multi-quarter formula. As shown in table 5.3, since that time fourteen states have tried this approach.

The multi-quarter alternative reflects a desire to balance the competing factors that influence fluctuations in average weekly earnings: time out of work due to unemployment and earnings in excess of the norm due to overtime hours. A multi-quarter formula is more likely to reflect usual full-time wages than is the high-quarter formula since, by considering a greater fraction of a calendar year, a better estimate of customary earnings will be provided.

Average Weekly Wage Formula

Only a half-dozen states compute the weekly benefit as a percentage of the claimant's average weekly wages in the base period, or in a part of the base period. In the calculation of the benefit, these states disregard weeks with no earnings or weeks in which earnings were below a stated amount. How a week of work or the average weekly wage are defined is crucial to whether or not the formula will yield a realistic benefit.

The average weekly wage formula has the advantage of making it possible to incorporate a base period immediately prior to the beginning of unemployment, thus permitting the use of recent wages as the basis for benefits. The wage data are usually obtained on a request basis from employers, as needed. In the late 1980s, several states with average weekly wage formulas switched to quarterly formulas, dropped request wage reporting, and forfeited the contiguous base period-benefit year. In large part, this was due to a 1984 federal law amendment that all states require employers to make quarterly reports of wages to a state agency.[13] The goal was to facilitate another requirement for a wider range of cross-checking among benefit and other programs for purposes of income and eligibility verification.

Annual Wage Formula

As of 1995, only five states compute the weekly benefit as a percentage of annual wages. The rationale for these formulas is the notion that a worker's annual earnings, rather than the weekly paycheck, determine the individual's standard of living. The first proposal for an annual wage formula was made by Frank B. Cliffe of the General Electric Company (Haber and Murray 1966, p. 176). He recommended that 1 percent of annual earnings be set as the weekly benefit amount. This would yield a 50 percent replacement of full-time wages only for workers who had 50 weeks of full-time work in the base period. Currently, the fractions range from 0.8 percent to 4.4 percent of annual wages.[14] Two states weight the schedules by providing claimants with lower annual earnings a higher percentage of annual wages.

Under the annual wage formula, it is not possible to ensure that the weekly benefit will be a fixed proportion of normal weekly wages. For example, a worker who earned $12,000 in the base period would qualify for a weekly benefit amount of $240 if the benefit is set at 2 percent of wages. The $240 benefit would represent 50 percent of the claimant's weekly wages only if the $12,000 represented 25 weeks of work. If the individual had worked more than 25 weeks to earn the $12,000, the $240 would be more than 50 percent of the weekly wage. If the claimant earned the $12,000 in fewer weeks, the benefit would be a percentage smaller than 50 percent of the weekly wage.

Annual wage formulas generally have the highest qualifying requirements of all states, but they also regularly provide the smallest weekly wage replacement ratio, particularly for workers with some unemployment or underemployment during the base period. Blaustein (1980, p. 194) showed that for half of the annual wage states examined, unless claimants had from 40 to 47 weeks of employment at a constant wage, individuals could not draw a weekly benefit amount representing half their weekly wages.

The Maximum Weekly Benefit Amount

On an individual level, the wage replacement ratio is a useful measure of benefit adequacy. For a given benefit formula, the maximum weekly benefit amount determines what proportion of claimants will receive the wage replacement ratio prescribed by the formula. There is little agreement on where the maximum should be set. Too high a maximum invites public criticism. Too low a maximum will prevent an excessive number of claimants from receiving a reasonable wage replacement. This is because, with a low maximum, the majority of claimants will receive the maximum rather than a benefit equal to half their lost wages (or whatever wage replacement ratio is intended by the benefit formula).

Benefit Maximums

Setting a maximum level on the weekly benefit amount is necessary to conserve the fund and to prevent inordinately high benefits being paid to any individual claimant. The Social Security Board (1938) suggested a maximum of $15 per week, which was in accord with the level

**Table 5.4 Percentage of UI Beneficiaries Eligible for the Maximum
Weekly Benefit Amount by State, Various Years 1975-1995**

State	1975	1980	1985	1990	1995
Alabama	35	55	50	44	39
Alaska	54	42	38	40	36
Arizona	50	63	66	50	57
Arkansas	14	20	17	13	16
California	30	26	26	20	25
Colorado	22	55	59	34	18
Connecticut	32	34	58	38	23
Delaware	49	43	34	--	37
District of Columbia	37	24	31	29	23
Florida	41	32	26	24	22
Georgia	41	52	44	37	38
Hawaii	35	36	29	35	40
Idaho	37	42	44	29	28
Illinois	41	50	40	81	48
Indiana	68	78	80	86	56
Iowa	56	53	54	54	50
Kansas	44	51	41	37	36
Kentucky	58	51	43	38	34
Louisiana	43	34	32	21	25
Maine	44	48	--	45	36
Maryland	50	51	39	49	48
Massachusetts	31	57	29	26	22
Michigan	62	75	42	38	36
Minnesota	38	33	32	34	35
Mississippi	44	41	41	35	37
Missouri	55	56	61	55	37
Montana	49	50	40	28	--
Nebraska	42	53	49	59	48
Nevada	42	48	41	45	--
New Hampshire	29	26	9	19	11
New Jersey	56	45	35	35	29
New Mexico	40	42	56	34	34
New York	38	35	41	32	30

State	1975	1980	1985	1990	1995
North Carolina	18	17	19	11	14
North Dakota	48	44	33	28	24
Ohio	59	54	65	53	22
Oklahoma	29	29	27	35	26
Oregon	43	45	31	31	22
Pennsylvania	32	30	20	23	22
Puerto Rico	33	27	31	28	27
Rhode Island	25	32	21	33	26
South Carolina	23	34	47	--	33
South Dakota	55	56	62	65	61
Tennessee	33	26	29	20	32
Texas	52	43	35	31	31
Utah	32	35	36	29	31
Vermont	29	30	38	44	37
Virginia	33	34	33	37	34
Virgin Islands	--	37	40	38	40
Washington	50	45	37	30	22
West Virginia	15	27	21	21	22
Wisconsin	31	27	33	38	35
Wyoming	55	35	38	41	59

SOURCE: Unpublished data provided by the Division of Actuarial Services, Unemployment Insurance Service, U.S. Department of Labor.

fixed by most states at the time. Some states adopted higher maximums: the maximum in Michigan was $16; in Wyoming, $18. The first UI check, issued August 17, 1936 by the Wisconsin agency to Neils B. Ruud, was for the $15 maximum.

Benefit maximums limit the extent to which the 50 percent concept, or other wage replacement rates intended by a benefit formula, can apply. With a 50 percent wage replacement rule, only those claimants with wage levels not more than twice the maximum will receive a 50 percent wage replacement. In most states, payments below the maximum are made at the rate of approximately 50 percent of lost wages; therefore, the proportion of beneficiaries receiving less than the maximum is a proxy for the proportion "adequately" compensated. Becker (1980, p. 13) found that roughly 34 percent of payments have been at the maximum, so that in broad terms the popular norm of adequacy—*one-half for four-fifths*—has not been met.

Table 5.4 lists the percentage of UI beneficiaries eligible for the maximum weekly benefit amount, by state, for various years since 1975. This table indicates that, over the past twenty years, there has been general improvement in the fraction of claimants receiving one-half wage replacement. It is interesting to note, by reference also to table 5.2 where statutory rules for setting state maximum weekly benefit amounts are listed, that the gain in the extent of benefit adequacy has been steadiest in states that currently adjust their maximum by statutory rule. Over the past twenty years the share of beneficiaries at the maximum weekly benefit amount has steadily declined in two states, Florida and Texas, which adjust their maximum by legislative discretion, as well as in three other states, Kentucky, North Dakota, and Washington, where the maximum is adjusted by statutory rule. Over the past ten years, among the sixteen states showing steady progress in this measure of adequacy, eleven adjust the maximum by rule and five adjust by discretion.[15]

The Level of the Maximum

The major issue is the level at which the maximum should be set. In this evaluation, one criterion of adequacy has been the percentage of claimants who are prevented from receiving at least a 50 percent wage replacement because of the maximum. Generally, the level is considered too low if a majority of claimants are eligible for the maximum.

With a maximum that equals 50 percent of the statewide average weekly wage, only claimants who earned the average wage in the state or less will receive half their lost wages. In most states, this will probably be fewer than half the number of claimants. Accordingly, if the majority of claimants are to receive half their lost wages rather than the maximum, the maximum will need to be set at *more* than 50 percent of the statewide average weekly wage. Table 5.2 provides a listing of the weekly benefit amount maximums by state and of the weekly benefit amount maximums as percentages of state average weekly wages.

A federal standard requiring the maximum weekly benefit amount to equal or exceed two-thirds of the statewide average weekly wage would allow a majority of covered workers to receive at least 50 percent wage replacement and would eliminate the wide variation among states in the proportion of workers eligible to receive such a percentage of lost wages. It would not, however, necessarily provide a 50 percent wage replacement to the "great" majority. Crosslin and Ross (1980) showed that a maximum equal to two-thirds of the statewide average weekly wage would not, with few exceptions, provide 80 percent of beneficiaries with a 50 percent wage replacement, regardless of whether the target group was covered workers, insured workers, claimants, or beneficiaries. The researchers found that the maximum weekly benefit amount would have to be set at 75 percent of average state wages if covered workers were the target group, 80 percent if insured workers were selected, and 85 percent for either claimants or beneficiaries (Crosslin and Ross 1980, p. 73).

The proportion of workers able to receive a 50 percent wage replacement is governed primarily by the level of the maximum, but it is also influenced by the benefit formula. The percentage of workers eligible for a 50 percent wage replacement *below* the maximum influences the effectiveness of the maximum. A state with a 1/20 high-quarter fraction, for example, will require a lower maximum to reach an overall wage replacement goal than would a state with a less generous fraction.

Another factor influencing the proportion of workers able to receive a 50 percent wage replacement is the distribution of income levels within a state. For example, although the 1980 maximums for Rhode Island and South Carolina were both set at 55 percent of the statewide average weekly wage, Crosslin and Ross (1980) showed that this would allow 70 percent of claimants in South Carolina to qualify for a 50 percent wage replacement, but only 63 percent of those in Rhode Island.

It has been recommended that the maximum weekly benefit amount equal two-thirds of the average wage in covered employment to meet the one-half for four-fifths standard. Presently, legislation in nine states specifies that the maximum weekly benefit amount shall be 2/3 or more of the average weekly wage in the state. Table 5.2 lists percentages of state average weekly wages at which the maximum weekly benefit must be set by statute, along with the actual maximum weekly benefit amount as of January 1996 and the ratio of that maximum to state average weekly wages in the prior year.[16] According to Papier the maximum weekly benefit amount should be tied to average base period earnings of beneficiaries (1974, p. 390). Papier estimated that to achieve one-half for four-fifths wage replacement, maximums would have to be set at 70 percent of average base-period earnings for beneficiaries without dependents and at 80 percent for beneficiaries with dependents.

Flexible Maximum

During the 1940s and into the 1950s, benefit maximums generally declined in relation to state average wage levels. Although wage levels rose rapidly, most states increased their maximums infrequently and by small amounts. Each increase required legislative action. Most legislatures convened only once every two years. Failure to increase the maximum at least every legislative year meant that the maximum lost ground in relation to wages.

As wages rise, proportionately more claimants qualify for the maximum, instead of a benefit related directly to their wages, unless the maximum also increases. To avoid the need for periodic legislative adjustments, by the mid-1950s several states turned to the "flexible maximum" concept, which sets the maximum as a specified percentage of the state average weekly wage in covered employment. Without further legislative action, the maximum amount is adjusted periodically, usually once a year, to maintain a constant relationship with wage levels.

As shown in table 5.2, thirty-three states specify that the maximum weekly benefit amount shall be adjusted annually to equal a fixed fraction of the state average weekly wage. It should be noted that this list does not include some large states such as New York, California, and Florida. Moreover, because of state trust fund conditions, the maximum has been "frozen" in several states either indefinitely or for specified periods (U.S. Department of Labor 1995a, table 305). Still other states have provisions that limit the statutory increase in the maximum weekly benefit amount if the state UI benefit trust is poorly funded.

Other Considerations in Setting the Maximum

Not all states accept the concept of the flexible maximum. Some states are reluctant to relinquish legislative control over the maximum, preferring to retain increases as legislative options. Others may fear the inflationary potential of indexing benefits to wage levels.

States are not uniformly willing to establish a maximum high enough to ensure that a majority of workers receive 50 percent wage replacement if they become unemployed. For some, cost is a barrier. For example, the National Commission on Unemployment Compensation estimated that the increase in costs in 1980 of setting all benefit maximums to at least 55 percent of statewide average weekly wages would have been about 15 percent in total. The cost impact would have ranged from no increase in several states that already provided a maximum that high, to an increase of more than 100 percent in Alaska. A rise in maximums to 60 percent would have meant an increment in national costs of about 19 percent, and, if the maximum had been set at two-thirds, national costs would have increased by about 25 percent over 1979 levels. The commission estimates were based on the assumption of a 7.5 percent unemployment rate (National Commission on Unemployment Compensation 1980, pp. 40-41).

Some state legislative provisions reflect the belief that claimants should share with employers the obligation for fund solvency, or at least for restoring depleted funds. A few states tie the maximum to a specific fund level, or condition any rise in the maximum on a solvency criterion. Opponents of these practices argue that unemployed claimants should not have to share the additional burden of ensuring that sufficient funds are available to maintain adequate benefits. Other states may simply oppose dollar figures that appear too high in relation to the wage levels of many workers. Some may prefer to focus on improvements in such priorities as benefit formulas or benefit duration, or they may opt for a program of minimum benefits.

Other Policy Issues

Minimum Weekly Benefit Amount

The original laws of almost all the states included a minimum weekly benefit of $5. Ignoring dependents' allowances, in 1995 the minimum ranged from $5 in Hawaii to $75 in New Jersey. A few states provide flexible minimums, established as either a percentage (10 percent or 15 percent) of the statewide average weekly wage, a percentage of the maximum weekly benefit amount (19 percent or 25 percent), or a percentage (4 percent) of the qualifying wages in the high quarter.

One simple objective explanation for why minimums on weekly benefits are set by states is to relieve the administrative burden of processing weekly payments smaller than some reasonable amount. A normative rationale for setting a minimum is based on benefit adequacy concerns. A 1962 Department of Labor recommendation urged that the minimum "be related to the weekly wages of the lowest wage group in the state for which the unemployment insurance program is considered appropriate" (U.S. Department of Labor 1962). In general, it is the minimum qualifying requirement that is set in relation to the lowest income group for whom the program is considered appropriate, and the minimum benefit is a by-product of that requirement.

The minimum weekly benefit and the state's minimum qualifying requirement are usually interrelated, and a change in one will often automatically provide a change in the other. For example, in a state with a high-quarter formula, where the minimum weekly benefit amount is set at 1/25 of the minimum qualifying income of $1,000 in high-quarter wages, a $200 increase in the high-quarter requirement will automatically result in increasing the $40 minimum benefit to $48. Conversely, a change in the minimum weekly benefit amount can result in an automatic change in the qualifying requirement. If Connecticut, for example, were to raise its $15 minimum to $25, its qualifying requirement of 40 times the weekly benefit amount would automatically increase its current $600 base-period minimum qualifying requirement to $1,000.

If the object is to key the minimum qualifying requirement (or the minimum benefit) to the needs of the lowest appropriate wage group, the goal may be defeated by the flexible minimums that have been described, which are tied directly or indirectly to changes in the state's average weekly wage. Increases in the state average wage may not be representative of the wage status of the lowest-wage group for whom the program is considered relevant.

Dependents' Allowances

The principal argument for dependents' allowances is simple: workers with dependents generally have less short-term flexibility for reducing expenditures than do other workers. While household heads have higher average wages than either single or married secondary workers, beneficiary studies also indicate that family heads devote a greater percentage of their earnings to meeting nondeferrable expenses (Haber and Murray 1966, p. 180).

The principal objection to dependents' allowances has been that they introduce an element of need into UI. Opponents argue that, although neither income nor means tests are involved, the payment of allowances and the required proof of dependents depart from the concept that benefits should be based solely on wages and payable to those who meet qualifying requirements as a matter of right.

Advocates, however, argue that allowances reflect only the general presumption, from a benefit adequacy perspective, that workers with dependents need more than do other workers:

> The vital difference that still exists between unemployment insurance and relief is that no individual inquiry and determination is made as to whether the claimant actually needs the dependents' benefit in order to house, feed, and clothe the dependent. The claimant merely has to establish that he has legal dependents; his personal affairs are not investigated (Haber and Murray 1966, p. 193).

Opponents have also contended that dependents' allowances have too often been used as substitutes for adequate basic benefits. Their position is that, since workers with dependents tend to have higher wages than those without, the "presumptive greater needs" of these workers can be met by higher benefit maximums, without the complexities and inequities of the allowances (Dahm and Fineshriber 1980, pp. 78-81).

Dependents' allowances tend to favor men over women claimants. Women are usually required to give more information and to answer more questions than men in claiming allowances. Generally, allowances are payable only to claimants who provide more than half of the support for a dependent. Working wives often earn lower wages than their husbands do and, consequently, qualify less frequently. Data for 10 states with dependents' allowances showed that, over a ten-year period (1968-1977), a far higher percentage of male claimants received such allowances. Except in two states where no allowances were payable to claimants at the maximum, about 17 percent of the women beneficiaries received allowances in 1977, in contrast to 48 percent of the men (Dahm and Fineshriber 1980, p. 89).

Originally, only the District of Columbia provided for dependents' allowances. In 1995, thirteen states paid higher weekly benefits to claimants with dependents. This compares with fourteen states in 1990, ten states in 1971, and five in 1948. The weekly benefit provisions of half of the ten largest states took account of dependents in 1995. The states vary in the definition of compensable dependent and in the amount of the allowance granted (U.S. Department of Labor 1995a, tables 307 and 308). All include children, usually under 18, typically encompassing stepchildren and adopted children. All but one include older children unable to work because of physical or mental disability. Most include a nonworking spouse. Three states include parents unable to work because of disability or infirmity. Three include a brother or sister under 18 orphaned or whose living parents are dependents.

Children and a nonworking spouse usually can be counted as dependents if the claimant provided more than half of their support and they are unemployed or have limited earnings. In almost all states, only one parent may draw allowances if both are receiving benefits simultaneously.

In seven states, the allowance for each dependent is a fixed amount. Two states make the allowance a percentage of the individual's weekly benefit amount. A few states base the allowance not only on the number of dependents but also on the amount of the claimant's earnings. In these states, the maximum weekly benefit amount and the earnings required to qualify for the maximum weekly benefit amount vary according to the number of dependents. The higher the number of dependents, generally, the higher the maximum weekly benefit amount and the higher the wage requirement for the maximum. All states have a limit on the total amount of dependents' allowances payable in any week, in terms of dollars, number of dependents, or the percentage of basic benefits, of high-quarter wages, or of average weekly wage. The dependents' allowance affects the maximum benefits payable on a claim in Alaska and Rhode Island where the fixed dependents' allowance is paid in any compensable week whether the claimant is fully or partially unemployed.

Recommendations of Federal Advisory Councils

In 1939, the scope of the Federal Advisory Council on Employment Security was broadened to include UI. As mentioned earlier, regarding pronouncements on benefit policy, Haber and Murray say that as early as 1955 the "Advisory Council recommended that the maximum should be equal to from three-fifths to two-thirds of the state-wide average weekly wage" (Haber and Murray 1966, p. 183). Few other recommendations of this council are noted elsewhere. In concluding their book, Haber and Murray recommend the following:

> A high level commission should be periodically appointed by the President, possibly in cooperation with congressional leaders, of persons of the highest standing in the ranks of management, labor, and the general public, to give a comprehensive view of the major policy issues regarding unemployment insurance (1966, p. 504).

Since that time, two such bodies have been created. Both have made clear proposals for benefit levels. The proposals are virtually identical.

The National Commission on Unemployment Compensation was established by Congress as part of Unemployment Compensation Amendments of 1976 (Public Law 94-566, Section 411, approved October 20, 1976). It was the first comprehensive review mandated by Congress. When making recommendations concerning the weekly benefit amount for federal guidelines to be specified in Federal Unemployment Tax Act (FUTA) amendments, the National Commission on Unemployment Compensation proposed the following two rules:

> (1) Each state must have a maximum weekly benefit amount which is not less than two-thirds of the average total weekly wages in covered employment in the state in the preceding year.

> (2) Each state must provide a weekly benefit amount between the minimum and maximum weekly benefit which averages at least 50 percent of the individual's average weekly wages (1980, p. 42).

Amendments to Section 908 of the Social Security Act, as contained in the Emergency Unemployment Compensation Act of 1991, provided for establishment of the Advisory Council on Unemployment Compensation. In its second annual report, presented in February 1995, the Advisory Council on Unemployment Compensation proposed the following:

> For eligible workers, each state should replace at least 50 percent of lost earnings over a six-month period, with a maximum weekly benefit amount equal to two-thirds of the state's average weekly wages (1995, p. 20).

Both the National Commission on Unemployment Compensation and the Advisory Council on Unemployment Compensation sought to ensure one-half wage replacement for at least 80 percent of beneficiaries. The popular standard of UI benefit adequacy first stated in the 1950s as one-half for four-fifths, continues to be the preferred norm.

Summary and Conclusion

A broad consensus has evolved that weekly UI benefits should replace about half of lost weekly earnings. This level of adequacy has been shown in numerous studies to satisfy the short-term spending needs of households. The states have chosen to determine weekly benefit amounts using various formulas; the most popular ones are based on earnings in the quarter of the base year when earnings are highest. If the unemployment compensation paid to beneficiaries were compared to the individuals' prior earnings, most states would be seen to meet the one-half wage replacement criterion of adequacy.

In all of the consumer expenditure studies of benefit adequacy, the level of the maximum appears to be the most important single factor in determining the average benefit-wage ratio and, consequently, the benefit-expense ratio. The level of the maximum also directly affects the proportion of claimants eligible for one-half wage replacement. Since the 1950s the publicly stated federal goal has been one-half for four-fifths, or 50 percent wage replacement for at least 80 percent of claimants. The most popular benefit maximum rule to help achieve this goal is to set the state maximum weekly benefit amount at two-thirds of the average weekly wage in UI-covered employment.

The issues of dependents' allowances and minimum weekly benefit amounts raise questions about whether aspects of need should be addressed by UI. Some argue that neither wage levels nor household composition should influence benefit rules. However, benefit adequacy studies show that low-wage workers and those with dependents suffer the greatest reductions in consumer expenditure when becoming unemployed. About one-quarter of the states provide additional benefits per dependent up to a certain limit, and several states provide minimum weekly benefits that exceed 50 percent wage replacement for low-wage workers. There is no real consensus on these aspects of benefit adequacy. However, these seem to be relatively low-cost areas where the social demands outweigh the insurance principles guiding the system.

Inadequacies and excesses occur with a wage-related benefit, regardless of what test of adequacy is applied. Benefits replace a portion of wages lost through unemployment, independent of the importance those wages have in the individual or in the family budget. For the wage earner with heavy family responsibilities, unemployment benefits often cover only a small portion of essential expenses. Precisely the same benefit amount may cover not only necessities, but also many incidentals, for a single wage earner, a worker with substantial income from investment or properties, or the member of a family with multiple wage earners.

The uneven results are inherent in a wage-related benefit that is not keyed to individual worker or family need. However, to criticize the benefit as inadequate or excessive in terms of meeting any particular individual's or family's circumstances is to ignore the objective of the program. The requirements UI addresses are not those of individual claimants, but the presumed need of all workers who become unemployed—for some degree of income replacement.

The program is not designed to relieve poverty. Such relief presupposes a means test to ensure the individual is indeed destitute and offers a benefit keyed to the individual's needs. Instead, UI seeks to *prevent* poverty, by sustaining, to a "substantial" extent, whatever standard of living the insured worker's former wage provided—until he or she manages to get back to work.

UI beneficiaries are not poor. They have significant attachment to the labor force and represent all income categories. The program has been criticized by some who contend that tax dollars should be limited to helping only those who are truly in need. The principal purpose of UI, however, is to prevent unemployed workers from descending into poverty before they can find suitable employment. The program thus seeks to prevent both drastic reductions in unemployed workers' living standards and further damage to their self respect and confidence. These are realistic and desirable goals. Like preventative medicine, UI can help avoid considerable welfare and psychological costs.

NOTES

This chapter incorporates previous work done by Murray Rubin. My work on this chapter benefited from valuable suggestions and guidance from Ronald Oaxaca, Michael Ransom, Paul Burgess, Stephen Woodbury, and Kenneth Kline. Insightful comments were offered by conference discussant Robert St. Louis. Claire Black and Ellen Maloney provided clerical support. Remaining errors are mine alone.

1. Sections 3304(a)(4), (h), Federal Unemployment Tax Act (FUTA); section 303(a)(5), Social Security Act (SSA).

2. Hoar (1934, p.26) writes that the 1934 Wisconsin law called for benefits to be "half the average weekly wage, but not less than $5, nor more than $10."

3. Raushenbush and Raushenbush (1979, chapter 2) discuss the evolution of the Wisconsin law and the influence of the earlier workers' compensation law enacted by Wisconsin in 1911.

4. It is reported quarterly by the U.S. Department of Labor in *UI Data Summary* and annually in updates to *UI Financial Data, ET Handbook No. 394.*

5. Under certain assumptions, this calculation could be done using sample data from the random audit benefits quality control program. Computation of the replacement rate recommended by the Advisory Council on Unemployment Compensation would impose a significant data processing burden on states. The process would involve weekly computations based on individual records.

6. Grossman considers the primary market worker in a household to be the one with the highest annual earnings; he labels other members with earnings as *secondary market workers* (Grossman 1973, p. 208).

7. Simulated levels of UI earnings replacement in the Panel Study of Income Dynamics data used by Gruber averaged around 50 percent. Relative risk aversion is the elasticity of the marginal utility of income with respect to income.

8. The full compensation triangle depicted in figure 5.3 is simply a two-dimensional representation of the quantity ($\underline{Y}$ - Y^1) represented by a vertical line in figure 5.2. Hurd (1980, p. 227-228) gives a full exposition of this idea.

9. The estimate is achieved by taking a second-order Taylor Series approximation of the difference between the exogenous cost of achieving the unconstrained utility level in the presence of the ration and the cost of achieving the same level in the absence of any constraint, around the fully employed point. The result is "a conventional Harberger (1971) type triangle measure of welfare loss" (Ashenfelter 1980, p. 553), which is applied to aggregate time series data.

10. Hurd (1980) estimated the parameters of a Taylor Series approximation of the substitution effect of a wage change on hours of work, integrated to find the compensated labor supply function, and then solved for the utility constant wage acceptance locus by inversion.

11. The results in O'Leary (1996) based on the Stone-Geary specification of utility are much more plausible than those based on a linear labor supply specification such as that used by Hurd (1980). It may be that the greater flexibility of the Stone-Geary form more fully captures underlying behavior.

12. This potentially long lag in how earnings influence benefits has not gone unnoticed by employers whose experience-rated tax liability can be shifted by specific short-term employment patterns.

13. Public Law 98-369, approved July 18, 1984. Michigan will soon switch from a wage request to a wage reporting state and simultaneously switch from an average weekly wage benefit computation to a high-quarter formula.

14. The 4.4 percent rate applies in Alaska, which creatively deals with a large population having a highly seasonal income pattern.

15. Steady reduction in the fraction at the maximum weekly UI benefit amount was achieved in the 1985-to-1995 period in Alabama, Florida, New York, Ohio, and Texas, which currently adjust the maximum by legislative discretion, and in Colorado, Connecticut, the District of Columbia, Idaho, Kansas, Kentucky, Massachusetts, Michigan, North Dakota, Puerto Rico, and Washington.

16. Even for states where the maximum weekly benefit amount is set by law to be a fraction of the average weekly wage in the state, the ratio of maximum weekly benefit amount to the average weekly wage may not appear to conform with the statute because of differences in the period over which state-covered wages are averaged and the date the adjustment is to be made. In table 5.2, there are thirty-three states indicted as having a statute for annually adjusting the maximum weekly benefit amount. Among these states, the most popular type of formula calls for averaging wages in the previous calendar year and adjusting the maximum in July. The figures in table 5.2 involve the maximum weekly benefit amount as of January 1996 and the average weekly wage in state UI-covered employment in calendar year 1995.

References

Abowd, John M., and Orley Ashenfelter. 1981. "Anticipated Unemployment, Temporary Layoffs, and Compensating Wage Differentials." In *Studies in Labor Markets,* Sherwin Rosen, ed. Chicago: University of Chicago Press.

Advisory Council on Unemployment Compensation. 1995. "Unemployment Insurance in the United States: Benefits, Financing, Coverage." ACUC, February.

_____. 1996. *Advisory Council on Unemployment Compensation: Background Papers*, Vol. 3. Washington, DC: ACUC, January.

Anderson, David A. 1994. "Compensating Wage Differentials and the Optimal Provision of Unemployment Insurance," *Southern Economic Journal* 60, 3 (January): 644-656.

Ashenfelter, Orley. 1980. "Unemployment as Disequilibrium in a Model of Aggregate Labor Supply," *Econometrica* 48 (April): 547-564.

Baily, Martin N. 1978. "Some Aspects of Optimal Unemployment Insurance," *Journal of Public Economics* 10 (December): 379-402.

Becker, Joseph M. 1960. "Twenty-Five Years of Unemployment Insurance," *Political Science Quarterly* 74 (December): 481-499.

_____. 1961. *The Adequacy of the Benefit Amount in Unemployment Insurance*. Kalamazoo, MI: W.E. Upjohn Institute.

_____. 1980. *Unemployment Benefits: Should There Be a Compulsory Federal Standard?* Washington, DC: American Enterprise Institute for Public Policy Research.

Blaustein, Saul J. 1980. "Diverse Treatment of Claimants by States." In *Unemployment Compensation: Studies and Research*, Vol. 1. Washington, DC: National Commission on Unemployment Compensation.

_____. 1993. *Unemployment Insurance in the United States: The First Half Century.* Kalamazoo, MI: W.E. Upjohn Institute.

Blaustein, Saul J., and Paul A. Mackin. 1977. "Job Loss, Family Living Standards, and the Adequacy of Weekly Unemployment Benefits." U.S. Department of Labor, Unemployment Insurance Service.

Burgess, Paul, Jerry Kingston, Robert St. Louis, and Joseph Sloane. 1980. "Benefit Adequacy and UI Program Costs: Simulations with Alternative Weekly Benefit Formulas." Unemployment Insurance Occasional Paper 80-4, U.S. Department of Labor, Employment and Training Administration.

Burgess, Paul, Jerry Kingston, and Chris Walters. 1978a. "The Adequacy of Unemployment Insurance Benefits: An Analysis of Weekly Benefits Relative to Preemployment Expenditure Levels." U.S. Department of Labor, Employment and Training Administration.

———. 1978b. "The Adequacy of Unemployment Insurance Benefits: An Analysis of Adjustments Undertaken Through Thirteen and Twenty-five Weeks of Unemployment." Unemployment Insurance Occasional Paper 78-6, U.S. Department of Labor, Employment and Training Administration.

Burtless, Gary. 1990. "Unemployment Insurance and Labor Supply: A Survey. In *Unemployment Insurance: The Second Half-Century,* W. Lee Hansen and James F. Byers, eds. Madison, WI: University of Wisconsin Press.

Congressional Research Service. 1980. "Federal-State Unemployment Compensation System." Study prepared for the Subcommittee on Public Assistance and Unemployment Compensation of the Committee on Ways and Means, U.S. House of Representatives, 100th Congress, 2d Session, Committee Print WMCP, 100-39 (September): 210-248.

———. 1998. "Unemployment Compensation: Problems and Issues." 88-597 EPW, CRS.

Corson, Walter, David Horner, Valarie Leach, Charles Metcalf, and Walter Nicholson. 1977. "A Study of Recipients of Federal Supplemental Benefits and Special Unemployment Assistance." Mathematica Policy Research, January.

Crosslin, Robert L., and William W. Ross. 1980. "Achieving Wage Replacement Goals." In *Unemployment Compensation: Studies and Research,* Vol. 1. Washington, DC: National Commission on Unemployment Compensation.

Dahm, Margaret M., and Phyllis H. Fineshriber. 1980. "Examining Dependents' Allowances; Appendix A: Entitlement to Unemployment Benefits Based on Considerations Involving Need: Conformity With Requirements of Federal Law." In *Unemployment Compensation: Studies and Research,* Vol. 1. Washington, DC: National Commission on Unemployment Compensation.

Davidson, Carl, and Stephen A. Woodbury. 1996. "Optimal Unemployment Insurance." In *Advisory Council on Unemployment Compensation: Background Papers*, Vol. 3. Washington, DC: ACUC, January.

Edgell, David, and Stephen A. Wandner. 1974. "Unemployment Insurance: Its Economic Performance," *Monthly Labor Review* 97, 4 (April): 33-40.

Feldstein, Martin S. 1974. "Unemployment Compensation: Adverse Incentives and Distributional Anomalies," *National Tax Journal* 27 (June): 231-244.

Flemming, J.S. 1978. "Aspects of Optimal Unemployment Insurance Search, Leisure, Savings and Capital Market Imperfections," *Journal of Public Economics* 10 (December): 503-525.

Gramlich, Edward M. 1974. "The Distributional Effects of Higher Unemployment," *Brookings Papers on Economic Activity* 2: 293-341.

Grossman, Michael. 1973. "Unemployment and Consumption," *American Economic Review* 63 (May): 208-213.

Gruber, Jonathan. 1994. "The Consumption Smoothing Benefits of Unemployment Insurance." Paper prepared for the Advisory Council on Unemployment Compensation, August.

Haber, William, and Merrill G. Murray. 1966. *Unemployment Insurance in the American Economy: An Historical Review and Analysis.* Homewood, IL: Richard D. Irwin.

Hamermesh, Daniel S. 1977. *Jobless Pay and the Economy.* Baltimore: Johns Hopkins University Press.

_____. 1982. "Social Insurance and Consumption: An Empirical Inquiry," *American Economic Review* 72, 1 (March): 101-113.

Hamermesh, Daniel S., and Daniel T. Slesnick. 1995. "Unemployment Insurance and Household Welfare: Microeconomic Evidence 1980-93." Working Paper 5315, National Bureau of Economic research.

Harberger, Arnold C. 1971. "Three Basic Postulates for Applied Welfare Economics," *Journal of Economic Literature* 9 (September): 785-797.

Hight, Joseph E. 1980. "Trends in Unemployment Insurance Wage Replacement, 1950 to 1977." In *Unemployment Compensation: Studies and Research,* Vol. 1. Washington, DC: Commission on Unemployment Compensation.

Hoar, Roger S. 1934. *Wisconsin Unemployment Insurance.* South Milwaukee: Stuart Press.

Hurd, Michael. 1980. "A Compensation Measure of the Cost of Unemployment to the Unemployed," *Quarterly Journal of Economics* 95 (September): 225-243.

Kingston, Jerry, Paul Burgess, Robert St. Louis, and Joseph Sloane. 1981. "Can Benefit Adequacy be Predicted on the Basis of UI Claims and CWBS Data?" Unemployment Insurance Occasional Paper 81-2, U.S. Department of Labor, Employment and Training Administration.

Lester, Richard A. 1962. *The Economic of Unemployment Compensation.* Princeton, NJ: Princeton University Press.

Munts. Raymond, and Irwin Garfinkel. 1974. *The Work Disincentive Effects of Unemployment Insurance.* Kalamazoo, MI: W.E. Upjohn Institute.

National Commission on Unemployment Compensation. 1980. Unemployment Compensation: Final Report." NCUC.

210

Oaxaca, Ronald L., and Carol A. Taylor. 1986. "Estimating the Impacts of Economic Programs on Urban Areas: The Case of Unemployment Insurance Benefits," *Journal of Urban Economics* 19 (November): 23-46.

O'Leary, Christopher J. 1990. "An Econometric Analysis of Unemployment Insurance Benefit Adequacy."W.E. Upjohn Institute Staff Working Paper 90-95, W.E. Upjohn Institute, November

_____. 1996. "The Adequacy of Unemployment Insurance Benefits." In *Advisory Council on Unemployment Compensation: Background Papers,* Vol 3. Washington, DC: ACUC, January.

Papier, William. 1974. "Standards for Improving Maximum Unemployment Insurance Benefits," *Industrial and Labor Relations Review* 27, 3 (April): 376-390.

Raushenbush, Paul A., and Elizabeth Brandeis Raushenbush. 1979. *Our U.C. Story.* Madison, WI: Raushenbush and Raushenbush.

Social Security Board. 1938. *Running Commentary on the January 1937 Draft Bill (Pooled-Fund Type).* Washington, DC: Bureau of Unemployment Compensation.

U.S. Department of Labor. 1962. "Unemployment Insurance Legislative Policy, Recommendations for State Legislation 1962. No. U-212a. Bureau of Employment Security.

_____. 1992. *Unemployment Insurance Financial Data.* ET Handbook 394. Employment and Training Administration.

_____. 1995a. "Comparison of State Unemployment Insurance Laws." Employment and Training Administration, Unemployment Insurance Service.

_____. 1995b. "UI Data Summary." Employment and Training Administration, Unemployment Insurance Service.

Vroman, Wayne. 1980. "State Replacement Rates in 1980." In *Unemployment Compensation: Studies and Research,* Vol. 1. Washington, DC: National Commission on Unemployment Compensation.

CHAPTER 6

The Duration of Benefits

Stephen A. Woodbury
Michigan State University and *W.E. Upjohn Institute for Employment Research*
Murray Rubin
Consultant

Unemployment insurance (UI) benefits have two dimensions: the weekly benefit amount and the potential duration of benefits. How much is paid per week and for how long are the two questions uppermost in the mind of an eligible UI claimant.

This chapter is concerned with issues involved in establishing both "regular" benefit duration and the duration of "extended" benefits. By "regular benefits," we mean the benefits provided by states during non-recessionary times. Regular state benefits are often referred to as the "first tier" of the UI system. By "extended benefits," we mean benefits that are paid in periods of high unemployment.

There have been two types of extended benefit programs in the United States. The first is the permanent standby Extended Benefit (EB) program enacted under the Federal-State Extended Unemployment Compensation Act of 1970. This program is supposed to activate automatically in a recession so as to provide extra weeks of unemployment benefits to workers who cannot find reemployment in hard times. The EB program is often referred to as the "second tier" of the UI system. The second type of extended benefit program is the federal "emergency" program. Congress has extended the duration of UI benefits on a temporary and discretionary basis during each of the last six recessions in the belief that the benefit durations provided by the first and second tier programs were insufficient. The various emergency programs are often referred to as the "third tier" of the UI system. The following two sections focus mainly on regular benefits, whereas the third section discusses the various extended benefit programs.

Three main questions arise in making policy on benefit duration. First, should benefits be offered to workers for a limited time or in perpetuity, and if they are offered for a limited time, what is the correct limit? Second, should all eligible workers face the same potential duration of benefits, or should potential duration vary with the work history and earnings of a worker? Third, should the duration of benefits be extended when labor markets are slack, and if so, what should be the relationship between labor market conditions and the potential duration of benefits?

We treat these questions from both institutional and analytical perspectives. In the first section, which follows, we review actual practice—how states set regular benefit durations—and briefly discuss some of the implications of that practice. We also discuss the waiting period and other interstate differences in potential duration. In the second section, we treat the adequacy and optimality of UI benefit duration, reviewing both the traditional institutional approach and modern analytical ways of examining duration adequacy. We discuss the historical and institutional reasons for existing practice in the states, empirical measures of duration adequacy such as the UI exhaustion rate and experience of UI exhaustees, the work disincentive effects of increasing the potential duration of benefits, and analytical work on optimal UI. Our goal is to provide a framework in which existing practice can be evaluated. In the third section, we address the matter of extending benefits during economic downturns. Along with issues of UI eligibility and coverage (treated by Bassi and McMurrer in chapter 2), benefit extensions have been the most visible source of contention and debate in UI during the last twenty-five years. Benefit extensions raise again many of the issues discussed in the next two sections, and provide a test of whether research on the duration of benefits has been fruitful. The final section provides a summary and some provisional conclusions.

How States Determine the Potential Duration of Benefits

From the beginning of the UI program in the United States, the generally accepted goal has been to provide a limited number of weeks of benefits, payable only long enough to tide an unemployed worker and household over a temporary spell of unemployment. Consensus on the meaning of "temporary" has changed over time—from 15 weeks, which was the most common potential duration at the beginning of the program in 1935, to 26 weeks, which is the maximum in all but two states today.

The apparent consensus in the United States that 26 weeks is a reasonable duration of benefits masks considerable variation among the states in how the duration of benefits is determined. Some states provide the same duration of benefits to all eligible claimants, whereas others vary benefit duration according to a claimant's past employment or wages. As a result, there are substantial differences among the states in the amount of prior work or wages required to qualify for different benefit durations. In the first part of this section, we review the various formulas used to compute benefit duration.

In addition, states differ in how long an unemployed individual must wait before receiving benefits. Originally, uncompensated waiting periods of two or more weeks were common. Currently, one week is required in most states and none in a few. Issues pertaining to the waiting period are reviewed in the second part of this section.

Finally, a few states provide benefits beyond the regular duration under special circumstances, for example, when workers are dislocated by a plant closing or by general permanent shrinkage of an industry. Also, two states have a regular maximum duration of 30 weeks, rather than the otherwise universal 26 weeks. These interstate variations are reviewed briefly in the last part of this section.

Potential Duration Formulas

Table 6.1 provides a summary of the practices used by the states to determine the potential duration of benefits. As can be seen in the first two columns, nine states currently provide the same potential duration of benefits to all who meet the minimum qualifying requirement (that is, the minimum and maximum potential durations are the same).

214

Table 6.1 Potential Duration of UI Benefits: Summary of State Practices, 1995

State	Potential duration (weeks)		Minimum requirement for maximum potential duration		a	b (%)	g	State minimum weekly benefit amount
	Minimum	Maximum	Base-period earnings ($)	High-quarter earnings ($)				
Alabama	15	26	1,716	516	0.33	4.17	7.91	22
Alaska	16	26	1,000	250-286	1.31	17.60	7.44	44
Arizona	12	26	3,120	1,000	0.33	4.00	8.25	40
Arkansas	9	26	3,588	897-1,183	0.33	3.85	8.57	46
California	14	26	2,080	900-920	0.50	4.35	11.49	40
Colorado	13	26	1,950	488-649	0.33	3.85	8.57	25
Connecticut	26	26	600	150	0.65	3.85	16.88	15
Delaware	23	26	2,184	966	0.50	4.35	11.49	21
District of Columbia	20	26	2,600	1.300	0.50	3.85	12.99	50
Florida	10	26	1,040	260	0.25	3.85	6.49	10
Georgia	9	26	3,848	962	0.25	4.00	6.25	37
Hawaii	26	26	130	32.5-105	1.00	4.76	21.00	5
Idaho	10	26	3,690	1,144	0.31	3.85	8.05	44
Illinois	26	26	1,600	400-1,160	0.83	3.77	22.02	51
Indiana	14	26	18,757	4,800	0.28	5.00	5.60	50
Iowa	11	26	2,496	740	0.33	4.34	7.60	32
Kansas	10	26	4,914	1,229-1,482	0.33	4.25	7.76	63
Kentucky	15	26	1,857	750	0.33	4.74	6.96	22

Louisiana	8	26	3,081	800	0.27	4.00	6.75	10
Main	21	26	2,730	683	0.33	4.55	7.25	35
Maryland	26	26	900	576	0.72	4.17	17.27	25
Massachusetts	10	30	2,000	500	0.36	3.85	9.35	14
Michigan	15	26	2,100	525-781	0.52	5.38	96.7	42
Minnesota	10	26	2,999	1,000	0.33	3.85	8.57	38
Mississippi	13	26	2,340	780	0.33	3.85	8.57	30
Missouri	11	26	3,510	1,000	0.33	4.50	7.33	45
Montana	8	26	4,469	1,117-1,375	0.32	4.00	8.00	55
Nebraska	20	26	1,575	394-400	0.33	5.00	6.60	20
Nevada	12	26	1,248	400	0.33	4.00	8.25	16
New Hampshire	26	26	2,800	1,200	0.30	4.40	6.82	32
New Jersey	15	26	4,375	1,094-1,623	0.45	4.62	9.74	75
New Mexico	19	26	1,777	1,068	0.60	3.85	15.58	41
New York	26	26	1,600	400	0.65	3.85	16.88	40
North Carolina	13	26	2,603	651-868	0.33	3.85	8.57	25
North Dakota	12	26	3,572	1,118	0.32	3.85	8.31	43
Ohio	20	26	6,864	1,716	0.25	3.85	6.49	66
Oklahoma	20	26	1,000	2,600	0.40	4.00	10.00	16
Oregon	4	26	5,304	1,326-1,360	0.33	5.00	6.60	68
Pennsylvania	16	26	1,357	900	0.69	4.00	17.25	35
Puerto Rico	26	26	280	75	0.58	9.30	6.24	7
Rhode Island	15	26	2,961	890	0.36	4.62	7.79	41

(continued)

Table 6.1 (continued)

State	Potential duration (weeks)		Minimum requirement for maximum potential duration		a	b (%)	g	State minimum weekly benefit amount
	Minimum	Maximum	Base period earnings ($)	High-quarter earnings ($)				
South Carolina	15	26	1,560	540	0.33	3.85	8.57	20
South Dakota	15	26	2,183	728	0.33	3.85	8.57	28
Tennessee	12	26	3,120	780	0.25	3.85	6.49	30
Texas	9	26	4,044	1,011–1,050	0.27	4.00	6.75	42
Utah	10	26	1,800	450–486	0.27	3.85	7.01	17
Vermont	26	26	1,628	1,163	0.42	4.44	9.46	25
Virginia	12	26	6,760	1,625	0.25	4.00	6.25	65
Virgin Islands	13	26	2,574	858	0.33	3.85	8.57	33
Washington	16	30	5,694	1,825	0.33	4.00	8.25	73
West Virginia	26	26	2,200	550–600	0.28	4.00	7.00	24
Wisconsin	12	26	3,250	1,250	0.40	4.00	10.00	50
Wyoming	12	26	3,467	1,000	0.30	4.00	7.50	16

NOTES: Parameter a is the maximum proportion of base-period earnings that can be paid in UI benefits during a given benefit year (see equation 3 in the text).

Parameter b is the proportion of high-quarter earnings paid as the weekly benefit amount (see equation 4 in the text).

Parameter $g = a/b$ and is an index of the state's potential duration generosity.

These are usually referred to as uniform duration states. The number of states providing uniform duration has fallen over the years, as Blaustein (1993, table 10.7, p. 304) has discussed.

The other forty-four states vary potential duration according to each claimant's past employment or earnings. These states use one of two methods to compute potential duration. In six states—Florida, Michigan, New Jersey, Ohio, Oklahoma, and Pennsylvania—potential duration is an increasing function of the number of "credit weeks" worked in the base period (roughly, the year preceding the spell of unemployment), up to the maximum 26 weeks. A credit week is a week in which earnings equal or exceed some specified minimum, so that,

(1) $D_{POT} = \min [f(credit\ weeks), 26]$

where D_{POT} denotes the potential duration of UI benefits and f is a function increasing in credit weeks. For example, in Ohio, a credit week is a week in which a worker earned at least 27.5 percent of the average weekly wage in the state. A worker qualifies for the minimum potential duration of 20 weeks of benefits by having 20 credit weeks in the base period. Then, the worker's potential benefit duration increases by 1 week for each additional credit week, up to the maximum of 26 weeks.

In thirty-eight states, the potential duration of benefits depends on the ratio of a claimant's base-period earnings to high-quarter earnings, up to the maximum 26 weeks. If we let BPE denote base-period earnings and HQE denote high-quarter earnings, then,

(2) $D_{POT} = \min [f(BPE/HQE), 26]$

where f denotes a function increasing in BPE/HQE. Note that BPE/HQE ranges from 1 for a worker whose entire base-period earnings were earned in a single quarter ($BPE = HQE$ for such a worker) to 4 for a worker who had identical earnings in all four quarters ($BPE = 4[HQE]$). The idea is that a worker with stable earnings throughout the base period will have a higher BPE/HQE and hence a higher potential duration of UI benefits.

In five states, the relationship between *BPE/HQE* and potential duration is explicit. For example, in North Carolina, potential duration is simply 8.67 times *BPE/HQE* (up to 26 weeks), so that a UI-eligible worker with *BPE/HQE* of 3 or greater is eligible for the maximum potential duration of 26 weeks of benefits.

In 33 states, however, the relationship between *BPE/HQE* and potential duration is masked by the formula used to calculate potential duration. In these states, potential duration is calculated as some fraction, *a*, of base-period earnings divided by the weekly benefit amount (*WBA*), up to the maximum:

(3) $D_{POT} = \min [a(BPE)/WBA; 26]$.

The parameter *a* limits the total UI benefits paid to a worker in the benefit year to some fraction of base-period earnings. In 18 states, $a = 1/3$, and, in the other 15 states, *a* ranges between .25 and .6. What needs to be noted is that in all of these states the weekly benefit amount is computed, in turn, as a fraction, *b*, of high-quarter earnings (or, in some cases, average earnings in the two highest quarters of the base period) up to some maximum:

(4) $WBA = \min [b(HQE), WBA_{MAX}]$.

Typically, *b* is 1/25 (.04), so that the weekly benefit amount equals one-half of average weekly earnings in the high quarter. (The parameter *b* ranges from 1/26 [.038] to 1/20 [.05] in these 33 states.) Substituting the *WBA* formula (4) into the potential duration function (3) yields

(5a) $D_{POT} = a(BPE)/b(HQE)$,   if $WBA < WBA_{MAX}$

or

(5b) $D_{POT} = a(BPE)/WBA_{MAX}$,   if $WBA = WBA_{MAX}$.

It follows that for eligible claimants whose *WBA* is less than the state's maximum,

(6) $D_{POT} = g(BPE/HQE)$

where

(7) $g = a/b$,

so the dependence of potential duration on BPE/HQE is clear for claimants whose WBA is below the maximum. For claimants whose WBA is at the maximum, potential duration will still depend on the relationship between base-period and high-quarter earnings. For example, a worker who obtains the maximum WBA as a result of high earnings in just one quarter may have potential duration below the maximum 26 (or 30) weeks, since that worker's base-period earnings will be low relative to his or her weekly benefit amount.

The parameter g can be usefully interpreted as an index of a state's duration generosity. Specifically, it gives the increase in the number of weeks of potential duration that result from a unit increase in BPE/HQE. In table 6.1, we have computed g for all 53 "states" (that is, UI jurisdictions). (For states that do not explicitly use the parameters a or b in computing the potential duration of benefits, we have calculated an implied g numerically.) Also in table 6.1, we have calculated the minimum base-period earnings and high-quarter earnings that an eligible claimant would need in order to receive the state's maximum potential duration of benefits.

An examination of g and of the minimum earnings required for maximum potential duration in table 6.1 shows that the variations in states' duration provisions are significant. Claimants with similar base-period work experience qualify for quite different potential durations depending on the state in which they reside, and the requirements for 26 weeks of regular benefits vary dramatically among the states. For example, to qualify for 26 weeks of regular benefits requires as little as $130 in the base period (with $32.50 to $105 in the high quarter) in Hawaii to as much as $18,757 in the base period (with $4,800 in the high quarter) in Indiana.

Variable duration reflects the notion that individuals "earn" their right to benefits by working, and that each week of benefits is earned by a given number of weeks of employment or earnings. The widespread use of variable duration also reflects two further concerns: first, that uniform duration is more expensive than variable duration, and second, that uniform duration can generate a high ratio of total benefits paid to base-period earnings, which could in turn lead to strong work disincentives.[1] We return to these issues in the discussion of extended benefits and again in the conclusion.

The Waiting Period

The waiting period has been debated since the beginning of the UI system in the United States. In all but a dozen states, a claimant must serve an uncompensated one-week period of unemployment before receiving benefits. At the beginning of the program, 31 of the state laws required a waiting period of two weeks, 17 required three weeks, and three required four weeks (Haber and Murray 1966, p. 200).

The waiting period was included in the early laws for reasons of both administration and financing. It allowed time for processing claims manually and for making determinations and contesting them before the end of the first compensable week. It also helped to conserve funds by avoiding compensation for short periods of unemployment. Over the years, however, experience showed that the waiting period was unnecessary for effective administration. Also, although a waiting period clearly increases fund solvency (other things being equal), the fact that several states have eliminated the waiting period shows that it is not essential for fund solvency.

Accordingly, some have argued that the waiting period should be eliminated entirely. The main argument for dropping the requirement is that it causes a delay in providing claimants with income in the early stages of their spell of insured unemployment. Since payment of a claimant's first benefit check usually occurs no earlier than three full weeks following the filing of the first claim, the existence of a waiting week means that the first check will represent compensation for only one week of unemployment. Eliminating the waiting week would not shorten the time it takes to deliver the first check, but that check would cover two weeks of unemployment instead of just one. This would be helpful if, as is often the case, a worker has delayed filing a claim until after being unemployed for some time.

Eliminating the waiting week requirement would be a relatively expensive step, however. In addition, an accumulating body of research and evidence suggests that it would be good public policy to extend the waiting period and to use the savings to finance a longer potential duration of benefits. O'Leary's (forthcoming) findings, which are discussed below, suggest that short spells of unemployment are overcompensated by UI, whereas long spells are under-compensated. Jacobson, LaLonde, and Sullivan (1993a, 1993b, 1993c) show clearly that dislocated workers suffer large losses of firm- and occupation-specific human capital that no existing program—including UI—even begins to address. This research provides a rationale for extending the waiting period and providing a longer potential duration of benefits.[2]

The number of states that impose a waiting week has been influenced strongly by a 1980 federal amendment to the federal-state Extended Benefits (EB) law. That amendment was one of several intended to reduce UI program costs by providing incentives for states to reduce the generosity of their regular UI benefit provisions.[3] It eliminated the federal 50 percent matching share for the first week of EB in any state that has no waiting week for regular benefits. The amendment also applies to states that have a waiting week for which the individual is later reimbursed if still unemployed after a specified period, and to states that waive a waiting week requirement if it would interrupt a continuous spell of insured unemployment.

The prospect of losing the federal share of funding for the first week of EB motivated some states to restore a waiting week and deterred others from eliminating it. Before the federal change in 1980, there had been a trend toward removing the waiting week, which peaked at twelve states with no waiting week and nine states that paid it after a specified number of weeks of unemployment. By 1984, the number was down to nine and six states, respectively. However, mainly because the EB program has become ineffective in recent years, the number of states without waiting week provisions has risen to twelve, although the number of states paying for the waiting week retroactively is now down to four.

A few states provide two exceptions to the waiting week requirement. The first exception applies when a claimant is unemployed and receiving benefits at the end of a benefit year. If the period of unemployment extends into the new benefit year, the individual may serve a waiting period for the new year either at the beginning or later in that new benefit year. The second exception allows claimants to serve a waiting period the week before beginning a new benefit year. This provision is advantageous to claimants who are unemployed for some time before they are able to begin a new benefit year; examples include claimants who exhaust benefits before the expiration of the first benefit year and remain unemployed or claimants who incur a second spell of unemployment before expiration of the first benefit year.[4]

As mentioned, a few states convert the waiting week into a compensable week after a specified period of unemployment. Since most unemployment is short-term, these states frequently never pay for the first week. However, such provisions could create an incentive to remain unemployed long enough to be paid for that week. No state currently provides for payment of the waiting week to individuals who find suitable, stable employment within a minimum period, although such a provision could create an incentive for quick reemployment, along the lines of a reemployment bonus.

Other Interstate Variations

Increased Duration under Special Conditions

A few states extend regular benefit duration for workers whose unemployment resulted from structural change such as shifts in demand or changing technology. Structural change usually manifests itself in plant closings or in the permanent shrinkage of an entire industry. Hence, these programs can be thought of as state-level dislocated worker extensions.[5]

A Hawaii law separate from the regular UI law provides an additional 13 weeks of benefits to individuals unemployed when a natural or other disaster causes damage that results in widespread unemployment. Puerto Rico provides up to 32 weeks of extended benefits to individuals who are dislocated as a result of technological change, closure of a plant or industry, or the elimination or reduction of sugar cane crops.[6]

In Iowa, potential benefit duration is normally computed as 1/3 of base-period earnings divided by the weekly benefit amount, up to a maximum of 26 weeks. However, for workers laid off because their employer went out of business, duration is computed as 1/2 of base-period earnings divided by the weekly benefit amount, up to a maximum of 39 weeks. In other words, the parameter a in table 6.1 increases from 1/3 to 1/2 for dislocated workers. Minnesota provides up to 6 weeks of extended benefits to workers affected by a mass layoff—defined as a permanent work force reduction of at least 50 percent in a facility employing 100 or more workers—when the county unemployment rate is at least 10 percent.

Other states also extend regular duration to dislocated workers but on a different basis. Massachusetts and Michigan have long provided additional weeks of benefits to claimants attending vocational retraining courses approved by the employment security agency. In both states, benefits may be extended up to 18 weeks.

State-level extensions such as these reflect a view that, at least for dislocated workers, regular benefits of 26 weeks are inadequate either to compensate a worker for permanent job loss and for the loss of firm- and occupation-specific human capital it implies, or to support a worker through a period of retraining that may be needed after permanent job loss. Of course, the enactment of such state-level extensions requires both a political consensus and favorable fiscal conditions, and the existing state-level extensions fall short of the comprehensive commitment to retraining advocated by some.

Maximum Duration

In 1979, twelve states paid more than 26 weeks of regular benefits. This represented the peak of a trend toward higher maximum durations that characterized the UI system in the United States into the 1970s. The trend was reversed in the 1980s, and, by 1989 (and still today), only two states (Massachusetts and Washington) provided regular benefit duration maximums in excess of 26 weeks. As can be seen in table 6.1, all other states have a maximum potential duration of regular benefits of 26 weeks.

Particularly in the 1960s and 1970s, there were several federal and other proposals to induce states to extend regular benefit duration beyond 26 weeks. In 1963 and 1965, for example, the Kennedy and Johnson administrations proposed a program of Federal Unemployment Adjustment Benefits (FUAB), payable in both good and bad times to those with long and substantial employment experience (Murray 1974, pp. 30-32). Thirteen weeks of FUAB would have been made available to individuals unemployed more than 26 weeks, provided they had at least 26 weeks of work in the base period and 78 weeks of work in the base period and the preceding two years. In that it would have provided extended benefits to workers with strong employment histories, the FUAB proposal resembled the types of dislocated worker programs that have been discussed recently (see, for example, Jacobson, LaLonde, and Sullivan 1993a, chapter 7), but no action was taken by Congress on the proposal.

In 1972, a committee of the Interstate Conference of Employment Security Agencies (ICESA) recommended to ICESA's Executive Committee that the federal government give a 50 percent subsidy for any week of regular benefits beyond the 26th week (up to 39) that any state saw fit to provide, under whatever conditions the state considered necessary (Murray 1974, pp. 25-26). ICESA took no action on the recommendation.

In 1973, it was reported that the Nixon administration was considering a proposal to require all states to set a maximum duration of at least 39 weeks (Murray 1974, pp. 26, 59). States would be reimbursed for 50 percent of the cost of benefits in excess of 26 weeks. Proportionately more work experience in the base period would be required for a claimant to qualify for benefits beyond 26 weeks: for example, 39 weeks would require 50 percent more than was required for 26 weeks. However, no proposal was actually introduced to Congress.

Thus, various proposals to extend regular benefit duration have been put forward and rejected over the years. It seems highly unlikely that proposals to increase regular state benefit durations would fare well today. An approach that provided federal financing without federal control would be more in keeping with the philosophy of the Republican Congress than an approach that dictated federal standards, but the budgetary implications of any such subsidy make it extremely unlikely.

The reluctance of states to extend benefits beyond 26 weeks has stemmed from at least three sources: first, the strains on state funds during the high unemployment of the mid-1970s and early 1980s; second, the federal conditions adopted in the 1980s for state repayment of federal advances; and third, enactment in 1970 of the federal-state EB program.

Adoption of EB in 1970 is arguably the major reason for the decline in the number of states with regular benefit durations in excess of 26 weeks. In brief, the EB program extends benefits in states where labor market conditions have deteriorated during the preceding one to two years. (We discuss EB in greater detail in the third section of this chapter.) EB extends potential duration by one-half of a claimant's regular benefit duration, up to a maximum of 13 weeks. Hence, when EB is in effect in a state, claimants gain no advantage from the availability of regular benefits beyond 26 weeks: the maximum weeks of combined regular benefits and EB is 39. In other words, when EB is in effect, claimants are eligible for the same 39-week potential duration whether the duration of regular state benefits in their state is 26 weeks or 30 weeks (or any other potential duration of regular benefits between 26 and 39 weeks). Moreover, EB is funded half from state UI trust funds and half from federal UI trust funds. Accordingly, EB results in a smaller drain on state UI trust funds than do benefits in excess of 26 weeks provided by a regular state program.

For the same reasons, adoption of EB is clearly the main reason for the decline in the number of states with their own extended benefit programs. In the mid-1970s, ten states had such programs, activated on the basis of particular state unemployment rates. By 1989, only three states (Alaska, California, and Connecticut) had such programs.

In sum, adoption of EB seems to have produced the acceptance of two ideas. The first is that unemployment beyond 26 weeks ceases to be solely a state responsibility. The second is that UI benefits should extend beyond 26 weeks only during periods of high unemployment.

Duration Adequacy and Optimality

The most obvious question in unemployment benefit duration is also the most difficult: What should be the potential duration of benefits? It is useful to think of the approaches to this question as either institutionalist or analytical, although the line between the two is not hard and fast. The institutionalist approach relies on historical observation, pragmatic considerations, and informal examination of data to gain an impression of whether benefit durations are adequate. The analytical approach makes explicit use of economic reasoning and modeling. In the first two parts of this section, we discuss the institutionalist approaches to benefit duration, describing the historical rationale for the existence of limited potential duration, and reviewing the literature on UI exhaustion rates and the experience of exhaustees. In the last two parts, we look at existing analytical work on the disincentive effects of increases in potential duration on the optimal duration of benefits.

We view the alternative approaches to duration adequacy as complementary rather than as competing ways of gaining insight into whether benefit durations are adequate. As will be seen, neither approach has progressed to the point where unequivocal or wholly convincing answers are supplied.

Historical Rationale for Limiting Potential Duration

Originally, financial concerns were the primary reason for limiting the duration of benefits. When the program began in 1935, actuaries argued that a 3 percent payroll tax could finance only 12 to 15 weeks of benefits. The actuaries' estimates were based on the unemployment experience of the 1930s, and, of course, such high rates of unemployment have not recurred. Indeed, actual payroll tax rates are now well below those originally contemplated (on average), yet the maximum benefit durations provided are now well above those originally contemplated.

In 1942, the Social Security Board acknowledged the importance of funding considerations in limiting benefit duration but also urged states to provide more weeks of benefits "unless fund conditions forbid."[7] In 1950, the U.S. Department of Labor reaffirmed the concept of limited potential duration, but for reasons that went beyond cost considerations. It concluded that potential duration should be limited mainly because UI is "short-term" insurance, intended to provide protection only to workers who are currently attached to the labor force and who are unemployed between jobs. UI is not intended for long-term unemployed workers for whom job search assistance, retraining, or relocation would be more appropriate.

Having reaffirmed the commitment to limited potential duration, the Department defined the limits of potential duration with respect to program goals:

> Whether the unemployment insurance program achieves its major objective of covering the nondeferrable expenses of insured workers during periods of involuntary unemployment without diminishing their savings appreciably or compelling them to draw on other community resources depends on the duration of payments as well as the amount of the weekly payments. To accomplish this purpose, the duration of benefits should be sufficient to enable the

great majority of insured workers to find suitable work before exhausting their benefit rights, under normal or recession conditions. In statistical terms, *the benefit period should be long enough to ensure that no more than 25 percent of the beneficiaries exhaust benefits under recession or better conditions* [emphasis added] (*Manual of State Employment Security Legislation* 1950, p. C-33).

By 1962, the Department of Labor's concept of limiting potential duration had translated into recommendations to the states: first, "that all eligible claimants be allowed a uniform potential duration of at least 26 weeks of benefits," and second, "that, if a State considers that it must vary duration in relation to base-period employment or wages, the variable potential duration should range from a minimum of 20 weeks to a maximum of at least 30 weeks" (*Unemployment Insurance Legislative Policy* 1962, p. 37). Thus, although federal adherence to the concept of limited duration remained constant over the years, the limit changed from 15 weeks in 1935 to double that in 1962. It is telling, perhaps, that there has been no comparable policy statement in the last 35 years.

Although duration maximums have increased over the years, there remains wide acceptance of the idea that the potential duration of benefits should be limited. This view seems to stem in part from the belief that under reasonably good economic conditions workers should be able to find reemployment reasonably quickly, and in part from concerns about moral hazard—that workers offered benefits of unlimited duration would extend their spells of unemployment to unacceptable lengths. Finite benefit extensions have been considered acceptable when labor markets are slack, but UI has been eschewed as a standing policy to assist long-term unemployed workers.

Two arguments have been made against extended benefits for long-term unemployed workers: first, such payments involve a drain on the trust fund, and second, they undermine the insurance character of the program (see Hansen and Byers 1990 for a cogent statement of the latter argument). The second of these arguments is important enough to deserve a brief restatement. When the UI system came into being in the United States, political considerations connected with financing the program dictated that it could cope only with brief spells of unemployment. Large industrial employers were induced to support UI legislation, with financing through an experience-rated payroll tax, by the promise that their workers on temporary layoff would receive benefits and hence would be available for recall when demand improved. It followed that the program could insure only against short-term unemployment. Dislocated workers and other long-term unemployed were not the object of the UI system, so to finance programs for such workers—such as retraining and income support during retraining—out of the UI trust fund would undermine the finances of the program.

The irony is that the main problems of the Great Depression were permanent job loss and long-term demand-deficient unemployment, not short-term or temporary layoff unemployment. So it really cannot be argued that UI, by insuring mainly against short-term spells of unemployment, met the needs of the 1930s, except that it was better than no system at all. There is also an element of ad hominem argument here: once we define UI as a program that is intended to insure workers against short spells of unemployment, then, by definition, providing benefits for longer spells of unemployment undermines the "integrity" and insurance character of the program. *Unemployment insurance was defined as a program for short-term unemployment out of financial and political expediency, not after consideration of whether permanent job loss or long-term unemployment are insurable risks that demand some form of social insurance.* Arguments that UI is a program for short-term unemployment—and that it should keep doing what it already does—do tell us what the program is, but they beg the question of what the program ought to be.

Much criticism of the UI system during the early 1990s amounted to a criticism of the failure of UI to assist dislocated and long-term unemployed workers. Indeed, the main change in the UI system that the Clinton administration has initiated—UI "profiling"—is intended to address this criticism and to assist workers who are likely to experience long spells of unemployment. The purpose of profiling (which is discussed further in the next section) is to speed reemployment of dislocated workers given that the political climate is so unfavorable to offering extended benefits to such workers.

However, traditional defenders of the system believe that the recent criticism of UI is based on a misunderstanding of its purpose; that is, they argue that the system is intended only to alleviate the hardship of short-term unemployment, particularly due to temporary layoffs. Again, it is clear that the system would have been politically infeasible in the 1930s had it provided more generous or long-term benefits and that the system has evolved so as to deal best with short-term unemployment. As the work discussed in the last part of this section suggests, on the other hand, it is unclear whether relatively generous compensation of short-term unemployment, and virtual neglect of long-term unemployment, is socially optimal. In other words, the goals of the system have been defined largely by looking at what the system has done and done well, rather than by examining what type of social insurance system (financed by a payroll tax) would improve the well-being of risk averse workers. The aims, it seems, have been set by circular reasoning—this is what the system does well; therefore, this must be its goal—rather than by thinking through the problem of insuring against the risk of job loss.

Exhaustion Rates and the Experience of Exhaustees

Past research has addressed whether the potential duration of UI benefits is adequate mainly by examining UI exhaustion rates—that is, the proportion of UI claimants who use up their entire regular state benefit entitlement[8]—and the experience of UI exhaustees. This has proven a useful approach, in that it has exposed the characteristics of state UI systems that tend to yield high or low exhaustion rates. However, in part because it lacks a normative framework, it has not led to a consensus about the proper duration of benefits.

Unemployment Insurance Exhaustion Rates

Ready availability of data to calculate the UI exhaustion rate has made it the most commonly used gauge of duration adequacy. In 1962, the U.S. Department of Labor last expressed the objectives of regular benefit duration:

> The program is intended to provide benefits for a sufficiently long period that, under reasonably normal business conditions and during short periods of recession, a high proportion of claimants can continue to receive benefits until they are called back to work or find other work (*Unemployment Insurance Legislative Policy* 1962, p. 35).

Although a "high proportion of claimants" has generally been considered as 75 percent (see the quote in the previous section from the *Man-*

ual of State Employment Security Legislation), it has never been defined carefully. Moreover, the terms "reasonably normal" and "short periods of recession" are quite vague. For example, "reasonably normal" meant higher rates of unemployment between the mid-1970s and late-1980s, when it was widely agreed that the natural rate of unemployment (that is, the rate of unemployment that is consistent with a constant rate of inflation) was higher than in earlier decades. In recommending an increase in the unemployment rates that activate the EB program, the Department of Labor argued in 1981 that "Structural changes in the labor force have contributed to a generally higher level of normal unemployment" (Rubin 1983, p. 125).

Table 6.2 displays the annual UI exhaustion rate (for the regular state program) from 1940 through 1994, along with the number of claimants who exhausted their regular UI benefits. The table also shows the total unemployment rate (for 1940 through 1994) and the average duration of unemployment in the economy (for 1948 through 1994).

Note that the regular exhaustion rate shown in table 6.2 is distinct from the total exhaustion rate, which is the proportion of UI claimants who use up both their regular state benefit entitlement and any extended benefits for which they qualify. The total exhaustion rate can never exceed the regular exhaustion rate and will be less than the regular exhaustion rate when an extended benefit program is in effect.

Not surprisingly, both the regular exhaustion rate and the number of exhaustees rise when aggregate economic conditions deteriorate—as reflected by increases in the unemployment rate and in unemployment duration. The main purpose of the extended benefit programs discussed in the following section has been to provide additional assistance to workers who exhaust their benefits under the regular UI program. Indeed, one of the main proposed goals of extended benefit programs has been to bring the *total* exhaustion rate (that is, the proportion of workers exhausting both regular and extended benefits) down roughly to the level of the regular exhaustion rate during nonrecessionary times (Hight 1975; Corson and Nicholson 1982). For example, Corson and Nicholson have estimated that the emergency extended benefit program that was implemented during the mid-1970s (Federal Supplemental Compensation) reduced the total exhaustion rate during the

Table 6.2 Regular UI Exhaustion Rate, Number of Regular UI Exhaustees, Total Unemployment Rate, and Unemployment Duration, United States 1940-1994

Year	Exhaustion rate (%) (1)	Number of regular UI exhaustees (000s) (2)	Total unemployment rate (%) (3)	Average duration of unemployment (weeks) (4)
1940	50.6	2,590	14.5	--
1941	45.6	1,544	9.7	--
1942	34.9	1,078	4.4	--
1943	25.5	194	1.7	--
1944	20.2	102	1.0	--
1945	18.1	250	1.6	--
1946	38.7	1,986	3.7	--
1947	30.7	1,272	3.5	--
1948	27.5	1,028	3.3	8.6
1949	29.1	1,935	5.3	10.0
1950	30.5	1,853	5.2	12.1
1951	20.4	811	3.2	9.7
1952	20.3	931	2.9	8.4
1953	20.8	764	2.8	8.0
1954	26.8	1,769	5.4	11.8
1955	26.1	1,272	4.3	13.0
1956	21.5	981	4.0	11.3
1957	22.7	1,139	4.2	10.5
1958	31.0	2,507	6.6	13.9
1959	29.6	1,676	5.3	14.4
1960	26.1	1,604	5.4	12.8
1961	30.4	2,366	6.5	15.6
1962	27.4	1,638	5.4	14.7
1963	25.3	1,872	5.5	14.0
1964	23.8	1,371	5.0	13.3
1965	21.5	1,087	4.4	11.8
1966	18.0	781	3.7	10.4
1967	19.3	867	3.7	8.7
1968	19.6	848	3.5	8.4

(continued)

232

Table 6.2 (continued)

Year	Exhaustion rate (%) (1)	Number of regular UI exhaustees (000s) (2)	Total unemployment rate (%) (3)	Average duration of unemployment (weeks) (4)
1969	19.8	811	3.4	7.8
1970	24.4	1,303	4.8	8.6
1971	30.5	2,057	5.8	11.3
1972	30.0	1,822	5.5	12.0
1973	27.7	1,508	4.8	10.0
1974	31.0	1,939	5.5	9.8
1974	37.8	4,195	8.3	14.2
1976	37.8	3,270	7.6	15.8
1977	32.5	2,850	6.9	14.3
1978	26.7	2,031	6.0	11.9
1979	26.7	2,037	5.8	10.8
1980	33.2	3,072	7.0	11.9
1981	32.4	2,989	7.5	13.7
1982	38.5	4,175	9.5	15.3
1983	38.4	4,180	9.5	20.0
1984	34.2	2,619	7.4	18.2
1985	31.2	2,575	7.1	15.6
1986	32.2	2,703	6.9	15.0
1987	30.6	2,409	6.1	14.5
1988	28.5	1,979	5.4	13.5
1989	28.0	1,940	5.3	11.9
1990	29.4	2,323	5.5	12.1
1991	34.8	3,472	6.7	13.8
1992	39.9	3,821	7.4	17.9
1993	39.2	3,204	6.8	18.1
1994	36.3	2,977	6.1	18.4

SOURCE: Columns 1 and 2 from *Unemployment Insurance Financial Data*, ET Handbook 394; columns 3 and 4 from *Handbook of Labor Statistics*, U.S. Department of Labor, Bureau of Labor Statistics, August 1989, and *Monthly Labor Review*, various issues.

1973-1975 recession to somewhat below the regular exhaustion rate during nonrecessionary times (Corson and Nicholson 1982, pp. 72-76).

In addition to cyclical ups and downs, however, there has been a secular rise in the regular exhaustion rate. For example, in 1994, which was not a recession year, 36.3 percent of UI claimants exhausted their regular benefits. This was only slightly below the exhaustion rates at the peak of the mid-1970s recession (37.8 percent) and of the early 1980s recession (38.5 percent). The regular exhaustion rate during the recession of the early-1990s, 39.9 percent, was a post-World War II high.

The secular increase in the regular exhaustion rate can be attributed partly to reductions over time in the generosity of state duration provisions and partly to the secular rise in unemployment spell durations. Although we do not explore these changes in detail here, some insight into the link between the generosity of state duration provisions and the exhaustion rate can be obtained from table 6.3, which displays the average potential duration of benefits (a proxy for duration generosity, in column 2) and the exhaustion rate (column 3) for each state in 1992. The most obvious point to note is that the nine states with uniform duration provide higher average potential duration than do any of the variable duration states.

The relationship between the generosity of state benefit formulas and the UI exhaustion rate can be seen more clearly in table 6.4, where we show the results of regressing the regular UI exhaustion rate on two variables: the average potential duration (which serves as a proxy for state duration generosity) and the total unemployment rate (as a proxy for labor market conditions). The data used in the regressions in table 6.4 come from table 6.3. A literal interpretation of the results is that states with greater average potential duration of benefits have lower exhaustion rates, so that a one-week increase in the average potential duration is linked to a 1.8 percentage point drop in the regular exhaustion rate. Also, states with higher total unemployment rates have higher regular exhaustion rates, so that a 1 percentage point rise in the unemployment rate is linked to a 3 percentage point rise in the regular exhaustion rate.

Table 6.3 (column 4) also shows the percentage of exhaustees eligible for fewer than 26 weeks of benefits. This is an alternative measure of duration adequacy, which Murray (1974) explored in some detail.

Table 6.3 Unemployment Rate, Average Potential Duration of UI, Exhaustion Rate, and Percentage of Exhaustees Drawing Fewer Than 26 Weeks of Benefits, by State, 1992

State	Total unemployment rate (%) (1)	Average potential duration of UI (weeks) (2)	UI exhaustion rate (%) (3)	Percentage of exhaustees drawing fewer than 26 weeks (4)
Alabama	7.3	24.1	24.7	45.6
Alaska	9.1	20.8	50.4	86.3
Arizona	7.4	23.0	39.9	51.4
Arkansas	7.2	22.8	35.7	56.8
California	9.1	24.2	44.2	26.2
Colorado	5.9	22.3	44.5	73.6
Connecticut	7.5	26.0	38.1	0.0
Delaware	5.3	25.6	27.1	10.9
District of Columbia	8.4	23.3	64.4	22.8
Florida	8.2	21.0	54.0	63.8
Georgia	6.9	21.5	39.8	74.3
Hawaii	4.5	26.0	34.5	0.0
Idaho	6.5	19.5	34.0	82.6
Illinois	7.5	26.0	42.0	0.0
Indiana	6.5	22.7	31.3	63.9
Iowa	4.6	22.4	30.0	64.2
Kansas	4.2	22.7	37.2	54.0
Kentucky	6.9	26.0	22.6	0.1

Louisiana	8.1	26.0	34.0	0.1
Maine	7.1	19.4	39.3	66.4
Maryland	6.6	26.0	21.1	0.0
Massachusetts	8.5	27.5	46.0	29.0
Michigan	8.8	22.7	35.0	54.0
Minnesota	5.1	23.4	33.3	51.3
Mississippi	8.1	23.4	33.3	50.8
Missouri	5.7	22.0	38.6	61.8
Montana	6.7	20.5	38.2	80.6
Nebraska	3.0	23.0	30.4	76.9
Nevada	6.6	22.7	39.7	50.6
New Hampshire	7.5	26.0	15.8	0.0
New Jersey	8.4	23.8	55.7	35.3
New Mexico	6.8	25.8	38.3	13.1
New York	8.5	26.0	51.5	0.0
North Carolina	5.9	23.0	21.1	61.8
North Dakota	4.9	19.9	38.5	78.4
Ohio	7.2	25.6	33.2	17.3
Oklahoma	5.7	21.6	43.6	78.0
Oregon	7.5	25.7	34.5	11.2
Pennsylvania	7.5	25.9	35.6	1.8
Puerto Rico	--	26.0	58.9	0.0
Rhode Island	8.9	21.7	44.8	59.0

(continued)

Table 6.3 (continued)

State	Total unemployment rate (%) (1)	Average potential duration of UI (weeks) (2)	UI exhaustion rate (%) (3)	Percentage of exhaustees drawing fewer than 26 weeks (4)
South Carolina	6.2	23.1	30.5	50.7
South Dakota	3.1	24.7	13.3	32.7
Tennessee	6.4	21.8	33.3	67.0
Texas	7.5	20.9	51.3	72.1
Utah	4.9	20.6	32.8	74.8
Vermont	6.6	26.0	26.5	0.0
Virginia	6.4	20.7	35.6	76.2
Virgin Islands	--	23.6	44.0	44.6
Washington	7.5	26.2	33.0	51.0
West Virginia	11.3	26.0	28.8	0.0
Wisconsin	5.1	24.5	22.0	67.8
Wyoming	5.6	22.4	32.2	68.7
Unweighted mean	6.8	23.5	36.6	42.6

SOURCE: Column 1 from *Employment and Earnings*; columns 2 and 3 from *Unemployment Insurance Financial Data*, ET Handbook 394; column 4 provided by Tom Stengel of Actuarial Services, U.S. Department of Labor, Employment and Training Administration, Unemployment Insurance Service.

The percentage of exhaustees eligible for fewer than 26 weeks is zero in the uniform duration states and is below 5 percent in three additional states—Kentucky, Louisiana, and Pennsylvania. However, in thirty states, over half of all regular exhaustees were eligible for fewer than 26 weeks of benefits, and in seven of these over three-quarters of all regular exhaustees were eligible for fewer than 26 weeks of benefits. Clearly, large proportions of regular UI exhaustees are eligible for fewer than the "standard" 26 weeks of benefits.

Table 6.4 Impacts of the Potential Duration of UI and the Unemployment Rate on the Exhaustion Rate and Percentage of Exhaustees Drawing Fewer Than 26 Weeks of Benefits, 1992

	Dependent variable	
Independent variable	Exhaustion rate	Percentage of exhaustees drawing fewer than 26 weeks
Average potential duration of UI benefits	-1.80 (.56)	-11.81 (0.92)
Total unemployment rate	3.17 (.76)	-2.52 (1.24)
Constant	56.66 (13.28)	337.99 (21.69)
R^2 (adjusted)	.299	.787
N	51	51

NOTES: OLS estimates using state-level data for 1992. Standard errors in parentheses. Data are displayed in table 6.3.

The link between the proportion of regular exhaustees eligible for fewer than 26 weeks of benefits and the generosity of state duration provisions can be seen more clearly in the last column of table 6.4, where we have regressed the proportion of exhaustees drawing fewer than 26 weeks on the average potential duration of benefits and the total unemployment rate, again using the state data in table 6.3. States with higher average potential duration of benefits have a lower percentage of regular exhaustees drawing fewer than 26 weeks; a one-week increase in average potential duration is linked to a nearly 11 percentage point drop in the percentage of regular exhaustees drawing fewer than 26 weeks, controlling for the unemployment rate. States with higher total unemployment rates have *lower* percentages of exhaustees drawing fewer than 26 weeks, which reflects the rise in long-term unemployment (and hence in 26-week exhaustees) that accompanies increases in the unemployment rate.

The regressions in table 6.4 illustrate the linkages between measures of regular UI exhaustion and both the generosity of duration provisions (represented by the average potential duration of benefits in a state) and labor market factors (represented by the unemployment rate). The average potential duration of benefits in a state plays a strong role in explaining both the regular exhaustion rate and the percentage of exhaustees who draw fewer than 26 weeks of benefits.

Based on this discussion, what are the pros and cons of using the regular exhaustion rate as a criterion of the adequacy of the potential duration of regular benefits? The main drawback of the regular exhaustion rate is its dependence on both labor market conditions and state benefit duration formulas. This mutual dependence makes it difficult to determine what an appropriate target for the regular exhaustion rate should be. Although short-run changes in the exhaustion rate may serve as an indicator of increasing or decreasing duration adequacy, even these short-run changes may be contaminated by cyclical variations in the UI take-up rate.

Also, as discussed in the first section of this chapter, there is a link between weekly benefit amounts and the potential duration of benefits that implies a trade-off between the two. For example, two states that both limit total benefits to one-third of base-period earnings (that is, $a = 0.33$ in table 6.1) will have much different average potential durations—and hence exhaustion rates—if one provides low weekly benefit amounts (and hence longer potential durations) whereas the other provides high weekly benefit amounts (and hence shorter potential durations). The regular exhaustion rate does not take account of the trade-off between the weekly benefit amount and the potential duration of benefits.

Finally, there is considerable empirical evidence that unemployment duration—and hence the exhaustion rate—can increase with increases in either the potential duration of benefits or in the generosity of weekly benefit amounts. However, if exhaustions rose due to greater UI generosity, we would clearly not want to interpret that increase as an indication that UI benefits had become less adequate.

These drawbacks notwithstanding, the intuitive appeal of the exhaustion rate is so strong that it will undoubtedly continue to be a widely used indicator of duration adequacy. In particular, the secular increase in the exhaustion rate, which has occurred during a period when both weekly benefit amounts and potential durations were being reigned in, is a rather clear indicator that the potential duration of regular UI benefits has become less generous in the last 15 years.

Experience of Exhaustees

As already noted, the regular exhaustion rate itself may or may not provide a meaningful measure of whether benefits are of adequate duration. A high regular exhaustion rate could, of course, reflect difficulty in gaining reemployment due to slack demand, but it could also reflect the disincentive effects of UI benefits on job search, among other things. The experience of UI exhaustees has been used to gain insight into which of these factors—supply or demand—is more important in generating exhaustions.

The length of time between benefit exhaustion and reemployment is a potentially useful gauge of the experience of UI exhaustees and duration adequacy. Table 6.5 summarizes what is known about the reemployment experience of UI exhaustees, based on four studies that have been conducted since the mid-1960s. Only one of these studies, the Atlanta-Baltimore-Chicago-Seattle (or "four-city") study from the mid-1970s, was performed during a time when labor markets were slack (Nicholson and Corson 1976). The others were done during nonrecessionary times (Burgess and Kingston 1979; Corson and Dynarski 1990; Murray 1974).

In all four studies, one-half or more of the exhaustees remained jobless 12 weeks after exhausting their benefits. However, the main inference to be drawn from these studies is that UI exhaustees are much less likely to find reemployment during recessionary times than during nonrecessionary times. That is, the percentages of workers reemployed at 4, 8, and 12 weeks are similar in the Pennsylvania, Arizona, and twenty-state studies but are much lower in the four-city study (the only study that drew a sample of claimants who exhausted their benefits during a recession).

Less is known about the experience of exhaustees more than 12 weeks after benefit exhaustion. Only the Pennsylvania and twenty-state

Table 6.5 Summary of Selected Studies of UI Exhaustees: Percentage of Exhaustees Reemployed after Benefit Exhaustion

| Weeks since exhaustion | Pennsylvania, 1966-1967 | | | Atlanta-Baltimore-Chicago-Seattle, 1974-1975 | | | | Arizona, 1976-1977 | Twenty-state survey, 1987-1989 |
| | All | Under 29 weeks | 29 weeks or more | White | | Nonwhite | | | |
				Men	Women	Men	Women		
2				5.6	5.3	3.5	2.3	11.5	18
4	24.5	32.9	17.9	11.1	9.8	6.1	5.3	18.3	24
6				15.2	12.5	8.5	7.9	24.4	31
8	33.0	43.0	25.1	18.7	15.3	10.1	9.9	30.2	35
10				21.9	18.9	14.4	11.9	37.0	40
12	35.5	45.7	27.5	25.3	20.8	18.4	13.5	40.0	44
14				27.0	23.7	20.3	15.5	42.1	48
16	37.5	49.1	28.1						51
22									57
26	36.4	49.5	25.8						61
34	35.6	47.5	26.0						67
44	35.6	45.4	27.6						72
48		44.0	30.4						75
52	36.5								
Sample size	11,511	5,039	6,472	493	561	375	303	235	1,920

SOURCE: Pennsylvania data from Murray (1974, table 5); Atlanta-Baltimore-Chicago-Seattle data from Nicholson and Corson (1976, tables V.8 and V.9); Arizona data from Burgess and Kingston (1979, table II.7); twenty-state data estimated from Corson and Dynarski (1990, figure III.6).

studies give data on the status of longer-term exhaustees, and comparing the two gives very different impressions of the percentage of exhaustees who remain jobless 6 months to one year after exhaustion. In each case, however, the percentage still jobless 6 months to one year after exhaustion is substantial.

The Pennsylvania study shows that there are variations in the reemployment experiences of exhaustees whose pre-exhaustion spells of unemployment were relatively short or long. Also, the four-city study shows differences in the reemployment experiences of white and nonwhite exhaustees and of men and women. The differences between white and nonwhite exhaustees are less pronounced than those between men and women.

Mainly because each has sampled a group of exhaustees at a single point in time, the studies leave unanswered whether UI exhaustees' difficulties in gaining reemployment are the result mainly of high unemployment, structural changes in the economy, inadequate regular benefit entitlement, or a combination of these. Further research, especially on how the experience of exhaustees changes over the business cycle, could be extremely useful.[9] Indeed, without such studies, the appropriate remedies for the reemployment problems of UI exhaustees—or whether remedies are needed—will remain unclear.

One obvious approach, increasing the potential duration of benefits, is actually more difficult than it appears on the surface, even if there were agreement that it would be appropriate. There are two main ways of lengthening the potential duration of benefits. The first is to change the duration formula in a variable duration state so that more workers are eligible for 26 weeks of benefits. This can be done by increasing the parameter a in table 6.1 so that a higher fraction of base-period earnings can be recovered during a benefit year with a given weekly benefit amount. The second is to increase the maximum regular benefit duration beyond the usual 26-week limit. This approach presents several issues: how far the maximum should extend beyond 26 weeks; whether benefits past 26 weeks should be available to all or only to those with substantial employment history; whether such benefits should be offered at all times, or only during a recession; whether the financing of benefits beyond 26 weeks should be a state, federal, or a shared responsibility; and how regular benefits beyond 26 weeks should interrelate with the permanent federal-state system of extended benefits. These issues are discussed further below.

The alternatives to increasing potential duration are retraining, relocation, or other (less costly, usually administrative) assistance to improve reemployment prospects. Because retraining generally requires income support during the period of training, it is extremely costly. Accordingly, the U.S. Department of Labor has opted for "profiling," the attempt to identify workers who are likely to exhaust their benefits and to refer them to relatively inexpensive reemployment services. Profiling with job search assistance can be viewed both as an effort to assist workers in gaining reemployment and (equally) as an effort to sort workers by their degree of commitment to gaining reemployment.[10] For example, evidence from at least two studies suggests that requiring workers to obtain reemployment services as a condition of continued UI benefit receipt induces some to drop out of the labor force and others to find reemployment even before the required services are provided (Corson, Long, and Nicholson 1985; Johnson and Klepinger 1991).

Profiling could change the character of exhaustees by weeding out those who are weakly attached to the labor force and by helping many of the rest to gain reemployment more quickly. Accordingly, profiling could change the nature of the problems faced by those who do exhaust their UI benefits. It follows that implementation of profiling will, if anything, increase the need for further research into the problems faced by exhaustees in gaining reemployment. Finally, for profiling to work, the demand for labor must be strong enough to absorb the workers who receive reemployment services. The need to discern whether exhaustees' troubles in gaining reemployment stem from slack demand or other sources will remain.

Work Disincentives

UI has come to be viewed as a program of trade-offs and balances: worker versus employer interests, federal versus state authority, and benefit adequacy versus work disincentives. The program's goal of providing adequate benefits may collide with the objective of preserving work incentives if the benefits are so generous that they reduce workers' motivation to gain reemployment.

The effect of UI on the duration of insured unemployment has been the subject of many studies in the last 25 years, although the impact of increasing weekly benefit amounts has been analyzed more often than has the impact of increasing the potential duration of benefits. Table 6.6 provides a summary of selected studies that have examined the relationship between the potential duration of benefits and the duration of various measures of unemployment. The table indicates the data used in each study, the summary estimate (or range of estimates) of the impact of an additional week of potential duration of UI benefits on the duration of unemployment, and provides remarks on the estimating technique.

It is clear that the estimates vary widely, from 0 in three cases to 0.9 in one case. This range, taken literally, would suggest that a 13-week benefit extension could have no impact on the expected duration of unemployment of workers, or could increase the expected duration of unemployment by nearly 12 weeks (13 weeks times 0.9). From the viewpoint of policy, such a wide range is not especially helpful. What factors can account for this dispersion of estimates?

First, as is almost always true in economic research, the data available to study the impact of potential duration on the expected duration of unemployment have limitations. Most of the studies summarized in table 6.6 have used UI administrative records, which are an excellent source of data on benefits and the duration of *insured* unemployment but do not track workers beyond their spell of insured unemployment. As a result, observed spells of unemployment are censored at the potential duration of benefits.

There are econometric methods for dealing with such data, although none is wholly satisfactory. A full treatment of these techniques and their various strengths and weaknesses is beyond the scope of this discussion, but it seems that studies that use UI exit rate models obtain lower estimates of the impact of increases in the potential duration of benefits than do studies that use maximum likelihood (including Tobit) duration models.[11] Given that the UI exit rate models impose less onerous distributional assumptions, they should probably be given greater weight than the other estimation methods.[12]

Second, the relationship between potential duration and the probability of reemployment (and hence the duration of unemployment) may vary with the tightness of the labor market. Even if an additional week

Table 6.6 Selected Estimates of the Impact of Increased Potential Duration of UI Benefits

Study	Data	Change in weeks of unemployment from 1 added week of potential UI	Remarks
Classen (1979)	UI claimants in Arizona and Pennsylvania, 1967-1969	0 - 0.12	Tobit duration estimates
Newton and Rosen (1979)	UI recipients in Georgia, 1974-1976	0.6	Tobit duration estimates
Katz and Ochs (1980)	Current Population Survey, individuals in 26 states, 1968-1970 and 1973-1977	0.17 - 0.23	Maximum likelihood duration esimates
Moffitt and Nicholson (1982)	Recipients of EB and FSC, 15 states, 1975-1977	0.1	Labor supply model, maximum likelihood estimates
Moffitt (1985a)	Continuous Wage Benefit History, 1978-1983	0.15	UI exit rate estimates
Moffitt (1985b)	Continuous Wage and benefit History, 1978-1983:		UI exit rate estimates
	White men	0.17	
	White women	0.10	
	FSC and EB recipients in 15 states, 1975-1978:		Maximum likelihood duration estimates
	Men	0.45	
	Women	0.28	
	UI recipients in Georgia, 1974-1976:		Maximum likelihood duration estimates
	Men	0.17	
	Women	0.37	
Solon (1985)	UI claimants in Georgia, 1978-1979	0.36	Maximum likelihood duration estimates

Study	Data	Change in weeks of unemployment from 1 added week of potential UI	Remarks
Ham and Rea (1987)	Canadian men, 1975-1980	0.26 - 0.35	UI exit rate estimates
Grossman (1989)	Continuous Wage and Benefit History, individuals in 3 states, 1981-1984	0.9	UI exit rate estimates of FSC impacts on UI exhaustees
Katz and Meyer (1990)	Continuous Wage and Benefit History, men in 12 states, 1978-1983	0.16 - 0.20	UI exit rate estimates
Davidson and Woodbury (1995)	UI recipients in: Illinois 1984-1985	0.2	Translation of reemployment bonus impacts using equilibrium search model
	Pennsylvania 1988-1989	0 - 0.2	
	Washington 1988-1989	0 - 0.2	

of benefits had the same effect on the intensity of a worker's job search regardless of the state of the labor market, that given change in search intensity would translate into a different reemployment probability depending on the availability of job offers. There have been few attempts to estimate how the impact of an additional week of potential duration varies with labor market conditions (but see Wandner 1975). There is a real need for further investigation of this issue.

Third, some studies have focused on the impact of increasing the potential duration of regular benefits, others have focused on the impact of EB, and still others have focused on the impacts of emergency extensions such as Federal Supplemental Benefits and Federal Supplemental Compensation. There is some evidence that the impacts of EB and emergency extensions are greater than the impacts of increasing the potential duration of regular benefits, but further work sorting out the various impacts and the reasons for them would clearly be useful.

Finally, there may simply be greater variation in the behavior of workers than economists are accustomed to considering. This is suggested, for example, by results derived from the reemployment bonus experiments, all of which were similarly designed, implemented, and monitored, but which nevertheless yielded results that varied over a substantial range (Davidson and Woodbury 1996).

If we eliminate the estimates that are obtained using duration models, then we significantly reduce the variation in the estimates. The exceptions are Grossman's study (1989), which differs from the others because it examines the impact of increasing the potential duration of benefits of workers who have already exhausted regular benefits, and Ham and Rea's study (1987) of the Canadian UI system, which differs in a variety of ways from the U.S. system. With these exceptions, all of the UI exit rate estimates are in the range of 0.1 to 0.2. Similarly, Moffitt and Nicholson (1982) obtain an estimate of 0.1 week, and translating the reemployment bonus impacts using an equilibrium search model yields estimates in the range of 0 to 0.2 (Davidson and Woodbury 1996). On the whole, then, the evidence suggests that increasing the potential duration of UI benefits by one week increases the expected duration of unemployment by one day (0.2 week) or less.

Optimal Unemployment Insurance

Efforts to use economic and econometric methods to gauge the optimal duration of UI benefits are relatively few and recent. Although the studies reviewed in this section have yet to point unambiguously toward conclusions about the optimal duration of benefits, the approach holds out hope of generating recommendations that are based on clearly articulated assumptions and observed behavior. Since benefit adequacy is reviewed in chapter 5, we focus on recent analyses that bear closely on the potential duration of benefits.

O'Leary's work on benefit adequacy (forthcoming) uses consumer theory informed by econometric estimates of the trade-off between income and leisure and concludes that short spells of unemployment are overcompensated by UI, whereas long spells are undercompensated. O'Leary's result stems from the assumption that the marginal utility of leisure diminishes. That is, an additional week of leisure (in the form of unemployment) has a far higher value to someone who works 50 weeks in a year (and has just 2 weeks of leisure) than to someone who works only 26 weeks in a year (and has 26 weeks of leisure). It follows that a much smaller weekly benefit amount is needed to compensate a worker for the first few weeks of unemployment (since the leisure implied by those first weeks is itself more valuable) than is needed to compensate a worker for later weeks of unemployment. However, since the weekly benefit amount is generally constant over the spell of insured unemployment, early weeks of unemployment (and short spells) are more fully compensated than are later weeks (and long spells).

Although the logic of O'Leary's findings is clear, the implications for policy are somewhat less so. Whenever there is moral hazard, as with UI, full compensation for the occurrence of a risky event is undesirable, since it raises the probability of the event (or its continuation). If the disincentive effect (that is, reduced job search intensity) of an additional week of potential benefits increases with the length of a spell of unemployment, then raising the weekly benefit amount as a spell of unemployment lengthens might be unattractive. The implications of raising the weekly benefit amount as a spell lengthens would need to be examined in a model that takes account of both the benefits and costs of doing so. An alternative way of correcting the overcompensation of short spells would be to extend the waiting period. This has the additional attraction of freeing funds that could be used to finance benefits beyond the usual limit of 26 weeks, in order to correct the undercompensation of long-term unemployed workers. Again, however, the implications of doing so need to be explored in a model that takes account of the response of unemployed workers to the proposed change in the pattern of unemployment compensation.

Gruber (forthcoming) has pointed out that appraising benefit adequacy by comparing UI benefits with pre-unemployment income is appropriate only if workers have no access to other sources of income, such as savings, loans, or the labor supply of other household members. If alternative income sources exist, then UI may substitute for the other ways of financing a spell of unemployment, crowd them out, and have no real effect on consumption. This insight highlights the importance of examining whether UI actually smoothes consumption, that is, whether unemployed workers who are eligible for more generous UI benefits experience smaller drops in consumption than do workers who are eligible for less generous UI benefits.

Gruber obtains conflicting results on whether UI smoothes consumption. Using data from the Panel Study of Income Dynamics, he finds quite strong evidence of consumption smoothing, whereas using data from the Survey of Consumer Expenditures, he finds far weaker evidence of smoothing. The latter result suggests that UI does crowd out other ways of financing a spell of unemployment, whereas the former result suggests that it does not. Until this empirical issue is resolved, it will be important to examine whether findings about benefit adequacy and optimal UI programs are sensitive to assumptions about the ability of workers to save and borrow, and the willingness of other members of the household to work more when the principal earner is unemployed.

We turn next to work on optimal UI that takes an equilibrium approach and incorporates both the benefits and costs (including those resulting from induced changes in behavior) of the UI system. There was a flurry of interest in this approach in the late 1970s—the contributions of Baily (1978) and Flemming (1978) are considered the classic treatments—although its complexity seems to have stalled further development. From our perspective, it is especially important that both Baily and Flemming assumed the potential duration of UI benefits to be infinite and derived an optimal replacement rate based on that assumption. Clearly, this assumes away the problem with which we are most concerned: the optimal potential duration of benefits.

Recently, Davidson and Woodbury (forthcoming) have extended the work of Baily and Flemming to examine the optimal potential duration of UI.[13] Surprisingly, they find that the optimal UI program is characterized by an infinite potential duration of benefits. The argument is as follows. Let WBA denote the weekly benefit amount and let T denote the potential duration of benefits. Suppose that we compare two UI programs (WBA_1, T_1) and (WBA_2, T_2) with $WBA_1 > WBA_2$ and $T_1 < T_2$ so that the second program offers lower benefits but a longer potential duration of benefits. Suppose further that these two programs cost the same amount to fund so that employed workers earn the same after-tax wage under the two programs. Then it can be shown that all risk-averse workers prefer the second program even though weekly benefit amounts are lower. The second program is preferred because the reduced probability that workers will exhaust their benefits more than offsets the reduction in weekly benefits. In the terminology of decision making under uncertainty, the second program is "less risky" than the first program and is therefore preferred by all risk-averse agents. Alternatively, to use the terminology that Rothschild and Stiglitz (1970) introduced in their classic paper on increasing risk, the second UI program, with longer potential duration and lower benefit amount, is a "mean-preserving spread," which reduces the risk associated with unemployment. Since the optimal UI program offers benefits indefinitely, while most states offer benefits for only 26 weeks, the model's results suggest that the potential durations in the U.S. system may not be generous enough.

Three remarks on this potentially controversial result need to be made. First, a likely objection to the finding that an infinite potential duration of benefits is optimal is that, if benefits were inexhaustible, workers would never return to work. It is true that lengthening the potential duration of benefits would lead workers to remain unemployed longer and to a higher unemployment rate. Davidson and Woodbury (forthcoming) show that increasing the potential duration of UI benefits from 6 months to an unlimited period with a UI replacement rate of 0.5 would raise the unemployment rate from 7 percent to 10 percent. However, this is not a shut down of the economy: workers would not collect UI benefits paying a replacement rate of 0.5 (or 0.75) forever. Also, the increase in the unemployment rate would result from voluntary behavior, not from economic hard times, and would connote an improvement in workers' well-being.

A second, more serious, objection is that extending benefits and lowering the benefit amount reduce the aggregate search effort of unemployed workers, which in turn could reduce employment. Lower employment would mean reduced tax revenues, so that the total amount paid to the unemployed would drop. If this occurred, the costs of the new program could outweigh its benefits (which stem mainly from reduced risk). It turns out, however, that this chain of events would not take place. The reason is that the reduction in aggregate search effort is almost fully offset by a change in the distribution of search effort across the spell of unemployment. That is, with a longer potential duration of benefits, search effort becomes more evenly distributed across the spell of unemployment, and this increases equilibrium employment. Davidson and Woodbury provide a simulation showing the net effects of the change in aggregate search effort and the change in the distribution of search effort: as the potential duration of UI benefits rises, unemployment rises by such a small amount that any loss in tax revenue is dominated by society's savings in aggregate search costs (the benefit of reduced aggregate search effort). Hence, changes in search effort do not erase the result that the optimal potential duration of benefits is infinite.

A third possible objection is that Davidson and Woodbury assume UI-eligible workers to be homogeneous; it is unclear whether the result that the optimal potential duration of benefits is unlimited is sensitive to this assumption. In future work, it will be important to consider that some UI-eligible workers may be weakly attached to the labor force, that some workers have a high probability of layoff with a low expected duration of unemployment (as do many blue-collar production workers), and that others face a low probability of layoff with a longer expected duration of unemployment (for example, white-collar nonproduction workers). It is an open question whether an unlimited potential duration of benefits would remain optimal in a model that accounts for these various types of workers.

Extended Benefit Programs

When unemployment rates rise in the wake of a recession, spells of unemployment tend to lengthen and more workers exhaust their UI benefits, that is, more workers experience spells of unemployment that exceed their potential duration of UI benefits. Whether these lengthened spells of unemployment occur because job separation rates rise or because reemployment rates fall is unimportant. As long as the lengthened spells result from slack demand and employer behavior (rather than from voluntary worker behavior), there is a justification for increasing the potential duration of UI benefits.

On six different occasions, beginning in 1958, Congress has reacted to slack labor markets by providing a limited number of weeks of federally financed "extended" benefits to workers who had exhausted their regular state benefits. In addition to these six temporary or discretionary programs, Congress in 1970 established a permanent or "standby" extended benefits program (under the Extended Unemployment Compensation Act), which in principle is activated automatically by conditions of high unemployment. The following discussion provides a brief history of the six temporary programs and of the standby extended benefits program.[14] We also discuss the three most controversial issues surrounding extended benefits: how these benefits should be activated, whether additional qualifying and eligibility conditions should be required, and how such benefits should be financed. Finally, we recommend two changes in extended benefit policy based on the evidence and discussion.

Federal Extended Benefit Programs: A Brief History

Currently, the maximum potential duration of unemployment benefits provided by regular state programs ("first-tier" programs) is 26 weeks in all states except Massachusetts and Washington, where the maximum potential duration is 30 weeks (see table 6.1 and the accompanying text). In ten states, the potential duration of benefits is 26 weeks for all claimants who qualify for any benefits (Illinois and New York are the only large states that provide such "uniform potential duration" of benefits). In every other state, the potential duration of benefits varies with a claimant's work experience in the base period, roughly the year preceding the claim for benefits (again, see the first section of this chapter).

Table 6.7 provides a summary of the main features of the six federal programs that have temporarily extended the potential duration of unemployment benefits beyond the duration provided by state programs. The permanent standby Extended Benefit program (EB) is also summarized in the table. The standby EB program has come to be called the "second tier" of the UI system, and temporary emergency extensions have come to be called the "third tier" of the system.

The first two federal temporary benefit extensions, Temporary Unemployment Compensation (TUC) and Temporary Extended Unemployment Compensation (TEUC), were enacted in 1958 and 1961. They were similar in that each lasted slightly over a year and extended the potential duration of benefits to workers who exhausted their regular state benefits by 50 percent, up to a maximum of 13 extra

Table 6.7 Federal Extended Unemployment Benefit Programs, 1958 to 1995

Program and enabling legislation	Effective dates and extensions	Potential duration of extended benefits provided	Financing	Notes
Temporary Unemployment Compensation Act, P.L. 85-441	6/58 - 7/59	50% of regular state duration, up to 13 weeks	Interest-free loans to 17 participating states	State participation voluntary
Temporary Extended Unemployment Compensation Act (TEUC), P.L. 87-6	4/61 - 6/62	50% of regular state duration, up to 13 weeks	Temporary increases in Federal Unemployment Tax (.4% in 1962, .25% in 1963)	
Extended Unemployment Compensation Act of 1970 (EB), P.L. 91-373, with major amendments in P.L. 96-364, P.L. 96-499, P.L. 97-35, P.L. 102-318	8/70 to present	50% of regular state duration, up to 13 weeks	One-half from Federal Unemployment Tax revenues paid to Extended Unemployment Compensation Account (EUCA); one-half from state UI reserves	EB activated in a state by an insured unemployment rate (IUR) trigger, 8/70 to present; EB could be activated in all states by a national IUR trigger, 8/70 to 8/81. Effective 1981, EB denied to claimants refusing to seek or accept suitable work and to claimants who had quit or been discharged. State triggers were made more restrictive 8/81. Eligibility for EB made more restrictive, effective 9/82. States permitted to adopt a total unemployment rate (TUR) trigger, 6/93

Program	Dates	Duration	Extended Unemployment Compensation Account (EUCA)	State-level triggers (different from EB triggers) used to activate program
Emergency Unemployment Compensation Act, P.L. 92-224 and P.L. 92-329	1/72 - 9/72, extended to 3/73	50% of regular state durations, up to 13 weeks		
Federal Supplemental Benefits (FSB), P.L. 93-572, P.L. 94-12, P.L. 94-45, P.L. 95-19	1/75 - 12/76, extended to 1/78	50% of regular state duration, up to 13 weeks (1/75-2/75 and 5/77-1/78); additional 50% of regular state duration, up to 13 weeks provided 3/75-4/77 (that is, up to 26 weeks of FSB total)	Repayable advances to EUCA from general revenues; general revenues after 3/77	EB program was activated in all states, so total potential benefit duration was 65 for those exhausting EB weeks between 3/75 and 4/77. State-level triggers applied starting 1/76. Uniform federal eligibility and disqualification standards implemented 4/77 (P.L. 95-19)
Federal Supplemental Compensation (FSC), P.L. 97-258, P.L. 97-424, P.L. 98-21, P.L. 98-135	9/82 - 3/83, extended to 9/83 and 3/85	FSC-I (9/82-1/83): 50% of regular state duration, up to 6 or 10 weeks. FSC-II (1/83-3/83): 65% of regular state duration, up to 8 or 16 weeks. FSC-IV (10/83-3/85): same as FSC-III, except entitlement did not vary once established	General revenues	Potential duration varied with state's EB status and separate FSC triggers. Except in FSC-IV, potential duration would vary when state's EB or FSC status changed. FSC-I and FSC-II exhaustees could collect FSC-III benefits, but not FSC-IV benefits. EB eligibility criteria applied to all phases of FSC. Available regular state benefits and EB (if activated) had to be exhausted to receive FSC

(continued)

254

Table 6.7 (continued)

Program and enabling legislation	Effective dates and extensions	Potential duration of extended benefits provided	Financing	Notes
Emergency Unemployment Compensation Act of 1991 (EUC), P.L. 102-164, P.L. 102-182, P.L. 102-244, P.L. 102-318, P.L. 103-6, P.L. 103-152	11/91 - 6/92, extended to 7/92, 3/93, 10/ 93, and 2/94	EUC-I (11/91-2/92): lesser of 100% of regular benefits, or 13 or 20 weeks EUC-II (2/92-7/92): lesser of 130% of regular benefits, or 26 or 33 weeks EUC-III (7/92-3/93): lesser of 100% of regular benefits, or 20 or 26 weeks EUC-IV (3/93-10/93): lesser of 60% of regular benefits, or 10 or 15 weeks EUC-V (10/93-2/94): lesser of 50% of regular benefits, or 7 or 13 weeks	EUC-I, EUC-II, and EUC-III from Extended Unemployment Compensation Account (EUCA); EUC-III and EUC-IV from general revenues	Potential duration determined at time of filing for EUC and depended on state's classification as high- or low-unemployment. EUC entitlement could be increased if state moved from low to high status, or if program became more generous; EUC entitlement could not be decreased. Claimants exhausting benefits between 3/91 and 11/91 could receive benefits under "reach-back" provisions (but no retroactive benefits paid). EB eligibility criteria applied to all phases of EUC. Once EUC was exhausted, a claimant needed to regain regular UI eligibility to receive additional EUC

weeks. They differed, however, in that TUC was a voluntary program financed by interest-free loans to 17 participating states. TEUC, on the other hand, was mandatory and was financed through increases in the federal unemployment tax.

If one accepts the need for extending benefits in a recession, then relying on temporary emergency extensions such as TUC and TEUC is clearly suboptimal. Temporary extensions are discretionary rather than triggered automatically. It takes time for Congress to recognize the onset of a recession and to enact legislation in response, so there may be a significant lag between the onset of slack labor markets and the availability of extended benefits. Also, temporary extensions have proven politically difficult to shut down, as we show below, so they are both slow to turn on and slow to turn off. Finally, temporary emergency extensions have usually been made effective on the date of enactment, leaving UI administrators little or no time to implement the new program.

In recognition of these problems with temporary extensions, in 1965 and 1966 Congress considered a proposal to create a permanent (or "standby") extended benefits program. The proposal was modeled on earlier temporary programs, in that it extended the potential duration of benefits by 50 percent, up to 13 weeks, for workers who exhausted their regular state benefits. However, the extended benefits would have been "triggered" automatically in a recession (rather than requiring congressional discretion and action) and would have been financed half-and-half by the states and the federal government. (Recall that regular UI benefits are financed out of state UI trust funds, whereas TEUC and most subsequent emergency extended benefits have been financed out of the federal UI trust fund.)

Although the proposal for a permanent standby extended benefits program failed in 1966, Congress enacted essentially the same proposal in 1970 as the Extended Unemployment Compensation Act, generally known as the Extended Benefits program, or EB. The intent of the permanent "standby" EB program was and is to extend automatically the potential duration of benefits when the economy slumps into recession, rather than to rely on a reaction from Congress. EB extends benefits to claimants who exhaust their regular state benefits by an amount equal to one-half of their regular benefit duration, up to 13 weeks. The weekly benefit amount is the same as the weekly benefit amount under the regular state program. Originally, EB was activated nationally whenever the national insured unemployment rate (IUR) averaged at least 4 percent for 13 weeks. Also, it was activated in a given state whenever the state's IUR averaged at least 4 percent for 13 weeks and was 20 percent above the state IUR of the corresponding 13-week period in either of the two previous years. The EB program is financed half-and-half from the federal and state UI trust funds. In the next part of this section, we discuss the activation (or "triggering") of EB, special qualifying and eligibility requirements, and financing.

States were allowed to adopt EB as early as October 1970 and were required to do so no later than January 1972. Even before EB became available in all states, however, Congress enacted the third temporary extension under the Emergency Unemployment Compensation Act (sometimes called "Temporary Compensation" or "TC"), which provided up to 13 weeks of extended benefits to claimants who either exhausted EB or exhausted regular benefits in states where EB was not available. Temporary Compensation was activated by special triggers that differed from the standby EB triggers. It was financed from Federal Unemployment Tax Act (FUTA) revenues. The program, which originally was set to run from January 1972 until September 1972, was extended through March 1973.

During the severe recession of the mid-1970s, the national trigger activated EB in all states, permitting workers to receive up to 26 weeks of regular unemployment benefits followed by up to 13 weeks of EB. Nevertheless, the recession was so severe that Congress enacted the fourth temporary emergency extension in January 1975, Federal Supplemental Benefits (FSB), which provided up to 13 additional weeks of benefits to those who exhausted regular benefits and EB.

In March 1975, the FSB program was extended and made more generous by providing yet another 13 weeks of benefits. As a result of this and further extensions of FSB, a claimant could receive up to 65 weeks of unemployment benefits for the period March 1975 through March 1977: 26 weeks of regular state benefits, 13 weeks of EB, and 26 weeks of FSB.

In April 1977, FSB was extended again (through January 1978), but the potential duration of benefits was reduced to 13 weeks from May 1977 through the end of the program. This extension also added special federal disqualifications for refusal of suitable work and for failure to actively seek work, defined suitable work for the FSB program, and added special penalty and repayment provisions for fraudulent acts on the part of both claimants and employers. This was the first time such disqualifications had been imposed as part of a temporary emergency extension.

In 1980 and 1981, Congress passed three changes that made it more difficult for the EB program to activate. First, the trigger that had activated EB nationally was eliminated. Second, the IUR needed to activate EB on a state-specific basis was increased. Third, the definition of insured unemployment was revised so as to omit EB claimants from the computation, reducing the IUR in times when EB was activated. In addition, more stringent eligibility and disqualifying conditions were imposed on EB claimants. All of these changes reflected a changed attitude toward extended benefits, one that reflected the intent of the new Reagan administration and Congress to reduce domestic programs. Corson and Nicholson's analysis (1985) concluded that the 1981-1982 changes in EB "had the effect of significantly reducing its overall size" (p. vii). Subsequent events suggest a stronger conclusion—that the changes virtually disabled the program.

Nevertheless, the parade of emergency unemployment benefit extensions continued in response to later recessions. In 1982, Congress enacted Federal Supplemental Compensation (FSC) as part of the Tax Equity and Fiscal Responsibility Act of 1982. FSC was different from previous emergency extended benefit programs in that the number of weeks payable in each state varied according to different criteria at different times. In fact, FSC went through four "phases," each of which provided different potential benefit durations for each state depending on the state's labor market conditions (see table 6.7, under "potential duration of extended benefits provided"). Under phase II, a UI claimant in a high unemployment state could be eligible for up to 55 weeks of benefits: 26 from the regular state program, 13 from EB (assuming the state had triggered on), and 16 from FSC.

Potential durations were somewhat shorter under phases III and IV of FSC, but the interstate differences in potential benefit durations were retained. Under FSC, then, there was more tinkering (or, more charitably, greater effort to fine-tune the program) than under previous emergency extensions in two senses. First, the idea that emergency extensions should provide different potential benefit durations to different states was wholly new. Second, the various phases of FSC led to frequent changes in potential benefit duration and created administrative difficulties for the states. Both of these aspects of FSC began to call into question the role of emergency extensions and seemed to be an admission that the standby EB program was already defunct.

The most recent emergency extension of unemployment benefits, Emergency Unemployment Compensation (EUC), was enacted in November 1991 after months of foot-dragging by the Bush administration, which had vetoed several earlier emergency extensions. EUC was the most complicated emergency benefit extension of all: it went through *five* phases, provided different potential durations across states at a given time, and had different potential durations within a state over time (see table 6.7 and Storey and Falk 1993). The potential duration of benefits within a state could change either because of congressional fiat (that is, a movement from one phase to another), or because a state changed its classification between high unemployment and low unemployment. By all accounts, EUC was a state UI administrator's nightmare. In Pennsylvania, for example, the potential duration of benefits changed *nine* times between November 1991, when EUC became effective, and February 1994, when phase V of EUC terminated. Five of these changes resulted from enactment of EUC or a movement from one phase to another, and four resulted because Pennsylvania was reclassified from low unemployment to high unemployment or vice versa. At one point, Congress let EUC lapse, but subsequently resuscitated it, and during the hiatus, state administrators and UI claimants were left hanging.

Activating Extended Benefits

We have already treated the rationale for limiting potential duration, the experience of exhaustees, the work disincentives of extending the potential duration of benefits, and the idea of optimal UI. These issues are important to the potential duration of regular and extended benefits alike. However, three issues are specific to extending benefits during a recession: how extended benefits should be activated, whether additional qualifying and eligibility conditions should be required for extended benefits, and how extended benefits should be financed. We discuss extended benefit triggers first and then turn to the latter two issues.

Activating Extended Benefits: National and State-Level Triggers

When the EB program began, extended benefits could be activated either nationally or on a state-specific basis. The national "trigger" activated the program in all states whenever the seasonally adjusted national IUR reached 4.5 percent for 13 weeks. The state-specific trigger activated the program in a state whenever a state's IUR reached 4 percent for 13 consecutive weeks and was at least 20 percent above the average state IUR of the corresponding 13-week period in either of the two previous years.

As shown in table 6.7 (see notes to Extended Unemployment Compensation Act of 1970), in 1980 and 1981, the national trigger was eliminated and the state-level trigger was raised from an IUR of 4 percent to 5 percent. In addition, the definition of the IUR was revised to exclude workers receiving extended and supplemental benefits, lowering the IUR. These changes made it less likely that EB would be activated in a recession. Combined with secularly falling insured unemployment rates, resulting mainly from decreased participation in UI,[15] the changes of 1981 led to a situation in which EB was nearly defunct by the time of the recession of the early 1990s. In fact, EB was activated in only 10 states during that recession and failed to be activated in several states where many observers felt labor market conditions were bad enough to warrant it.[16]

The decreasing availability of EB during recessions would seem to have been exactly the outcome desired by Congress in the early 1980s. However, in response to the failure of EB to be activated widely during the early 1990s recession, a later Congress passed legislation in July 1992 (and effective June 1993) allowing states to adopt an alternative trigger based on the total unemployment rate (TUR), that is, the conventionally defined unemployment rate estimated monthly by the Current Population Survey. The alternative trigger activates EB in a state if the state's three-month average TUR exceeds 6.5 percent and is 10 percent above the three-month average TUR in either of the two preceding years.

It is clear that, during the recession of the early 1990s, the alternative TUR trigger would have activated EB in many more states than did the old IUR trigger (Advisory Council on Unemployment Compensation 1994, chapter 6). The old trigger activated EB in ten states for an average of 6.2 months, resulting in benefit payments of $.9 billion. If the alternative TUR trigger had been in effect in all states throughout the recession, EB would have been activated in forty-three states for an average of 18.4 months, resulting in benefit payments of $11.8 billion.[17] Hence, nationwide adoption of the alternative TUR trigger would largely solve the problem of EB becoming defunct.

However, only seven states have adopted the alternative TUR trigger, and all did so shortly after the legislation was enacted. No additional state has since switched to the new TUR trigger. This suggests that the states are unwilling to take on the burden of funding even partially the second-tier or standby extended benefit program. Rather, they would prefer to rely entirely on temporary emergency extensions, wholly financed by the federal government.

During congressional debate on whether to extend the Emergency Unemployment Compensation program in 1992 and 1993, Republicans in Congress argued that if Congress continued its pattern of enacting emergency extensions whenever the economy went into recession, there would be no incentive for the states to switch to the new alternative EB trigger (that is, the trigger that is based on the TUR). Indeed, states have stalled in adopting the new TUR trigger because they do not really want EB to be activated in a recession. The old IUR trigger has become ineffective and rarely activates EB, whereas the alternative TUR trigger would be more effective. States, however, naturally prefer to have the federal government step in and provide emergency extended benefits, since emergency benefits have been financed wholly by the federal government. In contrast, only half of EB payments are financed by the federal government; the other half is financed out of states UI trust fund accounts. As long as the states can argue that EB is not providing adequate benefit durations, they can reasonably urge Congress to enact emergency extensions. Furthermore, as long as Congress accommodates the states with emergency extensions, the states have no incentive to switch to the alternative TUR trigger, which would be more effective but would also result in greater benefit payments from state UI trust funds.

A cynic might argue that Congress really does not want the standby EB program to work effectively, either—that members would prefer to step in and enact an emergency program whenever the economy slumps. An emergency program shows that Congress has "done something" in an economic downturn and offers the politicians a concrete program to point to when they stand for reelection. Such a cynical view may not be wholly unrealistic: the alternative TUR trigger *would* activate extended benefits in a recession (unlike the IUR trigger), and Congress *could* require the states to switch to the alternative TUR trigger. However, Congress has not done so.[18]

Activating Extended Benefits: Substate Triggers

An additional issue that has been considered repeatedly in Congress is substate triggers, that is, allowing EB to be activated in a depressed local area *within a state*, rather than requiring that EB be activated throughout a state when conditions in the entire state are severe enough. The logic underlying this notion is that, from the standpoint of labor markets, state boundaries may be quite arbitrary. There may be large differences in labor market conditions between urban areas within states (consider, for example, Philadelphia and Pittsburgh, or Los Angeles and San Francisco) or between the urban and rural parts of a state. Isn't it unfair to deny extended benefits to unemployed workers who live in a region that is experiencing high unemployment simply because they happen to live in a state where—overall—the unemployment rate is too low for the EB program to be activated? Wouldn't substate triggers allow more effective targeting of benefits to workers who are having real difficulty finding reemployment?

The arguments against adopting substate EB triggers are many and include considerations of administration, equity, and unavailability of appropriate data, as well as concerns about whether such a program would meet its intended goals (Czajka, Long, and Nicholson 1989; Advisory Council on Unemployment Compensation 1994, chapter 6). A major administrative stumbling block would be defining appropriate areas within states. Bills proposing the use of substate area triggers have provided a variety of regional definitions, including areas designated by the Secretary of Labor as contiguous population centers of at least 250,000, of at least 50,000, any county or equivalent of a county, any area designated as a Service Delivery Area under the Job Training Partnership Act, and any area designated as an economic area by the Bureau of Economic Analysis in the Department of Commerce.[19] As a geographical unit for activating EB, it is unclear whether any such local area would be less arbitrary than the state. Also, it is unclear whether individuals would be assigned to an area based on place of work or on place of residence. Whatever definitions of substate regions were adopted, it is clear that the potential for fraud would be greater and that it would be more difficult and costly to determine eligibility and process interstate (and interarea) claims. All of these issues raise concerns about the equity of substate triggers, since triggering EB in local areas could make it more likely that similar individuals facing similar labor market conditions and living near each other would receive different EB entitlements.

Another major problem in implementing substate triggers would be obtaining data for the substate triggers themselves. Accurate indicators of labor market conditions in each local area of the country are simply unavailable at present. The accuracy of substate TUR estimates is highly suspect. Data on employment levels are available only in 250 metropolitan areas and would need to be developed for places outside those areas. Developing either the TUR or local area employment statistics so that they could be used as an EB trigger would be difficult and costly.

Finally, in the most complete study of substate triggers, Czajka, Long, and Nicholson (1989) conclude that, although a substate program could be designed so as to improve the targeting of UI benefits to workers in slack labor markets during *non*recessionary times, the potential improvement in targeting during a recession is small. In other words, most of the increased benefit payments under a program of substate triggers would be made during nonrecessionary times, and the basic goal of a substate program, improved access to extended benefits during a recession, would not be achieved.

State boundaries have long been accepted for triggering extended benefit programs because the state has always been the basic operational unit for UI. Serious unemployment in local areas is clearly an appropriate concern of state and local governments, but it is more appropriately addressed through local economic development programs, or perhaps through individual state experiments with UI, than by means of the EB program (which has a significant federal component). Also, as discussed, the existing standby EB program no longer responds even to statewide unemployment problems because the old

IUR trigger no longer activates the program and states have dragged their feet in adopting the new TUR triggers. Fixing the existing EB program is clearly a more urgent priority of federal UI policy than trying to fine-tune the program to deal with the problems of localities.

Conclusions on Extended Benefit Triggers

The future of the EB program and emergency extensions is quite unclear at this time. Congress seems to pay attention to the UI system only when there is a recession, so the role of politics would seem to be more important than the role of economic (or any) analysis in determining the future of extended benefits. It needs to be noted that relatively little effort has been devoted to understanding what is (or would be) the socially optimal potential duration of benefits or to analyzing the extent to which the optimal potential duration should change with changing labor market conditions. These gaps, convincingly addressed, could have an impact on policy and on the future direction of extended unemployment benefits. Notwithstanding the gaps in our understanding of the optimal potential duration of benefits, we develop two sets of recommendations for extended benefit policy in the last part of this section.

Further Issues in Extended Benefits

Qualifying and Eligibility Requirements for Extended Benefits

In addition to making it more difficult for EB to trigger on, the 1980 and 1981 amendments to the standby EB program made eligibility for EB more restrictive. Whereas originally, all UI exhaustees were eligible for available extended benefits, the program now requires that workers have at least 20 weeks of work (or the equivalent) in the base period to qualify for EB.

The 1980 and 1981 amendments also require EB claimants to actively search for work and require the disqualification of EB claimants who failed to accept or apply for suitable work or training to which they were referred by the state Employment Service. This disqualification is for the duration of unemployment.[20]

The prevailing motivation behind the amendments was to reduce the size of the program, and the appeal for their enactment was made largely on that basis. It was also argued that the claimants affected were long-term unemployed persons lacking in initiative and hence less deserving of extended benefits (Rubin 1983, p. 115).

What are the merits of increasing the eligibility requirements for EB and of requiring EB claimants to satisfy the work search test? The research on benefit adequacy and optimal UI outlined in the second section of this chapter offers support for providing EB to all workers who exhaust regular UI when EB is in effect. Three arguments do favor setting more stringent eligibility requirements for extended benefits than for regular benefits, although their merits are debatable. The first is that individuals who have worked longer (and whose employers have contributed more) should have greater entitlement to benefits. Second, setting more stringent eligibility requirements for EB than for regular benefits reduces the financial cost of EB. Third, more stringent eligibility requirements for EB may limit the moral hazard of EB. For this third argument to be persuasive, there would need to be evidence that the work disincentive of an additional week of EB is greater for some workers—those who appear to be less strongly attached to the labor force—than for others. We are unaware of any such evidence, however.

Requiring EB claimants to satisfy a more stringent (and uniform) federal work search test makes little sense if indeed there are few job vacancies during periods when EB is activated. State UI administrators and employers alike would prefer to waive the work search test for EB in regions where it is clear that job vacancies are scarce. Imposing the work search test in such regions has little value and is costly to both administrators (who are expected to enforce the requirement) and to employers (who may get job inquiries from claimants who are merely trying to satisfy the work test without any serious hope of gaining reemployment). These findings are reflected in one of the recommendations of the Advisory Council on Unemployment Compensation, which suggested that "Each state should be allowed to determine an appropriate work search test, based on the conditions of its labor market" (Advisory Council on Unemployment Compensation 1994, p. 12).

Financing Extended Benefits[21]

There are three main issues in financing extended benefits: first, whether extended benefits should be funded out of payroll taxes (as are regular benefits) or from federal general revenues; second, whether extended benefits should be financed by the states, by the federal government, or by some combination of the two; and third, if EB is funded from a payroll tax, whether that payroll tax should be experience rated (as it is for regular benefits). A complete treatment of these issues would require a more detailed discussion of UI financing than is appropriate in this chapter. Briefly, though, regular benefits are funded fully by the states through a payroll tax that is experience rated (that is, dependent on each employer's past layoff experience) and collected on a taxable payroll limited to less than $15,000 a year (per worker) in all but eleven states.[22] This method of financing UI benefits creates economic incentives for firms to behave in ways that they otherwise would not. First, experience rating of the payroll tax reduces temporary layoffs and limits the extent to which employers in seasonal and cyclically sensitive industries are subsidized by employers in more stable industries (see Brechling and Laurence 1995, Levine's chapter 8 in this volume, and Topel 1990 for discussions and further references). Second, the cap on taxable payroll skews employers' demand for labor away from low-wage, less skilled workers and in favor of high-wage, more skilled workers. Also, the payroll tax cap creates an incentive for employers to assign extra hours of work (that is, overtime) to their existing work force rather than to hire additional workers.

Whether extended benefits should be funded by a payroll tax or by general revenues depends mainly on issues of tax equity. The available evidence suggests that the UI payroll tax is shifted partly to workers in the form of lower wages and partly to consumers in the form of higher prices. The part that is shifted to workers can be viewed as regressive, since low-wage workers bear a disproportionate share of the payroll tax as a result of the low taxable wage base. (This regressiveness would be blunted if low-wage workers received a disproportionate share of the benefits, which seems likely.) The part that is shifted to consumers can be viewed as proportionate if we assume that people with different incomes consume a mix of goods and services on which average UI taxes do not differ. On balance, then, the UI payroll tax is probably somewhat regressive (Hamermesh 1977, pp. 10-15). Federal general revenues, on the other hand, are somewhat progressive, given that (apart from social security payroll taxes) over 70 percent of those revenues are generated by the federal personal income tax. Tax equity, then, gives a slight edge to general revenues over payroll taxes as a funding source for extended benefits.

However, the overall question of tax equity ignores the issue of state-federal sharing of extended benefit expenses: should extended benefit payments that are made in a state be paid for by that state, by the federal government, or by some combination of the two? Currently, half the benefits under the EB program are paid out of the Extended Unemployment Compensation Account, which is funded from FUTA revenues (that is, the flat 0.8 percent of taxable payroll that the federal government charges for administration, extended benefits, and repayable advances). State UI trust fund reserves pay for the other half. Most emergency extensions, however, have been financed entirely from federal revenues, either from the EUCA or (increasingly) from general revenues (see table 6.7).

The existing state-federal sharing of EB funding appears to have wide acceptance and is based on the rationale that long-term unemployment is likely to be the result of macroeconomic conditions (both national and international) over which individual employers have little or no control (Murray 1974, chapter 5). Federal sharing of EB expenses, then, is a way of providing some assistance to states that are suffering disproportionately from long-term unemployment.[23] In addition, federal sharing has been seen as a way of reducing the resistance of states (and employers) to extended benefits. Although there appears to be no comprehensive economic analysis of the costs and benefits of federal sharing of EB funding, the arguments seem to favor the federal government assuming more, rather than less, of the funding burden for extended benefits.

There is no empirical evidence on whether experience rating of benefits paid under EB has the beneficial effects that have been estimated for experience rating of the regular program.[24] Obtaining such evidence would be difficult, given that the EB tax is such a small percentage of the overall UI tax. However, it seems likely that increasing the experience rating of EB would be far less beneficial than would increasing the experience rating of regular benefits. The main reason is that, although employers do have considerable discretion over the timing and incidence of temporary layoffs, they may have much less discretion over the incidence of permanent job losses, which often lead to long-term unemployment. Also, it has been argued that spells of unemployment that last beyond 26 weeks result more from general macroeconomic conditions than from the actions of a specific employer. As a result, there seems to be less scope for experience rating to have a positive effect in the case of EB than in the regular UI program, and less justification for its use in financing EB.

The Advisory Council on Unemployment Compensation (1994, pp. 11-12) recommended that any expansion of extended benefits be financed by raising the taxable wage base under the federal UI payroll tax (FUTA) from $7,000 to $8,500.[25] The Advisory Council believed that the two most attractive funding sources for EB are federal general revenues and FUTA, which is neither state-specific nor experience rated. Because the taxes that produce federal general revenues may be somewhat more progressive than the federal UI payroll tax, federal general revenues may have an advantage. However, the Advisory Council opted for reducing the regressiveness of the UI payroll tax by recommending an increase in the taxable wage base.[26] In any event, the Advisory Council believed the case for funding extended benefits out of an experience-rated payroll tax to be weak.[27]

Recommended Changes in the Extended Benefit Programs

The previous discussion suggests two recommendations for changes in extended UI benefit policy. First, *repair the EB triggers*. It is important that the standby EB program be made effective, so that the potential duration of benefits is lengthened in a timely manner when a recession hits. The importance of repairing the standby EB program follows from the available evidence that long spells of unemployment are underinsured and that the potential duration of regular state benefits may be suboptimal. Congress effectively disabled the triggers that activate EB in the early 1980s. Since then the program has often failed to be activated automatically in states that are experiencing slack labor markets during a recession. As a result, Congress has stepped in with increasingly complicated emergency programs that have significantly lagged the onset of recession, have been ad hoc in design, and have been difficult to administer. Compared with a well-designed standby EB program, these emergency programs have been far less effective in providing countercyclical stimulus and have been slower to provide benefits to unemployed workers.

Several recommendations have been advanced for repairing the triggers that activate the standby EB program. For example, a majority of members of the Advisory Council on Unemployment Compensation recommended that EB should be activated when a state's seasonally adjusted TUR exceeds 6.5 percent (Advisory Council on Unemployment Compensation 1994, p. 10). Similarly, as discussed, it is clear that several Republican members of Congress see adoption of the alternative TUR trigger by all states as the way to fix the problem.[28] Which of these recommendations is adopted is less important than ensuring that one of them is adopted. The EB program, which could be an effective, efficient, and socially useful program, is now all but a dead letter.[29]

Second, *design a third-tier temporary emergency program in advance of the next recession and have it ready to implement when and if Congress perceives that the standby EB program is not providing long-enough benefit durations.* Creating a model third-tier emergency program that can be put into effect at the discretion of Congress is important as a practical matter, since Congress has shown repeatedly a penchant for passing emergency extended benefit programs (at least after a delay) when the economy sinks into a recession—and did so even when the standby EB program was activated in most states that were experiencing slack labor markets (that is, during the recessions of the mid-1970s and early 1980s). Having an emergency program designed in advance would give the states time to set up the computerized information systems that are needed to implement the program quickly and to administer it effectively. Ultimately, the administrative costs of a well-designed emergency program would be lower than the costs of repeated ad hoc programs, and workers would be better served because benefits would be received in a timely manner. In other words, the net social benefits of a predesigned emergency extended benefit program would be far greater than the benefits of a program that has an ad hoc design and needs to be implemented on the fly.[30]

How should a ready-to-implement third-tier program be designed? We believe that there are three essential elements to such a program, which might be called the Federal Emergency Extended Benefits program. First, provide federal emergency benefits only in states in which the standby EB program has been activated, and only to workers who have exhausted both their regular and standby extended benefits. There are two main reasons for this feature of a federal emergency program. First, it would direct extended benefits to workers who face the most difficulty obtaining reemployment. Second, it would ensure that the standby EB program is taken seriously, that is, that effective EB triggers are established and maintained. Relatedly, it would create an incentive for states to adopt the alternative TUR trigger for EB (if it were not mandated by Congress), since federal funding for emergency benefits would be received only if EB were in effect. By ensuring the maintenance of an effective EB program, paying federal emergency benefits only to EB exhaustees would eliminate the need to implement "reach-backs" as part of emergency extensions.[31] If Congress preferred to provide extended benefits to all states in a recession, it would be appropriate first to reestablish the national trigger for the EB program. Consideration could then be given to providing federal emergency benefits to all states based on a similar national trigger for the federal emergency program.

Second, finance federal emergency benefits wholly out of federal revenues, either from FUTA funds or from general revenues. Federal funding of emergency extended benefits is in keeping with the widely accepted notion that increasingly long spells of unemployment, especially when induced by a recession, are more and more a federal responsibility (Murray 1974).[32]

Third, incorporate some bounded flexibility in the number of additional weeks of benefits provided by the federal emergency extended benefit program. Starting with the Federal Supplemental Benefits program (1975-1978), Congress has provided additional weeks of benefits in relation to the unemployment rate in a state. For example, under the Emergency Unemployment Compensation (EUC) program (1991-1994), each state was classified as either "high unemployment" or "low unemployment" based on its total unemployment rate. The number of weeks of emergency benefits provided in each state was then tied to the state's classification as "low" or "high" unemployment. Similarly, a ready-to-implement federal emergency program should provide for longer benefit extensions in states where conditions are worse. However, it is essential that there be flexibility in the number of weeks of benefits provided and in the unemployment rate that triggers each increment to extended benefits each time the program is enacted or reenacted. This would allow Congress to take account of current conditions and of changes in the relationship between UI exhaustions and the unemployment rate. Also, Congress would retain the sort of discretion it clearly prefers in fashioning extended benefit programs.[33]

Nevertheless, Congress should place two types of bounds on its flexibility in providing federal emergency benefits. First, for the purpose of determining how many weeks of these benefits to offer, states should be classified into at most two or three categories based on their total (quarterly) unemployment rate. For example, under EUC, states were classified as either high or low unemployment. Two or three categories should be enough, particularly if emergency extended benefits are provided in increments of eight or more weeks, as Corson, Grossman, and Nicholson (1986) suggest in their study of Federal Supplemental Compensation. Second, a state's assignment to a high or low unemployment classification should be on the basis of a calendar quarter, and Congress should not allow itself to change the number of weeks of emergency benefits provided to states in a given classification within a calendar quarter. In other words, it should be impossible to change the number of weeks of emergency benefits provided in a given state during a current calendar quarter. This recommendation is consistent with the findings of Corson, Grossman, and Nicholson (1986), who considered both administrative feasibility and program effectiveness in their research.

A fourth issue, the requirements that a worker would have to satisfy in order to be eligible for federal emergency extended benefits, would also need to be settled. We have no recommendation on this point. Since 1981, the eligibility requirements for standby EB have been set at the national level. In about 15 states, the eligibility requirements for EB are significantly more stringent than for regular state benefits, and, as a result, significantly fewer workers are eligible for EB than for regular state benefits. The available empirical evidence suggests that there is only a weak relationship between the characteristics that determine UI eligibility and a worker's expected duration of unemployment (Corson and Nicholson 1982, pp. 102-106; Pozo and Woodbury 1988). That is, using tighter eligibility requirements for EB than for regular state benefits reduces program expenses but does not screen out and deny benefits to workers who are weakly attached to the labor force. This supports dropping the uniform federal eligibility requirements for EB (and for any ready-to-implement federal emergency program) and allowing each state to set the eligibility requirements for all forms of UI benefits, first-, second-, and third-tier. On the other hand, an argument could be made that if federal revenues finance a program, the associated eligibility requirements should be set at the federal level. These arguments for and against setting eligibility requirements for EB and emergency benefits on a national basis would need to be weighed in fashioning a Federal Emergency Extended Benefits program.

The preceding recommendations for a ready-to-implement emergency extended benefit program are not intended merely to make the lives of UI administrators easier—although they would do that. Rather, such a program would result in more timely payment of emergency benefits to workers and would provide greater counter cyclical stimulus than past emergency extended benefit programs have done.

Some Provisional Conclusions

The adequacy of UI benefit duration has been debated since the beginning of the system, and the accepted norm for the potential duration of benefits, as expressed in policy, has changed significantly over the decades. When the program began in 1935, most states provided a maximum potential duration of 15 weeks of benefits. This norm gradually rose, until by 1979, the maximum potential duration of benefits was 26 weeks in most states and exceeded 26 weeks in twelve states. Augmenting this upward trend were the standby EB program, which came into existence in 1970, and a parade of temporary emergency benefit extensions. Both EB and the emergency extensions provided additional weeks of benefits during hard times. During the 1980s, the trend reversed, so that today, the maximum potential duration of regular state benefits is 26 weeks in all but two states. Also, in 1981 and 1982, Congress effectively scaled back the EB program. Whether this trend will continue or again reverse itself is to be seen. Pushing toward longer benefit durations are increasing concerns over dislocated workers and job insecurity; pushing toward shorter durations is the political obsession with reducing government programs without regard to social costs or benefits.

It seems fair to say that, as with other government programs, research and analysis have played a regrettably limited role in setting and changing the duration of UI benefits. There has, of course, been significant work on the disincentive effects of extended benefits (see the summary in table 6.6), and the U.S. Department of Labor has commissioned evaluations of the three most recent emergency extended benefit programs (Corson and Nicholson 1982; Corson, Grossman, and Nicholson 1986). However, it is also clear that the research thus far has not fully addressed some of the major issues that need to be investigated in forming policy on the duration of benefits, such as the optimal duration of benefits, how duration should change over the business cycle, and the merits of EB triggers other than the IUR and TUR. Whether further research along the lines described in the second section of this chapter will converge on a convincing and clear set of recommendations is yet to be seen, but the work that has been completed to date suggests that the current focus of the UI system on compensating only relatively short spells of unemployment may be unnecessarily narrow.

The findings that suggest this conclusion can be summarized as follows. First, the UI program in the United States was defined as a program for short-term unemployment mainly out of financial and political expediency, rather than after consideration of whether permanent job loss and long-term unemployment are insurable risks. The financial argument against covering longer spells of unemployment is not nearly as persuasive today as it was in the 1930s.

Second, existing studies suggest that increasing the potential duration of UI benefits by one week increases the expected duration of unemployment by one day (0.2 week) or less. This is a relatively small behavioral effect that suggests that the average UI recipient is not abusing or taking advantage of the availability of benefits (although a sizable minority of UI recipients could be doing so).

Third, work on consumption-smoothing and benefit adequacy suggests that short spells of unemployment are overcompensated by the UI system, whereas long spells are undercompensated. Also, research on optimal duration of benefits suggests that risk averse workers would willingly accept lower benefits early in a spell of unemployment in exchange for the promise of some nonzero level of benefits should their spell of unemployment turn out to be very long. It follows that reducing benefits to short-term unemployed workers (for example, through increasing the waiting period) in order to finance benefits to long-term unemployed workers would improve social welfare. Thus, considerations of consumption smoothing, benefit adequacy, and optimal insurance all suggest that it would be reasonable public policy to extend the potential duration of benefits beyond 26 weeks, perhaps even during nonrecessionary times.

These three findings apply equally to regular and extended benefits, in that they address the issue of potential duration in general. All three considerations suggest that the existing UI system has focused too narrowly on short spells of unemployment and that policy should pay greater attention to long-term unemployment. In fact, U.S. Department of Labor policy has recently moved in this direction. The UI profiling initiative is an attempt to identify new UI claimants who are likely to experience a long spell of unemployment and to exhaust their benefits. These claimants are then referred to intensive job search assistance. An alternative response would be to extend the waiting period by one or two weeks and to use the financial savings to fund a longer potential duration of regular state benefits.

Apart from setting the maximum potential duration of benefits, perhaps the most important general issue in the duration of benefits is whether potential duration should be the same for all workers who are eligible for benefits, or whether potential duration should vary with a worker's earnings prior to unemployment. This is a point that is equally significant to the regular and extended benefit programs. In the regular state program, the question is whether benefit duration should be uniform (in which case all workers who qualify for any benefits are eligible for the same potential duration) or variable (in which case recipients with different work histories are eligible for different potential durations). In extended benefit programs, the question is whether eligibility requirements should be higher for extended benefits than for regular benefits.

The research on benefit adequacy and optimal UI outlined in the second section of this chapter provides a justification for uniform potential duration of benefits to all eligible UI claimants and for provision of extended benefits (when such a program is in effect) to all workers who exhaust regular UI. In addition, it is clear that uniform duration in regular state programs results in a significant increase in the average potential duration of benefits in a state, which in turn reduces the UI exhaustion rate. The evidence suggests that the decline in average potential duration is at least partly responsible for the secular rise in UI exhaustions and that moves toward uniform duration would help to reverse the trend.

However, there are at least three arguments for varying the potential duration of benefits with a claimant's work history and, by implication, for setting more stringent eligibility requirements for extended benefits than for regular benefits. The first is that greater entitlement should be afforded to those who have worked (and whose employers have contributed) the longest. The counterargument is that weekly benefit amounts already reflect work history, so why should potential duration do so as well? The second argument is that variable duration and more stringent eligibility requirements for extended benefits result in lower program costs. Since lower program costs would, in this case, mean lower program benefits, this is hardly a persuasive argument. It begs the question whether lowering benefits can be justified by efficiency or equity criteria. A third argument in favor of variable potential duration of benefits and more stringent eligibility requirements for extended benefits is that they are ways of limiting the moral hazard of UI. In general, of course, limiting the duration of benefits is an effort to limit moral hazard. But variable duration and more stringent eligibility requirements for extended benefits take the further step of assuming that the work disincentive of an additional week of benefits is greater for some workers, those who appear to be less strongly attached to the labor force, than for others. The implicit argument is that it is possible to discern which eligible UI claimants are weakly attached to the labor force and hence are most likely to reduce their job search effort in response to an additional week of benefits. However, we are unaware of evidence that base-period earnings (or their pattern) provide an accurate measure of a worker's labor force attachment or that the disincentive effects of an additional week of benefits are greater for workers with lower or more variable base-period earnings. It seems likely that moral hazard can be handled more effectively by a work search requirement or intensive job search assistance than by limiting the potential duration of benefits.

Finally, the potential duration, triggering, and financing of extended benefits have been among the most contentious issues in UI during much of the program's history. The main rationale for extending UI benefits during a recession is that, during a recession, spells of unemployment lengthen and the number of UI beneficiaries who exhaust their benefits rises. As long as the lengthened spells result from slack demand and employer behavior (rather than being a result of voluntary worker behavior), there is a justification for increasing the potential duration of UI benefits. In fact, the evidence suggests that UI exhaustees are much less likely to find reemployment during recessionary times than during nonrecessionary times (see table 6.5), which tends to support the traditional rationale for extending benefits during a recession.

Work on the adequacy of extended benefits has relied primarily on the total UI exhaustion rate as a criterion for gauging duration adequacy. However, the exhaustion rate is an ad hoc criterion, since we really do not know what the "right" exhaustion rate is. Similarly, research on the merits of various "triggers" for extended benefits has been limited to comparing the amounts of benefits that would be paid under various triggers, without developing a normative framework that would provide real guidance as to which triggering mechanism would be optimal. In other words, although there has been much research on extended benefits—useful and competently done—the work has been developed without the sort of economic framework that would give convincing answers to some of the most pressing policy questions on extended benefits: What is the optimal potential duration of extended benefits? To what extent should potential benefit duration vary with changing labor market conditions? What are the best criteria for activating (and de-activating) extended benefits? What are the appropriate mechanisms for financing extended benefits?

Nevertheless, based on the existing research, as well as on pragmatic considerations, we offer two recommendations for extended benefit policy. First, we strongly recommend that the triggers for the standby EB program be repaired, so that the program will again be effective and the potential duration of benefits will be lengthened in a timely manner when the next recession hits. Second, and equally strongly, we recommend creation of a Federal Emergency Extended Benefits program in advance of the next recession. Such a program would be ready to implement when and if Congress perceived that the standby EB program is not providing sufficient benefit durations. A Federal Emergency Extended Benefits program would have three essential characteristics: it would provide federal emergency benefits only in states in which the standby EB program has been activated, and only to workers who have exhausted both their regular and standby extended benefits; it would be financed out of federal revenues; and it would give bounded flexibility in the number of additional weeks of emergency benefits provided. Compared with past emergency extended benefit programs, such a program would be easier and less costly to administer, result in more timely payment of emergency benefits to workers, and offer greater countercyclical stimulus.

NOTES

For helpful discussions and comments on earlier drafts, we are grateful to Laurie J. Bassi, Carl Davidson, Louis S. Jacobson, Peter Kuhn, Robert Pavosevich, Wayne Vroman, and Stephen A. Wandner. Rich Deibel, Ellen Maloney, and Claire Black assisted in preparing the manuscript.

1. See Advisory Council on Unemployment Compensation (1995, p. 129) for a discussion of replacement rates based on the administrative records of six states. Although the ACUC discussion is based on a different definition of the replacement rate (the ratio of weekly benefits to average base-period earnings) than the one used in the text, it does suggest that benefit durations in excess of base-period employment durations would imply strong work disincentives.

2. In addition, the waiting period serves the same function as a deductible in a standard insurance contract. Hence, it prevents very small claims (that is, short spells of unemployment) from being compensated and provides a mechanism for risk-sharing. See Davidson and Woodbury (1997) and the literature cited there, especially Raviv (1979) and Shavell and Weiss (1979).

3. The amendments were part of the Omnibus Budget Reconciliation Act of 1980 (P.L. 96-499, approved December 5, 1980). See also Rubin (1983, pp. 109-111).

4. See U.S. Department of Labor (1995, Section 315).

5. The UI payroll tax has been used as a vehicle to finance innovative programs (such as workplace-based training) for workers affected by structural change. For a review of these programs, see Leigh (1990).

6. The source for this and the next two paragraphs is U.S. Department of Labor (1995).

7. *Manual of State Employment Security Legislation* (1942), Employment Security Memorandum No. 13, p. 313.

8. The regular exhaustion rate is measured as the number of exhaustees in a given month divided by the number of initial claims for benefits that were filed six months before. This is an inexact measure of the exhaustion rate because not all initial claimants who exhaust their benefits do so six months later. Rather, some exhaust benefits in less than six months—for example, those whose potential duration of benefits is less than 26 weeks and who exhaust their benefits after a continuous spell of unemployment. Other exhaustees take more than six months to exhaust their benefits—for example, those who experience more than one spell of insured unemployment during the benefit year.

9. Given that only one of the four existing studies was performed during a recession, an additional study that sampled a group of exhaustees during a recession would be useful even if it did not continuously sample over a period of time that is long enough to include both tight and slack labor markets.

10. Profiling also reflects the view that most dislocated workers are job-ready.

11. Grossman's results (1989) are a glaring exception. They differ from any of the other estimates, however, because they are estimates of the impact of an additional week of emergency benefits for workers who have already exhausted their regular benefits.

12. Solving the data problems head-on might prove more satisfactory than econometric solutions to the data problems. there are ways of mitigating the limitation of administrative data, but to date these have not been pursued.

13. The remainder of this section draws liberally from Davidson and Woodbury (forthcoming).

14. For a more extensive narrative account, see Blaustein (1993, pp. 200-206 and 228-241).

15. On the drop in UI participation rates, see Bassi and McMurrer (in this volume) as well as Blank and Card (1991) and Vroman (1991).

16. EB was activated during 1990 in Alaska and Rhode Island. During 1991, EB was activated (in addition) in Maine, Massachusetts, Michigan, Oregon, Puerto Rico, Vermont, and West Virginia. In the first quarter of 1992, EB was activated in Louisiana. Notably missing from the list are California and northeastern states such as New York and Pennsylvania, all of which experienced a severe recession in the early 1990s.

17. These estimates are from Advisory Council on Unemployment Compensation (1994, chapter 6) and are for the period January 1990 through August 1993. For comparison, during the same time period the EUC program provided extended benefits in all states for 22 months, resulting in benefit payments of $23 billion. Advisory Council on Unemployment Compensation (1994, chapter 6) and Corson and Rangarajan (1994) provide estimated impacts of a variety of alternative EB triggers.

18. There is, however, a less cynical explanation of why Congress has not required the states to adopt the alternative TUR trigger. If the EB trigger were effective, EB would be activated in some states even during times of low national unemployment, since labor market conditions vary substantially across the states. So an ineffective EB program yields budget savings for the federal government.

19. See U.S. House of Representatives (1985), p. 91.

20. Congress suspended the disqualification for failure to search for work during 1991 through 1995; however, the disqualification is now back in effect.

21. This discussion draws on Advisory Council on Unemployment Compensation (1994, chapter 6).

22. Of the eleven states that have a payroll tax base exceeding $15,000, only one (New Jersey) is among the ten largest states. See Advisory Council on Unemployment Compensation (1996, table 5-1, p. 67).

23. If some states specialize in industries that tend to generate long-term unemployment, such interstate assistance could turn into interstate subsidies that have efficiency consequences.

24. In 1994, thirty-four states charged some percentage of benefits paid under EB back to the employer (Advisory Council on Unemployment Compensation 1994, chapter 6).

25. In 1996, the Advisory Council on Unemployment Compensation recommended (with some dissent) raising the payroll tax base to $9,000 and adjusting the base annually by the Employment Cost Index (Advisory Council Unemployment Compensation 1996, p. 19).

26. From a political standpoint, of course, the payroll tax has the distinct advantage that it is dedicated to the payment of UI benefits.

27. In contrast to the reasoning of the Advisory Council on Unemployment Compensation, Brechling and Laurence (1995) have recently offered a theoretical case for funding the costs of permanent job loss by taxing employers who permanently reduce their employment. Brechling and Laurence argue that a socially optimal rate of adjustment can be obtained by forcing the agent who controls the rate of adjustment to pay for the adjustment costs. This argument can be

extended to suggest that EB should be funded by employers who contract and are responsible for long-term unemployment. In other words, EB should be funded out of experience-rated payroll taxes, not out of general revenues. The debatable point in this argument is whether employers in contracting industries really are able to control the rate at which they contract.

28. As discussed earlier in this section, the alternative TUR trigger activates EB in a state when the state's three-month average TUR exceeds 6.5 percent and is 10 percent above the three-month average TUR in either of the two preceding years.

29. Once the triggers have been repaired in this basic way, attention could be paid to whether greater potential duration of benefits should be activated if the unemployment rate rose significantly above 6.5 percent. For example, Hight (1975) and Corson and Nicholson (1982, chapter 5) investigated how the total UI exhaustion rate could be kept constant by triggering additional benefit extensions with increases in the insured unemployment rate. They found that the exhaustion rate is held constant by adding about 3.5 to 5.1 weeks to potential duration for each 1 percentage point increase in the insured unemployment rate. With a TUR trigger, the relationship between exhaustion rates and the TUR would need to be investigated.

30. See Corson, Grossman, and Nicholson (1986) for a discussion of the administrative difficulties encountered during the Federal Supplemental Compensation program.

31. Reach-backs have provided emergency extended benefits to workers who exhausted their benefits before adoption of the emergency extension program. For example, under the Emergency Unemployment Compensation program (1991-1994), most individuals who received reach-back EUC benefits had exhausted their regular state benefits between March and November 1991 but had never received benefits under the standby EB program. With an effective EB program, these workers would already have received some weeks of extended benefits, and there would be no need for a reach-back.

32. However, Brechling and Laurence (1995) have offered quite a different set of recommendations. See note 27.

33. Obviously, Congress would have the discretion to ignore any ready-to-implement third-tier program and to fashion an entirely new one, as it has done (in effect) in the past. However, the purpose of creating such a third-tier program is to shorten the time needed to react to a recession and to ease and rationalize administration of the program.

References

Advisory Council on Unemployment Compensation. 1994. "Report and Recommendations."ACUC, February.

_____. 1995. "Unemployment Insurance in the United States: Benefits, Financing, Coverage." ACUC, February.

_____. 1996. "Defining Federal and State Roles in Unemployment Insurance." ACUC, January.

Bailey, Martin N. 1978. "Some Aspects of Optimal Unemployment Insurance," *Journal of Public Economics* 10 (December): 379-402.

Bassi, Laurie J., and Daniel P. McMurrer. 1997. "Coverage and Recipiency: Trends and Effects." Chapter 2 in this volume.

Blank, Rebecca M., and David E. Card. 1991. "Recent Trends in Insured and Uninsured Unemployment: Is There an Explanation?" *Quarterly Journal of Economics* 106 (November): 1157-1189.

Blaustein, Saul J. 1981. *Job and Income Security of Unemployed Workers.* Kalamazoo, MI: W.E. Upjohn Institute.

_____. 1993. *Unemployment Insurance in the United States: The First Half-Century.* Kalamazoo, MI: W.E. Upjohn Institute.

Brechling, Frank, and Louise Laurence. 1995. *Permanent Job Loss and the U.S. System of Financing Unemployment Insurance.* Kalamazoo. MI: W.E. Upjohn Institute.

Burgess, Paul L., and Jerry L. Kingston. 1979. "Labor Market Experiences of Unemployment Insurance Exhaustees." Unemployment Insurance Occasional Paper 79-3, U.S. Department of Labor, Employment and Training Administration.

Classen, Kathleen P. 1979. "Unemployment Insurance and Job Search." In *Studies in the Economics of Search*, S.A. Lippman and J.J. McCall, eds. Amsterdam: North-Holland.

Corson, Walter, and Mark Dynarski. 1990. "A Study of Unemployment Insurance Recipients and Exhaustees: Findings from a National Survey." Unemployment Insurance Occasional Paper 90-3, U.S. Department of Labor, Employment and Training Administration.

Corson, Walter, Jean Grossman, and Walter Nicholson. 1986. "An Evaluation of the Federal Supplemental Compensation Program." Unemployment Insurance Occasional Paper 86-3, U.S. Department of Labor, Employment and Training Administration.

Corson, Walter, David Long, and Walter Nicholson. 1985. "Evaluation of the Charleston Claimant Placement and Work Test Demonstration." Unemployment Insurance Occasional Paper 85-2, U.S. Department of Labor, Employment and Training Administration.

Corson, Walter, and Walter Nicholson. 1982. *The Federal Supplemental Benefits Program*. Kalamazoo, MI: W.E. Upjohn Institute.

_____. 1985. "An Analysis of the 1981-82 Changes in the Extended Benefit Program." Unemployment Insurance Occasional Paper 85-1, U.S. Department of Labor, Employment and Training Administration.

Corson, Walter, and Anu Rangarajan. 1994. "Extended UI Benefit Triggers." Unemployment Insurance Occasional Paper 94-2, U.S. Department of Labor, Employment and Training Administration.

Czajka, John I., Sharon K. Long, and Walter Nicholson. 1989. "An Evaluation of the Feasibility of a Substate Area Extended Benefit Program: Final Report." Unemployment Insurance Occasional Paper 89-5, Department of Labor, Employment and Training Administration.

Davidson, Carl, and Stephen A. Woodbury. 1996. "Unemployment Insurance and Unemployment: Implications of the Reemployment Bonus Experiments." Staff Working Paper 96-44, W.E. Upjohn Institute.

_____. 1997. "The Optimal Dole with Risk Aversion, Job Destruction, and Worker Heterogeneity." Staff Working Paper 97-49, W.E. Upjohn Institute.

_____. Forthcoming. "Optimal Unemployment Insurance," *Journal of Public Economics*.

Flemming, John S. 1978. "Aspects of Optimal Unemployment Insurance." *Journal of Public Economics* 10 (December): 403-425.

Green, David A., and W. Craig Riddell. 1993. "The Economic Effects of Unemployment Insurance in Canada: An Empirical Analysis of UI Disentitlement," *Journal of Labor Economics* 11 (January, part 2): S96-S147.

Grossman, Jean Baldwin. 1989. "The Work Disincentive Effect of Extended Unemployment Compensation: Recent Evidence," *Review of Economics and Statistics* 71 (February): 159-164.

Gruber, Jonathan. Forthcoming. "Unemployment Insurance, Consumption Smoothing, and Private Insurance: Evidence from the PSID and CEX," *Research in Employment Policy* 1.

Haber, William, and Merrill G. Murray. 1966. *Unemployment Insurance in the American Economy*. Homewood, IL: Richard D. Irwin.

Ham, John C., and Samuel A. Rea, Jr. 1987. "Unemployment Insurance and Male Unemployment Duration in Canada," *Journal of Labor Economics* 5 (July): 325-353.

Hamermesh, Daniel S. 1977. *Jobless Pay and the Economy*. Baltimore, MD: Johns Hopkins University Press.

Hansen, W. Lee, and James F. Byers. 1990. "Unemployment Compensation and Training: Can a Closer Link Be Forged?" In *Unemployment Compen-*

sation: The Second Half-Century, W. Lee Hansen and James F. Byers, eds. Madison, WI: University of Wisconsin Press.

Hight, Joseph E. 1975. "Insured Unemployment Rates, Extended Benefits, and Unemployment Insurance Exhaustions." Twenty-Eighth Proceedings of the Industrial Relations Research Association.

Jacobson, Louis, Robert LaLonde, and Daniel Sullivan. 1993a. *The Costs of Worker Dislocation.* Kalamazoo, MI: W.E. Upjohn Institute.

_____. 1993b. "Earnings Losses of Displaced Workers," *American Economic Review* 83 (September): 685-709.

_____. 1993c. "Long-Term Earnings Losses of High-Seniority Displaced Workers," *Federal Reserve Bank of Chicago Economic Perspectives* 17 (November/December): 2-20.

Johnson, Terry R., and Daniel R. Klepinger. 1991. "Evaluation of the Impacts of the Washington Alternative Work Search Experiment." Unemployment Insurance Occasional Paper 91-4, U.S. Department of Labor, Employment and Training Administration.

Katz, Arnold, and Jack Ochs. 1980. "Implications of Potential Duration Policies." In *Unemployment Compensation: Studies and Research*, Vol. I. Washington, DC: National Commission on Unemployment Compensation, July.

Katz, Lawrence F., and Bruce D. Meyer. 1990. "The Impact of the Potential Duration of Unemployment Benefits on the Duration of Unemployment," *Journal of Public Economics* 41 (February): 45-72.

Leigh, Duane E. 1989. *Assisting Displaced Workers: Do the States Have a Better Idea?* Kalamazoo, MI: W.E. Upjohn Institute.

_____. 1990. *Does Training Work for Displaced Workers?* Kalamazoo, MI: W.E. Upjohn Institute.

Levine, Phillip B. 1997. "Financing Benefit Payments." Chapter 8 in this volume.

Manual of State Employment Security Legislation. 1942. Washington, DC: Social Security Board, Bureau of Employment Security.

Manual of State Employment Security Legislation. 1950. Washington, DC: U.S. Department of Labor, Bureau of Employment Security.

Miller, Mike, Robert Pavosevich, and Wayne Vroman. 1997. "Trends in Unemployment Insurance Benefit Financing." Chapter 9 in this volume.

Moffitt, Robert. 1985a. "Unemployment Insurance and the Distribution of Unemployment Spells," *Journal of Econometrics* 28 (April): 85-101.

_____. 1985b. "The Effect of the Duration of Unemployment Benefits on Work Incentives: An Analysis of Four Data Sets." Unemployment Insurance Occasional Paper 85-4, U.S. Department of Labor, Employment and Training Administration.

Moffitt, Robert, and Walter Nicholson. 1982. "The Effect of Unemployment Insurance on Unemployment: The Case of Federal Supplemental Benefits," *Review of Economics and Statistics* 64 (February): 1-11.

Murray, Merrill G. 1974. *The Duration of Unemployment Benefits*. Kalamazoo, MI: W.E. Upjohn Institute.

Newton, Floyd C., and Harvey S. Rosen. 1979. "Unemployment Insurance, Income Taxation, and Duration of Unemployment: Evidence from Georgia," *Southern Economic Journal* 45 (January): 773-784.

Nicholson, Walter, and Walter Corson. 1976. "A Longitudinal Study of Unemployment Insurance Exhaustees: Waves I and II." Report prepared for the Employment and Training Administration, U.S. Department of Labor, January.

_____. 1985. "An Analysis of the 1981-82 Changes in the Extended Benefits Program." Unemployment Insurance Service Occasional Paper 85-1, U.S. Department of Labor, Employment and Training Administration.

O'Leary, Christopher J. Forthcoming. "The Adequacy of Unemployment Insurance Benefits," *Research in Employment Policy* 1.

Pozo, Susan, and Stephen A. Woodbury. 1988. "Tightening Eligibility Requirements for Unemployment Insurance." Paper presented at the Midwest Economics Association Annual Meeting, Chicago, April.

Raviv, Arthur. 1979. "The Design of an Optimal Insurance Policy," *American Economic Review* 69 (March): 84-96.

Rothschild, Michael, and Joseph E. Stiglitz. 1970. "Increasing Risk: A Definition," *Journal of Economic Theory* 2: 225-243.

Rubin, Murray. 1983. *Federal-State Relations in Unemployment Insurance: A Balance of Power*. Kalamazoo, MI: W.E. Upjohn Institute.

_____. 1990. "State-Federal Relations in Unemployment Insurance." In *Unemployment Compensation: The Second Half-Century*, W. Lee Hansen and James F. Byers, eds. Madison, WI: University of Wisconsin Press.

Shavell, Steven, and Laurence Weiss. 1979. "The Optimal Provision of Unemployment Insurance over Time." *Journal of Political Economy* 87 (December): 1347-1362.

Solon, Gary. 1985. "Work Incentive Effects of Taxing Unemployment Benefits," *Econometrica* 53 (March): 295-306.

Storey, James R., and Gene Falk. 1993. "Unemployment Compensation: The Emergency Unemployment Compensation (EUC) Program." CRS Report to Congress 93-367 EPW. Congressional Research Service, March 25.

Topel, Robert H. 1990. "Financing Unemployment Insurance: History, Incentives, and Reform." In *Unemployment Compensation: The Second Half-Century*, W. Lee Hansen and James F. Byers, eds. Madison, WI: University of Wisconsin Press.

Unemployment Insurance Legislative Policy: Recommendations for State Legislation. 1962. BES No. U-212A. U.S. Department of Labor, Bureau of Employment Security.

U.S. Department of Labor. Various years."Comparison of State Unemployment Insurance Laws." Employment and Training Administration, Unemployment Insurance Service.

U.S. House of Representatives. Committee on Ways and Means. 1985. "The Feasibility of Using Substate Areas for the Payment of Unemployment Benefits." In Hearings before the Subcommittee on Public Assistance and Unemployment Insurance, February 20.

Vroman, Wayne. 1991. "The Decline in Unemployment Insurance Claims Activity in the 1980s." Unemployment Insurance Occasional Paper 91-2, U.S. Department of Labor, Employment and Training Administration.

Wandner, Stephen A. 1975. "Unemployment Insurance and the Duration of Unemployment in Periods of Low and High Unemployment." U.S. Department of Labor, Employment and Training Administration, Unemployment Insurance Service.

CHAPTER 7

Work Incentives and Disincentives

Paul T. Decker
Mathematica Policy Research

The unemployment insurance (UI) system must address a fundamental trade-off between two important factors: (1) the need to provide unemployed workers with benefits that are "adequate," as discussed in Chapter 5, and (2) the need to minimize the disincentive to rapid reemployment implicit in the provision of UI benefits. The intent to provide adequate benefits tends to encourage more generous ones, which would ensure that the economic needs of a larger proportion of claimants are met. However, more generous benefits tend to strengthen the reemployment disincentive. Given this trade-off, states have been urged to provide benefits high enough to replace a substantial portion of lost wages, but not so high as to significantly dilute the incentive to return to work. As a result, a "rule-of-thumb" that has guided UI policy since the inception of the system is that weekly UI benefits should replace roughly 50 percent of workers' weekly wages.

This chapter reviews the theory and empirical evidence on the effects of UI policy on the behavior of unemployed workers in order to investigate the following issues:

- Whether and the extent to which more generous benefits act as a disincentive to reemployment, thus prolonging unemployment and increasing the unemployment rate
- Whether prolonged unemployment can have a positive impact by leading to higher-paying work if claimants use the period of unemployment to select the best possible job
- Whether the negative effects of UI on reemployment are offset by effects of UI on labor market transitions other than the unemploy-

ment-to-employment transition or by spillover effects of claimants' behavior on unemployed workers who do not receive UI
benefits

The discussion then turns to policy options that have evolved in
response to the reemployment disincentive that is inherent in UI and
concludes with a consideration of the task faced by policy makers in
light of the theoretical and empirical evidence on the effect of UI on
employment.

Direct Effects of Unemployment Insurance on Claimants: Disincentives to Reemployment

Theoretical studies have demonstrated that more generous benefits
create an incentive for claimants to remain unemployed, and empirical
studies have shown that UI does indeed tend to lengthen unemployment spells of claimants. Increases in either the amount of benefits or
in the potential duration of benefits induce longer spells, but the magnitude of these effects is still uncertain. In this section, both the theory
and empirical findings related to this effect are reviewed.

Theory

The theory supporting the disincentive effect of UI is based on the
premise that UI tends to prolong unemployment spells because it lowers the cost of unemployment. Unemployed workers who receive UI
benefits tend to consume more leisure, to reduce the intensity (and
therefore the cost) of their job search, or to be more selective in accepting a job offer than they would be in the absence of UI. All of these
tendencies will generate longer unemployment spells. Increasing the
two key parameters of the UI system—the amount and potential duration of benefits—would tend to exacerbate this effect.

Two general theoretical models, the labor-supply model and the job-
search model, have been used to describe the disincentive to reemployment inherent in UI. Moffitt and Nicholson (1982) utilized a labor-supply model to represent the effect of UI on the duration of
unemployment spells. In this model, a newly unemployed individual is

assumed to plan his or her activities over a fixed period, deciding how to divide his or her time between work and leisure in the form of unemployment. During the period, the individual may either consume the maximum amount of leisure by remaining unemployed for the full interval or accept a job that is to begin at a particular point, remaining unemployed until that point.

In the labor-supply model that includes UI, the budget constraint relevant to individuals who are eligible for UI and are planning employment-related activities over period T is represented by line ABC in figure 7.1. For an unemployment spell that exceeds the point at which UI benefits are exhausted, which is typically 26 weeks after the initial claim, the cost of an additional week of unemployment is the foregone earnings for that week. The individual worker is assumed to receive a fixed weekly wage, w, when employed, and this fixed wage represents the earnings foregone for a week of unemployment. For an unemployment spell that is less than 26 weeks, the net cost of an additional week of unemployment is $w-b$, where b is the weekly UI benefit received by the claimant. The relatively lower cost of unemployment during periods of benefit receipt represents the unemployment subsidy of UI.

The labor-supply model can be used to show that making UI benefits more generous (by increasing either the amount or potential duration of benefits) will increase unemployment spells of claimants. An increase in the weekly benefit amount tends to lengthen unemployment spells because it lowers the net cost of unemployment. The effect of the weekly benefit increase is represented in figure 7.1 by the shift of the budget constraint out to line $AB'C'$. For claimants who would exhaust benefits if the weekly benefit were not increased—that is, those between B and C on the original line—the increase in the benefit amount causes a pure income effect that raises consumption of leisure/unemployment, as long as leisure is a normal good. For claimants who would not exhaust benefits if the weekly benefit were not raised—those located between A and B on the original line—the benefit expansion generates both substitution and income effects in the same direction, thus increasing unemployment.

As is true for an increase in the amount of benefits, an increase in potential duration of benefits tends to lengthen unemployment spells, by extending the period in which the cost of unemployment is lowered by the availability of benefits. If, for example, the potential duration of benefits were increased from 26 to 39 weeks, the budget constraint in figure 7.1 would shift to line $AB''C''$. The only claimants who would be affected by the shift are those who would have exhausted benefits in the absence of the shift. For these claimants, the income and substitution effects of the shift are also in the same direction—toward greater unemployment—so the impact of a longer potential benefit period is to unambiguously increase unemployment.

Figure 7.1 Impact of Increases in UI Benefit Parameters on the Budget Constraint for UI Claimants

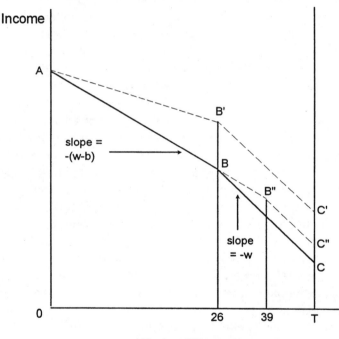

Weeks of Unemployment

The labor-supply model further implies that many claimants will return to work near the time that they exhaust their benefits. Reemployment is likely to occur at this point because of the sudden increase in the cost to claimants of an additional week of unemployment when benefits are exhausted. This is represented by the kink in line *ABC* in figure 7.1. Many claimants will respond to this increase in the cost of unemployment by accepting a job or at least by searching more actively.[1]

An alternative approach to modeling the effect of UI on unemployment spells is based on the job-search model (Burdett 1979 and Mortensen 1977). In this model, it is assumed that the search occurs in an environment in which claimants are uncertain about the wage offers they will receive from one week to the next. Given such uncertainty, unemployed workers set their search intensity and their minimum acceptable wage so as to maximize the present value of lifetime income. It follows that claimants will end their unemployment spell when they receive a wage offer that exceeds their minimum acceptable wage.

In the job-search model, UI lowers the cost of unemployment and therefore encourages claimants to reduce the intensity of their search or to raise their minimum acceptable wage. Either response tends to prolong unemployment spells. In addition, an increase in the amount or potential duration of benefits will strengthen the reemployment disincentive. The resulting impact on rates of reemployment is illustrated in figure 7.2, which presents the time pattern of reemployment for UI claimants. The top panel shows that an increase in the benefit level tends to lower reemployment rates early in unemployment spells and to increase reemployment rates near and beyond the point of benefit exhaustion, *P*. The bottom panel shows that an increase in potential duration of benefits from P_0 to P_1 also decreases reemployment rates early in the unemployment spell and increases subsequent reemployment rates. The overall impact of these changes in reemployment rates would be to raise average unemployment spells.

Although both the labor-supply theory and the job-search theory imply that UI is likely to prolong unemployment spells, the job-search theory also suggests that prolonged unemployment spells can have a positive impact. Because UI provides financial assistance to claimants, they can presumably be more selective in taking a new job than they would be in the absence of UI. That is, because of UI, claimants can spend more time searching for the best possible job opening. If, as a result, claimants obtain more stable or higher-paying jobs than they would in the absence of UI, the prolonged unemployment spell has

Figure 7.2 Impact of Increases in UI Benefit Parameters on Reemployment Rates

been productive. Hence, if the job-search model is valid, and UI constitutes a subsidy to job search rather than to leisure, a full evaluation of UI must weigh the benefits of increased search against the costs of increased unemployment.

The reemployment disincentives inherent in UI are intended to be offset somewhat by partial benefit schedules that allow claimants to accept part-time work and to still retain a portion of their UI benefits. However, partial benefit schedules, which vary by state, have been criticized because they do not create clear incentives for partial benefit claimants to work as much as possible. The effect of the typical partial benefits schedule on the relationship between a worker's earnings and income (earnings plus benefits) is shown in figure 7.3. Claimants with zero earnings have income equal to their full weekly benefit amount (WBA). A small amount of earnings, up to one-quarter of WBA in figure 7.3, is disregarded in computing the partial benefit amount, so a one-dollar increase in earnings generates a one-dollar increase in income over this range. For earnings above the disregard, the benefit payment is reduced by a dollar for each additional dollar of earnings; the earnings-income function in figure 7.3 is flat over this section, as earnings simply displace benefits. Benefits are eliminated altogether if earnings exceed WBA. The effect of this elimination of benefits, combined with the earnings disregard, is to create a point where a marginal increase in earnings causes a decline in income. This is reflected in the discontinuity in the earnings-income function at the point where earnings equal WBA in figure 7.3.

Two aspects of the partial benefit schedule can be criticized for impeding work incentives. First, workers on the flat section of the earnings-income function have no incentive to increase earnings at the margin, since the gain in earnings has no effect on income. Second, the discontinuity where earnings equal WBA creates a disincentive to raise earnings at the margin, since that increment will generate a decrease in income. Munts (1970) presents data from Wisconsin on benefit receipt that suggest that claimants are responsive to the work disincentives created by partial benefits schedules.

The simplest way to maintain work incentives is to construct a partial benefits schedule without an earnings disregard that reduces benefits by a fraction of one dollar for every one-dollar increase in earnings. A benefits schedule of this type will create a relatively smooth, upward-sloping earnings-income function, ensuring that as earnings increase income will also increase and benefits will be phased out gradually. This type of benefits schedule is used in Kentucky, where claimants lose 80 cents in benefits for every additional dollar of earnings.

Figure 7.3 Example of a Partial UI Benefits Schedule

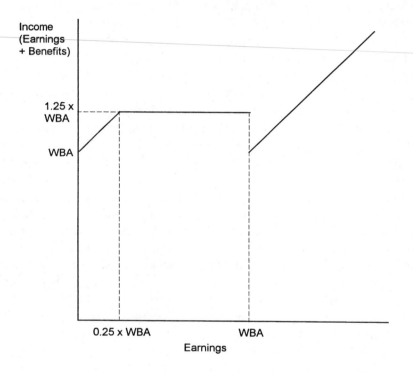

WBA = Full weekly benefit amount

Empirical Evidence

Over the past twenty years, many researchers have studied empirically the impact of UI benefits on unemployment spells. Danziger, Haveman, and Plotnick (1981), Gustman (1982), Burtless (1990), and Atkinson and Micklewright (1991) summarize the literature before the

Table 7.1 Estimated Impacts of UI Benefit Parameters

Study	Data used	Estimation methods	Impact of weekly benefit amount	Impact of potential benefit duration
Newton and Rosen (1979)	UI records on Georgia claimants (1974-1976)	Tobit	--	A one-week increase in potential duration increases unemployment spells by 0.4 - 0.5 weeks
Moffitt and Nicholson (1982)	Survey of FSB claimants (1974-1976)	Maximum likelihood with kinked budget constraint	A 10 percentage-point increase in the replacement rate increases unemployment spells by 0.98 weeks for men and 0.84 weeks for women	A one-week increase in potential duration increases unemployment spells by 0.1 weeks for men and women
Moffitt (1985a)	CWBH administrative records, men only (1978-1983)	Proportional hazards model	A 10 percent increase in the benefit amount increases unemployment spells by half a week	A one-week increase in potential duration increases unemployment spells by 0.15 weeks
Moffitt (1985b)	CWBH (1978-1983), JSARP survey data (1979-1981), UI records on Georgia claimants (1974-1976)	Proportional hazards model	--	A one-week increase in potential duration increases unemployment spells by 0.17 to 0.45 weeks for men, 0.10 to 0.37 weeks for women
Solon (1985)	CWBH-Georgia (1978-1989)	Proportional hazards model, based on taxation of benefits imposed in 1979	A 10 percentage-point increase in the replacement rate increases unemployment spells by between half a week and a full week	A one-week increase in potential duration increases unemployment spells by 0.3 weeks

(continued)

Table 7.1 (continued)

Study	Data used	Estimation methods	Impact of weekly benefit amount	Impact of potential benefit duration
Meyer (1989)	CWBH (1979-1984)	OLS, based on increases in state WBA minimums and maximums	A 9 percent increase in benefits increases weeks of UI benefits by one-and-a-half weeks	--
Meyer (1990)	CWBH, men only (1978-1983)	Proportional hazards model	A 10 percentage-point increase in the replacement rate increases unemployment spells by one-and-a-half weeks	--
Katz and Meyer (1990)	CWBH, men only (1978-1983)	Proportional hazards model	--	A one-week increase in potential duration increases unemployment spells by between 0.16 and 0.20 weeks
Davidson and Woodbury (1995)	Estimates from UI bonus experiments	Simulations based on estimated impacts of bonus experiments	A 10 percentage-point increase in the replacement rate increases unemployment spells by 0.3 to 1.1 weeks	A one-week increase in potential duration increases unemployment spells by 0.05 to 0.20 weeks

NOTE: FSB = Federal Supplemental Benefits. CWBH = Continuous Wage and Benefit History. These data were extracted from UI administrative records in thirteen states. JSARP = Job Search Assistance Research Project (also known as the Employment Opportunity Pilot Project). The project was conducted in twenty sites. FSC = Federal Supplemental Compensation.

1980s. Therefore, the following discussion focuses primarily on estimates that have appeared in the literature over the past ten to fifteen years, as summarized in table 7.1. The estimated impacts of the two main UI parameters on unemployment spells will be considered, as well as recent findings related to the timing of reemployment as associated with the point of benefit exhaustion, and the research on the potential impact of UI on reemployment wages.

Impact of Changes in the Benefit Amount

Studies of the effect of changes in the weekly benefit amount have consistently demonstrated that there is a disincentive to reemployment associated with UI. Almost uniformly, the research has generated estimates showing that higher weekly benefit amounts lengthen the duration of unemployment spells. The magnitude of this effect, however, is uncertain. Based on the studies completed as of 1977, Hamermesh (1977) concludes that the best estimate is that a 10 percentage-point increase in the wage replacement rate (the ratio of the weekly benefit amount to the pre-UI after-tax weekly wage) raises the average unemployment spell by half a week. However, this conclusion is founded on studies that present estimates ranging from zero to about 1.5 weeks. Danziger, Haveman, and Plotnick (1981) report a similarly wide range of estimates.

Recent research on the effect of increasing the two main parameters of the UI system has attempted to refine estimates of these effects by using new data or new methodologies. The Continuous Wage and Benefit History (CWBH), which combines administrative data from several states, has been used in many studies over the past 10 years. The CWBH includes accurate administrative data on levels of UI benefits, potential duration of benefits, and weeks of UI receipt, thereby precluding the measurement errors associated with survey data on unemployment spells.[2] Recent studies also tend to use hazard models to control for the use of incomplete, or censored, measures of unemployment spells. A measure of unemployment is said to be "censored" if the unemployment spell is not completed at the point of observation. This happens either because observed spells are measured by UI receipt, which cannot account for unemployment beyond benefit exhaustion, or because survey data measure unemployment as of the time of the survey and cannot measure spells that continue beyond the time of the survey. Since weeks of UI receipt are often used in recent studies, censoring can be a major issue because the measure itself can introduce bias into the estimates—especially since substantial rates of benefit exhaustion imply that a large proportion of observed unemployment spells are, in fact, incomplete. Hazard models allow researchers to control for the biases introduced by censored measures of unemployment by explicitly treating censored spells differently than completed spells in the estimation procedure.

The recent studies that use new data and more appropriate methods find that the estimated impact of increased benefit amounts on unemployment spells tends to be higher than the half-week response to a 10 percentage-point increase in the replacement rate cited by Hamermesh (1977). Moffitt and Nicholson (1982) estimate that a 10 percentage-point increase in the replacement rate extends unemployment spells by slightly less than one week (table 7.1). Moffitt (1985a) reports that estimates based on the CWBH data imply that a 10 percent increase in the weekly benefit amount (which represents an increase in the average replacement rate of about 6 percentage points) raises unemployment spells by half a week. In terms of replacement rate impacts, this suggests that a 10 percentage-point increase in the replacement rate would raise unemployment spells by about 0.8 weeks. Meyer (1990), using the same data as Moffitt but somewhat different estimation methods, finds an even greater impact. His findings suggest that a 10 percentage-point increase in the replacement rate lengthens unemployment spells by one-and-a-half weeks.

Because the evidence shows that the benefit amount significantly affects unemployment spells, it seems clear that disincentives to reemployment are inherent in the UI system and should not be ignored in setting the benefit amount. If benefits are increased because of concerns about adequacy, the result will be longer unemployment spells for claimants. Although the exact magnitude of the response is uncertain, the lengthening in average unemployment spells is likely to be in the range of 0.5 weeks to 1.5 weeks for every 10 percentage-point increase in replacement rates.

Impact of Changes in the Potential Duration of Benefits

Studies have generally shown that, as predicted, increases in the potential duration of benefits lengthen unemployment spells, although the magnitude of the impact is not clear. The recent estimates shown in table 7.1 suggest that a one-week rise in potential duration extends unemployment by between 0.1 and 0.5 weeks. This is a fairly wide range of estimates, which suggests, for example, that increasing potential duration from 26 weeks to 36 weeks would lengthen average unemployment spells by between 1 week and 5 weeks. Even estimates near the lower end of the range imply that the impact of an increase in potential duration is important. Katz and Meyer (1990) show, for example, that a given cut in UI expenditures achieved by reducing the potential duration of benefits shortens unemployment spells by twice as much as a similar cut achieved by reducing benefit levels. Regardless, policy prescriptions based on estimates of such uncertain magnitudes need to be evaluated with great care.

Research has also addressed the issue of the timing of reemployment relative to the timing of benefit exhaustion. Both the labor-supply and job-search theories imply that the probability of reemployment increases near the point of benefit exhaustion. These predictions are confirmed by empirical research (Katz and Meyer 1990), which shows that the rate at which claimants secure work increases substantially just before they exhaust their benefits. Katz and Meyer conclude from these findings that the potential duration of benefits has a strong effect on either recall policies of firms or on job-search strategies of workers.

In a different study based on a nationally representative sample of UI claimants, Corson and Dynarski (1990) also detect a jump in the probability of reemployment near the point of benefit exhaustion, but, contrary to Katz and Meyer, they argue that the magnitude of the effect is modest.[3] They emphasize that 75 percent of workers who exhausted their benefits were still unemployed more than a month after receiving their final UI payment, and that 60 percent were still unemployed 10 weeks after their final payment.

While the estimates from these studies apply to the UI claimant population as a whole, researchers have recently emphasized the importance of distinguishing between claimants who eventually return to their previous job and claimants who accept a new job. Data drawn from the Panel Study of Income Dynamics (PSID, 1980-1981) for a sample of unemployed workers (both UI claimants and nonclaimants) show that 52 percent of unemployment spells in that sample ended in a return to the previous employer (Katz and Meyer 1990). Research has shown that at the time of their layoff, workers are generally able to accurately predict whether or not they will be recalled. Among a nationally representative sample of UI claimants from 1987 and 1988, 92 percent of those who were given definite recall dates returned to work for their pre-UI employers. About 70 percent of claimants who expected to be recalled but who were not given definite recall dates returned to work for their pre-UI employers. In contrast, only 9 percent of claimants who did not expect to be recalled returned to work for their previous employers.

One would predict that claimants who expect to be recalled are likely to differ in their job-search behavior from claimants who do not expect to be recalled. The possibility of being recalled may prompt claimants to invest less time and money in the search for a new job. Claimants who anticipate recall may also respond differently to changes in UI than do other claimants. The models presented in the preceding section on theory may not apply to claimants who expect to be recalled and who have little control over the timing of their recall. Hence, the predicted effects of UI based on these models may apply best to claimants who do not anticipate being recalled.

Recent estimates tend to support this prediction. Corson and Dynarski (1990) find that, as postulated, increases in the replacement rate and in the potential duration of benefits lead to longer unemployment spells for claimants who do not expect to be recalled. However, increases in the replacement rate are associated with significant decreases in UI receipt for claimants who expect to be recalled, and variations in potential duration of benefits have a small and insignificant impact on these claimants. Corson and Dynarski attribute the reduction in UI spells of claimants who expect to be recalled to the layoff and recall policies of firms.

Impact of Unemployment Insurance on Reemployment Wages

The preceding empirical studies suggest that the availability of UI tends to prolong unemployment spells. Despite these findings, we cannot determine whether the additional periods of unemployment due to UI represent leisure time or extra job-search time. Presumably, if UI gives claimants extra time to search for a job, and the search is productive, then reemployment outcomes should, on average, be more favorable with UI than in the absence of UI.

One important outcome that can be used to test this hypothesis is the wage at reemployment. UI may have a positive impact on reemployment wages by inducing claimants to be more selective in their acceptance of wage offers. Several studies that have attempted to estimate the impact of UI on reemployment wages provide only mixed evidence that such an effect exists. In an early study of the relationship between UI and reemployment wages, Ehrenberg and Oaxaca (1976) estimated that a 10 percentage-point rise in the wage replacement rate increased the reemployment wage by 7.0 percent for men and 1.5 percent for women. These results suggest that the growth in unemployment associated with increases in UI represents, to some extent, productive job search. However, subsequent studies have failed to support this finding (Classen 1977, 1979; Moffitt 1985b; and Meyer 1989). Most recently, Meyer (1989) found no evidence that increases in state minimum and maximum benefit levels have caused claimants to have higher reemployment earnings. His point estimates imply a decline in wages in response to benefit increases, but the large standard errors of these estimates make it impossible to say anything conclusive about the actual sign of the effect.

Several factors may complicate the potentially positive link between UI and higher reemployment wages. First, claimants may use their UI to search longer for jobs that have better benefits or other desirable characteristics, but not necessarily higher pay. Second, claimants may use their UI to search longer for jobs with better training opportunities but with relatively low pay in the short run. Both of these factors imply that even if claimants use UI to look for a better job, the effect on reemployment wages may still be ambiguous.

Institutional Factors Affecting the Job-Search Behavior of Claimants

To counteract the reemployment disincentives inherent in UI, state UI systems refer claimants to the Employment Service (ES) and impose various work-search requirements on them.[4] Most states require all new claimants who are not employer-attached to register with the state ES. These claimants can use job placement assistance and other ES services, such as employment counseling. The ES may also refer claimants to particular jobs if their skills match the requirements of positions listed with the ES. In this case, state laws generally require individuals to accept the referral to "suitable work," or they may be denied benefits. However, the ES does not have the resources or the appropriate job listings to provide job referrals to the majority of claimants.

Claimants are also expected to document their work search as part of the UI claims process. In many states, they must provide UI with a minimum number of names of potential employers contacted for each claims week. Nevertheless, state agencies usually do not aggressively validate the information provided, which leads one to question the effectiveness of the current work-search requirements in offsetting the reemployment disincentive of UI. On the other hand, evidence from a recent demonstration of alternative work-search policies shows that standard work-search requirements do reduce benefit receipt as compared with a system in which claimants do not have to document their work-search efforts (Johnson and Klepinger 1994). New legislation requires claimants identified as likely to exhaust UI benefits to participate in mandatory job-search assistance services, which have the potential to further offset the reemployment disincentive effects of UI. These requirements are discussed later in this chapter.

Other Effects of Unemployment Insurance

Although it seems clear that UI tends to prolong the unemployment spells of claimants, its impact on the unemployment rate or on the proportion of the population that is employed is unclear. UI prolongs unemployment spells because it negatively affects the transition of UI claimants into jobs. While this particular consequence would tend to decrease employment at any given time, it could be offset by UI impacts on other labor market transitions. Furthermore, UI may have spillover effects on individuals who do not respond directly to UI but are nonetheless affected by the behavior of UI claimants.

Effects on Labor Market Transitions

The effects of UI may extend to labor market transitions beyond that from unemployment to employment, which has been the focus of most research on UI. Figure 7.4 shows the predicted impact of UI on transitions between three different situations: employment, unemployment, and not being in the labor force. The effect discussed so far, the reemployment disincentive faced by benefit claimants, is represented by the negative sign next to the arrow from unemployment to employment. This shows that, given the reemployment disincentive inherent in UI, one would predict that UI has a negative impact on the rate at which workers move from unemployment to employment. However, the existence of UI may also affect the flow of individuals in the opposite direction. For example, UI may increase the transitions from employment to unemployment because the protection it offers makes jobs with a high risk of layoff more attractive than they would be in the absence of UI. If workers are more likely to take high-risk jobs, the layoff rate for the labor force in general should rise, expanding the flow from employment to unemployment. Furthermore, UI may cause firms to increase the use of temporary layoffs to manage their workforce, which would also increase the rate at which individuals move from employment to unemployment.[5]

In addition to the effect on the transitions between employment and unemployment, UI may influence the transitions in and out of the labor force. First, the existence of UI should decrease the flow of people out of the labor force. Employed workers are less likely to leave the labor force directly because they can receive UI benefits by moving to unemployment instead. Similarly, unemployed workers are reluctant to leave the labor force because such a move would entail the loss of their benefits. Hence, both employed and unemployed individuals are less likely to leave the labor force than they would be in the absence of UI.

The existence of UI should increase the flow of individuals from outside the labor force into both employment and unemployment. The insurance value of UI increases the movement of individuals into the labor force because it makes work more attractive.[6] This effect tends to increase the flow into both employment and unemployment because some workers move directly into jobs while others begin searching for work and are therefore classified as unemployed. Hamermesh (1979) studied the effect of UI on flows into employment and found that, for married women, the estimated rise in employment because of UI was nearly large enough to fully compensate for the increase in unemployment due to the UI-related reemployment disincentive.

Figure 7.4 Theoretical Effect of UI on Labor Market Transitions

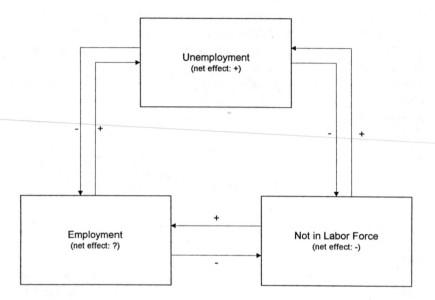

Accounting for the effects of UI on all labor market transitions generates some clear hypotheses on the net effects of UI on unemployment and labor force participation. First, as shown in figure 7.4, UI is predicted to generate a net increase in labor force participation because it positively influences both of the flows into the labor force and negatively influences both of the flows out of the labor force. Similarly, unemployment should rise because the existence of UI increases both of the flows into unemployment and decreases both of the flows out of unemployment. Only the net effect on employment is ambiguous given the impacts shown in figure 7.4.

Clark and Summers (1982), who have conducted the only comprehensive empirical study of the effects of UI on labor market transitions, present findings that are largely consistent with figure 7.4. They estimate that UI has a positive and significant impact on the transition from employment to unemployment, a strong negative effect on the transition from employment out of the labor force, and a positive and significant effect on the transition to unemployment from outside the labor force. However, they find that UI has a negative effect on the transition to employment from outside the labor force, contrary to what is shown in figure 7.4. In addition, the estimated effects on the transitions out of unemployment are small and insignificant.

Taken together, the estimated impacts of UI on all labor market transitions imply that UI increases unemployment, but that it also raises labor force participation and employment. Clark and Summers estimate that UI, as it existed in 1978, caused a net increase in the unemployment rate of 0.65 percentage points, a net increase in the employment ratio of 0.62 percentage points, and a net decrease in the labor force nonparticipation ratio of 1.11 percentage points.[7] These estimates are consistent with the predicted net effects shown in figure 7.4.

These findings suggest that studies that focus solely on UI claimants in evaluating the incentive effects of UI may overstate the impacts of the program on net unemployment. However, so far, the issues addressed by Clark and Summers have not been examined by other empirical studies. More evidence is needed before we can declare that UI increases employment.

Effects of UI on Nonrecipients

A majority of unemployed workers do not receive UI benefits either because they are not eligible or because they do not choose to receive them. In addition, the rate of benefit receipt among the unemployed has declined in recent years.[8] The ratio of claims to unemployment averaged 0.35 in the 1980s, compared with 0.41 in the 1970s (Corson and Nicholson 1988).

Recent discussions of the disincentive impacts of UI have addressed the possibility that the behavior of recipients has spillover effects on unemployed workers not receiving UI. If UI recipients and other unemployed workers are competing for a limited number of job vacancies, the ability of the other unemployed workers, or nonrecipients, to find a job may be affected by the actions of the UI recipients. If UI reduces the job-search intensity or the rate of job acceptance among recipients, it may enhance the reemployment opportunities available to nonrecipients, allowing the nonrecipients to return to work faster than they would have in the absence of UI. This would shorten the average unemployment spells of nonrecipients. The size of this effect would depend partly on the degree to which nonrecipients are substitutable for recipients with regard to filling the existing job vacancies. Given the potential for substitutability, a full analysis of the net effect of UI on unemployment spells must address potential impacts on average spells of nonrecipients as well as of recipients.

Initial empirical evidence suggests that these spillover effects are important. Levine (1993) estimates that the effects are substantial: a 10 percentage-point increase in the replacement rate shortens unemployment spells of nonrecipients by one week or more. Since the majority of unemployed workers are nonrecipients, a spillover effect this large would completely offset the increase in unemployment caused by the rise in UI benefits, according to the estimates discussed earlier in this chapter. In fact, the magnitude of the effect suggests that an increase in UI benefits would probably generate a *decrease* in aggregate unemployment. Levine supports this conclusion by estimating that a 10 percentage-point increase in the replacement rate would lead to a 0.4 percentage-point reduction in the unemployment rate, although the estimate is not statistically significant. This finding appears to contradict Clark and Summers (1982), who showed that a rise in UI benefit amounts would increase the unemployment rate; however, they did not explicitly control for unemployed nonrecipients. Given that the Levine study represents the first direct analysis of spillover effects, further research will be required before we can draw firm conclusions on this potentially important outcome.[9]

Potential Policy Responses to Reemployment Disincentives

The UI system has traditionally promoted rapid reemployment through work-search requirements and referrals to the ES. However, for many years, policy makers have discussed the possibility of changing the program in such a way as to create new financial incentives for reemployment or to provide additional job-search assistance or other employment services that would expedite claimants' return to work. The policy option related to financial incentives that has received the most attention is a reemployment bonus, a lump-sum paid to those who become reemployed quickly. Several social field experiments were conducted over the past decade to rigorously test this concept in an operational UI environment.[10] Two other sets of field experiments evaluated a more service-oriented approach to encouraging reemployment. The first set tested different strategies for providing employment services, especially enhanced job-search assistance, to make claimants more employable or to make their job search more effective. The second set offered services and benefits to claimants interested in starting their own business. While these experiments focused primarily on providing claimants more services, they also affected reemployment incentives. Both the bonus experiments and the enhanced services experiments were based on a random assignment design in which claimants were part of a control group that received existing services or were part of a treatment group that received the service package or the bonus offer being tested.

This section presents a discussion of the bonus and enhanced-services experiments and of how they affect the reemployment incentives faced by claimants.[11] Also included is a description of how legislation, based on the findings from these experiments, has changed the UI system.

The Reemployment Bonus Experiments

Three bonus experiments were conducted between 1984 and 1989. They were designed to counteract the reemployment disincentives inherent in UI by offering a direct financial incentive for reemployment. The first experiment, the Illinois UI Claimant Bonus Experiment, was conducted in 1984 by the Illinois Department of Employment and Security. In this experiment, eligible UI claimants were assigned randomly to the treatment group, which received a bonus offer, or to the control group, which received no offer. A bonus of $500 was paid to claimants in the treatment group who started work at a full-time job within 11 weeks of filing their initial UI claim and who remained employed for at least four months. The difference in average UI receipt between the treatment and control groups implies that the bonus offer reduced the average spell of UI benefit receipt by more than one week. Furthermore, the bonus was cost effective from the perspective of the UI system: for every dollar spent on bonuses in Illinois, UI benefit payments were reduced by more than two dollars (Spiegelman and Woodbury 1987).

The Illinois findings led the U.S. Department of Labor to sponsor additional field experiments to further test the hypothesis that a reemployment bonus offer could significantly shorten spells of insured unemployment and save the UI system money. In 1988 and 1989, two other experiments were conducted in Pennsylvania and Washington to test a variety of reemployment bonus offers. The findings from these experiments are similar.[12] Bonus offers in the two experiments tended to reduce benefit payments, but the effect was more modest than that found in Illinois.[13] Moreover, for nearly all of the bonus offers that were tested, the amount of bonus payments plus the administrative costs associated with making the offers exceeded the estimated savings in UI payments generated by the offers (Decker and O'Leary 1995). These results from Pennsylvania and Washington therefore contradict those from Illinois and suggest that reemployment bonuses are unlikely to be a cost-effective method for speeding reemployment, at least from the standpoint of the UI system.[14]

Overall, the outcomes from the bonus experiments clearly demonstrate that claimants respond to financial incentives for reemployment, and that a reemployment bonus can at least partly counteract the reemployment disincentives in the UI system. However, the findings also preclude us from being optimistic about the possibility of using reemployment bonuses to generate net savings for the UI system. The estimated impacts are generally not large enough to generate such net savings.

Two other factors not reflected in the estimates of the bonus impacts may cast further doubt on the potential for net savings from reemployment bonuses. First, the behavior of claimants who are offered a bonus may have displacement effects on other UI claimants and unemployed workers who are not offered a bonus. Second, the availability of reemployment bonuses may increase entry into UI.

If all unemployed workers generally compete for a limited number of job vacancies, claimants who find positions more quickly because they receive a bonus offer may displace other unemployed workers from these jobs. The increase in employment among the bonus claimants may therefore be partly or fully offset by decreased employment among other unemployed individuals. Consequently, the impact estimates cannot be used to determine the full effect of a bonus on the total unemployment rate because they do not account for displacement.[15]

In terms of how the availability of reemployment bonuses affects entry into UI, unemployed workers who previously did not apply for UI might be induced to do so once they know they can receive a special payment upon reemployment. For example, individuals who expect to be unemployed for a few weeks might not apply for UI under normal circumstances. However, a reemployment bonus would make applying for UI considerably more valuable to them, since they are likely to receive that payment when they return to work. The potential for entry effects would add to the net costs of offering a permanent reemployment bonus, and entry effects are not accounted for in the estimated impacts from the bonus experiments.[16] One way to address increased entry would be to tie the bonus offer to an increase in the waiting period for filing an initial benefit claim. The longer waiting period would discourage the short-term unemployed from filing a claim that establishes potential eligibility for the reemployment bonus.

An alternative to a bonus as an incentive for reemployment would be a wage supplement for claimants who take a job. Wage supplements may encourage some claimants to accept job offers that they otherwise would not take, thus shortening average unemployment spells. The impact of such a supplement would probably vary according to its size and duration and how eligibility for it is defined. The displacement effect of changing the incentives for reemployment is an issue for a wage supplement as it is for reemployment bonuses. Claimants who take jobs more readily in response to a wage supplement may displace unemployed workers who are not offered a wage supplement. To date, there have been no experiments to test the effect of wage supplements on UI claimants,[17] but the findings from the bonus experiments suggest that the effect would probably be modest.

Enhanced Services Experiments

Two types of services for unemployed workers, job-search assistance and self-employment assistance, have been tested in recent experiments. This section presents the results from these experiments and describes the UI legislation based on these findings. The discussion focuses particularly on the relationship between the tested services and the reemployment incentives faced by UI claimants.

The Job-Search Experiments

The UI system has traditionally encouraged reemployment of claimants through work-search requirements and referrals to the ES. Over the past 15 years, there has been a trend toward relaxing work-search requirements, and some states have eliminated them altogether. However, federal policy makers have recently moved toward requiring claimants to participate in employment services as a condition of UI receipt. In the final extension of the federal Emergency Unemployment Compensation program,[18] states are required to implement a system for evaluating claimants as they enter the UI system and to provide permanently displaced claimants with mandatory job-search assistance or other employment services. The states must use a set of characteristics to create a "profile" of each claimant and to identify claimants who are unlikely to become reemployed quickly.[19] These individuals are then provided a set of mandatory services intended to help them prepare for and find a new job. The mandatory nature of these services suggests that, in addition to preparing claimants for a new job, they may increase the perceived costs of collecting UI benefits and therefore affect the reemployment incentives faced by claimants.

The impetus for the creation of a worker profiling and reemployment services system is a set of findings from the New Jersey Unemployment Insurance Reemployment Demonstration. As with the bonus experiments, the New Jersey demonstration was based on a classical design in which claimants were assigned to the control group, which received existing services, or to a treatment group, which was required to participate in a set of job-search assistance activities.[20] The package of job-search assistance offered to treatment group members was intended to speed reemployment by encouraging claimants to search more aggressively and more effectively for a new job. The findings from this demonstration show that claimants who received mandatory job-search assistance returned to work more quickly than claimants who did not receive such help. Because claimants resumed work more quickly, they also claimed one-half of one week less of UI benefits over the year after their initial claim, and the decrease in UI payments generated by mandatory job-search assistance was large enough to pay for the provision of the services (Corson et al. 1989). Job-search assistance therefore appears to be a cost-effective method for encouraging reemployment. Two other random-assignment studies that tested the effects of alternative job-search assistance policies, the Charleston Claimant Placement and Work Test Demonstration (Corson, Long, and Nicholson 1984) and the Washington Alternative Work Search Experiment (Johnson and Klepinger 1994), also show that mandatory job-search assistance can help expedite reemployment.

Most discussions about the impacts of mandatory job-search assistance focus on the magnitude of the impacts rather than on the process through which they occur. We can consider at least three different ways in which assistance can have an effect on reemployment. First, job-search assistance can make claimants more effective job searchers, resulting in quicker reemployment. I refer to this influence as the *skills effect* of mandatory job-search assistance because it occurs as claimants take the skills that they learn from the job-search workshop and related services and apply them in looking for a new job.

Second, job-search assistance can lead to more rapid reemployment by encouraging claimants to begin searching for work sooner than they otherwise would. The help may give claimants a psychological boost that inspires them to begin looking for work immediately. I refer to this impact as the *encouragement effect* of mandatory job-search assistance. Like the skills effect, the encouragement effect is related to the substance of services designed to help claimants cope with the psychological aspects of unemployment and to stimulate claimants to search aggressively for a new job.

Finally, mandatory job-search assistance may also affect the incentives for reemployment. As is true for the financial parameters of UI, its nonfinancial aspects, such as administrative requirements or mandatory services, have important influences on reemployment incentives. Regarding mandatory job-search assistance, claimants may return to work more quickly in order to avoid participating in job-search assistance services. Because this behavior is caused by the incentives created by the services rather than by the services themselves, I refer to this impact as the *incentive effect* of mandatory job-search assistance.

Indirect evidence of the potential importance of these different effects of mandatory job-search assistance can be obtained by examining the impact of assistance on the rates at which claimants exit the UI system, focusing especially on the timing of these impacts. If the skills effect is dominant, and claimants exit UI because the services make their job search more effective, we would expect the impact on the exit rate to occur either after the services are received, or possibly near the end of services if claimants apply their new search skills immediately. If the encouragement effect is important, we would expect the impact on the exit rate to occur somewhat earlier than with the skills effect. This is because the encouragement effect could occur as services are beginning, such that claimants are inspired to immediately begin searching for a new job. Of course, even if claimants begin looking right away, it may take them some time to find a new job. Hence, the encouragement effect may increase the exit rate both during and after the services. The incentive effect would generate earlier impacts than would either the skills effect or the encouragement effect. Claimants who return to work and exit UI to avoid participating in services would do so after being informed of the services, possibly before such assistance even begins. The incentive effect may continue as services are being delivered if claimants want to avoid participating in additional services. Thus, it is impossible to disentangle the incentive effect from the encouragement effect because both impacts would increase the UI exit rate throughout the period of service delivery.

Evidence from the UI demonstrations on the timing of exit from UI suggests that the encouragement and incentive effects play important roles in the impact of assistance on employment and on UI receipt. Corson and Decker (1989) show that, in the New Jersey demonstration, a significant part of the impact of mandatory job-search was due to an increased UI exit rate in the first seven weeks after the initial claim. The timing of this result corresponds to the periods in which claimants were notified about services (generally in week four after the initial claim) or were required to participate in services (generally weeks five to seven after the initial claim).[21] Johnson and Klepinger (1994) detected a similar effect of mandatory services in the Washington Alternative Work Search Experiment. This early impact implies that mandatory job-search assistance encouraged some claimants to return to work quickly, before the services were completed or, in some cases, even before services began.

Although the early impacts suggest that the incentive and encouragement effects are important, we do not know whether they account for most of the impact of job-search assistance or whether the skills effect is also key. In addition, regardless of the source of the impact of job-search assistance, the service had important long-run benefits. In an evaluation of the long-run impacts of the New Jersey demonstration, Corson and Haimson (1996) find that job-search assistance reduced UI benefit receipt not only in the initial benefit year but in subsequent years as well. They conclude that claimants who were assigned to mandatory job-search assistance found employment that was more stable than that found by control group members.

The Self-Employment Experiments

Self-employment assistance is another policy option that expands the services available to UI claimants and expedites reemployment. Under the traditional UI system, claimants must be available for work and conduct an active job search. Therefore, an individual who "works" full-time on starting a business is generally ineligible for UI. This policy creates a disincentive to self-employment, but recent legislation gives states the option to change this policy. Title V of the North American Free Trade Agreement (NAFTA) Implementation Act (P.L. 103-182) allows states to offer self-employment assistance to help speed the transition of dislocated workers into new employment. Under this service option, eligible claimants who want to establish their own business are paid a self-employment allowance that is equivalent to their UI benefit. They are expected to work full-time on starting their business, and they are exempted from UI work-search requirements. In addition, they are allowed to retain any earnings from self-employment. In effect, the new law removes the barrier to full-time self-employment by allowing payments to self-employed claimants. States are also required to provide self-employment assistance services to claimants receiving self-employment allowances.[22] Participation in these services, which is mandatory for recipients of the allowance, is limited to no more than 5 percent of regular UI claimants. So far, four states are operating self-employment programs for their UI claimants.[23]

This legislation is a response to the relatively positive findings from random-assignment self-employment demonstrations conducted in Washington and Massachusetts. The results indicate that self-employment is a viable reemployment option for a small proportion of UI claimants. Both demonstrations provided self-employment allowances and additional assistance to claimants who completed a set of initial intake activities. In Washington, the self-employment allowance was offered as a lump-sum payment equal to the amount of the claimant's remaining UI entitlement, while, in Massachusetts claimants were offered weekly allowances equal to their UI benefit amount. Of targeted claimants, 4 percent in Washington and 2 percent in Massachusetts completed the initial intake activities and were determined to be eligible for participation in the program (Benus, Wood, and Grover 1994). In terms of the impact on economic outcomes, the availability of self-employment assistance shortened unemployment spells among claimants in both demonstrations and increased earnings in one of the demonstrations (Washington).[24] Only in Massachusetts did the self-employment program reduce total benefits (regular UI payments plus self-employment allowances) paid during the benefit year, by about $700 per eligible claimant. The program in Washington, which paid lump-sum self-employment allowances, increased total benefits paid by about $1,100 per eligible claimant. Self-employment assistance may also decrease the probability that individuals file claims in the future, which would generate savings in UI benefits in the long run. At this time, the data to investigate this potential long-run impact on new claims are not available.

Conclusion

Changes in the parameters of the UI system affect unemployment as predicted by theory: increases in the amount and potential duration of benefits tend to prolong unemployment spells. These effects should therefore be considered in evaluating any proposals to alter UI parameters. In fact, work disincentives were an important consideration in the move to apply the federal income tax to UI benefits beginning in 1979, which reduced the after-tax benefit paid to claimants.[25]

Despite evidence of the presence of disincentive effects, researchers disagree on the importance of these effects. This dispute arises partly because estimates of the impacts of changing UI parameters cover a wide range, and partly because researchers describes similar estimates in different ways. Where one researcher characterizes an effect as "substantial," another views it as "modest." Regardless, work disincentives of some magnitude are implicit in UI insofar as it pays claimants for staying unemployed. The task of policy makers, therefore, is to balance the need for adequate benefits with the need to limit the disincentive to work.

Other potential effects of UI beyond work disincentives should also be considered in setting benefit parameters. Although higher benefits prolong unemployment, they may generate better reemployment outcomes if the period of additional unemployment is spent finding the best possible job. The most obvious implication of this argument is that higher UI benefits should cause higher reemployment wages, but empirical studies of this issue have thus far provided only mixed evidence that such an effect exists.

Even though UI benefits prolong unemployment spells of claimants, they may not necessarily lead to lower aggregate employment or to higher aggregate unemployment for the population. Individuals are probably more likely to enter the labor force and less likely to leave it because of the availability of UI. As the labor force expands, aggregate employment would tend to increase. UI benefits may also have an indirect effect on those unemployed workers not receiving benefits. If all unemployed individuals tend to compete for a limited number of job vacancies, greater unemployment among claimants might be matched by a drop in unemployment among other jobless persons who would otherwise be crowded out of work opportunities by claimants. To date, not enough empirical research has been conducted to fully assess the impact of UI on all possible labor market transitions.

NOTES

I thank Ronald Oaxaca, Christopher O'Leary, Stephen Wandner, Walter Corson, Sheena McConnell, and Daryl Hall for their comments on earlier drafts of this chapter.

1. Another reason for an increase in the probability of reemployment near the point at which benefits are exhausted is that firms who have temporarily laid off workers have an incentive to recall them while they are still receiving benefits. Otherwise, some portion of those laid off will accept other jobs after benefits are exhausted. This is expensive for the firm if the workers have skills or training that are specific to that firm. See chapter 8 for a discussion of the effect of UI on layoff and hiring incentives for firms.

2. For example, Sider (1985) discusses errors in measuring unemployment spells using Current Population Survey data.

314 Work Incentives and Disincentives

3. Corson and Dynarski also note that the precision of the estimates does not allow them to reject the hypothesis that the increase in reemployment probabilities in weeks near benefit exhaustion was due to chance.

4. Chapters 4 and 11 discuss the effect of UI work-search requirements.

5. See chapter 8 for a full discussion of employer behavior under UI.

6. The insurance value of UI that makes work more attractive may be somewhat offset by UI taxes, depending on whether the incidence, or the true burden, of the tax falls on employees or employers. If the incidence falls on employees, their net wage will be reduced, which will make work somewhat less attractive.

7. The employment ratio is the proportion of total employment to the total working-age population. The nonparticipation ratio is the proportion of working-age individuals who are neither employed nor unemployed to the total working-age population.

8. Corson and Nicholson (1988), Blank and Card (1991), and Vroman (1991) discuss this trend and its causes.

9. Davidson and Woodbury (1995) present preliminary findings, based on a simulation model calibrated using estimates from the UI bonus experiments (see the following section), which suggest a much smaller spillover effect than that found by Levine (1993). They estimate that a 10 percentage-point increase in the benefit amount would shorten unemployment spells of nonrecipients by one-half to one day, and that a one-week increase in the potential duration would shorten spells by one-quarter of a day.

10. Laboratory experiments can also be used to investigate the factors that affect job search in a setting with UI benefits. Cox and Oaxaca (1989) discuss how laboratory experiments can test some of the principles that underlie the existing research on UI.

11. Meyer (1995) provides a detailed summary of many of the UI experiments discussed in this chapter.

12. O'Leary, Spiegelman, and Kline (1995) discuss the findings from the Washington experiment, and Corson et al. (1992) discuss the findings from the Pennsylvania experiment.

13. A reemployment bonus was also tested as part of the New Jersey UI Reemployment Demonstration. Since the design of this bonus was different from that of the bonuses offered in Illinois, Washington, and Pennsylvania, I exclude it from my discussion. However, as is true for the results from Pennsylvania and Washington, the findings from the New Jersey bonus experiment suggest that a bonus has a smaller impact than that found in Illinois. See Decker (1994) for a detailed comparison of the Illinois and New Jersey findings.

14. Davidson and Woodbury (1991) argue that the relatively larger impact in the Illinois experiment was due to the inclusion of a subset of claimants who were eligible for an additional 12 weeks of UI benefits through Federal Supplemental Compensation. Analysis based on claimants eligible only for regular UI benefits generates impact estimates similar to those found in Pennsylvania and Washington. These findings suggest that the potential savings from a reemployment bonus increase when potential benefit durations are longer.

15. Corson et al. (1992) make an effort to account for displacement in their estimates of the impacts of the Pennsylvania Reemployment Bonus Demonstration, but the imprecision of the estimated displacement effect renders the estimate essentially meaningless. Dynarski (1993) describes the general problem in trying to detect displacement effects in a demonstration setting. Davidson and Woodbury (1993) present an alternative approach to investigating displacement effects based on a simulation model.

16. A reemployment bonus could also tend to increase entry into the labor force by making UI and therefore employment more valuable. This is in addition to the general effect of UI benefits on labor force entry discussed in the previous section of this chapter.

17. Corson and Haimson (1994) review issues related to the design of a wage supplement. The use of wage supplements to encourage employment among low-income individuals is currently being tested in two demonstrations: the Canada Self-Sufficiency Project (Mijanovich, Gurr, and Vernon, forthcoming) and the New Hope Project in Milwaukee (Kerksick 1993).

18. The relevant legislation is the Unemployment Compensation Amendments of 1993 (Public Law 103-152), section 4 on worker profiling. U.S. Department of Labor (1994) provides a description of the system requirements.

19. Chapter 11 discusses claimant profiling.

20. Mandatory activities included orientation, vocational testing, a one-week job-search workshop, an assessment interview, and follow-up contacts.

21. The primary service, the job-search workshop, generally occurred in week six or seven after the initial claim, depending on the individual.

22. The self-employment activities that must be offered include entrepreneurial training, business counseling, and technical assistance.

23. The four states operating UI self-employment programs are New York, Maine, Oregon, and Delaware.

24. These measures include combined employment and earnings from either wage and salary employment or self-employment.

25. In 1979, UI benefits were made taxable for single individuals whose income exceeded $20,000 and for married taxpayers filing jointly whose incomes exceeded $25,000. Further legislation in 1982 lowered these income limits to $12,000 and $18,000, respectively. The Tax Reform Act of 1986 made all UI benefits taxable.

References

Atkinson, Anthony B., and John Micklewright. 1991. "Unemployment Compensation and Labor Market Transitions: A Critical Review," *Journal of Economic Literature* 29, 4: 1679-1727.

Benus, Jacob, Michelle L. Wood, and Neelima Grover. 1994. "Self-Employment as a Reemployment Option: Demonstration Results and National Legislation." Unemployment Insurance Occasional Paper 94-3, U.S. Department of Labor, Employment and Training Administration.

Blank, Rebecca, and David Card. 1991. "Recent Trends in Insured and Uninsured Unemployment: Is There an Explanation?" *Quarterly Journal of Economics* 106, 4: 1157-1189.

Burdett, Kenneth. 1979 "Unemployment Insurance Payments as a Search Subsidy: A Theoretical Analysis," *Economic Inquiry* 17, 3: 333-343.

Burtless, Gary. 1990 "Unemployment Insurance and Labor Supply: A Survey." In *Unemployment Insurance: The Second Half Century*, W. Lee Hansen and James F. Byers, eds. Madison: University of Wisconsin Press.

Clark, Kim B., and Lawrence H. Summers. 1982. "Unemployment Insurance and Labor Market Transitions." In *Workers, Jobs, and Inflation*, Martin Neil Baily, ed. Washington, DC: Brookings Institution.

Classen, Kathleen P. 1977. "The Effect of Unemployment Insurance on the Duration of Unemployment and Subsequent Earnings," *Industrial and Labor Relations Review* 30, 4: 438-444.

_____. 1979. "Unemployment Insurance and Job Search." In *Studies in the Economics of Search*, S. A. Lippman and John J. McCall, eds. Amsterdam: North-Holland Press.

Corson, Walter S., and Paul T. Decker. 1989. "The Impact of Reemployment Services on Unemployment Insurance Benefits: Findings from the New Jersey Unemployment Insurance Reemployment Demonstration." Unpublished manuscript, Mathematica Policy Research.

Corson, Walter, Paul Decker, Shari Dunstan, and Stuart Kerachsky. 1992. "Pennsylvania Reemployment Bonus Demonstration: Final Report." Unemployment Insurance Occasional Paper 92-1, U.S. Department of Labor, Employment and Training Administration.

Corson, Walter, and Joshua Haimson. 1996. "The New Jersey Unemployment Insurance Reemployment Demonstration Project: Six-Year Folllowup and Summary Report" (revised edition). Unemployment Insurance Occasional Paper 96-2, U.S. Department of Labor, Employment and Training Administration.

Corson, Walter, Shari Dunstan, Paul Decker, and Anne Gordon. 1989. "New Jersey Unemployment Insurance Reemployment Demonstration Project: Final Evaluation Report." Unemployment Insurance Occasional Paper 89-3, U.S. Department of Labor, Employment and Training Administration.

Corson, Walter, and Mark Dynarski. 1990. "A Study of Unemployment Insurance Recipients and Exhaustees: Findings from a National Survey." Unemployment Insurance Occasional Paper 90-3, U.S. Department of Labor, Employment and Training Administration.

Corson, Walter, and Joshua Haimson. 1994. "Wage Supplements for Dislocated Workers: The TAA Wage Supplement Demonstration." Mathematica Policy Research.

Corson, Walter, David Long, and Walter Nicholson. 1984. "Evaluation of the Charleston Claimant Placement Work Test Demonstration." Mathematica Policy Research.

Corson, Walter, and Walter Nicholson. 1988. "An Examination of Declining UI Claims During the 1980s." Unemployment Insurance Occasional Paper 88-3, U.S. Department of Labor, Employment and Training Administration.

Cox, James C., and Ronald L. Oaxaca. 1989. "Unemployment Insurance: The Worker's Perspective." In *Investing in People: A Strategy to Address America's Workforce Crisis*. Washington, DC: U.S. Department of Labor, Commission on Workforce Quality and Labor Market Efficiency.

Danziger, Sheldon, Robert H. Haveman, and Robert Plotnick. 1981. "How Income Transfer Programs Affect Work, Savings, and the Income Distribution: A Critical Review," *Journal of Economic Literature* 19, 3: 975-1028.

Davidson, Carl, and Stephen A. Woodbury. 1991. "Effects of a Reemployment Bonus under Differing Benefit Entitlements, or, Why the Illinois Experiment Worked." Unpublished manuscript, Michigan State University and W.E. Upjohn Institute.

_____. 1993. "The Displacement Effects of Reemployment Bonus Programs," *Journal of Labor Economics* 11, 4: 575-605.

_____. 1995. "Unemployment Insurance and Unemployment: Implications of the Reemployment Bonus Experiments." Draft paper prepared for the Advisory Council on Unemployment Compensation.

Decker, Paul T. 1994. "The Impact of Reemployment Bonuses on Insured Unemployment in the New Jersey and Illinois Reemployment Bonus Experiments," *Journal of Human Resources* 29, 3: 718-741.

Decker, Paul T., and Christopher J. O'Leary. 1995. "Evaluating Pooled Evidence from the Reemployment Bonus Experiments." *Journal of Human Resources* 30, 3: 534-550.

Dynarski, Mark. 1993. "The Effects of Displacement on Measures of Reemployment Bonus Impacts." *Evaluation Review* 17, 1: 47-59.

Ehrenberg, Ronald G., and Ronald Oaxaca. 1976. "Unemployment Insurance, Duration of Unemployment, and Subsequent Wage Gain," *American Economic Review* 66, 5: 754-766.

Feldstein, Martin. 1974. "Unemployment Compensation, Adverse Incentives, and Distributional Anomalies," *National Tax Journal* 37: 231-244.

Gustman, Alan. 1982. "Analyzing the Relation of Unemployment Insurance to Unemployment." In *Research in Labor Economics*, Vol. 5, Ronald G. Ehrenberg, ed. Greenwich, CT: JAI Press.

Hamermesh, Daniel. 1977. *Jobless Pay and the Economy.* Baltimore: Johns Hopkins University Press.

_____. 1979. "Entitlement Effects, Unemployment Insurance and Employment Decisions," *Economic Inquiry* 17, 3: 317-332.

Johnson, Terry R., and Daniel H. Klepinger. 1991. "Evaluation of the Impacts of the Washington Alternative Work Search Experiment." Unemployment Insurance Occasional Paper 91-4, U.S. Department of Labor, Employment and Training Administration.

_____. 1994. "Experimental Evidence on Unemployment Insurance Work-Search Policies," *Journal of Human Resources* 29, 3: 695-717.

Katz, Lawrence F., and Bruce D. Meyer. 1990. "The Impact of the Potential Duration of Unemployment Benefits on the Duration of Unemployment," *Journal of Public Economics* 41, 1: 45-72.

Kerksick, J. 1993. "Implementing the New Hope Project." Paper presented at the Association for Public Policy Analysis and Management Annual Conference.

Levine, Phillip B. 1993. "Spillover Effects between the Insured and Uninsured Unemployed," *Industrial and Labor Relations Review* 47, 1: 73-86.

Meyer, Bruce D. 1989. "An Event Study Approach to the Effects of Unemployment Insurance." Unpublished manuscript, Northwestern University.

_____. 1990. "Unemployment Insurance and Unemployment Spells," *Econometrica* 58, 4: 757-782.

_____. 1995. "Lessons from the U.S. Unemployment Insurance Experiments," *Journal of Economic Literature* 33, 1: 91-131.

Mijanovich, T., S. Gurr, and S. Vernon. Forthcoming. "The Self-Sufficiency Report: A Report on the First Year of a Program to Make Work Pay for Income Assistance Recipients." Social Policy Research Demonstration Corporation, Vancouver, Canada.

Moffitt, Robert. 1985a. "Unemployment Insurance and the Distribution of Unemployment Spells," *Journal of Econometrics* 28, 1: 85-101.

_____. 1985b. "The Effect of the Duration of Unemployment Benefits on Work Incentives: An Analysis of Four Data Sets." Unemployment Insurance Occasional Paper 85-4, U.S. Department of Labor, Employment and Training Administration.

Moffitt, Robert, and Walter Nicholson. 1982. "The Effect of Unemployment Insurance on Unemployment: The Case of Federal Supplemental Benefits," *Review of Economics and Statistics* 64, 1: 1-11.

Mortensen, Dale T. 1977. "Unemployment Insurance and Job Search Decisions," *Industrial and Labor Relations Review* 30, 4: 505-17.

Munts, Raymond. 1970. "Partial Benefits Schedules in Unemployment Insurance: Their Effect on Work Incentives," *Journal of Human Resources* 5, 2: 160-176.

Newton, Floyd C., and Harvey S. Rosen. 1979. "Unemployment Insurance Income Taxation and Duration of Unemployment: Evidence from Georgia," *Southern Economic Journal* 45, 3: 773-784.

O'Leary, Christopher J., Robert G. Spiegelman, and Kenneth Kline. 1995. "Do Bonus Offers Shorten Unemployment Insurance Spells? Results from the Washington Experiment," *Journal of Policy Analysis and Management* 14, 2: 245-269.

Sider, Hal. 1985. "Unemployment Duration and Incidence: 1968-82." *American Economic Review* 75,3: 465-472.

Solon, Gary. 1985. "Work Incentive Effects of Taxing Unemployment Benefits," *Econometrica* 53, 2: 295-306.

Spiegelman, Robert G., Christopher O'Leary, and Kenneth J. Kline. 1992. "The Washington Reemployment Bonus Experiment Final Report." Unemployment Insurance Occasional Paper 92-6, U.S. Department of Labor, Employment and Training Administration.

Spiegelman, Robert, and Stephen A. Woodbury. 1987. "Bonuses to Workers and Employers to Reduce Unemployment: Randomized Trials in Illinois," *American Economic Review* 77, 4: 513-530.

U.S. Department of Labor. 1994. "Worker Profiling and Reemployment Services System: Legislation, Implementation Process and Research Findings." Unemployment Insurance Occasional Paper 94-4, U.S. Department of Labor, Employment and Training Administration

Vroman, Wayne. 1991. "The Decline in Unemployment Insurance Claims Activity in the 1980s." Unemployment Insurance Occasional Paper 91-2, U.S. Department of Labor, Employment and Training Administration.

CHAPTER 8

Financing Benefit Payments

Phillip B. Levine
Wellesley College and *National Bureau of Economic Research*

Roughly thirty years ago, Haber and Murray (1966) published a volume on the condition of the Unemployment Insurance (UI) system in the United States. In terms of financing UI, the main controversies of the day included the financial stability of the system and the nature of the tax structure, called experience rating, that charged a higher tax rate to firms with greater layoff experience. They wrote the following:

> The recent indication of weaknesses in many state [UI trust] funds has given new importance to the consideration of measures to protect the adequacy of state unemployment insurance funds (Haber and Murray 1966, p. 318)

In addition, they posed the question:

> In what ways could experience rating systems be improved or modified so as to contribute toward sounder financing? (p. 319).

Today, these issues continue to be some of the main controversies in financing UI. Concern about the potential for financial problems in the system was almost prophetic. The financial condition of the UI system continued to deteriorate and, during the recessions of 1973-75 and the back-to-back recessions of the early 1980s, many states had to borrow funds from the federal government to cover their benefit payments. The situation improved somewhat over the long economic expansion of the middle and late 1980s. However, following this long expansion and a relatively mild recession in 1990-1991, the financial condition of the UI system in 1993 was considerably weaker than at virtually any time since its inception in 1938.

One potentially important contributor to the changing financial status of the UI system is the taxable wage base. Over the past thirty years, the rapid rate of price increases considerably eroded the taxable wage base, or the maximum amount of earnings upon which UI taxes are levied. The relatively small growth in the nominal wage base has been considerably more than offset by inflation. Tax rates were required to rise correspondingly to finance higher and higher benefits. The wisdom of this approach is certainly open to question today.

The issue of experience rating has also received considerable attention over the past three decades, particularly in the academic literature. Experience rating means that a firm's UI taxes are set so that its tax burden increases as it lays off more workers. The focus of recent research regarding experience rating is its potential effect on temporary layoffs. Because the current financing system is only imperfectly experience rated (i.e., additional layoffs do not always result in a higher tax burden), some have argued that this provides firms with an incentive to lay off workers. The financial condition of the UI system will be weakened if firms follow through on this incentive to a significant degree.

This chapter reviews the financial condition of the UI system, the taxable wage base, and the effects of an experience-rated UI tax. To begin, a brief discussion of the financial structure of the UI system will be presented. This will be followed by a report on the results of an analysis of over fifty years of financial data from the UI system, taking into consideration some of the consequences of a low taxable wage base. The experience-rated nature of the UI tax will then be analyzed. Institutional features that create imperfections in experience rating and the economics literature that has examined the effects of these imperfections on temporary layoffs will be discussed. Finally, conclusions and implications for policy will be drawn.

Financial Structure of the Unemployment Insurance System

The system of financing UI benefits in the United States is controlled at both the federal and state levels of government. Some aspects of the system are dictated directly by the federal government, and some are determined entirely by the states. This part of the chapter will briefly describe the role played by each level in financing the system.[1] A flow chart displaying this information is presented as an appendix to the chapter.

Financing Regular Benefits

To pay for regular UI benefits, all employers are subject to a federal unemployment insurance tax equal to 6.2 percent of their federal taxable payroll. A federal tax credit of 5.4 percent is available, however, for firms in states that have met a series of federal guidelines. These guidelines require that, among other things, states have in place their own tax system with some form of experience rating, charging a lower tax rate to firms who lay off fewer workers. Since all states meet these guidelines, the de facto federal component of the UI tax is 0.8 percent of federal taxable payroll.[2] This federal component of the tax is primarily used for administrative expenses and to pay for the federal share of extended benefits. Federal revenues collected in excess of these expenses go into a trust fund used to finance loans to states whose trust funds have become insolvent.

Although state tax systems are required to meet certain guidelines, these standards are generally quite broad. For instance, the federal tax credit is awarded to firms in states that have an experience-rated tax system, but the type of system employed is chosen at each state's discretion. In addition, the federal taxable wage base is currently set at $7,000 per covered worker, but states have the option to set a higher taxable wage base. As a result of the latitude allowed in the guidelines, state tax systems often exhibit substantial differences. The variation across states in taxable wage bases and in experience-rating systems, in particular, is explored in greater detail later in this chapter.

Financing Extended Benefits

Extended benefits (EB), or benefits paid to unemployed workers beyond the regular benefit exhaustion date during periods of recession, are financed differently than are regular UI benefits. The cost of providing benefits of this type is split equally by the federal and state governments. As indicated, part of the federal component of the UI payroll tax contributes to a trust fund that accumulates during periods of prosperity to pay for the federal component of extended benefit costs during an economic downturn. The state component of EB is paid for with reserves in the state's UI trust fund.

This system of financing extended benefit payments became quite important during the most recent recession in 1990-1991. Problems in the methods that trigger EB prevented the system from making payments to workers in many locations during the downturn, as described in chapter 6 of this volume. As a result, a stopgap measure, the Emergency Unemployment Compensation Act (EUCA), temporarily provided benefits with the same intent. In those locations where EB had been triggered, states had the option to terminate these payments and to replace them with EUC benefits. The program, however, was financed entirely by the federal government, as opposed to being split by the state and federal governments. As a result, state UI reserves were depleted to a far lesser extent over this period than they had been in previous recessions.

Loans to State Governments

The strain imposed during recessions has often led to insolvency in state trust funds, particularly following the 1975 and 1982-1983 recessions. To provide assistance in such a crisis, the federal government established a system of loans that can be made to the states to finance these temporary shortages in reserves. When the system was instituted in 1954, it was very generous to the states. States had up to four years to repay the loan with no interest. If the loan were not repaid during that period, payment would be made by reducing the credit allowed against the federal UI payroll tax until the repayment took place. This system amounted to a several year interest-free loan from the federal government to the states. The incentive to borrow eventually became apparent as loans became quite common by the late 1970s; by 1979, 25 states had borrowed over $5.6 billion (Blaustein 1993). As a result, loan provisions have been restricted over time. The biggest change in the system took place in 1981, when the federal government started charging interest on funds borrowed.

Trends in Funding and the Taxable Wage Base

The financial condition of the UI system has weakened considerably over the past several decades. This section of the chapter will more fully explore the financial difficulties experienced by the system and then move on to address a potential cause of the problem, a low and largely unindexed taxable wage base. For this purpose, financial statistics will be examined that are aggregated over all states between the years 1938 and 1993.[3] Although each state administers its own UI system and some generalizations may not be appropriate for all states, the decision to use aggregated data is driven by the desire to draw conclusions regarding the UI system as a whole.

Financial Condition of the Unemployment Insurance System

Over the years, state UI trust funds have fallen dramatically and have become increasingly likely to experience a deficit during a major recession. Figure 8.1 represents this pattern. It depicts the ratio of the balance in state UI trust funds (net reserves) to total annual wages paid over roughly the past half century.[4] This ratio provides an indicator of the health of the UI trust fund, such that larger ratios indicate larger reserves. As trust funds are depleted, the ratio will approach zero, and a negative ratio indicates a deficit in the funds. A strong cyclical component is apparent in figure 8.1, with the ratio of net reserves to wages paid increasing during expansions and falling during recessions. This makes sense because, during an expansion, relatively high employment leads to larger tax revenues and fewer UI recipients while, in a downturn, relatively high unemployment leads to smaller tax revenues and more UI recipients.

The overriding trend apparent in the figure, however, is towards lower fund reserves. In fact, the relatively large recessions of 1975 and 1983 led many state funds to run deficits that required loans from the federal government to pay for UI benefits. The extent of the problem was so severe in 1983 that the aggregate of all state trust funds was in deficit. Prior to this, state trust funds never came close to running out of money.

Many changes were made over the last two decades in an attempt to restore solvency to the system. In 1981, the federal government pro-

Figure 8.1 Ratio of Net Reserves to Taxable Payroll, 1938-1993

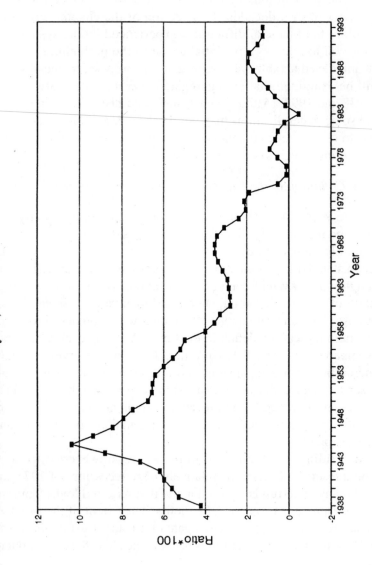

vided a strong incentive to states to keep their individual UI trust funds solvent by legislating that interest would be charged on future loans. To reduce UI expenditures, some states restricted eligibility so that fewer people could receive benefits. In addition, in the highly inflationary period of the late 1970s and early 1980s, many states did not increase UI benefits, leading to a benefit cut in inflation-adjusted dollars. In New York State, for example, the ratio of average weekly benefits to average weekly wages, sometimes referred to as the replacement ratio, fell from 0.326 in 1979 to 0.279 in 1982.

The biggest change in the states, however, was observed in the tax rates assigned to the payrolls of employers. The time series of the average employer tax rate is depicted in figure 8.2. Again, a strong cyclical pattern is observed in this figure. During and just after a recession, tax rates rise to cover the additional liabilities accrued by the system during the downturn. Ignoring the cyclicality, the trend is towards higher tax rates since the early 1950s. For example, the average employer tax rate (as a percentage of taxable payroll) following the economic expansion of the late 1960s and early 1970s was under 1.5 percent. In 1990, after another long expansion, the average rate was about 2 percent.

The increase in average tax rates masks some of the variability across firms. Those firms at the maximum tax rate have faced a large rise in tax payments. This pattern in the data can be seen in figure 8.3, which represents the average tax schedule for states employing the reserve ratio method of financing over the period 1978-1987. The beginning and end points of this time span follow the end of a major recession by a few years and represent roughly comparable points in the business cycle. The schedules show that there has been a secular increase in tax rates for those firms who lay off a lot of workers, leading to a negative reserve ratio. The maximum rate increased from about 4.5 percent in 1978 to almost 7 percent in 1987.[5] There has been some change in tax rates faced by firms with lower reserve ratios, but there is no obvious pattern to these changes. The conclusion apparent from this figure is that states have attempted to recoup some of their increased UI expenditures from the firms with the greatest layoff history.

Although these changes have improved the financial picture of the UI system over the past decade, its condition is still relatively weak by historical standards. Referring back to figure 8.1, the economic expansion of the middle and late 1980s restored UI trust funds to a level not

328

Figure 8.2 Average Employer Tax Rates, 1938-1993

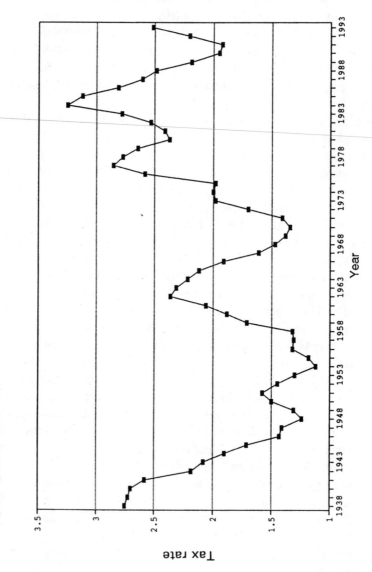

Figure 8.3 Tax Schedules Averaged over All Reserve Ratio States, Selected Years, 1978-1987

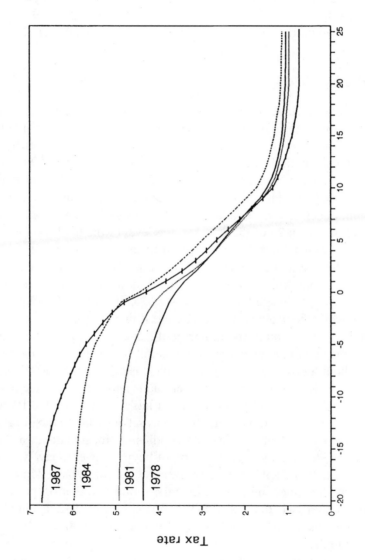

seen since 1974. The mild recession of 1990-1991 led to a relatively small reduction in the size of the fund.[6] However, a severe recession could again lead to insolvency in many states. Reductions in the trust find equal to those encountered in either the 1973-1975 or 1981-1982 recession would once more exhaust aggregate reserves in state UI trust funds.

The Taxable Wage Base

The taxable wage base is another component of the UI financing system subject to federal regulation. The federal government sets a minimum wage base, currently $7,000, which must be met by all states. Thus, employers only pay UI taxes on the first $7,000 of each worker's earnings. States have the option of setting a taxable wage base above the federal minimum. In 1994, thirty-nine states and the District of Columbia elected to set a higher taxable wage base, although it was $11,000 or less in 24 of these states (the level of the tax base for each state is presented in table 8.1). In addition, seventeen states have indexed their wage base, usually as a fraction of the average earnings level in the state. Most of the bigger states, however, have not done so. For example, the wage base in New York, California, and Florida is $7,000, while the wage base in Texas and Illinois is $9,000.

With the exception of the minority of states that have indexed their taxable wage base, adjustments are generally made in an ad hoc manner; without legislation specifying an increase, the wage base remains constant. Adjustments have only been made sporadically since it was first established in 1939, and inflation has severely eroded its real value. In 1940, the taxable wage base was set at $3,000, equal to average annual earnings at that time. After adjusting for inflation, this base would provide roughly $31,000 worth of buying power today, which is about four and one-half times the current $7,000 wage base. Moreover, this method of financing stands in stark contrast to that of the social security system, where legislation was first passed in 1972 to automatically adjust its taxable wage base to keep pace with inflation. In 1940, the base in the social security system also equaled $3,000. As of 1972, the social security taxable wage base had climbed to $9,000, and the UI taxable wage had risen to $4,200. Today, the comparable figures are $53,400 and $7,000 for social security and UI, respectively.

Table 8.1 The Taxable Wage Base in 1994, by State

State	Taxable wage base	Indexed	State	Taxable wage base	Indexed
Hawaii	$25,000	Yes	Ohio	$8,750	No
Alaska	$23,800	Yes	Delaware	$8,500	No
Idaho	$20,400	Yes	Georgia	$8,500	No
Washington	$19,000	Yes	Louisiana	$8,500	No
Oregon	$19,000	Yes	Maryland	$8,500	No
New Jersey	$17,200	Yes	Missouri	$8,500	No
Rhode Island	$16,400	Yes	Alabama	$8,000	No
Utah	$16,200	Yes	Kansas	$8,000	No
Nevada	$15,900	Yes	Kentucky	$8,000	No
Minnesota	$15,100	Yes	New Hampshire	$8,000	No
Montana	$15,000	Yes	Pennsylvania	$8,000	No
Iowa	$13,900	Yes	Vermont	$8,000	No
North Carolina	$13,200	Yes	Virginia	$8,000	No
New Mexico	$13,100	Yes	West Virginia	$8,000	No
North Dakota	$13,000	Yes	Arizona	$7,000	No
Wyoming	$11,400	Yes	California	$7,000	No
Massachusetts	$10,800	No	Florida	$7,000	No
Oklahoma	$10,700	Yes	Indiana	$7,000	No
Wisconsin	$10,500	No	Maine	$7,000	No
Colorado	$10,000	No	Mississippi	$7,000	No
District of Columbia	$9,500	No	Nebraska	$7,000	No
Michigan	$9,500	No	New york	$7,000	No
Arkansas	$9,000	No	South Carolina	$7,000	No
Connecticut	$9,000	'No	South Dakota	$7,000	No
Illinois	$9,000	No	Tennessee	$7,000	No
Texas	$9,000	No			

These patterns are shown in figure 8.4, which presents the fraction of covered earnings taxable by both the UI and social security systems. Throughout the 1940s, both systems taxed the same proportion of earnings. A series of ad hoc adjustments to the social security taxable wage base in the 1950s and 1960s maintained the wage base at a roughly constant level while the UI wage base continued to fall. Indexation and other tax increases actually raised the relative size of the Social Security taxable wage base while a few ad hoc increases only temporarily slowed the continued decline in the 1970s and 1980s in the UI system.

Problems with the Current System

A major deficiency in the current system of UI financing is that the infrequent, ad hoc adjustments to the taxable wage base lead to a continual erosion of its financial stability. The problem rests in a few simple accounting identities:

1. revenues collected are equal to the product of the tax rate and taxable wages paid in the state,

2. benefits paid out are equal to the product of the number of unemployed, insured workers and the amount of benefits they collect, and

3. if the benefits paid out exceed the revenues collected, the balance in the UI trust fund must fall.

Even in the absence of severe cyclical downturns, these basic relationships indicate that the current system of UI financing will drift towards insolvency. This is because benefit levels, for the most part, rise to keep pace with inflation, but taxable wages do not. As a result, benefit payments will continually increase more than revenues do and the trust fund will persistently decline. Short-term benefit reductions, penalties imposed for borrowing, and short-term tax rate increases cannot solve this problem in the long run. Moreover, this difficulty is unrelated to the outcome of the debate regarding the merits of a "forward-funded" UI system (i.e., a system that finances large benefit payments made during recessions by accumulating large reserves during booms rather than by borrowing), discussed in chapter 9 of this volume. Regardless

333

Figure 8.4 Fraction of Covered Earnings Taxable by UI and Social Security, 1938-1993

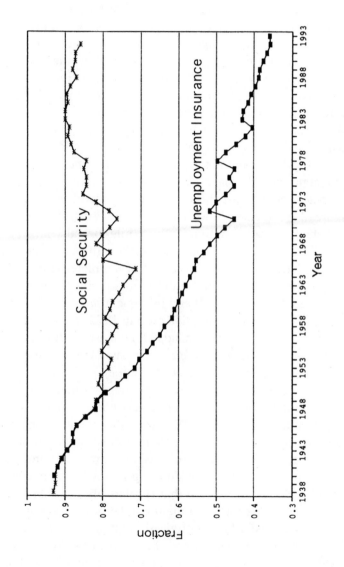

of the level of trust fund reserves deemed adequate, the accounting
identities suggest that reserves will slip lower and lower and will eventually fall below that level.

To illustrate these concepts, figure 8.5 displays one measure indicating the generosity of UI benefits and one measure indicating the tax burden imposed on workers' wages, where both measures are aggregated
across states. The generosity gauge is the ratio of average weekly benefits to average weekly wages.[7] It expresses the fraction of the average
worker's wage that would be replaced by the average weekly benefit and
is therefore sometimes called the replacement ratio. The tax burden
gauge is the ratio of taxable wages to total wages paid in the state. It indicates what fraction of wages earned are taxed by the UI system.

Figure 8.5 shows that the generosity of UI benefits has remained
fairly constant over the past fifty years. The average weekly benefit
would replace roughly one-third of the average worker's weekly wage.
This figure also indicates, however, that the fraction of wages taxed by
the UI system has fallen dramatically. While virtually all wages paid
were taxable fifty years ago, only around one-third are currently taxable. The decline in this ratio is a result of the increase in total wages
paid at roughly the rate of inflation while taxable wage growth has
been restricted due to the small and infrequent increases in the taxable
wage base. The discrete rises in this ratio in 1972, 1978, and 1983 cor-
respond exactly with federally mandated increases in the taxable wage
base. This pattern in the UI taxable wage base stands in stark contrast
to the experience of the Social Security system.

The evidence presented in the figure suggests that, while the real
generosity of the UI system has been largely constant over time, the tax
burden falls almost unabatedly. Therefore, the simple accounting relationships clearly indicate that the system must move towards insolvency unless changes are made. Increasing tax rates continually is one
approach to providing adequate funding for the system, even in the
presence of a taxable wage base that is relatively constant in nominal
dollars. Increasing tax rates can maintain the basic accounting identities if rates are raised fast enough to keep pace with the inflation
adjustments made to UI benefits. In fact, a pattern like this has taken
place over the past two decades, as shown in figure 8.2 and 8.3, and as
discussed earlier in the chapter. This approach, however, creates different problems, which are explored in the following section.

335

Figure 8.5 The Ratio of Taxable to Total Wages and the Replacement Ratio, 1938-1993

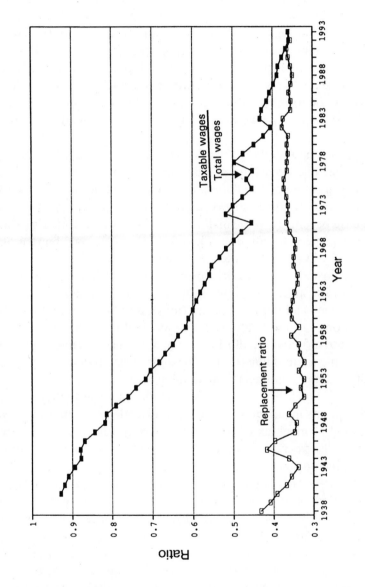

Tax Rates and Low-Wage Workers

A payroll tax that only applies to earnings up to a specific level results in a greater proportion of earnings being taxed for low-wage workers than for high-wage workers. Both social security and UI taxes share this feature, whose effect depends upon the incidence of the payroll tax.[8] If the tax is paid largely by firms, it provides a disincentive for firms to hire relatively less skilled workers. If the tax is passed along to workers in the form of lower wages, it is a form of regressive taxation. Either way, low-wage workers are hurt disproportionally by this type of tax.

The problem with the UI tax is that it has historically had a roughly constant taxable wage base and an increasing tax rate. As the taxable wage base is eroded by inflation, only lower- and lower-wage workers remain taxed on all or most of their earnings. Similarly, the taxable wage base becomes a very small part of a high-wage worker's earnings as wages grow with inflation. Therefore, the additional burden of the tax borne by low-wage workers is growing over time.

Again, historical characteristics of the UI system aggregated across states will illustrate this point. Table 8.2 considers three hypothetical workers: one is a low-wage earner (making $5,000 per year in current dollars), one is a moderate-wage earner (making $25,000 per year in current dollars), and the third is a high-wage earner (making $75,000 per year in current dollars). The Consumer Price Index is used to convert these dollar amounts to comparable levels of purchasing power in 1954, 1969, and 1989. These years are chosen because they all represent low points in tax rates following an extended economic expansion. Using the historical tax rates and the federally mandated taxable wage base for those years, an estimate is obtained of the percentage of each worker's income paid to UI taxes.[9]

The results presented in table 8.2 demonstrate quite clearly the increasing tax burden faced by low-wage workers or by the firms that employ them. In 1954, a firm employing a low-wage worker paid 1.12 percent of the individual's wage as UI taxes, about five times the percentage (0.22) paid by a firm employing a high-wage earner. A firm employing a moderate wage earner paid 0.65 percent. Regressiveness in the system grew somewhat during the relatively low inflation years between 1954 and 1969. In the latter year, the tax burden for a low-wage worker increased slightly to 1.38 percent, while the high-wage worker's burden fell to 0.2 percent, one-seventh the rate for the low-wage worker. The middle-wage worker's tax burden stayed roughly constant. By 1989, however, the inflation of the 1970s and early 1980s led to vastly different tax burdens. The tax imposed upon a firm employing a low-wage worker increased to 2.18 percent of his/her earnings. This is about 20 times the percentage paid by a firm employing a high-wage worker, which dropped to 0.09 percent. Between 1954 and 1989, the tax burden facing low-wage workers doubled, while the burden facing high-wage workers was cut in half.

Table 8.2 UI Tax Payments as Percentage of Earnings for Representative Workers, Selected Years

Year	Earnings in 1990 $s	Earnings in nominal $s	Tax rate	Taxable wage base	Taxes due in nominal $s	Percentage of nominal earnings
Low-wage worker						
1954	5,000	1,029	1,12	3,000	11.52	1.12
1969	5,000	1,348	1.38	3,000	18.60	1.38
1989	5,000	5,000	2.18	7,000	109.00	2.18
Middle-wage worker						
1954	25,000	5,145	1.12	3,000	33.6	0.65
1969	25,000	6,738	1.38	3,000	41.4	0.61
1989	25,000	25,000	2.18	7,000	152.6	0.61
High-wage worker						
1954	75,000	15,435	1.12	3,000	33.6	0.22
1969	75,000	20.213	1.38	3,000	41.4	0.20
1989	75,000	75,000	2.18	7,000	65.4	0.09

Thus, disproportionate costs may be borne by low-wage workers or by the firms that employ them as a result of the historical pattern of maintaining a relatively constant taxable wage base while increasing tax rates to finance inflation-adjusted benefits. Low-wage workers either become more and more expensive employees relative to high-wage workers or are subject to an increasingly regressive tax, depending upon the incidence of the tax. This effect will continue until the taxable wage base is indexed.

Experience Rating and Employment Fluctuations

Another area in which state financing systems differ is in the way they implement experience rating. Recall that an experience-rated state tax system is required for firms to take a credit against the federal UI tax. The method by which taxes are experience rated, however, is left to the discretion of the states and has led to differences across states. This part of the chapter will explore the various types of systems used and will then proceed to review the evidence regarding claims that the current system provides firms with an incentive to lay off workers.

State Tax Systems

The two most common ways of computing the tax rate a firm will be charged are the reserve ratio and benefit ratio methods. Financing systems of these types are in place in thirty-three states and seventeen states, respectively. The remaining states have systems that are less common and will not be described here.[10]

Under a reserve ratio financing system, a "bank account" is established for each firm, with tax payments added to the account and UI benefits drawn from it. The reserve ratio is the ratio of the reserves in the firm's account to the average taxable payroll of the firm over, typically, the past three years. Firms with a high reserve ratio have contributed considerably more in taxes than they have paid out in benefits. In contrast, firms with a negative reserve ratio have paid out more in benefits than they have paid in taxes.

Tax rates are assigned according to a tax schedule that relates a firm's reserve ratio to a specific tax rate. A simplified version of a tax schedule is presented in figure 8.6. A firm's UI tax rate is a decreasing function of its reserve ratio, subject to a minimum and a maximum rate. When a firm lays off workers, the benefits paid to that worker are charged to the firm's account. Its reserve ratio, therefore, falls. For a firm with a "moderate" reserve ratio (i.e., those firms located on the sloped portion of the tax schedule) laying off an additional worker will increase its tax rate. This represents the experience-rating feature of the UI tax system. On the other hand, if the firm lays off enough workers, its reserve ratio will fall beyond the point where the tax rate rises above the maximum rate. At this point, laying off more workers will not lead

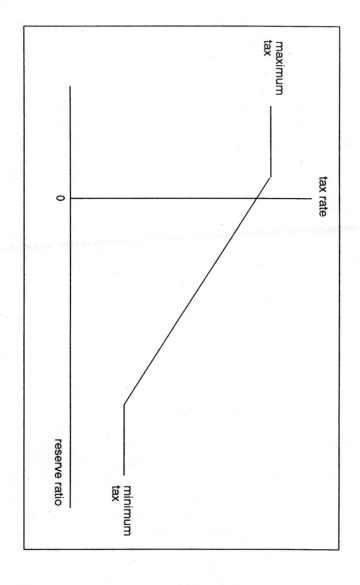

Figure 8.6 Typical Tax Schedule

to an increase in the tax rate charged to the firm. Moreover, a firm that lays off relatively few workers and has a high reserve ratio will still pay the minimum tax rate if it lays off an additional worker. It is for these reasons that the system is said to be imperfectly experience rated.

Tax rates in a benefit ratio system are more directly linked to the level of benefits received by a firm's laid-off workers. This system ties a firm's UI tax rate to the ratio of the benefits drawn by its employees, typically over the past three years, to the size of its taxable payroll during those years. A tax schedule then relates the firm's benefit ratio to a tax rate that it must pay. The tax schedule is similar in nature to that presented in figure 8.6, with the obvious exception that the benefit ratio rather than the reserve ratio belongs on the x-axis. Again, moderate layoff firms face tax rates that increase with their layoff experience. The existence of a minimum and maximum tax rate indicates that the system is only imperfectly experience rated.

Across states, tax levels vary dramatically. Table 8.3 presents the minimum, maximum, and average tax rates for all states in 1993. Maximum tax rates range from 5.4 percent in several states (the minimum allowed by federal law) to 10 percent in Michigan. Average tax rates range from 0.5 percent in South Dakota to 4.8 percent in Pennsylvania and New York.

Tax Systems and Experience Rating

In describing the reserve ratio and benefit ratio systems, the feature of imperfect experience rating shows up quite clearly because of the presence of the minimum and maximum tax rates. Imperfect experience rating creeps into the system in more subtle ways as well. This section will more fully explore this aspect of the tax system.

One method of assessing the degree of experience rating across states is the Experience Rating Index (ERI). This measure takes into account benefits paid out that do not increase the tax imposed upon firms because (a) the firm is at the minimum or maximum tax rate (ineffectively charged benefits), (b) the firm is no longer operating in the state (inactive charges), or (c) the benefit payments are not charged back to the employer's account for some other reason (noncharged benefits). Noncharged benefits may result, for instance, if a state elects

Table 8.3 Minimum, Maximum, and Average Tax Rates as a Percentage of Taxable Wages in 1993, by State

State	Maximum tax rate	Minimum tax rate	Average tax rate	State	Maximum tax rate	Minimum tax rate	Average tax rate
Alabama	6.0	0.4	1.6	Montana	6.4	0.3	1.4
Alaska	5.4	1.0	2.0	Nebraska	5.5	0.1	1.2
Arizona	6.4	0.1	1.5	Nevada	5.4	0.3	1.5
Arkansas	6.0	0.1	3.0	New Hampshire	6.5	0.1	2.2
California	5.4	1.1	3.6	New Jersey	5.8	0.5	1.2
Colorado	5.4	0.0	1.3	New Mexico	5.4	0.6	1.5
Connecticut	6.4	1.5	3.4	New York	7.0	2.5	4.8
Delaware	9.5	1.0	2.6	North Carolina	5.7	0.0	1.0
District of Columbia	7.5	2.0	4.0	North Dakota	5.4	0.4	1.4
Florida	6.4	0.2	1.8	Ohio	8.5	0.7	2.9
Georgia	8.6	0.1	1.6	Oklahoma	5.5	0.1	1.2
Hawaii	5.4	0.0	10.	Oregon	5.4	1.6	2.6
Idaho	5.4	0.5	1.8	Pennsylvania	10.5	2.1	4.8
Illinois	7.7	0.6	2.9	Rhode Island	8.3	2.2	3.7
Indiana	5.5	0.2	1.2	South Carolina	5.4	1.2	1.8
Iowa	7.5	0.0	1.6	South Dakota	7.0	0.0	0.5
Kansas	6.4	0.1	2.4	Tennessee	10.0	0.2	2.0
Kentucky	9.0	0.3	2.1	Texas	6.4	0.3	1.3
Louisiana	6.0	0.3	1.9	Utah	8.0	0.4	1.0
Maine	7.5	2.4	3.8	Vermont	5.9	0.6	2.7

(continued)

Table 8.3 (continued)

State	Maximum tax rate	Minimum tax rate	Average tax rate
Maryland	8.1	1.8	2.9
Massachusetts	8.1	2.2	3.9
Michigan	10.0	1.0	4.1
Minnesota	9.1	0.6	1.8
Mississippi	5.4	1.2	2.1
Missouri	7.8	0.0	2.3

State	Maximum tax rate	Minimum tax rate	Average tax rate
Virginia	6.3	0.2	1.2
Washington	5.4	0.5	2.3
West Virginia	8.5	1.5	3.0
Wisconsin	9.8	0.0	2.2
Wyoming	8.8	0.3	2.1

to make payments to workers who quit their job after a disqualification period or if the payments represent extended benefits.

Formally, the ERI is computed as

$$\text{ERI} = 100 - \%\text{IEC} + \%\text{IAC} + \%\text{NNC}$$

where %IEC represents the percentage of benefit payments that are ineffectively charged benefits, %IAC indicates the percentage of benefit payments that are charged to inactive firms, and %NNC is the percentage of payments that are not charged to firms. An ERI of 100 indicates that all benefits are charged to firms and that the degree of experience rating is complete. An ERI of zero would show that no benefits are charged to firms and that there would be no experience rating. Table 8.4 presents the ERI and its components for all states in 1994. A significant degree of variation is present in these data. For example, the ERI in North Carolina is only 31 percent compared to 84 percent in New York.

Although the ERI is a comprehensive source of data regarding the current status of experience rating, it does have some limitations, as highlighted by Vroman (1986, 1994). First, the ERI is just a snapshot of the relationship between benefit payments and tax liabilities. It does not take into account the fact that benefits incurred today will lead to higher future tax payments by experience-rated firms. Second, the lag between benefit charges and tax increases leads to cyclicality in the ERI. When a recession begins, benefit charges increase, but taxes for experience-rated firms do not rise until the following year. Therefore, the fraction of benefits that are ineffectively charged will appear to increase. At the end of the recession, this lag will lead tax payments to grow more rapidly than benefit payments and will reduce the ERI. This cyclical component has nothing to do with structural changes in the UI financing system and may provide policy makers with misleading data.

Recent empirical research in the academic literature has utilized an alternative indicator of the degree of experience rating a firm faces through a concept called the marginal tax cost (MTC). The MTC is designed to measure the additional tax burden for a firm if it lays off a worker and that worker receives one dollar in UI benefits. For firms at the minimum or maximum tax rate in either type of system, the MTC is zero since tax rates would be unaffected.

Table 8.4 Components of the Experience Rating Index (ERI) in 1994, by State

State	Ineffectively charged (%)	Inactive charges (%)	Noncharged (%)	ERI	State	Ineffectively charged (%)	Inactive charges (%)	Noncharged (%)	ERI
Alabama	27	7	14	52	Montana	15	9	13	63
Alaska	NA	NA	NA	NA	Nebraska	10	8	27	55
Arizona	4	1	14	81	Nevada	14	1	13	72
Arkansas	NA	NA	NA	NA	New Hampshire	11	7	5	77
California	26	15	6	53	New Jersey	52	10	0	38
Colorado	18	9	5	68	New Mexico	7	9	17	67
Connecticut	26	2	14	59	New York	8	7	2	84
Delaware	0	17	1	83	North Carolina	38	12	19	31
District of Columbia	15	19	1	64	North Dakota	17	6	12	64
Florida	6	4	15	75	Ohio	12	6	9	73
Georgia	9	10	7	75	Oklahoma	6	13	15	66
Hawaii	23	5	39	33	Oregon	20	11	22	48
Idaho	31	2	17	50	Pennsylvania	16	11	10	64
Illinois	16	2	11	71	Rhode Island	9	8	7	75
Indiana	5	8	11	75	South Carolina	12	6	23	58
Iowa	13	8	12	66	South Dakota	27	7	19	47
Kansas	18	8	15	59	Tennessee	1	14	12	73
Kentucky	13	8	2	77	Texas	NA	13	18	NA
Louisiana	1	9	15	75	Utah	4	8	22	66

Maine	11	3	26	60
Maryland	NA	NA	NA	NA
Massachusetts	21	6	15	58
Michigan	12	8	2	77
Minnesota	17	1	12	69
Mississippi	17	14	19	50
Missouri	10	1	19	70

Vermont	21	9	20	51
Virginia	5	8	10	77
Washington	10	9	42	39
West Virginia	20	16	5	59
Wicsonsin	14	4	12	70
Wyoming	NA	10	11	NA

For firms between the minimum and maximum rates, however, the MTC is probably not equal to unity (i.e., the firm's tax burden will not increase by one dollar) in either the reserve ratio or benefit ratio financing systems. Consider a firm in a reserve ratio state that has constant employment.[11] If this firm is located along the sloped portion of the tax schedule and it pays out a one-dollar UI benefit, its reserve ratio will fall and its taxes will increase in the following year. If the additional tax liability in the next year is less than one dollar, then the firm will not have yet fully repaid the dollar in benefits. Its reserve ratio will still be higher than it was before the benefit payout and it will again face a somewhat higher tax rate in the following year. This pattern will repeat itself until the full dollar is repaid.

Although full repayment would indicate perfect experience rating, that repayment may have taken place over several years. Therefore, the present discounted value (PDV) of the additional taxes paid will actually be less than one dollar, indicating imperfect experience rating. Since the "imperfection" rests in the PDV calculation, two factors that influence the degree of experience rating become apparent. First, the slope of the tax schedule will influence how quickly the dollar is repaid. If the slope is steep, the dollar will be repaid more quickly and the MTC will be closer to unity.[12] Second, the interest rate used in the PDV calculation will influence the MTC. Higher interest rates will reduce the degree of experience rating.

This approach to calculating the MTC and incentives for firms is based upon a small change in benefit payments that is, perhaps, appropriate in examining temporary layoffs. A reduction in the size of a firm's workforce through permanent layoffs, however, may similarly be subsidized by the UI system. Brechling and Laurence (1995) point out that large changes in employment not only alter the tax rate, but the size of the payroll upon which that tax has to be paid. Because the total tax burden decreases in response to such downsizing, they argue that this type of system encourages firms to lay off workers in this context as well. Limited empirical research has considered the response of employers to this incentive, and the remaining discussion will focus on the effect of experience rating on temporary layoffs.

Experience Rating and Temporary Layoffs

The employment effects of imperfect experience rating have generated a significant amount of research over the last two decades. The approaches taken to examine this issue have developed considerably over the period and will be summarized in this section of the chapter. The survey provided here is not intended to be complete but is presented as an overview of developments in the literature. Previous surveys can be found in Brechling (1977), Topel and Welch (1980), and Hamermesh (1990).

Theoretical foundations for this research were laid by Feldstein (1976), Baily (1976), and Brechling (1977). The effect of imperfect experience rating on layoffs was addressed in the context of an implicit contract model. In this type of model, there is some form of long-term attachment between firms and workers. Imperfect experience rating leads to layoffs because layoffs are subsidized. If a firm lays off a worker, the UI benefits received by that worker are greater than the additional tax costs faced by the firm. If firms and workers have a long-term attachment, both firms and workers can benefit from this subsidy if the firm cycles workers through temporary spells of unemployment. The firm will benefit because it can pay the workers a little less. Workers will benefit because their total compensation, equal to wages and UI payments, will be higher. Therefore, firms will use temporary layoffs to extract the subsidy regardless of demand conditions, but particularly during periods of low demand.

Initial attempts to empirically test this proposition typically analyzed the effects of differences in parameters of the UI system on layoffs. Feldstein (1978) used microdata from the 1975 Current Population Survey to examine the probability of being on temporary layoff on the survey date as a function of the average weekly UI benefit in the worker's state. Since the absolute size of the subsidy created by imperfect experience rating grows with the benefit level, he hypothesized that benefits should be positively correlated with the probability of temporary layoff. The results from Feldstein's analysis supported this hypothesis and led to the conclusion that a large share of temporary layoff unemployment is created by imperfect experience rating. Brechling (1981) used aggregate industry level data by state for the years 1962-1969 to examine the impact of parameters of the tax schedule itself, such as the maximum tax rate and the slope. As discussed earlier, a higher maximum or a steeper slope will increase the degree of experience rating and should reduce layoffs. Support for this relationship is observed, particularly in response to differences in the maximum tax rate.

The next major advance in this literature came in a series of papers by Topel (1983, 1984, 1985). A significant contribution made by Topel was his parameterization of the degree of experience rating. Rather than bringing specific components of the UI system into his empirical work, Topel introduced the concept of the marginal tax cost, measuring the amount of a one-dollar benefit that is repaid by the firm in the form of higher taxes. This parameterization provided a convenient approach to observing that experience rating is imperfect even for firms between minimum and maximum tax rates. Moreover, it provided a useful way to simulate what would be the effect on temporary layoffs if the experience rating were complete. Changing the MTC from its current level to unity would approximate the effects of instituting a UI system with perfect experience rating.

Topel's research computed the degree of experience rating aggregated across firms in twenty-nine different industries for several states and a few years. Using microdata from the Current Population Survey, he estimated models of the probability of being on temporary layoff as a function of the MTC. Findings from this research uniformly showed that workers employed in states and industries with a lower degree of experience rating were significantly more likely to be temporarily laid off. Movement from the current system to one with complete experience rating would lead to approximately a one-third to one-half reduction in temporary layoff unemployment, according to Topel's estimates.

A problem with the research completed to this point was that it ignored the effects of imperfect experience rating on layoffs at different times in the business cycle. The theoretical literature based on implicit contract models indicated that an effect should be observed in all periods but that it should be stronger during cyclical downturns. The next advance in this literature explicitly incorporated differences over the business cycle in the analyses.

The theoretical basis for much of this work also changed from an implicit contract model, stressing long-term attachments between firms and workers, to adjustment cost models that place importance on the costs of changing the size of a firm's workforce (Anderson 1993; Card and Levine 1994). An experience-rated UI tax is treated as an adjustment cost. Firms that want to reduce the size of their workforce will have to incur a greater firing cost the greater the degree of experience rating. Importantly, firms that want to *hire* workers must also take this cost into consideration because they will face a higher cost should they decide to lay off those workers sometime in the future. Therefore, not only does a greater degree of experience rating reduce the incentive to lay off workers during an economic downturn, it reduces the incentive for firms to hire workers during an expansion. In other words, the greater the degree of experience rating, the less the variability in employment over the business cycle. This pattern is depicted in figure 8.7.

Depending upon the data set employed, there are significant differences in the empirical tests of this proposition. Card and Levine (1994) use 10 years of data from the Current Population Survey; estimate MTC measures by state, industry, and year; and assign these measures to each individual in the sample. Their approach is similar to the one taken by Topel, except that they explicitly model the effect of the MTC on temporary layoffs in each year over the 10-year span from 1978-1987, which included a severe recession and two periods of economic growth. They find that imperfect experience rating may be linked to as much as 50 percent of temporary layoffs during the recessionary years of 1982-1983, but that there are considerably smaller effects at the peak of the business cycle in 1979 and 1986-1987. Similar results are observed for temporary layoffs over seasonal patterns of employment demand throughout the year. The advantage of the approach employed by Card and Levine is that it utilizes a largely nationally representative source of data over a long time period.

An alternative approach, implemented by Anderson (1993) and Anderson and Meyer (1994), is to use the information available in a unique source, the Continuous Wage and Benefit History (CWBH) data. The CWBH represents quarterly UI administrative records on firms and individuals in eight states between 1978 and 1984. The advantage of this data source is that an MTC measure can be created for individual firms and can then be applied to the employees of that firm. Although use of the CWBH data allows for firm-level analysis, it

Figure 8.7 Effect of Imperfect Experience Rating (ER) over the Business Cycle

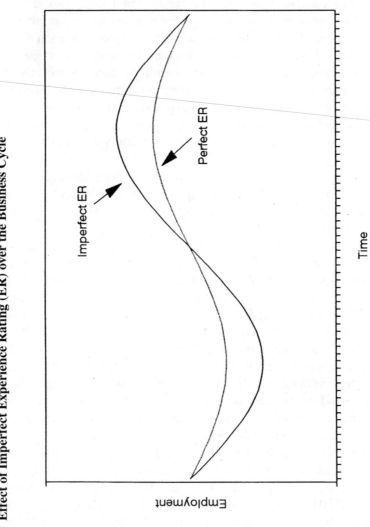

introduces other problems; results may only pertain to those states included in the survey and may not be nationally representative, and personal characteristics are not available in this data source and cannot be controlled for in the empirical work.

Using a subsample of firms in the retail trade industry from the CWBH data, Anderson (1993) examines the cyclical pattern of employment over a quarterly demand cycle as a function of the individual MTCs of the firms. Consistent with an adjustment cost model, she finds that the peak-to-trough change in employment levels is smaller among firms that face a higher MTC (i.e. a greater degree of experience rating). Over the entire cycle, employment is shown to be slightly higher in firms facing a higher MTC.

Quite recently, Anderson and Meyer (1994) have used the CWBH data to carefully examine two potential problems that may have affected previous empirical work. First, they consider problems that may be present in the work by Topel (1983, 1984, 1985) and Card and Levine (1994), who utilize measures of the MTC evaluated at the state/ industry level. Previous research indicates that this approach masks a considerable degree of variability occurring across firms within states and industries (Anderson and Meyer 1993) and may result in biases in the estimated impact of imperfect experience rating. The results presented by Anderson and Meyer indicate that aggregation has only a small impact on the estimated effect of imperfect experience rating on temporary layoffs.

Possibly a more important problem addressed by Anderson and Meyer (1994) is the potential endogeneity of the MTC cost measures in models of temporary layoffs.[13] Since a firm's MTC is determined by its past layoff history, previous empirical models have estimated how temporary layoffs are affected by MTC, which is a function of lagged temporary layoffs. Serial correlation in a firm's layoff history will therefore lead to endogeneity bias. Moreover, in prior research estimating MTC measures aggregated to the state level, state tax schedules may have shown a response to the aggregate layoff behavior of firms in the state. If firms lay off many workers, state tax schedules may adjust to provide the necessary revenue to pay for the additional benefits.[14] Anderson and Meyer find that, even after controlling for this source of bias, over 20 percent of temporary layoffs can be attributed to imperfect experience rating.

Summary and Conclusions

This chapter has addressed two major developments in UI financing since Haber and Murray's 1966 volume. First, the financial condition of the system has been examined, along with the role that the structure of the taxable wage base has had on this condition. The system was shown to be financially weak and subject to insolvency should a major recession occur. Moreover, the low taxable wage base, which is mainly constant in nominal dollars, will continue to threaten the financial stability of the system unless continually rising tax rates provide an offset. This alternative may produce the necessary funds but will require the system to place a larger and larger tax burden on low-wage workers.

These factors highlight the need to index the taxable wage base.[15] Although an increase in the wage base before instituting indexation may be desirable to help assure the solvency of the fund, it appears that such a tax increment would be impossible in the current political environment. Indexation, on the other hand, is not a tax increase; it merely prevents inflation from eroding the current tax base.

The second goal of this chapter was to examine the effects of imperfect experience rating on temporary layoffs. The literature addressing this issue has developed considerably over the period. Additional econometric problems, more complicated statistical techniques, and more detailed data have emerged. However, empirical results have been remarkably consistent; a movement to a financing system with perfect experience rating will eliminate 20-50 percent of all temporary layoffs. Although there is relative consistency in these findings, recent evidence indicates that increasing the degree of experience rating will not come without a price. Treating the UI tax as an adjustment cost, it becomes clear that fewer layoffs during a downturn in economic activity may be matched by fewer new hires during periods of economic expansion. Some empirical research has supported this view.

These results provide no clear policy recommendations regarding experience rating. A system with a greater degree of experience rating may lead to less variability in employment over the business cycle than would a system with a lower degree of experience rating. An evaluation of which approach is preferable should, therefore, depend upon the average level of employment over the entire business cycle in the two systems. A higher level of employment, on average, in a system with less experience rating may compensate for the greater employment variability. Unfortunately, not enough research has been conducted to date to fully inform a policy conclusion here.

NOTES

I would like to thank Patty Anderson, Rob Pavosevich, and Bruce Vavrichek for comments on a draft of this chapter, Tara Gustafson for outstanding research assistance, and Mike Miller of the Unemployment Insurance Service for his help in obtaining some of the data used in the analysis.

1. For more thorough discussions of the institutional features of UI financing, see Blaustein, Cohen and Haber (1993) or Vroman (1986, 1994).

2. Of this federal tax, 0.2 percent was originally imposed in 1977 as a temporary surcharge to build up reserves in an extended benefit trust fund. It has been in place ever since.

3. These statistics are obtained from the U.S. Department of Labor, Employment and Training Administration (1983 and more recent supplements).

4. An alternative measure of the UI system's financial status is the high cost multiple, which expresses the fund reserves as a fraction of the highest 12-month benefit payout in the state's history. Trends in this measure are similar to those shown in figure 8.1 and are discussed in chapter 9 of this volume.

5. Part of this increase may be explained by 1985 changes in federal guidelines that raised the federal unemployment tax to 6.2 percent and the tax credit to 5.4 percent for those states whose maximum tax rate was at least 5.4 percent. This change came in response to the large number of state systems that were insolvent, indicating that many states would have had to increase tax rates anyway. Therefore, a hypothetical illustration of changes in state tax schedules over this period without the alteration in federal policy would have likely looked similar.

6. As noted earlier, this experience is partly attributable to short-term problems in the EB system that imposed the entire cost of benefits paid beyond the standard exhaustion period on the federal government. In recent recessions, the cost was split by the state and federal governments, imposing a far greater burden on state trust funds; this will probably also be true in the future.

7. Other measures of generosity, which are not explored in detail here, include the potential duration of benefits and the percentage of unemployed workers receiving UI benefits. On these scales, benefits have become less generous over time.

8. Anderson and Meyer (1994) examine the incidence of the UI payroll tax and find that most of the tax is borne by firms.

9. Results would be somewhat different for states that have chosen to increase their taxable wage base above the federally mandated level. One can interpret the numbers provided here as representing workers who live in states like California or New York that have maintained their taxable wage base at this level.

10. Details regarding other types of systems and an extended discussion of many issues in UI financing can be found in Becker (1972).

11. A similar analysis could be reported for a firm in a benefit ratio state but is omitted in this case for the purposes of brevity. See Card and Levine (1994) for a more formal treatment of the material presented here.

12. In fact, if the slope is "steep enough," it is possible for the MTC to be greater than unity.

13. Card and Levine (1992) also present an analysis of this problem, although one which is not as complete as that in Anderson and Meyer (1994).

14. In fact, this effect is institutionalized in many states that have adopted a series of tax schedules. The particular tax schedule in effect at a point in time is a function of the size of the UI trust fund at that time. As the trust fund is drawn down during a recession, tax schedules increase.

15. The implications of increasing the federal taxable wage base have been addressed in detail by Cook et al. (1995).

Appendix to Chapter 8
The Role of Federal Financing
in the Unemployment Insurance System

Mike Miller

U.S. Department of Labor

Although state unemployment insurance (UI) taxes pay the greater share of the overall costs of the UI system (approximately 75 percent over the 1988-1995 period), there is also a key role for federal financing. The overall funding flow of the system is summarized in appendix figure 8.1. Federal funding sources include both payroll taxes and general revenues. The three areas of the system that are federally funded are state and federal administration of employment security programs, various federal and extended benefits, and loans to insolvent States.

Federal Unemployment Tax Act

The Federal Unemployment Tax Act (FUTA) tax is a national payroll tax collected by the Internal Revenue Service. The FUTA tax plays three different roles in the UI system. The first one, as has been discussed, is to provide a powerful incentive for states to legislate a UI system that conforms to federal requirements. This is accomplished by giving a large tax credit to employers in states with approved systems. The second role, which will be discussed further, is to provide a repayment mechanism for loans to states.

The third role is to provide financing for certain costs of the system. The items funded by the FUTA tax include UI administration, at both the federal and state levels, most federal and state Employment Service costs, veterans employment programs, labor market information programs, collection of the FUTA tax, management of the Unemployment Trust Fund, the federal share of federal-state Extended Benefits (EB), a portion of outlays under temporary recessionary benefit extensions, and loans to states.

The current FUTA tax rate is 6.2 percent, payable on the first $7,000 of a worker's wages in a calendar year. Under normal conditions, employers receive a 5.4 percent tax credit, leaving a net effective tax rate of 0.8 percent of taxable wages. Appendix table 8.1 shows the history of the FUTA rate and taxable wage base. The current rate includes a 0.2 percent surcharge first implemented in 1977 to repay a general fund debt caused by heavy outlays for EB and Federal Supplemental Benefits (FSB). When the debt was repaid in 1987, the surcharge was scheduled to trigger off. However, Congress has chosen to

Appendix Figure 8A.1 Federal-State UI System Sources of Funds

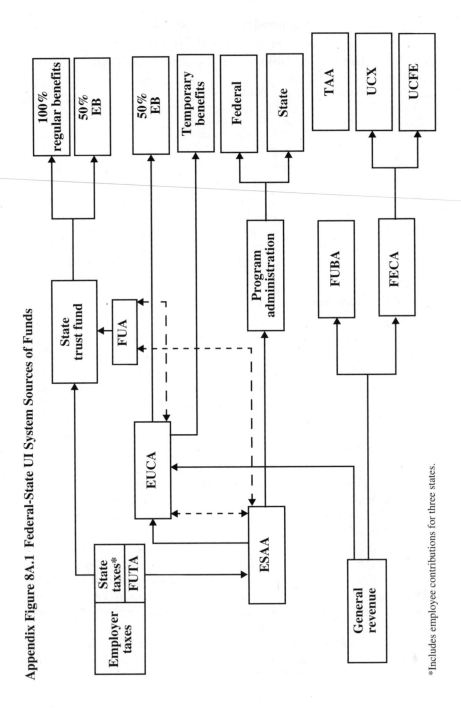

*Includes employee contributions for three states.

extend this tax several times, usually for the purpose of federal deficit reduction. Currently, the effective rate is scheduled to drop from 0.8 percent to 0.6 percent on January 1, 1999. No change has been made in either the effective tax rate or the taxable wage base since 1983.

Appendix Table 8A.1 FUTA History

Calendar years	Tax rates (percent)				Taxable wage base ($)
	Total effective rate	ESAA share	EUCA share	FUA share	
1936-1939	0.3				All wages
1940-1960	0.3				3000
1961	0.4				3000
1962	0.8				3000
1963	0.65				3000
1964-1969	0.4				3000
1970-1971	0.5	0.45	0.05		3000
1972	0.5	0.45	0.05		4200
1973	0.58	0.45	0.13		4200
1974-1976	0.5	0.45	0.05		4200
1977	0.7	0.45	0.25		4200
1978-1982	0.7	0.45	0.25		6000
1983-1987	0.8	0.48	0.32		7000
1988-1990	0.8	0.52	0.18	0.10	7000
1991-1992	0.8	0.72	0.08		7000
1993-1996	0.8	0.64	0.16		7000

General Revenues

Although the UI system is basically an employer-financed program, federal general revenues also play a role. In terms of size, one of the most important items funded from general revenues is all or part of the cost of temporary benefit extensions, which are enacted by the Congress to provide additional benefits during economic downturns. These benefits, which are typically 100 percent federally funded, may be financed by either the FUTA tax or general revenues or both. The deciding factor usually has been whether or not sufficient FUTA funds are available in the extended benefit account. General revenues are used indirectly to pay for benefits for ex-federal workers and ex-servicemen, via reimbursements by the affected agencies. General revenues are used to pay for special programs that affect targeted groups, such as benefits under the Trade Adjustment Assistance (TAA) program. General revenues also come into play as a borrowing source when the federal accounts are insolvent. In the past, general revenues were also used to pay for such temporary programs as Special Unemployment Assistance (SUA) in the mid-1970s.

The Federal Accounts

There are four federal accounts in the Unemployment Trust Fund (UTF) that are used to provide federal financing. Some funding is also done directly through an appropriation.

Employment Security Administration Account

The Employment Security Administration Account (ESAA) account is used to fund the administrative costs of the UI system and of other related employment security programs. Virtually all of the income to this account is from the FUTA tax. Items funded include all costs of UI administration at both federal and state levels. At the state level, in addition to UI administration, this account funds 97 percent of state Employment Service costs, two veterans employment programs, and labor market information programs run by the states for the Bureau of Labor Statistics. At the federal level, this account pays for all Department of Labor activities related to employment security programs. In addition, Treasury administrative costs related to collecting the FUTA tax and to managing and investing the UTF are charged to the ESAA account.

Extended Unemployment Compensation Account

The Extended Unemployment Compensation Account (EUCA) pays for the federal share (50 percent) of benefit outlays under the permanent federal-state EB program. FUTA receipts are used for this purpose. EUCA is also used to fund temporary recessionary benefit programs, such as the recent Emergency Unemployment Compensation (EUC) program. Whether FUTA or general revenues are used to fund these programs, all funds flow through this account.

Federal Unemployment Account

The Federal Unemployment Account (FUA) provides loans to states under Title XII of the Social Security Act. All state loan repayments, either voluntary or through FUTA credit reductions, are deposited in this account, as are interest payments.

Each of these first three accounts (ESAA, EUCA, and FUA) earns interest at the same rate as is true for the state trust fund accounts. When any of these three accounts becomes insolvent, it may borrow interest-free from one of the other two. Interaccount borrowing first became effective in 1993. If the other accounts do not have sufficient balances to allow this, funds may be borrowed from general revenues, with interest.

Federal Employees Compensation Account

The Federal Employees Compensation Account (FECA) acts as a revolving fund to pay for two federal programs, Unemployment Compensation for Federal Employees (UCFE) and Unemployment Compensation for ex-Servicemen (UCX). States draw from this account to pay benefits, then provide information to the U.S. Department of Labor, which in turn bills the appropriate agencies on a quarterly basis. Reimbursements from the agencies then flow into the FECA. General revenue advances may be made to the account if it becomes insolvent. These do not have to be repaid until the FECA balance is considered to exceed future needs.

Federal Unemployment Benefits and Allowances

Federal Unemployment Benefits and Allowances (FUBA) is an appropriation, rather than a trust fund account. Currently, this appropriation is used to fund benefits (after UI exhaustion) and training for import-impacted workers under the Trade Act. This appropriation has in the past been used to pay for a variety of federal benefit programs, including benefits for workers displaced by Redwood Park expansion, and benefits to Public Service Employment participants.

Account Flows and Ceilings

FUTA receipts currently flow into two accounts, ESAA and EUCA (appendix figure 8.2). FUA also took in a share of FUTA receipts for three years, calendar years 1988-1990, but currently gets only those receipts attributable to reduced credits for loan repayment. Eighty percent of FUTA receipts are retained in ESAA, with the remaining 20 percent going to EUCA. The distribution of FUTA receipts has been changed a number of times over the years. Appendix table 8.1 shows the history of this distribution since EUCA was established in 1970.

At the end of each fiscal year, a ceiling is applied to every account, and excess balances are transferred out (appendix figure 8.2). For ESAA, the ceiling is 40 percent of the spending of the current year from the account. For EUCA and FUA, the ceilings are percentages of total UI-covered wages, one-half and one-quarter of 1 percent, respectively. The procedure for transferring excess balances is that first, EUCA and FUA balances are checked and any excesses are transferred to ESAA. Then, if ESAA has an excess, that excess is transferred to EUCA to the extent that account is below its ceiling. The remaining excess, if any, is transferred to FUA to the extent that account is below its ceiling. In the event that all three accounts are at their ceilings at the end of a fiscal year, the remaining excess is distributed to state trust fund accounts in proportion to FUTA taxable wages by state. This is called a Reed Act distribu-

360

Appendix Figure 8A.2 Flow of FUTA Funds

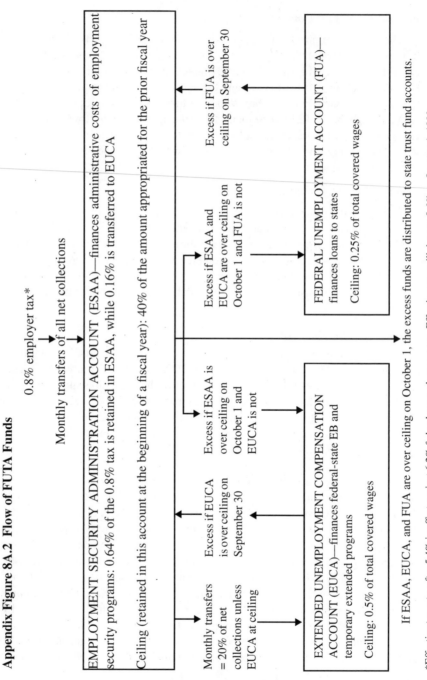

0.8% employer tax*

Monthly transfers of all net collections

EMPLOYMENT SECURITY ADMINISTRATION ACCOUNT (ESAA)—finances administrative costs of employment security programs: 0.64% of the 0.8% tax is retained in ESAA, while 0.16% is transferred to EUCA

Ceiling (retained in this account at the beginning of a fiscal year): 40% of the amount appropriated for the prior fiscal year

Monthly transfers = 20% of net collections unless EUCA at ceiling

Excess if EUCA is over ceiling on September 30

Excess if ESAA is over ceiling on October 1 and EUCA is not

Excess if ESAA and EUCA are over ceiling on October 1 and FUA is not

Excess if FUA is over ceiling on September 30

EXTENDED UNEMPLOYMENT COMPENSATION ACCOUNT (EUCA)—finances federal-state EB and temporary extended programs

Ceiling: 0.5% of total covered wages

FEDERAL UNEMPLOYMENT ACCOUNT (FUA)—finances loans to states

Ceiling: 0.25% of total covered wages

If ESAA, EUCA, and FUA are over ceiling on October 1, the excess funds are distributed to state trust fund accounts.

*Effective tax rate, after 5.4% is offset against 6.2% federal unemployment tax. Effective rate will drop to 0.6% on January 1, 1999.

tion. A Reed Act distribution has occurred only three times, all in the mid-1950s. These funds, although residing in the state trust fund accounts, may be used for UI program administration.

Title XII Loans

An important aspect of federal financing is the Title XII loan system. Loans are available to states without any qualifying requirements other than insolvency. States apply to the U.S. Department of Labor and are approved for specific amounts, but loans are made only to the extent a state's balance falls below zero on any given day. Loan funds come from the FUA account. Since 1982, interest has been charged on loans, except those that are repaid within the same fiscal year. The interest rate is equal to the average rate earned by the UTF during the last quarter of the prior year.

Repayments are made in one of two ways. The state may transfer monies from its trust fund account to the FUA account. Alternatively, there is an automatic repayment mechanism that operates via the FUTA credit. In the third year of a loan, the 5.4 percent tax credit is reduced by 0.3 percent, making the effective FUTA tax rate 1.1 percent for employers in the affected state. The amount of receipts attributable to the credit reduction goes to the FUA account and reduces the state's outstanding loan balance. In subsequent years, as long as there is a loan outstanding, the credit is reduced by greater and greater amounts. The basic increment is 0.3 percent per year, but this can be varied using a calculation involving the state's average tax rate and benefit cost rate. To add further complexity, there are provisions for several types of tax relief. To receive relief for its employers, the state must apply to the U.S. Department of Labor and meet certain criteria related to solvency.

References

Anderson, Patricia M. 1993. "Linear Adjustment Costs and Seasonal Labor Demand: Evidence from Retail Trade Firms," *Quarterly Journal of Economics* 108 (November): 1015-1042.

Anderson, Patricia M., and Bruce D. Meyer. 1993. "Unemployment Insurance in the United States: Layoff Incentives and Cross-Subsidies," *Journal of Labor Economics* 11 (January): S70-S95.

_____. 1994. "The Effects of Unemployment Insurance Taxes and Benefits on Layoffs Using Firm and Individual Data." Mimeo, Dartmouth College Department of Economics, December.

_____. 1995. "The Incidence of a Firm-Varying Payroll Tax: The Case of Unemployment Insurance." Mimeo, Dartmouth College Department of Economics, April.

Baily, Martin. 1976. "On the Theory of Layoffs and Unemployment," *Econometrica* 45 (July): 1043-1063.

Becker, Joseph M. 1972. *Experience Rating in Unemployment Insurance: An Experiment in Competitive Socialism*. Baltimore: Johns Hopkins University Press.

Blaustein, Saul J. 1993. *Unemployment Insurance in the United States: The First Half Century*. Kalamazoo, MI: W.E. Upjohn Institute.

Brechling, Frank. 1977. "Unemployment Insurance Taxes and Labor Turnover: Summary of Theoretical Findings," *Industrial and Labor Relations Review* 30 (July): 483-494.

_____. 1981. "Layoffs and Unemployment Insurance," In *Studies in Labor Markets*, Sherwin Rosen, ed. Chicago: University of Chicago Press.

Brechling, Frank, and Louise Laurence. 1995. *Permanent Job Loss and the U.S. System of Financing Unemployment Insurance Benefits*. Kalamazoo, MI: W.E. Upjohn Institute.

Card, David, and Phillip B. Levine. 1992. "Unemployment Insurance Taxes and the Cyclical and Seasonal Properties of Unemployment." National Bureau of Economic Research Working Paper No. 4030.

_____. 1994. "Unemployment Insurance Taxes and the Cyclical and Seasonal Properties of Unemployment," *Journal of Public Economics* 53 (January): 1-29.

Cook, Robert F., Wayne Vroman, Joseph Kirchner, Anthony Brinsko, and Alexandra Tan. 1995. "The Effects of Increasing the Federal Taxable Wage Base for Unemployment Insurance." Unemployment Insurance Occasional Paper 95-1, U.S. Department of Labor, Employment and Training Administration.

364

Feldstein, Martin S. 1976. "Temporary Layoffs in the Theory of Unemployment," *Journal of Political Economy* 84 (October): 937-957.

_____. 1978. "The Effect of Unemployment Insurance on Temporary Layoff Unemployment," American Economic Review 68 (December): 834-846.

Haber, William, and Merrill G. Murray. 1966. *Unemployment Insurance in the American Economy: An Historical Review and Analysis.* Homewood, IL: Richard D. Irwin.

Hamermesh, Daniel S. 1990. "Unemployment Insurance Financing, Short–Time Compensation, and Labor Demand," *Research in Labor Economics* 11: 241-269.

Topel, Robert H. 1983. "On Layoffs and Unemployment Insurance." *American Economic Review* 73 (September): 541–559.

_____. 1984. "Experience Rating of Unemployment Insurance and The Incidence of Unemployment," *Journal of Law and Economics* 27 (April): 61-90.

_____. 1985. "Unemployment and Unemployment Insurance," *Research in Labor Economics* 7: 91-135.

_____. 1990. "Financing Unemployment Insurance: History, Incentives, and Reform." In *Unemployment Insurance: The Second Half Century,* W. Lee Hansen and James F. Byers, eds. Madison: University of Wisconsin Press.

Topel, Robert H., and Finis Welch. 1980. "Unemployment Insurance: Survey and Extensions," *Economica* (August): 351-379.

U.S. Department of Labor. 1983 and Annual Supplements. *Unemployment Insurance Financial Data, ET Handbook 394,* Employment and Training Administration.

Vroman, Wayne. 1986. Experience Rating in Unemployment Insurance: Some Current Issues." Final report to the United States Department of Labor, Contract No. 99-4-3214-04-010-01, April.

_____. 1994. "Some Issues in Financing Unemployment Insurance." Mimeo, Urban Institute, August.

CHAPTER 9

Trends in Unemployment Benefit Financing

Mike Miller
UI Service, U.S Department of Labor
Robert Pavosevich
UI Service, U.S. Department of Labor
Wayne Vroman
Urban Institute

State unemployment insurance (UI) programs in the middle of the 1990s have aggregate trust fund balances totaling more than $30 billion. Most state UI programs passed through the 1990-1992 recessionary period without needing to borrow from the U.S. Treasury. This stands in sharp contrast to the recessions of 1973-1975, 1980, and 1981-1982, when borrowing was widespread and large-scale and indebtedness extended over multi-year periods.

This chapter reviews the history of UI trust fund financing with particular attention to recent developments. It is divided into six main sections. The first provides a long-run overview of UI trust fund reserves from the program's inception through the mid-1990s. The next section reviews the history of borrowing and loan repayments with particular attention to changes caused by revised debt repayment provisions of the early 1980s. Without attempting to be definitive, this part also discusses the question of trust fund adequacy and some common measures of trust fund adequacy. The third section introduces the topic of flexible financing as a benefit funding strategy. Individual elements of flexible financing are identified and their growth and prevalence are described. The fourth section undertakes several investigations of flexible financing. These help in an assessment of its overall quantitative importance. The fifth section discusses policy implications of flexible financing, and the final section provides a summary and conclusions.

The main conclusions of the chapter can be stated quite simply.

1. The state UI trust funds are now more healthy than at the end of the 1970s and start of the early 1980s, but not so large that the risks of insolvency and debt are merely matters of historical interest. The fact that borrowing during 1990-1994 was so modest is partly attributable to the mild nature of the recession.

2. There is a continuing need for states to maintain reserves to avert large-scale borrowing during a future recession. We note and express concern for the comparatively modest pace of trust fund rebuilding during 1993-1994. It appears likely that reserves available for the next recession will be less adequate than they were prior to the 1990-1992 recession.

3. While flexible financing provisions are now more prevalent in UI, we were not able to demonstrate an increased quantitative importance of such provisions compared to the situation, for example, twenty years ago.

4. The speed and strength of automatic financing responses built into current UI statutes appear inadequate to the needs that would arise in a future downturn if its depth and severity equaled the average of the eight post-World War II recessions.

Trends in Aggregate Unemployment Insurance Reserves

Following the establishment of state UI programs in 1937, the history of aggregate trust fund reserves falls into three distinct periods. Sustained and large accumulations occurred during the earliest years. This was caused by two factors: lower benefit costs than originally anticipated and the effects of full employment during World War II. As a fraction of covered payrolls, aggregate reserves reached their all-time peak at the end of 1945 (10.4 percent). Modest absolute growth in reserves continued through the end of 1948, when the $7.60 billion total represented 7.91 percent of covered payrolls.

These years of trust fund accumulations clearly were helped by the strong macroeconomic environment associated with World War II. Aggregate benefit payments, which had averaged about 1.5 percent of covered payrolls during 1938-1940, averaged only about 0.5 percent of payrolls during 1941-1945, with payout rates especially low during 1943 and 1944. Despite large reductions in average tax rates (from 2.69 percent of payrolls in 1938 to 1.50 percent in 1945), tax revenues exceeded benefits in every year through 1945.

The early years of the program also witnessed changes that effectively increased the average duration of benefits. In the initial years of UI, nearly all states imposed a two- or three-week waiting period and limited the maximum benefit duration to 15 or 16 weeks.[1] These limitations were premised on actuarial expectations that benefit payouts would average 3 percent of payrolls. In fact, actual payout rates during this period were much lower, especially during World War II. As experiences with low payout rates persisted, states modified their laws to shorten the waiting period and to lengthen maximum duration. These changes occurred mainly in the 1940s and 1950s.

During the thirty-two years from 1948 to 1979, growth in UI trust fund reserves lagged substantially behind the growth in the economy. Table 9.1 helps illustrate this situation, showing aggregate net reserves, covered payrolls, and net reserves as a percentage of payrolls (commonly termed the reserve ratio) for selected years.[2] Of the nine individual years displayed in the table the first eight represent prerecession years for the individual post-World War II recessions, with the back-to-back recessions of 1980-1983 and 1990-1992 treated as single episodes. The most interesting feature of the 1948-1979 period is the continuous decline in aggregate reserves measured as a percentage of payrolls, from 7.91 percent in 1948 to 0.91 percent in 1979. Even during the long continuous expansion of the 1960s, when aggregate reserves nearly doubled, growing from $6.67 billion to $12.64 billion, there was a small decline in net reserves relative to total payrolls.

Since state trust funds were so large at the start of the 1948-1979 period, the decline in reserves did not present financing problems for many states until the mid-1970s. Alaska, Michigan, and Pennsylvania were the only states that obtained loans to finance benefits during the 1950s and 1960s. All of these loans were fully repaid by the late 1960s.

Table 9.1 Aggregate UI Trust Fund Reserves for Selected Years, 1948 to 1994

Year	End-of-year net trust fund balance	Annual covered payrolls	Net reserves as a percentage of payrolls
1948	7.603	96.1	7.91
1953	8.913	139.2	6.41
1957	8.659	173.6	4.99
1959	6.674	186.9	3.57
1969	12.636	365.7	3.46
1973	10.882	510.0	2.13
1979	8.583	938.4	0.91
1989	36.871	1,918.0	1.92
1994	31.344	2,368.5	1.32

SOURCE: Data from the U.S. Department of Labor, Unemployment Insurance Service. Data on reserves measured in billions of dollars. Data refer to all fifty-three programs. Payroll data for 1994 are preliminary.

Substantial drawdowns of state trust funds occurred in the early 1970s. The first states to require loans were Connecticut, Vermont, and Washington during 1972-1974, with reductions in defense-related procurement causing especially high unemployment in both Connecticut and Washington during 1970-1972.

Large-scale borrowing from the U.S. Treasury first became widespread in 1975 as the 1974-1975 recession caused financing problems for many states. Nearly half of all UI programs required loans during 1975-1978, and total borrowing exceeded $5.0 billion. Furthermore, the post-1975 recovery was not sufficiently robust to fully restore trust fund balances by the end of the 1970s. Note in table 9.1 that net reserves at the end of 1979 totaled only $8.58 billion, about $2.3 billion less than at the end of 1973. The reserve ratio at the end of 1979 was only 0.91 percent, roughly one-fourth of the reserve ratio at the end of 1969, and the lowest prerecession reserve ratio shown in Table 9.1.

Because state programs entered the 1980-1983 recessionary period with historically low reserves, borrowing was even more widespread and of larger scale during the early 1980s than in the previous decade. Table 9.1 shows that substantial net trust fund accumulations occurred between 1979 and 1989. This ten-year interval is appropriately divided into an initial four years of recession (1980-1983) followed by six years of substantial trust fund building. Net reserves were actually negative at the end of 1983 (-$5.8 billion, not shown in table 9.1) so that the 1984-1989 period had a total accumulation of more than $42 billion.

Despite the reserve buildup of 1984-1989, note in table 9.1 that the 1989 net reserve balance of $36.87 billion represented only 1.92 percent of covered payrolls. As a fraction of covered payrolls this level was only slightly more than half the levels of 1959 and 1969 and somewhat smaller than the balance at the end of 1973. Despite net reserves being relatively lower in 1989 than in 1973, state borrowing during the most recent recession was much smaller than during the mid-1970s. A discussion of the contrasting pattern of borrowing in the two periods is reserved for the next section.

The final aspect of table 9.1 to note is the aggregate reserve position of the states at the end of 1994. Net reserves of $31.34 billion represented 1.32 percent of covered payrolls, roughly midway between the reserve levels of 1979 and 1989 when measured as a percent of covered payrolls. The $31.34 billion represents an increase of $5.50 billion in net reserves from two years earlier, the low point of the most recent recession. It should be noted that the $2.75 billion annual rate of trust fund accumulations during 1993 and 1994 stands in contrast to an annual accumulation rate that averaged $7.0 billion during 1984-1989. If one were to speculate on the net reserve position of the states at the start of the next recession, it would appear that reserves will be smaller relative to covered payrolls than they were prior to the 1990-1992 recession.

To summarize, the history of aggregate net reserves since the inception of unemployment insurance falls into three periods: (1) 1937-1948—substantial reserve accumulations; (2) 1948-1979—substantial losses of reserve adequacy; and (3) 1979 to the present—trust fund building, although the high point of the period (1989) did not reach the level of 1973. Furthermore, based on data from 1993 and 1994, recent reserve accumulations have occurred at a substantially slower pace than during the 1984-1989 period. This has obvious implications for potential borrowing by the states during the next recession.

A Brief History of State Borrowing

Funding Concepts

Revenues that fund regular state UI programs are obtained mainly from payroll taxes on covered employers. Tax receipts are deposited into state UI trust fund accounts maintained at the U.S. Treasury. These accounts are the source for benefit payments to eligible claimants.

The funding strategy for regular UI is usually characterized as pre-funding (or advance funding or forward funding). Trust fund balances are built up prior to recessions, drawn down during recessions, and then rebuilt during the subsequent recoveries. This funding arrangement means that the program acts as an automatic stabilizer of economic activity, i.e., it makes larger injections than withdrawals into the spending streams during recessions and larger withdrawals than injections during economic recoveries. The preceding characterization was less accurate during the recessions of the mid-1970s and the early 1980s because the trust fund balances were not adequate to pay regular UI benefits to all claimants. Large-scale and persistent state borrowing took place.

During the most recent downturn, state UI trust funds were generally adequate to meet demands for benefit payments. For the five full years of 1990 to 1994, only seven states required loans from the Federal Unemployment Account (FUA), the federal trust fund loan account, and only two states (Connecticut and Massachusetts) engaged in "large-scale" borrowing.[3] As noted, this recent situation stands in sharp contrast to the recessions of 1974-1975 and 1980-1983. In both earlier periods, borrowing was much more widespread and larger in relative scale.

To place 1990-1994 trust fund borrowing experiences into more of a historical perspective, table 9.2 provides summary data that extend back over the 1970s and 1980s. The top panel in table 9.2 summarizes

371

Table 9.2 Number of States by High-Cost Multiple and Borrowing Activity

End of year	High-cost multiples (HCMs)							National HCM
	Negative	0.0 - 0.5	0.5 - 1.0	1.0 - 1.5	1.5 - 2.0	2.0+	Total	
1969	0	0	1	16	15	20	52	1.68
1973	1	4	14	12	12	9	52	1.04
1979	9	13	16	12	2	0	52	0.41
1989	0	9	22	18	3	0	52	0.87
State borrowing activities, 1979-1979								
Initial HCMs	1	4	14	12	12	9	52	
States with loans	1	4	12	5	2	0	24	
States with "large" loans	1	4	8	1	1	0	15	
State borrowing activities, 1980-1987								
Initial HCMs	9	13	16	12	2	0	52	
States with loans	8	11	10	2	0	0	31	
States with "large" loans	2	6	5	1	0	0	14	
State borrowing activities, 1990-1994								
Initial HCMs	0	9	22	18	3	0	52	
States with loans	0	4	3	0	0	0	7	
States with "large" loans	0	2	0	0	0	0	2	

SOURCE: Data from the U.S. Department of Labor, Unemployment Insurance Service. Data exclude the Virgin Islands. Large loans are defined as total borrowing over the indicated periods equal to 1 percent or more of total payrolls for a single year, 1975, 1984, and 1991, respectively

state UI trust fund reserve balances at the end of four separate years: 1969, 1973, 1979, and 1989. These four dates were selected (as in table 9.1) because they precede the onset of recessions and recession-related increases in the demand for UI benefit payments.

The information summarized in table 9.2 involves the concept of the high-cost multiple (HCM), also known as the reserve ratio multiple. This is a UI actuarial concept that assesses state reserve adequacy by taking into consideration three important factors pertinent to the state: the balance in its UI trust fund, the scale of its economy, and its own past experiences in paying UI benefits. The denominator in the HCM is the highest cost benefit payout period in the state's history. This is total benefit payout over a twelve-month period expressed as a percentage of covered wages for the same period. The interstate range of high-cost percentages extends from a low of 1.04 percent (in South Dakota between January and December 1964) to a high of 4.37 percent (in Rhode Island between January and December 1975). The highest cost period for the U.S. as a whole was 2.24 percent (between January and December 1975).

The numerator of the HCM, the reserve ratio, is the end-of-year trust fund balance divided by covered wages for the year and expressed as a percentage.[4] The ratio of these two ratios, the HCM, is thus a measure whose numerator incorporates information on both the UI trust fund balance and the on scale of the state's economy (as approximated by covered wages) while the denominator is a measure of risk, the highest previous twelve-month payout rate.

In the past, some have advocated that states build trust fund reserves to levels that produce an HCM of 1.5. This level implies that the fund balance would equal eighteen months of benefits if paid out at the historically highest payout rate. As a measure of trust fund adequacy, the HCM has its critics. Many practitioners feel that the 1.5 HCM is too conservative as a standard, i.e., that a prudent state could function with a much lower trust fund balance with little or no risk of fund insolvency.[5]

While trust fund financing has been practiced since the inception of UI, there is no consensus over the appropriate measure of trust fund adequacy. The recently disbanded Advisory Council on Unemployment Compensation (ACUC) examined funding issues in its February 1995 Report.[6] Chapter 5 of the report analyzed the funding situation of the states as of the end of 1993 under three alternative potential solvency standards. Table 5.3 in the report shows the number of states meeting HCM solvency standards ranging from 0.25 to 1.75 using seven measures of high costs: one involving the highest twelve-month costs ever experienced, three involving the highest twelve-month cost periods over the past ten years and three involving the highest twelve-month cost periods over the past twenty years.

The ACUC recommended that states meet an HCM standard of 1.0, where the state's high cost rate is measured as the average of the three highest-cost twelve-month periods over the past twenty years. The ACUC also recommended that the federal partner provide four specific financial incentives to the states to meet forward funding goals, e.g., preferential interest rates for achieving large balances and lower interest rates on recession-related borrowing if prerecession balances equaled or exceeded solvency standards.[7] The ACUC's financing recommendations, if instituted, would improve the solvency of many state UI programs.

Summary of State Borrowing

Because UI trust fund balances were so large during the initial post-World War II decades, there was a very limited need for state borrowing from the U.S. Treasury. As noted, just three states, Alaska, Michigan and Pennsylvania, required loans before 1970, and only Alaska actually used its loans to pay benefits. These loans were secured mainly during 1958 and 1959, and repayments were completed during 1967 and 1968.

The post-1970 experiences have been much different. The top panel of table 9.2 displays the distribution of HCMs prior to the four most recent economic downturns.[8] Each row shows multiples for fifty-two UI programs (all except the Virgin Islands). The final entry for each row is the national HCM. From this last column as well as from the distributions of state multiples, it is clear that reserves were most ample at the end of 1969 and lowest at the end of 1979. Between 1979 and 1989, most states increased reserves substantially, and the national high-cost multiple roughly doubled, increasing from 0.41 to 0.87.

The lower three panels in table 9.2 then summarize state borrowing experiences in the three most recent downturns. Each panel shows how many states needed loans and how many needed "large" loans, i.e., loans that totaled 1.0 percent or more of covered payrolls. The twenty-four states that needed loans during 1974-1979 borrowed a total of $5.5 billion. Between 1980 and 1987, a total of $24.0 billion was borrowed by thirty-one programs. In contrast, borrowing by seven states during 1990-1994 totaled only $4.4 billion, less in absolute value than during 1974-1979. The comparative scale of borrowing during the three recessionary episodes is vividly illustrated when total loans are expressed as a percentage of payrolls for one year during each period: 0.95 percent during 1974-1979, 1.75 percent during 1980-1987, but only 0.21 percent during 1990-1994.[9] Table 9.2 also shows the number of states needing large loans during the three episodes. These respective counts are fifteen, fourteen and two.

The purpose of prefunding (or advance funding) UI programs is to have adequate reserves in the state trust funds to make benefit payments during recessions without resorting to borrowing (or at least large-scale borrowing). By ranking states according to their HCMs, the bottom panels of table 9.2 provide a convenient summary of the prevalence of borrowing according to an indicator of prerecession reserve adequacy. In each episode, borrowing and large-scale borrowing were most prevalent among states with low prerecession fund balances. States with HCMs of 1.0 or larger generally have been successful at avoiding borrowing. Conversely, those with multiples below 0.5 have been most likely to need loans and to need large loans.

Table 9.2 also illustrates that the 1.5 HCM guideline is not a foolproof indicator of reserve adequacy. There have been states that entered recessions with multiples above 1.5 that subsequently needed loans. Conversely, not all states with prerecession multiples below 0.5 have needed loans. However, for identifying states at risk of needing loans and of needing large loans, the HCM is a useful indicator.[10]

An interesting contrast emerges when borrowing during the 1980-1987 and 1990-1994 periods is compared. For HCMs in the 0.0 to 0.5 and 0.5 to 1.0 ranges, note that the proportions that borrowed were much lower during 1990-1994 than during 1980-1987. In addition, the proportions needing large loans were also much lower during 1990-1994.[11] One important reason for reduced borrowing activity among states with comparable prerecession HCMs was the relative mildness of the recent downturn when compared to the back-to-back recessions of the early 1980s.

Borrowing Provisions

State UI programs are required to make timely payments to eligible claimants regardless of current balances in their trust fund accounts held at the U.S. Treasury. If state reserve balances are inadequate there are statutory provisions for borrowing from the Treasury. These provisions, in Title XII of the Social Security Act, are important to review.

Treasury loans for purposes of making benefit payments are available to states on essentially an as-needed basis. Interest charges accrue if advances are still outstanding after certain mandatory repayment dates. These are levied at the interest rate applicable to medium-term U.S. debt but are capped at 10.0 percent. Interest accrues on the average daily indebtedness. States that borrow after January 1 of a given year can avoid interest charges altogether if loans are fully repaid by September 30 of the same year. Loans taken and fully repaid in the same fiscal year are commonly referred to as cash-flow loans.[12]

The states also face debt repayment requirements under Title XII. If debt has been outstanding on January 1st of two consecutive years and has not been fully repaid by November 10th of the latter year, an automatic debt repayment process is activated. On January 1 of the following year, 0.3 percent is added to the federal part of each employer's UI tax obligation under the Federal Unemployment Tax Act (FUTA) tax: i.e., 1.1 percent is levied rather than 0.8 percent on the first $7,000 of earnings for each employee. The proceeds of the 0.3 percent penalty tax go toward repaying the oldest part of the state's debt. Higher penalty tax rates apply in later years.

Because FUTA penalty taxes are levied at a single flat rate, a state may prefer to make voluntary repayments of experience- rated state UI taxes. These must be levied as new tax obligations (not withdrawals from the state's UI trust fund), and their yield must at least equal the yield of the federal penalty tax. Voluntary repayment can also be accomplished by a special assessment levied on top of regular employer state UI taxes.

Prior to 1982, debt repayment provisions differed from current provisions in several ways. Two especially important contrasts should be noted: (1) loans did not carry interest charges, and (2) automatic debt repayment through mandatory FUTA penalty taxes was suspended by emergency federal legislation. In short, debt burdens before 1982 were lighter.

The increase in the cost of indebtedness has affected state attitudes towards debt, as shown by their debt repayment behavior.[13] Debts incurred in the late 1970s were repaid slowly, whereas post-1982 debts were repaid rapidly. Post-1982 debts have often been held for such short periods that no interest has been due.

Tables 9.3A and 9.3B summarize national details on loans, debt and debt repayments from 1972 to 1994. Interest-free and interest-bearing debts are distinguished, with the changeover to interest-bearing advances taking place on April 1, 1982. Note in table 9.3A that borrowing during the 1990s never exceeded $1.5 billion per year.

Probably the most interesting feature of table 9.3B is the contrast in loan repayment patterns for the two types of loans. Of the $10.48 billion of interest-free loans, $6.44 billion (over 60 percent of the total) was repaid as FUTA penalty taxes (credit reductions). In contrast, the fraction was only 1.2 percent ($0.29 billion) for the interest-bearing advances repaid in this manner with the rest made as voluntary repayments. The vivid contrast in repayment patterns is also indicated by the annual repayment rates for the two types of debt. The all-year weighted averages of the two repayment rates are 14 percent for interest-free debt and 56 percent for interest-bearing debt.

The fast pace of debt repayment, apparent from 1983, has also characterized the loans of the 1990s. Under current debt repayment provisions, debtor states have demonstrated strong sensitivity to interest charges, and the prospect of these charges has led to faster corrective actions by the states.

Changes in state-level patterns of borrowing and loan repayment mean that debts are now held for shorter periods.[14] However, part of the explanation for shorter periods of indebtedness is an increased willingness of states with financing problems to reduce UI benefits even before the economy has recovered from a recession.[15] This greater inclination dates from the early 1980s. Both macro and income distribution considerations suggest this timing of benefit reductions is not appropriate.

Table 9.3A Summary of State UI Debt and Debt Repayment Activities, 1972 to 1994 ($ billions)

	State UI debt, December 31			Loans to states		
Year	Total	Interest free	Interest bearing	Total	Interest free	Interest bearing
1972	0.07	0.07	NA	0.07	0.07	NA
1973	0.09	0.09	NA	0.03	0.03	NA
1974	0.11	0.11	NA	0.02	0.02	NA
1975	1.59	1.59	NA	1.49	1.49	NA
1976	3.40	3.40	NA	1.85	1.85	NA
1977	4.58	4.58	NA	1.29	1.29	NA
1978	5.09	5.09	NA	0.84	0.84	NA
1979	3.83	3.83	NA	0.05	0.05	NA
1980	4.99	4.99	NA	1.47	1.47	NA
1981	6.27	6.27	NA	1.61	1.61	NA
1982	10.63	7.57	3.07	5.18	1.76	3.42
1983	13.37	6.93	6.40	6.63	NA	6.63
1984	9.49	5.74	3.75	3.01	NA	3.01
1985	6.11	4.54	1.58	2.55	NA	2.55
1986	4.81	3.40	1.41	2.29	MA	2.29
1987	2.05	1.54	0.51	1.23	NA	1.23
1988	0.78	0.78	0.00	0.23	NA	0.23
1989	0.60	0.60	0.00	0.00	NA	0.00
1990	0.42	0.42	0.00	0.00	NA	0.00
1991	1.01	0.42	0.80	0.77	NA	0.77
1992	1.27	0.21	1.06	1.48	NA	1.48
1993	0.19	0.00	0.19	1.37	NA	1.37
1994	0.00	0.00	0.00	0.80	NA	0.80
All years				34.26	10.48	23.78

SOURCE: Based on data from the U.S. Department of Labor, Unemployment Insurance Service.
NA = not applicable.

Table 9.3B Summary of State UI Debt and Debt Repayment Activities, 1972 to 1994 ($ billions)

		Loan repayments[a]			Loan repayment rate[b]		
		Interest free					
Year	Total	Credit reductions	Voluntary repayments	Interest bearing	Total	Interest free	Interest bearing
1972	0.00	0.00	0.00	NA	0.00	0.00	NA
1973	0.00	0.00	0.00	NA	0.00	0.00	NA
1974	0.00	0.00	0.00	NA	0.00	0.00	NA
1975	0.01	0.01	0.00	NA	0.01	0.01	NA
1976	0.04	0.00	0.04	NA	0.01	0.01	NA
1977	0.11	0.01	0.10	NA	0.02	0.02	NA
1978	0.33	0.00	0.33	NA	0.06	0.06	NA
1979	1.31	0.00	1.30	NA	0.25	0.25	NA
1980	0.31	0.06	0.25	NA	0.06	0.06	NA
1981	0.33	0.32	0.01	NA	0.05	0.05	NA
1982	0.83	0.47	0.00	0.36	0.07	0.06	0.11
1983	3.93	0.63	0.01	3.30	0.23	0.08	0.34
1984	6.84	0.88	0.31	5.65	0.42	0.17	0.60
1985	5.93	0.99	0.21	4.74	0.49	0.21	0.75
1986	3.59	0.80	0.34	2.45	0.43	0.25	0.63
1987	3.99	0.93	0.93	2.13	0.66	0.55	0.81
1988	1.50	0.56	0.20	0.74	0.66	0.49	1.00
1989	0.18	0.18	0.00	NA	0.23	0.23	NA
1990	0.18	0.18	0.00	NA	0.30	0.30	NA
1991	0.18	0.00	0.00	0.18	0.15	0.00	0.23
1992	1.22	0.20	0.00	1.01	0.49	0.49	0.44
1993	2.45	0.21	0.00	2.24	0.93	1.00	0.92
1994	0.98	NA	NA	0.98	1.00	NA	0.99
All years	34.26	6.44	4.03	23.78	0.30	0.14	0.56

SOURCE: See table 9.3A. NA = not applicable.
a. Voluntary repayments accounted for all but $0.29 billion of interest-bearing loan repayments.
b. Annual repayment rates measured as repayments divided by the sum of debt at the start of the year plus loans received during the year. All-year averages are weighted averages of annual repayment rates, where weights are annual loans plus annual start-of-year debt.

State Trust Funds, Borrowing, and Unemployment during 1990-1994

State-level information on UI trust fund reserves and unemployment for 1990-1992 is displayed in table 9.4A. For each of the fifty-three UI programs, the table shows reserves and HCMs at the end of 1989 and 1992 and three-year changes. Also included is a measure of recession-related unemployment growth, i.e., each state's 1990-1992 unemployment rate is shown as a ratio to its 1987-1989 unemployment rate.

Note the national aggregates at the bottom of table 9.4A. Total net reserves declined by about $11 billion over these three years, and the national HCM decreased by about one-third, from 0.87 to 0.56. At the end of 1992, however, only four states had negative net reserves.

Observe the large drawdowns of reserves in California and New York, both exceeding $2.5 billion, and the losses in Massachusetts, Connecticut and Pennsylvania. Combined, these five states accounted for $8.6 billion of reserve losses or 78 percent of the national total.[16] One indicator of the comparative shallowness of the 1990-1992 downturn is the national unemployment rate ratio of 1.156, i.e., the national unemployment rate during 1990-1992 was only 15.6 percent higher than the 1987-1989 prerecession average.

The state-level information can be organized in alternative ways to illustrate different points about recent trust fund reserve losses. Table 9.4A arrays the states according to the level of their 1989 HCMs. During 1991 and 1992, four UI programs borrowed from the FUA: Michigan, Connecticut, the District of Columbia and Massachusetts. Arranging the 1989 state HCMs in ascending order as in table 9.4A, these states ranked 1st, 2nd, 5th, and 8th, respectively. The three other states needing loans during the 1991-1994 period (Missouri, New York, and Maine) ranked 10th, 21st, and 29th, respectively, in table 9.4A. Thus, while borrowing was related to initial reserve balances, it had other determinants as well.[17]

One informative way to examine the loss of reserves during 1990-1992 is to note changes in state-level unemployment rates. Table 9.4B rearranges the information from table 9.4A to emphasize recession-related increases in state unemployment. The largest proportional increase in state-level unemployment occurred in New Hampshire, where the 1990-1992 average rate was 6.80 percent while the 1987-1989 average was 2.83 percent, yielding a ratio of 2.400. States are

Table 9.4A Summary of Net Reserves by State, December 1989 and December 1992
(States Arrayed by 1989 High-Cost Multiples)

	Net reserves ($ millions)			High-cost multiple			Unemployment rates 1990-1992/ 1987-1989
	Dec. 1989	Dec. 1992	Change	1989	1992	Change	
Michigan	370	-72	-442	0.13	-0.02	-0.15	1.116
Connecticut	274	-653	-927	0.22	-0.53	-0.75	1.947
Ohio	778	602	-176	0.30	0.21	-0.09	1.037
Arkansas	131	81	-50	0.40	0.20	-0.20	0.934
District of Columbia	76	-19	-95	0.40	-0.09	-0.49	1.405
West Virginia	146	141	-5	0.41	0.35	-0.06	1.019
Louisiana	306	601	295	0.43	0.72	0.29	0.693
Massachusetts	909	-380	-1,289	0.45	-1.08	-0.63	2.236
Illinois	1,268	848	-421	0.47	0.28	-0.19	1.035
Missouri	372	3	-369	0.50	0.00	-0.50	1.028
Minnesota	359	224	-135	0.52	0.27	-0.25	1.093
Pennsylvania	1,616	808	-808	0.55	0.25	-0.30	1.297
Montana	80	96	16	0.63	0.62	-0.01	0.970
South Carolina	415	433	18	0.66	0.60	-0.06	1.154
Kentucky	393	364	-29	0.69	0.54	-0.15	0.877
North Dakota	45	50	5	0.70	0.65	-0.05	0.909
Wyoming	54	110	56	0.71	1.23	0.52	0.756
Texas	989	586	-402	0.73	0.36	-0.37	0.902

State						
Maryland	598	146	-452	0.75	0.17	-0.58	1.387
Colorado	239	339	100	0.75	0.87	0.12	0.796
New York	3,181	214	-2,967	0.76	0.05	-0.71	1.476
Arizona	493	372	-120	0.84	0.55	-0.29	1.037
California	5,419	2,787	-2,633	0.89	0.42	-0.47	1.380
New Hampshire	204	130	-74	0.89	0.55	-0.34	2.400
Tennessee	657	603	-54	0.90	0.69	-0.21	1.041
Nebraska	127	161	34	0.92	0.97	0.05	0.671
Rhode Island	304	104	-199	0.92	0.32	-0.60	2.227
Alaska	180	232	52	0.93	1.06	0.12	1.005
Maine	206	35	-171	0.94	0.15	-0.79	1.632
Georgia	1,018	966	-52	0.96	0.79	-0.17	1.032
Washington	1,364	1,766	402	0.97	0.99	0.02	0.937
Indiana	770	942	171	1.04	1.11	0.07	1.083
New Jersey	2,795	2,440	-355	1.06	0.85	-0.21	1.664
Nevada	321	234	-87	1.12	0.65	-0.47	1.047
Wisconsin	1,041	1,195	154	1.17	1.13	-0.04	1.007
Virginia	718	507	-212	1.17	0.74	-0.43	1.366
Delaware	207	219	11	1.19	1.13	-0.06	1.685
North Carolina	1,471	1,387	-83	1.20	0.98	-0.22	1.362
Iowa	518	615	98	1.20	1.21	0.01	0.943
Alabama	623	550	-72	1.21	0.90	-0.31	0.965
Utah	239	342	104	1.25	1.40	0.15	0.885

(continued)

Table 9.4A (continued)

	Net reserves ($ millions)			High-cost multiple			Unemployment rates 1990-1992/ 1987-1989
	Dec. 1989	Dec. 1992	Change	1989	1992	Change	
Florida	2,041	1,444	-597	1.30	0.80	-0.50	1.345
Oklahoma	323	419	96	1.34	1.53	0.19	0.910
Oregon	804	1,055	251	1.35	1.47	0.12	1.070
Kansas	472	606	134	1.35	1.47	0.12	0.943
Idaho	220	240	20	1.37	1.16	-0.21	0.967
Hawaii	340	362	22	1.40	1.35	-0.05	1.058
New Mexico	174	239	65	1.48	1.69	0.21	0.857
South Dakota	45	50	5	1.49	1.29	-0.20	0.811
Vermont	197	181	-16	1.59	1.37	-0.22	1.783
Mississippi	388	345	-43	1.67	1.26	-0.41	0.916
Puerto Rico	564	749	186	1.82	2.15	0.33	NA
Virgin Islands	28	47	19	1.92	3.21	1.29	NA
U.S. total	36,871	25,847	-11,029	0.87	0.56	-0.31	1.156

NA = not applicable.

arrayed in descending order of their unemployment rate ratios in table 9.4B.

A striking feature of the table is the geographic concentration of the increases in unemployment. As noted, the national average increase for 1990-1992 relative to 1987-1989 was 15.6 percent or a ratio of 1.156. There are sixteen states whose unemployment rate ratios exceed the national average. Fifteen of these are located along the eastern seaboard of the United States, and the sixteenth is California.[18]

The most dramatic increases in unemployment occurred in New England, whose constituent states occupy the five top rows and the eighth row in table 9.4B. All three Middle Atlantic states had above-average increases, with ratios of 1.664, 1.476 and 1.297 in New Jersey, New York and Pennsylvania, respectively. Of the nine states in the South Atlantic division, six also experienced above-average increases, while a seventh (South Carolina) roughly matched the national average. Thus, Georgia and West Virginia were the only South Atlantic states not to experience a major increase in unemployment during 1990-1992.

Note also in table 9.4B that nineteen states actually had lower average unemployment rates during 1990-1992 than in 1987- 1989. An additional twelve states with higher unemployment during 1990-1992 experienced increases that were less than half the national average increase, i.e., their ratios lie between 1.000 and 1.078. Thus, for thirty-one of fifty-one states, unemployment rates either declined during 1990-1992 or increased only moderately. This "fact" provides much of the explanation for the limited borrowing by state UI programs during the 1990-1992 downturn.

Yet another perspective on trust fund reserve adequacy and reserve losses during 1990-1992 is provided in table 9.4C. Here the state-level information has been arranged to focus on reductions in HCMs between 1989 and 1992. Maine led the nation with a reduction in its multiple of 0.79. The multiples in thirteen states decreased by 0.40 or more, and nine of the thirteen are located along the Atlantic coast.[19] As with the increases in unemployment, the decreases in reserves were concentrated mainly along the eastern seaboard.

Table 9.4C is also useful for showing the full range of reductions in state HCMs during 1990-1992.[20] Not one of the reductions equaled or exceeded -1.0, and only five equaled or exceeded -0.60. The five states

**Table 9.4B Summary of Net Reserves by State, December 1989 and December 1992
(States Arrayed by Unemployment Rate Ratios)**

	Net reserves ($ millions)			High-Cost Multiple			Unemployment rates 1990-1992/ 1987-1989
	Dec. 1989	Dec. 1992	Change	1989	1992	Change	
New Hampshire	204	130	-74	0.89	0.55	-0.34	2.400
Massachusetts	909	-380	-1,289	0.45	-0.18	-0.63	2.236
Rhode Island	304	104	-199	0.92	0.32	-0.60	2.227
Connecticut	274	-653	-927	0.22	-0.53	-0.75	1.947
Vermont	197	181	-16	1.59	1.37	-0.22	1.783
Delaware	207	219	11	1.19	1.13	-0.06	1.685
New Jersey	2,795	2,440	-355	1.06	0.85	-0.21	1.664
Maine	206	35	-171	0.94	0.15	-0.79	1.632
New York	3,181	214	-2,967	0.76	0.05	-0.71	1.476
District of Columbia	76	-19	-95	0.40	-0.09	-0.49	1.405
Maryland	598	146	-452	0.75	0.17	-0.58	1.387
California	5,419	2,787	-2,633	0.89	0.42	-0.47	1.380
Virginia	718	507	-212	1.17	0.74	-0.43	1.366
North Carolina	1,471	1,387	-83	1.20	0.98	-0.22	1.362
Florida	2,041	1,444	-597	1.30	0.80	-0.50	1.345
Pennsylvania	1,616	808	-808	0.55	0.25	-0.30	1.297
South Carolina	415	433	18	0.66	0.60	-0.06	1.154
Michigan	370	-72	-442	0.13	-0.02	-0.15	1.116

Minnesota	359	224	-135	0.52	0.27	-0.25	1.093
Indiana	770	942	171	1.04	1.11	0.07	1.083
Oregon	804	1,055	251	1.35	1.47	0.12	1.070
Hawaii	340	362	22	1.40	1.35	-0.05	1.058
Nevada	321	234	-87	1.12	0.65	-0.47	1.047
Tennessee	657	603	-54	0.90	0.69	-0.21	1.041
Ohio	778	602	-176	0.30	0.21	-0.09	1.037
Arizona	493	372	-120	0.84	0.55	-0.29	1.037
Illinois	1,268	848	-421	0.47	0.28	-0.19	1.035
Georgia	1,018	966	-52	0.96	0.79	-0.17	1.032
Missouri	372	3	-369	0.50	0.00	-0.50	1.028
West Virginia	146	141	-5	0.41	0.35	-0.06	1.019
Wisconsin	1,041	1,195	154	1.17	1.13	-0.04	1.007
Alaska	180	232	52	0.93	1.06	0.12	1.005
Montana	80	96	16	0.63	0.62	-0.01	0.970
Idaho	220	240	20	1.37	1.16	-0.21	0.967
Alabama	623	550	-72	1.21	0.90	-0.31	0.965
Kansas	472	606	134	1.35	1.47	0.12	0.943
Iowa	518	615	98	1.20	1.21	0.01	0.943
Washington	1,364	1,766	402	0.97	0.99	0.02	0.937
Arkansas	131	81	-50	0.40	0.20	-0.20	0.934
Mississippi	388	345	-43	1.67	1.26	-0.41	0.916
Oklahoma	323	419	96	1.34	1.53	0.19	0.910

(continued)

Table 9.4B (continued)

	Net reserves ($ millions)			High-Cost Multiple			Unemployment rates 1990-1992/ 1987-1989
	Dec. 1989	Dec. 1992	Change	1989	1992	Change	
North Dakota	45	50	5	0.70	0.65	-0.05	0.909
Texas	989	586	-402	0.73	0.36	-0.37	0.902
Utah	239	342	104	1.25	1.40	0.15	0.885
Kentucky	393	364	-29	0.69	0.54	-0.15	0.877
New Mexico	174	239	65	1.48	1.69	0.21	0.857
South Dakota	45	50	5	1.49	1.29	-0.20	0.811
Colorado	239	339	100	0.75	0.87	0.12	0.796
Wyoming	54	110	56	0.71	1.23	0.52	0.756
Louisiana	306	601	295	0.43	0.72	0.29	0.693
Nebraska	127	161	34	0.92	0.97	0.05	0.671
Puerto Rico	564	749	186	1.82	2.15	0.33	NA
Virgin Islands	28	47	19	1.92	3.21	1.29	NA
U.S. total	36,871	25,847	-11,029	0.87	0.56	-0.31	1.156

NA = not applicable.

Table 9.4C Summary of Net Reserves by State, December 1989 and December 1992 (States Arrayed by Changes in High-Cost Multiples)

	Net reserves ($ millions)			High-Cost Multiple			Unemployment rates 1990-1992/ 1987-1989
	Dec. 1989	Dec. 1992	Change	1989	1992	Change	
Maine	206	35	-171	0.94	0.15	-0.79	1.632
Connecticut	274	-653	-927	0.22	-0.53	-0.75	1.947
New York	3,181	214	-2,967	0.76	0.05	-0.71	1.476
Massachusetts	909	-380	-1,289	0.45	-0.18	-0.63	2.236
Rhode Island	304	104	-199	0.92	0.32	-0.60	2.227
Maryland	598	146	-452	0.75	0.17	-0.58	1.387
Florida	2,041	1,444	-597	1.30	0.80	-0.50	1.345
Missouri	372	3	-369	0.50	0.00	-0.50	1.028
District of Columbia	76	-19	-95	0.40	-0.09	-0.49	1.405
California	5,419	2,787	-2,633	0.89	0.42	-0.47	1.380
Nevada	321	234	-87	1.12	0.65	-0.47	1.047
Virginia	718	507	-212	1.17	0.74	-0.43	1.366
Mississippi	388	345	-43	1.67	1.26	-0.41	0.916
Texas	989	586	-402	0.73	0.36	-0.37	0.902
New Hampshire	204	130	-74	0.89	0.55	-0.34	2.400
Alabama	623	550	-72	1.21	0.90	-0.31	0.965
Pennsylvania	1,616	808	-808	0.55	0.25	-0.30	1.297

(continued)

Table 9.4C (continued)

	Net reserves ($ millions)			High-Cost Multiple			Unemployment rates 1990-1992/ 1987-1989
	Dec. 1989	Dec. 1992	Change	1989	1992	Change	
Arizona	493	372	-120	0.84	0.55	-0.29	1.037
Minnesota	359	224	-135	0.52	0.27	-0.25	1.093
Vermont	197	181	-16	1.59	1.37	-0.22	1.783
North Carolina	1,471	1,387	-83	1.20	0.98	-0.22	1.362
New Jersey	2,795	2,440	-355	1.06	0.85	-0.21	1.664
Idaho	220	240	20	1.37	1.16	-0.21	0.967
Tennessee	657	603	-54	0.90	0.69	-0.21	1.041
Arkansas	131	81	-50	0.40	0.20	-0.20	0.934
South Dakota	45	50	5	1.49	1.29	-0.20	0.811
Illinois	1,268	848	-421	0.47	0.28	-0.19	1.035
Georgia	1,018	966	-52	0.96	0.79	-0.17	1.032
Michigan	370	-72	-442	0.13	-0.02	-0.15	1.116
Kentucky	393	364	-29	0.69	0.54	-0.15	0.877
Ohio	778	602	-176	0.30	0.21	-0.09	1.037
West Virginia	146	141	-5	0.41	0.35	-0.06	1.019
South Carolina	415	433	18	0.66	0.60	-0.06	1.154
Delaware	207	219	11	1.19	1.13	-0.06	1.685
North Dakota	45	50	5	0.70	0.65	-0.05	0.909
Hawaii	340	362	22	1.40	1.35	-0.05	1.058

Wisconsin	1,041	1,195	154	1.17	1.13	-0.04	1.007
Montana	80	96	16	0.63	0.62	-0.01	0.970
Iowa	518	615	98	1.20	1.21	0.01	0.943
Washington	1,364	1,766	402	0.97	0.99	0.02	0.937
Nebraska	127	161	34	0.92	0.97	0.05	0.671
Indiana	770	942	171	1.04	1.11	0.07	1.083
Colorado	239	339	100	0.75	0.87	0.12	0.796
Kansas	472	606	134	1.35	1.47	0.12	0.943
Oregon	804	1,055	251	1.35	1.47	0.12	1.070
Alaska	180	232	52	0.93	1.06	0.12	1.005
Utah	239	342	104	1.25	1.40	0.15	0.885
Oklahoma	323	419	96	1.34	1.53	0.19	0.910
New Mexico	174	239	65	1.48	1.69	0.21	0.857
Louisiana	306	601	295	0.43	0.72	0.29	0.693
Puerto Rico	564	749	186	1.82	2.15	0.33	NA
Wyoming	54	110	56	0.71	1.23	0.52	0.756
Virgin Islands	28	47	19	1.92	3.21	1.29	NA
U.S. total	36,871	25,847	-11,029	0.87	0.56	-0.31	1.156

NA = not applicable.

at the top of table 9.4C are particularly relevant because each state experienced a major increase in unemployment. The lowest unemployment rate ratio for these five states was 1.476 for New York. Observe that fifteen programs actually had HCMs at the end of 1992 than at the end of 1989, a unique development during a recessionary period and largely attributable to the shallowness of the recession.

To help place the 1990-1992 downturn into a greater perspective, table 9.5 displays state-level summary information for the four most recent recessions. The top half of the table focuses on increases in unemployment while the bottom half summarizes reductions in HCMs.

The most important inference to be drawn from the table is very simple: the 1990-1992 downturn was mild relative to the previous three downturns. Consider first the increases in state unemployment rates. Of the fifty states and the District of Columbia, the number with ratios of 1.25 or larger were as follows: 1971-1973 (thirty-seven), 1974-1976 (thirty-two), 1981-1983 (thirty-six), and 1990-1992 (sixteen). Both summary measures at the end of each line (the state median and the U.S. total) convey the same message: the 1990-1992 downturn was comparatively mild in terms of the increase in the average unemployment rate.

Turning to the reductions in HCMs shown at the bottom of table 9.5, the same point emerges. The numbers of states whose multiples decreased by 0.5 or more were as follows: 1969-1973 (thirty-four), 1973-1976 (forty-four), 1979-1983 (twenty-five), and 1989-1992 (eight). Finally, the state medians and U.S. totals at the ends of these four bottom lines reemphasize the small reductions in HCMs during 1989-1992.[21]

From the information in table 9.5, one main conclusion emerges: the increases in unemployment and losses of trust fund reserves were unusually small during the most recent recession. Also contributing to the modest amount of state borrowing during 1990-1994 were the comparatively high levels of reserves present in many states prior to the downturn.

One additional factor linked to emergency UI benefits contributed to the low level of state borrowing during 1990-1994. The Emergency Unemployment Compensation (EUC) program paid benefits to large numbers of claimants from late 1991 through early 1994.[22] This program compensating regular UI exhaustees was fully federally financed.

Table 9.5 Recession-Related Changes in Unemployment and UI Trust Fund Reserves

Ratios of average state unemployment rates for indicated periods

Annual averages	Less than 0.75	0.75 - 0.99	1.0 - 1.24	1.25 - 1.49	1.5 - 1.74	1.75 - 1.99	2.0+	State median	U.S. total
1971-1973 over 1967-1969	0	2	12	15	12	3	7	1.45	1.51
1974-1976 over 1971-1973	0	6	13	21	8	3	0	1.33	1.33
1981-1983 over 1977-1979	0	2	13	12	12	11	1	1.52	1.42
1990-1992 over 1987-1989	2	17	16	8	3	2	3	1.11	1.16

Changes in state UI high-cost multiples

End-of-year changes	Increase	Decreases 0.0 - 0.24	0.25 - 0.49	0.5 - 0.74	0.75 - 0.99	1.0 - 1.49	1.5+	State median	U.S. total
1969 to 1973	1	4	12	13	9	10	2	-0.66	-0.65
1973 to 1976	1	4	2	10	12	13	9	-0.92	-0.98
1979 to 1983	10	6	10	9	3	10	3	-0.49	-0.62
1989 to 1992	13	19	11	6	2	0	0	-0.20	-0.31

SOURCE: Calculations performed at the Urban Institute using data from the U.S. Department of Labor. State unemployment rate estimates prior to 1976 for several small states made at the Urban Institute. Calculations are shown for the fifty states and the District of Columbia.

However, after August 1992 there was a feature of EUC, known as optional EUC, which allowed claimants to utilize their EUC base period if it yielded a larger weekly benefit than the base period preceding their more current spell of unemployment. Thus, new claimants for state-financed regular UI were able to collect added weeks of federally-financed EUC even though they experienced substantial intervening periods of employment. Furthermore, the utilization of these EUC benefits did not preclude receipt of any regular UI benefits (based on the later base period) after exhausting EUC. In effect, the U.S. Treasury paid some weeks of what otherwise would have been state-financed regular UI benefits.

While EUC was operating it paid total benefits of $27.9 billion. State reporting of EUC captured only one element of optional EUC, the number of initial claims, which totaled 12.6 percent of all EUC initial claims. It is almost certain that optional EUC benefits were received for shorter periods than other EUC benefits. To estimate the savings to state UI trust funds, an algorithm was developed to project weeks compensated and benefits for optional EUC claims at the national level. The algorithm was then applied to state-level data on optional EUC initial claims to estimate state-level payouts. Because identical durations for the two groups of EUC claimants were assumed, the algorithm probably exaggerates payouts under optional EUC. Nationwide, optional EUC was estimated to total $3.12 billion. However, assuming these amounts reduced state reserves dollar for dollar and assuming no response of experience-rated taxes, only $0.475 billion in added state borrowing was projected during 1992-1994 had optional EUC not been available. Interestingly, all of the added borrowing estimated by the model was concentrated in the seven states that did borrow from the U.S. Treasury, i.e., no other states would have borrowed in the absence of optional EUC benefits.

Thus, without optional EUC, we estimate that seven states would have borrowed a total of $4.89 billion (rather than $4.42 billion) and that the aggregate state UI trust fund balances at the end of 1994 would have been $28.21 billion (rather than $31.34 billion). As a factor explaining the low level of state borrowing during 1990-1994, optional EUC was not important.

A final detail regarding loan repayments during 1991-1994 should be noted. In August-September 1993 Connecticut repaid $0.818 billion of Title XII advances using the proceeds of state-issued bonds, the major part of a bond issuance that totaled $1.0 billion. These bonds are scheduled to be fully repaid by 2002. The first of fourteen scheduled semiannual repayments occurred in February 1995, so that very little of this state-issued debt has been repaid.[23] Thus, for Connecticut, most of the state UI debt might be appropriately counted as still outstanding.

To summarize, the low amount of state borrowing during 1990-1994 can be attributed to two major factors: (1) more adequate trust fund balances at the end of 1989 compared to 1979, and (2) the mild nature of the recession across most of the country. Optional EUC was not an important factor explaining the low level of borrowing.

One other concluding observation from this section is to note the low annual rates of trust fund rebuilding during 1993 and 1994. It appears that states will have less adequate reserves (as suggested by solvency indicators such as HCMs) when they enter the next recession than they did prior to the 1990-1992 downturn.

Perhaps states currently require fewer reserves than in the past because their financing systems are now much more responsive to trust fund drawdowns. The historical descriptions from this section did not try to assess the quantitative importance of so-called flexible financing features or their growth in recent years. The next two sections address this important topic.

Flexible Financing Provisions

The key factors that make UI benefit financing a complex and important issue are that benefit outlays are highly sensitive to the business cycle and that the timing and severity of cyclical downturns are difficult to predict. Each state must develop a funding strategy to deal with these elements. In the early years of the UI program, as demonstrated in the first section, the focus of financing strategy was on building up sufficient reserves to handle a worst-case recession, using the HCM or similar measure as a benchmark. However, over the years it has been increasingly recognized that determining the appropriate level of reserves is more complex than just looking at potential future outlays. A state must also assess the responsiveness of its tax system to changes in benefit outlays and fund balance, as well as take into account the level of borrowing risk that is deemed acceptable. The more responsive the tax system, the lower the reserve level required for a state's needs. Likewise, the greater the acceptable risk of borrowing, the lower the adequate reserve level. From a pure fund adequacy perspective, as opposed to other goals of the UI system, it is recognized that having a low fund balance coupled with a responsive tax system is a legitimate strategy.

Tax responsiveness refers to the level and speed of the automatic response to benefit increases built into state UI tax systems. This automatic response occurs in two ways. First, experience-rating systems assign tax rates to individual employers based on some measure of experience with unemployment, usually related to the amount of UI benefits paid. As benefit costs rise, average tax rates also rise. Second, every state has some triggering mechanism whereby a declining fund balance leads to higher tax rates for all firms, either through multiple rate schedules or surcharges or both. Beyond taxes, some states also have mechanisms that tie benefit restrictions to low threshold levels of trust fund balances. The combination of tax and benefit features automatically triggered by the condition of the trust fund is sometimes referred to as flexible financing.

The origins and evolution of flexible financing in the individual states reflect varied historical developments. In some states, ad hoc arrangements were created during periods of trust fund inadequacy and were intended as temporary fixes. Others have implemented flexible financing as permanent changes. At least two states, Illinois and Pennsylvania, overhauled their tax and benefit statutes in the late 1980s with the intention of reducing the average trust fund balance over the business cycle and adding flexibility features. Recession-related drawdowns would be countered by automatic tax increases and benefit reductions as the fund balance descended past certain thresholds towards zero. We have not attempted to follow the individual motivations leading to state actions but have tried to document the changing prevalence of flexibility features.

Despite the awareness of flexible financing as a component of a funding strategy, little has been written about the determinants of flexible financing and there has been even less quantitative analysis. These topics are the focus here and in the following sections.

There is a general perception that states have increased their reliance on flexible financing over time, especially since 1980. Several events occurred in the early 1980s that may have caused this. First, during the back-to-back recessions of 1980-1983, thirty-one states borrowed from the federal loan account to pay benefits. Second, federal loan policy became significantly tighter, as previously discussed. Deferrals of FUTA credit reductions (for loan repayment) were eliminated in 1980 and the interest-free feature (except on a very short-term basis) of the loan system was eliminated in 1982. At the same time that borrowing has become a less attractive option for states, there has been a growing recognition that carrying large trust fund balances may have undesirable effects. As a result, states have an incentive to make their tax systems more responsive.

This section discusses features that make a system more responsive and examines changes made by states since 1980. We also compare and contrast a responsive and a nonresponsive state. The next section undertakes some quantitative analysis of responsiveness and tries to determine whether or not responsiveness has increased in the last decade or so. Also, the results of a simulation analysis of the flexible financing system in Pennsylvania are reported. The subsequent discussion addresses some pros and cons and policy issues associated with flexible financing.

Flexibility Features and Trends

Since 1980, although they have often acted hesitantly, many state legislatures faced with problems of insolvency in their UI trust fund accounts have moved to increase the responsiveness of their UI systems. They have enacted legislation meant to increase UI taxes and to lower UI benefits during recessionary periods. These states are, in effect, making up for the lack of forward funding in their systems by working to avoid insolvency at low levels of trust fund reserves. States have done this primarily by:

• making tax table triggers more sensitive,
• adding or strengthening existing solvency taxes, and
  linking changes and/or levels of benefits to trust fund reserves

The most significant revisions in these features have come from states with relatively severe solvency problems. Tables 9.6A and 9.6B display the changes since 1980 in selected tax features for fifty-one programs.

In the past fifteen years, eleven states have raised the fund balance triggers that activate the highest tax rate schedule, while either holding constant or raising tax rates for the top schedule. This change alone means that the state will respond with higher rates on employers at an earlier time for a given benefit drawdown. For example, in 1991, Indiana raised the fund balance required to trigger on its highest employer tax rate schedule from 0.85 percent of wages to 1.5 percent, making it easier to activate that schedule when the balance falls.

Table 9.6A 1996 Flexible Tax Features (Part 1)

	Solvency tax	Change since 1980	Responsive social tax	Change since 1980	Highest tax schedule trigger (Change since 1980)	Lowest tax schedule trigger	Array method	Change since 1980
Alabama			x	x	-	-		
Alaska	x	x	x	x		-	x	
Arizona								
Arkansas	x				-			
California	x	x			-	-		
Colorado	x		x		+			
Connecticut	x				+			
Delaware	x							
District of Columbia					+			
Florida								
Georgia	x					+		
Hawaii					-			
Idaho					+		x	
Illinois	x	x						
Indiana					-	+		
Iowa							x	
Kansas							x	
Kentucky								
Louisiana	x	x	x					
Maine	x							
Maryland	x	x			-			
Massachusetts			x	x	+	-		

	Solvency tax	Change since 1980	Responsive social tax	Change since 1980	Highest tax schedule trigger (Change since 1980)	Lowest tax schedule trigger (Change since 1980)	Array method	Change since 1980
Michigan	x		x					
Minnesota	x	x			+	+		
Mississippi	x		x					
Missouri	x				+	+		
Montana					+			
Nebraska								
Nevada								
New Hampshire	x							
New Jersey	x	x			-			
New Mexico								
New York	x				-	-		
North Carolina	x				-	-		
North Dakota					+	-	x	x
Ohio	x		x					
Oklahoma	x							
Oregon								
Pennsylvania	x	x			+			
Rhode Island	x		x		+			
South Carolina	x							
South Dakota	x	x				+		
Tennessee					+			
Texas	x	x	x			+		
Utah			x		-			
Vermont					-	+	x	
Virginia	x	x	x		-			
Washington							x	x
West Virginia								
Wisconsin			x					
Wyoming	x				+	+		
Total	28	11	13	3	13+/11-	8+/8-	7	2

SOURCE: U.S. Department of Labor, Unemployment Insurance Service.
NOTE: For trigger change columns, "+" indicates a move to more responsiveness and "-" means the opposite. The responsive social tax is an explicit recoupment of noncharges and ineffective charges. The array method assigns tax rates to employers ranked by experience factor, such that each tax rate applies to an equal amount of taxable wages.

Table 9.6B 1996 Flexible Tax Features (Part 2)

	Indexed tax base	Change since 1980	Flexible tax base	Change since 1980	Benefit ratio	Change since 1980	Flexible employee tax	Change since 1980
Alabama					x	x		
Alaska	x	x					x	
Arizona								
Arkansas								
California								
Colorado								
Connecticut					x			
Delaware								
District of Columbia			x	x				
Florida					x			
Georgia								
Hawaii	x							
Idaho	x							
Illinois					x	x		
Indiana								
Iowa	x				x	x		
Kansas								
Kentucky								
Louisiana								
Maine								
Maryland					x			
Massachusetts								
Michigan					x			
Minnesota	x	x			x			
Mississippi					x			
Missouri			x	x				
Montana	x	x						
Nebraska								
Nevada	x							
New Hampshire								
New Jersey	x						x	
New Mexico	x							
New York								
North Carolina	x	x						
North Dakota	x	x						
Ohio								
Oklahoma	x	x						

	Indexed tax base	Change since 1980	Flexible tax base	Change since 1980	Benefit ratio	Change since 1980	Flexible employee tax	Change since 1980
Oregon	x				x			
Pennsylvania					x		x	x
Rhode Island	x	x						
South Carolina								
South Dakota								
Tennessee								
Texas					x			
Utah	x				x	x		
Vermont					x			
Virginia					x	x		
Washington	x	x			x	x		
West Virginia								
Wisconsin								
Wyoming	x	x			x			
Total	17	9	2	2	17	6	3	1

SOURCE: U.S. Department of Labor, Unemployment Insurance Service.
NOTE: A flexible tax base is one that increases or decreases with solvency conditions. An indexed tax base is one that increases with average wages.

The addition or strengthening of an existing solvency tax can have the same effect as increasing the sensitivity of a tax table trigger. Though states have various names for these taxes, they are primarily meant to increase revenues at low levels of trust fund reserves.

As of 1995, twenty-eight states had a solvency tax. Since 1980, eleven states added a solvency tax specifically triggered by low trust fund levels and designed solely to boost contributions. Most solvency tax rates range from 0.1 to 1.0 percent and are levied as additions to existing experience-rated tax rates.

Many of the solvency taxes were added as part of more comprehensive law reforms to deal with incidents of insolvency but now remain in place and contribute to the eroding degree of countercyclicality of the UI system. As an illustration, after having severe solvency problems in the early 1980s, Minnesota, in 1988, raised the trigger on its highest tax schedule from $80 million to $200 million, effectively activating the top schedule sooner in the face of a trust fund drawdown. Furthermore, the state removed a rate limiter that had been in place to prevent an employer's rate from increasing or decreasing by more than 2.5 percentage points in one year.

Also added to the Minnesota system was an unusual feature that contributes significantly to responsiveness. This is a solvency tax, which can change on a quarterly basis, adding 10 percent to scheduled tax rates when the trust fund falls below $150 million and 15 percent when the fund falls below $75 million.

In addition to solvency taxes, many states add a "social tax" to the basic tax rate. These social taxes can have a significant effect on the degree of tax responsiveness. During the 1980s, three states joined the existing thirteen that had social taxes constructed to specifically recoup the dollar amount of the previous year's uncollectible benefit charges, i.e., ineffective charges and noncharges. Other states either account for social charges indirectly in their tax rate schedules or through solvency taxes based on the fund balance. By attempting to account for each dollar of the previous year's total benefits, these sixteen states increase the responsiveness of taxes to current outlays. Without this accounting, the fluctuating number of employers at the maximum and minimum tax rates, which determines a large share of social charges, can cause noticeable differences between total benefits paid out and tax revenues. In particular, the volume of social charges may cause the tax system to respond inadequately during periods of trust fund drawdowns.

Massachusetts has perhaps the most comprehensive computation of social charges. The state accounts for each dollar of unattributed benefit costs by adding together noncharged benefits, benefits charged to inactive firms, ineffective charges, and dependents' benefits, and then subtracting interest earned and the balances of minimum-rated employers. A portion of the resulting amount is assigned to each employer as a deduction from each one's reserve ratio. In effect, employers are credited with lower reserves, resulting in higher taxes.

Part of this trend has also included making levels of benefit payments to UI claimants contingent on the size of the trust fund. Table 9.7 provides additional details on this feature and on the trigger mechanism that activates flexible benefits.

Twelve states enacted some form of flexible benefit provision between 1983 and 1991, and these features are still present in nine states as of 1995. Eleven of the twelve states provided for benefit freezes or benefit reductions.[24] All states but Delaware target these automatic features on high-wage claimants. Ten states have done this through automatic limits on the annual growth in the maximum weekly benefit amount (WBA) and/or reductions in the maximum. Three states provide for variation in the wage replacement rate, but two of the three (Pennsylvania and Wyoming) hold low-wage beneficiaries harmless when the reductions are in effect.

Table 9.7   Flexible Benefit Features

	First year	Last year	Flexible replacement rate	Flexible maximum WBA	Fund balance	Reserve ratio	Employer taxes	All other
Alabama								
Alaska								
Arizona								
Arkansas								
California								
Colorado								
Connecticut								
Delaware	1988		x	x	x			
District of Columbia								
Florida								
Georgia	1989	1991		x	x			
Hawaii								
Idaho								
Illinois	1991			x	x		x	x
Indiana								
Iowa								
Kansas								
Kentucky	1987			x	x		x	
Louisiana								
Maine								
Maryland								
Massachusetts								
Michigan								
Minnesota	1983			x	x			
Mississippi								
Missouri								
Montana								
Nebraska								
Nevada								
New Hampshire								
New Jersey								

(continued)

Table 9.7 (continued)

	First year	Last year	Flexible replacement rate	Flexible maximum WBA	Fund balance	Reserve ratio	Employer taxes	All other
New Mexico								
New York								
North Carolina	1984	1987		X		X		
North Dakota	1991			X	X		X	
Ohio								
Oklahoma	1984			X			X	
Oregon								
Pennsylvania	1990		X			X		
Rhode Island								
South Carolina								
South Dakota								
Tennessee								
Texas								
Utah								
Vermont	1987			X				X
Virginia								
Washington	1985	1993		X		X		
West Virginia								
Wisconsin								
Wyoming	1984		X		X			
Total			3	10	7	3	4	2

SOURCE: Data taken from U.S. Department of Labor, Unemployment Insurance Service publications such as "Significant Provisions of State Unemployment Insurance Laws" and from Commerce Clearing House summaries of state UI laws.

In ten of the twelve states, the trigger for the automatic benefit feature has been either the absolute level of the state trust fund or the trust fund balance measured as a ratio of covered wages (as a ratio of benefit payouts in Pennsylvania). Other components of the triggers have been almost always related to financing variables, e.g., employer tax rates (four states) or outstanding Title XII loans (Vermont). The trigger mechanism in three states involves more than a single indicator, with the Illinois trigger having three separate components.[25]

Additional Flexibility Features

There exist several other important tax provisions that also act to quicken the response of UI taxes and that have increased in number in the last fifteen years. Tables 9.6A and 9.6B provide an overview of these features. The following elements tend to contribute to the faster response of systems:

- Benefit ratio experience rating,
- Indexed taxable wage base, and
- Array method of assigning tax rates

Experience-rating formulas—reserve ratio, benefit ratio, benefit wage ratio, and payroll decline—are designed to assess the amount of benefit payments attributable to an individual firm and to recoup a portion through the assignment of a yearly tax rate.[26] Several factors in the way experience-rating mechanisms have been constructed lead to greater responsiveness in some states than in others.

The benefit ratio and benefit wage ratio formulas are considered as responding faster because of their shorter memory[27] and lack of reserve accounting. The crediting of contributions to employer accounts in a reserve ratio system actually creates a drag on responsiveness after the first year. How much faster benefit ratio systems respond is difficult to measure because of the different intervals within tax schedules and the varying employer mix in each state. However, taking just a sample of states that incurred similar benefit payouts during the last recession, a general comparison can be made in the amount of movement by employers into and out of the minimum and maximum tax rates for the different formulas. The following table helps to illustrate the contrasting behavior.

Table 9.8 Comparison of Movement in Distributions of Wages by Tax Rate

Percentage at each tax category	Reserve ratio states	Benefit ratio states
1990 percentage of wages taxed at minimum rate	10.3	38.6
1993 percentage of wages taxed at minimum rate	7.8	25.1
1990 percentage of wages taxed at maximum rate	4.6	5.5
1993 percentage of wages taxed at maximum rate	6.0	6.4

SOURCE: Based on U.S. Department of Labor, Employment and Training Administration, ES-204 reports, section C. Data refer to three reserve ratio states (Arizona, Hawaii, and Rhode Island) and three benefit ratio states (Alabama, Maryland, and Virginia).

In this sample of states, the greatest difference was in the number of employers moving away from the minimum rate under the benefit ratio as opposed to under the reserve ratio system. Reserve ratio states went from an average of 10.3 percent of wages being taxed at the minimum rate to 7.8 percent, while the benefit ratio states went from 38.6 percent of wages to 25.1 percent. Thus, a much larger share of wages moved to higher tax rates in the benefit ratio states than in the reserve ratio states.

The number of employers at the minimum and maximum tax rates is an important determinant of the responsiveness of any state system. The more firms there are at the minimum and maximum tax rates the less responsive the tax system is to benefit shocks, because those employers will exhibit less movement in their tax rates. Maximum-rated employers will be bounded by the highest tax rate, and minimum-rated employers often have large previous balances or low previous benefit levels.

In a review of all state tax schedules for rate year 1993, there was an average of 4 percent of employers located at the maximum tax rate. This ranged from a high of 14 percent in California to a low of less than 1 percent in New Hampshire. There was an average of 16 percent of employers located at the minimum rate, ranging from a high of 58 percent in Nevada to less than 1 percent in New Jersey.

In order to avoid the congregation of employers at the minimum and maximum tax rates, a few states actually fix the number of employers that will receive each rate by ranking employers against each other, rather than by setting rates in preassigned intervals. In 1987, North Dakota joined six other states in using this type of so-called "array" allocation system for employer tax rate determinations.[28] Array allocation rate setting, which is independent of the type of experience rating formula, places a specific percentage of aggregate taxable wages in each tax rate interval. This not only allows states to determine total contributions more precisely, since the percentage of wages at each tax rate is predetermined, but also can be more effective in responding to changes in benefit levels.

Possibly the most significant change in state financing laws that affects responsiveness in experience rating is a rise in the state taxable wage base or indexing the base. Note in table 9.6B that since the 1982 increase in the federal taxable wage base to $7,000, nine states have passed laws to index their wage bases to a proportion of total wages, bringing the sum to seventeen indexed states (plus the Virgin Islands). Another seventeen states increased their taxable wage base somewhere between $500 and $3,800 during this period.

In a benefit ratio state, increasing the taxable wage base extends the range of effective experience rating to high-unemployment firms, as compared to a state that maintains a much lower base. In a reserve ratio state, however, the immediate effect is not as clear and will depend more on the distribution of employers along a given state tax schedule. For a much higher base, reserve ratio employers will have a tendency to move away from the maximum and minimum rates and towards the experienced-rated portion of the tax table. However, the higher contributions will also help some employers build up significant balances, allowing them to remain in the more unresponsive portions of the tax schedule.[29]

Additionally, six states have had a provision that varies the wage base according to the trust fund balance. Of these, two states (see table 9.6B) currently have such a provision. Since 1985, Missouri has automatically raised its taxable wage base by $500 per year whenever the trust fund balance has fallen below $100 million and lowered it by $500 per year (but not below $7,000) whenever the balance has exceeded $250 million. Between 1992 and 1995, Ohio provided for $250 annual increments in its tax base ($8,000 in 1991), but the base would have automatically increased to $9,000 if the trust fund had fallen below a predetermined threshold. Iowa implemented special additions to its indexed tax base in the three years of 1984 to 1986. Montana had a similar provision between 1975 and 1977. Hawaii experimented with a trigger-activated flexible tax base in the single year 1988. The District of Columbia instituted a trigger-activated tax base provision in 1995.

All of these provisions, together with several others that are perhaps quantitatively less significant,[30] have been adopted during periods of insolvency and now remain as features contributing to the faster response of UI taxes.

A Comparison of Texas and New York

To better assess how particular features of state laws affect responsiveness, two states were chosen for closer examination. As the following table illustrates, tax revenues in Texas were clearly more responsive to benefit increases than were tax revenues in New York during and after the 1990-1991 recession.

Table 9.9 Annual Trust Fund Data for Texas and New York ($ billions)

	Texas			New York		
Year	Balance	Benefits	Taxes	Balance	Benefits	Taxes
1988	$0.27B	$0.75B	$1.49B	$3.26B	$1.03B	$1.34B
1989	0.99	0.71	1.36	3.18	1.32	0.94
1990	1.29	0.74	0.93	2.55	1.76	0.89
1991	0.94	0.96	0.52	1.19	2.46	0.98
1992	0.59	1.12	0.71	0.21	2.44	1.37
1993	0.45	1.04	0.84	0.13	1.99	1.97
1994	0.48	0.98	0.99	0.19	2.00	2.06

SOURCE: U.S. Department of Labor (1992).

Although the recession was mild in Texas, contributions responded strongly to the growth in benefits. The first large benefit increase did not occur until 1991, when benefits rose by 30 percent, followed by a further 17 percent increase in 1992, before declining slightly in 1993. Contributions, which had reached a low point in 1991, responded quickly, with an increase of 37 percent the first year and 18 percent in each of the next two years. The fund balance dropped three years in a row but in 1994 started to rise again.

New York, on the other hand, experienced a very large growth in benefit outlays during this recession, with the first significant increase occurring in 1989. Benefits rose by 28 percent in 1989, 33 percent in 1990, and 40 percent in 1991. Contributions, however, went *down* in 1990. The first significant increase occurred in 1992, three years after the beginning of the recession. New York eventually exhausted its once-large fund balance and needed cash-flow loans in both 1992 and 1993.

We compared and contrasted the laws of these two states to see if we could identify factors that made their tax systems more or less responsive. Although Texas and New York cannot be compared directly on all dimensions of their legislation, three key differences stand out.

First, Texas has a benefit ratio system, and New York has a reserve ratio system. A benefit ratio system reflects benefit increases quickly, because the employer's experience factor is not affected by current and past contributions. Changes in employer experience factors accounted for approximately the same average tax rate change in both states during this time period, even though the recession was much more severe in New York.

Second, Texas explicitly and immediately covers its nonchargeable and ineffective charges by reflecting them in the following year's tax rates through its "replenishment ratio" and "replenishment tax rate." New York has no analogous mechanism.

Third, Texas makes a direct link between the level of its solvency surcharge and the amount of contributions needed to restore the fund balance to the desired level. New York, in contrast, has a single solvency rate no matter how low the fund balance drops.

Quantitative Analysis of Flexible Financing

This section summarizes our empirical analyses of the quantitative importance of flexible financing. Measures of the response of contributions to increased benefit outflows are derived. One-, two-, and three-year response measures are calculated, and changes dating back to the early 1950s are documented. Tax responsiveness in 1970 and 1990 is then examined for a subset of states that had recessions centered on both dates. Regressions also are fitted to estimate possible changes in tax responsiveness. Finally, a simulation analysis of flexible financing in Pennsylvania is reviewed.

Empirical Tax Responsiveness Measures

Since the preceding section shows that many states have added flexible financing features in recent years, we attempted to test empirically whether tax responsiveness has increased quantitatively, particularly in the years following the loan policy changes of the early 1980s. An important practical difficulty is that the economy has experienced only one, fairly mild, recession since 1980-1983 from which to make inferences.

Using annual data from 1950 through 1994, we first constructed empirical measures of tax responsiveness. Recessions were identified on a state-by-state basis rather than nationally to account for differential timing of business cycles across states as well as localized economic downturns. Recessionary periods were defined as those in which the increase in the benefit cost rate (benefits as a percentage of total wages) from the base year to the peak year was 35 percent or greater. The beginning year of the recessionary period was identified as the first year with a 20 percent increase over the prior year (which then became the base year). An additional criterion was to eliminate recessions that started within three years of the previous recession, to avoid overlapping of the response measures. The total number of periods meeting these criteria was 303, or about 6 per state, with 47 occurring since 1982.

We then computed one-year, two-year, and three-year tax responses for each recessionary period, as follows:

$$\text{one-year response} = \frac{(C_{t+1} - C_t)}{(B_t - B_{t-1})}$$

$$\text{two-year response} = \frac{((C_{t+1} - C_t) + (C_{t+2} - C_t))}{((B_t - B_{t-1}) + (B_{t+1} - B_{t-1}))}$$

$$\text{three-year response} = \frac{((C_{t+1} - C_t) + (C_{t+2} - C_t) + (C_{t+3} - C_t))}{((B_t - B_{t-1}) + (B_{t+1} - B_{t-1}) + (B_{t+2} - B_{t-1}))}$$

where
  C = contributions
  B = benefits, and
  t = first year of recessionary period

There appear to be several difficulties in measuring responsiveness accurately. First, benefit cost rates exhibit frequent fluctuations, even in nonrecessionary periods; thus, tax rates are never in equilibrium. Second, the pattern of benefit increases, e.g., slow buildup versus steep increase, has an impact on the measured response, except for the one-year measure. For example, for a given cumulative rise in benefits, the three-year measure would be higher for a recessionary period in which the first year had the largest gain than for a period in which the increases started modestly and then gradually became greater. Third, using annual data obscures the precise timing of benefit increases.

Probably as a direct result of these assessment problems, the measured responses exhibited a wide spectrum of values, including many outside the expected range of 0.0 to 1.0. In particular, there were many negative responses. Assuming that these values were due to the measurement problems that have been discussed, rather than representing true responses, the extreme values were eliminated before any analysis was done. We included only those recessionary periods for which all three measures fell within the range of acceptable values (including some negatives for the one-year and two-year measures). This reduced the number of recessionary periods to 236, of which 33 occurred since 1982.

The first analysis examined simple averages of the measures across states, without regard to state size or other factors, for three different time periods. These averages are shown below.

Beginning year	Number of periods	One-year response	Two-year response	Three-year response
1952-1968	88	0.11	0.31	0.43
1969-1981	115	0.14	0.36	0.54
1982-1991	33	0.15	0.34	0.62

Several observations can be made about these averages. First, the 1952-1968 period has the lowest average responsiveness for all three measures. Second, the 1982-1991 period has a clear edge over the 1969-1981 period only for the three-year measure, even falling slightly below it for the two-year measure. Third, the differences in responsiveness are the clearest between the first two time periods, indicating that most of the increase in responsiveness over the years occurred in the 1970s rather than in the 1980s. Finally, the biggest gains in responsiveness over time are in the three-year measure.

The second analysis of the response measures compared the 1990 recession to the 1970 recession. This comparison was made because the 1990 downturn was closer in size to that in 1970 than to the more recent recessions. A key difference between the 1970 and 1990 recessions, however, was that aggregate reserves as a percentage of total payroll were almost twice as large in 1969 as in 1989 (table 9.1).

Twenty-three states met the various criteria for inclusion in both time periods. Responsiveness measures for the two recessions were compared for each of those states. Among states for which all three response measures were higher in one time period than in the other, nine states were more responsive in 1970 than in 1990, and only seven states were more responsive in 1990 than in 1970.

An interesting point to note is that the two recessions varied significantly in size for many states, which may affect the responsiveness comparison. Of the twelve states where there was both a clear difference in the severity of the two recessions and a clear variation in responsiveness, eight states were more responsive in the milder of the two recessions.

A third analysis was done by fitting regressions to the data to control for factors that might affect the measured responsiveness. The results are shown in table 9.10. Three regressions are displayed, using the one-year, two-year, and three-year response measures, respectively, as dependent variables. The explanatory variables include the reserve ratio at the beginning of the recessionary period, the change in the benefit cost rate for each of the recessionary years, and binary variables for unmeasured state differences. Time effects were measured with two binary variables, one for the period 1969-1992 and one for the period 1982-1992.

One observation based on the results in table 9.10 is that responsiveness is clearly related to reserve levels, with greater responsiveness at lower reserve ratios. The magnitude of the reserve effect does not appear to be very large, however, with the impact of a 1 percentage-point decline in the reserve ratio ranging from a 3 percentage-point increase in the one-year response to a 5 percentage-point increase in the three- year response.

A more important observation is that none of the time effects are significant. The largest coefficients are, in fact, negative, possibly indicating a reduction in tax responsiveness over time after controlling for reserve levels. The conclusion to be drawn from these regressions and the other analyses of response measures is that we have been unable to show empirically that tax responsiveness has increased since the early 1980s.

**Table 9.10 Regressions on Responsiveness Measures
1952-1992**

	One-year response	Two-year response	Three-year response
Intercept	.495	.789	1.054
Reserve ratio	-.034**	-.035**	-.053**
	(.010)	(.011)	(.014)
1969-1992 dummy	-.079	-0.47	.006
	(.047)	(.053)	(.067)
1982-1992 dummy	.008	-.083	-.003
	(.048)	(.053)	(.067)
First-year BCR increase			.00097*
			(.00050)
Second-year BCR increase		-.00043**	
		(.00015)	
Third-year BCR increase			-.00140*
			(.00026)
R^2	.338	.458	.476
Mean of dependent variable	.13	.33	.51

NOTE: All regressions include state dummies. Standard errors are in parentheses. Sample size is 236.
BCR = benefit cost rate.
*Significant at the .05 level.
**Significant at the .01 level.

Flexible Financing in Pennsylvania

A second type of quantitative analysis was to simulate the impact of flexible financing features for a specific state. Pennsylvania enacted UI legislation in 1988 designed to increase the automatic responsiveness of taxes and benefits, thus reducing the potential need for borrowing during recessions. The 1988 law followed earlier solvency legislation of 1980 and 1983 and a history of large-scale borrowing from the U.S. Treasury. Of the thirty-seven state UI programs that borrowed sometime during the 1970s and 1980s, Pennsylvania's $5.5 billion total was the largest.

Pennsylvania's 1988 solvency measures provide for additional employer taxes, variable employee taxes, and benefit reductions. All adjustments to taxes and benefits are activated by a single trigger. The trigger is calculated as the ratio of the fund balance at the end of the current fiscal year (June 30) to the average benefit outlay for the current and the two previous fiscal years, and the ratio is expressed as a percentage. Thus a trigger value of 100 indicates that the fund balance is equal to one year's worth of benefits.

There are two flexible employer taxes. An employer surcharge is imposed as a flat amount that can assume seven different values. Trigger ratios of 150 or larger cause a tax reduction while the largest surcharge is levied when the trigger falls below 50. Employers are also subject to graduated "additional contributions" when the trigger falls below 95. The trigger-activated employee surcharge has a range of possible values from 0.0 to 0.2 percent of total covered wages. Finally, weekly benefits (for claimants paid more than half of the maximum WBA) are reduced by 5 percent whenever the trigger ratio falls below 50. Many of these flexible financing provisions have effects specified as fixed dollar amounts. Thus as economic growth occurs, their size automatically declines relative to macroeconomic variables such as covered employment and total wages.

The impacts of these automatic provisions were studied using a simulation model that included detailed equations for the determination of UI taxes and UI benefits.[31] Model simulations were conducted for the years 1991 to 1999. The analysis specified a series of unemployment-inflation scenarios and simulated benefits, taxes, and trust fund balances with the automatic provisions first "off" and then "on." The time paths of unemployment reproduced state unemployment from earlier periods as well as specifying successively higher unemployment rates. Differing inflation rates were also simulated.

Perhaps the most interesting results were yielded by a series of simulations that successively raised the average total unemployment rate by 0.5 percentage point increments. The simulations showed that total benefit outlays grew consistently for successive increments but that additional taxes reached upper limits, causing the fund balance to decline further and cumulative borrowing to increase, despite the presence of the flexible financing provisions. Even when all provisions were fully turned "on," benefit outflows exceeded taxes by wide margins.

The distribution of worker and employer sacrifices was found to be sensitive to the assumed rate of inflation.[32] At low inflation rates, the burden of the flexible financing provisions was roughly 50-50, with most of the employee burden arising from employee taxes. At higher inflation rates, the employee share rose to more than half, with the employee taxes accounting for most of the increased employee share. This results from the combination of an unlimited tax base for employees and a limitation on employer taxes caused by the fixed tax base. Additional simulations suggested that indexing both the employer tax base and the solvency features (rather than using fixed absolute dollar amounts) would substantially enhance the effectiveness of flexible financing in preventing indebtedness and reducing the scale of insolvency.

Three of the principal findings were straightforward. First, the presence of flexible financing provisions in Pennsylvania reduces the scale of borrowing but does not prevent insolvency. Second, the flexible financing features were more effective in small downturns than in more serious recessions (measured in terms of the increase in the average total unemployment rate for 1991-1999). Finally, inflation weakened the effectiveness of the flexible financing features in the later years of the simulation period.

Implications of Flexible Financing

State Choices

In choosing whether or not to implement a funding strategy that relies on a strong element of flexible financing, it is important for a state to look at the trade-offs involved. The chief argument in favor of flexible financing is that trust fund reserves can be kept low and, at the same time, the risk of borrowing can be minimized. The negative aspects of large balances have become more widely recognized in recent years. First, states may perceive that the opportunity cost of holding balances exceeds the interest earnings on reserves. For any given level of benefit payouts, a state may prefer to hold smaller trust fund balances now than in the past on the argument that the rate of return is higher for funds held by employers.[33] Second, large trust fund balances may increase pressures for benefit liberalization or for diversions of UI taxes to other purposes. Either use of the trust fund is easier to do politically if the fund balance is perceived to be larger than necessary.[34]

It is clear that, in the aggregate, states now have smaller desired trust fund levels than in the past. Although prerecession balances in 1989 were high relative to those of the preceding decade, as a percent of payroll they were only about half of 1969 balances (table 9.1). This is an appropriate comparison because 1969 and 1989 were both at the end of long periods of economic growth, presumably allowing reserves to be accumulated to desired levels.

A second impetus towards flexible financing is that, even if a state chooses to have a low trust fund balance, there are incentives to avoid or minimize borrowing. Since 1982, interest has been charged on loans (except those repaid the same year they are made). This interest must be paid from sources outside the trust fund, either through a separate tax or from state general revenues. A further disincentive is the automatic repayment feature of the FUTA tax, which is activated after two years of borrowing. This tax repays the loan via a flat surcharge on the low federal tax base, rather than through the experience-rated state UI tax.

The chief argument against flexible financing is that the timing of benefit decreases and tax increases hurts both claimants and employers. Claimants are faced with reduced benefits at a time when their need is the greatest. Businesses are faced with tax increases before they have fully recovered from the recession.

Two additional arguments against relying on flexible financing can also be noted. First, a state may implement flexible financing features, but the provisions may not act with enough strength to prevent insolvency. Flexible tax features, for example, simply may not generate sufficient added revenues in a timely manner to counteract the effects of a serious recession. Second, there is a question of the presence of enough political will to let strong flexible features operate as intended. When the time comes, the state executive and/or legislature may decide to nullify the automatic response to satisfy preferences of the claimant and/or business community. Absent a large trust fund reserve, the result could be that the state needs large-scale loans.

National Perspective

While flexible financing may be an attractive option for some states, widespread use of flexible financing would be a cause for concern from a national economic perspective. The main problem with flexible financing from this viewpoint is that it reduces the countercyclical performance of the UI system. One of the original objectives of the UI system was to act as an automatic stabilizer of the macro economy, primarily through maintenance of consumer purchasing power. Flexible benefit provisions directly reduce this stabilization effect. Taxes that respond too quickly also may curtail business spending at the wrong time and adversely affect the recovery. The stabilization role of UI is already diminished because of the long-term decline in the proportion of the unemployed who receive benefits. Increased use of flexible financing would further erode this position.

During the 1950s, when UI trust fund balances were much greater, there was a good deal of debate and experimentation on ways to make tax rates more countercyclical. In the past ten or fifteen years, with relatively low trust fund balances, there has been considerable state legislative movement in the opposite direction, towards quicker recovery of benefit costs in the form of flexible financing features. It appears, however, that the shift towards flexible financing has not been of sufficient quantitative importance to have had a significant effect.

Summary and Conclusions

This chapter has reviewed the history of state UI reserves and borrowing as well as recent trends. A key finding is that states have been slow to rebuild their trust funds since the recessionary trough of 1992. At the observed fund-building rates of 1993 and 1994, it appears that states will enter the next recession with less adequate reserves than they had prior to the 1990-1992 recession.

We have examined flexible financing. As documented, many states have added flexible financing features to their UI laws in recent years, consistent with the common perception that pay-as-you-go financing has increased. We estimated the quantitative effect of flexible financing provisions and found that, in the aggregate, the impact of these provisions is rather small.

One finding was common to two separate investigations of flexible financing. First, for the twelve states for which responsiveness in both the 1970 and 1990 recessions could be compared, eight showed greater responsiveness in the milder of the two downturns. Second, in the simulation analysis of Pennsylvania's 1988 law, its flexible financing features were found to be more effective in countering the effects of mild recessions. Thus, as currently structured, flexible financing qualities may be more effective during mild as opposed to severe downturns. If this finding is corroborated by other research, it may point to a need to enact solvency taxes and other flexible features that have more "bite" than those presently in place. Otherwise, the inadequacy of such mechanisms for maintaining solvency would be discovered at the most inappropriate time, i.e., during a major recession.

Several conclusions can be drawn from the analysis. First, state UI trust funds are now more healthy than at the end of the 1970s and start of the early 1980s, but they are not so large that the risks of insolvency and debt are merely matters of historical interest. The fact that the borrowing during 1990-1994 was so modest is partly attributable to the mild nature of the recession. Second, there is a continuing need for states to maintain reserves to avert large-scale borrowing during a future slowdown. We note and express concern for the comparatively modest pace of trust fund rebuilding during 1993-1994. It appears likely that reserves available for the next recession will be less adequate than they were prior to the 1990-1992 recession. Third, while flexible financing provisions are now more prevalent and possibly of greater significance than they were twenty years ago, our empirical results did not suggest that the change has been of large quantitative importance. Fourth, the speed and strength of automatic financing responses appear inadequate to the needs that would arise in a future downturn if its depth and severity equaled the average of the eight post-World War II recessions.

NOTES

Any opinions expressed in this chapter are solely those of the authors and do not necessarily reflect the positions of the U.S. Department of Labor or the Urban Institute.

1. See chapter 12 in Haber and Murray (1966).

2. The term "net reserves" refers to total state reserves less outstanding loans from the U.S. Treasury at the end of the indicated years. The term "aggregate payrolls" refers to taxable employ-ets only and does not reflect employers who finance benefit payments on a reimbursable basis.

3. Connecticut and New York also borrowed small amounts during the first six months of 1995. The definition of a "large" loan, as the term is used in this chapter, is given shortly.

4. Thus, table 9.1 shows reserve ratios for the entire United States for nine individual years.

5. Two criticisms are frequently made. First, the highest cost period is often so far in the past, e.g., January-December 1964 for South Dakota, that it may no longer be relevant as an indicator of risk. Second, because the multiple is a static concept, it does not adequately recognize the dynamic response of taxes when trust funds are being depleted. A fast response of taxes can allow a state to function successfully with a lower trust fund reserve. The validity of the second argu-ment motivates this chapter.

6. See chapters 2 and 5 and appendix E in Advisory Council on Unemployment Compensation (1995).

7. The recommendations are numbers 2-6 in chapter 2 of the Advisory Council on Unemploy-ment Compensation report. Several of the ACUC recommendations for providing financial rewards to states that build large reserves previously appeared in a book by one of the authors. See chapter 6, pages 145-146, in Vroman (1990).

8. Table 9.2 displays similar information to that previously displayed in table 9.1, but for a shorter time period and with attention to state-level as well as to aggregate detail.

9. The single years within each period used as the numerieres for the borrowing totals were respectively 1975, 1984, and 1991.

10. Regression analysis of the probability of a state needing a loan during a recession consis-tently shows a negative and highly significant coefficient on the prerecession HCM.

11. Clearly, the passage of a longer period of time can affect cumulative measures of borrow-ing activities. However, of the 31 programs that needed loans between 1980 and 1987, twenty-nine borrowed between 1980 and 1983. Because the 1980-1987 borrowing was heavily concen-trated early in that time span, the 1980-1987 and 1990-1994 periods are more comparable than might initially be imagined.

12. There are other conditions for interest avoidance, e.g., no borrowing between October 1 and December 31. Also, if a states does owe interest, repayment of these financing charges can be deferred for up to 15 months following the September 30 due date, with additional interest accru-ing on the unpaid balance.

13. Debt repayment behavior also changed as a result of the Social Security Amendments of 1983 that gave debtor states strong financial incentives to improve solvency and repay debt through a combination of benefit reductions and tax increases. Three distinct financial incentives were offered: deferred payment of interest, lower interest rates, and reduced FUTA penalty taxes.

14. One summary of the changes in state repayment patterns during the 1980s is given in chapter 1, tables 1.5 and 1.6, of Vroman (1990).

15. Specific details of the benefit reductions enacted by states with the biggest financing prob-lems in the early 1980s are provided in chapter 2 of Vroman (1986).

16. The concentration of reserve losses among a few big states is not unique to the 1990-1992 downturn. During the recession of the early 1980s, four large industrial states (illinois, Michigan, Ohio, and Pennsylvania) accounted for about 80 percent of total borrowing.

17. A partial list would include: (1) state legislative actions to improve solvency, (2) automatic changes in taxes and benefit payments activated by reductions in trust fund balances, and (3) the size and persistence of the increase in unemployment (a proxy for the depth of the recession in the state).

18. The recession might be characterized as bicoastal simply because California is so large relative to other states on the West Coast. Note in table 9.4B that for the other four states in the Pacific division the ratio of unemployment rates ranges from low to high as follows: Washington (0.937), Alaska (1,005), Hawaii (1.058), and Oregon (1.070). None of these four states had its unemployment rate ratio increase by even half of the national average increase.

19. The other four are California, Mississippi, Missouri, and Nevada.

20. Because the recent recession was comparatively mild, it should be kept in mind that larger reductions in HCMs would take place during a more serious downturn.

21. Note in the bottom panel of table 9.5 that ten states increased their HCMs during the 1979-1983 period. While we have not attempted to explain this pattern, it should be observed that several states with low and negative balances enacted solvency legislation during 1982 and 1983 with the specific objective of reducing indebtedness. State-level legislation contributed to these increases in reserves.

22. EUC benefits exceeded $250 million in every month between December 1991 and April 1994. Payments exceeded $1.0 billion in eighteen of these twenty-nine months. During 1992 and 1993, annual EUC benefits totaled more than half of regular UI benefits.

23. Connecticut was the only state to finance its 1991-1994 borrowing with state-issued bonds. The state's motivation was to save on interest costs since state debt is tax-free ,and interest rates are lower than for U.S. Treasury debt. During the mid-1980s, Louisiana and West Virginia also used this method to repay Title XII debts. See Vroman (1993) for an analysis of state bond issuance and a comparison with traditional borrowing from the U.S. Treasury.

24. Minnesota provides for a higher maximum benefit amount when the trust fund balance falls. Thus, its flexible benefit provision is not a flexible financing provision in the sense that it does not contribute to trust fund solvency.

25. The three elements of the Illinois trigger mechanism are the level of the trust fund, average employer tax rates, and the growth in first payments.

26. Experience-rating systems are of two general types: stock-based and flow-based. Stock-based systems (reserve ratio systems) use the employer's account balance (measured relative to either total or taxable payrolls) to gauge experience and to set individual employer tax rates. Flow-based systems 9benefit ratio, benefit wage ratio, and payroll decline systems) use measures of benefit payouts and/or payrolls of liable employers to set individual employer tax rates. In both types of systems, the indicator of experience causes taxes to increase following recession-related benefit payouts.

27. Reserve ratio calculations take into account the entire experience (contributions minus benefits charged) since the employer was in existence, while benefit ratio formulation uses only the last three years of benefits.

28. The other states are Alaska, Idaho, Iowa, Kansas, Vermont, and Washington.

29. How much the size of the tax base affects responsiveness depends also on the number of payroll years that reserve ratio and benefit ratio states use to measure their experience rate. Interestingly, adding years to the denominator of the reserve ratio will increase responsiveness, while the opposite is true for a benefit ratio calculation. During recessions, taxable payroll for some employers decreases quickly, pushing the reserve ratio up and thus causing a lowering of the tax

rate. In a benefit ratio calculation, the declining wages tend to increase the tax rate on employers. Previously, six states used only the last year of taxable wages in the denominator of the reserve ratio calculation. This number had declined to three states in 1995: Massachusetts, South Carolina, and wisconsin.

30. Among these are a short lag between computation date and effective date of new tax rates, narrow intervals between tax schedule triggers and between tax rate triggers within schedules, trust-fund-activated employee taxes, not crediting solvency taxes to employer reserve accounts, and not limiting year-to-year rate or schedule changes.

31. See Worden and Vroman (1991). Appendix A of their paper shows the model's equations.

32. Worker sacrifices have two components: increased employee taxes and reduced benefits to claimants.

33. We do not know of research to formalize the rates of return calculations that support arguments for maintaining funds with employers as opposed to holding reserves in trust funds. Certainly, arguments to lower taxes on employers would be weakened if trust fund reserves were invested in assets with higher rates of return than U.S. government debt.

34. Again, rhetoric and casual observation provide much of the basis for this assertion. It would be useful to investigate the issue within a formal statistical (regression) framework.

References

Advisory Council on Unemployment Compensation. 1995. "Unemployment Insurance in the United States: Benefits, Financing, Coverage." ACUC, February.

Commerce Clearing House. 1995. *Topical law Reports: Unemployment Insurance Reporter.* Chicago: Commerce Clearing House.

Haber, William, and Merrill Murray. 1966. *Unemployment Insurance in the American Economy.* Homewood, IL: Richard D. Irwin.

U.S. Department of Labor, 1992. *Unemployment Insurance Financial Data, ET Handbook 394,* Employment and Training Administration.

_____. 1995. "Significant Provisions of State Unemployment Insurance Laws, July 3, 1994," and earlier issues. Unemployment Insurance Service.

Vroman, Wayne. 1986. *The Funding Crisis in State Unemployment Insurance.* Kalamazoo, MI: W.E. Upjohn Institute.

_____. 1990. *Unemployment Insurance Trust Fund Adequacy in the 1990s.* Kalamazoo, MI: W.E. Upjohn Institute.

_____. 1993. "Alternatives for Financing State Unemployment Insurance Trust Fund Debts: Final Report." Report to the U.S. Department of Labor, Unemployment Insurance Service, July.

Worden, Kelleen, and Wayne Vroman. 1991. "Flexible Financing in State Unemployment Insurance Laws." Urban Institute, April.

CHAPTER 10

Fraud, Abuse, and Errors in the Unemployment Insurance System
Extent, Measurement, and Correction

Burman Skrable
UI Service, U.S. Department of Labor

This chapter examines the extent of financial losses or leakages in the federal-state system of unemployment insurance (UI) in the United States. "Leakages" or "losses" will be used interchangeably to refer to funds due the UI system that it failed to receive, benefits wrongly paid out, and other resources lost. Where possible, the chapter attempts to distinguish losses resulting from intentional (fraudulent) actions by claimants, employers and UI agency staff from those occurring for nonfraudulent reasons.

The UI system is a major social insurance program in the United States. In fiscal year (FY) 1995, a year of relatively low unemployment, total UI program benefit payments amounted to $21 billion, state tax collections (contributions) were $23 billion, federal collections for various federal and federal-state extended benefit programs and administration were $5.5 billion, and allocations to state employment security agencies (SESAs) for administration were $3.6 billion. Due to the size and complexity of the system, the incentives facing claimants and employers, and the limited administrative funding available to enforce compliance, the UI system contains many areas of opportunity for the inappropriate use of funds. Policy makers, as well as other stakeholders in the system, want to know the causes of errors and misuses as well as the scale of fraud and abuse, so that these problems can be minimized.

In a discussion of the loss of funds from a social insurance system due to error or fraud, the legal and economic views are related but not identical, and both are of interest. The law's main concern is whether the losses are fraudulent or erroneous. Legally, the question is the following: did the person *willfully or intentionally* misrepresent facts affecting benefit eligibility or tax liability? Although state laws vary considerably in whether any given action involving the UI system involves fraud, all states have much more severe penalties and can exercise a greater variety of recovery options in the case of fraud. The range of state fraud laws must be kept in mind whenever a national estimate of "UI fraud" is offered.

The economic view is broader and concerned more with knowing why payment errors occur so that they can be prevented. Economists also want to know the size of errors, so that the costs and benefits of prevention or recovery strategies can be determined. Economists tend toward a threefold classification of overpayments. First, there are small random mistakes due to inadvertence by both UI staff and claimants or employers. Second, in complex programs such as UI, characterized by many involved provisions for benefit eligibility and tax liability, the range of errors due to lack of knowledge or the time to make thorough determinations is considerable. Such errors would be systematically related to the complexity of the program but can be reduced by better training of staff, systematizing procedures, and educating claimants and employers. Third, some claimants and employers will intentionally cheat. Economists go beyond merely calling this "fraud" to analyzing the extent to which the system provides incentives and disincentives for such behavior. They reason that certain individuals weigh the benefits of cheating against its "cost" in terms of the likelihood of being detected and the penalty they face if caught and act accordingly to maximize their incomes. In the case of UI, the balance of incentives certainly appears to favor fraudulent behavior. The rules are complex. Claimants and employers provide crucial information that is expensive to verify. Administrative budgets to process tax and benefit actions are spare. Because of the desire to ensure customer service and to meet promptness standards, timeliness has been emphasized over accuracy. Thus, the chance of detection is low. Penalties are relatively light in most cases.[1]

This chapter is organized around a description of the major UI resource flows, since these constitute the potential sources for misuse through errors and fraud. At each critical point in the review, the size of the basic funding flow is identified, and the potential for leakage at the point is explained. If leakages at that point are regularly measured by the current system of monitoring, current practice is described, and a brief historical sketch is provided of the development of the present measurement or assessment approach. The most recent estimate of leakages at that point will also be given, along with what has been done or is being done to stanch the outflows, recover overpayments, or collect outstanding debts.

The chapter concludes with a discussion of some technical issues and measurement gaps. The main ones involve measuring: (1) the extent to which current estimates from the Benefits Quality Control (BQC)[2] program of dollar overpayments actually represent true dollar losses to the UI system, (2) the accuracy of claims denial decisions, and (3) the degree to which employers comply with contributions (payroll tax) laws.

Major Financial and Information Flows in the Unemployment Insurance System

Figure 10.1 outlines the principal financial and information flows that characterize the UI system. In nearly all cases, each financial flow is accompanied by a counterflowing stream of information from claimants and employers. Very often, the information is essential to determining the proper size of the corresponding financial flow. In fact, the opportunity for fraud or other abuse often arises from the fact that the beneficiary or taxpayer controls the information. This is the essential *moral hazard* problem in principal-agent relations. The six important flows depicted in figure 10.1 are each described in the following subsections.

The Benefits Flow

In the UI process, the state employment security agency (SESA) obtains information from individuals when they file an initial or continued claim for benefits. This is combined with data from employers on the person's base-period earnings and/or weeks of work and reason for

Figure 10.1 Major Financial and Information Flows in the United States Unemployment Insurance System

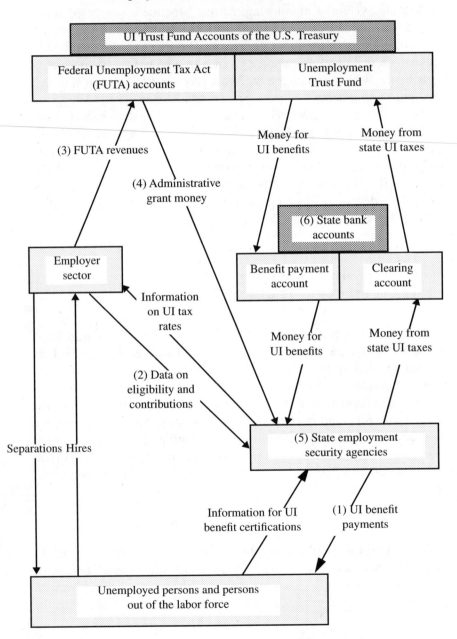

separation. Together, this material allows the SESA to determine initial monetary and nonmonetary eligibility for UI benefits and subsequently to make benefit payments. In fourteen of the past twenty-five years, benefit payments were the largest financial flow in the UI system. In calendar year (CY) 1994, the UI benefit payment outflow was approximately $22.6 billion. Benefit payments included the following main components:

• Regular state UI	$21.657 billion
• Federal-state extended	0.220
• Ex-Federal Employees UCFE)	0.275
• Ex-Servicemembers (UCX)	0.347
• Disaster Unemployment Assistance	0.114
• Trade Readjustment Allowances	0.130
Total	$22.743 billion

State Contributions and Reimbursements

Over 98 percent of the 6 million employing units covered by the system are subject to UI payroll tax contributions and are referred to as "contributory employers." They make quarterly contributions (tax payments) to the UI trust fund based on their taxable quarterly wages and their SESA-determined tax rate. Most employer tax rates are experience rated: after a lag of one to three years, depending on the state, the UI tax rates of employers reflect the benefits paid to their former employees. For purposes of UI financing, the remaining 2 percent of UI-covered employers are referred to as reimbursing employers. This group includes mostly state and local governmental units and nonprofit agencies. From the standpoint of UI, these employers are self-insured; they repay benefit charges dollar-for-dollar and are not subject to a state experience-rating tax scheme.

In CY 1994, the sources of funds were as follows:

• State Contributions	$21.975 billion
• State Reimbursements	1.140
Total	$23.115 billion

Federal Unemployment Tax Act Revenues

In addition to making state UI tax payments, contributory employers remit a flat federal tax on wages paid to each employee. This tax, paid to the IRS, is 0.8 percent of annual wages up to the maximum of the federal taxable wage base, presently set at $7,000 per calendar year. These collections were approximately $5.5 billion in FY 1995. The revenue is apportioned by formula among the Employment Security Administration Account (ESAA), the Extended Unemployment Compensation Account (EUCA), and the Federal Unemployment Account (FUA). (See the appendix to chapter 8.) In FY 1995, 85 percent of Federal Unemployment Tax Act (FUTA) revenue went to the ESAA.

Administrative Grants

From the ESSA, the federal government provides grants to states to administer the state and federal unemployment compensation programs, the Employment Service (ES), and the Veterans Employment and Training Service (VETS). The UI administrative grants are tied to the UI workload—benefit payment and tax collection activities. Each quarter, states receive a formula-driven *base* amount to fund their continuing program level. If their workload exceeds a certain amount, they may also claim additional *contingency* funding. In FY 1995, these costs amounted to $3.6 billion:

- State UI $2.3 billion
- Federal programs   0.2
- ES, VETS   1.1

UI Administration

As listed, in FY 1995 SESAs received $2.3 billion to administer their state UI programs and another $200 million to administer federal unemployment compensation programs. There is potential for fraudulent state use of funds allocated to pay for administration.

Trust Fund Operations

As noted, in FY 1995 the federal-state UI system collected some $23 billion from employers and paid out roughly the same amount in benefits to claimants. Money deposited to and withdrawn from the Unemployment Trust Fund (UTF) accounts at the U.S. Treasury passes through state bank accounts called the UI Clearing Account on the way to the Treasury and the UI Benefit Payment Account on the way from the Treasury. Although states are legally required to deposit employer contributions and other monies for the unemployment fund (e.g., benefit overpayment recoveries) and any interest earnings on those funds into the UTF, state treasurers and banks have an obvious financial motive for leaving unemployment funds in state bank accounts as long as possible, to defray bank charges through earnings on compensating balances.

The following sections describe the main risks of financial *loss* that may be encountered because of fraud or errors at each of the six points that have been summarized. Also reviewed is how the federal-state UI system now attempts to assess the risks and to measure the losses. A brief history of the development of the assessment approach is given, together with recent estimates of losses. The summary and conclusions section reviews how data have been used to prevent future losses and suggests further steps that might be taken.

Types of Benefit Payment Errors

UI provides temporary, partial wage replacement as a matter of right to involuntarily unemployed workers with substantial attachment to the labor force. States evaluate labor force attachment by reviewing the extent of work and/or earnings in a twelve-month *base period* preceding the application for unemployment benefits. Furthermore, states closely scrutinize reasons for separation from work, as well as the claimant's continuing ability, availability, and degree of active work-search to ensure that the claimant is truly unemployed and not actually out of the labor force.

Determining UI eligibility thus involves tests at three levels: (1) monetary, (2) separation, and (3) continuing eligibility. Risks for wrong payments or payments to ineligible persons exist at all stages. The common thread linking these risks is that of *moral hazard*: potential beneficiaries supply some of the information needed to determine benefit eligibility and therefore have the ability to withhold critical facts. Realities of time and cost force the UI system to accept information provided by claimants and employers as valid, especially in the short term. This leaves the system open to many risks of improper payment. The following reviews the main risks at each eligibility level.

Losses Based on Monetary Eligibility

In all but two states, monetary eligibility is determined through examining computerized agency wage record data. These data are also used to set the weekly benefit amount for claimants deemed monetarily eligible. There are two main kinds of risks.

- A *fictitious employer* is an imaginary enterprise that establishes an employer account with the SESA. It submits bogus wage records for imaginary employees on whom it initially pays UI taxes. The ostensibly laid-off workers then file claims based on those fictitious wage payments. This practice is clear and intentional fraud.

- *Routine monetary errors* due to inaccurately maintained and/or submitted payroll data by employers are numerous. Most cause small dollar mistakes in claimants' weekly benefit amounts, but when added together they are important sources of error, and both underpayments and overpayments from this source probably exceed fictitious employer losses. In the aggregate, base-period wage errors tend to result in just about the same dollars overpaid as underpaid.

Losses Due to Separation Violations

Claimants must have been separated from work through no fault of their own. Such separations include various categories of quits for good cause and discharges without cause. In six states, even claimants who quit or were discharged for disqualifying reasons become eligible for UI benefits if they remain unemployed long enough. The main type of fraud under this category occurs when claimants who quit or were legitimately discharged for improper workplace behavior file for benefits alleging "lack of work" and their claims go unchallenged by their separating employer.

Leakages Due to Continuing Eligibility Violations

Claimants must be able, available, and actively seeking work, and may not refuse an offer of suitable work during each period of unemployment claimed (usually one week). States consider refusal of suitable work to be the most serious of these violations and typically penalize it by stopping benefits for the remainder of the benefit year and canceling wage credits. In practice, this seems to happen infrequently. Most continuing eligibility violations occur because claimants are unable to work or are unavailable for the week claimed, fail to make a proper search for work, or fail to meet the test of being unemployed because of excess earnings or other income. The claimants then either fail to inform the agency that they have not met the eligibility conditions or consciously give wrong information. In the broadest sense, the latter is fraudulent behavior, although, depending on the state, much of it may not be considered fraud.

Measurement and Detection of Benefit Payment Errors

The UI program has two principal kinds of systems for identifying, estimating, and/or detecting improper benefit payments. These are: (1) Benefit Payment Control (BPC) activities and systems, designed to detect and deter fictitious employers and individuals who have disqualifying income while in claims status and, where feasible, to recover overpaid amounts; and (2) the Benefits Quality Control (BQC) program, a sample-based system for estimating the extent and nature of improper payments so that deficient processes may be improved.

Benefit Payment Control

All detection and recovery systems come under the common rubric of BPC. The systems attempt to detect specific instances of error and abuse, and, where the dollar amount involved is large enough to justify the cost of pursuit, to initiate recovery procedures. SESAs are encouraged to publicize prosecutions for fraud widely to discourage others from engaging in such practices.

Systems for Fictitious Employers

For some twenty years, there has been continuing concern about detecting—and, more importantly, preventing—the various kinds of fictitious employer schemes that could defraud the UI system of massive sums. The mainstay is the Fictitious Employer Detection System (FEDS). It comprises two subsystems. The New Employer/Employee Tracking System (NETS) uses data in SESA records to determine within 15 weeks of a claim being filed against a new account whether that account is legitimate. The Legitimate Employer Claims Analysis System (LECAS) identifies for review employers engaging in certain suspicious claims patterns, e.g., both the employer and claimant addresses were post office boxes.

Because of the age of the FEDS systems, administrators in some states believe that sophisticated thieves have identified ways of avoiding detection. Other techniques to spot fictitious employers and similar, fictitious claims include monitoring and following up on frequent claimant address changes, looking for multiple UI benefit checks mailed to a single address, verifying that claimants are not ineligible illegal aliens through the Systematic Alien Verification for Entitlement (SAVE) program, and using the Enumeration Verification System (EVS) to identify persons filing claims with other than their own social security numbers.

Systems for Detecting Disqualifying Income

The BPC system also includes mechanisms designed to detect disqualifying income. A person with more than a certain amount of income in a week, whether from earnings or most other sources, is ineligible for a UI benefit that week. The most significant type of tool used for detection is the crossmatch and postaudit. To find claimants with disqualifying earnings within their states, most SESAs use the Model Crossmatch system, a computer match of the prior six months of claimant records with employer wage records. Five states use the more extensive Benefit Audit, Reporting, and Tracking System (BARTS), which allows a full one-year match. Nearly all states use a similar crossmatch, called the Interstate Crossmatch/Claimant Locator, each quarter to detect individuals making claims in one state while working in another. It also allows them to locate persons with outstanding overpayment balances who have left the state. Because they rely on wage records, these crossmatches can detect only private sector work. Depending on their laws and economies, some states use similar crossmatches to detect ineligible workers in government jobs, including federal, state, county, municipal, National Guard, and the military reserves.

All crossmatching systems first detect potential violators, then apply variable dollar screens to indicate those with the greatest recovery potential. BPC staff verify week-by-week earnings of the indicated claimants with employers. The last step is to audit claimants and to set up overpayments for recovery as warranted.

Other Crossmatches

States have at their disposal a variety of other systems that use crossmatching to detect specific types of disqualifying income or disqualifying conditions. There are social security, workers' compensation, and Railroad Retirement crossmatch systems for disqualifying income. Some states also review or match prison data, death records, Job Service hires, and special employer new-hire reports to detect other disqualifying conditions.

Less Systematic Approaches

BPC also relies on tips, referrals, and border checks to obtain allegations of fraud and abuse. Staff follow up with audits or investigations.

Estimating the Extent of Improper Payments: The Benefits Quality Control Program

The Benefits Quality Control (BQC) program is a system in place since 1987 to estimate the extent, kind, causes and responsibilities of dollars overpaid by the federal-state UI system. BQC also provides estimates of the dollar value of underpayments. Its design evolved in three main stages.

In the late 1970s, the UI Service developed measures of initial and continued claims accuracy as part of the Performance Standards

Project. Between 200 and 300 randomly sampled claimants were interviewed about both initial and continued claims activities in a review "designed to establish that the SESA made proper payments with the information that was available or which could have been obtained by utilizing proper interviewing techniques" (U.S. Department of Labor 1976-1977, p. II-8). Measures of initial and continued claims performance became part of the UI Quality Appraisal system for assessing program performance but were not used to estimate dollars overpaid or underpaid.

In 1979, the National Commission on Unemployment Compensation (NCUC) funded a pilot test in six cities of a new approach to determining payment accuracy. Randomly selected samples of UI benefits were thoroughly analyzed for accuracy to estimate the "true" level of improper payments. The examination included in-person contacts with the claimant, employers, and third parties to verify pertinent information. The investigation also involved a postaudit, similar to the current BPC crossmatch, to detect earnings during the claim period. This study estimated overpayments at several times the rate BPC detected.[3] The U.S. Department of Labor then funded a replication of this random audit (RA) study in five states. When statewide findings confirmed the results obtained in the pilot study conducted in cities, the Department of Labor began extending RA to other states. By 1984, forty-six states were conducting random audit investigations, each on a minimum of 400 sampled cases per year. Estimated overpayments averaged about 12 percent of benefits, implying some $1.5 billion overpaid for the system at the time.

In 1983, in response to overpayment issues raised by the U.S. Department of Labor Inspector General in connection with RA findings, the department convened an interagency Benefit Payment Oversight Committee. The committee recommended that the department establish a formal BQC system. The BQC program was phased in voluntarily and became mandatory in 1987. Its methodology was adapted from RA experience. However, BQC sample sizes were larger and varied by size of state to enable more precise estimates of error types and causes. BQC also adopted an explicit commitment to using the data for program improvement and compiled a more extensive record on each case sampled for this purpose.

Since 1987, all SESAs except the Virgin Islands have been required by regulation to operate BQC programs to assess the accuracy of their UI benefit payments. The BQC programs operate as follows: each state draws a weekly sample of payments. Annual samples presently average slightly over 800 cases per state, with a range of 480 to 1,800. A specially trained staff reviews SESA records and contacts the claimant, employers, and third parties to verify all the information pertinent to the benefit amount for the sampled week. Initially, all verifications were done in person. Since July 1993, after a pilot test showed that certain aspects of claims could be verified more efficiently with little loss of thoroughness by telephone, investigators have been allowed to use a mix of in-person and telephone/fax contacts. Using the verified information, investigators determine what the benefit payment should have been to accord fully with state law and policy. Any differences between the actual and reconstructed amount are underpayment or overpayment errors and are recorded in a specially provided computer along with their types, causes, and responsibilities. This information is used to estimate the extent of improper payments in the state to guide possible future program improvements. In FY 1995, states received approximately $26 million to operate the BQC program.

Estimated and Detected Overpayments

Table 10.1 presents data on estimated and detected benefit overpayments during CY 1994. The BQC estimate covered a $21.2 billion universe—some 93 percent of all benefit payments, with interstate benefits the main area outside its review. In the aggregate, approximately $1.82 billion, or 8.6 percent, was overpaid. State overpayment rates ranged from 1.9 percent to 17.7 percent. About 11 percent of BQC-detected overpayments occurred at the monetary determination level, 16 percent resulted from separation decisions, and the remaining 73 percent were due to various continuing eligibility violations. Of the eligibility violations, excess earnings during the benefit period and other failures to maintain eligibility, principally neglecting to register with the Job Service, were most important. Overpayments classified as fraud totaled an estimated $390 million (not shown in table).

**Table 10.1 Fiscal year and Calendar Year 1994 Estimated and Detected
Leakages by Source ($millions)**

	Estimated	Detected	Recovered
A. Benefit payments	$1,820	$543	$257
1. Monetary eligibility	201	NA	NA
a. Fictitious employers	---	6	NA
2. Separation	294	10	NA
3. Continuing eligibility		NA	NA
a. Work search	321	NA	NA
b. Other (fail to register)	431	NA	NA
c. Benefit yr. earnings	437	173	NA
d. Other disqualifying income	137	NA	NA
4. Not attributable to stage of eligibility determination	---	354	257
B. Contributions and reimbursements	935	311	53
1. Tax rate errors	NA	NA	NA
2. Underreported contributions	935	53	53
3. Hidden employers	NA	NA	NA
4. Uncollected receivables	NA	258	NA
C. FUTA tax payments	NA	NA	NA
D. Administrative fund allocations			
1. Overstated workload	NA	NA	NA
E. Agency administrative operations	0.7	1.0	NA
UI staff losses involving:			
1. Benefits	0.3	0.1	
2. Contributions	0.3	0.4	
3. Administrative funds	0.1	0.5	
F. Trust tund operations	4.6	NA	NA
1. Clearing account	4.6	NA	
2. Benefit payment account	NA	NA	
G. Total—all sources	$2,760	$855	$310

NOTE: NA = not available.

For the same time period, BPC activities identified $543 million in actual overpayments potentially subject to recovery, of which $220 million constituted fraud. Since BQC and BPC report data in somewhat different formats, and the methods used to detect 58 percent of overpayments ($312 million) were not specified, it is not possible to provide the same breakdowns of data on estimated, detected, and recovered overpayments. It may be presumed that most of BPC detections involve excess earnings and other income during the benefit year, the aggregate of which BQC estimated at $574 million in 1994.[4] Fictitious employer detections were $6 million, and overpayments identified through employer protests (mostly involving reason for separation) were only $10 million.

Types of Errors in Employer Contributions

UI contributing employers pay a quarterly tax on the wages (up to the state's annual maximum wage base) of their covered employees. Typically, they receive a quarterly form containing their tax rate from the SESA. Employers report total and taxable wages of employees paid during the quarter on this form, and return it with the tax payment due. Annual earnings exceed the taxable wage base for most workers. In 1994, earnings taxable for UI amounted to only 36.2 percent of all wages paid to workers covered by the UI system. For these taxable wages, the main sources of losses in contributions have been (1) errors in the tax rate, (2) underreported employees or wages per employee, (3) *hidden employers*, and (4) unpaid or uncollected contributions due.

Errors in the Tax Rate

The fifty-three UI jurisdictions each use one of four basic experience-rating approaches. The actual rate formulas can be very involved. Complexities increase when firms merge or hire workers through employee-leasing companies. The U.S. Department of Labor presently has no data on the extent of errors in experience-rated taxes or on the degree to which such mistakes might cancel one another out in the aggregate. A recent internal security panel did, however, identify tax rate errors as a major UI risk area.[5] Procedures implemented in 1996 to assess the quality of tax operations will judge tax rate accuracy. The approach adopted involves evaluating the SESA's controls designed to ensure tax rate accuracy and determining whether these are operative by drawing a small (60 accounts) acceptance sample. However, the acceptance sample is not designed to yield an estimate of tax rate errors.

Underreported Employees and Wages

Since early in the history of the federal-state UI program, SESAs have been required to audit covered employers. The Quality Appraisal system set a Desired Level of Achievement (DLA) for the fraction of employers audited each year. Remaining at 4 percent for many years, it was recently reduced to 2 percent when audit quality standards were tightened. Similar to BPC operations, these audits were principally designed as an efficient means of ensuring compliance with UI laws and timely collection of taxes. During CY 1994, SESAs audited 129,000 firms, identifying $53 million in underreported contributions and $8 million in overreported contributions.

Although existing field audits tend to be cost-effective, SESAs select firms for audit in many ways; none of them permit states to estimate the extent of underreporting as BQC does for benefit overpayments. Estimating underreporting has, however, been considered by the U.S. Department of Labor and remains under consideration. A model for this approach has been tried. In 1989, Illinois estimated 1987 employer compliance by carefully auditing 875 randomly selected firms. Nearly 45 percent of firms had some underreporting error; 13.6 percent of employees were unreported, with most of them having been misclassified as independent contractors. The researchers who conducted the project estimated that covered wages were underreported by $1.18 billion (4.2 percent) and contributions by $45 million. Although it was a one-time sample and included only firms headquartered in Illinois, the authors nevertheless concluded that "since reporting requirements as well as noncompliance detection probabilities and penalties in Illinois are typical of those in other states" the findings may have national applicability.[6] An underreporting rate of 4.2 percent for taxable wages, at the 2.6 percent U.S. average tax rate in 1994, implies leakages of about $935 million.

Hidden Employers

SESAs routinely pursue many avenues to identify firms that choose not to register. These include scanning yellow page listings, reviewing business license lists and other tax filings, and conducting additional forms of outreach. Many employers are only spotted when claimants file for benefits and the agency has no wage records: these are called *blocked claims*. There are no estimates of the potential number of hidden employers.

Unpaid Tax Liabilities

Each quarter, about 11 percent of employers provide late wage reports and tax payments or fail to report at all. At the end of CY 1994, the states had about $1.8 billion in due but uncollected UI taxes. As a rule of thumb, most amounts not collected within 15 months will not be obtained. At the end of 1994, uncollected taxes of $1.37 billion were at least 15 months old. The bulk of receivables remains in SESA accounts due to state laws that prohibit removal regardless of age. (Some indebtedness can be as much as fifty years old.) In 1994, states accrued $2.264 billion in new accounts determined receivable (ADR), and collected (liquidated) $2.007 billion, a difference of $257 million. Also during that year, they wrote off $239 million as uncollectible, so total amounts due grew by only $18 million. It must be noted that ADRs, write-offs and liquidations relate to different time periods. Most ADRs are terminated within a quarter or two, but some liquidations and most write-offs pertain to receivables established years earlier.

Federal Taxes

How well the conclusions of the previous section apply to FUTA payments is not known. The two taxes have one major difference: the FUTA tax is not experience rated, and thus fewer rate errors should be involved. Most employers pay a net FUTA tax rate of 0.8 percent of each employee's first $7,000 in annual wages.[7] It should also be noted that the FUTA tax base of $7,000 applies to the earnings of all workers. By contrast, in 1994, thirty-nine states had higher taxable wage bases for determining their state UI tax, ranging up to $25,500 in Hawaii.

Administrative Grants

The U.S. Department of Labor provides SESAs with funds for UI administration based on forecasts of workload (benefit payment and tax collection activities). After a completed quarter, states determine whether their workload was high enough to have earned their projected funds. If the workload exceeded the amount needed to fund the base allocation, states may be entitled to additional contingency funds. Fund claims are based on a series of key "workload items," such as initial and continued claims taken, nonmonetary determinations made, number of subject employers, and lower authority appeals. The risk of funding misuse arises mostly from inaccurate workload reports. For many years, these data have been validated against federal definitions through the Workload Validation program to minimize losses through overreporting; data from the program are not amenable for use in assessing potential leakages from this source.

SESA Administrative Operations

Within SESAs, the bulk of UI administrative effort is directed toward accomplishing the primary mission of paying benefits and collecting taxes. The remaining effort is spent on the various housekeeping or overhead functions supporting that mission: personnel activities, computer operations, procurement, research and analysis, and evaluation. The major vehicle for examining all of these operations is called Internal Security, which comprises a variety of "risk assessments" of all SESA functions, including those involving its chief mission. As such, Internal Security often overlaps with other assessment or quality assurance activities, including BPC, Revenue Quality Control, investigations or studies spawned by the findings of BQC and various audit efforts. Internal Security assessments often lead to internal investigations and/or audits.

The U.S. Department of Labor recently funded a risk-assessment project. In it, Internal Security experts from fifteen states identified and ranked internal risks of various sources. Principal risks to benefit payment integrity involved centralized check-printing and the possibility for SESA employees to process UI benefit claims for friends and family members. In the tax area, the experts noted numerous weaknesses in current centralized cashiering processes, lack of audit trails, lack of intact deposits in the field, and poor physical security for staff and buildings in the field. In other aspects of agency operations, the report noted numerous risks to computer systems: lack of passwords and identification numbers or infrequent changes to them, lack of backups of key systems and files, ability of dial-up users to change the state UI data bases or to obtain information without identifying themselves and a general lack of computer controls.

In FY 1995, states reported detecting approximately $1 million in UI employee fraud through their internal security operations. Half involved SESA administrative funds, most of this lost through embezzlement. A total of about $150,000 in misappropriated UI benefits was detected, mostly involving improper claims for others. The remainder involved contributions, of which misappropriated refunds was the largest source. In addition, SESA staff estimated undetected losses of $650,000 and that their controls prevented another $1.7 million from being lost.

Trust Fund Operations

The Secretary of the Treasury is trustee for the Unemployment Trust Fund (UTF) established under section 904 of the Social Security Act (SSA). The UTF contains a separate subaccount for each state. These accounts increase with the deposit of UI tax collections from employers and from interest accruals, and they decrease as states withdraw funds to make benefit payments. To avoid having to borrow or to delay benefits in recession years when UI payments are high, states are encouraged to build up reserve balances in years of low unemployment. Ideally, reserves would be accumulated by drawing contributions from employers when the economy is expanding, and reserves would be drawn down by increasing benefit payments that maintain aggregate spending during recessions. In chapter 9, the macroeconomic stabilizing aspect of ideal UI financing is examined.

Funds going into and out of the UTF pass through operational accounts for each state: the Clearing Account for tax receipts and Benefit Payment Account for payments. The main risk of losses to or leakages from the trust fund, and therefore to the UI system, comes from states that retain balances in operational accounts longer than permitted under applicable federal law (SSA, FUTA, Cash Management Improvement Act [CMIA]). In doing this, states are tempted to use interest accruals for purposes other than paying benefits or refunding employers, proscribed by the so-called "withdrawal standard." Actual diversion of funds is always a theoretical risk but in practice is fairly easy to detect and would occasion an immediate conformity action.

Inflows into the trust fund through the Clearing Account are subject to the "immediate deposit" requirement (FUTA section 3304[a][3] and SSA section 303[a][4]). In practice, the U.S. Department of Labor has interpreted this by establishing a DLA of two days for transfers from the Clearing Account to the trust fund. In FY 1994, thirty-six states met or exceeded this DLA: eight typically made transfers within one day. Data show that fourteen states failed to meet the DLA (Virgin Islands data are unavailable). Their deposits, totaling nearly $7.0 billion, took an average of 5.6 days to be deposited in the UTF. This is almost four days longer than the standard. At the average interest rate the funds would have earned (6.76 percent), this implies losses of $4.6 million to the UTF.[8]

Until the CMIA of 1990 became effective in 1993, the U.S. Department of Labor monitored a DLA for withdrawals from the Benefit Payment Account, similar to the one for Clearing Account transfers. Since 1993, payment account withdrawals have been managed according to individual draw-down agreements between the states and the U.S. Treasury. These allow many states to retain cash balances amounting to a few days of UI benefit payments in order to defray bank charges. Nevertheless, balances for thirteen states averaged only 0.5 days worth of payments or less: six states had zero balances. Among the fifty-one states that reported, the median balance was 1.6 days of UI benefit payments, with the maximum being 12 days.

Some Qualification and Measurement Issues

The decision environment of the federal-state UI system is ever changing. The general tightness of government budgets has affected the availability of UI administrative funding. States have been forced to reexamine priorities and to seek less expensive means of paying benefits and collecting taxes. At the same time, technology seems to be offering simpler, more convenient, and less costly ways for states to make benefit payments. Following the lead of Colorado, several states have begun to take UI benefit claims over the telephone. Other states have experimented with different alternatives to paying by check. The effect of these changes on program integrity and on the willingness and ability of states to assess risk is unknown. In the short run, tighter budgets are inducing states to emphasize their basic mission at the expense of monitoring integrity. Under the newly proposed comprehensive improvement system called UI Performs, the U.S. Department of Labor has suggested reducing the benefit payment accuracy sample to about half the size used by the BQC program, and allowing states complete flexibility to verify information for sampled units by telephone, mail, and fax instead of in person.

The previous sections of this chapter have reviewed the comprehensive range of efforts taken to identify and correct financial leakages from the UI system. To identify or measure actual or potential losses, states use detection and recovery systems such as BPC and employer field audits, as well as estimation systems such as BQC. Nonetheless, some gaps and measurement issues remain. Four of these principal issues are discussed in the following subsections: (1) the meaning of overpayments as measured by the BQC system, (2) the effect of inaccurately denied claims, (3) the estimation of noncompliance with contribution reporting requirements, and (4) the size of interest losses due to excess state cash balances.

The Meaning of Benefits Quality Control-Estimated Overpayments

The Random Audit BQC methodology estimates proper, under- and overpaid continued weeks claimed by extrapolating from estimates based on samples of individual weeks paid. The samples are drawn so as to provide an accurate cross-sectional picture of payments made in every state in every week. Each payment sampled is painstakingly reconstructed in accordance with written state law and policy. For 1994, BQC estimated that, if all payments had been made correctly, UI outlays would have been $19.58 billion. That is, actual outlays of $21.21 would have been reduced by $1.85 billion of overpayments and increased by $0.19 billion of underpayments.

The $1.85 billion estimate of overpayments produced by the quality control group needs to be qualified. On the one hand, as a measurement vehicle it probably understates overpayments. Over the past three years, BQC was unable to verify half of worksearch contacts; according to BQC procedures, these are counted as proper. Also, as indicated in note 4, the BQC methodology is not as well suited as that of the BPC crossmatch and post audit to detecting concealed or underreported claimant earnings. Conceptually, on the other hand, BQC estimates tend to exaggerate overpayments. Maintaining continuing UI eligibility involves the joint fulfillment of two requirements: remaining unemployed and satisfying various eligibility conditions imposed by state UI law. Although the two conditions coincide closely, the fit is not perfect. BQC estimates the numbers of weeks and dollars that should not have been paid because eligibility conditions were not fulfilled. Many of those claims involving continuing eligibility violations would, however, have been paid eventually for individuals with long unemployment terms.

The BQC methodology estimates overpayments by applying state UI eligibility provisions and the applicable state penalty structure. This approach implies that if claimants, employers, and SESA staff fulfilled all program requirements, overpayments and underpayments would be eliminated and trust fund outlays would be reduced by the difference between the two—which amounted to $1.6 billion in 1994. While this assumption is valid for certain kinds of overpayment mistakes, e.g., monetary and most separation errors, it is not true for some other types.[9] Prime examples are failure to register with the Job Service and failure to make work search contacts. As an illustration, the typical penalty for neglecting to register with the Job Service for a particular week is loss of benefit eligibility for the week in question. Following state rules, BQC methodology assigns such an improperly paid week as an overpayment. However, this penalty typically does not reduce the total benefits payable on a claim; it simply delays payment. Further, available evidence is clear that relatively few UI claimants become reemployed through the Job Service, so the expected reduction in length of unemployment from one week's registration with the Job Service is much less than one week. The BQC method therefore over-estimates the savings to the UI Trust Fund if the spell of unemployment continues beyond the improperly paid week. The case of worksearch violations is a similar example, although not as extreme. Other, analogous situations could be cited.

The Accuracy of Benefit Denials

The UI system does not assess the accuracy of decisions to deny claims with the same intensity as benefit payments are investigated. In part, this is because denials are relatively infrequent: in 1994, only one in ten initial claims was denied for monetary reasons, one in eight monetarily eligible claims was denied for separation reasons, and one in sixty-one continued claims was denied for continuing eligibility reasons. Using data in claims files, each year the Quality Performance Index (QPI) rates adherence to procedures and application of law and policy for separation and continuing nonmonetary eligibility determinations. No field checking is done nor is accuracy per se determined. Claims denied for failing monetary eligibility conditions are not assessed at all. Thus, BQC's estimate of underpayments remains incomplete.

In 1987, the U.S. Department of Labor conducted a five-state pilot test of measuring denied claim accuracy using the BQC methodology. Initial errors in monetary denials averaged 23 percent and in nonmonetary denials about 15 percent before correction through redetermination or appeal. No dollar estimates could be attached to these findings. As part of the redesign of benefit and tax performance measures to be implemented through UI Performs, the accuracy of denial decisions will be assessed. In all probability, this will be done using the BQC field-verification approach. Pilot testing, due to start in 1997, will precede nationwide implementation.

Estimating Compliance with Contribution Reporting Requirements

As noted, the accuracy of contribution reports could be estimated by a general application of the Illinois model, in which a random sample of firms in each state is drawn and audited. An inference could then be made about overall compliance. Furthermore, noncompliance profiles developed in the process could be used to guide sample selection for future audits. Unfortunately, to achieve what is considered reasonably satisfactory precision, large audit samples would be needed because of the large firm-to-firm variation inherent in audit findings.

Design work by Abt Associates has suggested that stratified random samples of approximately 1,600 subject employers should be drawn in most states.[10] In the Illinois employer compliance pilot conducted in 1988, nearly 900 firms were sampled. Taking these as the range for a nationwide measurement effort, somewhere between 49,000 and 85,000 employers would have to be audited. This is a significant share of the 129,000 audits actually performed in 1994. The benefits and costs of mounting such a measurement effort are still being considered within the U.S. Department of Labor.

The Measurement of Foregone Interest from Unemployment Trust Fund Transfers

In the section on trust fund operations, an estimate of $4.6 million was given as the amount of funds lost by the UTF for fourteen states in 1994 that failed to meet the DLA of allowing at most two days for funds to reside in the clearing account before their transfer into the UTF. As noted, there is no comparable DLA for the maximum number of days payments should be retained in the Benefit Payment Account. A glance at U.S. Department of Labor data shows, however, wide variation across states in both series. Two states are able to transfer funds to the Clearing Account within 0.1 day, and seven states performed this task in 1 day or less, but one state took nearly 49 days. In the case of the Benefit Payment Account, six states held zero balances and the median was 1.6 days, but eight states exceeded 4.5 days with the highest being 12.1 days. Current banking technology permits both swifter transfer into the trust fund and much smaller balances in the Benefit Payment Account. In light of present technology—as shown by performance in many states—foregone interest would seem to be much greater than the estimate presented.

Summary and Conclusions

The estimates reported in this chapter suggest that losses to the UI system during CY 1994 were approximately $3 billion. This total amounted to about 7 percent of total system financial flows in 1994. Leakages from benefits were $1.9 billion, over 8 percent of benefit outlays. Leakages from the tax stream were composed primarily of estimated underreported contributions ($935 million) and known but uncollected contributions ($258 million). These leakages totaled approximately $1.2 billion, or 5 percent of state tax collections. For reasons outlined earlier in the chapter, estimates of leakages from both streams are probably somewhat low.

Despite some underestimates and missing data, the figures for UI system financial leakages given in this chapter seem to be in the right ballpark. The two largest missing components are underreported FUTA taxes and underreported state and FUTA taxes by "hidden" employers. A total of some $5.5 billion in FUTA taxes was actually paid in 1994. The fixed taxable wage base and tax rate for FUTA suggest that the rate of underreporting might be lower than for state UI taxes. If FUTA underreporting is of the same magnitude as state contributions, losses to the federal Treasury (not UI trust funds) could be on the order of $200 million. Hazarding a guess at how large the "hidden employer" problem might be is difficult, but for several reasons it might be assumed to be rather small. States routinely use many devices to identify subject employers—various checks with taxing and licensing agencies, reviewing classified ads, and the like. Blocked claims investigations turn up others as former employees claim benefits only to find their wages not on file with the UI agency. No estimates of these or of two other sources—misreporting due to improperly set state tax rates, or overpayments in administrative allocations due to overstated work-load data—have been attempted. Both can be expected to be small.

The UI system's partners tend to have different degrees of concern about leakages, with the federal partner, particularly the U.S. Department of Labor, tending to have a higher level. It is vested with oversight responsibilities, more detached from operational involvement, and more subject to concerns about fraud and abuse in the national political arena. It has thus tended to push or induce states to put more effort into performance measurement and other forms of integrity activities than they would generally select on their own.

Each state sees its response as involving a weighing of responsibilities, benefits, and costs. The first balance the state must strike is between operating the basic program and attempting to ensure its integrity. The typical SESA sees its primary duty as serving its customers by paying benefits and collecting taxes. The numerous opportunities and incentives for leakages created by the interaction of complex UI laws and policies and sparse administrative funding levels were noted earlier.

In this environment, integrity must be pursued by balancing various activities. The first involves integrity or performance measurement. The UI agency must have reliable assessments of the extent of under-collected or underpaid taxes and of over- and underpaid benefits to know how serious are its losses, where they occur, and why. Understanding the seriousness of its problem allows it to decide on the relative balance between operations and integrity activities. It must then assess how much energy to devote to further measurement and balance initiatives to change its legal framework, improve operational processes within a given legal framework, conduct activities designed to detect and deter leakages, and recover outstanding balances. At all levels, the U.S. Department of Labor has tried to increase states integrity efforts.

In the short run, UI agencies can often do little to change "the system"—the complex rules affecting benefit eligibility and tax liability—within which they work. For a number of historical reasons, most state UI systems have accrued a variety of subtle distinctions defining equitable treatment. Students of UI integrity, chief among them Kingston and Burgess, have pointed out that program complexity is quite costly, especially in terms of administrative effort, inequities among similarly situated claimants and employers, and incentives for fraud. They have urged states to consider simplifying their UI programs where possible.[11]

Despite the difficulties of altering the system, the results of performance measurements have led to changes in this environment. Both the Random Audit and BQC programs identified worksearch violations as a prime cause of benefit overpayments. (In the early years of Random Audit, worksearch issues accounted for an about half of measured overpayments.) In response, many states changed their worksearch requirements, generally to make them more liberal or to require claimants to receive a formal warning before a worksearch disqualification could be assessed. In 1994, work search accounted for only 17 percent of national average dollars overpaid, and the decline in work search overpayments represented most of the decrease in average overpayments. Changes in law accounted for much of the reduction in errors due to work search.

Changes in worksearch laws and policies have reduced worksearch-related errors, but the basic structure of incentives and disincentives making noncompliance attractive for many claimants and employers remains. BQC attributed half of its 1994 estimated overpayments solely to intentional or accidental claimant actions. This amounts to over $900 million. Adding in joint responsibilities with the UI agency or employers raises the figure to $1.2 billion. Employers are responsible for underreported taxes ($935 million). In addition, over $250 million of unpaid taxes could not be collected in 1994. Even though these losses largely reflect behavior UI agencies cannot affect directly, their size challenges the states and the U.S. Department of Labor to continue to address their causes.

Within a given system, states must next decide how much effort is warranted to prevent leakages by improving the efficiency of various processes. These decisions are generally guided by estimates of the size and causes of leakages and should be shaped by considerations of cost versus probable effectiveness. Performance measurements have played a noticeable role in process change. A salient example comes from Random Audit experience. Random Audit findings showed convincingly that states using computerized wage records made more accurate monetary determinations than those who requested monetary data from employers at the time of initial claims. Partly as a result, the number of wage-request states has gone from about a dozen in the early 1980s to two at present. Under the Quality Control program, states have conducted nearly 150 program improvement studies, funded either with grants or supported with BQC staff temporarily released from verification duties. They have implemented over 40 of the recommended improvements.

State efforts notwithstanding, BQC data suggest a slowing pace of improvement in accuracy. When states were first implementing Random Audit in the early 1980s, the national average overpayment rate was on the order of 12 to 15 percent. The first BQC report was for CY 1988; overpayments averaged 10.1 percent for the country. They have since fallen to about 8.6 percent, as of 1994. If Michigan is excluded, however, the decline is from 9 percent in 1988-1989 to 8.1 percent in 1990-1994.[12] The drop in overpayments due to worksearch violations has accounted for the entire decrease in BQC overpayments between 1988-1989 and 1992-1994, as it seems to have for the decline in Random Audit days as well.

Still, BQC data suggest a fertile area for further improvements in accuracy does lie within the agencies' direct control. Of the $1.82 billion overpayments estimated for 1994, SESAs were totally responsible for over $400 million. They shared accountability with others, mostly claimants, for another $290 million. The extent to which these "costs of complexity" can be reduced by process improvements is a direct challenge for the future. Many errors involve failure to register claimants with the Job Service. Even perfect registration of claimants would have only limited value in shortening unemployment durations for claimants.

Again using the calculus of costs versus expected benefits, states must decide how much effort should go into detecting and recovering overpaid benefits and underpaid taxes. As with many performance measurement systems, U.S. Department of Labor assistance, requirements, and funding have exerted an important influence on this integrity activity. Although such efforts "clean up" after leakages occur, making the system aware of them and their effectiveness is also intended to deter claimants and employers from committing fraudulent actions in the future. In 1994, BPC activities detected some $540 million in actual overpayments, about 30 percent of what BQC estimated in total. Of this, some $260 million was recovered. Field audits are the main tax equivalent to BPC activities. In 1994, field staff audited about 130,000 subject employers and identified and recovered $53 million in underreported contributions. This is about 6 percent of our rough estimate of the total. Recent experience shows the effect of federal targets on this process. In 1990, with a DLA to audit 4 percent of subject employers (versus the 1994 DLA of 2 percent, reduced to phase in more stringent auditing standards), states conducted 177,000 audits and detected $84 million of underreported contributions.

As noted, most estimated overpayments and underreported taxes involve evasive behavior by claimants and employers. Massive efforts to restructure the UI system's incentives are unlikely. Narrowly defined process improvements, at least to improve benefit payment administration, have had, overall, slight effects on payment accuracy. The most productive avenue remaining might thus be more, and more intelligent, detection and recovery efforts. Students of UI integrity have concluded that much evasive behavior is systematic, and thus liable to detection and deterrence by computerized profiling. They have urged this for increasing employer compliance with tax reporting laws and for screening claimants to focus scrutiny on those persons statistically more likely than average to violate various UI eligibility provisions (Blakemore et al. 1996; Burgess 1992; Burgess and Kingston 1987, p. 256). Such work could build on the profiling systems developed to identify laid-off individuals who are prone to need extensive reemployment assistance and implemented in the past two years. Benefits profiling could use the extensive BQC records. Employer profiling would require each state to mount one-time, if not continuing, random audit programs of employers as was done in Illinois. The targeted selections of workers would help SESAs focus enforcement efforts, information, and job search assistance on workers most likely to need them. Targeted employer audits would increase yield. Both should also provide more effective deterrence if the activity and results are publicized (Kingston, Burgess, and St. Louis 1986, p. 334; Blakemore et al. 1996, p. 22).

In the fall of 1995, a joint state-U.S. Department of Labor work group proposed a new approach to performance management called UI Performs. It is intended to address all dimensions of quality and to improve the system's balance between measuring performance and taking actions to raise it. UI Performs is built around more federal-state cooperation, an explicit commitment to continuous improvement, and stronger joint performance planning. When fully implemented in 1998, it should provide the system with improved performance measures, including an indicator of the accuracy of decisions to deny benefits. It also incorporates initiatives nearing completion to improve benefits timeliness, quality measures, and tax performance. The incentive to analyze experience and make program improvements will be strengthened by a more comprehensive planning process. By inducing the U.S. Department of Labor and states to look more broadly and in a balanced way at total performance, UI Performs has the potential to help stanch leakages at all levels, possibly through such innovative approaches as greater targeting of compliance efforts.

NOTES

The author would like to express his appreciation to reviewer Paul Burgess for his helpful comments on earlier drafts of the chapter. He is also grateful to Steve Wandner and Chris O'Leary for their extensive editorial assistance.

1. For a concise, thorough statement of the incentives and disincentives for compliance with benefit eligibility provisions, see Burgess (1992). A more complete treatment is Burgess and Kingston (1987), especially chapter 6. A review of incentives for employers to comply with contribution reporting requirements is given in Blakemore et al. (1996).

2. In 1996, the BQC was renamed the Benefit Accuracy Measurement (BAM) program.

3. See Kingston and Burgess (1981), especially table 15.

4. Conceptually, the BPC wage record crossmatch is a more thorough mechanism for detecting benefit-year earnings than BQC. BQC identifies earnings directly through the claimant interview (and so depends on claimant honesty) and indirectly through various employer verifications. The BPC crossmatch obtains positive matches on all work reflected in wage record data. In practice, however, crossmatch programs screen out instances where abuse is likely to involve small dollar amounts; additionally, agency staff cannot afford to investigate many other low-potential "hits." The 1979 pilot that developed Random Audit included a crossmatch and postaudit. Based on one quarter's crossmatch, these raised detected overpayments by 0 to 20 percent (average: 7 percent). Because of the small average effect, and the large delay it occasioned in case completions, this feature was not included in either Random Audit or BQC.

5. See California Employment Development Department (1995).

6. See Blakemore et al. (1996). The authors note that the Illinois study could not help but underestimate the rate of underreporting. Illinois could not audit firms headquartered out of state, and this knowledge may have affected their compliance. Of course, the study also included only registered employers, so noncompliance by "hidden" employers could not be estimated.

7. The actual FUTA tax rate is 6.2 percent. Employers pay 0.8 percent if they remit the correct amount of state taxes in a timely manner and the state is eligible for the offset credit of 5.4 percent.

8. The U.S. Department of Labor is now investigating an additional avenue by which interest may be lost by the UTF. In some states, additional accounts may be maintained by non-UI agencies that collect UI taxes. These accounts can be the repository of UI funds before they are trans-

ferred to the standard clearing account. Such accounts can therefore both delay the deposit of monies into the fund and affect how accurately the timeliness of transfer from the Clearing Account can be measured.

9. This general issue was first raised by Burgess, Kingston, and St. Louis (1982, pp. 37-39) in the context of how much tighter UI administration might reduce trust fund outlays.

10. See Marcus and Battaglia (1990) and subsequent analyses.

11. See Burgess and Kingston (1987), especially chapters 3 and 8.

12. Michigan data, although questionable, were published in 1988; publication was suspended in 1989-1992 and only resumed in 1993 when the state achieved adequate BQC quality. The bulk of Michigan overpayments involve "other eligibility" failures, mostly failure to register claimants with the Job Service.

References

Blakemore, Arthur E., Paul L. Burgess, Stuart A. Low, and Robert D. St. Louis. 1996. "Employer Tax Evasion in the Unemployment Insurance Program," *Journal of Labor Economics* (April): 210-230.

Burgess, Paul L. 1992. "Compliance with Unemployment Insurance Job-Search Regulations," *The Journal of Law and Economics* 35, 2 (October): 374-396.

Burgess, Paul L., and Jerry L. Kingston. 1987. *An Incentives Approach to Improving the Unemployment Compensation System.* Kalamazoo, MI: W.E. Upjohn Institute.

Burgess, Paul L., Jerry L. Kingston, and Robert D. St. Louis. 1982. *The Development of an Operational System for Detecting Unemployment Insurance Payment Errors Through Random Audits: The Results of Five Statewide Pilot Tests.* Prepared under Contract No. 99-9-2322-29-40, U.S. Department of Labor, Employment and Training Administration, Unemployment Insurance Service, December.

California Employment Development Department. 1995. "Unemployment Insurance National Risk Analysis Project, Current and Future Vulnerabilities." Report prepared for the U.S. Department of Labor, Unemployment Insurance Service, November.

Kingston, Jerry L. and Paul L. Burgess. 1981. "Unemployment Insurance Overpayments and Improper Payments in Six Major Metropolitan Areas." Report prepared for the National Commission on Unemployment Compensation, May.

Kingston, Jerry L., Paul L. Burgess and Robert D. St. Louis. 1986. "Unemployment Insurance Overpayments: Evidence and Implications," *Industrial and Labor Relations Review* 39, 3,(April): 323-336.

_____. 1986. "Unemployment Insurance Overpayments: Evidence and Implications," *Industrial and Labor Relations Review* 39, 3 (April): 323-336.

Marcus, Steven S., and Michael P. Battaglia. 1990. "Revenue Quality Control Employer Compliance Audits." Report prepared for U.S. Department of Labor, Unemployment Insurance Service, April.

U.S. Department of Labor. 1976-1977. "Unemployment Insurance Program Performance Standards Project." Individual state reports, Employment and Training Administration, Unemployment Insurance Service, Office of Program Management.

_____. 1995a. "Unemployment Insurance Quality Appraisal Result FY 94." Employment and Training Administration, Unemployment Insurance Service, Office of Program Management.

_____. 1995b. "Unemployment Insurance Quality Control 1994 Annual Report." Employment and Training Administration, Unemployment Insurance Service, Office of Program Management.

CHAPTER 11

The Role of the Employment Service

David E. Balducchi
U.S. Department of Labor
Terry R. Johnson
Battelle
R. Mark Gritz
Batttelle

> I had told [President Roosevelt] that the Employment Service was practically nonexistent although its name was still on a letterhead. . . . He said, "Resurrect the Employment Service right away. . . ."
>
> Frances Perkins describing Employment Service revitalization in 1933

The U.S. Employment Service, U.S. Department of Labor, is the agency responsible for establishing and maintaining a federal-state system of local public employment offices. There are nearly 1,800 offices of the Employment Service (ES), also referred to as the Job Service, located in fifty-four states and territories of the United States, which provide a free public labor exchange to assist individuals seeking employment and employers seeking workers.[1] The ES is at a crossroads in its Labor Department history, both in terms of its relationship to the unemployment insurance (UI) program and its role in the formulation of a new workforce development system that can better meet the needs of job seekers and employers in a dynamic global economy.[2] Devised in the midst of the Great Depression, the federal-state ES system was established to address the recruitment requirements of New Deal public works programs. With the creation of the UI program, the ES system was subsequently organized as part of the employment security system, which includes both ES and UI programs, to mitigate the vagaries of cyclical unemployment that characterized the U.S. labor market.[3] This model of the ES as a free public labor exchange worked well for about a half-century, until the nature of work began to change rapidly. The structural shift in America's economic engine that began in the late 1970s has caused more workers to be permanently laid off, as the jobs they held disappeared, leaving them without the skills needed to obtain their next job. Moreover, the new "information economy" of the 1990s is continuing to transform the nature of work and will most likely lead to more frequent job changes, many of which will also involve significant career moves, for new and experienced workers. This heightened and increasing problem of structural unemployment requires new public and private reemployment solutions and an examination of the relationship between the ES and the UI program.

The attitudes of policy makers towards the ES, and the roles it should play in a new workforce development system, have been largely influenced by anecdotal evidence, as well as by the findings from more formal evaluations. In its early years, the ES received praise for its key role in aiding economic recovery from the Great Depression and for its postwar efforts to help in the transition from a wartime to a civilian economy. In contrast, over the last 30 years, the ES has been criticized as being ineffective and antediluvian. Much of this perspective is based largely on anecdotal information and (mis)perceptions, rather than on the evidence from more formal evaluations of its effectiveness. For example, the ES is often criticized because employers generally seem to list only relatively low-skill, low-wage jobs with the service, and only as a last resort after they are unable to find workers through other mechanisms. Similarly, in some circles, the ES has developed the image of an "unemployment office" due to its formal "business" relationship with the UI program and because it is often co-located with the UI office. The ES has also been criticized for serving relatively disadvantaged workers and others who only use the ES after other job-finding methods have failed. Finally, critics have pointed to relatively low and declining ES placement rates, and to even lower placement rates for UI claimants, as evidence of ineffectiveness. In contrast, as will be described, the results of formal evaluations of the ES paint a very different picture of its effectiveness, recognize the potentially valuable role the ES can play as a last resort, and note that the decline in placement rates must be adjusted for factors outside ES control and viewed in the broader context of its changing mission and the target groups it serves, the level of funding provided, and shifts in labor market conditions.

In this chapter, we examine the past, present, and future role of the ES in the reemployment process, including the historical and projected linkages between the ES and the UI program. Understanding the future role of the ES in a new workforce system requires a knowledge of the formal ties between the ES and the UI programs, as well as a historical perspective on the evolving mission of the ES over more than sixty years. Also, in understanding how effectively the ES has operated in the past, how it works today, and how it is likely to function in the future, it is important not to rely on anecdotes and perceptions but, as much as possible, to draw on reliable quantitative research that measures the outcomes achieved compared to what would have happened if the program or particular service had not been available.

The remainder of this chapter is organized into four sections. In the next section, we describe the key linkages between the ES and the UI program, including the "work test" and the different types of reemployment services that the ES has provided UI claimants over the years. This is followed by a discussion of the major changes in the mission of the ES, including alterations in programs and policies, target groups (including UI claimants), and resources. For the most part, we briefly describe the early years and focus on major shifts during the past ten years. The third section summarizes the available research evidence on the effectiveness of the work test and of various ES services provided to job seekers. The final section offers our view as to how the ES is likely to function in the near term as part of a new workforce development system, with a particular focus on the relationship to the UI program and the services that will be provided to UI claimants. We draw inferences about the probable effectiveness of the labor exchange system in the future. We also identify the major gaps in our knowledge of the effectiveness of certain aspects of the likely future system, which, if filled, could help shape labor exchange policies and services.

Linkages between the Employment Service and the Unemployment Insurance Program

The ES has played an integral part in the UI program since the inception of the federal-state UI program in the Social Security Act (SSA) of 1935. In the two years between the passage of the Wagner-Peyser Act of 1933, which established the federal-state ES, and the creation of the UI program, the primary mission of the ES was to function as a labor exchange by obtaining information on the skills and qualifications of unemployed workers and referring qualified applicants to appropriate job openings that were listed by employers. With the creation of the UI program, the functions of the ES were expanded to add work registration of UI claimants to the original job-matching goal. Although the mission of the ES has spread far beyond labor exchange activities over the last sixty years, the relationship of the ES with the UI program has historically focused on two fundamental roles: the work test and reemployment services.

Work Test

A leading role played by the ES system in the UI program is to administer the work test requirement as a condition for continuing UI benefits eligibility to ensure that UI claimants are actively seeking jobs. To offset the disincentive to search for work resulting from the availability of UI benefits and to guarantee that claimants are exposed to the job market, the UI program imposes various administrative standards to encourage claimants to seek work. In particular, all federally approved state UI programs must include able-to-work and available-for-work eligibility requirements that claimants must satisfy on a continuing basis in order to receive UI benefits.[4] For example, in most states, UI claimants who are not job-attached (i.e., are not on temporary layoff and expect to be recalled by their former employer, or do not obtain employment through a union hiring hall) are usually required to register for work with the ES, which affirms their labor force attachment and availability for work, and are required to accept a suitable job referral or an offer of suitable work.[5] In addition, UI claimants who are not job-attached are required to search actively for work and, in many states, to document the employers they contact as part of the continuing claims process.

The ES assists the UI program in its efforts to monitor compliance with the able-to-work and available-for-work requirements, and this function is commonly referred to as the work test for continuing UI benefits eligibility. Typically, in most states, the ES administers the work test requirement by identifying claimants who neglect to register with the ES, fail to accept suitable job referrals, or refuse offers of suitable employment. In such cases, it then refers these issues to the UI program for a determination as to whether UI benefits should be denied. Although the enforcement of the work test has varied considerably over time, as well as across states, the underlying concept of the work test has remained relatively constant throughout the sixty years that the ES has been performing this function for the UI program. The new UI requirement relating to worker profiling, for claimants likely to experience long unemployment spells to participate in reemployment services, imposes additional work test responsibilities upon the ES. In certain cases, new work test responsibilities are also put upon Economic Dislocation and Worker Adjustment Assistance (EDWAA) service providers.

Reemployment Services

The other fundamental role of the ES in the UI program is to provide UI claimants with exposure to job openings and employment services. In fact, during its first forty years of operation, ES was the *only* public agency that offered labor exchange and employment services to the unemployed and others seeking new jobs. The role of the ES in assisting UI claimants to find jobs has primarily involved job-matching services. Historically, the four major job-matching services provided by the ES to unemployed workers have been job referral, counseling, testing, and job development. Despite the many revisions in mission and focus over its first sixty years, the changes in the provision of such services have been primarily in terms of which individuals have been targeted to receive them. Each of these services will be described briefly.

Job Referral

The original mission of the ES was to provide basic labor exchange services through referrals of registrants to job openings listed with the service. This is still one of its current roles and involves matching the skill requirements listed by the employer with the qualifications of applicants. Traditionally, this has occurred through a combination of activities: sometimes individuals identify potential job openings of interest and discuss them with an ES placement interviewer, or ES interviewers, using manual or computerized search methods, identify a job opening that may be appropriate for an applicant. In most offices today, this may involve review of available openings through individual state job banks or throughout the United States by way of a computer search of a national job listings data base, which is called America's Job Bank (AJB). More recently, in response to the job-seeking needs of customers and to reduced staff resources, many states are streamlining their placement assistance process and adopting a "self-service" philosophy for the mainstream job seeker. This approach allows those who are job-ready to find their own work of interest, freeing up staff resources to focus on unemployed job seekers who face employment barriers and need more intensive services.

Available evidence indicates that a minority of all ES registrants, 30 to 40 percent, receive at least one job referral, and the rate is usually considerably lower for UI claimants.[6] A "successful" referral that results in a job placement requires several additional steps: the applicant must contact the employer, be offered the job, and accept the job offer. Among those individuals who receive a job referral, approximately 30 to 40 percent are placed in a job.[7] Hence, only about 10 to 15 percent of all ES registrants are placed in a job by the ES and the rate for UI claimants is lower.[8]

Counseling

Over the last sixty years, the ES has placed varying levels of emphasis on the provision of employment counseling services, such as assistance to individuals in making occupational choices, changes, or adjustments. Employment counselors help people make these decisions by providing access to employment information; by interpreting the results of aptitude, interest, and skills tests; and by providing other employment or training assistance. For the most part, counseling has been traditionally given to individuals facing various types of employment barriers, who are not currently job ready, whereas work referrals are provided to job-ready applicants. During the middle-to-late 1960s, when the ES began focusing on serving the disadvantaged, roughly 20 percent (or more) of all new applicants received at least one employment counseling interview. More recently, the proportion of registrants receiving counseling has been falling steadily as the number of ES counselors has declined, and, in the 1990s, only 3 to 4 percent of ES registrants receive employment counseling.

Testing

Aptitude and interest tests have historically been an important part of the services provided by the ES and, in particular, by ES counselors. Various tests have been used in different ES offices, including the General Aptitude Test Battery (GATB),[9] the Specific Aptitude Test Batteries (SATB), the Interest Check List, and the Basic Occupational Literacy Test, among others. ES counselors use these tests to help youth make career decisions. In addition, test results are used to assess specific job qualifications and to screen out applicants who are not qualified for a particular job opening.

The trends in the extent of test administration over time have, for the most part, mirrored trends in counseling services. In the middle 1960s, roughly 20 to 25 percent of all applicants received testing. This compares to less than 5 percent of all applicants by 1980, with the majority of tests given to women or used primarily for skills evaluation for clerical positions (Johnson et al. 1983). Currently, approximately 2 to 3 percent of all ES applicants receive testing services, and it appears that the likelihood that UI claimants receive testing services is even lower.[10]

Job Development

Job developments are similar to job referrals except that there are no existing openings listed with the ES. In an effort to help individuals find jobs, ES interviewers, recognizing that an applicant has specific work skills, may contact employers who hire individuals with similar skills, even though a vacancy has not been listed with the ES. Through this process, the ES interviewer may arrange an appointment for the applicant with an employer, and some of these job development interviews result in job placements.

There is relatively little information on the extent of job development services and trends over time. Available evidence (Johnson et al. 1983) that relates to the operation of the ES around 1980 indicates that approximately one out of ten registrants received a job development. However, the use of job developments is highly cyclical and likely to depend on the availability of staff resources.

Other Job Search Assistance Services

In addition to these basic labor exchange services, some ES offices offer more intensive ways to help unemployed workers find jobs. These services include job finding clubs or job search assistance workshops that are usually offered on a periodic basis (e.g., weekly, monthly) and may be designed for specific groups. There is, however, considerable variation across sites in the intensity of the service and in the groups targeted to receive assistance. For example, the service can range from a single, brief (one to three hour) meeting/workshop, to a week-long intensive program of job finding, skill development and resume preparation. Some workshops are targeted to UI claimants or to specific subsets of claimants (e.g., dislocated workers), while others are targeted to occupational groups (e.g., white-collar workers, blue-collar workers).

Job-finding clubs originated in the late 1960s. Many of the early clubs were developed for white-collar or professional workers who tended to experience particular difficulties in finding new employment. The clubs are essentially peer-support groups of unemployed individuals, who meet to share their experiences and lessons learned in looking for work.Usually the meetings are facilitated by an ES staff member, often the local employment counselor. We are aware of no job-finding clubs, prior to the Worker Profiling and Reemployment Services (WPRS) initiative, that required claimants to participate in order to receive UI benefits.

The goal of job-search workshops is generally to ensure that each unemployed worker can define his or her job search objectives and can develop an employability or job search plan. Workshops vary in the time devoted to specific subjects, but most job-search workshops include such topics as how to effectively handle losing your job, self-assessment, developing realistic employment goals, organizing a job-search strategy, preparing a resume, filling out a job application, and job interview techniques. Job search workshops tend to combine a classroom lecture style with extensive group discussion. Several different types of job-search assistance workshops have been tested as part of federal or state demonstration programs. In some cases, attendance at the workshops has been mandatory; in these instances, this service also introduces a work test feature because failure to report to the workshop as directed could lead to denial of UI benefits.

Summary

As indicated, the primary linkages between the ES and UI programs concern the administration of the work test and the provision of labor exchange and reemployment services to claimants. In contrast to the relative stability of the work-test function of the ES, job matching has shifted focus several times. To understand the reasons behind these shifts, it is essential to have a more in-depth knowledge of the history of the ES. As will be described in more detail, the functional shifts are due to changes in the central mission of the ES, in the target groups to be served, and in administrative structure and program resources. Moreover, these shifts in the mission of the ES, as they relate to providing reemployment services, have intensified in the last decade. A significant part of the next section is devoted to understanding the role of the ES in the creation of a new workforce development system that can effectively serve Americans in the emerging "information economy" of the 1990s and beyond.

The Employment Service: The First Sixty Years

To fully understand how the ES functions today and to provide a context for interpreting ES evaluation results, it is important to know how the mission and corresponding focus of the job-matching services of the ES have evolved over time. Because of the host of changes that have occurred in ES operations over the years, it is not feasible to document them all in detail. Instead, we summarize what we consider to be the major modifications in policy, program emphasis, and program resources. This section draws from previous books, reports, and papers concerned with the ES, including Adams (1969), Johnson et al. (1983), and Kulik (1994).

In 1933, the Wagner-Peyser Act established the federal-state ES with the mission of coordinating state employment agencies that provide free services to "men, women and juniors who are legally qualified to engage in gainful occupations."[11] During the Great Depression, the ES primarily functioned as a placement agency to refer applicants to newly created jobs in public works programs and work relief projects; the scarcity of private sector jobs limited the role the ES initially played in that part of the labor market. Title III of the Social Security Act of 1935 created the UI program and directed that benefits be paid through public employment offices or other agencies as approved by the Social Security Board (now the Secretary of Labor).[12] Throughout the UI program's sixty-year history, public employment offices have been the only agency authorized to administer the payment of UI benefits. Under federally approved state UI laws, states have also been required to pay UI benefits only to claimants who were able to work and available for work and who met state-specific work-search requirements.

The ES registered claimants for work, referred qualified claimants (and other applicants) to suitable job openings, and informed the UI program when claimants did not meet the registration requirements, refused a referral to suitable employment, or refused a job offer. This role of performing the work test formed the cornerstone of the initial relationship between the ES and UI programs and, at the same time, introduced a new dimension to ES responsibilities. Specifically, it marked the first time that the ES was faced with serving individuals who were *required* to register for work.[13] As such, it put the same ES staff members who were referring applicants to jobs in the potentially awkward position of also being responsible for reporting on the work test.

Although the ES and UI programs had been operated as federal-state partnerships,[14] state ES agencies were put under direct federal control during World War II and served as a local labor market for workers in the war industries. After World War II, the operations of the ES were returned to the states, and priority was placed on providing services to returning veterans and to those workers who were dislocated through the process of shifting from a war economy to a civilian economy. The postwar period also created two new responsibilities for the ES in the areas of compliance and special services to additional target groups. First, the ES provided certification of foreign labor and was required to show that employment opportunities and wages for U.S. workers would not be harmed if foreign workers were admitted. Second, in addition to offering preferential counseling and placement opportunities for veterans, by the mid-1950s, the target groups for special assistance had expanded to include youth, older workers, and the disabled.

The linkages between the ES and the UI program were strengthened during the late 1950s. During this period, the UI trust fund—the primary source of funding for local ES offices—exceeded the legal maximum, and these excess monies were distributed to individual state accounts. Under special conditions known as "Reed Act" provisions, these monies could be used by states to obtain, among other things, new buildings to administer employment security programs. As new offices were acquired, many state UI claims offices were located "in the same building as the employment offices" (Haber and Murray 1966, p. 426). At that time, critics charged that co-locating unemployment and employment offices would damage the image of the ES. They contended that good jobs and high-quality job seekers would not be attracted to co-located employment offices, and that physical separation of ES and UI would also encourage formal communication between the two agencies (Haber and Murray 1966). At one level, they may have been correct, as many American job seekers view the local employment office as a place to go when they are out of work—that is, as the "unemployment office"—not a place to look for a job. However, this co-location of ES and UI offices in post-World War II America has resulted in UI claims filing and work registration being available at a single location in many states and has spurred a number of policy initiatives centered around the development of one-stop services.

The 1960s brought a host of new responsibilities for the ES. In 1961, the Area Redevelopment Act required the ES to help establish training programs in depressed areas and called for a large expansion of its efforts in collecting labor market information. For example, it directed the ES to collect information on unemployment levels by labor market area to determine whether disadvantaged areas qualified for federal assistance. It also established a role for the ES to work with state and local educational programs to provide data on occupational trends that would be useful in curriculum development and career counseling.

A new era for the ES was initiated with the passage of the Manpower Development and Training Act in 1962 and the Economic Opportunity Act of 1964, which increased the involvement of the ES in training programs and human resource development activities. Taken together, these pieces of legislation greatly de-emphasized the job matching and labor exchange role of the ES and resulted in the ES becoming the lead public agency in the design and delivery of job training and human resource development programs. The ES provided outreach, screening, and referral services for various training programs and other social programs established through the Great Society legislation; many of these programs were targeted to disadvantaged groups (e.g., Job Corps, Neighborhood Youth Corps). The ES also offered job readiness services for new labor force entrants and placed individuals who completed training programs in jobs. By 1965, these changes had shifted the major mission of the ES to serving low-income and disadvantaged workers through human resource development services; consequently, the ES grew considerably during this period as additional resources were allocated to meet the challenge of providing needed services to the disadvantaged. In addition, this shift in the mission of the ES resulted in a 1967 Labor Department initiative to facilitate a dialogue around the development of an integrated delivery system for human services at central locations (U.S. Department of Labor 1967, p. 3), which is surprisingly similar to the current one-stop services concept described below.

The ES reached a program zenith in the 1960s as substantial funding increases were provided to meet the needs of the disadvantaged. However, the era where the ES was the sole public provider of reemployment services ended in the early 1970s, with the passage of the Comprehensive Employment and Training Act (CETA) of 1973. CETA fundamentally changed the institutional infrastructure for employment and training assistance by fragmenting the delivery of employment and training services to economically disadvantaged and permanently laid-off job seekers. Under the CETA, the institutional infrastructure emphasized local design and delivery of employment and training programs,[15] and the primary mission of the ES returned to its focus on the basic labor exchange functions of referral to job openings and job placement. As a result of this return to its original mission, funding for the ES remained relatively constant over the 1970s in real dollars. Although the ES was expected to conduct assessment activities and to provide placement services for local employment and training programs, CETA did not give the ES a clear-cut role in the employment and training system, and conflicts over "turf issues" appear to have limited the integration of service delivery between the two agencies (Levitan and Taggart 1976).

The gradual decline in the role of the ES continued through the 1980s with the next two shifts in national employment and training policy: the replacement of CETA with the Job Training Partnership Act (JTPA) in 1982, and the replacement of the JTPA dislocated worker program with the EDWAA Act in 1988.[16] Both JTPA and EDWAA, which amended JTPA Title III, continued the movement toward local control of the delivery of employment and training services to unemployed workers. In an effort to refocus the ES on its basic labor exchange mission, and to foster cooperation and linkages between ES and JTPA programs, the 1982 JTPA legislation amended the Wagner-Peyser Act to give states expanded authority to reshape state labor exchange programs through federal special purpose block grants. Moreover, although EDWAA specified that the ES should have a role in the provision of services to dislocated workers, states were allowed considerable discretion in the structure of the service delivery process. In addition to devolving much authority for the ES from the federal level to the states, the amendments also altered the ES grants funding formula by allocating resources to states based on need, as measured by various indicators of unemployment.[17]

Although modifications in the reporting requirements that accompanied the 1982 Wagner-Peyser Amendments make it difficult to accurately measure the change in overall ES program funding, Kulik (1994) estimates that the level of resources (in real dollar terms) for the basic labor exchange activities declined by about 20 percent from 1984 to 1992. As a result, some states augmented federal ES funding through manipulation of their UI tax laws or special assessments to maintain or enhance labor exchange activities for special target groups. For example, in 1982, Montana assessed a separate surcharge on top of employer UI taxes to shore up ES operations. Since then, other states have taken steps to buttress their labor exchange systems through the collection of special taxes that are used to provide ES services to job seekers.[18] Still other states have combined local office ES and UI job descriptions and have cross-trained staff to perform claims taking and labor exchange functions; these actions were taken to cut costs or prod more "case-managed" services and, in some cases, have complicated the work test role of the ES.

The new federalism of the last three decades achieved its objective of strengthening local control of reemployment services. However, the lengthy stepwise progression of this process has often resulted in fragmented, and sometimes in contradictory, local delivery of employment and training programs to unemployed workers, including UI recipients. Moreover, during the same period, the rapid pace of global competition, the downsizing of old-line American industries, and the emergence of the information economy have created a need to revamp the employment security system and the delivery of employment and training services to job seekers. In 1991, the U.S. General Accounting Office (GAO) reported:

> While ES programs in some states have flourished without Labor's technical assistance, wide variations in local office performance indicate that active assistance from Labor may help to improve the effectiveness of their programs....GAO recommends that the Secretary of Labor work with the states to identify and solve problems affecting ES program quality and performance.[19]

During the last few years, federal and state policy makers have perceived the need to design new workforce development systems to improve services to incumbent and potential workers and have introduced a number of alternative legislative proposals that have important implications for the future of the employment and training system and for the role of the ES in that process. Several such state proposals have been implemented. For example, Indiana, Iowa, and New Jersey each enacted legislation to revamp their employment and training systems. In large measure, these early state workforce development system changes were achieved with little federal assistance.

After a year of development, in March 1994, President Clinton announced the administration's workforce development proposal, called the Reemployment Act, to overhaul the country's fragmented employment and training system. The bill was designed to "reinvent" America's splintered job-finding system using an approach based upon service provider collaboration and competition. Under the bill's provisions, state and local governments, community colleges, and private service providers could be designated as operators, as long as they met "chartering" service criteria of the ES and other employment and training programs.

Throughout the Reemployment Act's development and short legislative life, three fundamental policy issues emerged: customer service, choice, and competition. The issue of enabling both public and private labor exchange operators to compete for customers divided the bill's natural allies and dominated every discussion of the bill's worth. As the 103rd Congress ended, the Clinton administration could not even obtain waiver authority to experiment with state employment and training programs, and the bill died. Nevertheless, the Labor Department began to press forward with its vision of building a comprehensive workforce development system.

There are four common themes that appear to be widely recognized as essential components of an effective workforce development system:

1. a reemphasis on meeting the job-finding needs of the system's customers, which the ES has dubbed "ES Revitalization";

2. the early identification of individuals who are likely to be out of work for long periods and the provision to them of job-search assistance services, often referred to as "Worker Profiling and Reemployment Services";

3. the provision of information needed by job seekers to make informed labor market choices, which is embodied in the concept of "America's Labor Market Information System"; and

4. the implementation of a seamless delivery system for all employment and training services, such as nationwide "One-Stop Career Centers."

ES Revitalization

An essential element of an effective workforce development system is a focus, and concern, on the part of ES staff that the program is meeting the needs of the people who seek out employment services, that is, its customers. Recognizing the necessity to improve the ES customer focus, states, the Labor Department, and others developed an "ES Revitalization Work Plan" designed to strengthen the capacity of the ES to deliver quality information and services to its customers.[20] The goal of ES revitalization is to transform the traditional labor exchange model characterized by bureaucratic rules, standardized services, and dispassionate staff into a new vision of the labor exchange process that promotes universal access, permits consumer choice, provides customized services, and enables staff to either facilitate customer self-service or provide more intensive employment interventions.

To achieve this goal, the ES developed a long-term agenda and identified short-term improvements, including steps to be taken within the existing resources to enhance ES customer service. The long-term agenda envisions three tiers of ES service levels, each focusing on meeting individual customer needs, and would provide employers the ability to select job seekers from any tier. Specifically, the plan categorizes the services into the following tiers:

- Tier I: Self-Help (resource center and automated self-help system containing information on jobs, and job search assistance);

- Tier II: Basic Intervention (basic assessment and services, such as referral to jobs, job search assistance, and training);

- Tier III: Intensive Services (job seekers could be served by ES or referred to other workforce development programs).

In the short term, the United States Employment Service established cooperative agreements with six states to develop and share the latest knowledge and practices in areas that will enhance ES customer service: staff capacity building (Iowa), best practices clearinghouse (West Virginia), customer satisfaction (Rhode Island), job matching (Ohio), leadership exchange (Texas) and local office redesign (Maryland).[21] A description of several key products includes the following:

- **Clearinghouse**. Gives SESAs an on-line computer resource, called *The Workforce ATM*, that contains federal and state workforce development information. The Internet address for *Workforce ATM* is http://www.icesa.org.

- **Customer Satisfaction**. Provides SESAs with customer satisfaction measurement tools for employers, job seekers/claimants, and staff, and staff training to utilize customer feedback. Customer satisfaction is increasingly viewed as a leading gauge of success in workforce development programs and a main source of guidance for labor exchange service improvements.
- **Job Matching**. Offers SESAs technical information about effective methods to match job seekers with employers by identifying and documenting SESA automated job-matching systems and by identifying alternative systems (e.g., resume-based, skill-based, text-retrieval). Intelligent job matching technology is likely to play an increasing role in future labor exchange systems.

Worker Profiling and Reemployment Services

Based on findings from Labor Department-sponsored demonstration programs, it is widely believed that the early identification of, and provision of reemployment services to, individuals who are likely to be long-term unemployed should be a key component of any effective workforce development system. Thus, in March 1993, an amendment to the Social Security Act directed the Labor Department to establish and encourage state participation in a profiling screening program to identify likely UI exhaustees needing reemployment services.[22] In November 1993, additional amendments to the Act made state participation in the profiling screening program mandatory and required UI claimants identified by the profiling program to participate in reemployment services or risk being disqualified from receiving UI benefits.[23]

Although the profiling screening process and the identification of targeted claimants are the responsibility of the UI program, the WPRS system increases the work test responsibilities of the ES and EDWAA service providers. Specifically, the WPRS system contains four basic components: (1) early identification, (2) selection and referral, (3) reemployment services, and (4) feedback to the UI program. The UI program is responsible for the first two components, while ES and EDWAA substate grantees share responsibilities for the other two components. For example, in most states, claimants selected by the state profiling screening program are referred to ES or EDWAA substate grantee service providers by their fifth week of unemployment for orientation and assessment. The assessment process is designed to identify the reemployment needs of each claimant, through vocational testing, interest inventories, and counseling, and to result in the development of an individualized service plan.[24] Claimants who have the skills and experience to fill openings that are currently available receive job referrals, while others are required to participate in a program of reemployment services customized to suit the claimant's reemployment situation. The potential reemployment services that meet the requirements include job search workshops, interview or resume preparation classes, or other job search assistance services.[25] Claimants who do not have marketable skills are referred to occupational training providers through the EDWAA program or through other training programs.

The WPRS system not only strengthens the mission of the ES to provide reemployment services to UI claimants, it further expands the work-test responsibilities that are performed by the ES or the EDWAA service provider, depending on state referral arrangements. These expanded work-test responsibilities include feedback to the UI system relating to the claimant's week-to-week participation status, completion of reemployment services, or failure to participate in reemployment services.

To ensure that there was sufficient capacity within the states to provide reemployment services and feedback information to UI, approximately $20 million in program years (PYs) 1994-1995 EDWAA supplemental funds was made available to support the capacity building and implementation efforts of states. These EDWAA supplemental funds were distributed through the existing substate grantee structure to local EDWAA service providers and the ES. In states where the ES is the WPRS service provider, supplemental funds were used to revitalize assessment, counseling, and job search programs for dislocated workers and feedback systems to UI, which helped to build ES staff capacity and to partially offset the declining resources received in recent years.

America's Labor Market Information System

Labor market information is a critical element of any new workforce development system designed to meet the needs of workers and employers in an information economy, including workers and employers who must adapt to the educational and training requirements of this different economy. A comprehensive and easily accessible national labor market information system will provide the data necessary to make informed choices about jobs and to maintain U.S. global competitiveness. For example, such a system will enable workers to adjust more rapidly to structural changes in the economy and help them make informed career choices minimizing the amount of structural unemployment. This type of system is also needed to support the development of One-Stop Career Centers, which will facilitate job seeker and employer access to employment, training, and income support programs.

A network of this sort has been included in most proposed workforce development programs, including the Clinton administration's vision of a truly comprehensive labor market information system, which has been dubbed America's Labor Market Information System (ALMIS). The purpose of ALMIS is to help labor markets function more efficiently. Reflecting a philosophy similar to that underlying the concept of One-Stop Career Centers, ALMIS will offer one-stop access to information. As such, it will give anyone—job seekers, students, employers—direct access to a wide range of labor market information from a variety of sources. ALMIS will also include valuable program evaluation data, such as on customer satisfaction, and information about the performance of education and training providers.

A companion of ALMIS is AJB, a nationwide electronic labor exchange of job orders shared by states and operated by the AJB Service Center in Albany, New York, which currently lists over 600,000 job openings daily. In the past, access to individual state job banks was limited, and available only to those who used ES offices. To address this issue, in 1995, the job listings in AJB and affiliated state job banks were made available to the Internet, and in a way so that employer listings can be easily reviewed and searched electronically.[26] To further support an enhanced electronic labor exchange, federal-state ES cooperation has made it possible for employers to enter job orders directly into the AJB system, and a nationwide ALMIS talent bank network of job seekers is being tested, which can be easily searched by employers.[27] These technological advances will provide employers and job seekers with new nontraditional ways to tap into the labor market.

One-Stop Career Centers

A central feature of the Clinton administration's efforts to replace the splintered employment and unemployment structure with a comprehensive workforce development system is in the formation of One-Stop Career Centers.[28] The vision of such centers is to transform the fragmented employment and training system and afford all job seekers easy access to reliable, up-to-date information on jobs, skills in demand, performance records of training institutions, and UI benefits, as well as to provide employers access to the talent and skills they need to successfully manage their businesses. The four tenets that underpin the goals of these centers are as follows:

- **Universality**. To integrate the delivery of services from existing unemployment, employment and job training programs and to provide customers with an array of job finding and employment development assistance
- **Customer Choice**. To provide customers with options and choices of where to get the services that best meet their needs
- **Integrated System**. To offer a comprehensive and accessible "one-stop shop" for employment and educational with integrated programs, services, and governance structures including access to Labor Department-funded employment and training programs
- **Performance-Driven/Outcomes-Based**. To measure system performance and to determine if it actually achieved outcomes, including a strong connection to whether the customer is satisfied with the services received (U.S. Department of Labor 1994a).

In 1994, the Labor Department provided grants to implement One-Stop Career Centers to six states[29] and gave planning grants to nineteen other states totaling $34 million. In 1995, an additional ten states received $40.5 million to implement One-Stop Career Center systems.[30] Finally, in early 1996, all remaining states received grants totaling approximately $4 million to develop One-Stop systems.[31] Further

Labor Department investments are planned.[32] Each state will offer state and federally funded employment and training services to customers at single points of delivery, and performance measures will be linked to customer satisfaction, cross-program indicators, and continuous improvement. Thus far, most of the states that are implementing One-Stop Career Centers are using the ES as the centerpiece of their new systems.

Summary

As has been indicated, the roles and responsibilities of the ES during its first sixty years have changed considerably. Although the initial charter to match unemployed workers to job openings listed by employers was complicated by the addition of numerous responsibilities and by multiple target groups with different needs, by the mid-1970s, the focus had returned to providing basic labor exchange services for applicants. In addition, the role of the ES as a player in the employment and training arena changed, as other programs were introduced that were responsible for a broad range of employment and training functions, and as federal authority for operating the program was replaced by state authority. Consequently, the emphasis placed on the administration of the work test tended to vary depending on unemployment conditions. Also, as more disadvantaged target groups were added to the list of ES responsibilities, services to claimants—who were required to register for work at the ES—were not a priority.

In contrast, over the last several years, the ES has become involved in a major initiative to respond to structural changes in the workplace and to utilize advanced information systems. Both the structural change and advanced technologies require innovative ways to organize and provide services and are leading to a different role for the ES in serving structurally unemployed customers, mostly UI claimants, who are likely to need more intensive assistance. This new way to organize and provide services should lead to a new labor exchange system "without walls" where job seekers obtain services and find jobs, and employers find high-qualify workers through a variety of computer-assisted tools and integrated delivery systems.

Evidence of the Effectiveness of the Employment Service in Assisting Unemployed Workers

As described, the two main roles of the ES in serving UI claimants involve (1) helping in the administration of the work test, and (2) providing basic labor exchange and job search assistance to UI claimants. In this section, we summarize evidence concerning the impacts and cost-effectiveness of the ES in performing the work test and in helping unemployed workers to find jobs. Whenever possible, we focus on the evidence as it pertains specifically to UI claimants.

The evidence on the effectiveness of the ES and of specific ES services varies considerably in terms of validity. Here, we distinguish between two types of validity: internal and external. Internal validity refers to obtaining unbiased estimates of the effects of ES services on employment and earnings outcomes. External validity refers to the ability to generalize the findings to a broader population.

In some cases, the evidence is based on carefully designed and implemented field experiments, which randomly assigned individuals to groups that were offered specific services or to a control group that was not. In these instances, differences in the outcomes between the groups have high internal validity and provide very strong and convincing evidence of the effects of the services in question, at the sites where the field experiments are conducted. If the sites are representative, and meet the external validity criterion, then the findings can be generalized to a broader population.

In other cases, the evidence is based on statistical comparison group designs, where outcomes for individuals who receive the service are compared to outcomes for individuals who do not, using multivariate methods that (whenever possible) control for demographic and other personal characteristics and labor market conditions. In these situations, the internal validity of the evidence depends critically on the degree of similarity between the groups being compared, and on the effectiveness of the statistical procedures in adjusting for potential systematic differences between the two groups.

Still other cases have evidence that consists simply of information bits, and inferences are drawn without a real benchmark for comparison purposes. Finally, in certain cases, the effectiveness of the service is for all practical purposes completely unknown, as it has never been evaluated.

Effects of the Work Test

Individuals receiving UI benefits must demonstrate that they are able to work and available for work. In most states, claimants who are not job-attached are required to actively search for work, to register for work with the ES, to participate in assigned work-search activities, and to accept suitable job referrals. Claimants who are found not to comply with this requirement are disqualified from receiving UI benefits for the period they are out of compliance, or possibly longer.

The administration of the ES work-test requirement involves ES staff effort (and hence incurs costs) and provides potentially important benefits to society.[33] These benefits arise from the potential reductions in UI payments, as claimants leave the unemployment rolls sooner than they would have done in the absence of the work test. Reduced weeks of UI payments could occur because claimants return to work more quickly or because even though they continue to claim additional weeks of benefits, some of their claims are denied for not meeting the work test. Reductions in UI payments could also occur if, because of the perceived higher costs of collecting UI payments due to the work test, claimants choose to no longer receive benefits but do not immediately return to work. Since these outcomes generate different benefits from the social perspective, in order to fully assess the overall impact of the work test it is important to understand whether it affects the subsequent wage rates or earnings of claimants.

There is considerable evidence concerning the administration and effects of the work test requirements for UI claimants. This includes descriptive information reported in Johnson et al. (1981b) of how the work test operated in a national sample of thirty ES offices in 1980; evidence based on an analysis of time series of cross sections of 1964-1981 state data concerning variation in UI nonmonetary eligibility determination rates, as reported in Corson et al. (1984a); and descriptive information from a national survey of recipients of unemployment benefits and exhaustees reported in Corson and Dynarski (1990). It also includes findings from two demonstration programs. We will first highlight the evidence from the nonexperimental studies, which are all based on nationally representative data:

- There are extensive differences across UI/ES offices in the requirements claimants must meet to be viewed as able to work and available for work; as to whether claimants are required to register with the ES; and in the degree of enforcement of the work test. Office managers and ES staff consistently reported that staff spent modest amounts of time in activities related to the work test for UI claimants, and that such time did not generally detract from their ability to provide labor exchange services to other registrants. The large majority of ES staff also did not consider their role in the work test as "monitoring" or "policing," but simply as a provider of information to the UI program that was obtained through the normal part of the ES process of following up with employers on the status of job openings.

- Nonmonetary determination rates vary considerably from UI office to UI office and depend on differences in agency practices and behaviors, as well as on differences in eligibility regulations and criteria across states. States with formal requirements that claimants search for work, and with detailed instructions regarding the documentation necessary to meet the requirements, have higher nonmonetary determination rates, and states with more severe disqualification penalties have fewer denials. It also appears that higher sanctions reduce the number of individuals seeking unemployment benefits.

- Results from a national survey reveal that most job-attached claimants who expect to be recalled by their previous employer are recalled, indicating that the limited work-search requirements imposed for job-attached claimants by most states are appropriate. In contrast, 16 percent of individuals receiving UI benefits who did not expect to be recalled reported that they did not look for work while receiving UI benefits, and 18 percent of exhaustees found a job within two weeks of receiving their last payment.

This nonexperimental evidence, which suggests that the costs of conducting the work test are not large and that strict work-search requirements could be effective in reducing UI outlays, is strongly supported by the experimental evidence obtained from two demonstration programs conducted in the 1980s. These two projects—the Charleston Claimant Placement and Work Test Demonstration, and the Washington Alternative Work Search Experiment—provide a good contrast, in that the Charleston demonstration evaluated an approach that strengthened the work test, and the Washington demonstration assessed an approach that streamlined (or weakened) the work test. The work test component of the Charleston demonstration implemented in three ES offices involved a comparison of two groups of claimants who received a first UI payment: claimants randomly assigned to a control group that had their work registration requirement waived (which essentially formalized the policy that was previously in effect), and claimants randomly assigned to a treatment group that was instructed to register with the ES no later than the end of the week following the week in which they received their first check. Based on a cross-matching of ES and UI data files, claimants who did not comply with the strengthened work test were called in by the UI program for a fact-finding interview to determine whether a disqualification should be imposed until the requirement was met.

In contrast, the Washington demonstration, which was conducted in a single large urban ES office, examined the effectiveness of the work test by comparing the outcomes of two groups of monetarily and non-monetarily eligible claimants that were randomly assigned to different work test approaches. One group was assigned to the standard work search policy, traditionally used in most states, of requiring claimants to make at least three employer contacts each week and to report those contacts on their continued claim form. The other group was randomly assigned to a streamlined work search approach that did not require claimants to report work search contacts and had UI payments automatically sent to claimants in a sum equal to the weekly benefit amount, unless the claimant called the local office to report changes in circumstances that affected the benefit amount. The following brief summary of highlights from these two experimental evaluations of the impacts and cost-effectiveness of the work test is based on the results reported in Corson, Long, and Nicholson (1984) and in Johnson and Klepinger (1994):

> The experimental evidence from the demonstration projects is consistent and clearly indicates that strong work test requirements

are effective in reducing UI payments and that weak work search and work test policies have large and adverse consequences for the UI trust fund. For example, evidence from the Charleston demonstration indicates that a strengthened work test requirement that claimants must register with the ES or else will be denied benefits, coupled with rigorous enforcement, reduces UI payments by 0.5 weeks per claimant, and does not affect claimants' likelihood of working or average earnings. Moreover, evidence from the Washington demonstration indicates that a weak work search policy has very large and adverse consequences for the UI trust fund. Specifically, relative to the standard approach to work search, the weaker policy resulted in longer durations of unemployment benefit receipt of over 3 weeks and increased total UI payments by over $250 per claimant, but did not significantly affect claimants' subsequent earnings.[34]

The consistency of results from these two demonstration projects, each with high internal validity, indicates that the role of the ES in performing the work test for UI claimants is very significant. In particular, the findings suggest that UI/ES offices that require claimants to search for work and to register with the ES and that have an effective mechanism to follow-up and enforce this requirement, can bring about significant savings to the UI trust fund, without adversely affecting other outcomes for claimants. However, there appears to be wide variation in work test policies and practices across offices, which limits the overall effectiveness of the ES in this role nationwide.

Effectiveness of Services

The second major role the ES plays for UI claimants (and for other registrants) involves the provision of basic labor exchange services or services to assist in the matching of qualified applicants with job openings. This includes the fundamental services such as job referrals, employment counseling, testing, and job development. It also includes other, more intensive, services, such as job search workshops, which are offered periodically in some offices. In this section, we summarize the available evidence on the effectiveness of ES services, with particular attention, whenever possible, on the evidence as it pertains to serving claimants.

Because the ES is mandated to serve all individuals who request assistance, attempts to use experimental methods of random assignment to evaluate the ES have previously been rejected by the Labor Department as inappropriate or infeasible.[35] As a result, the evidence of the overall effectiveness on the main ES labor exchange services is based on comparison group methodologies that statistically control for potential differences between the groups of applicants who receive services and those who do not. Because comparison group designs, regardless of the rigorous statistical methods used, have less internal validity and provide inherently less convincing results on program effectiveness, there are *no* studies that provide incontrovertible evidence on the overall effectiveness of the main ES labor exchange services. Moreover, most of the available evidence corresponds to how the ES program was operating in the late 1970s to the mid 1980s. Despite these potential limitations, we will summarize the lessons learned from the most rigorous of these studies.

There is, however, extensive and quite convincing evidence concerning the impacts of job search workshops on the labor market outcomes of unemployed workers and, in particular, of UI claimants. This is primarily because of several demonstration projects undertaken by the U.S. Department of Labor at a variety of sites, in which claimants were randomly assigned to a treatment group that included a mandatory job search workshop, or to a control group that was not eligible for the workshop. Classical experimental evaluation methods were viewed as appropriate in these instances, as the workshop was considered to be something "extra, and in addition to" the basic labor exchange activities, and in most instances, was not part of the regular set of ES services offered prior to the demonstration.[36] The findings from these studies will also be summarized.

Primary Labor Exchange Services

Of the various labor exchange and job-matching services provided by the ES—job referral, counseling, testing, job development—there is no reliable research evidence on the impacts of testing or of job development. Moreover, there is no reliable evidence on the effects of the labor market information services provided by the ES. In contrast, there has been one comprehensive national evaluation (Johnson et al. 1983) that examined the impacts of ES labor exchange services, primarily job referrals, on the short-term labor market outcomes of ES applicants in a representative sample of ES offices. In addition, research by Katz (1978), Romero, Cox, and Katz (1991), and work in progress by Katz and Jacobson examine the job search outcomes of individuals who use the ES versus the outcomes of those who do not, using a rich data base for unemployed workers in a single state, Pennsylvania. There has also been one (pilot) experimental evaluation of the effectiveness of counseling in the ES (Benus et al. 1977), and there has been a national survey of the counseling program (Johnson et al. 1981). The main highlights from these studies are as follows:

- Women who receive ES job referrals are estimated to return to work more quickly (about three weeks sooner) and to obtain higher earnings (by nearly 25 percent) in the short term than otherwise similar individuals who did not receive referrals. Because the wage rates of women who received referrals and those who did not are very similar, the earnings gains are due to women with referrals spending more time in employment; however, they do not trade earlier employment for lower wage rates.

- The positive effects of ES job referrals for women are widespread and are not concentrated on specific subgroups. In particular, the effects of ES referrals for women are similar for both mandatory and nonmandatory registrants.

- In part because the cost of serving ES registrants is so low, the benefits that accrue to women in the short term are sufficiently large to conclude that the ES is an efficient use of public resources, even without considering long term outcomes or other potential benefits of the ES.

- Many unemployed workers (and particularly dislocated workers) use the ES as a "last resort" or as a "backstop," and turn to the ES only after other job- finding methods have failed. After controlling for when dislocated workers choose to use the ES, results indicate that ES services (placements and referrals that do not lead to placements) significantly reduce the remaining unemployment duration. Although the effects are significant for both men and women, the effects are larger for women who were dislocated, and for those who wait longer to use the ES.

• A pilot study of the impacts of ES counseling concluded that it had no significant impact on duration of unemployment, earnings, or job satisfaction.[37] This is consistent with findings from a national survey of the counseling program, in which counseling supervisors reported that counselors were primarily evaluated on the quality of the counseling records kept, the size of their caseload, and their communication and relationship skills; many fewer indicated that counselors were evaluated on ES services provided to job seekers or on the results of those services.

Although these results indicate that job referral services provided by the ES to unemployed workers may be cost-effective, the conclusions apply primarily to how the ES operated 15-20 years ago. Moreover, a recent national survey of UI recipients and exhaustees (Corson and Dynarski 1990) reported that only 4 percent of all recipients and exhaustees found their jobs through the ES. New information is needed to assess the effectiveness of the ES overall and in providing job-matching services to claimants.

Job Search Assistance Services

In addition to these analyses of the basic labor exchange services, there have been a number of demonstrations in recent years designed to test the effects of enhanced job search assistance services (and other services) in improving the labor market outcomes of UI claimants. These efforts include three demonstration projects completed in the 1980s—the Charleston Claimant Placement and Work Test Demonstration, the New Jersey UI Reemployment Demonstration, and the Washington Alternative Work Search Experiment—all of which were rigorously conducted using random assignment to treatment or control status. In addition, the success of these projects and the need to better understand the behavioral response to different service delivery packages have spawned other ongoing, rigorous demonstrations testing various packages of enhanced job search services in Maryland,[38] Florida, and the District of Columbia. We will briefly describe the key features of these programs and highlight the lessons learned from the demonstrations completed to date.

The Charleston, New Jersey, and Washington demonstrations shared several key design features. For example, all three programs adopted an "early intervention" philosophy and offered enhanced ES job search assistance services relatively early in the unemployment spell (i.e., generally four-to-six weeks). Moreover, the additional services provided were all considered "mandatory," and claimants who did not report could be denied benefits. Finally, the enhanced services all included a job search workshop that was conducted by ES staff. Despite these common elements, there were also important differences in the population of claimants targeted for assistance, and in the intensity and content of the specific services offered:[39]

- In Charleston, the job search workshop lasted only approximately three hours and was offered to all claimants (except those with mass layoff claims) who had been collecting UI benefits for four weeks. Moreover, the claimants randomly assigned to take the workshop also received strengthened work test services and a detailed ES interview along with a job referral or job development attempt.

- The New Jersey demonstration was designed to serve the subset of claimants who were likely to be dislocated workers.[40] Further, all treatment group members assigned to take the workshop were first interviewed and tested (in about the fifth week after filing the claim), and they were also required to make follow-up periodic contacts with the ES office. The workshop was designed to last three hours each morning for a week.

- The demonstration in Washington tested a "pure" job search workshop treatment that involved a two-day intensive workshop about five-to-six weeks after filing the claim. Workshop participation was required except for union members and employer-attached claimants.

Despite the differences in design and target groups, the results from the three demonstrations, reported in Corson et al. (1984b), Corson et al. (1989), and Johnson and Klepinger (1991, 1994), are quite consistent. Highlights from these demonstrations indicate the following:

- There is strong and statistically significant evidence on the effectiveness of enhanced job search assistance services in reducing the duration of UI benefits. On average, claimants in the group directed to the job search workshop received about one-half week less of UI payments during the benefit year than those assigned to the control group. This corresponds to about $50-$70 per claimant on average.

- There is no evidence that the relatively rapid reemployment of claimants in the enhanced services group occurs at the cost of lower earnings or hourly wage rates. That is, the wage rates and earnings of the treatment and control groups are similar.

- Extensive benefit-cost analysis indicates that the enhanced services approach in each demonstration was very cost-effective.

- It appears that the shorter durations of receipt of UI payments for the workshop groups are primarily due to the effect of being required to attend the workshop, which raises the costs to the claimant of remaining on UI, and are not due to the enhanced job search abilities derived from participating in the workshop.

The consistency of the findings across sites from these experimental evaluations, each with internal validity, provides strong evidence that mandatory job search assistance workshops for claimants early in their unemployment spell are a cost-effective method of reducing the duration of unemployment and of promoting more rapid reemployment, without compromising the level of pay.[41] These findings lead Meyer (1995) to conclude that policy makers "should consider making enhanced job search assistance services universal." However, because of the difficulty of isolating the effects of the job search assistance workshop from the effects of other changes that were made, it is unclear how the best combination of enhanced services should be designed.

The Current and Future Role of the Employment Service in a New Workforce Development System

The ES has undergone numerous changes in recent years and is at a crossroads in its history, both its relationship with the UI program and in its role in a new workforce development system. Moreover, although the preceding discussion has identified valuable information concerning the impacts and cost-effectiveness of the ES in general and in its roles in serving UI claimants, much of this information is becoming somewhat dated, and there are many gaps in our understanding of the effectiveness of certain ES services. Some of the knowledge gaps will be filled by evidence from recently completed or ongoing research demonstration programs; in other areas, there is much to learn, and there are no research efforts we are aware of to address those issues.

In this concluding section, we first offer our view as to how the ES will probably function in the near future as part of a new workforce development system. Then, based on the available research evidence, we discuss how effective the new system is likely to be, particularly as it relates to the work test and reemployment services. As part of this discussion, we identify the major knowledge gaps, describe what information is anticipated to be obtained from recent/current demonstrations to fill these gaps, and outline potential areas that should be considered for research that could be used to help shape future ES policies and services.

Writing in 1966, Haber and Murray concluded that it was premature to indicate how far the process of separation between the UI and ES components would or should be. In the thirty years since they reached this conclusion, there has been an unprecedented amount of structural change in the U.S. and world economies. In today's information economy, the proposition of separate UI, ES, and training systems is incompatible with the speed and methods with which information is conveyed and work is performed. Twenty-first century job seekers will need integrated—not fragmented—programs and systems to manage their work lives. They also will need easy access to comprehensive information concerning occupations, labor market trends, and availability of education, employment and training services.

The role of the ES in the information age will be quite different from its past missions. Computerization has allowed several states, such as Colorado, Wisconsin, and North Carolina, to permit unemployed workers to file for benefits over the telephone, to use voice response units to provide weekly claims and job information, and to capitalize on artificial intelligence software to determine benefit eligibility. The future UI program will rely more and more on automated claims processes that will require fewer staff resources. This may allow the ES to devote increased staff efforts to providing quality reemployment services for dislocated UI claimants in a more "case-managed" environment.

The information age is also reshaping the labor exchange functions of the ES. Currently, numerous individuals search for job openings through ES automated job banks linked to the AJB through local ES offices or from personal computers in their own homes. Many states are converting local office areas where UI claimants once stood in lines for services into "resource centers" where job seekers sit to browse computer job listings, prepare resumes, or access a variety of labor market and training "consumer reports." By the end of the century, the expansion of ALMIS and AJB will likely enable all job seekers to provide information about their talents and to obtain data about job openings, reemployment services, and training through full-service career centers and a network of self-access systems via telephones, personal computers, and kiosks. By providing mainstream unemployed workers with an unbounded labor exchange system, easy access to critical information to help them find their own jobs should be commonplace. Thus, more ES staff resources should be available to focus on structurally unemployed workers who face more severe employment barriers and who require more intensive services.

Future full-service labor exchange offices may replicate features of the prototype one-stop Plymouth Career Center in Plymouth, Massachusetts,[42] or Employment Service Center in Tampa, Florida. The Plymouth office stations all local workforce development partners in a one-stop Career Center, where customers receive job information through an advanced computer resource library and a comprehensive menu of services. Located in the former Plymouth Job Center office, the Career Center was completely remodeled to meet the needs of new workforce development partners and customers. The design and implementation of the Plymouth Career Center resulted from a partnership between local area employers, the community college, and employment and training providers.

The Tampa center is located in a former shopping mall where all Florida employment and training programs, as well as other community agencies, are housed to serve area customers. The Tampa Employment Service Center includes eight employment and training organizations, formerly located at thirteen different public employment and training office locations. All job seekers who enter the facility are greeted by a knowledgeable Service Center staff member, as UI and ES staff are cross-trained. Center staff members think of themselves as "old UI claims takers" or "old ES interviewers," and they provide job seekers with all the assistance needed at a single service point.

It is likely that the workforce development system of the next decade will include one-stop services that are tailored to customer needs and are provided in such a way that both the employer and the job seeker have access to the information necessary to make better employment and reemployment choices. Instead of the archaic "one size fits all" approach of providing similar services to all unemployed workers, the future system will offer multiple levels of assistance that range from access to valuable self-service tools to more intensive services. Within this system, individuals with certain requirements will receive what they need, not a service designed for the average unemployed worker. In addition, the job-matching function will continue to become more automated, with new information systems giving individual job seekers and employers the opportunity to increase their involvement in the process. Finally, the WPRS initiative mandates the participation in designated reemployment services of claimants identified through a profiling screening program as likely UI exhaustees. This will ensure that the ES expands its work test function.

The preceding discussion briefly summarizes a widely held view of the direction the workforce development system is headed, including its likely key features, and the labor exchange functions that will be performed. Despite this perspective, a key question still remains to be answered. How effective will such a system be in meeting the needs of unemployed workers in the rapidly changing global economy? We will address this question based on the available research evidence and will highlight the major issues that need to be addressed in future research.

The increase in the use of automated and remote processes for filing initial and continuing UI claims will result in more efficiency in that fewer staff resources will be required to conduct these functions. At the same time, however, the use of more automated claims filing processes is also likely to lead to less contact between the average claimant and the ES system, which may focus the work test role of the ES on an exclusive subset of the population of UI recipients—dislocated workers—who are referred to the ES as a result of a profiling screening system. Moreover, many states seem to be reducing the work search requirements for claimants, and some are considering eliminating the requirement that claimants register for work at the ES.[43] However, there is no indication that states are modifying their availability for work requirements for refusing a suitable job referral or an offer of suitable work. The research evidence strongly indicates that UI programs that require claimants to search for work and to register with the ES and that follow through and enforce these standards produce significant savings to the UI trust fund through reduced UI payments. Moreover, there is good evidence that streamlined registration and work search policies have adverse consequences for the UI trust fund. As such, to the extent that the future workforce development system includes a UI program that relies more heavily on automated and distant processes and streamlined registration and work search requirements, the value of the ES will be limited in performing the work test, contributing to higher UI outlays.

There is also reasonably strong evidence on the likely effects of the WPRS initiative. Specifically, results from the New Jersey UI Reemployment Demonstration indicate that identifying individuals early in their unemployment spell who are likely to be displaced and who will experience difficulty in becoming employed, and providing intensive (mandatory) services to those individuals, is a cost-effective way to reduce UI payments and facilitate reemployment. Although the program tested in New Jersey has been the model on which many states are designing their early intervention program, it is also clear that there are potentially important differences between the New Jersey model and how WPRS may be implemented that could affect the effectiveness of the WRPS initiative. For example, the New Jersey model used a highly structured and standardized approach for claimants who were referred to services (e.g., orientation, testing, job-search workshop, assessment interview), as opposed to the new focus on customized service that is likely to prevail as these programs develop. Moreover, the New Jersey model required that claimants report to the ES office at several specific points following the assessment interview; it is too early to tell whether many states are adopting the same feature in their profiling and reemployment services programs. The ongoing Labor Department-sponsored Job Search Assistance Demonstration in Florida and the District of Columbia and an evaluation of the WPRS systems in Delaware, Florida, Kentucky, Maryland, New Jersey, and Oregon will provide evidence on the effects of a standardized versus a customized service-delivering strategy for claimants who are profiled

and referred to reemployment services. However, it is difficult to estimate how much difference changes to the New Jersey model will make
in the likely benefits from the WPRS process.

Perhaps the two most important changes in the workforce development system concern the movement to integrated one-stop services and
the expansion of labor market information. Although the evaluation of
the New Jersey demonstration concluded that the success of the project
was in no small part due to the well-developed linkages between UI,
ES, and JTPA and the coordinated efforts of their staff, this belief was
based on qualitative judgments and not on formal quantitative evidence. The New Jersey demonstration did not test a one-stop service
approach, and we are aware of no other research projects underway
that will provide valid evidence on the effectiveness of one-stop services. This is an important research gap. Specifically, it is important to
understand the overall effectiveness of the one-stop approach and
whether this success varies depending on the service mix/levels offered
(e.g., information broker, job matching service, job search assistance,
training).

Moreover, there is no research evidence on the cost-effectiveness of
providing labor market information; it is assumed that improvements
in the access to and quality of information will lead individuals to use
the data and to make better employment and career decisions.
Although it is often thought to be difficult to experimentally test the
effects of increased information, the Departments of Labor and Education are currently implementing a demonstration project that uses
experimental techniques to assess the effects of providing information
to experienced workers on investment in lifelong learning. Similar
efforts should be considered to test the effects of improved labor market information on reemployment decisions of unemployed workers.

In spite of the lack of concrete evidence, one-stop systems are likely
to serve as the organizing vehicle for providing access to a wide range
of customized employment services. In the end, one-stop services may
provide only street-level consolidation of local offices, rather than of
programs. At this juncture, it is not clear whether the bundling of services in many states at physical sites in each labor market area will
provide job seekers with more than co-located programs. Without federal legislative changes, current employment and training programs
retain separate eligibility and funding streams that limit consolidation.

Beyond program consolidation, a one-stop delivery system is still no pie-in-the-sky job seeker panacea. Unless state one-stop systems are built upon integrated computer structures, their value in today's information economy will be short term. The road to a unified one-stop services system is a long one. Ultimately, the issue for federal and state ES policy makers may be what role the state ES is to play in one-stop system development.

As the Labor Department and its state partners shape a long-term strategy for the ES based upon the needs of employers and job seekers, it may be that future Wagner-Peyser resources of states will fund workforce development systems and not an old-line institution—the ES. Irrespective of what moniker is used to describe state labor exchange functions, a new look at performance standards is sorely needed to ensure state-to-state program quality and expansion of unmediated job listing and seeking technologies. Before the end of the century, a Labor Department goal should be to examine national labor exchange performance standards that improve access, increase job listings, promote service satisfaction, and reduce job transition time. An examination of labor exchange performance standards for UI claimant services should include the degree of early intervention, the receipt of quality reemployment services, the analysis of job transition time standards for claimants who are experiencing different (i.e., frictional, cyclical, structural) unemployment circumstances, and the resultant UI trust funds' savings.

Each chamber of the 104th Congress has passed legislation that could have dramatically altered the entire employment and training system as it has evolved since the days of the New Deal. The Consolidated and Reform Education, Employment, and Rehabilitation Systems Act (CAREERS Act, H.R. 1617), which was passed in the House of Representatives on September 19, 1995, and the Senate version of H.R. 1617, called the Workforce Development Act (passed October 10, 1995), consolidated a large number of education, and employment and training programs into a limited number of block grants to states. The House bill would have fused about 100 programs into three block grants to states. The Senate bill would have consolidated about 80 programs into a single block grant to states. Both bills created a one-stop delivery system for the provision of employment and training services; amended the Wagner-Peyser Act to establish a more "state-led" labor exchange system; and required the ES to integrate its programs into the one-stop system.

In the House bill, the federal ES functions would have been administered by the Secretary of Labor. Under the Senate bill, the federal ES functions would have been administered by a Workforce Development Partnership under the joint control of the Secretary of Labor and the Secretary of Education. There are other areas of the Senate bill which, if enacted into law, would have produced marked change to the existing federal-state labor exchange system. Section 1 of the current Wagner-Peyser Act reads, in part, "to promote the establishment and maintenance of a national system of public employment offices. . . ." In the Senate bill, the word "public" modifying "employment offices" was deleted. This change could have resulted in the privatization of labor exchange services, which in turn would have raised a host of accountability and continuity-of-service issues. In addition, the Senate bill would have apportioned to states 25 percent of the single block grants (including Wagner-Peyser funds) for workplace employment activities or Wagner-Peyser activities. The issue of separate FUTA funding to provide for the administration of ES programs counting toward the 25 percent workforce employment apportionment could have sharply limited state resources for occupational training. Further, the House bill promoted private sector labor exchange services and authorized federal incentive grants through which one-stop centers and labor market information implementation would have been accomplished. The Senate bill provided for no similar federal incentive funding to states.

In summary, both bills promoted the development of one-stop delivery systems, folded employment services into them, created options for public and private operators, ensured customer choice, and drastically shifted government control to the states. As such, they contained several key features of the failed 1994 Reemployment Act and its policy successor, the proposed G.I. Bill for America's Workers.[44] In July 1996, a House-Senate conference committee voted out along party lines the Workforce and Career Development Act, but Congress failed to take further action.

The ES system in the United States is likely to experience manifold changes in the next few years. As the federal ES role diminishes, state ES agencies may be catapulted to leadership positions that they may not have expected. At what may be the most decisive crossroads in its history, ES finds itself headed in several new directions:

- **U.S. Employment Service**. Its title may still be listed on a federal "letterhead," but its partnership role is likely to be more "consultative."

- **State Employment Services.** They are likely to continue merging their labor exchange programs into broader workforce development systems. Federal block grants to states for employment, training, education and welfare programs may be more flexible and also increase the demand for the ES to serve welfare customers.

- **Local Employment Services.** They may be operating in a more deregulated environment, where the lines between public and private labor exchange service providers are increasingly blurred.

- **Employers and Job Seekers**. They are likely to be provided with job and training services and with "consumer reports" about labor markets at multiple service points using distant and self-accessed technologies—in an electronic labor exchange "without walls." Those who need them are likely to receive comprehensive and mediated services that are customized to their requirements.

Throughout this century, despite sometimes conflicting public policy directions, the ES has provided vital labor exchange services to the American workforce. As we enter the next century, the signposts of the new directions point to likely shifts in the federal-state ES partnership and in the ES public charter. However, the fate of a national electronic labor exchange system may be tied as much to its popularity and growth as to any legislative reform.

NOTES

The authors wish to thank Louis Jacobson for his helpful comments in preparation of this chapter.

1. There are offices in fifty states, the District of Columbia, the Commonwealth of Puerto Rico, Guam, and the Virgin Islands.

2. On January 3, 1918, the Division of Information in the Labor Department was renamed the U.S. Employment Service and reorganized to facilitate war production. The economic prosperity that followed World War I left little policy sentiment for retaining a national ES system until the tumult of the Great Depression. In 1933, the ES was at a similar crossroads, and President Roosevelt decided to revitalize it.

3. The employment security system is a national network of state agencies, called state employment security agencies (SESA), that today operates a public ES, a UI system, a foreign labor certification program, labor market information programs, including the collection of employment and unemployment statistics carried out under cooperative agreements with the Bureau of Labor Statistics, and may also include other employment and wage loss programs, such as temporary disability insurance.

4. Although it is a federal requirement that approved UI programs include "able-to-work and available-for-work" continuing eligibility criteria, states have substantial latitude in setting the specific standards to meet this requirement. For example, when a claimant is unable to work because he or she is ill or otherwise incapacitated, benefits are not payable, albeit state laws vary on what constitutes incapacity. Further, in some states, claimants who are not job-attached are required to contact at least three potential employers during each week they claim benefits, while other states require fewer contacts per week, or do not require the contacts to be listed when claiming benefits. In addition, the work search requirements placed on claimants who expect to be recalled differ, depending on whether there is a known recall date.

5. Availability for suitable work means work "which is ordinarily performed in (the claimant's) chosen locality in sufficient amount to constitute a substantial labor market for his services" (U.S. Department of Labor, 1962, p. 57).

6. Johnson et al. (1983) find that UI claimants are much less likely to obtain a job referral than are other ES registrants. Specifically, after adjusting for other characteristics, they estimate that regular ES registrants are roughly 50 percent more likely to obtain a job referral than are UI claimants. More recent data confirm that regular ES registrants are considerably more likely to obtain a job referral than UI claimants. However, ES services to UI claimants have increased to claimants over the last few years. Specifically, national program data for the three-year period of program year (PY) 1992-1994 indicate that the proportion of all UI claimants who registered with the ES who received at least one referral increased from 23.4 to 29.0 percent.

7. Over PY 1992-1994, the proportion of individuals who received ES referrals who were placed ranged from 32.6 to 33.8 percent.

8. In PY 1994, the proportion of all ES registrants who were placed in a job was 14.3 percent. This compares to 7.5 percent for all UI claimants who registered with the ES.

9. In the early 1990s, based upon a National Academy of Sciences report, *Fairness in Employment Testing* (May 1989), the Labor Department advised states to terminate the use of within-group conversion scoring or other race- or ethnicity-based adjustments to GATB scores in making selection and referral decisions. States are permitted to use the GATB and its variants, as one of a variety of criteria, for referring customers to job vacancies (U.S. Department of Labor, 1991).

10. For example, from PY 1992 to 1994, the proportion of all eligible claimants who were tested ranged from 1.4 to 2.1 percent.

11. Section 3(a) of the Wagner-Peyser Act of June 6, 1933, 29 U.S.C. 49 et seq.

12. Section 303(a)(2) of the SSA, 42 U.S.C., and section 3304 (a)(1) of the Federal Unemployment Tax Act (FUTA), 26 U.S.C.

13. Many years later, in 1971, the ES took on a similar function for certain recipients of food stamps and Aid to Families with Dependent Children (AFDC).

14. In these partnerships, the federal government has traditionally been responsible for establishing broad policy and program guidelines, for payroll taxes to finance the administration of programs, and for allocating operating budgets to the states, who were in turn responsible for the day-to-day operations of the programs.

15. This relationship was characterized as a federal-local partnership and labeled "New Federalism." Under this federal-local governance structure, the Nixon administration and subsequent administrations initiated federal block grants to states and local areas.

16. We believe that the SESA should have been designated to administer the EDWAA program. Dislocated workers are, in large measure, a subset of SESA UI and ES customers.

17. Originally, administrative funds to operate state ES programs were based upon a federal-state match. Since 1938, the principal revenue source for funding state ES programs is employer contributions under FUTA, 26 U.S.C. The amount of ES funds derived from FUTA revenues has varied, and, currently, is 97 percent from FUTA and 3 percent from federal general revenue. Administrative grants to operate state ES programs are allocated under a mandated formula (section 6 of the Wagner-Peyser Act) that distributes 97 percent of the available ES funds to states according to relative shares of the civilian labor force and number of unemployed. The Secretary of Labor distributes 3 percent of the total available ES funds to assure that all states maintain a statewide ES.

18. Twenty states utilize employer surtaxes to fund administrative and program costs of employment and training programs (U.S. Department of Labor 1995, pp. 2-39 to 2-44).

19. U.S. General Accounting Office (1991, p. 5). In the report, GAO also recommended that the Labor Department develop performance standards for the ES labor exchange system. While some federal-state ES steps to develop standards were taken, no ES performance standards have been implemented.

20. ES Revitalization partners include the Labor Department, State Employment Security Agencies (SESAs), organized labor, Interstate Conference of Employment Security Agencies (ICESA), and the International Association of Personnel in Employment Security.

21. The cooperative agreements are operated in conjunction with the Center for Employment Security Education and Research, an affiliate of ICESA.

22. Public Law (P.L.) 103-6, section 4, Profiling New Claimants (March 4, 1993).

23. P.L. 103-152, section 4, Worker Profiling (November 24, 1993).

24. The service plan contains a description of the specific set of services that will be provided and for which participation is required as a condition of continuing UI eligibility. It is to serve as a reemployment compact between the claimant, service provider, and the UI program, and may form the basis for feedback to the UI component. In many states, ES staff prepare the service plan and provide reemployment services in cooperation with other service providers.

25. Some of the states that received Labor Department assistance to implement early WPRS systems are providing a broader range of reemployment services. For example, Delaware includes money management in the assessment process, and New Jersey places emphasis on direct placement referrals for job-ready claimants and provides in-depth assessment and job clubs as follow-up to a job-search workshop.

26. As of this writing, twenty-nine states have voluntarily placed their state job banks on the Internet. The Internet address is http://www.ajb.dni.us.

27. A twenty-state Talent Bank Consortium, led by Michigan and Missouri, was formed to pilot test an electronic on-line resume system.

28. Over the years, various proposals to provide one-stop services have been introduced. In April 1992, the Bush administration sponsored the Job Training 2000 Act (S. 2633), which included creation of a local Skill Center network to provide "one-stop shopping' for vocational and job training services. The bill received scant congressional attention.

29. Connecticut, Iowa, Maryland, Massachusetts, Texas, and Wisconsin. Under the Massachusetts proposal, One-Stop Career Center development is based upon market competition, which is unique among One-Stop implementation states. Massachusetts One-Stop operators are selected through a competitive process open to public and private service providers.

30. Arizona, Illinois, Indiana, Kentucky, Louisiana, Minnesota, Missouri, New Jersey, North Carolina, and Ohio.

31. In fiscal year (FY) 1994, Congress appropriated $50 million for ALMIS and One-Stop Career Centers under existing Wagner-Peyser Act authority. In FY 1995, Congress approved the Labor Department's request to expand ALMIS and One-Stop systems and appropriated $100 million.

32. After a lengthy debate, in April 1996, the administration and Congress reached an overall FY 1996 budget agreement that included $110 million for ALMIS and One-Stop systems. The president's FY 1997 budget requests $150 million toward the continued growth of ALMIS and One-Stop systems.

33. As indicated earlier, the ES plays a role in administering the work test requirements for other income support programs, as well as for UI. In this chapter, we focus on the evidence concerning the UI program.

34. If such a weak work test were implemented nationwide, the results suggest that the adverse consequences for the UI trust fund could exceed $2 billion. In interpreting this evidence, it is important to note that the specific streamlined policy tested in Washington differed from normal services both in that the work search requirements were reduced and the UI payment process was altered, as claimants were automatically sent a check for their full benefit amount unless they contacted the office to report a change in circumstances that affected their benefit payments. As such, it is likely that a significant part of the overall impact is due to the changes in the payment process, and that only part is due to the streamlined work search requirements. A recently completed demonstration in Maryland was designed to overcome this problem and to provide direct evidence on the efficacy of work search requirements per se.

35. The only exception of which we are aware is a pilot study of the effects of ES counseling, in which individuals in need of counseling were randomly assigned to receive it or not; both groups received normal placement services, as appropriate. The results of that study, reported in Benus et al. (1977), are summarized in the following text.

36. As job search workshops become more entrenched as part of the basic set of reemployment services offered, it will be interesting to see whether this limits the ability of researchers to use classical experimental evaluation methods to test the effectiveness of such services.

37. Although the sample sizes of ES registrants in need of counseling and included in the pilot study were relatively small, the estimated impacts were also consistently small and did not approach conventional levels of statistical significance.

38. The demonstration in Maryland is also testing the effects of alternative work search requirements, including increases in the number of employer contacts, as well as testing the effects of verifying the reported contacts.

39. As a result of these design differences, it is difficult to separate the effects of the mandatory job search workshop from the effects of the other job search assistance and requirements provided in some of these demonstrations.

40. A series of eligibility screens was used to target the services to likely dislocated workers. The most important screen was a tenure requirement, which excluded all claimants who had not worked for their previous employer for at least three years. In addition, individuals younger than age 25 and those with a definite recall date were excluded. Only about one-quarter of all UI claimants who received a first payment were eligible for the demonstration.

41. Very preliminary results from the Job Search Assistance Demonstration, currently being tested in Florida and the District of Columbia, appear to be consistent with the results reported from the earlier demonstrations and indicate that enhanced job search assistance services reduce UI benefit payments.

42. The Plymouth Career Center was awarded the 1995 National Awards Pyramid Prize sponsored by the U.S. Department of Labor and the ICESA, for collaboration in improved customer

service. Inaugurated in 1994, the SESA National Awards program was based upon recommendations from ICESA and other ES Revitalization partners.

43. While we know of no quantitative evidence that identifies the causes for relaxation of registration and work search requirements by states, we suggest one reason may be that federal implementation in the 1980s of a nationwide UI quality control program influenced states to relax formal registration and work search policies to improve measured payment accuracy rates.

44. In December 1994, President Clinton proposed a Middle Class Bill of Rights designed to help Americans meet the challenges of the new economy. One of its elements, a G.I. Bill for America's Workers, would restructure federal job training programs by giving the resources directly to workers to learn new skills, and would provide information, advice, and job search assistance.

References

Adams, L.P. 1969. "The Public Employment Service in Transition." In *Cornell Studies in Industrial and Labor Relations*, Vol. 16. Ithaca, NY: New York State School of Industrial and Labor Relations.

Benus, Jacob, Arden Hall, Patricia Gwartney-Gibbs, Marilyn Coon, Christine Cole, Diane Leeds, and Douglas Brent. 1977. "The Effectiveness of Counseling in the U.S. Employment Service: A Pilot Study." Report prepared by SRI International under Contract No. 20-06-75-48 for the U.S. Department of Labor, Employment and Training Administration, August.

Corson, Walter, Paul T. Decker, Sharie M. Dunstan, Anne R. Gordon, Patricia Anderson, and John Homrighausen. 1989. "New Jersey Unemployment Insurance Reemployment Demonstraiton Project." Unemployment Insurance Occasional Paper No. 89-3, U.S. Department of Labor, Employment and Training Administration.

Corson, Walter, and Mark Dynarski. 1990. "A Study of Unemployment Insurance Recipients and Exhaustees: Findings from a National Survey." Unemployment Insurance Occasional Paper No. 90-3, U.S. Department of Labor, Employment and Training Administration.

Corson, Walter, Alan Hershey, and Stuart Kerachsky. 1984. "Application of the Unemployment Insurance System Work Test and Nonmonetary Eligibility Standards." Report prepared by Mathematica Policy Research.

Corson, Walter, David Long, and Walter Nicholson. 1984. "Evaluation of the Charleston Claimant Placement and Work Test Demonstration." Report prepared by Mathematica Policy Research under Contract No. 20-34-82-07 for the U.S. Department of Labor, Employment and Training Administration.

Haber, William, and Merrill G. Murray. 1966. *Unemployment Insurance in the American Economy: An Historical Review and Analysis*. Homewood, IL: Richard D. Irwin.

Jacobson, Louis. 1994. "The Effectiveness of the U.S. Employment Service." Draft report by Westat, prepared for the Advisory Commission on Unemployment Compensation, March.

Johnson, Terry R., Katherine P. Dickinson, and Richard West. 1985. "An Evaluation of the Impact of ES Referrals on Applicant Earnings," *Journal of Human Resources* 20, 1 (1985): 117-137.

Johnson, Terry R., Katherine P. Dickinson, Richard W. West, Susan E. McNicholl, Jennifer M. Pfiester, Alex L. Stagner, and Betty, J. Harris. 1983. "A National Evaluation of the Impact of the United States Employment Service." Final report prepared by SRI International under Contract No. 23-

06-79-04 for the U.S. Department of labor, Employment and Training Administration, June.

Johnson, Terry R., and Dan H. Klepinger. 1991. "Evaluation of the Impacts of the Washington Alternative Work Search Experiment." Unemployment Insurance Occasional Paper 91-4, U.S. Department of Labor, Employment and Training Administration.

_____. 1994. "Experimental Evidence on Unemployment Insurance Work-Search Policies," Journal of Human Resources 29, 3 (Summer): 695-717.

Johnson, Terry R., C. Eric Munson, Samuel Weiner, Asi Cohen, Marilyn L. Coon, and Susan E. McNicoll. 1981a. "Findings from a Survey of the U.S. Employment Service Counseling Program." SRI International, March.

Johnson, Terry R., C. Eric Munson, Gary L. Steiger, Samuel Weiner, Marilyn L. Coon, and Susan E. McNicoll. 1981b. "A National Evaluation of the U.S. Employment Service: A Description of Monitoring and Community Service Activities Performed by Local ES Offices." Report prepared by SRI International, March.

Johnson, Terry R., C. Eric Munson, Jennifer M. Pfiester, Gary L. Stieger, Marilyn L. Coon, and Susan E. McNicoll. 1981c. "A National Evaluation of the Impact of the United States Employment Service." Report prepared by SRI International under contract to the U.S. Employment Service, April.

Katz, Arnold. 1978. "Exploratory Measures of Labor Market Influences of the Employment Service." Unpublished manuscript, Department of Economics, University of Pittsburgh.

Kulik, Jane. 1994. "The U.S. Employment Service: A Review of Evidence Concerning its Operations and Effectiveness." Report prepared for the Advisory Council on Unemployment Compensation under Contract No. B9A34914, May.

Levitan, Sar, and Robert Taggart. 1976. The Promise of Greatness. Cambridge, MA: Harvard University Press.

Meyer, Bruce D. 1995. "Lessons from the U.S. Unemployment Insurance Experiments," Journal of Economic Literature 32 (March): 91-131.

Perkins, Frances. 1946. The Roosevelt I Knew. New York: Viking.

Romero, Carol, Donald Cox, and Arnold Katz. 1991. "The Potential Effectiveness of the Employment Service in Serving Dislocated Workers Under EDWAA: Evidence From the 1980s." Research Report 91-02, National Commission for Employment Policy.

"The States Labor Market Information Review." 1995. Report from the Interstate Converence of Employment Security Agencies.

U.S. Department of Labor. 1962. "Unemployment Insurance Legislative Policy, Recommendations for State Legislation 1962." BES No. U-212A, Bureau of Employment Security.

_____. 1967. Improving Communications and Service to the Public. MA Manual Transmittal Sheet No. 13, Manpower Administration, December 8.

_____. 1991. "Policy on Selection and Referral Techniques for Employment and Training Progrtams." Federal Register 56, 243 (December 18).

_____. 1994a. "Notification of Availability of Program Year 1994 Grants for the Planning/Development and Implementation of the One-Stop Career Center System." Field Memorandum No. 47-94, Employment and Training Administration, May 13.

_____. 1994b. Employment Service Revitalization Work Plan." Employment and Training Administration. U.S. Employment Service Program Letter 15-94, October 3.

_____. 1995. "Comparison of State Unemployment Insurance Laws," Comparison Revision, No. 5, Employment and Training Administration, September 3.

U.S. General Accounting Office. 1991. "Employment Service: Improved Leadership Needed for Better Performance." GAO/HRD-91-88, August.

CHAPTER 12

Intersection of Unemployment Insurance with Other Programs and Policies

Walter S. Corson
Mathematica Policy Research, Inc.

A primary objective of the unemployment insurance (UI) system is to insure experienced workers against the risk of unemployment by providing limited replacement of lost wages to those who become unemployed through no fault of their own. Earlier chapters have addressed the question of whether the UI system achieves this objective adequately, and these chapters have identified some deficiencies in the degree to which UI provides income support to the unemployed. Chapter 2, which focuses on the coverage of jobs and the unemployed, points to the recent decrease in the proportion of the unemployed receiving UI, despite increased coverage of jobs, as evidence of a decline in the insurance value of the system. The chapter also points out that low-wage workers are least likely to qualify for UI despite the fact that they work in jobs that are included in the system. Chapter 5, which looks at the adequacy of the weekly benefit amount, concludes that, while weekly benefits satisfy the short-term needs of most claimants, benefit levels may be less adequate for low-wage workers and those with dependents. Finally, chapter 6, which examines the duration of benefits, concludes that short spells of unemployment may be overcompensated and that an optimal system would have longer benefit durations.

These conclusions about the adequacy of the income support provided by the UI system are reexamined in this chapter in light of the fact that this system, while the primary source of income support for unemployed workers, is not their only source. UI is one piece of a larger public and private social insurance and welfare system that also provides some income support to unemployed workers. For example, jobless individuals may, depending on their age, disability status, or family income, receive income from public programs, such as social security, workers' compensation, and the welfare system. Similarly, they may receive termination pay from their employers or other types of payments from private sources as a result of their job loss.

More specifically, this chapter analyzes whether the gaps in UI coverage identified in earlier chapters are addressed by other social insurance and welfare programs. That is, does the existing social insurance and welfare system as a whole provide adequate income support to unemployed workers, or are there gaps in coverage that the UI system or other programs should address? In particular, are the gaps in coverage of long-term unemployed and low-wage unemployed workers addressed by other programs? This question raises the issue of whether there is adequate coordination between UI and other public and private social insurance and welfare programs. Are there, in fact, extensive overlaps in recipient populations among income support programs? Should UI benefits or benefits from other programs be adjusted to consider such overlaps or other sources of income support?

UI's focus on income support also gives rise to questions about whether reemployment services for UI claimants should receive more emphasis. Historically, the UI system has relied on the labor exchange function of the Employment Service (ES) to help claimants become reemployed. Evidence that increasing numbers of claimants suffer permanent job separations and long spells of unemployment, however, suggests that it might be useful to provide more reemployment services, particularly to dislocated workers. Furthermore, findings from recent demonstrations suggest that providing reemployment services or other assistance to these claimants can lead to more rapid reemployment, and the UI system has moved in this direction. The Unemployment Compensation Amendments of 1993 require state UI programs to profile claimants as they enter the system, to identify dislocated workers and refer them to reemployment services. States have recently completed implementing programs to support this requirement.

Two other relatively recent changes in the UI system that restructure benefits or provide additional services to claimants are also designed to promote their employment. First, beginning in 1978, a number of states introduced short-time compensation schemes that restructure the UI benefit calculation to permit payment of UI to groups of workers for partial weeks of unemployment. The idea is to encourage firms to respond to business fluctuations by shortening the work week for a larger group of workers than would otherwise have been laid off, thus promoting the continued employment of workers. Second, based on the results of two demonstrations, states are now permitted to provide UI claimants with self-employment allowances and services as a way of promoting self-employment as a reemployment option.

This chapter addresses these issues. It reviews the way in which the UI system intersects with other income support programs, to identify gaps in the social safety net and to examine how these programs are coordinated. It then discusses recent changes in the UI system to promote reemployment services to claimants and the rationale behind these changes. Finally, it reviews two recent initiatives—short-time compensation and self-employment assistance—that also attempt to promote claimant employment.

Unemployment Insurance and Income Support Programs

Benefit Trends

Social insurance and public assistance programs have grown tremendously in the last forty years. As shown in table 12.1, social insurance programs—that is, programs designed to maintain incomes for individuals who can no longer work because they are elderly, disabled, or unemployed—grew fivefold between 1950 and 1990 as a percentage of GDP (from 1.85 percent to over 9 percent). Public programs that provide assistance to low-income individuals and families also grew during this period although not by as large an amount. In 1950, expenditures for these programs equaled .94 percent of GDP, and, in 1990, they equaled 2.67 percent.

Table 12.1 Social Welfare Expenditures, Selected Fiscal Years 1950-1990 ($ millions)

	Fiscal year						
	1950	1960	1970	1975	1980	1985	1990
Social insurance[a]	$4,946	$19,307	$54,691	$123,013	$229,754	$369,595	$510,616
OASDI	784	11,032	29,686	63,649	117,119	186,151	245,556
Medicare	0	0	7,149	14,781	34,992	71,384	106,806
UI/ES[b]	2,310	3,045	3,858	13,878	18,482	18,482	20,036
Disability/workers' compensation	697	1,656	3,669	7,469	14,835	24,207	41,583
Cash benefits	502	1,196	2,621	4,926	10,960	17,072	26,191
Medical benefits	195	460	1,048	2,543	3,875	7,135	14,392
Public aid[c]	2,496	4,101	16,488	41,447	72,703	98,356	145,642
Cash and in-kind benefits	2,445	3,608	11,275	27,896	45,133	54,497	70,275
Medical benefits	51	493	5,213	13,551	27,570	43,860	75,367
As percentage of GDP							
Social insurance	1.85	3.81	5.55	8.14	8.69	9.31	9.35
OASDI	0.29	2.18	3.01	4.21	4.43	4.69	4.50
Medicare	0.00	0.00	0.73	0.98	1.32	1.80	1.96
UI/ES	0.87	0.60	0.39	0.92	0.70	0.47	0.37
Disability/workers' compensation	0.26	0.33	0.38	0.50	0.56	0.61	0.74
Cash benefits	0.19	0.24	0.27	0.33	0.41	0.43	0.48
Medical benefits	0.07	0.09	0.11	0.17	0.15	0.18	0.26

Public aid						
Cash and in-kind benefits	0.94	0.81	1.67	2.74	2.75	2.48	2.67
Medical benefits	0.92	0.71	1.14	1.85	1.71	1.37	1.29
	0.02	0.10	0.53	0.90	1.04	1.11	1.38

SOURCE: Bixby (1993, pp. 70-76).

NOTE: Numbers include expenditures from federal, state, and local revenues and trust funds under public law and include capital outlays and administrative expenditures.

a. Includes railroad and public employee retirement funds in addition to the listed programs.

b. Includes unemployment compensation under state programs, programs for federal employees, and railroad unemployment insurance; trade adjustment assistance; payments under extended, emergency, disaster, and special unemployment insurance programs; and employment services.

c. Includes cash payments and medical assistance under the Aid to Families with Dependent Children, Medicaid, emergency assistance, Supplemental Security Income, Food Stamps, WIC, and General Assistance programs. Also includes social services, work relief, work-incentive and work experience activities, surplus food, repatriate and refugee assistance, and low-income home energy assistance.

This overall growth in social insurance and public assistance expenditures has, however, not been uniform among programs or over time. For example, programs that provide medical benefits grew the fastest, while the growth in public assistance expenditures for nonmedical benefits leveled off in the last fifteen years. Most important for our purposes, expenditures for unemployment insurance and employment services did not grow over this period as a percentage of GDP. The data in table 12.1 suggest, in fact, that there has been a decline in expenditures relative to GDP in recent years, but comparisons among individual years can be misleading since UI benefits fluctuate widely with the unemployment rate. To address this analytic problem, UI benefits as a percentage of GDP were regressed on the unemployment rate and a time variable for the 1950-1993 period to control for the state of the economy. The results of this regression suggest that there has been a small but statistically significant long-run decline in UI benefits as a percentage of GDP, of about .077 percent every ten years.

Workers who become unemployed or who are otherwise unable to work may receive private as well as public support, with most private assistance provided through employee benefit plans. Data on the prevalence of these plans for medium and large private firms (table 12.2) suggest that many workers in these firms participate in income continuation, retirement, or disability plans.[1] For example, in 1993, 42 percent of workers had severance pay provisions, 78 percent participated in retirement income plans, 87 percent had short-term disability protection via sick pay or sickness and accident insurance, and 41 percent had long-term disability insurance. Based on the data in table 12.2, participation in these plans appears to have declined slightly in the past ten years, although some of this measured decrease may have been due to changes in the sample frame used for the survey.

Overall, these data suggest that workers who become unemployed currently are likely to receive slightly less in terms of UI benefits than they would have twenty or more years ago and that any gaps in UI coverage of unemployed workers are likely to have grown rather than to have been closed. However, the growth in other social insurance and to a lesser extent in public assistance programs could potentially fill these gaps or overlap with UI if unemployed workers qualify for these benefits. Similarly, data on employee benefits show that substantial numbers of workers in private employment participate in income continuation, retirement, and disability plans. These plans could also provide benefits to UI claimants or other unemployed workers.

Table 12.2 Selected Employee Benefits, Medium and Large Private Firms, Percentage of Full-Time Employees Participating

	1983	1988	1993
Income continuation plans			
Severance pay	50	42	42
Supplemental unemployment benefits	NA	6	4
Retirement income plans	82	80	78
Disability benefits			
Short-term protection	94	89	87
Paid sick leave	68	69	65
Sickness and accident insurance	49	46	44
Long-term disability insurance	45	42	41
Medical insurance	96	90	82

SOURCE: U.S. Department of Labor, "Employee Benefits in Medium and Large Firms," Bulletin 2213 (August 1984); Bulletin 2336 (August 1989); Bulletin 2456 (November 1994).
NOTE: Comparisons between years may be misleading because of major changes in the sample frame used for the survey.
NA = not available.

Supplemental Unemployment Benefits and Termination Pay

Some workers who lose their jobs receive income support while unemployed through Supplemental Unemployment Benefit (SUB) plans. These plans provide a supplemental weekly payment to laid-off workers that, in conjunction with the UI weekly benefit, equals a specified percentage of the pre-layoff weekly wage. The plans are supported through employer-financed trust funds that have been established in some labor-management contracts, particularly in the automobile, steel, and rubber industries. All states except New Mexico, Puerto Rico, South Carolina, and South Dakota have ruled that these payments do not affect UI benefit payments.[2]

Workers who lose their jobs may also receive various kinds of severance or termination payments from their employers. Generally, these termination payments fall into two categories: (1) wages in lieu of notice; and (2) severance payments, which are generally based on years of service. As of 1994, thirty-three states counted wages in lieu of notice as disqualifying income for UI purposes. In twelve of these states, claimants receiving wages in lieu of notice were disqualified from UI for the weeks in which they received payments. In the remaining twenty-one states, the UI benefit was reduced by the amount of the wage payment. Since weekly wages will in most cases exceed the UI weekly benefit amount, few claimants would receive payments under the latter provision. Twenty-two states had the same disqualifying income provisions for all types of severance payments.

The availability of severance pay and SUB payments to some workers will not, however, fill gaps in UI coverage for the long-term unemployed or for low-wage workers. While a significant fraction of UI claimants may receive severance pay (in 1993, 42 percent of full-time employees in medium and large firms were eligible for severance pay), these payments generally amount to a limited number of weeks of wages, and they are primarily available to individuals with higher wages, generally professional and technical workers. While SUB payments are more available to production than to professional and technical workers, they are primarily available to relatively high-wage production workers (union workers in manufacturing). Moreover, only a few UI claimants are likely to receive SUB payments (in 1993, only 4 percent of employees in medium and large firms were eligible for SUB if they were laid off).[3]

Additionally, the treatment by some states of wages in lieu of notice and severance payments as disqualifying income for UI seems inconsistent. There does not appear to be a rationale to handle income from these sources any differently than income from other private sources, such as SUB or prior savings, which provide support to individuals who have lost their jobs. Instead, just as in these other cases, the UI work test could be used to determine if individuals who are receiving wages in lieu of notice or severance payments are looking for work and hence are eligible for UI.

Pensions and Social Security Retirement Income

Some workers who are laid off from a job may already be receiving social security old age assistance or a private or government pension, or they become eligible for and begin receiving retirement income from these sources. If these workers are interested in finding a new job and they have sufficient prior earnings, they are also potentially eligible for UI. The question then arises as to whether or not UI should be paid. One could argue that receipt of social security or other retirement income should be viewed as evidence that the individual is not in the labor force and hence is not eligible for UI, even though he or she expresses a desire to become reemployed. Under this argument, no UI benefits would be paid to claimants who receive retirement income. Alternatively, one could contend that social security old age assistance and UI are part of a unified public social insurance system and that individuals should not receive duplicate benefits from this system. Under this argument, the UI benefit would be reduced by the amount of the social security benefit (or vice versa), so that the individual would receive only the maximum amount available from either system. A similar rationale could apply to private or other government pensions. In this case, one could argue that employer contributions to retirement funds and the UI Trust Fund are part of a unified insurance system and that the payment of duplicate benefits is inappropriate. Finally, one could maintain that there is no connection between receipt of retirement income and UI. An individual who is looking for work and meets UI work test requirements should be eligible for UI.

Currently, UI policy regarding retirement income is generally consistent with the second of these three approaches. Under a federal law that went into effect in 1980, benefits from social security and Railroad Retirement benefits are to be deducted dollar for dollar from the UI benefit amount, as are private or other government pension payments if they are made under plans contributed to by a base-period employer. However, states can reduce UI benefits at less than a dollar-for-dollar rate to account for employee contributions to social security, Railroad Retirement, or a pension. States can also disregard pensions if base period employment did not affect eligibility for or the amount of the pension, but this provision does not apply to social security or Railroad Retirement. As of 1994, fifty states deducted pension payments for base-period employers only, while three states deducted all pension payments. The majority of states (thirty-eight), however, adjust the deduction for social security, Railroad Retirement, and pension income for employee contributions; fewer states (twenty-four) exclude pensions not affected by base-period work.

Before the passage of the federal requirement, states could treat pension and social security income as they wished. During the 1960s and 1970s, many states deducted pension income for base-period employers from the UI benefit, but many fewer deducted social security. For example, in 1973, thirty-five states deducted pension income, and twelve deducted social security. Early in the history of the UI program, however, the majority of states denied UI to individuals receiving social security. These changes over time in the treatment of pension income, particularly social security, reflect some ambivalence about whether individuals receiving social security can be considered to be attached to the labor market and a concern that the UI work test cannot be applied well enough to make this determination.

The federal requirement to deduct pension income has affected the composition of the UI claimant population and the likelihood that individuals are receiving both UI and social security, Railroad Retirement, or pension income. In 1988, about 1.5 percent of the UI population was age 65 or over (Corson and Dynarski 1990), while in 1978, before passage of the requirement, 4.4 percent of claimants were age 65 or over (U.S. Department of Labor 1979). The data for 1988 also show that 6.2 percent of UI recipients received payments from social security or Railroad Retirement, and that 5.7 percent received other pension income (9.4 percent received income from one or both of these sources). Data for the general UI population are unavailable for the 1970s, but data for claimants who received extended UI benefits under the Federal Supplemental Benefits (FSB) program in the mid-1970s show that the rate of social security or pension benefit receipt was very high among this population. Among FSB recipients, 18.2 percent received funds from social security or Railroad Retirement and 10.8 percent received pensions (Corson et al. 1977). Since a higher proportion of FSB recipients were age 65 or older than was true for regular UI recipients, these recipiency rates for social security and pensions should be viewed as upper bounds for the rates for the general UI population. Nevertheless, it appears that there has been a decline in the rate of receipt of retirement income among UI claimants.

In summary, the availability of income from social security, Railroad Retirement, or pensions provides a source of long-term support to some UI recipients. Since relatively few UI recipients receive income from these sources, however, they do not, in general, fill any gaps in UI coverage of the long-term unemployed.

Workers' Compensation and Disability Insurance

Workers in the United States are insured through workers' compensation and, in some cases, through disability insurance against the risk of job loss resulting from injury or illness. Specifically, separate workers' compensation programs in each state and for federal employees provide income maintenance payments and medical and hospital care to workers with job-related disabilities. The income maintenance payments, like UI, offer partial replacement of lost wages, but the replacement rate is generally higher than for UI benefits. Payments can also be made to the dependents of deceased workers whose deaths result from job-related accidents or occupational diseases. The majority of workers' compensation claims involve a temporary total disability—that is, the claimant cannot work while recovering from an injury but is expected to recover. A small number of claims (less than 1 percent) become permanent total disabilities, but most of the rest are for partial disabilities. In most cases, benefit payments continue for the duration of the disability. As of 1991, about 87 percent of wage and salary workers were covered by workers' compensation (Nelson 1993). Workers' compensation payments, particularly medical payments, have grown rapidly in the past ten to fifteen years.

Those who can no longer work because of an injury or illness that is not job-related are often provided financial assistance, in the short run, by temporary disability programs and, in the long run, by the Social Security Disability Insurance program.[4] Temporary disability programs, which are the relevant ones for the UI system, are mandated in five states—California, Hawaii, New Jersey, New York, and Rhode Island—and in Puerto Rico. Most workers in these states are covered by Temporary Disability Insurance (TDI) plans that are administered directly by the state or by private insurance carriers. TDI eligibility requirements and benefit payments are similar, although not always identical, to UI eligibility requirements and benefit payments. In states in which TDI programs are not mandated, many employers provide temporary disability coverage through private programs or through sick leave provisions. In 1993, most full-time workers (87 percent) in medium and large establishments were covered by TDI plans and/or paid sick leave, although only about half of these workers had sickness and accident insurance plans (see table 12.2). Coverage for state and local employees is similar, although paid sick leave is relatively more important as a benefit for this group.

Those who are out of work because of an injury or illness, whether temporary or permanent, that results in total disability are not likely to be eligible for UI because they will not be "able and available to work," as UI eligibility rules require in most instances. When the disability is partial, however, the individual may be able to work in some type of job and could qualify for both UI and workers' compensation.

Conceptually, one might argue that UI and workers' compensation, and potentially TDI, should operate in concert to replace lost income for a worker who loses a job involuntarily. If an individual qualifies for both UI and workers' compensation or TDI, it makes sense to offset the benefits from one program with the benefits from the other. An alternative view is that an individual who receives disability benefits to compensate for the loss of one job, but qualifies for UI because he or she is able and available to work at some other job, should be paid UI benefits. According to this view, anyone who is involuntarily unemployed and seeking work is entitled to UI if he or she has had sufficient base-period earnings to qualify for benefits.

In practice, state UI programs reflect a mix of these views. Twenty-eight states have no explicit offset requirements for workers' compensation and presumably permit payment of UI to a worker who meets the able and available requirements. The remaining twenty-five states have provisions to offset UI benefits if an individual is eligible for workers' compensation. In seventeen of these states, UI benefits are reduced by the amount of the Workers' Compensation benefit; in the other seven, no UI is paid at all. This latter approach seems to carry the concept of benefit coordination to an inappropriate extreme. The policy may have no practical consequences, however, because the replacement rates for the weekly benefit and the maximum benefit under workers' compensation exceed those under UI.

The six existing TDI programs appear to be well coordinated with UI, since TDI benefits are paid when an individual is unable to work and hence not eligible for UI.[5] In these programs, TDI benefits are paid when an individual becomes ill or injured, both while employed and while unemployed. Ten additional states have provisions that permit continued payment of UI to claimants who become ill or injured while collecting UI. These provisions appear to be a way of covering such workers in states that do not have mandated TDI programs. This coverage is unavailable in other states, however. In these states, a UI claimant who becomes ill or injured is not eligible for UI while he or she is unable to work.

As the discussion here suggests, the number of UI claimants who also receive workers' compensation or disability benefits is quite small. Although no recent statistics are available, data from the mid-1970s collected for a study of extended UI benefit recipients showed that only about 1 percent of this population collected workers' compensation (Corson et al. 1977). Given the growth in workers' compensation in recent years, this number is likely to have grown, but it is probably still the case that there is very little overlap between workers' compensation, disability, and UI.

Health Insurance

The UI system provides income support to workers, but it does not provide for the continuation of any fringe benefits, including health insurance. Hence, coordination of UI benefits with health insurance coverage is not an issue. Instead, the likelihood that UI recipients are covered by health insurance and whether coverage should be made available to this population become important.

Although direct evidence on the degree of health insurance coverage for the UI population is not available, we can examine various ways in which claimants could be covered. Specifically, workers who lose their jobs could be covered by employer-provided health insurance that continues for some period after layoff. They could also be covered through insurance provided by another family member or by a public program such as medicare or medicaid, and they could purchase coverage on their own.

Health insurance coverage from a pre-UI job will probably continue after layoff, but the duration is likely to be short. Information on group health plans collected for the National Commission on Unemployment Compensation and published in 1980 indicates that, at the time, about 80 percent of unemployed workers covered by these plans could retain coverage for a time, but the average period was only a month (Malhotra and Wills 1980). Very few health insurance plans extend coverage for four or more months after a job loss. This pattern suggests that few long-term UI recipients are likely to have this type of health insurance coverage.

UI recipients can also obtain health insurance coverage through other family members or through public programs, such as medicare or medicaid. Data on the characteristics of recipients, however, suggest that these sources do not provide coverage for most claimants (Corson and Dynarski 1990). About 40 percent of claimants have working spouses, who might have health insurance coverage through their jobs, but not all spouses have coverage nor would all spouses have elected family coverage. In addition, few UI recipients are likely to be covered by public programs. Medicare is not an option for most recipients: less than 2 percent are age 65 or older, and 6 percent receive social security or Railroad Retirement. Medicaid is probably also not an option for most recipients because only 3 percent receive Aid to Families with Dependent Children (AFDC), Supplemental Security Income (SSI), or other welfare benefits.

The final way in which UI recipients can obtain health insurance is by purchasing coverage on their own. Workers who leave a job with health insurance coverage are allowed, through the Consolidated Omnibus Budget Reconciliation Act of 1985 (COBRA), to pay for extending their existing coverage for up to 18 months. However, many UI recipients are not likely to have the financial resources needed to purchase insurance when they are unemployed. Many had low-paying jobs and low family incomes prior to receiving UI. Even for other recipients, the cost, which equals 102 percent of the combined employer-employee premium, may be prohibitive. For example, in 1992, the average annual cost of employer-provided health insurance in mid-sized companies was $3,865 (Johnson & Higgins 1992); in weekly terms this is equivalent to about 40 percent of the average weekly UI benefit amount.

In summary, the evidence reported here suggests that substantial numbers of UI recipients, particularly long-term ones, are likely to lack health insurance coverage. Coverage under most employer-sponsored health plans does not extend long enough to provide for the long-term unemployed. Less than half of UI recipients have working spouses who might have health insurance. Few recipients are likely to be eligible for medicare or medicaid. Many recipients do not have the financial resources needed to purchase insurance under the COBRA provisions.

Providing health insurance to the UI population would probably best be accomplished through general reforms in the health insurance system leading to more universal coverage. However, an alternative, more targeted approach was proposed in the 1997 administration budget. Under this plan, unemployed workers would receive premium subsidies to purchase private insurance for up to six months with funds provided from general revenues. Individual states would design and administer the programs, but the details of who would be eligible and how the programs would work were unspecified.

Welfare Programs

Some UI recipients with low family incomes are eligible for benefits from welfare programs—AFDC, SSI, General Assistance (GA), and food stamps—or for assistance through the Earned Income Tax Credit (EITC), a refundable tax credit. These benefits are coordinated with UI by requiring applicants for welfare benefits to apply for and collect any UI for which they are eligible. Income from UI is considered in the welfare benefit calculation. UI income is also counted as part of taxable income used in the EITC calculation.

UI recipients may be eligible to obtain benefits from welfare programs, but relatively few do so. For example, data for 1988 indicate that under 3 percent of UI recipients received cash welfare benefits (AFDC, SSI, or other welfare), and only 4 percent received food stamps (Corson and Dynarski 1990).[6] Rates of welfare benefit receipt rose following UI benefit exhaustion (to 4 percent for cash benefits and 7.5 percent for food stamps), but not by substantial amounts.

In contrast, a greater proportion of UI recipients receive income from the EITC. For example, 1993 data from the Internal Revenue Service indicate that about 22 percent of the tax returns that had income from unemployment compensation programs also had tax credits or payments under the EITC. However, these same data show that the average annual EITC benefit was relatively small ($1,024).[7]

The low rates of welfare benefit payments among UI recipients and exhaustees occur for several reasons. First, some UI recipients have sources of family income other than UI—for example, their spouse's earnings—that make them ineligible for welfare. Second, welfare programs have asset as well as income eligibility requirements that may disqualify UI recipients. For example, families with liquid assets that exceed $2,000 are not eligible for food stamps. Third, AFDC and SSI benefits are available only to specific categories of families or individuals—families with children, in the case of AFDC, and individuals who are age 65 or older, blind, or disabled, in the case of SSI. Finally, UI recipients may be reluctant to apply for welfare benefits, because they are likely to be newly eligible and unlikely to view themselves as long-term welfare recipients. They do, however, appear to apply for the EITC.

Although few UI recipients or exhaustees actually collect welfare program benefits, a number have family incomes that are below the poverty line or likely to be below the poverty line if UI were not available. For example, a Congressional Budget Office study found that 20 percent of long-term UI recipients had family incomes below the poverty line, and another 27 percent would have had family incomes below the poverty line if they were not receiving UI benefits (Congressional Budget Office 1990).[8] This study found further that 16 percent of long-term UI recipients continued to have family incomes below the poverty line three months after UI benefit exhaustion. Similar results were found in a study of extended benefit recipients in the mid-1970s (Corson and Nicholson 1982).

While not the main objective of the UI program, the importance of UI as an antipoverty mechanism has played a role in debates about extended UI benefits. The current welfare system does not provide much support to UI recipients or exhaustees, so some policy makers have argued that UI should be extended because of its antipoverty effects, particularly during recessionary times. Extending UI benefits, however, is an inefficient way to meet an antipoverty objective, because benefits are paid not only to poor but also to nonpoor families. In fact, the same tabulations that illustrate the antipoverty effects of UI show that a substantial share of benefits is paid to individuals with family incomes well above the poverty line. Targeting UI extensions better to poor families could be achieved by means-testing extended UI benefits, but this process would imply a major departure from the fundamental design of the UI program, which is based on an individual concept of eligibility. Means-testing extended UI would require that eligibility be recomputed based on family income. An alternative approach, which is used in several other countries (see chapter 14), is to provide UI exhaustees with means-tested unemployment assistance through a separate program. However, unless a separate assistance program is developed, the current welfare system is expanded, or the duration of UI benefits is extended, the present gap in income support to the long-term unemployed, including low-income individuals, is likely to remain.

Unemployment Insurance and Programs for Dislocated Workers

Since the 1980s, attention has focused on the reemployment problems of workers who are laid off from their jobs permanently and who must find a new job. The number of these workers, who have been called "dislocated" or "displaced," has been sizable. For many, labor market experiences following layoff have included long spells of unemployment and a reduction in wages after reemployment.

Since 1984, the Bureau of Labor Statistics of the U.S. Department of Labor has identified and tracked dislocated workers through biannual supplements to the Current Population Survey. In this survey, workers who report "having lost or left a job because of a plant closing, an employer going out of business, a layoff from which they were not recalled, or other similar reason" are classified as dislocated. The 1994 survey found that about 5.5 million workers were dislocated in the 1991-1992 period. Nearly half of this group had been employed in their jobs for three or more years (Gardner 1995).

An earlier analysis of data on these dislocated workers by the Congressional Budget Office (CBO) found that about two million individuals were dislocated each year during the 1980s (Congressional Budget Office 1993). Although the numbers were higher than average during the early 1980s recession,[9] substantial numbers were dislocated in all years, including those in which the unemployment rate was relatively low. The CBO study also found that workers in goods-producing industries—agriculture, mining, construction, and manufacturing—

and in blue-collar occupations were at greater risk of dislocation than workers in service-producing industries and in white-collar occupations. Substantial fractions of the dislocated worker population were from service-producing industries and white-collar occupations, however. Moreover, differences in the risk of dislocation for these groups narrowed during the 1980s, a trend that continued in the early 1990s (Gardner 1995).

The CBO study also showed that many dislocated workers have long spells of unemployment and reductions in wages after reemployment. One to three years after losing their jobs, half of the individuals were not working or had new jobs with weekly earnings of less than 80 percent of their prelayoff earnings. The workers with the largest losses had the least education, were the oldest, and had the longest tenure with the previous employer. Furthermore, dislocated workers who held a job at the time of the survey had endured relatively long jobless spells: the average duration was just under 20 weeks.

Additional studies of dislocated workers based on individual-level data sets have also demonstrated that worker dislocation is costly. Topel (1993) cites three studies that, depending on the point of observation, estimated wage losses of 10 to 30 percent as a result of dislocation—that is, dislocated workers who became reemployed earned about 10 to 30 percent less than they earned in their predislocation job.[10] Even five years after their job loss, the wages of dislocated workers in these studies were still about 15 percent lower than their predislocation levels. The large loss in wages, together with the relatively long jobless spells experienced by dislocated workers, implies that the total cost of dislocation is high. This is confirmed by estimates based on a sample of dislocated workers in Pennsylvania (Jacobson, LaLonde, and Sullivan 1993). Total discounted earnings losses for these workers over the six years after their job loss were equal to an average of $41,000 per worker.

Many dislocated workers enter the UI system. Furthermore, many UI recipients can be classified as dislocated workers. The CBO study found that 70 percent of dislocated workers who were jobless for at least five weeks reported receiving UI benefits. In addition, more than half of the dislocated workers who received UI reported exhausting their benefits. Data from a study of UI recipients in 1988 show that more than half of the UI recipient population had no recall expectations at the time they entered the UI system, and about 36 percent could be characterized as dislocated, under a definition similar to that used in the CBO survey (Corson and Dynarski 1990). Not surprisingly, these figures were higher among UI exhaustees: 67 percent had no recall expectations and 52 percent could be classified as dislocated.

Dislocated workers who enter the UI system, like dislocated workers in general, have longer-than-average spells of unemployment and a greater likelihood of wage reductions than other claimants. Corson and Dynarski (1990) used their sample of UI claimants from 1988 to compare employment and UI benefit outcomes of dislocated and nondislocated workers.[11] They found that dislocated workers, particularly those with substantial job tenure, had lower reemployment rates, longer spells of unemployment, higher UI exhaustion rates, and a lower ratio of post-UI to pre-UI weekly wages than other claimants. For example, only 81 percent of the dislocated workers with three or more years of job tenure had become reemployed during the first twenty months after their initial claim, compared with 92 percent of the nondislocated workers.

Data from a demonstration program in New Jersey, in which claimants were followed for six years, showed that individuals targeted for demonstration services—permanently separated claimants with three or more years of job tenure—experienced large reductions in annual earnings relative to their UI base-period earnings throughout the six-year period (Corson and Haimson 1996). This drop in earnings was considerably larger than that experienced by other claimants. Even claimants who became reemployed had substantial earnings losses; average earnings for employed individuals did not reach pre-UI levels until the fourth year after the initial claim. By the sixth year, annual average earnings for employed individuals exceeded the base-period average by $1,889, but this 10.5 percent increase in nominal earnings did not keep pace with inflation (the Consumer Price Index for the Northeast rose approximately 34 percent in this period) or with the average weekly earnings of manufacturing workers in New Jersey (average weekly earnings rose by approximately 25 percent in this period).

UI claimants who exhaust their benefits also have especially high earnings losses. These losses, at least for manufacturing workers, are illustrated by findings based on a sample of UI exhaustees from manufacturing drawn from 10 states for an evaluation of the Trade Adjustment Assistance program (Corson et al. 1993). The findings show that the costs of dislocation among UI exhaustees from manufacturing, as measured by earnings losses, were about $35,000 (undiscounted) over the first three years after the initial UI claim. Furthermore, since average earnings were still relatively low among the sample three years after the initial claim, we can conclude that the full earnings losses would be significantly larger if we were able to expand the post-layoff period of observation.

Trends in Unemployment and Dislocation

Trends in three unemployment measures suggest that an increasing proportion of the unemployed population is made up of dislocated workers. These measures include the proportion of unemployed workers on temporary layoff, the proportion of unemployed workers with long unemployment spells, and the proportion of UI claimants who exhaust their benefits. The trend in the proportion of job losers from the Current Population Survey (CPS) who report that they are on temporary layoff is shown in figure 12.1. Although the series has been relatively volatile between 1967 and 1994, the long-run trend is clearly a decrease in the proportion of job losers on temporary layoff and, hence, a corresponding increase in the proportion on permanent layoff. The trend line in figure 12.1 implies that the proportion of job losers on temporary layoff declined by nearly three-tenths of a percentage point per year over the observation period. This downward trend is statistically significant at the 99 percent confidence level. Further evidence on the relative decline in temporary layoffs is provided by comparing the average proportion of temporary layoffs early in the observation period with the proportion later in the observation period. The average annual proportion over the first ten years of the series is 32 percent, compared with about 27 percent over the last ten years of the series.

At the same time that the share of temporary layoffs has declined, the proportion of unemployed workers who are jobless for 15 or more weeks has increased. Figure 12.2 shows the data on unemployment, which are drawn from the CPS, between 1950 and 1994 and the estimated trend in the unemployment data over this period. The trend line indicates that an increasing percentage of unemployed workers have remained so for at least 15 weeks. The highest rate of long-term unemployment shown in figure 12.2 occurred not in recent years but during the recession of the early 1980s, when the proportion of long-term to total unemployed reached 39 percent in 1983. Nevertheless, the general trend since 1950 has been for long-term unemployment to become more prevalent. The estimated trend suggests that the proportion of unemployed workers who were unemployed for at least 15 weeks increased annually by a quarter of a percentage point over the observation period; this estimated trend is statistically significant at the 99 percent confidence level.

Figure 12.1 Percent of Job Losers on Temporary Layoff, 1967-1994

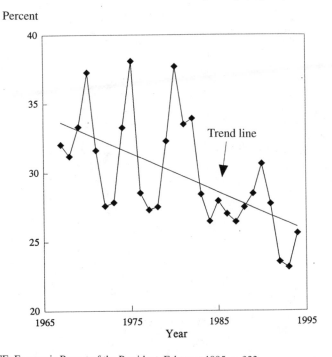

SOURCE: Economic Report of the President, February 1995, p. 322.
NOTE: Job losers on temporary layoffs are individuals who were laid off and are expecting to be recalled.

The findings on UI benefit exhaustion parallel those on long-term unemployment. The benefit exhaustion rate, which is shown in figure 12.3, applies only to unemployed workers who file for and begin to

Figure 12.2 Percent of Unemployed Who Are Unemployed 15 Weeks or More, 1950-1994

Percent

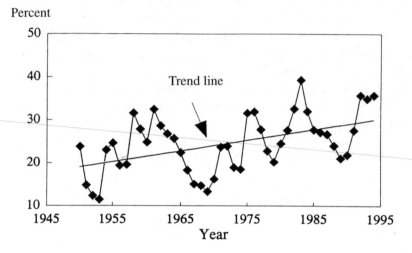

SOURCE: Economic Report of the President, February 1995, p. 322.

Figure 12.3 UI Exhaustion Rate, 1950-1994

Percent

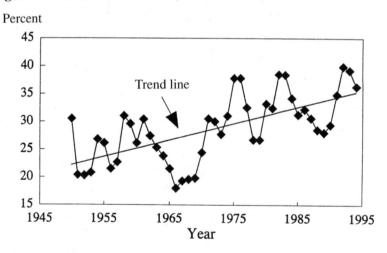

SOURCE: U.S. Department of Labor, *Unemployment Insurance Financial Data*, ET Handbook 394, Employment and Training Administration.

collect UI benefits. Although the trend in benefit exhaustion may respond to changes in the type of workers filing for UI, it is still a useful indicator of the reemployment difficulties of unemployed workers who are receiving UI benefits. As expected, the pattern over time of the exhaustion rate is similar to that of the long-term unemployed measure. Estimates of the long-term trend in benefit exhaustion suggest that the exhaustion rate increased annually by an average of three-tenths of a percentage point between 1950 and 1994.

Trends in the three measures illustrated in the figures show that a growing number of job losers do not expect to return to work with their previous employer, that unemployed individuals are increasingly likely to remain unemployed for at least 15 weeks, and that UI claimants are increasingly likely to exhaust their benefits. These developments suggest that unemployed workers are more likely now than in the past to face long unemployment spells with uncertain reemployment prospects, and, accordingly, that more of them could be characterized as dislocated workers.

Programs to Aid Dislocated Workers

The federal/state system of unemployment compensation is the primary source of cash benefits for dislocated workers. Most dislocated workers who receive UI are also registered with the ES, but relatively few receive substantive reemployment services. For example, a recent study of long-term recipients found that just 6 percent were receiving job search assistance that was more intensive than simple ES work registration (Richardson et al. 1989). Rates of service receipt reported in a 1988 survey of UI recipients were considerably higher (64 percent said they received some services), but a substantial number (36 percent) still received no services, and few received intensive services, such as assessment, counseling, or job search workshops (Corson and Dynarski 1990).

Dislocated workers may receive reemployment services and training through several other programs explicitly targeted to them. The largest of these, the Economic Dislocation and Worker Adjustment Assistance (EDWAA) program, which operates as Title III of the Job Training Partnership Act (JTPA), provides funding to states and through states to substate grantees to provide training (occupational classroom and on-the-job training) to dislocated workers.[12] In addition, grantees may provide related services—orientation and assessment, job search assistance (generally provided through group workshops), counseling, and relocation assistance. As part of EDWAA, states also conduct rapid response activities, to inform dislocated workers of available services as soon as a plant closing or mass layoff is announced. Funding under this program has grown in recent years, from under a half billion dollars in 1990 to more than one billion dollars in 1995. Nevertheless the total number of dislocated workers served under EDWAA is a relatively small proportion of the total number of dislocated workers. For example, approximately 300,000 individuals per year received assistance under EDWAA between 1990 and 1993 as compared to the over 2 million dislocated workers per year identified in the Bureau of Labor Statistics dislocated worker survey.

Other programs provide services to specific groups of dislocated workers. The Trade Adjustment Assistance (TAA) program seeks to aid individuals who lose their jobs because of trade liberalization. In the 1970s this program emphasized compensating workers for lost income by adding a supplement to the weekly UI benefit and by extending weekly benefits from the 26 provided by UI to 52 or to 78 weeks for individuals in training or age 60 or older. In 1981, the supplement to the UI weekly benefit amount was dropped, as was the extension for individuals age 60 or older. Separate funds for training were also made available in 1982. These funds were expanded substantially in 1988, and training was made mandatory unless the requirement is waived. As a result, the focus of the program has shifted toward providing adjustment services, and the likelihood that recipients receive reemployment services, especially training, has increased (Corson et al. 1993). This program is, however, quite small, with approximately 20,000-50,000 recipients per year. Various amendments to JTPA have also authorized new programs for special categories of workers, including special reemployment assistance for workers who lost their jobs after the Clean Air Act was implemented and for workers dislocated because of reductions in defense expenditures. Services under these special initiatives are provided through the EDWAA program. A number of earlier programs to aid workers dislocated by federal policy initiatives (such as the enlargement of Redwoods National Park, railroad reorganizations, and airline deregulation) were also targeted on specific groups of workers.

Despite the large number of special programs, the overall number of workers served by EDWAA and other dislocated worker programs is relatively small. The 1988 UI study data suggest that under 5 percent of UI recipients and under 10 percent of exhaustees receive any services from these programs (Corson and Dynarski 1990).

Evidence from Program Evaluations

Formal evaluations of four major demonstration projects during the 1980s assessed the extent to which reemployment services helped enhance the reemployment prospects of dislocated workers. Three of these demonstrations addressed layoffs at specific industrial plants in Detroit (Kulik, Smith, and Stromsdorfer 1984), Buffalo (Corson, Long, and Maynard 1985), and Houston and El Paso (Bloom and Kulik 1986). Although these demonstrations had relatively small samples and used different research methodologies,[13] one general finding emerged: the reemployment outcomes for workers who received special assistance in looking for work tended to be more favorable than those for workers in the comparison/control groups, but additional benefits from participating in a training program were either ambiguous or small, relative to program costs. For example, the evaluation of the Buffalo project found that job search assistance had significant effects on reemployment rates and on average weekly earnings, but classroom and on-the-job training had statistically insignificant effects (Corson, Long, and Maynard 1985). Because the per-participant costs of training were approximately four times the cost of job search assistance alone, the report concluded that only the job search assistance treatment was cost-effective.

A fourth major evaluation—the New Jersey UI Reemployment Demonstration Project—had a somewhat broader focus than the plant-based projects described earlier. The goal of the New Jersey demonstration was "to examine whether the Unemployment Insurance system could be used to identify workers early in their unemployment spells and to provide them with alternative, early intervention services to accelerate their return to work" (Corson et al. 1989). Overall, 8,675 UI claimants were assigned randomly to one of three treatments (job search assistance only, job search assistance combined with training or relocation assistance, and job search assistance combined with a cash bonus for early reemployment) and then compared with a randomly selected control group of 2,385 claimants who received only regular services. Demonstration services were targeted to dislocated workers through a series of eligibility screens that excluded workers who (1) did not receive a UI first payment within five weeks after their initial claim, (2) were collecting partial UI benefits, (3) were younger than twenty-five years of age, (4) had fewer than three years of employment experience on their last job, (5) had a specific recall date from their employer, or (6) were usually hired through union hiring-hall arrangements. As a whole, these screens excluded approximately 73 percent of all workers who received a first payment from UI during the sample period.

Each treatment in the New Jersey demonstration had a statistically significant effect on reducing the collection of UI benefits and on raising subsequent employment and earnings (Corson et al. 1989; Corson and Haimson 1996). UI benefits were reduced in both the initial benefit year and in subsequent years. The total benefits of the treatments also exceeded their total costs from the perspectives of both society and the individuals involved. From the viewpoint of government alone, however, only the job search and reemployment bonus treatments were unambiguously beneficial. No clear evidence emerged that providing training or relocation help in addition to job search assistance led to cost-effective gains. Evaluations of demonstration programs similar to the New Jersey one in Minnesota, Nevada, South Carolina, and Washington support the notion that stronger links between UI recipients and the reemployment service system are a cost-effective way to promote rapid reemployment among UI recipients (see Meyer 1995 and U.S. Department of Labor 1995 for reviews).

Current Policy Initiatives: Profiling and Reemployment Services

The UI system is a logical avenue for identifying workers who might be helped by reemployment services, because the majority of dislocated workers collect UI benefits, and they usually begin to receive these payments early in their unemployment spells. Other targeting mechanisms (such as the rapid response program outreach efforts under EDWAA) are important but more limited than a UI-based approach, because they tend to focus on specific groups of dislocated workers (such as those from plant closings or mass layoffs, in the case of EDWAA). Identifying workers early in their unemployment spells has several advantages. By beginning the adjustment process more quickly, claimants can use UI benefits as income support during training, if training is necessary. For workers who do not need training, the risk of exhausting UI benefits can be lessened, and income can be increased through more rapid reemployment. Because many dislocated workers collect UI benefits for a substantial period of time, potential program savings from more rapid reemployment can also be achieved.

This reasoning, combined with evidence from the New Jersey demonstration that long-term UI recipients can be identified early in their unemployment spells, resulted in the Unemployment Compensation Amendments of 1993, which require state UI programs to *profile* claimants as they enter the UI system so that dislocated workers can be identified. Subsequent interpretations of this requirement by the U.S. Department of Labor provide guidance on how states should implement a profiling mechanism.[14] Specifically, states are encouraged to adopt and adapt an approach developed by the Labor Department (U.S. Department of Labor 1994). This method uses a two-step process to identify dislocated workers. In the first step, non-job-attached claimants are identified; in the second, a probability of exhaustion is estimated for each claimant, on the basis of education, job tenure, industry, occupation, and other variables. Those with the highest probabilities of exhaustion are considered the target group. States that do not have sufficient data to estimate such models are expected to use a fixed set of screens to identify dislocated workers (as was done in the New Jersey demonstration), but they are encouraged and provided with technical assistance to develop statistical profiling models as more data become available.

Identifying dislocated workers is the first step in helping these individuals become reemployed; strengthening linkages to reemployment services is the second step. For this reason, the worker profiling legislation requires state UI systems to refer profiled claimants to reemployment services. Referred claimants are expected to participate in reemployment services as a condition of eligibility for UI unless they

have already done so or have a justifiable cause for failure to participate.

To make these requirements operational, states are expected to
establish agreements between the UI system and service providers (the
ES or EDWAA programs), so that profiled claimants can be referred to
a provider and receive services. Service providers in each locality generally hold initial orientation sessions with claimants, followed by
assessment sessions in which individual assistance plans are developed
for each claimant. Participation in reemployment services identified in
the plans is a condition for continued UI eligibility. In addition to orientation and assessment, reemployment services can include counseling, job search assistance (such as workshops), referrals to jobs and job
placement, and other similar types of help, but they do not include
training or education. Claimants can be referred to training or educational services; if they participate, they do not have to take part in other
reemployment services. However, engaging in training or education is
not a mandatory component of the service plans. So that UI can monitor and evaluate the reemployment services participation requirement
and continuing eligibility, states are expected to develop feedback
mechanisms to provide UI with information about whether referred
claimants participate in and complete mandated services.

All states have now put these Worker Profiling and Reemployment
Services (WPRS) systems into effect. In late 1994, Delaware, Florida,
Kentucky, Maryland, New Jersey, and Oregon began implementing
WPRS systems, while other states began implementation in 1995 and
early 1996. Each of the initial six states successfully developed partnerships among the UI, ES, and EDWAA systems, a method to profile
and refer long-duration claimants to reemployment services, and a way
to provide feedback to the UI system from the service providers
(Hawkins et al. 1996). In most localities, the ES is the primary provider
for mandatory reemployment services, with short duration services
being emphasized on individual service plans. Lengthier, more extensive assistance is given less frequently and generally on a voluntary
basis. Such help is often provided through referrals to EDWAA.

Unemployment Insurance Benefit Restructuring Initiatives

Two other relatively recent UI system initiatives are, like the WPRS systems, designed to promote employment of claimants.[15] These initiatives—short-time compensation and self-employment assistance—restructure the UI benefit system to increase employment and, in the second case, to provide additional services to claimants.

Short-Time Compensation

Short-time compensation (STC) allows firms to adjust their workforce in response to business fluctuations without resorting to layoffs.[16] Under STC, firms reduce use of their workforce simply by requiring a group of employees—typically more than would otherwise be laid off—to work shorter weeks. These workers are compensated for their lost work time with partial UI benefits. STC may neutralize what some have viewed as a pro-layoff bias in regular state UI programs, which tend to be relatively restrictive in the payment of partial benefits (Feldstein 1976).[17] Under STC, UI benefits can be paid under a much broader set of conditions than in the normal program. As implemented in the United States, STC is viewed as a workforce stabilization plan, used during periods of economic downturn that are expected to have only short-term effects on the labor needs of employers.

STC programs were introduced in the United States in 1978, when California implemented its Work Sharing Unemployment Insurance program as an experimental effort to mitigate the public-sector employment problems that were expected to accompany declines in state revenue resulting from tax reductions. The California plan has been the prototype for other STC initiatives in this country. The 1981-1982 recession acted as a catalyst for expansion of STC programs, which were established by states throughout the 1980s. As of 1994, STC programs had been implemented in seventeen states, although many of these programs have modest activity.

Because state STC programs were grafted onto the existing UI system, and because many followed model legislation prepared by the U.S. Department of Labor, the programs have many similarities. All are implemented by a work-sharing plan for a given employer that, once approved, remains in effect for a set period. These plans specify the hours reduction and the handling of fringe benefits during the period. State laws limit the number of weeks STC can be collected and indicate how benefits are to be calculated, usually as a proportion of the weekly UI benefit for which the worker is eligible. State plans also specify how STC benefits are charged to an employer. In many states, they are charged in exactly the same way as regular UI benefits. Early concern about the budgetary impact of STC on state trust funds, however, caused some states to adopt special charging provisions and even surtaxes for firms using the program. However, because of the modest use of STC, only a few states retain these provisions.

Participation in STC is low in states with a program. Kerachsky, Nicholson, and Hershey (1986) showed that firm participation in STC was less than 0.5 percent of all employers in the three states (Arizona, California, and Oregon) studied. Work by Vroman (1992) indicated that STC use continued to be low, generally accounting for no more than 0.3 percent of UI claimants.

Findings from the Kerachsky, Nicholson, and Hershey (1986) study also suggest that STC has a clear but limited impact on layoffs. As expected, participation in STC did reduce layoffs: approximately 13 percent fewer hours were spent on layoffs by workers in STC firms than by workers in comparison firms. Even firms using STC continued to use layoffs as their primary method of work force reduction, however. Nearly 80 percent of all the compensated hours of unemployment among workers in these firms were spent on layoff rather than on STC-compensated hours reduction. In addition, total compensated unemployment was nearly 11 percent higher among STC users than among otherwise similar employers. These findings tend to refute the notion that STC hours simply substitute for hours spent on regular UI. Instead, the effect of STC on the trade-off between layoffs and hour reductions appears to be more complex. An ongoing study is currently evaluating this effect and related issues associated with STC.

Self-Employment Assistance

Another policy option that expands services to UI claimants and encourages reemployment is self-employment assistance. Under the traditional UI system, claimants must be able and available for work and must conduct an active job search for wage and salary employment, so those who work full-time on starting their own business are generally ineligible for UI. Clearly, this policy creates a disincentive to self-employment. However, recent legislation has offered states the option of changing this situation. Title V of the North American Free Trade Agreement (NAFTA) Implementation Act (Public Law [P.L.] 103-181) allows states to offer self-employment assistance as an additional tool to help speed the transition of dislocated workers into new employment.[18] Under this option, eligible claimants who want to establish their own business are paid a self-employment allowance equivalent to their UI benefit. These claimants are expected to work full-time on starting their own business and are exempted from UI work search requirements. In addition, they are allowed to retain any earnings from self-employment, without losing their self-employment allowance. The effect of the new law is to remove the barrier that disallowed payment of UI benefits to claimants pursuing full-time self-employment. States are also required to provide self-employment assistance activities to claimants receiving self-employment allowances.[19] Participation in these services is mandatory for recipients of the allowance, and total participation cannot exceed 5 percent of regular UI claimants. To date, ten states have enacted self-employment programs for UI claimants, and programs are operational in Maine, New York, Oregon, Delaware, Maryland, New Jersey, and California.

The legislation allowing self-employment was a response to the relatively positive findings on impacts from two random assignment demonstrations conducted in Washington and Massachusetts. These results indicated that self-employment is a viable reemployment option for a small proportion of UI claimants. Both demonstrations provided self-employment allowances and additional assistance activities to claimants who completed a set of initial intake activities. In Washington, the self-employment allowance was offered as a lump-sum payment equal to the amount of the claimant's remaining UI entitlement; in Massachusetts, claimants were offered weekly allowances equal to their UI benefit amount.[20] Four percent of targeted claimants in Washington and 2 percent in Massachusetts completed the initial intake activities and were determined eligible for participation in the program. In terms of impacts on economic outcomes, the availability of self-employment assistance generated an increase in self-employment and an increase in time employed among claimants in both demonstrations. Impacts on total earnings (from self-employment and wages and salaries) and on total benefits paid (regular UI payments plus self-employment allowances) were mixed. In the Washington program, total earnings did not rise—the increase in self-employment income was offset by a reduction in wage and salary income—while in Massachusetts both self-employment and wage and salary income rose. The Washington program, which paid lump-sum allowances, also increased total benefits paid by about $1,000 per eligible claimant while the Massachusetts self-employment program reduced total benefits paid during the benefit year by about $900 per eligible claimant. Both programs were cost effective from the participant and societal perspectives, but only the Massachusetts program was cost effective from the governmental perspective. The Massachusetts model of paying weekly allowances equal to the UI weekly benefit amount has been adopted in the national legislation.

Conclusion

The UI system is intended to provide income support to experienced workers who become unemployed involuntarily and, through referrals to the ES, assistance in becoming reemployed; however, other public and private programs also provide income support and reemployment assistance to jobless workers. The presence of this wider set of social insurance, public assistance, and reemployment programs must be considered in an assessment of the adequacy of the income support and reemployment assistance provided to unemployed workers. The existence of these other programs also raises the question of whether they are well coordinated with UI. These issues have been examined in this chapter.

Income Support

The examination of social insurance, public assistance, and private programs that may provide income support to unemployed workers showed that, in general, overlaps in coverage are small. Few UI claimants appear to be eligible for or to receive income from social insurance, public assistance, or private programs designed to provide income to older, disabled, or low-income individuals or families. However, a substantial percentage of unemployed workers appear to be eligible for severance or termination pay (in 1993, 42 percent of full time employees in medium and small firms were eligible for severance pay). In addition, a significant share receives income from the EITC (in 1993, 22 percent of the tax returns reporting unemployment compensation income also reported tax credits or payments under the EITC).

These findings indicate that the gaps in the income support provided by the UI system to low-wage workers and the long-term unemployed identified in earlier chapters, are not filled by other income support programs. Severance pay is more often available to workers with higher than with lower wages, and it tends to have a short duration; further, the amount of income provided by the EITC is modest (the annual average payment or tax credit in 1993 was about $1,000). Other than UI, sources of income support are generally not available to the UI population.

The analysis in this chapter also suggests that another important gap in support to the unemployed is for health insurance. Relatively few unemployed individuals, particularly among the long-term unemployed, are likely to have health insurance coverage. While current legislation requires employers to permit laid-off workers to purchase health insurance coverage for up to eighteen months at a cost equal to 102 percent of the employer-employee premium, few UI claimants are likely to be able to afford this increasingly costly benefit.

Finally, rules providing for the coordination of benefits from UI and other programs have been established for state UI programs. For public programs, these regulations often offset the benefits from one program by those from another so that an individual will not receive multiple benefits, although certain states permit the payment of some multiple benefits if the individual meets UI able and available requirements. Rules for the coordination of private sources of income with UI have also been established. These criteria vary by state as well and are similar to the stipulations governing income from public programs. However, in some states, the treatment of different kinds of private income seems inconsistent. For example, certain states treat wages in lieu of notice and severance payments as disqualifying income for UI while income from SUB payments is ignored in the UI benefit calculation.

Instead, it seems more reasonable to ignore all private sources of income in the benefit calculation and to use the UI work test to ensure that claimants are available and looking for work and are hence eligible for UI.

Reemployment Assistance

Historically, the UI system has provided reemployment assistance to UI claimants through the ES and through referrals from the ES to programs like EDWAA for dislocated workers. However, in the past, few claimants received intensive reemployment assistance from the ES or from other sources, despite the fact that increasing numbers of claimants are permanently separated from their pre-UI employers and might benefit from services. Growth over the years in other indicators of worker dislocation, such as the proportion of the jobless who are long-term unemployed and the UI exhaustion rate, also points to a greater need for reemployment assistance for UI claimants.

There has also been evidence from recent demonstrations that an increased level of reemployment services coupled with a participation requirement could lead to more rapid reemployment of UI claimants and to lower UI benefit payments. The combination of factors that have been described has led to legislation requiring states to implement WPRS systems. Under these systems, states are expected to identify permanently separated claimants who are likely to experience long spells of unemployment and to refer them to reemployment services from the ES or another service provider. Referred claimants are supposed to participate in reemployment services such as job search assistance as a condition of continued UI eligibility, unless they have already done so or have a justifiable cause for failure to participate. States are also expected to develop feedback mechanisms to provide UI with information about whether referred claimants participate in required services.

Early indications suggest that these WPRS systems can be implemented successfully. If sufficient resources are available to provide reemployment services, these systems should lead to an increase in the level of reemployment services provided to UI claimants and to increased coordination between UI and reemployment service providers. Other recent UI initiatives—short-time compensation and self-employment allowances—are also aimed at promoting the employment of claimants. Short-time compensation is intended to strengthen ties with existing employers by providing an alternative to temporary layoffs, and self-employment assistance is designed to help claimants develop an alternative to wage and salary work.

NOTES

I am grateful to Sheldon Danziger, Walter Nicholson, and the editors for their comments on this paper and to Cindy Castro for her help in producing the paper.

1. These firms account for approximately one-quarter of all employment.

2. For convenience, the fifty-three UI jurisdictions—the fifty states, the District of Columbia, Puerto Rico, and the Virgin Islands, are called "states."

3. The decline in employment in automobile and other manufacturing industries has also led to a decline in the number of workers covered under SUB plans. Haber and Murray (1966) report that over 2.5 million workers were covered by SUB plans in 1962, while the 1993 survey of benefits in medium and large firms reports that 1.2 million workers are covered.

4. The Social Security Disability Insurance program provides monthly cash benefits to workers under age 65 who become disabled and can no longer work because of the disability. Benefits become available after a five-month waiting period.

5. In four states, the same agency administers TDI and UI.

6. Conversely, few Food Stamp and AFDC program recipients receive UI. In 1988, 2.3 percent of Food Stamp households (U.S. Department of Agriculture 1990) and 4.3 percent of AFDC families (U.S. Department of Health and Human Services 1990) had income from UI.

7. These numbers were computed from data reported by the Internal Revenue Service (1995, table 2) and from data reported in testimony on the earned income tax credit by the Commissioner of Internal Revenue (Richardson 1995, table 1).

8. This latter estimate assumed that individuals would not respond to a loss of UI benefits by increasing job search activities or by lowering the wage at which they would accept a job. Thus, this estimate provides an upper-bound poverty rate in the absence of UI.

9. As indicated in the previous paragraph, the annual number of dislocated workers was also higher during the recession of the early 1990s than in the 1980s.

10. The three studies are Topel (1990, 1991) and Ruhm (1991).

11. Corson and Dynarski use the BLS definition of dislocated workers, which includes workers who lose their jobs because their plants close, their employer went out of business, or they were laid off and not recalled.

12. EDWAA uses a relatively broad definition of dislocated workers. Workers are eligible for EDWAA if they have been laid off or have received a notice of termination, are UI eligible, and are unlikely to return to their previous industry or occupation; they have been laid off or received a notice of termination as a result of a plant closing or substantial layoff; or they are long-term unemployed individuals with limited opportunities for reemployment in their occupation.

13. The Detroit evaluation used a comparison plant methodology, whereas the Buffalo and Texas evaluations used random assignment methods that differed according to how nonparticipants were treated.

14. Unemployment Insurance Program Letter No. 45-93, Field Memorandum No 35-94, and other documents in U.S. Department of Labor 1994.

15. A third initiative to promote reemployment—reemployment bonuses—has been tested experimentally, but legislation permitting states to incorporate reemployment bonuses in their UI programs has not been enacted. For a discussion of reemployment bonuses, see chapter 7.

16. Short-time compensation is also referred to as work sharing or shared-work compensation.

17. Most states have partial benefit schedules that specify a dollar-for-dollar reduction in benefits for wages in excess of a modest weekly earnings disregard. For a typical worker, these schedules usually mean that no benefits are paid if the employee works two or more days per week.

18. This legislation has a five-year time limit, but pending legislation would make permanent the provisions permitting states to provide self-employment allowances and assistance.

19. Self-employment activities that must be offered include entrepreneurial training, business counseling, and technical assistance. This assistance is most often provided through state economic development agencies.

20. For a description of the Washington and Massachusetts demonstrations and a discussion of the results, see Benus et al. (1995). See also Wilson (1995) for comparisons to programs in other countries.

References

Benus, Jacob, Terry Johnson, Michelle Wood, Neelima Grover, and Theodore Shen. 1995. "Self-Employment Programs: A New Reemployment Strategy. Final Report on the UI Self-Employment Demonstration." Unemployment Insurance Occasional Paper 95-4, U.S. Department of Labor, Employment and Training Administration.

Bixby, Ann Kallman. 1993. "Public Welfare Expenditures, Fiscal year 1990." *Social Security Bulletin* 56, 2 (Summer): 70-76.

Bloom, Howard S., and Jane Kulik. 1986. "Evaluation of the Worker Adjustment Demonstration: Final Report." Unpublished manuscript, Abt Associates, July.

Congressional Budget Office. 1990. "Family Incomes of Unemployment Insurance Recipients and the Implications for Extending Benefits." Congress of the United States, Congressional Budget Office.

_____. 1993. "Displaced Workers: Trends in the 1980s and Implications for the Future." Congress of the United States, Congressional Budget Office.

Corson, Walter, Paul Decker, Shari Dunstan, and Anne Gordon. 1989. "The New Jersey Unemployment Insurance Reemployment Demonstration Project: Final Evaluation Report." Unemployment Insurance Occasional Paper 89-3, U.S. Department of Labor, Employment and Training Administration.

Corson, Walter, Paul Decker, Phillip Gleason, and Walter Nicholson. 1993. "International Trade and Worker Dislocation: Evaluation of the Trade Adjustment Assistance Program." Unpublished manuscript, Mathematica Policy Research.

Corson, Walter, and Mark Dynarski. 1990. "A Study of Unemployment Insurance Recipients and Exhaustees: Findings from a National Survey." Unemployment Insurance Occasional Paper 90-2, U.S. Department of Labor, Employment and Training Administration, April.

Corson, Walter, and Joshua Haimson. 1996. "The New Jersey Unemployment Insurance Reemployment Demonstration Project: Six-Year Followup and Summary Report." Unemployment Insurance Occasional Paper 96-2, U.S. Department of Labor, Employment and Training Administration.

Corson, Walter, David Horner, Valerie Leach, Charles Metcalf, and Walter Nicholson. 1977. "A Study of Recipients of Federal Supplemental Benefits and Special Unemployment Assistance." Unpublished manuscript, Mathematica Policy Research, January.

Corson, Walter, Sharon Long, and Rebecca Maynard. 1985. "An Impact Evaluation of the Buffalo Dislocated Worker Demonstration Project." Unpublished manuscript, Mathematica Policy Research, March.

Corson, Walter, and Walter Nicholson. 1982. *The Federal Supplemental Benefits Program: An Appraisal of Emergency Extended Unemployment Insurance Benefits*. Kalamazoo, MI: W.E. Upjohn Institute.

Feldstein, Martin. 1976. "Temporary Layoffs in the Theory of Unemployment," *Journal of Political Economy* 84, 5 (October): 937-957.

Gardner, Jennifer M. 1995. "Worker Displacement: A Decade of Change," *Monthly Labor Review* 118, 4 (April):48-57.

Haber, William and Merrill G. Murray. 1966. *Unemployment Insurance in the American Economy*. Homewood, IL: Richard D. Irwin.

Hawkins, Evelyn K., Suzanne D. Kreutzer, Katherine P. Dickinson, Paul T. Decker, and Walter S. Corson. 1996. "Evaluation of Worker Profiling and Reemployment Services Systems." Unemployment Insurance Occasional Paper 96-1, U.S. Department of Labor, Employment and Training Administration.

Internal Revenue Service. 1995. *Statistics of Income Bulletin* (Fall).

Jacobson, Louis, Robert J. LaLonde, and Daniel G. Sullivan. 1993. *The Costs of Worker Dislocation*. Kalamazoo, MI: W.E. Upjohn Institute.

Johnson & Higgins. 1992. "A Special Report from the Foster Higgins Health Care Benefits Survey, 1992." New York: Johnson & Higgins.

Kerachsky, Stuart, Walter Nicholson, and Alan Hershey. 1986. "An Evaluation of Short-Time Compensation Programs." Unemployment Insurance Occasional Paper 86-4, U.S. Department of Labor, Employment and Training Administration.

Kulik, J., D.A. Smith, and E. Stromsdorfer. 1984. "The Downriver Community Conference Economic Readjustment Program: Final Evaluation Report." Unpublished manuscript, Abt Associates, May 18.

Malhotra, Suresh, and John Wills. 1980. "Employer-Provided Group Health Plans and the Unemployed." In *Unemployment Compensation: Studies and Research*, Vol. 3. Washington, DC: National Commission on Unemployment Compensation, July.

Meyer, Bruce D. 1995. "Lessons from the U.S. Unemployment Insurance Experiments," *Journal of Economic Literature* 33, 1 (March): 91-131.

Nelson, William J. "1993. Workers' Compensation: Coverage, Benefits, and Costs, 1990-91," *Social Security Bulletin* 56, 3 (Fall): 68-74.

Richardson, Margaret Milner. 1995. Testimony before the Subcommittee Oversight, Subcommittee on Human Resources, House Committee on Ways and Means, June 15.

Richardson, Philip, Albert Irvin, Arlen Rosenthal, and Harold Kuptzin. 1989. "Referral of Long-Term Unemployment Insurance Claimants to Reemployment Services." Unemployment Insurance Occasional Paper 89-2, U.S. Department of Labor, Employment and Training Administration.

Ruhm, Christopher J. 1991. "Are Workers Permanently Scarred by Job Displacements?" *American Economic Review* 81 (March): 319-324.

Topel, Robert. 1990. "Specific Capital and Unemployment: Measuring the Costs and Consequences of Worker Displacement," *Carnegie-Rochester Series on Public Policy* 33: 181-214.

_____. 1991. "Specific Capital, Mobility, and Wages: Wages Rise with Job Seniority," *Journal of Political Economy* 99 (February): 145-176.

_____. 1993. "What Have We Learned from Empirical Studies of Unemployment and Turnover?" Paper presented at the ASSA meetings, Anaheim, California, January.

U.S. Department of Agriculture. 1990. "Characteristics of Food Stamp Households, Winter 1988." Food and Nutrition Service, Office of Analysis and Evaluation.

U.S. Department of Health and Human Services. 1990. "Characteristics and Financial Circumstances of AFDC Recipients: FY 1988." Office of Family Assistance, Division of Program Evaluation, Information and Measurement Branch.

U.S. Department of Labor. 1979. "Unemployment Insurance Statistics, January-March 1979." Employment and Training Administration.

_____. 1994. "The Worker Profiling and Reemployment Services System: Legislation, Implementation Process, and Research Findings." Unemployment Insurance Occasional Paper 94-4, U.S. Department of Labor, Employment and Training Administration.

_____. 1995. "What's Working (and what's not): A Summary of Research on the Economic Impacts of Employment and Training Programs." Office of the Chief Economist, January.

U.S. Department of Labor. Various years. "Employee Benefits in Medium and Large Firms." Bureau of Labor Statistics.

Vroman, Wayne. 1992. "Short Time Compensation in the U.S., Germany, and Belgium." Unpublished manuscript, Urban Institute, June.

Wilson, Sandra. 1995. "Self-Employment Programs Provide Alternative to UI," *Workforce Journal* 4, 3 (Summer): 36-43.

CHAPTER 13

Federal-State Relations

Thomas E. West
Michigan Employment Security Agency
Gerard Hildebrand
UI Service, U.S. Department of Labor

Almost sixty years after its inception, following over 340 million first payments of unemployment insurance (UI) to individuals, significant problems with benefit fund solvency in many states,[1] and after substantial growth in program complexity, the UI program continues to be the initial point of contact for someone who becomes unemployed. Although the program has experienced a number of pivotal problems, some inherent in its basic structure and some beyond its control, it continues to be a model of federal-state interaction and cooperation. The purpose of this chapter is to examine the dynamics that established the original federal-state UI system and to discuss how this unique relationship has evolved over the last sixty years. Some of the issues that will be discussed, notably administrative financing, are shared by the employment service program that works to find jobs for UI claimants; however, this chapter will be limited to UI.

Program Inception

The initial discussions involving the development of the UI program in the United States focused on three primary issues: (1) whether an exclusively national system was appropriate, (2) to what extent state legislatures should have discretion about program requirements, and (3) the degree to which states should be required to meet minimum federal standards. The federal-state UI program came about as a result of the need for income protection in the political and economic climate of the Great Depression of the 1930s. Attempts in 1916 and again in 1921 to pass federal UI legislation had failed. Between 1917 and 1933 thirteen unemployment benefit or guaranteed employment plans were developed by individual companies. President Franklin D. Roosevelt had hoped that either private insurance programs or individual states would provide for temporary income coverage to help offset the unpredictability of unemployment. Although private insurance programs had developed slowly in the early 1930s, many had failed and, prior to 1935, only Wisconsin had enacted a UI law. States were reluctant to enact UI laws at their level since they would be at a competitive disadvantage relative to states without UI programs. The Wagner-Lewis bill of 1934 solved some of the state concerns by proposing a federal tax with an offsetting credit for employers if the state met certain requirements. Although President Roosevelt supported the proposal, he requested that consideration be delayed until further study could be completed.[2]

To examine the matter, President Roosevelt created the Committee on Economic Security which eventually recommended a federal-state system calling for a federal tax with provisions for credit against that tax, similar to that put forward in the Wagner-Lewis proposal. With its recommendation for a federal-state system, the committee also expressed its apprehension about the compromise:

> A federally administered system of unemployment compensation is undoubtedly superior in some respects, particularly in relation to employees who move from state to state . . . . We recognize also that in other respects State administration may develop marked inadequacies. Should these fears expressed by the champions of a federally administered system prove true, it is always possible by subsequent legislation to establish such a system . . . . Accordingly, the Congress can at any time increase the requirements which state laws must fulfill and may, as it sees fit, at some future time, substitute a federally administered system for a cooperative Federal-state system we recommend (Report of the Committee on Economic Security 1935).

The arguments used to support a totally federal system involved uniformity of protection and coverage, consistency for employers who had multistate operations, the ability to pool trust fund resources and collect taxes centrally, and less administration. Those who favored a federal-state system countered with the following: a national system would be cumbersome to operate; the decision process would function better if states could enact laws complying with broad federal requirements; there would be more accountability of state and local officials under a federal-state system to develop a program responsive to individual state needs and conditions; and, rather than proposing changes to the federal laws which may not work throughout the country, a federal-state system would mean that states could experiment with new ideas, which could then be exported to other states.

The committee's unanimous recommendation for a federal-state system was made primarily for three reasons: (1) it was known that President Roosevelt preferred that approach, (2) there was a significant question as to whether a wholly federal system was constitutional, and finally (3) Congress was apparently unwilling to relinquish all state authority over this issue to the U.S. government. Although the committee's report did not detail federal or state duties, it did outline general recommendations for incentives to states to enact laws adopting minimum state standards, providing for the control of trust fund reserves, establishing substantive program provisions, and providing effective administration. In most cases the responsibilities were to be shared and collaborative.

The 1935 Social Security Act (SSA), which created the federal-state system, did not end discussions about the basic structure of the program. By the end of 1937, concerns about the constitutionality of the federal-state system were resolved by the U.S. Supreme Court. Even by then, states had developed their own vested interest in the program and were prepared to strongly resist any attempts to change it to an exclusively federal system.[3] With the possibility of an exclusively federal system reduced, proponents for more uniformity switched their attention to active support for federal benefit standards. Although benefit standards have been proposed by a number of different administrations, they have never been adopted.

The 1935 SSA addressed UI in two ways. First, Title III provided for grants to states for the administration of their UI programs. The receipt of these grants was conditioned on state law meeting the requirements of Title III and Title IX of the SSA. Second, certain sections of Title IX (since recodified as that part of the Internal Revenue Code called the Federal Unemployment Tax Act [FUTA]) created the cornerstone of the federal-state system: a federal tax with a significant tax credit offset for employers in states with UI laws meeting federal law requirements. Although the basic concept of a gross versus a net FUTA rate has remained the fundamental incentive feature in the system, the amounts of the gross and net rates have changed. (When the program began, the gross FUTA rate was 3 percent with a net FUTA rate of 0.3 percent. In 1996, the gross FUTA rate was 6.2 percent, including a temporary tax of 0.2 percent). Employers who have paid their full state unemployment tax obligations can receive a 5.4 percent offset credit on their FUTA rate if their state law meets federal requirements, provided the state has had no outstanding loans from the federal government for more than two years and provided the services are covered under state law. Based on a taxable wage base of $7,000, most employers pay no more than $56 (0.8 percent of $7,000) per employee. However, if the state is ruled out of conformity or compliance with federal law, then an employer's cost per employee would increase to $434 (6.2 percent of $7,000).[4]

The Federal-State Partnership

Rather than a simple federal-state partnership, the UI system embodies a whole host of interested parties, with each affecting the operation of the program at both the state and national level. Although within the UI program the federal government is referred to as the "federal partner," this federal partner is really comprised of the U.S. Congress and the executive branch, including the U.S. Department of Labor, at both the national and regional office levels, and the Office of Management and Budget. Not surprisingly, the federal partner will not always present a consistent view on issues relating to the UI system, primarily because different interests in the program are represented. Congress has several times rejected efforts by different administrations to impose benefit standards on states. As federal UI law involves other federal agencies, the U.S. Department of Labor may disagree with those agencies and has sometimes participated in judicial action, as friend of the court on behalf of the states in cases concerning whether states have complied with federal requirements.

The "state" partner is comprised of the fifty different states, the District of Columbia, Puerto Rico, and the Virgin Islands. Each has its own legislature, UI advisory councils, business and labor organizations that protect the interests of their constituents, and state courts. Like the federal partner, the state partner is comprised of different entities with widely divergent interests and opinions.

As the UI program has evolved since the 1930s, the state UI agencies have served to explain both the mechanics and history of the program to state legislatures. State agency staff also commonly assist the legislatures in explaining how proposals to change state law might conflict with federal law, which could result in the loss of federal tax credits and the ability of the state UI agency to receive administrative grants. Similarly, staff members at the U.S. Department of Labor are called upon to provide the explanations of program administration to Congress, to testify regarding economic shifts that necessitate program modifications, and to estimate the impact of legislative changes. Without this institutional knowledge, legislative changes could not be made at either the state or federal level.

The federal-state partnership ranges from a system that functions as a model of cooperation to a contentious program with widely divergent problems and proposed remedies. An example of how the federal-state partnership works cooperatively in accomplishing its basic mission can be shown in the programs enacted by Congress to address prolonged spells of unemployment during national recessions. A permanent Extended Benefits (EB) program was required of the states by Congress in 1970 to provide for a "second tier" of income protection for individuals exhausting entitlement to regular state unemployment benefits during a period of high state or national unemployment. Unlike regular state UI, the federal government pays about one-half the cost of EB payments. Congress has also authorized a number of "third tier" programs (these programs are sometimes referred to as "emergency benefit programs"), usually on short notice and usually 100 percent federally funded, either in the midst of or towards the end of a national economic downturn. These third tier programs may involve a variety of triggering mechanisms, qualifying requirements and complex "reach-back" provisions which provide additional income protection to individuals who have exhausted both regular state benefits and all available EB prior to the creation of the new program. Such initiatives are generally implemented with very little time to develop the administrative procedures necessary to pay benefits to millions of workers. Without cooperation at the federal and state levels, these third tier benefits might never come into existence, much less reach the unemployed.

The U.S. Department of Labor works with the states to formulate program operation, to provide access to both the program dollars and administrative grants for the states, and to provide guidance on program administration. States generally have the responsibility to announce eligibility, to contact individuals who have exhausted entitlement, and to develop reporting and payment systems accommodating these program requirements.

By contrast, as discussed later in this chapter, the problems associated with administrative financing in the 1980s and 1990s have caused many states to advocate more state control over funding and program issues. These discussions result in disagreements among states and between states and the federal partner; these controversies, while sometimes divisive, highlight state problems and provide an opportunity for strengthening the system. However, since states represent their individual interests, the solutions proposed by some states could be detrimental to others.

Conformity and Compliance

Two types of issues exist when the U.S. Department of Labor believes a state UI program does not meet the requirements of federal law: conformity and compliance. A conformity issue arises when the state law does not agree with federal law. This may occur because the state law contains a provision inconsistent with federal law or because it does not contain a provision required by federal law. The conflict may be created by the law itself, or by administrative or judicial interpretation. A compliance issue exists when actual state practice conflicts with federal law. Whereas conformity is directed at the state law itself, compliance is directed at the proper administration of state law. Put another way, conformity relates to law while compliance relates to performance. Conformity and compliance issues arise under both the SSA and the FUTA. If the state does not conform and comply with the provisions of the FUTA, employers in the state will lose tax credits, and the state will not be eligible for administrative grants under the SSA. Failure to meet the requirements of the SSA, however, results only in the loss of administrative grants.

Federal Law Requirements

Originally, there were few federal requirements.[5] The President's Committee on Economic Security (1935) in its report to the President, recommended that federal standards apply only to matters on which uniformity was absolutely essential and that states share in the development of those standards. Another recommendation was to require that the federal government grant administrative funds to states "under conditions designed to insure competence and probity" (President's Committee on Economic Security 1935). This approach ensured some uniformity among states while providing sufficient latitude for states to enact provisions suitable for their area. The intent was to avoid interstate competition by requiring, as a condition for the credit, that all states have the same basic structure.

The Senate Finance Committee's 1935 report on the legislation that eventually was enacted emphasized that the legislation "does not set up a federal unemployment compensation system" and that "[e]xcept for a few standards which are necessary to render certain that the state unemployment compensation laws are genuine unemployment compensation acts and not merely relief measures, the states are left free to set up any unemployment compensation system they wish, without dictation from Washington." The 1935 SSA followed the pattern of the Tenth Amendment to the Constitution by implicitly providing that all UI responsibilities not expressly delegated or implied to the federal government are reserved for the states (Rubin 1983, p. 64).

The original SSA created 12 requirements:

1. Methods of administration reasonably calculated to insure full payment of UI when due. This provision has become perhaps the most important in the federal-state relationship due to its broadness and its litigation in federal courts.

2. Payment of UI through public employment offices or other agencies that the Secretary of Labor may approve. This assures that UI

claimants receive any employment services that may assist their return to work.

3. A fair hearing for all claimants who have been denied UI. Since this requirement was added prior to the explosion in administrative law, one might question whether this stipulation would be included if the SSA were created today. The first requirement listed would appear to mandate a fair hearing as a basic element of determining whether payment of UI is made when due.

4. All receipts for the unemployment fund must be immediately transferred to its account in the Unemployment Trust Fund in Washington. This requirement assures that UI monies are immediately turned over to the federal government for investment in federal, rather than in state securities. This system was given impetus by fears that mass liquidation of state-held securities on a falling market would further an economic downturn and cause the value of a state fund to decline.

5. All amounts withdrawn from the state unemployment fund may be used only for the payment of UI, i.e., cash payments to individuals with respect to their unemployment. This requirement assures that trust monies are used only for the purpose of the trust, which is the payment of UI. Along with the stipulation that payments be made through public employment offices, it is the basis of the "able and available" requirement.[6]

6. States must make reports required by the U.S. Secretary of Labor.

7. States must provide information to any agency of the United States charged with the administration of public works or assistance through public employment. This provision is obsolete.

8. States are prohibited from denying benefits to individuals entitled to UI. In hindsight, this provision seems superfluous given that states follow their laws, and, if they do not, the state courts would become involved.

9. UI may not be paid until two years after the first day of the first period with respect to which contributions are required. This

assured that states had adequate reserves on hand prior to commencing the payment of UI. Once a state commenced its UI program, it was no longer affected by this provision.

10. UI may not be denied due to a failure to accept a job if the position is vacant because of a strike or lockout; if the wages, hours, or other conditions of work offered are substantially less favorable than those prevailing in the locality; or if, as a condition of employment, the individual is required to join or to refrain from joining any bona fide labor organization. These provisions were added to assure that UI would not be used to deflate wages as well as to keep the UI program neutral in matters of labor-management relations.

11. All the rights, privileges or immunities conferred by state law shall exist subject to the power of the state legislature to repeal the power of the law at any time. This provision was included as the creation of an entirely federal UI system still appeared possible in 1935. It provides protection to states in the event their laws are repealed and replaced with a federal system.

12. To receive the additional credit against the federal unemployment tax, any reduced rate of contribution assigned an employer must be based on the employer's experience with unemployment. Although states do not have to receive the additional credit, this provision has the effect of a requirement, since early in the history of the program, almost all states chose to adopt experience rating. Currently, all states use experience rating.

The preceding requirements merely established a skeletal framework for the system. They did not mention base periods, benefit years, or waiting weeks. They did not mandate anything in terms of eligibility except that the individual be able and available for work and that the individual may not be denied benefits due to certain refusals of work. They did not compel states to have provisions relating to voluntary quits, discharges for misconduct, or the individual's suitability for refused work. They did not address duration of benefits. A state need not cover services if choosing to lose tax credit on those services. Conversely, nothing prohibited states from having broader coverage.

This lack of specificity may be surprising since current state UI programs are similar in many ways. Such commonality results from a consensus concerning what constitutes an effective UI program.[7] For example, in 1945, ten years after the enactment of the SSA, twenty-three states did not have any provisions relating to quits, misconduct or refusals of suitable work; today, all states have these provisions. As another example, in 1940, most states had maximum durations of 16 or fewer weeks. By 1955, most states had durations of around 20 weeks. Today, fifty-one states have maximum durations of 26 weeks.

Following the enactment of the SSA, thirty-five years went by with few changes in federal law. In 1939, those provisions of the SSA relating to federal tax credits were moved to the FUTA, a part of the Internal Revenue Code. In the early 1940s, two requirements were added concerning the use of UI-granted funds. In the 1950s coverage was broadened. However, in 1970 and 1976, many new requirements were created. Since 1980, new requirements have been added through the budget reconciliation process rather than through legislation concerned with the UI system itself. Although this approach has sped up legislation, it also means that laws are enacted without hearings or much deliberation and that UI program decisions are made due to budgetary instead of program concerns.

Some of the requirements added since 1970 are matters of national interest probably appropriate for the federal partner to address. Among these requirements are the following:

1. States may not deny or reduce UI to individuals who live in or filed from another state. This provision assures equal treatment by prohibiting state law provisions discriminating against such individuals.

2. States must participate in a combined-wage plan created with their participation and approved by the Secretary of Labor. Prior to this amendment, there were several combined-wage plans, with the result that some individuals still could not establish eligibility.

3. States must cover services performed for state and local governments and certain religious, charitable, and educational nonprofit organizations.[8] Under this extension of coverage, UI must be paid

on the same terms and conditions as other services covered under state law. These provisions were added since the governmental and nonprofit entities were not subject to the federal tax. Therefore, states did not have the incentive to cover these services, and large numbers of unemployed individuals might never have received UI. The amendment changed this. (Two other provisions related to this coverage provision were not quite as clearly a matter of national interest. First, states were required to give the governmental and nonprofit entities the option to reimburse the state unemployment fund rather than to pay taxes. Second, certain school services may not be used to establish UI eligibility between and within academic periods.)

4. States must pay UI to claimants in training approved by the states. The notion here was that UI should not act as an impediment to training that may help the individual return to employment.

5. States must participate in the federal-state EB program. This assured that no state would be discouraged from extending the duration of UI during periods of high unemployment. Further, it presumably would obviate the need for Congress to create special benefit programs during recessions.

6. States were prohibited from using services performed by an alien in establishing a claim unless the alien was in one of three specified categories. Since the federal government oversees efforts related to aliens such as admission and granting of work authorization, this interest was integrated into the UI program. The notion behind the amendment was to deny UI to "illegal" aliens who should not have been working and who were, in some cases, replacing Americans.

Other requirements added since 1970 are more difficult to characterize. For example, due to the way state eligibility criteria were structured, it was possible for an individual with only one separation from work to exhaust the first benefit year and to later establish a second benefit period. Congress amended FUTA to require that UI could not be paid in a second benefit year unless the claimant had worked since the beginning of the first benefit year. Congress did not say how much work was required. As a result, states could require as little as one hour of work. It is not clear why Congress felt this area had to be addressed nor is it clear why the provision was left open to manipulation due to the lack of a minimum standard. On the other hand, leaving the minimum standard to the states was entirely appropriate to the federal-state system.

Purely political considerations seem to have been the rationale for some requirements. As the result of a television show depicting individual abuses of the UI program, Congress amended federal law to require states to deny benefits to certain athletes between sports seasons and to reduce UI due to receipt of pensions and other retirement pay. Both of these provisions were, in effect, statutory assumptions of unavailability. Since many retirees were in fact looking for work, the original pension provision was later amended to apply only to pensions 100 percent financed by base-period employers. This creates a situation where only a relatively few pension recipients are prohibited from simultaneously collecting a pension and UI. Although the athlete provision has been less controversial, it has served to deny UI to low-income minor league athletes who are looking for work during the off-season. To the states, the pension and athlete provisions symbolize inappropriate federal intervention since neither seems to address any national concern.

Further requirements came about in an effort by Congress to save money. For example, as part of the reconciliation process in 1980 and 1981, the EB program was amended. Whereas state eligibility conditions had previously applied to EB claims, federal requirements were created concerning work search, suitable work, monetary qualifying requirements, and requalifying following a disqualification. Federal sharing was denied for any amount that was rounded up to the next whole dollar and for the first week of EB unless the state had a non-compensable waiting week. Finally, the amendments changed the trigger levels in such a way that the program has not since served to pay EB even during recessionary times. Under more recent amendments, Congress attempted a legislative fix to this trigger problem by giving the states the option of paying EB when the total unemployment rate in a state reached a certain level.

The two most recent requirements are also attempts to help balance the budget. Public Law (P.L.) 103-6 encourages the creation of a system of profiling all new claimants for regular UI to determine those claimants most likely to exhaust UI and to need reemployment services. In P.L. 103-152, Congress changed this to a mandate. The congressional history of this mandate indicates concern that individuals were not fully utilizing available reemployment services. Full utilization would presumably reduce UI costs by accelerating reemployment. However, from the perspective of the federal unified budget, the UI costs savings attributable to profiling were actually used to pay some of the costs of prolonging the Emergency Unemployment Compensation program.

The second example of budgetary concerns resulting in a conformity requirement is found in P.L. 103-465. In this legislation, Congress requires states to withhold federal income taxes from UI when the claimant so elects. The purported reason was that taxpayers found it burdensome to make quarterly estimated tax payments. While there was merit to that argument, the immediate impetus was accelerated tax collection, thereby helping to pay for costs of implementing the General Agreement on Tariffs and Trade, which was generally unrelated to the UI program.

This mixing of what is purportedly an expansive benefit program with restrictive eligibility conditions, reduced federal sharing of benefit costs, and high state triggers sends conflicting signals since the UI program works only when it pays benefits. States generally view federally mandated restrictive eligibility provisions as being inappropriate to the federal-state relationship and sometimes as being just plain wrong. For example, some states waive work search requirements for regular benefits when there are no jobs during a recession. However, the EB work search provision takes exactly the opposite approach by requiring claimants to search for work that does not exist.

Another issue in the relationship is that, as the years have gone by, Congress has grown more specific in legislating in most areas. This, of course, has the result of limiting state discretion. One example of these limitations is the self-employment program. As a rule, states may withdraw amounts from their unemployment funds only for payment to unemployed individuals. This means that self-employed persons normally will not collect UI. As a result, Congress amended federal law to permit withdrawals to pay for self-employment assistance programs. The authorizing provision in federal law lays down, by our count, eleven restrictions that states must follow. This is compared with only twelve requirements for the entire original UI program!

In other cases, Congress has granted the U.S. Department of Labor wide authority in implementing new requirements. For example, the profiling legislation stipulates that states must "meet other requirements" that the department determines to be appropriate. The Labor Department issued extensive operational direction and required states to submit detailed plans in order to obtain start-up funding. Similarly, when Congress compelled states to give individuals the option of having federal income tax withheld, it required approval of a state plan by the Labor Department. This time the department took a different approach: any state following the department's broad draft legislative language would automatically have its plan approved.

It should be noted that changes in federal law have not been limited only to conformity and compliance matters (Hight 1982, pp. 617-618). Prior to 1970, there were sixteen changes to federal UI provisions. Since then, there have been forty-four separate changes to UI provisions, including eighteen separate ones involving extending duration, such as EB, Emergency Unemployment Compensation, Federal Supplemental Benefits, and Federal Supplemental Compensation. Although these programs respond to the needs of the jobless during periods of high national unemployment, they also add to the complexity of the system and often create confusion when they are extended or expire. More important, the ability of states to deal with these changes exemplifies the strength of the partnership in making frequent adjustments. This collaborative adaptability is essential to the operation of the UI system in a dynamic economy.

We will now put aside the question of whether current federal requirements are appropriate to the federal-state relationship or even appropriate for the UI program itself. In this section, we will look at these requirements to determine how provisions are administered and which, in terms of the federal-state system, are more easily administered than others. For this purpose, we group federal law requirements into three categories: "methods of administration," minimums, and absolutes.

Methods of Administration

The SSA requires state law to provide for "such methods of administration . . . as are found by the Secretary of Labor to be reasonably calculated to insure full payment of unemployment compensation when due" (42 U.S. Code § 503[a][1]). This provision is unique in that, on its face, it requires nothing unless the U.S. Department of Labor sees fit to create a requirement. Looking back on this 1935 provision in 1982, a longtime department employee concluded that it "is sufficiently broad to permit virtually any federal control over administration that USDOL sees fit to impose" (Rubin 1983, p. 42). On the other hand, if the Labor Department chooses not to determine a method of administration, states need do nothing. It has been argued that the department has exercised considerable restraint in applying this provision, coming out with few major interpretations since about 1950.[9]

The discretionary nature of this provision has made it the subject of litigation for advocacy groups representing UI claimants. Indeed, it seems that, notwithstanding the considerable federal legislation enacted since 1970, this litigation has rechanneled the efforts of the U.S. Department of Labor mainly into performance oversight. The issues of litigation and performance oversight are sufficiently important that they will be treated in more detail later.

Minimum Requirements

Minimum requirements recognize the original spirit of the federal-state relationship: states are free to develop their own requirements within a framework set by federal law. The degree of flexibility, of course, varies with each minimum requirement. Examples are the pension, alien, and approved training provisions. The U.S. Department of Labor follows two general rules in interpreting and applying these minimums: (1) if the requirement impinges on areas otherwise left to the states, it is construed as narrowly as possible while reasonably effectuating its purpose, and (2) any language that may be construed as leaving discretion to states is broadly construed, unless there are compelling reasons for a narrow construction.[10] Of course, unless the requirement is completely clear, there will be disagreement as to what reasonably effectuates its purpose.

Some minimum requirements create little or no tension in the federal-state relationship. For example, the "double dip" provision gives states such latitude that, once the provision is placed in state law, there will likely be no conformity or compliance issues raised. Similarly, the approved training provision allows the states to determine what training will be approved. Again, once the state has an approved training provision, few issues will be raised.

Other minimum federal requirements are not as easily administered. To illustrate, the alien provision uses a very broad phrase—"permanently residing in the United States under color of law"—to describe certain aliens. States are not required to have this phrase in their laws and states that do have the provision can interpret it more restrictively than does the U.S. Department of Labor. The problem with administering the provision is that the phrase invites differing interpretations. Based on federal court decisions in other programs such as Supplemental Security Income, claimant advocacy groups have in many cases successfully argued that aliens who have made themselves known to the Immigration and Naturalization Service (INS) are permanently residing in the United States under color of law. The Labor Department and the INS, however, take the position that only aliens with written acknowledgment from the INS meet this definition. Since state UI agencies do not control state courts or advocacy groups, the Labor Department almost always has an issue concerning the alien provision pending with at least one state.[11]

Absolute Requirements

The third and last category involves the absolute requirements. These requirements are framed in such a way that they provide no latitude to the states or the U.S. Department of Labor in administering them. Some absolute requirements are so clear that they create little friction in the federal-state system. For example, if federal law sets a numeric standard such as the 20 weeks of work requirement for EB, then states simply incorporate that standard into their laws. Another example involves the mandatory coverage and equal treatment requirements for services performed for state and local governments and certain nonprofit organizations. States either cover the services and provide equal treatment, or they do not. Perhaps the most important examples are the "immediate deposit" and "withdrawal" standards.

The between and within terms denial of UI benefits for services performed for these governmental and nonprofit schools is, in part, an absolute. UI may not be paid based on services performed by a teacher, researcher, or administrator if the individual has a contract or reasonable assurance of performing services in the following period. States must deny UI based on these services. Administration of this denial has been a problem. The provision assumes that, given the same set of facts, all states would reach the same conclusions. This, of course, simply will not happen. Even two UI appeals referees from a given state will not always reach the same conclusion given the identical set of facts. As a result, differences between the U.S Department of Labor and the states will inevitably arise. Although many times the issues are significant, other times the problematic state interpretation concerns a very minor point and affects very few individuals. The U.S. Department of Labor frequently does not know about situations that it should address until states, due to timeliness considerations, have already made a determination. In short, this ostensibly "absolute" requirement is not entirely absolute.[12]

Some absolute requirements are needed in the federal-state system. For example, the deposit and withdrawal standards frame the nature of the entire system and implement its trust fund aspect by assuring that monies are used only for the payment of UI. The requirements relating to interstate and combined-wage claims assure equal treatment of claimants and cooperation between states. Others likely exist due to political considerations. For example, without the between and within terms denial, Congress might have been unable to extend coverage to governmental entities and nonprofit organizations. Regardless of the reason for its existence, when an absolute requirement assumes that every state eligibility determination in a given area is consistent with federal law, it places heavy burdens on both the U.S. Department of Labor and the states. The Labor Department often cannot effectively monitor such requirements; the monitoring that does occur is after the fact, with the result that states must amend their laws or ignore their own administrative decisions. Such requirements are better framed as minimum requirements, which give states considerable latitude. For example, the between and within terms denial could simply require states to have a denial provision relating to school services. The schools, the employees and the state agency could negotiate the appropriate denial, perhaps using any draft legislative language provided by the Labor Department. Similarly, the EB work search could mandate that states require EB claimants to have a more stringent work search than that stipulated for regular benefits; the details of this policy could be left to the states.

This approach is not new. Haber and Murray (1966) discussed the degree of strain new requirements might place on the federal-state relationship:

> If the standards are specific and conformity with them can be easily verified, no difficulties in the federal-state relations should arise. If the standards are subject to different interpretations or compliance with them is difficult to verify, strained relations could result (Haber and Murray 1966, p. 446).

The Federal Courts Move In

Timeliness

Starting with the U.S. Supreme Court's 1970 decision in the *Java*[13] case, the federal courts have played a major role in the federal-state program. The *Java* decision addressed a provision of California law that stopped payment of UI to otherwise eligible individuals when an appeal was filed. In other words, the possibility of a reversal of an individual's eligibility was used as the basis for suspending payments. The Court interpreted the "methods of administration" provision to require payment at the time "when payments are first administratively allowed as a result of a hearing of which both parties and are permitted to present their respective positions." As a result of the *Java* case in effect creating a new conformity requirement, forty-seven states had to amend or reinterpret their laws.[14] Although *Java* had many implications, the emphasis on timeliness is probably its primary legacy.

Although the U.S. Department of Labor had always stressed promptness, it became an overwhelming concern following *Java*. Suits concerning the timeliness of appeals and first payments were frequent in the 1970s and suits regarding payment on continued claims continue into the 1990s. The promptness of first level appeals was also an issue in another case decided by the U.S. Supreme Court. While this case was being litigated, the Labor Department issued regulations concerning the timeliness of appeals. Regulations concerning the timeliness of first payments followed.

State Eligibility Criteria

Since the inception of the UI program, the U.S. Department of Labor has, in the absence of a federal law requirement, left all eligibility matters to the states. In the department's view, *Java* stands for the limited proposition that a state law provision that does nothing but delay payment of benefits is an administrative consideration inconsistent with federal law.

The U.S. Court of Appeals in the Seventh Circuit took a different view in the *Pennington* case.[15] In Illinois, as in all states, employment performed during the base period determines whether the individual has sufficient attachment to the labor force to qualify for UI. As do most states, Illinois uses a base period consisting of the first four of the last five completed calendar quarters. In most states, employment during the "lag" quarter between the end of the base period and the filing of the claim is not used to establish a claim, even if its use would qualify the individual.

In the *Pennington* case, the court said that, since the base period was founded on administrative considerations related to the method used by the state of obtaining employment history, it was subject to the federal "methods of administration" requirement. The court only briefly addressed the fact that the only reason the base period exists is for eligibility purposes and did not reconcile the tension between administrative and eligibility provisions. In any event, *Pennington* effectively creates a new conformity requirement for the states in the Seventh Circuit.

Court decisions such as *Pennington* cause sharp disruptions in state UI programs when state laws, acceptable for sixty years, must be amended. Since the U.S. Department of Labor is often in agreement with state provisions, even to the extent of filing friend of the court briefs, it should be no surprise when the department does not embrace such decisions. As a result, sometimes federal law may be interpreted and applied differently in different areas of the country. The Labor Department is, however, required to treat all decisions handed down by federal courts located in the District of Columbia, including the U.S. Supreme Court, as conformity requirements.

Oversight

The nature of federal oversight has changed considerably over the years. In the early decades of the program, the federal partner approved furniture acquisition, salary levels for administrators, and state organizational structure. Those days are long gone. States are free to spend their UI grants as they see fit without direction from the U.S. Department of Labor. The only restriction is that the grant be necessary for the proper and efficient administration of state UI law. The Department of Labor now only very rarely advises a state that its grant may not be spent for a specific UI activity.

To some extent, the changing nature of oversight is driven by shifts in staffing patterns of the Labor Department. For fiscal year 1994, there were only about 310 federal staff members nationwide compared to over 40,000 state staff members. In the national office, there were fewer than 100 individuals on staff whereas, about ten years earlier, there were over 130. Despite this shrinkage, the U.S. Department of Labor has had to pick up additional responsibilities whenever Congress enacts new legislation. One might question whether staffing is sufficiently low to constrain the ability of the department to adequately perform its activities.

In the 1970s, as a result of the action occurring in federal courts, the main concern of the U.S. Department of Labor with the states shifted to the performance of UI activities. Promotion of timeliness was institutionalized in the late 1970s, when the department, in consultation with the states, created a performance measurement system, called the "Quality Appraisal," to the present day.[16] States not meeting designated performance levels are required to submit corrective action plans as a condition of receiving the following year's UI grant.

The Department of Labor believed that, if it did not establish an oversight system emphasizing timeliness, the federal courts probably would. Since there are many types of UI claims (intrastate, interstate, UI for ex-military personnel, UI for ex-federal employees, and combined-wage), the department created performance levels for each. In some cases, two different performance levels were created. For example, timeliness for first payments was measured 14 days following the end of the first compensable week (21 days for states with no waiting week) and then again after 35 days. The department also measured the timeliness of certain combined-wage functions, the handling of unemployment fund monies, and the determination of whether an employing unit was an "employer" subject to state UI law.

The bulk of the performance levels emphasizes timeliness. Although Java is one reason, the main factor is that timeliness is objective and easy to assess, unlike quality and accuracy. Quality performance measures exist for nonmonetary determinations and appeals and for some tax functions.

The nature of the performance measures differs in another regard. Numeric criteria for first payment promptness (for both intrastate and interstate claims) and for the disposition of lower authority appeals are found in regulations.[17] Meeting these criteria indicates that state programs comply with federal law. Other measures do not have criteria in regulations. They have "desired levels of achievement," (DLAs), which by definition are merely "desired." Still other measures do not have any numeric goal attached to them.

Has this measurement approach had an impact on the UI system? If statistics alone are any indicator, the answer is yes. From the early to mid-1970s first payments made within 14/21 days fluctuated around 80 percent of total first payments. When the timeliness criteria of the U.S. Department of Labor became effective, there was a dramatic improvement in performance. There were, however, periods when timeliness dropped below 70 percent. (See figure 13.1.) On April 1, 1979, the current criterion of 87 percent paid timely came into effect. Since then, the national average has more often than not been above 87 percent. In fact, the national average has not dipped below that level since early 1979. Only a small number of states have had chronic problems, as shown in table 13.1.

Federal oversight is certainly one reason for this consistent performance. Another is that automation allows first payments to be made more rapidly and allows the states to better handle the increases in UI workloads occurring during recessions. (There is, however, a continued need for more claimstakers when workload increases. This is generally accommodated through overtime, moving workers from support to frontline work, and hiring temporary employees.) Also, since the mid-1980s, almost all states have converted to systems using employer quarterly wage reports to determine eligibility. As a result, few claims are delayed due to an employer's failure to respond.

Figure 13.1 Timeliness of First Payments, Impact of Standards Created by Secretary of Labor, 1971-1995 U.S. Average, All States

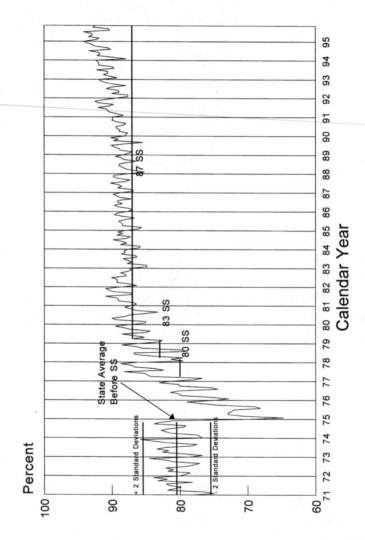

NOTE: 80% SS effective 4/1/77 to 3/31/78; 83% SS effective 4/1/78 to 3/31/79; 87% SS effective 4/1/79 forward.

Table 13.1 First Payment Timeliness, 1990-1994

Number of states	Number of years criterion met
34	All 5 years
7	4 of 5 years
8	3 of 5 years
1	2 of 5 years
2	1 of 5 years
1	Never met criterion

SOURCE: U.S. Department of Labor, *Unemployment Insurance Quality Appraisal Results,* published annually.

This level of sustained performance is not always matched in other areas. For example, states are required to dispose of 60 percent of all lower authority appeals within 30 days of the date of appeal. In the early 1970s, the national average was only 20 percent. (See figure 13.2.) From calendar year 1977, two years after the 60 percent criterion first took effect, through 1994, there was a decided and permanent rise in the national average. Even so, this average has not consistently met the 60 percent criterion. As shown in table 13.2, the failure to meet the criterion is persistent for some states.

Table 13.2 Lower Authority Appeals Timeliness, 1990-1994

Number of states	Number of years criterion met
18	All 5 years
7	4 of 5 years
9	3 of 5 years
6	2 of 5 years
4	1 of 5 years
9	Never met criterion.

SOURCE: U.S. Department of Labor, *Unemployment Insurance Quality Appraisal Results*, published annually.

On the other hand, for the 1994 performance year, thirty states exceeded the 60 percent criterion by 10 percent or more. This suggests that the criterion should be raised. Even for the 1992 performance year,

Figure 13.2 Promptness of Disposition of Lower Authority Appeals: Introduction of Standards Created by U.S. Secretary of Labor, 1971-1995, U.S. Average, All States

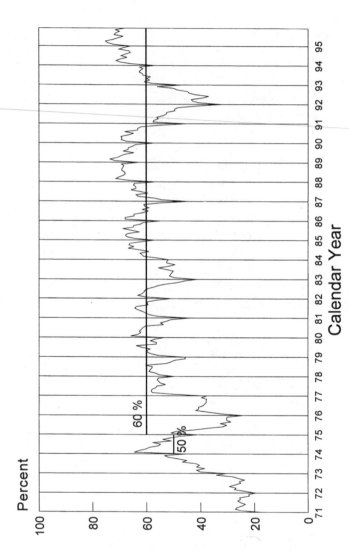

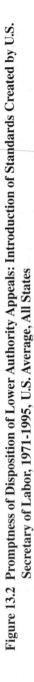

NOTE: 50% SS effective calendar year 1974; 60% SS effective

when recessionary effects resulted in most states not meeting the criterion, this number was seventeen.

Part of the problem in achieving the 60 percent criterion is that appeals referees have very specialized skills. When vacancies exist or increases in workload create the need for additional positions, most new referees cannot immediately be shunted into hearings. Instead, considerable training is necessary. Also, the appeals process itself is not greatly amenable to automation. Even so, automation has assisted in scheduling appeals, in easing research by making precedent decisions available, and by speeding the issuance of decisions once the appeal is heard. While this performance measure results in a rapid conclusion to the contested issue, it may mean that the parties are required to participate in a hearing process even if they are not fully prepared. It may also mean that the hearings are abbreviated in order to achieve a prompt disposition of the next scheduled case.

Although there have been concerns in some states about the effect of timeliness on accuracy of payment and on due process, others have exceeded the federal performance levels without the perception that accuracy and due process have been compromised. Some states seem overwhelmed by workload changes; others seem better equipped to handle such changes.

The preceding timeliness standards are almost without exception viewed as being beneficial to the UI program. However, this is not the case with all measures. According to a U.S. General Accounting Office report (1989, p. 44), some of the performance levels "may be inappropriate and provide misleading indications of service quality." The report noted the "overemphasis on promptness of service" and said "some DLAs measure inappropriate or misleading aspects of service quality, wherein an improvement in the measure could actually be indicating a decline in service quality." The DLA specifically targeted in the report was for field audit effectiveness. Meeting the DLA may require states to divert staff that might otherwise be used to collect delinquent tax payments. Another example is the DLA for recovery of overpayments to claimants. Since the DLA measures the percentage of overpayments recovered, states may meet the goal by concentrating on collecting dollars instead of on detecting overpayments. As a result, the state's performance will look good, even though relatively few overpayments are established.

The Quality Appraisal never claimed to measure the entire system. Consequently, it is not surprising that Burgess and Kingston found that the approach did not constitute a comprehensive or valid way of measuring the total quality of the program (Burgess and Kingston 1987, p. 137). Not assessed are how long claimants must wait for service or how far they must travel to file a claim. On the employer side, there are no measurements involving the length of time needed to resolve a tax dispute or to calculate new tax rates when the experience of a business is transferred to a successor employer. Surveys are not widely used to assure that both claimants and employers are being served in a professional, consistent, efficient, and fair manner. Changes to the DLAs have been relatively minor even though the U.S. Department of Labor has always had the ability to unilaterally add or delete both performance measures and DLAs. Recently, however, work on updating the benefit measurements found in the Quality Appraisal has been completed. There is an ongoing effort to revise the measures related to the handling of unemployment funds by the states, from the moment the monies are received until they are used for the paying of UI.

In the 1980s, the U.S. Department of Labor developed a Quality Control program, independent of its Quality Appraisal system. Originally, Quality Control consisted of an exhaustive postaudit of payments for purposes of determining accuracy. Every year, the Department of Labor publishes the results, including an error rate for each state. Since the procedures and laws differ in each state, it is difficult to draw any comparisons between them, with the result that no performance level has been established. Beginning in 1996, all states are also required to operate a revenue Quality Control program to measure state UI functions related to collecting employer contributions. This program replaces some of the revenue measures in the Quality Appraisal.

A workgroup made up of federal and state UI program managers has developed a new approach to performance measurement. The goal of this approach is to improve performance over the long run by emphasizing program outcomes and customer service. All measures would exist under a single measurement and oversight system called "UI Performs."

With the exception of the original benefit Quality Control program, all of these measurement efforts have had heavy participation from the states. State input helps the U.S. Department of Labor to determine whether a proposed measurement is necessary or useful as well as the effort in implementing the measurement in each state. The UI Performs workgroup operated on the assumption that its members would reach consensus on each point. At the time of this writing, most of these endeavors are in the implementation stage; we should soon be able to look at the new oversight system and, a little later, to consider what effect it has on state performance and federal-state relations.

Enforcing Federal Law Requirements

States often view the federal presence in the state legislative process as a mixed blessing. Federal law requirements are often seen as intrusive, and both state legislatures and state agencies resent having to implement provisions without the opportunity to debate their merits. The U.S. Department of Labor hears these objections each time Congress adds new federal requirements. However, the state agencies also recognize that the federal presence has prevented many undesirable state proposals from being enacted. As a result, the UI program is less subject to passing state legislative whims than are other state programs, such as workers' compensation.

Each year, the U.S. Department of Labor reviews hundreds of proposed state bills. Also reviewed are procedures, regulations and court cases. In most instances, the bills do not create any problems with federal law. In fact, many of the areas covered by the bills do not fall under any federal requirement. The problems that do exist are generally resolved prior to enactment. Certain such initiatives are enacted, however, and the federal partner is required to take some steps to correct the problem. Most issues that arise are resolved through negotiation rather than direct confrontation (Haber and Murray 1966, pp. 450-451). At any given time, the Labor Department unit responsible for conformity tracks between thirty and sixty issues.

Issues not resolved through negotiation result in conformity and compliance hearings. An oral hearing before a U.S. Department of Labor administrative law judge may be requested by the state(s). The judge issues a recommended decision which the Secretary of Labor may adopt, modify or reverse. If the Secretary determines that a state is not in conformity/compliance, the state may appeal to the U.S. Court of Appeals in the circuit in which the state is located or with the U.S. Court of Appeals for the District of Columbia.

Since 1982, there have only been three conformity hearings involving the regular UI program.[18] In the first proceeding, the Secretary decided against the Department of Labor by finding that an appeals practice used by the District of Columbia was consistent with federal law. Specifically, the District of Columbia automatically ruled in favor of the claimant when the employer failed to appear at an appellate hearing involving a discharge for misconduct. In the second hearing, the Secretary found that the use of hypothetical, rather than actual, experience by the State of Washington for a certain group of employers was inconsistent with federal law. In the third hearing, the Secretary found that Minnesota law was inconsistent with federal law when it allowed reduction of an individual's UI to offset amounts the individual owed the unemployment fund in unpaid taxes due to his or her previous status as an employer. The unfavorable decisions were not appealed to the courts, and in neither case were administrative grants or tax credits actually withheld.

In one instance, there was an actual withholding of administrative grants where the state did not request a hearing. The Virgin Islands lost several days worth of administrative grants due to a late payment of interest on amounts borrowed from the federal government to pay UI.

The most recent experience in conformity/compliance hearings is that clear issues, such as the late payment of interest by the Virgin Islands, are resolved informally. Issues that go to hearing address areas where states feel that the federal law does not clearly prohibit state practice. In one of the preceding cases, the state was proven right. In addition to giving states an opportunity to air their views, the hearing process helps assure that the U.S. Department of Labor does not interpret federal law to create requirements not inherent in that law.

Concerning performance issues detected through its measurement systems, such as timely payment of UI and timely disposition of appeals, the U.S. Department of Labor has never initiated steps to withhold certification. The reason most frequently offered is an unwillingness to hold back administrative grants since that would only increase performance problems. (This seems somewhat at odds with the department's regular reminders to states that withholding of grants/tax credits will occur if a state law is inconsistent with federal law.)

Another reason is that performance does not change overnight. The Department of Labor, through its regional offices, tends to emphasize incremental improvements in performance. Slightly enhanced performance or the taking of steps that should lead to better performance indicates that eventually the problem may be resolved without initiating withholding actions.

A mixed blessing for both the federal and state partners is created by the potential loss of the FUTA tax credit or the total withholding of administrative funds as an enforcement tools. On the one hand, even when they feel their position is correct, states may yield due to their own political situations, to avoid litigation, and to avoid any risk of losing credits or grants. On the other hand, for political, economic, and programmatic reasons, the U.S. Department of Labor is reluctant to initiate withholdings. As a result, tax credits have never been withheld, and grants only rarely. Sometimes states believe that withholdings will never occur and have become belligerent or have failed to respond to the Labor Department's conformity efforts, even on obvious conflicts. Although lesser enforcement measures have been suggested from time to time, no such measures have been adopted. A lesser measure may have no additional effect if it requires the same amount of Labor Department time and effort to enforce as withholding grants/employer tax credits. This is because providing notice for opportunity and hearing, documenting a case, and facing the prospect of appeals to the courts require the department to undertake a major effort. However, if lesser enforcement measures can be more easily carried out, states and employers may resist their use.

The principal question in discussing the nature of conformity and compliance is the following: Do they work for the betterment of the system? In the main, the answer is "yes." Although one might question the need for some of the federal requirements, or the lack of others, the system has assured that UI monies are protected and that it fulfills its fundamental purpose of providing income support for individuals unemployed through no fault of their own. The hearing process assures that the U.S. Department of Labor takes state concerns seriously. That only three matters have gone to hearing since 1982 suggests that, more often than not, the states and the Labor Department are in agreement about how federal law should be applied to the states.

Administrative Financing

The conformity and compliance requirements establish the frame-work for the UI system and, as a result, have perhaps been the primary focus of the federal-state relationship during the first fifty years of the program. However, state concerns about the adequacy of administrative funding have resulted in many skirmishes in the relationship and now is perhaps the primary issue.

Since administrative funding affects both the quality and timeliness of services, it is of great importance and has been an issue for states since the inception of the program. The debate that occurred during the 1930s about the basic structure of the system also included questions about how state programs should be funded. Since then, discussions regarding funding problems have resulted in debates about whether the UI program would operate better as a federalized system, whether it should be "devolved" to state control, or whether the original structure works best.

As noted in the first section, the FUTA tax pays for state administrative costs. The basic premise, shared by employers and states, is that these revenues should pay the full costs of the UI program. The result is that costs of administration are pooled and redistributed according to state need. Some states receive more in administrative grants than their employers paid in, while others receive less. Federal administrative monies not appropriated by Congress are transferred to other federal accounts in the Unemployment Trust Fund, primarily to the account paying for the federal share of EB.

The first step in distributing money to the states is the appropriation by Congress of monies from the Unemployment Trust Fund for administrative purposes. The next step is the allocation of monies to the states by the U.S. Department of Labor. We will discuss each separately and then consider whether the system should be changed.

The Federal Appropriation

When the UI program was first created, the FUTA tax was deposited into and UI administrative funds were paid from federal general revenues, apparently to address constitutional concerns. However, not all FUTA revenues were appropriated, as Congress was using these receipts to help balance the federal budget. In 1952, a comparison of the revenues generated from the FUTA tax with the administrative appropriation showed a difference of between $500 million and $1.1 billion, depending upon which estimates were used.[19]

In response, the Employment Security Administration Financing Act (P.L. 83-567) of 1954 was passed. It provided for earmarking federal unemployment taxes. Although the taxes continued to be deposited into general revenues and appropriations were paid out of general revenues, any excess tax collections (the difference between revenues and expenditures) would be credited to the Federal Unemployment Trust Fund. The legislation established a loan fund of $200 million for states and also provided that when that fund's ceiling was reached, the states would share in the surplus collections. States could then use the funds for the payment of UI, or a state legislature could under certain conditions appropriate them for administrative purposes. In 1960, Congress required the deposit of the FUTA tax in a specific account in the Unemployment Trust Fund and provided for appropriations from this fund. This ostensibly meant that UI appropriations would not be subject to budget balancing or other fiscal policies.

This was in fact the case for several years. Then, in 1967, a Commission on Budget concepts, appointed by President Johnson, recommended a single unified budget that included the transactions of all trust funds.[20] As a result, in 1969 Congress enacted the Unified Budget Act, which placed all federal trust funds, including the Unemployment Trust Fund, within the federal budget process. UI appropriations became subject to the budget-balancing preoccupation of Congress, and state UI administrative appropriations suffered.

The Balanced Budget and Emergency Deficit Control Act of 1985, generally known as Gramm-Rudman-Hollings, established an automatic process to reduce federal deficits by "sequestering" funds from all federal programs not specifically exempted. These actions resulted in reductions in administrative funding for federal fiscal years 1986, 1987, 1989, and 1990. (Regular UI benefits were not affected because they are state funds held in trust by the U.S. Treasury. The federal share of EB was, however, reduced.) Even though the assets of the Unemployment Trust Fund are dedicated under federal law, these amounts are classified as "discretionary" for federal budget purposes. This means that UI grants can be used in reconciling the federal budget.

Ironically, the administrative costs of other entitlement programs (e.g., medicaid and food stamps) are treated as "mandatory" even though these costs are funded through general revenues. UI, with its dedicated trust fund, would seem to be in a better position to claim mandatory status.

Still another problem in the process was created when, in the 1980s, Congress appropriated amounts based on inaccurate low estimates of unemployment. As a result, insufficient funds were available to administer the system, and Congress sometimes enacted a supplemental appropriation. This approach has fortunately been eliminated by the creation of an automatic funding provision (called "contingency reserve" language) built into current appropriation bills.

In sum, the UI program has frequently received across-the-board spending reductions without regard to program need. This has happened even during periods of rising unemployment, when additional administrative funds are normally provided to states to process the increase in claims. Except for a brief period, the history of administrative financing has been a chapter in the history of balancing the federal budget.

Allocation of the Appropriation to the States

Under the Social Security Act, the U.S. Department of Labor (USDOL) provides, out of appropriated funds, amounts "necessary for the proper and efficient administration" of state UI law.[21] The state allocations are to be based on an estimate of the cost of proper and efficient administration using: (1) the state population, (2) an estimate of the number of persons covered by the state law, and (3) other factors that the Secretary of Labor considers relevant.

Initially, state UI programs were funded using a "line item" budget justification for each staff person and piece of equipment needed. By 1941, budgeting was accomplished by estimating the workload and functions necessary to support that workload (Haber and Murray 1966, p. 402). The state allocations were made on the basis of a "work load time factor" system that required work measurement studies for routine activities such as processing tax returns, and national averaging for nonstandard activities such as benefit appeals. By 1963, the allocation process had evolved into "position allocations based on functional areas." In the first twenty-five years of the program, the determination of administrative resources involved an inexact method that used historic funding experience to establish the annual administrative grant for each state (Haber and Murray 1966, pp. 402-403).

A new system developed in the 1970s, called the Cost Model, measured the amount of time required to complete various units of work. The Cost Model used 700 different activity codes and seventeen separate workload measurements. Each state was allocated a specific amount of time to complete a certain activity. For example, a given state might be alloted five minutes to process each continued claim. These "minutes per unit" (MPUs) would be multiplied by the anticipated workload and ultimately converted to a certain number of staff-year positions based on the annual number of hours worked in each state. Each state would be assigned a different time factor based on the actual time necessary to complete the workload item. The Cost Model program was designed to be updated every three years so that state efficiencies and changes in the law could be factored into the time allocations. However, in 1984, the restudies were discontinued because of their cost and because of questions as to whether the MPUs derived from the studies were being used to inflate costs.

Perhaps the most basic criticism of the Cost Model was the lack of incentives for states to improve operations. That is, if a state were to implement new procedures that resulted in increased administrative efficiencies and, consequently, lower program costs, the state grant would be reduced by the amount of savings. In the late 1980s, changes were made by the U.S. Department of Labor, giving states more bottom line authority over determinations of spending of administrative resources. These actions shifted more responsibility for controlling costs to the states and also signaled that future state allocations would focus more on workload changes rather than on the actual costs of processing the workload.

Even so, more than twenty years after the initial application of the model, states continue to be primarily compensated for their administrative costs on the basis of Cost Model MPUs. These MPUs may, however, be prorated downward by the U.S. Department of Labor to balance the workload with the congressional appropriation. The MPUs in use in the mid-1990s are based on the studies completed more than ten years earlier, with the result that the MPUs do not bear a strong relationship to current state administrative costs. However, states now have "bottom-line authority" to use their administrative grants. For example, where once amounts received for initial claims had to be used for initial claims, they can now be used for any UI task, including appeals and tax functions. This method of allocation, therefore, bears less relationship to actual program costs but gives states more flexibility to initiate their own costs savings.

State Treatment of Federal Administrative Grants

Employers pay the FUTA tax primarily to support the administrative costs of UI and the employment service and to obtain labor market information at the national, regional, and state levels. Congress appropriates administrative funds annually, and those resources are allocated to states by the U.S. Department of Labor. However, there are two additional steps in the process before the administrative grants are actually spent on direct employer and claimant services. These activities bring a variety of "state partners" into the process of deciding state priorities and methods of determining service delivery.

In most states, the legislatures must also appropriate the federal administrative grants before the state agency can spend the funds on services. Although the legislatures generally approve the grants with minimal review as part of legislative oversight activities, state agencies are required to justify their expenditures in terms of service delivery and performance. In theory, the federal grant can only be expended for "proper and efficient administration"; however, in practice state agencies are subject to some political pressures involving the use of federal grants.

When a state has satisfied all the federal and state requirements, it can address the budgetary allocation to the local level. Employers may want to know why the FUTA taxes that support administrative costs are unavailable to provide more local services. Claimants (who often erroneously believe that their taxes pay for both benefit and administrative costs) want to know why local staff is unavailable to respond to concerns about the complexity of the UI system or to provide assistance with problems. Finally, local agency personnel want to know why they are impacted by decisions made at the federal level, which affect their ability to provide the service that they believe is justified locally.

The state allocation of administrative resources results in many difficult choices between direct service delivery, central support and overhead expenditures. Sometimes states must manage declining administrative resources by implementing new technologies. Although these strategies make sense in the long run, there are initial capital investment choices and resistance to changes in service delivery which must be factored into the short-term decisions.

Should the Administrative Funding System be Changed?

Since states are unhappy with both the appropriation process and the allocation methodology of the U.S. Department of Labor, some are questioning, at least with regard to administrative financing, whether the federal-state partnership is the best approach. Proposals to revise the 100 percent federal funding concept were made as early as the 1940s, and today the original concept has been modified without any federal law change, as many states rely on state resources to supplement their federal UI grants. Even more have been relying on state resources to fund their employment service programs. For example, in 1980, eight states received supplemental state funds amounting to $1.1 million for administrative purposes (U.S. General Accounting Office 1989). Although some states obtained funds from general revenues or new taxes, the most frequent source was state "penalty and interest" funds consisting of amounts employers pay when they are delinquent in making tax payments and reports. By 1987, thirty-three states were using $54 million in state funds for UI or the employment service. A survey of states showed that although the number of states receiving state funds for administration was about the same in 1993 as it was in 1987, the aggregate funding exceeded $162 million.[22] At that level (and there are some indications that the reported use of state funds is understated), states were providing approximately 5 percent of their administrative resources. Since the distribution of funds bore little resemblance to the taxes that employers in a given state paid or to the actual costs of operating the program in that state, employers felt that they were paying for administrative costs twice.

All of these factors indicated that the system was ripe for a change in funding methods. A number of bills introduced in 1982, known as the Bliley-Warner bills, would have allowed a state, subject to agreements with the Secretaries of Labor and Treasury, to collect FUTA taxes and to retain a portion to fund the administrative costs of its UI program. Although the bills never received a hearing, they were indicative of growing state discontent with the federal appropriation and allocation system.

In the 1986 Budget of the United States Government, the *devolution* of administrative financing was discussed:

> Working with the states, the Administration will develop and propose legislation to devolve to the states the responsibility for managing and financing their employment services and unemployment insurance services. The federal unemployment tax will be reduced accordingly, freeing tax resources for the states . . . This proposal would encourage efficiency in state administration by increasing the flexibility with which states carry out their programs (Executive Office of the President 1986, section 5, pp. 5-98 to 5-99).

This proposal was based on the theory that, although under the current UI program states can legislate their own policy, federal appropriations for administration may not meet state needs.

The discussions that developed, which involved the federal government and many states, brought out complaints that the existing appropriation mechanism had two major deficiencies: underfunding (insufficient resources) and cross-subsidies (inadequate return of FUTA taxes to some states). Proponents argued that devolving the system would create self-insurance for purposes of administrative costs, requiring states to do everything possible to reduce program costs. The opponents of devolution argued that the national system would not survive. Their concerns were that (1) states would effectively compete by offering lower cost services, which would result in wide variations in service delivery from state to state, and (2) states would be unable to fund their programs through the full economic cycle, which was very unpredictable in many states and which occurred more frequently in some states than in others. In other words, the pooling of risk was desirable.

In 1986, a proposal known as the Equity Act was developed by a group of thirteen states, but was never introduced. This plan would have resulted in the collection of federal UI tax by states and their retention of 0.5 percent of their taxable payrolls to operate their programs. Each state would be required to abide by a "maintenance of effort" provision to ensure that state programs would conform to minimum federal requirements. The National Governors' Association also developed a proposal that increased the overall federal appropriation and guaranteed that a state would receive a minimum return of the taxes that employers in that state pay to the federal government to operate UI, the Employment Service and Labor Market Information programs (Committee on Ways and Means 1988, pp. 324-328).

The theory behind allowing states to receive a guaranteed percentage of state revenues is that FUTA revenues are really taxes paid by employers in that state for administration of UI within the state. This assumption divides the states into two groups: the "winner" states, which currently receive more in administrative funds than employers in that state pay in FUTA taxes for administrative costs, and the "loser" states, which receive less. In theory, if the "loser" states were able to retain a larger share of the FUTA taxes paid by employers in their state, their administrative funding problems would be resolved.

This theory is not new and will likely never completely vanish. We share the view of Haber and Murray, who addressed the issue of administrative funds not being returned to the states where the employers paid the FUTA taxes:

> We are not impressed with the argument that federal unemployment taxes are state money that should be returned to the state. The federal unemployment tax, like all federal taxes, is a national tax, to be used for national purposes. ...The pooling of the tax on a national basis and allocation of funds on the basis of needs for proper and efficient administration meets the state needs better than if each state were given what their employers contributed. Actually, most of the complaints as to allocation of state grants are due to inadequacy in the total federal appropriations (Haber and Murray 1966, p. 417).

Administrative funds are pooled and allocated to states on the basis of need, using workload as the primary factor. If the congressional appropriation were greater and if the Unemployment Trust Fund were not part of the unified federal budget, the problems of states would perhaps be resolved.

Although the appropriation is the main problem, the method of allocating resources is also significant. Recognizing this, in 1991, Congress required the Secretary of Labor to undertake an "Administrative Financing Initiative" (P.L. 102-164, Section 304). As a result, the U.S. Department of Labor began discussing with states a proposal that attempted to equalize state funding by using more objective criteria to increase predictability and facilitate budget planning. By using its own experience, combined with the application of national cost factors, a state could be in a better position to develop multi-year budget plans. On the negative side, the total funds appropriated would be approximately the same, so about half the states would be worse off, while half the states would be better off.

When discussing allocation, several issues arise. One is the lack of a consistent relationship between the actual cost of administering state programs and the amounts received. On the one hand, the SSA provides that the Secretary of Labor allocate funds to states for "proper and efficient administration" of state UI law. What is "proper and efficient" is debatable. While most states desire more administrative funding, even they do not agree among themselves on what is proper and efficient. If state A argues that its law is more expensive to administer, then state B, looking out for its own appropriation, will respond that state A is inefficient and should, therefore, receive a smaller allocation. UI programs are far from homogeneous. Some are large, some small, some are susceptible to high unemployment, and some are more insulated from economic downturns.

Because administrative funds are obtained from federal grants, state legislatures and interest groups often do not focus on the costs of administering new state provisions, but on the provisions themselves. Employers and state legislators share the view that to the extent that employers pay FUTA taxes to support the costs of program administration, they should be able to structure state provisions as they wish, as long as there is no conflict with federal law.

However, does this mean that a state should expect federal grants for administration of its law regardless of complexity or cost? For example, if a state chooses to enact a very complex approach involving benefit disqualifications, is it reasonable to anticipate that the costs of processing will be paid by federal grants regardless of the cost as compared with other states? Alternatively, should the U.S. Department of Labor pay only "normal processing costs" for basic provisions, with the states paying for more complex or cumbersome provisions? With state legislatures passing benefit and tax provisions that do not necessarily reflect administrative efficiency and static or declining federal appropriations, state UI agencies are caught in the middle. Also caught in the middle is the Department of Labor, which must still make determinations on how an appropriation is allocated. That a state chooses to enact a costly new provision does not mean Congress will increase the appropriation, nor does it mean that another state's allocation should be reduced.

The administrative funding issue has an obvious and significant impact on the federal-state relationship. States have noted that without adequate administrative resources, they must struggle in their ability to deliver services. To the extent that Congress does not appropriate sufficient funds for the system to operate, states have less discretionary authority. As a result, states view the administrative funding issue as increasing the power of the federal partner to influence program delivery. Alternatively, if states are able to argue that adequate administrative resources must be granted to support provisions enacted at the state level, irrespective of their cost-effectiveness, then the balance shifts towards the states. Until the Unemployment Trust Fund is removed from the federal Unified Budget, Congress will continue to limit expenditures, even though employers will continue to pay taxes dedicated to a specific use and even though the program suffers in states with inadequate funding.

Federal-State Interaction: Fund Solvency

Conformity issues define the basic structure of the federal-state UI program, and the administrative financing provisions make the resources available to deliver the services. This section will review the involvement and interaction of the federal-state partnership in addressing and settling the problems of state Unemployment Trust Fund insolvency. The U.S. Department of Labor provides oversight, and financial and program support. States have the responsibility and authority through their legislatures to decide benefit and tax levels and to provide direct services to both employers and claimants consistent with the basic objectives of the program.

Before the 1970s, insolvency was not a recurring problem, and fund reserves were generally adequate, with only a handful of states borrowing. However, the severe recession in the mid-1970s required twenty-five states to secure loans from the federal partner in order to continue to pay state unemployment benefits. (Although some of this loan money came from a loan account in the Unemployment Trust Fund, the federal partner was also required to borrow from general revenues.) At the end of 1982, twenty-three states still had outstanding loans amounting to $10.6 billion. During that eight-year period, state insolvency became a significant problem that influenced the direction of the program (Rubin 1983, pp. 240-241). This problem also exemplifies how Congress, the U.S. Department of Labor, state legislatures, and state UI agencies address and resolve new challenges on a collaborative basis as the issues arise.

In the early 1980s, the magnitude of the loans, which in a few states exceeded $1 billion, and the condition of the national economy necessitated congressional action. At first, Congress responded with the elimination of most interest-free loans by imposing interest charges on new borrowing. However, Congress later adopted less restrictive terms for loan repayment if certain states made changes to improve their solvency. These incentives to reduce federal loans influenced state legislative changes to lower benefit costs and to increase state taxes, as a condition of getting the relief on debt repayment and interest charges. Efforts to eliminate insolvency sometimes resulted in more stringent state qualifying requirements for benefits, lower wage replacement percentages, and freezes in benefit increases. These efforts to restore solvency also contributed to the declining percentage of persons receiving benefits as compared to the total number of unemployed (U.S. General Accounting Office 1993, p. 4).[23] Clearly, the magnitude of the insolvency problem mandated that states initiate major changes in the benefit financing schemes in order to repay prior loans, pay current benefit obligations, and begin accumulating some cash reserves as a buffer against future downturns.

A report by the House Ways and Means Committee (1989, p. 296) noted that funding for state benefits had significantly improved since the recession in 1981-1982. This was partly due to long periods of economic growth and partly due to federal incentives for states to improve their fund balances. However, the report indicated that there will be trouble maintaining solvency for state funds in the future. One example of the basis for that concern is the way states respond to wage growth, that is, by increasing benefits without correspondingly raising the taxable wage base. Another sign, the comparatively low reserve levels that states are maintaining in their funds, shows the increased probability of future borrowing. See chapter 9 for a more complete discussion of this phenomenon.

One central issue in the federal-state partnership is the degree of responsibility of the federal partner in maintaining state solvency. Congress could regulate state balances in one of three ways. First, states could be compelled to maintain certain reserves. However, there would be considerable difficulty in establishing a single standard that would minimize borrowing and reflect efficient measurements for all state situations. For example, the ability of a state to maintain a solvent fund cannot be defined in terms of reserve levels only. Consideration must also be given to the responsiveness of the tax system to increased benefit payments, the potential to recover the benefits paid, the nature of the economy, and the ability to build reserves before the next recession causes a new drain on the fund. Even if it were possible to develop reasonable reserve standards, some would advocate that the standards themselves would compromise the ability of states to control their own system.

Secondly, Congress can change the taxable wage base to encourage all states to adjust a powerful component of the state experience-rating systems. The problem with increasing the taxable wage base is that it also forces uniformity among states, which runs contrary to the original intent to make states accountable for their own tax provisions and schedules. Efforts to increase the federal taxable wage base can impact the balance within the state experience-rating systems by changing the share of UI costs borne by low-wage-paying employers (who have most of their payrolls taxed) relative to that of high-wage employers.

As a third possibility, Congress could adopt a method of benefit financing that addresses economic situations that are clearly beyond the ability of a state to fund. For example, when national recessions have a prolonged impact on certain regions of the country, it is reasonable to support a catastrophic insurance program. These national insurance proposals have been considered in the past under the names of "reinsurance" or "cost-equalization." The difference in those philosophies involves whether the individual experience of the state is the triggering mechanism or whether some absolute level of unemployment determines eligibility. One problem with these proposals is that they result in a redistribution of federal taxes that would cause some states to qualify, while others would not. As a result, discussions break down for the same reasons that certain states object to the administrative funding idea of devolution.

Since states have the responsibility to decide on both tax and benefit provisions for their citizens, it is logical that the primary responsibility for benefit financing should rest with the states. The problem of state benefit financing raises three issues in the federal-state relationship:

- First, states must insure their own unemployment risks. However, to a large extent, unemployment is beyond the ability of the state to control.

- Second, states can determine their own tax and benefit levels based on local needs. On the other hand, confrontations will develop between local business and labor groups as businesses try to lower UI tax costs while organized labor struggles to maintain benefit levels that adequately replace wages.

- Third, if state funds become insolvent, monies can be borrowed from the Federal Unemployment Account which in turn is funded through FUTA revenues. However, if states rely too heavily on the federal loans, the interest on the loans becomes a general obligation of the state. Although the prospect of finance charges on outstanding loans gives states the option to either maintain solvency or to face the consequences by paying interest, requiring such payments in the midst of an economic downturn can be viewed as an additional tax due to high levels of unemployment.

Who then bears the primary burden for fund solvency? The answer is that, as with other provisions, there must be a shared responsibility. State decision making must balance benefit levels and eligibility criteria for the regular UI program with the degree of taxation and experience rating that a state accepts and with its overall solvency philosophy. Meanwhile, the federal partner needs to continue to bear a portion of the burden for extended benefits or other continuations of benefits. The responsibility of the U.S. Department of Labor would include guidance, training of state staff, and the development of solvency measurements that are more comprehensive than those currently available. With the establishment of interest on federal loans to states, Congress has required states to be more responsible in maintaining solvency. Although the incentive approach used in the early 1980s to encourage states to repay their loans and to accumulate necessary reserves worked in restoring state solvency, Congress, the Labor Department, and the states must exercise care to ensure that the basic program objectives are not compromised for the sake of solvency concerns.

Summary

The UI program has the advantage of being self-financing and of being based on a workload-driven formula. As a result, it has survived during periods when the lack of program funding in other areas has resulted in extreme reduction or outright elimination of services. It has a proven record of responding to social and economic need by providing temporary wage replacement for those who have lost their jobs through no fault of their own. By means of mutual cooperation at the federal and state levels, the system has survived many challenges: a series of regional recessions, which tested the ability of states to finance benefit costs; recurring budget reductions unrelated to either program needs or to the dedicated revenues paid; criticisms of benefit payments to some groups of workers (such as those receiving retirement pay); and state delivery systems that are sluggish or that pay benefits to ineligible claimants. In 1995, debates raged in Congress over whether programs such as Aid to Families with Dependent Children or food stamps should be substantially modified or entirely replaced. Meanwhile, congressional discussions of UI were close to nonexistent. (Although it should be noted that, in 1996, the governor of Virginia presented a devolution plan to the National Governors' Association, and a congressional hearing on devolution and a variety of other issues occurred in mid-1997.) Even if it has not been an outright success in every regard, neither can the UI program and the federal-state system be considered as having failed.

Some of the disagreements that existed when the program was established in the 1930s continue to be discussed. The degree of federal control, the extent of state flexibility, and issues concerning administrative funding are still debated. Almost every state cites shortages of administrative dollars as a reason for closing local offices. The lack of benefit standards raises questions about the national equity of the program. It has been criticized for inaccurate and delayed benefit payments and for failure to collect taxes from delinquent employers. There is a considerable duplication of effort. For example, UI computer systems differ between states; sometimes this results in inefficient programming and in systems that have been frequently modified but never redesigned to function well.[24]

The system is administratively complex and difficult to explain to claimants, employers, and the general public. It is also debatable whether the federal partner has exerted too much or too little influence over states or whether the federal partner has abdicated its responsibility to ensure that states are administering their laws consistent with federal requirements.

Most of the original architects of the program, both in Washington, D.C., and in the states, are now gone. Millions of individual recipients of unemployment benefits do not know about the nature of the federal-state system. Although UI is a major concern to employers, labor unions, and legal aid groups, there is no specific "UI lobby" for all individuals who might become unemployed. As a result, the UI program does not always seem focused nor does it receive the political or moral support that it once did. Compared to other programs, such as social security, medicare, and medicaid, it is infrequently in the public eye.

State UI and employment service agencies have responded to this situation by continuing to support an organization that, since 1937, has acted as an institutional memory, serves as a historical bridge, and strives to maintain the balance between the state and federal partners. The Interstate Conference of Employment Security Agencies (ICESA) acts as the advocate for states to Congress and the U.S. Department of Labor and has performed an essential role in preserving the federal-state partnership. On an ongoing basis, ICESA facilitates networking and the exchange of information between all fifty states, the District of Columbia, Puerto Rico, and the Virgin Islands. ICESA provides an essential link between the federal and state partners in assisting the development of UI policy and in acting as a liaison between the states, the Labor Department, and Congress. Although ICESA is a positive force, it should be noted that ICESA is not a lobbyist organization. ICESA is not chartered to advocate the interests of either employers or claimants.

The federal partner's response has been less apparent. Into the 1950s, it was not unusual to find the Secretary of Labor actively involved in UI program decisions. Today, this is uncommon. The federal UI service resides in the Employment and Training Administration (and previously in the Manpower Development Administration), which mainly focuses on job training programs. (This aspect is mirrored at the state level, as UI agencies are combined with other agencies having distinctly different missions.) Decisions by the U.S. Department of Labor concerning the UI program are often made by individuals relatively inexperienced with UI and with greater interest in other programs. Meanwhile, congressional UI determinations are frequently made on the basis of budget balancing and politics, and not on what makes program sense.

In spite of those concerns, the system continues to pay benefits each year while maintaining generally solvent funds for the state. There are differing philosophies that result in varying laws and procedures, and there are points of contention with the U.S. Department of Labor, but the existing infrastructure is well-positioned to provide service to employers and claimants in the future. The system will function best if there is a continuing dialogue between the federal and state partners that fully acknowledges the fundamental mission of the UI system. Both partners will be better able to develop innovative approaches to service delivery by incorporating the efficiencies of data processing systems and other developing technologies and by taking human ecology into account. It is vitally important that states focus on eliminating all barriers to getting UI payments to those who are qualified.

No doubt the system will meet a variety of new challenges in the future. Its strength and its ability to respond to such challenges, are in the dialogue and interaction that occur between the federal and state partners. We hope the federal-state partnership will find ways to resolve its current problems. An individual in need of income support depends on the program and on its fulfillment of the vision established by its original architects—that there be a system that provides temporary income support to those who lose their jobs through no fault of their own.

NOTES

The authors would like to acknowledge and thank Dr. Joseph Hight of the U.S. Department of Labor for his contribution to this chapter.

1. For purposes of this chapter, the terms "state" or "states" refer to the fifty states, the District of Columbia, Puerto Rico, and the Virgin Islands.

2. Haber and Murray (1966) provide a complete description of the discussions in their chapters 6, 7, and 20.

3. See Hight (1982, p. 616).

4. Failure by a state to cover FUTA-taxable services means that employers in that state could not claim the FUTA credit on those services. As a result, most states currently have "recapture" provisions, which extend coverage to services defined in federal law, to avoid employers having to pay additional FUTA taxes.

5. A complete list of federal law requirements and the year in which they were first added may be found in the appendix.

6. The legislative history indicates that UI is only to be paid to individuals "who cannot find other work: (Senate Reports No. 628, 74th Congress, 1st Sess., 1935, 11.)

7. The U.S. Department of Labor has, however, encouraged states to change their laws in particular ways. For example, in 1962, it issued a book entitled *Unemployment Insurance Legislative Policy: Recommendations for State Legislation.\

8. This requirement did not take its final form until 1976.

9. Hildebrand (1995, 1996) discusses this and other aspects of how the U.S. Department of labor applies federal law.

10. Hildebrand (1995 and 1996) states this thesis and provides a more thorough explanation of how the U.S. Department of Labor applies federal laws.

11. A more basic issue is whether the "permanently residing in the United States under color of law test" is appropriate for the UI program. Congress established this test for several programs, including Supplemental Security Income, Aid to Families with Dependent Children, and medicaid. That the UI program is uniquely employment based is lost in this definition.

12. As it has learned about factual situations not covered by the original between and within terms denial, Congress has often amended the denial with the consequence that the statute is clumsily written and sometimes leads to unexpected results. In the case of "nonprofessional" services—that is, those services not performed by a teacher, researcher, or administrator—Congress seems completely at sea. At first, denials for those services were optional on the part of the states; than they became mandatory; currently, they are again optional. Now that the provisions are once more optional, states have considerable latitude in implementing them, as the U.S. Department of Labor views them as the outer limit of what is permissible. States did not have this latitude when the provisions were mandatory.

13. *Java* v. *California Department of Human Resources Development*, 402 U.S. 121 (1971).

14. Java also stood for the proposition that, even though federal UI law does not purport to require anything of the states since it is an incentive-based system, the federal courts will still find jurisdiction.

15. *Pennington* v. *Didrickson*, 22F.3d 1376 (1994), cert. denied, 115 U.S. 613 (1994).

16. The Advisory Council on Unemployment Compensation (1996) discusses these oversight programs in chapter 6 of its January 6, 1996 report.

17. 20 C.F.R., parts 640 and 650.

18. Rubin (1983, pp. 171-214) discusses the major conformity hearings held prior to 1982.

19. Haber and Murray (1966, p. 404).

20. See Blaustein (1993, p. 216).

21. Section 302(a), SSA; 42 U.S.C. 502(a).

22. Interstate Conference of Employment Security Agencies (ICESA) Employment Security Funding Survey 1991-1993. Prepared by the ICESA Board of Directors.

23. The General Accounting Office analysis concluded that state concerns about declining or insolvent trust funds resulted in state changes making it more difficult for claimants to qualify for benefits.

24. This problem is not unique to the UI system. According to the U.S. General Accounting Office (1995, p. 17), federal administrative funding to a variety of means-tested programs encourages state automation, but no innovation.

Appendix to Chapter 13
Federal Law Requirements

Approval for Tax Credits

Sections 3303 and 3304 of the Internal Revenue Code of 1986 (also know as FUTA) contain the minimum federal requirements that states must meet for employers to obtain the normal and additional tax credits. The year the requirement was first added to federal law is in parentheses.

- Compensation is paid through public employment offices or other approved agencies (1935).

- No compensation is paid until two years after the first period with respect to which state contributions are payable (1935).

- All of the funds collected under the state program are deposited in the federal Unemployment Trust Fund (UTF). Title IX of the Social Security Act prescribes the distribution of the tax among the various accounts of the UTF (1935).

- All of the money withdrawn from the UTF is used to pay unemployment compensation, to refund amounts erroneously paid into the fund, or for other specified activities (1935).

- Compensation is not denied to anyone who refuses to accept work because the job is vacant as the direct result of a labor dispute, or because the wages, hours, or conditions of work are substandard, or if, as a condition of employment, the individual would have to join a company union or resign from or refrain from joining any bona fide labor organization (1935).

- Compensation is paid to employees of state and local governments; there are required limitations on benefit entitlement during vacation periods for certain employees in education (1935).

- Compensation is paid to employees of FUTA tax exempt nonprofit organizations, including schools and colleges that employ four or more workers in each of 20 weeks in the calendar year (1970).

- State and local governments and nonprofit organizations may elect to pay regular employer contributions or to finance benefit costs by the reimbursement method (1970).

- Compensation is not payable in two successive benefit years to an individual who has not worked after the beginning of the first benefit year (1970).

- Compensation is not denied to anyone solely because the individual is taking part in an approved training program (1970).

- Compensation is not denied or reduced because an individual's claim for benefits was filed in another state or Canada (1970).

- The state participates in arrangements for combining wages earned in more than one state for eligibility and benefit purposes (1970).

- Compensation is not denied by reason of cancellation of wage credits or total benefit rights for any cause other than discharge for work-connected misconduct, fraud, or receipt of disqualifying income (1970).

- Extended compensation is payable under the provisions of the Extended Unemployment Compensation Act of 1970 (extended benefit program).

- No individual is denied compensation solely on the basis of pregnancy or termination of pregnancy (1976).

- Compensation is not payable to a professional athlete between seasons who is under contract to resume employment when the new season begins (1976).

- Compensation is not payable based on services performed by an alien unless the alien was (1) lawfully admitted for permanent residence, (2) legally available to work in the United States, or (3) permanently residing under color of law (1976).

- The benefit amount of an individual is reduced by that portion of a pension or other retirement income (including income from social security and Railroad Retirement) funded by a base-period employer (1976).

- Wage information in the agency files is made available, upon request and on a reimbursable basis, to the agency administering transitional assistance to needy families (1977).

- Wage and claim information is disclosed to the Secretary of Health and Human Services for the National Directory of New Hires and for child support and other purposes (1996).

- Any interest required to be paid on advances is paid in a timely manner and is not paid, directly or indirectly (by an equivalent tax reduction in such state) from amounts in the trust fund of the state (1983).

- Federal individual income tax is withheld if a claimant so requests (1995);.

- All the rights, privileges, or immunities conferred by state UI law exist subject to the power of the state legislature to amend or repeal such law at any time (1935).

- Reduced tax rates for employers are permitted only on the basis of their experience with respect to unemployment (1935).

Approval for Grants for Costs of Administration

Title III of the SSA provides for payments from the federal UTF to the states to meet the necessary costs of administering the unemployment compensation programs in the states and the major proportion of the cost (97 percent) of operating their public employment offices. Under this title, the grants are restricted to those states that have a UI law approved under the FUTA and that have been certified by the Secretary of Labor as providing the following provisions (some are also included in the FUTA):

- methods of administration (including a state merit system) that will insure full payment of unemployment compensation when due (1935);
- unemployment compensation payment through public employment offices or through other approved agencies (1935);
- fair hearings for individuals whose claims for unemployment compensation have been denied (1935);
- payment of all funds collected to the federal UTF (1935);
- that all of the money withdrawn from the state trust fund account will be used either to pay unemployment compensation benefits, exclusive of administrative expenses, to refund amounts erroneously paid into the fund, or for other specified activities (1935);
- reports required by the Secretary of Labor (1935);
- information to federal agencies administering public works programs or assistance through public employment (1935);
- limitation of expenditures to the purpose and amounts found necessary by the Secretary of Labor for proper and efficient administration of the state law (1939);
- repayment of any funds the Secretary of Labor determines were not spent for unemployment compensation purposes or have exceeded the amounts necessary for proper administration of the state unemployment compensation law (1939);
- that, as a condition of eligibility, any claimant referred to reemployment services pursuant to the profiling system participate in such services (1993);
- information to the Railroad Retirement Board as the board deems necessary (1938);

- reasonable cooperation with every agency of the U.S. charged with the administration of any unemployment insurance law (1938);

- the stipulation that any interest on advances be paid by the date on which it is required to be paid and is not paid directly or indirectly (by an equivalent reduction in state unemployment taxes or otherwise) by such state from amounts in its trust fund account (1983);

- information to the Department of Agriculture and state food stamp agencies with respect to employee wages, UI benefits, home address, and job offers (1980);

- employee wage information to any state or local child support agency (1980);

- the requirement that a claimant disclose whether or not he/she owes child support obligations; deductions from benefits shall be made for any such child support obligations, and the amount of such deduction shall be paid by the state UI agency to the appropriate child support agency (1981);

- information for purposes of income and eligibility verification be requested and exchanged in accordance with a state system meeting the requirements of Title XI of the SSA; the UI wage record system may, but need not, be the required state system (1984);

- wage and claim information is disclosed to the Department of Health and Human Services and the National Directory of New Hires for child support enforcement and other purposes (1996);

- for establishment and use of a system of profiling new claimants of regular compensation to identify those likely to exhaust such compensation and to need job search assistance (1993).

References

Advisory Council on Unemployment Compensation. 1994. "Report and Rec-
ommendations." ACUC, February.
_____. 1995. "Unemployment Insurance in the United States: Benefits,
Financing, Coverage." ACUC, February.
_____. 1996. "Defining Federal and State Roles in Unemployment Insur-
ance. ACUC, January.
Blaustein, Saul J. 1994. *Unemployment Insurance in the United States: The
First Half Century.* Kalamazoo, MI: W.E. Upjohn Institute.
Burgess, Paul L., and Jerry L. Kingston. 1987. *An Incentives Approach to
Improving the Unemployment Compensation System.* Kalamazoo, MI:
W.E. Upjohn Institute.
Executive Office of the President. Office of Management and Budget. 1986.
Budget of the United States Government: Fiscal Year 1986. Washington,
DC: Government Printing Office.
Haber, William, and Merrill G. Murray. 1966. *Unemployment Insurance in the
American Economy.* Homewood, IL: Richard D. Irwin.
Hight, Joseph E. 1982. "Unemployment Insurance: Changes in the Federal-
State Balance," *University of Detroit Journal of Urban Law* 59, 4: 615-630.
Hildebrand, Gerard. 1995 and 1996. "Federal Law Requirements for the Fed-
eral-State Unemployment Compensation System: Interpretation and Appli-
cation," *University of Michigan Journal of Law Reform* 29, Issues 1 and 2
(Fall 1995 and Winter 1996): 527-584.
Interstate Conference of Employment Security Agencies (ICESA). 1992.
"Employment Security Funding Survey 1991-1993. Prepared for the
ICESA Board of Directors, March.
National Commission on Unemployment Compensation. 1980. "Final
Report." NCUC, July.
National Foundation for Unemployment Compensation and Workers' Com-
pensation. 1994. "Highlights of Federal Unemployment Compensation
Laws."
President's Committee on Economic Security. 1937. "Social Security in
America." Social Security Board Publication No. 20.
Report of the Committee on Economic Security. 1935. Reported in the
Employment Security Act, Hearings before the Committee on Finance on
S. 1130, Senate, 74th Congress, 1st session.
Rotherham, James A. 1993. "Budgetary Treatment of Unemployment Trust
Fund Programs and the Employment Service: Options for Reform." Cham-
bers Associates.

598

Rubin, Murray. 1983. *Federal-State Relations in Unemployment Insurance.* Kalamazoo, MI: W.E. Upjohn Institute.

U.S. Department of Labor. 1962. *Unemployment Insurance Legislative Policy: Recommendations for State Legislation.* Washington, DC: Government Printing Office.

U.S. General Accounting Office. 1989. "Unemployment Insurance: Administrative Funding Is a Growing Problem for State Programs." GAO/HRD-89-72BR.

_____. 1993. "Unemployment Insurance Program's Ability to Meet Objective Jeopardized." GAO/HRD-93-107, September.

_____. 1995. "Means-tested Programs: An Overview of Problems and Issues." GAO/T-HEHS-95-76.

U.S. House of Representatives. Committee on Ways and Means. 1988. "Federal-State Unemployment Compensation System." Subcommittee on Public Assistance and Unemployment Compensation, September.

_____. 1989. "Federal-State Unemployment Compensation System." Subcommittee on Public Assistance and Unemployment Compensation, September.

Vroman, Wayne. 1990. *Unemployment Insurance Trust Fund Adequacy.* Kalamazoo, MI: W.E. Upjohn Institute.

CHAPTER 14

Unemployment Compensation in the Group of Seven Nations
An International Comparison

James R. Storey
Congressional Research Service
Jennifer A. Neisner
Congressional Research Service

In considering U.S. unemployment compensation (UC) policy issues, it is useful to examine how other nations aid their jobless, since UC systems vary greatly. This chapter compares UC among the Group of Seven (G-7) nations: Canada, France, Germany, Italy, Japan, the United Kingdom, and the United States. These seven nations are the industrialized countries with the largest economies. They meet annually to review their economic policies and to consider policy changes that might be mutually beneficial.

The main body of this chapter describes major events in the development of each of the seven systems, analyzes how they differ along several dimensions, and provides examples of how other national systems differ from the G-7 programs. Appendixes to this chapter provide a description of the UC system in each of the G-7 countries and a chronological chart of how each system developed. Program rules and benefit amounts discussed in this report are those that applied in 1993 unless otherwise indicated.

The term unemployment compensation is used in this chapter to refer to a nation's overall system of unemployment benefits. Unemployment insurance (UI) is used in connection with the components of these systems that base benefits on insured work histories. Unemployment assistance (UA) is used in relation to programs that do not tie benefits explicitly to work history or that extend UI benefits to the unemployed who meet a test of financial need.

The reader should be aware of three limitations of this chapter. First, need-related aid for the unemployed is included in the discussion only where it is offered as an integral part of a UC system. All seven nations have need-related assistance programs outside their UC systems, but they are not covered here. Second, employment services are discussed only to the extent that they are explicitly a part of a UC system. Third, special arrangements that may exist for unemployed public sector workers are not discussed except to the degree that such arrangements are integrated with provisions for compensation of jobless private sector workers.

In comparing program rules across nations, this chapter cannot describe the full historical, economic, and political contexts that determine international variations. However, the reader should keep in mind that such factors as unionization, government relationships to industries, labor force diversity and mobility, and economic trends are important in understanding the significance of the program differences that are highlighted.

Monetary figures used in the chapter usually are stated in the national currency, with the U.S. dollar equivalent shown in parentheses.[1] Dollar equivalents were calculated using the currency exchange rates in effect for July 1993.[2]

Major Events in the Development of Unemployment Compensation

By the end of the 19th century, unemployment protection schemes were organized in several countries through trade unions, mutual benefit societies, and other worker associations. Under these plans, members contributed to funds from which benefits were provided.[3] Organizations in France, Germany, and the United Kingdom provided unemployment benefits, which in some cases (notably France) were subsidized by government contributions. The inadequacies of such funds led to a recognition that broader measures would be needed to protect more of the populace and that national governments would have to be involved.

In 1911, the United Kingdom became the first country to legislate a national compulsory UI program with the passage of the National Insurance Act. In 1919, Italy instituted a UI program covering most manual workers. Although these programs were limited in coverage and benefits, they were soon expanded. In the period following World War I, several countries instituted unemployment programs, the majority of which were compulsory insurance schemes, notably the German UI system in 1927. In addition, six countries employed subsidized voluntary schemes.

The economic depression of the 1930s and the risk of high unemployment following World War II led several countries to develop comprehensive social insurance programs for the unemployed. This development included the improvement of existing schemes, as in Italy and the United Kingdom, and the establishment of new programs, in the United States with passage of the Social Security Act of 1935, which contained a UI program, in Canada with enactment of the Unemployment Insurance Act of 1940, and in Japan with enactment of the Unemployment Insurance Law of 1947.

During the postwar period until the recessions of the early 1970s, most countries modified their systems by extending coverage and increasing benefit durations and rates. In the late 1960s and early 1970s, UC programs were overhauled in several countries in response to changes in the objectives held for UC. An emphasis was placed on integrating the income maintenance aspects of UC with a wider human resources policy, one that emphasized job training and related provisions. In Germany, UI was integrated into the Employment Promotion Act of 1969. Japan adopted the Employment Insurance Act in 1974. This act, which replaced the Unemployment Insurance Act, emphasized the concept of lifetime employment as opposed to temporary aid. Canada passed a new Unemployment Insurance Act in 1971 that included job training provisions as well as benefits in case of sickness, maternity, and retirement. Likewise, the United Kingdom restructured UI under the Social Security Act of 1975. The United States enacted a trade adjustment assistance (TAA) program in 1962 and expanded it in 1974 to provide workers displaced by import competition with compensation and employment services. A 1970 law established a permanent extended benefits (EB) program to provide federal support for UI benefit extensions in states with high unemployment rates.

The 1980s saw several countries revoke or cut back on program reforms of the 1970s. The United Kingdom eliminated its earnings-related benefit in 1982, returning to a flat-rate UI benefit. France restored its dual UI-UA system in 1984 following disappointment with a unified system. The United States tightened eligibility for EB and TAA in 1981 and made all UI benefits taxable in 1986. In 1988, TAA claimants were required to accept retraining unless specifically waived by the government.

In the past few years, UC systems have not changed dramatically, but there were substantial modifications in several G-7 countries. Germany, faced with large-scale unemployment since reunification, offered special extended UI benefits in the former German Democratic Republic (GDR) in 1990 for a temporary period. Canada passed Bill C-21 in 1990, the most important provision of which ended government contributions to UI. The United States, confronted with increasing unemployment due to the 1990-1991 recession, enacted Emergency Unemployment Compensation (EUC) in November 1991 and extended its life several times until it expired in April 1994. (This marked the third time that Congress enacted *temporary* extended benefits since creation of the *permanent* EB program in 1970.) The U.S. system was also changed to place more emphasis on early intervention for claimants likely to experience long-term jobless spells, and states were authorized to use an optional unemployment measure for activation of EB to make it more available during downturns. TAA was expanded to deal with potential dislocations from the North American Free Trade Agreement (NAFTA). Italy tightened the rules for use of its special UI benefits by firms experiencing downsizing. France made major changes to its UI benefit structure and tightened UA eligibility.

Comparison of Unemployment Programs in the G-7 Nations

The UC systems of the G-7 nations are detailed in appendix 14.A. This section compares these seven systems using the same structure as the appendix: objectives, administration, financing, coverage, eligibility, benefits, and employment services.

Objectives

The formally stated objectives of the seven systems are similar. All are intended to provide income support to the jobless and to promote stability of employment. However, the relative emphasis given to different objectives varies substantially. The systems of Canada and Japan specify reentry into employment as a main objective of UC. Italy and Japan attempt to prevent unemployment through temporary wage subsidies of workers in depressed industries. France, Germany, and the United Kingdom have designed their systems to aid workers experiencing long-term unemployment. The U.S. system, through decentralization, bases policy more on subnational decisions about labor market issues.

The following sections describe variations among the seven systems, including the

- degree of national control over the system;
- division of program funding among employees, employers, and government;
- work history required for eligibility;
- relationship between benefit amounts and past wages;
- adjustment of benefit duration according to economic conditions;
- extension of benefit duration for hard-to-employ workers;
- coverage of new labor force entrants and reentrants;
- availability of means-tested benefits for the long-term jobless; and
- inclusion of job training activities in the UC system.

Administration

Each of the seven systems is supervised nationally by an executive department or ministry of the national government. However, delegation of authority by the supervising organization varies substantially across nations. Collection of program revenue is handled differently from administration of benefit claims in six of the seven nations. Only

Japan collects revenue through the same local agencies that administer benefit payments.

The revenue earmarked for UI is collected by the national revenue agency in Canada, Italy, and the United States, although most U.S. revenue is collected by state agencies and then deposited with the U.S. Treasury. The United Kingdom relies on its Department of Social Security for tax collection, and Japan on its Labor Ministry. In France, financial management is the responsibility of employer associations known by the acronym of ASSEDICs. The payroll tax in Germany is collected through the Social Security tax collection system by sickness funds serving specific localities, enterprises, or occupational groups.

Five of the G-7 countries administer claims through a local office network under the direct management of the national agency responsible for employment matters. The two exceptions are France and the United States. Administration in France is the responsibility of UNEDIC, an acronym for an employee organization. Municipalities perform payment functions where there is no UNEDIC office. Local administration in the United States is handled by the local office networks of fifty-three distinct state employment security agencies,[4] which operate under the general guidance of the U.S. Department of Labor.

Financing

Program financing methods vary among the G-7 nations in regard to who pays, how much each party pays, and for what they pay. Funding arrangements are summarized in table 14.1. All seven nations use a payroll tax to fund UI benefits. While Japan pays one-fourth of UI benefits with general government funds, the other six countries rely on the payroll tax exclusively (figure 14.1). Five of the seven apply the tax to both employee and employer; Italy and the United States (except for three states) do not tax employees.[5] Japan taxes all covered wages, France and the United Kingdom apply their employer taxes to all wages, and Italy taxes all wages above an exempt amount. The other three nations have ceilings on taxable wages. The United States taxes wages less than do the other six nations (figure 14.2A).

Four of the seven nations have fixed payroll tax rates, with the employee rates ranging from 0.55 percent (Japan) to 3.25 percent (Ger-

Table 14.1 Funding Sources for UC Benefits in the G-7 Nations, 1993

| Nation/program | Proportion of benefit cost paid from | | | Level of tax on | | | |
| | Payroll tax on | | Government subsidy (%) | Employee | | Employer | |
	Employee (%)	Employer (%)		Tax rate (%)	Wage base[a] ($)	Tax rate (%)	Wage base[a] ($)
Canada UI	42	58	0	3.0	30,178	4.2	30,178
France							
UI	42	58	0	2.97[b]	111,102	4.18	All wages
UA	0	0	100	--	--	--	--
Germany							
UI	50	50	0	3.25	49,680[c]	3.25	49,680[c]
UA	0	0	100	--	--	--	--
Italy							
Basic benefit	0	100	0	--	--	1.61-1.91[d]	[e]
Special benefit	0	100	0	--	--	0.3-0.8[f]	[e]
Wage supplement	0	NA	NA	--	--	1.92-2.2[g]	[e]
Japan UI	37.5	37.5	25	0.55[h]	All wages	0.55[i]	All wages
United Kingdom							
UI	NA	NA	0	2.0-9.0[j,k]	32,345[k]	4.6-10.4[j,k]	All wages[k]
UA	0	0	100	--	--	--	--
United States							
UI	2[l]	98[l]	0	0.0-0.125[m]	0-23,200[m]	0.6-4.2[n]	7,000
TAA	0	0	100	--	--	--	23,900[n]

(continued)

Table 14.1 (continued)

NOTE: NA indicates not available.

a. Wage base figures were annualized and converted to U.S. dollars using July 1993 exchange rates.

b. Tax rate is 2.42 percent on first $25,270 of earnings.

c. The taxable wage ceiling is $36,570 in the former GDR.

d. Lower rate applies to industrial managers and higher rate to other jobs.

e. Taxable wage base is wage in excess of $34 a day. No upper limit.

f. Lower tax rate applies to industrial firms and higher rate to construction firms.

g. Tax rate is 1.9 percent for firms with fewer than 50 employees.

h. Construction workers and seasonal workers pay 0.65 percent of wages.

i. Employers of seasonal and construction workers pay 0.65 percent. Employers pay an additional 0.35 percent (0.45 percent for construction firms) to fund employment services.

j. The first employee tax rate applies to the first $4,313 of annual earnings, and the second rate to additional earnings. A range of rates is shown for employers because ther ate is higher at higher wage levels.

k. The United Kingdom payroll tax funds other social security programs in addition to UI. In 1992, UI benefits accounted for 4.1 percent of all benefit costs financed by this tax.

l. Employee share was estimated by the Congressional Research Service. It represents an upper bound on the actual employee share of UI financing.

m. Only three states tax employees. Rates range from 0.1 percent in Pennsylvania to 1.125 percent in New Jersey. Taxable wages range from $8,000 in Pennsylvania to $23,200 in Alaska.

n. Tax rates and taxable wages vary by state, and tax rates vary by firm in each state. The rates shown are the lowest and highest average state rates. The national average tax rate applied to taxable wages in covered employment was 2.3 percent state and 0.8 percent federal. If all covered wages had been taxable, the national average rate would have been 0.9 percent. The taxable wage base for the median state was $8,500.

many) and the employer rates from 0.55 percent (Japan) to 4.2 percent (Canada). Of the systems with variable tax rates, the United Kingdom rates vary with wage level. Tax rates in Italy are differentiated by industry, job type, and firm size. The U.S. rates vary by state and by firm within state. The latter variation reflects the efforts of states to "experience-rate" program financing so that employers creating larger unemployment costs pay more taxes. The other six nations do not vary rates for experience. Japan applies a higher tax rate to seasonal and construction jobs. The average state tax rate in the United States in 1993 was 2.3 percent, and the federal tax rate was 0.8 percent. Measuring state taxes as a percentage of all U.S. wages, the effective state tax rate was 0.9 percent. Figure 14.2B compares nominal payroll tax rates.

Figure 14.1 Shares of UI Benefits Financed by Employer Taxes, Employee Taxes, and General Government Funds, 1993

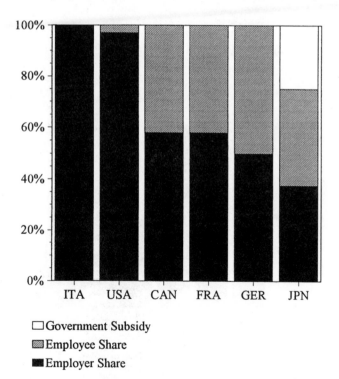

NOTE: United Kingdom not shown because employee share could not be determined.

608

Figure 14.2A Taxable Wage Base for UI, 1993

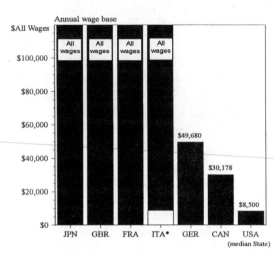

*Italy taxes all wages above an exempt amount ($34 per day, annualized to $8,840).

Figure 14.2B Nominal UI Payroll Tax Rates, 1993

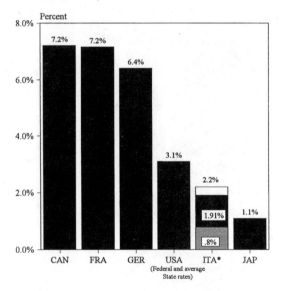

NOTE: Chart does not include figures for the United Kingdom as its payroll tax funds other social security programs in addition to UI and no UI rate is specified.
*Includes figures for the special benefit (0.3 - 0.8%), basic benefit (1.61 - 1.91%), and wage supplement (1.9 - 2.2%) components of the Italian UI system.

Germany relies most heavily on employee taxes (covering 50 percent of UI benefit costs), with Canada and France (42 percent) next. The least reliant on employee taxes are the United States (less than 2 percent) and Italy (0 percent).[6]

The non-UI parts of these seven UC systems are supported by general government revenue. The three nations with UA programs (France, Germany, the United Kingdom) pay for UA entirely with government funds, as does the United States for the TAA program that extends benefits to workers dislocated by import competition.[7] Italy has a wage supplement that is supported partly by government funds and partly by the employer payroll tax. Canada stands alone among the G-7 in its lack of any general government financing for its UC system.

The level of expenditure supported by these financial arrangements is shown in figure 14.3 for each G-7 nation as a percentage of gross domestic product (GDP) for selected fiscal years 1985 through 1993. Three systems (those of Canada, France, and Germany) have consistently cost more than 1 percent of GDP, and the system of the United Kingdom has returned to that level after a decline during the late 1980s. The other three systems are much smaller relative to the respective national economies. The Japanese system is the smallest at 0.26 percent of GDP, which is only about three-fifths of the size of the U.S. program (0.45 percent). The U.S. program has not exceeded 1 percent since the recession year of 1975 (not shown).

Figure 14.4 shows this expenditure data adjusted for the level of unemployment by dividing each GDP percentage by the corresponding unemployment rate. The resultant statistic indicates that relative program cost has diverged since 1990. The German program is by far the most expensive; the U.S. and Italian programs are the least expensive. By this adjusted measure, the U.S. program is only one-fifth the size of the German one. The U.S. program ranked either sixth or seventh among the G-7 throughout the period shown.

Coverage

All seven systems provide broad coverage to wage and salary workers. Three UC systems (in France, Germany, and Japan) coordinate coverage with national pension systems by excluding workers over pensionable age. The U.S. program usually reduces UC benefits for

610

Figure 14.3 Public Expenditures for UC as a Percentage of GDP

Percentage of GDP

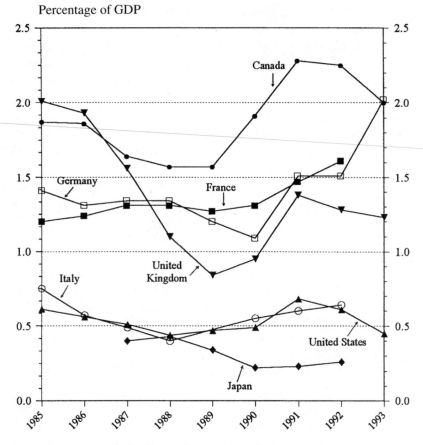

NOTE: Data not available for all years. See Appendix C for backup table.
*Data before 1991 for Germany excludes the eastern states. For 1991 and later years, data are for the unified Germany.

Figure 14.4 Public Expenditures for UC as a Percentage of GDP per Percentage Point of Unemployment

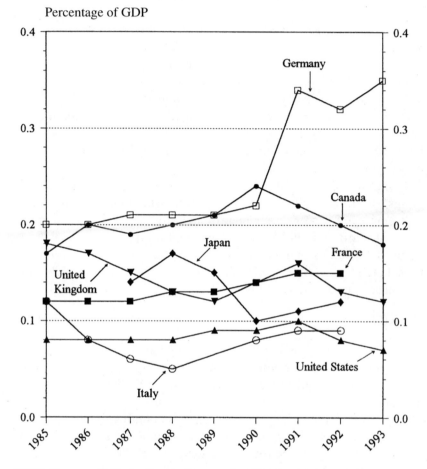

NOTE: Data not available for all years. See appendix 14.C for backup table.
*Data before 1991 for Germany exclude the eastern states. For 1991 and later years, data are for the unified Germany.

pension recipients. Three systems (in Canada, Germany, and Japan) specifically exclude certain part-time workers based on a weekly threshold for hours worked. Italy excludes managerial personnel from basic UI eligibility.

Some systems have special arrangements for seasonal workers. Canada has particular rules for self-employed fishermen. France has certain rules for construction workers, the merchant marine, longshore workers, and aviators. Germany excludes seasonal workers employed less than 180 days in the past three years. Italy excludes seasonal workers. Japan excludes those working six months or less in a year and covers small firms in selected industries only on a voluntary basis. In the United States, seasonal workers whose work spells fall below thresholds set by each state are excluded.

France and the United Kingdom provide coverage through UA programs for virtually all unemployed persons who do not qualify for UI. Self-employed persons are generally not eligible for UI, although the State of California covers them on a voluntary basis. Workers on reduced schedules may receive partial UI benefits in all seven countries. In the United States, this "short-time" compensation is only available in seventeen states, however.

Eligibility

Eligibility for UI depends on a person's having worked in covered employment for some minimum time during a base period. The extent of employment required varies widely, however. These requirements are summarized for the G-7 programs in table 14.2.

The requirement in Italy is the strictest, amounting to half of the past two years, 13 weeks of which must be continuous to receive full benefits. Japan requires work for half of the past year, but the base period can be extended to up to four years for those out of the workforce because of illness, injury, or pregnancy. Germany has the longest base period (three years) and requires covered work for at least 360 days during that time. The Canadian requirement calls for work for at least 40 percent of a one-year base period, although this criterion is more lenient in regions with high unemployment. The requirement in France calls for covered work for one-fourth of the prior year.

Table 14.2 Minimum Employment Needed in Covered Job for UI Eligibility in the G-7 Nations, 1993

Nation	Minimum amount of covered employment required		Reference period for required work
	Duration	Earnings[a]	
Canada			
Low-unemployment region	20 weeks	$116/week	Prior 52 weeks
High-unemployment region	10 weeks	$116/week	Prior 52 weeks
New entrant/reentrant	20 weeks	$116/week	Prior 52 weeks
France	91 days or 520 hours	None	Prior 12 months
Germany			
Seasonal workers	180 days	None	Prior 3 years
Other workers	360 days	None	Prior 3 years
Italy			
Basic benefits	(1) 52 weeks, and (2) 2 years	None	(1) Prior 2 years, and (2) Any period
Special benefits	Same as above, but 13 weeks must be continuous	None	Same as above
Japan			
Workers out of labor force because of illness, injury, or pregnancy	6 months	None	Past 48 months
Other workers	6 months	None	Past 12 months
United Kingdom			
Full benefits	None	$4,147/ year	Prior tax year
Reduced benefits	None	$2,073/ year	Prior tax year
United States			
UI	[b]	$1,390/year	First 4 of last 5 quarters[c]
TAA	26 weeks[d]	$30/week[d]	Prior 52 weeks

a. Currency figures were converted to U.S. dollars using July 1993 rates.

b. Nine states required covered employment for 15-20 weeks. Other states had no explicit work duration requirement. The minimum earnings requirement shown ($1,390) was the median for the fifty-three state programs. The required minimums ranged from $130 (Hawaii) to $4,280 (Oklahoma).

c. In forty-eight of the fifty-three state programs.

d. To be eligible for TAA, claimant must also meet state UI eligibility requirements.

Minimum work requirements in the United Kingdom and United States are primarily earnings based and are relatively low. The United Kingdom requires a year's earnings to exceed $4,147 for full benefits. The rule in the United States varies by state, but the median state requires only $1,390 in covered wages (equivalent to 41 days of full-time work at the minimum wage) over four quarters to qualify for a minimum benefit. However, nine states do have requirements for work duration, ranging from 15 to 20 weeks in four quarters, and the majority of states require a minimum earnings amount in the worker's highest-paid quarter. Of the states with this latter stipulation, the median state high-quarter earnings requirement is 61 percent of the earnings required over four quarters.

Each of the G-7 nations has rules that disqualify claimants whose unemployment results from voluntary quitting, misconduct, refusal of a suitable job, involvement in a labor dispute, or failure to accept training. Those jobless because of labor disputes are generally disqualified for the duration of the dispute. However, the length of disqualification for other causes of unemployment varies among the seven programs. Italy has a thirty-day disqualification for job quitters, those fired for misconduct, and those who refuse jobs. Canada disqualifies individuals for up to 12 weeks, as does Germany, but Canada disqualifies job quitters and those fired for misconduct indefinitely until they requalify through subsequent jobs. In Japan, disqualifications last as long as three months. France disqualifies job quitters for 3 months and denies eligibility for misconduct or job offer refusals, although job quitters may become eligible after 121 days of job search. Disqualifications for voluntary quits and misconduct last for 26 weeks in the United Kingdom. The United States has the strictest rules on disqualification, which are set by each state. For example, the disqualification for voluntary quitting is for the duration of the unemployment spell in forty-seven of the fifty-three state programs (figure 14.5).

Eligibility rules for UA in the three G-7 nations that have these programs are also tied to work history. France requires employment in at least five of the past ten years but reduces this requirement by up to three years for periods spent rearing children. the German program requires at least 150 days of insured employment during the past year. The United Kingdom has no specific work history stipulation. UA claimants have to comply with work registration rules similar to those

for UI claimants. UI exhaustees are eligible for UA in all three countries. A means test is used to limit UA eligibility to those in financial
need.

Figure 14.5 Maximum Disqualification Period for Voluntary Quits, 1993

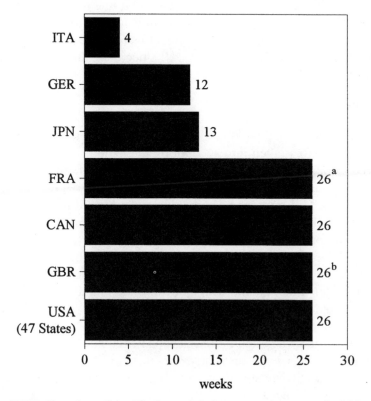

NOTE: Chart shows disqualification periods for an unemployment spell of 26
weeks.
a. Claimant can become eligible after 121 days if work search requirement is met.
b. Claimant can become eligible if jobless spell lasts more than 26 weeks.

The proportion of unemployed workers assisted by the U.S. program in the mid-1980s was low relative to the proportions helped in
Canada, France, and Italy. The U.S. figure was similar to those for UI
in Germany and the United Kingdom, but the figures in those countries
were much higher with UA recipients counted. In 1985, 34 percent of

U.S. jobless workers received UI. Comparable statistics for five of the other nations were as follows: Canada, 80 percent; France, 55 percent (72 percent including UA recipients); Germany, 39 percent (68 percent with UA recipients included); Italy, 60 percent (for 1981-1983); and the United Kingdom, 32 percent (as of 1984), (90 percent with UA recipients included).[8] It should be noted that unemployment rates in Canada, France, and the United Kingdom were 1.5 times the U.S. rate in the mid-1980s. Higher unemployment usually means that a greater proportion of the jobless qualify for UI since there are relatively more job losers than job quitters during downturns.

Benefits

The method of calculating UI benefits is unique to each program. The main factors taken into account by the benefit formulas are displayed in table 14.3. Of the seven programs, only the U.S. program lacks a national benefit formula.

All of the G-7 programs except that of the United Kingdom relate benefits to past wages. Germany replaces 63 percent of after-tax wages; the other systems base benefits on gross pay. The formula in Japan is the only one that provides a more generous rate of wage replacement, the lower the wage level.[9] Canada, France, Japan, and the United States limit benefits with monetary maximums, the maximums in the United States being the lowest except for a few states. The wage replacement rate in Japan of 80 percent at low wage levels is the highest rate, but the wage figure used in Japan excludes overtime pay and bonuses, which account for nearly one- third of cash compensation in Japan. UI benefits are subject to income taxes in all of the G-7 nations except Germany and Japan.

Age is generally not used as a factor in computing UI benefits, but Japan does pay lump-sum benefits to persons over 65, and the United Kingdom has higher benefit levels for unemployed workers who are over pensionable age. Benefits are more generous for workers with dependents in Germany, the United Kingdom, and fourteen U.S. states. The United Kingdom awards lump-sum "redundancy" benefits to long-term employees who have been dismissed. Italy uses a higher wage replacement level for those dismissed by firms that are undergoing planned workforce reductions or reorganizations. The U.S. system is

Table 14.3 Major Determinants of UI Benefit Amounts in the G-7 Nations, 1993

Nation	Past wages	Age[a]	Relationship of UI benefit formula Work history[a]	Region[a]	Dependents
Canada	57% of average gross wage, max. of $313/week	None	None	None	None
France	57.4% of average gross wage, min. of $22.34/day, max. of $52.54/day[b]	None	None	None	None
Germany	63% of average net wage	None	None	None	68% of average net wage for claimant with children
Italy					
Basic benefit	20% of average wage	None	None	None	None
Special benefit	80% of average wage	None	None	None	None
Japan	80% of average gross wage at low wage levels, 60% at high wage levels, max. of $85/day	Lump-sum benefit for workers over 65	None	None	None
United Kingdom	None: benefit is $66/week	$83/week if over pension age, plus $50 for spouse and $16/child	Lump-sum benefit for workers dismissed after 104 weeks of continuous employment	None	Additional $41/week with dependents

(continued)

Table 14.3 (continued)

Nation	Past wages	Age[a]	Relationship of UI benefit formula Work history[a]	Region[a]	Dependents
United States	50% of average gross wage in most states, max. of $133 to $335/week[c]	None	None	Different formula in each state	14 states had dependents' allowances, which added up to $156/week

NOTE: Currency figures were converted to U.S. dollars using July 1993 exchange rates.

a. Benefit amounts naturally vary with age, work history, and region since these factors are often related to wage levels and, therefore, benefit amounts. However, this table displays only the relationship of each factor to a program's benefit *formulas*.

b. Benefits in France are reduced 8 to 17 percent after the initial benefit period and every four months thereafter.

c. The maximum in the median state was $223 a week.

the only one without a national benefit formula, its UI benefits being determined by fifty-three different state formulas that produce widely varying benefit amounts.

Figure 14.6 compares weekly UI benefit amounts across the seven nations for three hypothetical cases. For the United States, amounts are shown for the states with the highest (Massachusetts) and lowest (Mississippi) benefit maximums.[10] Case 1 is a single worker age 25 who has worked six months at an annual salary rate of $10,000. Case 2 is a 31-year-old married worker with one child who has worked three years and was earning $28,000 a year at the time of job loss. Case 3 is a married worker age 55 with two children who has worked twenty-five years and was earning $50,000 a year.

Case 1 would be ineligible in Germany and Italy. In the other countries, the weekly benefit ranges from $48 (25 percent of the weekly wage) in Massachusetts to $156 (81 percent of wages) in France. For case 2, benefits vary more, exceeding $500 a week in Italy (100 percent wage replacement) and $300 in Canada (57 percent wage replacement), France (57 percent), Germany (68 percent), Japan (65 percent), and Massachusetts (59 percent), while amounting to only $165 (31 percent) in Mississippi and $107 (20 percent) in the United Kingdom. The weekly benefit for case 3 is over $900 in Italy (100 percent wage replacement), ranges around $600 in Japan (60 percent) and Germany (68 percent), and falls between $300 and $500 in Canada (33 percent), France (38 percent), and Massachusetts (49 percent). However, the benefit is the same as for case 2 in Mississippi (17 percent) and the United Kingdom (11 percent).

Maximum benefit durations also vary widely across the G-7 nations, as shown in table 14.4. The first column shows the maximum duration for full-time workers with substantial work histories. For such workers, UI benefits generally last about half a year in Japan and the United States, two-thirds of a year in Canada, a full year in Germany, Italy, and the United Kingdom, and two-and-a-half years in France. However, maximum durations can vary considerably from these benchmark figures in every country except the United Kingdom. Table 14.4 illustrates how four key factors (work history, age, unemployment rate, and region) affect maximum benefit durations.

620

Figure 14.6 UI Benefit Amounts for Three Hypothetical Cases, 1993

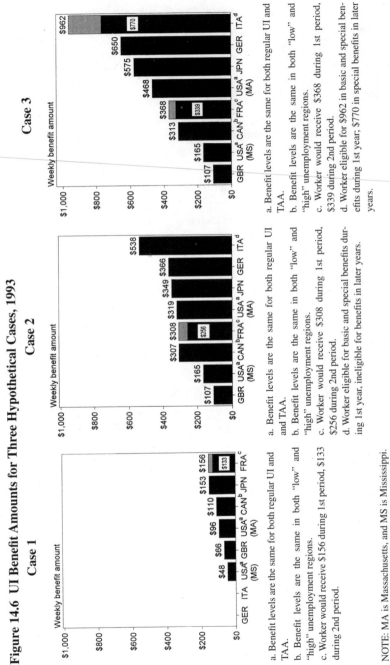

Case 1

a. Benefit levels are the same for both regular UI and TAA.
b. Benefit levels are the same in both "low" and "high" unemployment regions.
c. Worker would receive $156 during 1st period, $133 during 2nd period.

Case 2

a. Benefit levels are the same for both regular UI and TAA.
b. Benefit levels are the same in both "low" and "high" unemployment regions.
c. Worker would receive $308 during 1st period, $256 during 2nd period.
d. Worker eligible for basic and special benefits during 1st year, ineligible for benefits in later years.

Case 3

a. Benefit levels are the same for both regular UI and TAA.
b. Benefit levels are the same in both "low" and "high" unemployment regions.
c. Worker would receive $368 during 1st period, $339 during 2nd period.
d. Worker eligible for $962 in basic and special benefits during 1st year; $770 in special benefits in later years.

NOTE: MA is Massachusetts, and MS is Mississippi.
Case 1: Age 25, single, worked 6 months at $10,000 annual rate.
Case 2: Age 31, married with 1 child, worked 3 years, earning $28,000 in last year.
Case 3: Age 55, married with 2 children, worked 25 years, earned $50,000 in last year.

Table 14.4 Determinants of Maximum UI Benefit Durations in the G-7 Nations, 1993

Nation	Maximum benefit duration for full-time workers	Variation in maximum duration in relation to			
		Work history	Age	Unemployment rate	Region
Canada	35 weeks (worked all year)	17 weeks with 20 weeks of work in 1 year	None	Up to 50 weeks in regions with high unemployment	Varies for regions with unemployment over 6%
France First period	275 days	122 days if less than 426 days of work in last 2 years (214 days if 50 or older)	214 days if under 25; 457 days if 50 or older; 610 days if 50 to 54 and worked at least 821 days in last 3 years; 822 days if 55 or older	None	None
Second period	637 days	334 days if worked less than 426 days in last 2 years (425 days if 50 or older; 91 days if worked less than 243 days in last year; 0 days if worked less than 192 days in last year	699 days if under 25; 913 days if 50 or older; 759 days if 50 to 54 and worked at least 821 days in last 3 years; 1,003 days if 55 or older	None	Extensions granted by employer groups

(continued)

Table 14.4 (continued)

	Maximum benefit duration for full-time workers	Variation in maximum duration in relation to			
Nation		Work history	Age	Unemployment rate	Region
Germany	52 weeks (worked at least 24 of last 36 months)	35 weeks with 16 months of work; longer durations for combination of age and service (see next column)	78 weeks for workers 42 or older with 36 months of work; 95 weeks for workers 44 or older with 44 months of work; 113 weeks if 49 or older within 52 months of work; 139 weeks if 54 or older with 64 months of work	None	None
Italy Basic benefit	180 days	90 days for construction workers, less than 180 days for some farm workers	None	None	None
Special benefit	12 months	None	24 months for workers 40 to 49; 36 months if 50 or older	None	None

Japan	180 days (age 30-44 and worked 5-9 years; under 30 and worked over 9 years; 45-54 and worked 1-4 years)	90 days for less than 1 year of work; 210-300 days for certain age and service combinations; 90-day extension for claimants awaiting training	90 days if under 30 unless worked over 9 years; 210-300 days for certain age and service combinations	90-day extension if uninsured unemployment over 4%	90-day extension in remote areas and for industries in recession
United Kingdom	52 weeks	None	None	None	None
United States					
UI	26 weeks (30 in 2 states) (must have worked certain amount in 42 states)	4-30 weeks for minimum work required by state in 42 states[a]	None	39-46 weeks when extended benefits triggered by high unemployment in a state	None[b]
TAA	52 weeks (including UI duration)	78 weeks if in training (including UI duration)	None	None	None

a. Median minimum duration for these forty-two states is 13 weeks.
b. Durations may vary by state as indicated elsewhere.

France, Germany, and Japan vary maximum durations by age and length of service in combination. Basic benefit periods can be extended for these factors as follows:

- In France, the benefit duration can be as long as five years for workers age 55 and older who have worked at least two-and-a-quarter of the last three years;
- In Germany, the regular 52-week period can be increased to 139 weeks for workers 54 and older who have worked at least 64 months;
- In Japan, the regular 180-day period can be increased to as much as 300 days for workers 55 and older who have worked more than nine years.

In Canada and the United States, age is not a factor in determining duration, nor is service occurring before the base period. However, the level of unemployment is a determinant of duration in Canada, Japan, and the United States. Benefit extension periods in France result in a claimant's original UI benefit amount being reduced by 8 percent to 17 percent when such extensions occur. These reductions are repeated every four months.

Canada and the United States provide longer benefit periods based on unemployment rates in labor market regions and states, respectively. Canada also takes weeks of insured employment into account; its normal 35-week benefit period can be as long as 50 weeks for full-year workers in regions with unemployment above 10 percent. The usual U.S. maximum benefit duration of 26 weeks is extended to 39 weeks in states where the insured unemployment rate for a 13-week period exceeds 5 percent and is at least 120 percent of the corresponding rates in the two preceding years.[11] In forty-one states, an insured rate of 6 percent or higher will trigger the extension without regard to the rates in the preceding two years. States have authority to trigger 13 weeks of extended benefits when their total unemployment rate exceeds 6.5 percent and is at least 110 percent of the corresponding rate in one of the two preceding years.[12] Total unemployment of 8 percent can trigger 20 weeks of extended benefits. However, only seven states had authorized this more liberal trigger mechanism as of July 1995.

A temporary benefit extension had effectively supplanted the permanent EB program with benefits that totaled as much as 52 or 59 weeks depending on the total unemployment rate in a state, but the program expired in April 1994. The United States has enacted temporary benefit extensions during each major recession since 1958. The other six nations have changed permanent law in reaction to economic change, but they have not relied on temporary programs for benefit extensions.

Figure 14.7 compares maximum UI benefit durations for the same three cases for whom benefit amounts were shown in figure 14.6. The typical 26-week initial U.S. benefit period (30 weeks in Massachusetts) is relatively generous for the youngest worker (case 1), representing a longer duration than would be available from UI in France or Japan, or in Germany and Italy, where this case would be ineligible. For case 2, however, the initial benefit duration in the United States would be shorter than in all the other nations but Japan. Eligibility for EB could make the U.S. duration longer than the duration in Canada for its regions of low unemployment. For case 3, all six nations would provide benefits for a longer time than would the United States, but EB would make the U.S. duration similar to that in a low-unemployment Canadian region. However, the relatively few U.S. claimants eligible for TAA have a maximum duration longer than that shown in figure 14.7 for Canada, Japan, and the United Kingdom. The benefit periods could be well in excess of 100 weeks for case 3 in France, Germany, and Italy.

Figure 14.7 does not show UA durations, which can extend benefits at a lower rate indefinitely in France, Germany, and the United Kingdom. While eligibility for UA is indefinite, it is subject to a means test. France pays a flat-rate benefit of F72.92 ($12.18) a day, with larger benefits for eligibles who meet criteria for old age and length of service. The German UA benefit is 56 percent of net wages (58 percent for claimants with children). The UA benefit in the United Kingdom for claimants with no other income is £44.00 ($65.16) a week, £69.00 ($102.19) for couples.

Employment Services

All seven nations have public programs to provide job training and other employment services to those with employability problems. This discussion is limited to those services that are integral to each national UC system.

626

Figure 14.7 UI Maximum Benefit Durations for Three Hypothetical Cases, 1993

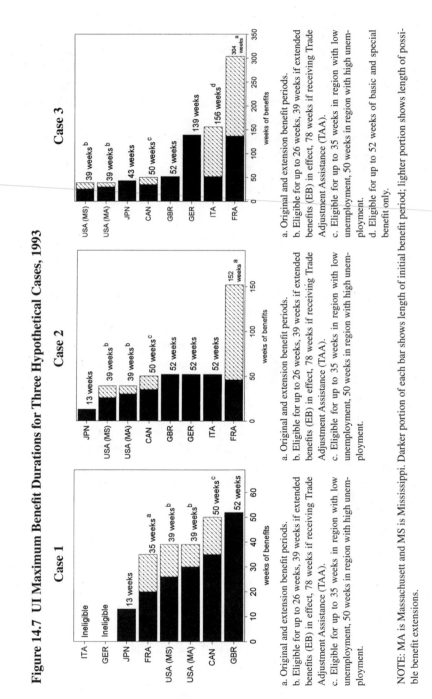

a. Original and extension benefit periods.
b. Eligible for up to 26 weeks, 39 weeks if extended benefits (EB) in effect, 78 weeks if receiving Trade Adjustment Assistance (TAA).
c. Eligible for up to 35 weeks in region with low unemployment, 50 weeks in region with high unemployment.

a. Original and extension benefit periods.
b. Eligible for up to 26 weeks, 39 weeks if extended benefits (EB) in effect, 78 weeks if receiving Trade Adjustment Assistance (TAA).
c. Eligible for up to 35 weeks in region with low unemployment, 50 weeks in region with high unemployment.

a. Original and extension benefit periods.
b. Eligible for up to 26 weeks, 39 weeks if extended benefits (EB) in effect, 78 weeks if receiving Trade Adjustment Assistance (TAA).
c. Eligible for up to 35 weeks in region with low unemployment, 50 weeks in region with high unemployment.
d. Eligible for up to 52 weeks of basic and special benefit only.

NOTE: MA is Massachusett and MS is Mississippi. Darker portion of each bar shows length of initial benefit period; lighter portion shows length of possible benefit extensions.

The G-7 countries all require UC claimants to register with employment offices where information is provided on available jobs. Service provision to UC claimants beyond this basic help varies a great deal. Italy and Japan use wage supplements and subsidies to firms to permit them to retain employees during downturns. Canada, France, Germany, and Japan provide skills development training as part of their UC systems. In the United States, states are required to identify claimants who are likely to experience long-term unemployment so that these individuals can receive employment services early in their jobless spells. Job training is not available within the U.S. program, but TAA claimants must enroll in approved training unless this requirement is waived. Claimants in approved training usually continue to receive weekly benefits and may be eligible for special allowances for job search and relocation.

Unemployment benefits can be used to help claimants start new businesses in Canada, France, Germany, Italy, and the United Kingdom. The United States has tested this idea in two state demonstration projects, and 1993 legislation authorized all states to allow UI claimants to start businesses while receiving benefits.

Public expenditures in 1993 for employment services and training, including programs outside the UC systems, are shown in table 14.5.

Table 14.5 Public Spending for Employment Services and Training by the G-7 Nations, 1993

	Spending as a percentage of	
Nation	**GDP**	**UI benefits**
Canada	0.60	30
France (1992)	0.48	30
Germany	0.78	39
Italy (1992)	0.10	16
Japan	0.06	23
United Kingdom	0.33	27
United States	0.14	31

SOURCE: OECD (1994, table 1.B.2).

NOTE: The public spending figures shown here include employment services and administration, training for unemployed adults, and support of unemployed persons starting enterprises.

Spending as a percent of GDP was highest in Canada, France, and Germany. The lowest expenditures relative to size of economy were registered by Italy, Japan, and the United States (ranked fifth). German spending was more than five times that of the United States relative to GDP.

When spending for employment services and training is viewed in relationship to UC spending (table 14.5, right column), there is less variation across the G-7. The German ratio of 0.39 is highest, and the Italian of 0.16 is lowest. Thus, these nations represent the most and least aggressive in applying active labor market measures in relation to the size of their income support for the jobless. The ratios of the other five countries fall in the range of 0.23 (Japan) to 0.31 (United States).

Recent Trends

Several trends since 1990 can be identified across the G-7 UC programs. Some programs have lengthened the periods during which claimants are disqualified for voluntary unemployment. Eligibility has been tightened in two countries (for UA in France, for special UI benefits in Italy). On the other hand, none of the G-7 has liberalized eligibility rules. Benefit amounts have been lowered relative to wages in Canada; no G-7 country has raised them. Benefit periods have been lengthened in some cases. Prolonged benefits were tied to age and work history in France and Italy. The U.S. program has adopted a more liberal measure of unemployment for the activation of EB but has left its implementation up to the states. Several of the G-7 programs have attempted better integration of UI with employment services.

Conclusions

While all of the G-7 nations have UC systems that mandate coverage of most workers and that finance most of the costs with payroll taxes, the seven systems differ widely in their details. The variations are particularly striking when the U.S. system is compared with the other six. The U.S. system is the only one that

- has most of its rules set by subnational governments;
- uses experience rating to set tax rates on employers;

- bases extended benefit periods on unemployment levels in its political subdivisions;
- relies on temporary programs to augment UI in coping with recession-related unemployment increases; and
- provides additional unemployment benefits for dislocated workers whose joblessness can be linked to national trade policy.

The UC systems of the other six G-7 nations also vary widely among themselves, but there are some common trends. National spending on UC as a percentage of GDP has tended to converge since 1990 except for Germany, which had to absorb the unemployment costs of the former GDR after reunification. All of the G-7 countries are placing greater emphasis on reemploying the jobless in one way or another. Finally, recent program changes have generally been in the direction of retrenchment as unemployment and the associated costs have risen in Canada and western Europe.

Other Types of Unemployment Compensation Systems

Overview

This section presents an overview of the types of UC systems found worldwide and describes three systems that contrast sharply with the programs of the G-7 nations. The 1993 edition of *Social Security Programs Throughout the World* (U.S. Department of Health and Human Service 1994) describes the programs of 163 countries. Of these, 75 countries had a formal public law authorizing compensation for jobless workers. These 75 laws can be classified as follows:

- compulsory social insurance—fifty countries;
- voluntary social insurance—three countries;
- means-tested assistance—nine countries (plus seven countries that also operate social insurance programs);
- severance pay—twelve countries; and
- compulsory self-insurance—one country.

All of the G-7 nations and forty-three others operated compulsory social insurance programs in 1993. These programs are characterized generally by broad coverage and by some linkage of funding and/or benefit amounts to covered wages. However, the program in Chile is funded entirely from general government revenue and pays flat-rate benefits. In Estonia, the program is government-funded and ties benefits to the minimum wage. Latvia also ties benefits to the minimum wage. Malta pays flat-rate benefits. The forty-three countries in addition to the G-7 nations that operated compulsory social insurance schemes as of 1993 were as follows:

Albania	Cyprus	Kyrgyzstan	Russia
Argentina	Czech Republic	Latvia	Slovakia
Armenia	Egypt	Lithuania	South Africa[13]
Austria	Estonia	Luxembourg	Spain
Azerbaijan	Georgia	Malta	Switzerland
Bangladesh	Greece	Moldova	Turkmenistan
Barbados	Hungary	Netherlands	Ukraine
Belarus	Iceland	Norway	Uruguay
Belgium	Iran	Poland	Uzbekistan
Chile	Ireland	Portugal	Venezuela
China	Israel	Romania	

Three Scandinavian countries (Denmark, Finland, and Sweden) had voluntary social insurance systems operated through labor unions. Union participation in UC is not compulsory.

Means-tested assistance programs apply means tests to unemployed workers to determine their eligibility. Benefit amounts may be related to need as well. Some of these programs stand alone, while others are components of larger UC systems. Nine countries had only a means-tested program. They were the following:

Australia	Hong Kong	New Zealand	Slovenia
Brazil	Mauritius	Serbia	Tunisia
Bulgaria			

Seven countries used means-tested assistance to augment a social insurance program, either for selected unemployed workers with little or no recent work experience, or for those exhausting their UI benefits, or both. Three of the G-7 nations (France, Germany, and the United Kingdom) had such arrangements. The other four countries with dual UI and UA programs were Austria, Finland, Ireland, and Portugal.

Twelve countries offered only severance pay to unemployed workers. Usually this benefit is paid by the employer under a labor law that specifies the employer and employee types to which it applies and the amount of the severance pay. The countries with severance pay only were as follows:

Bolivia	Ecuador	Libya	Solomon Islands
Botswana	Honduras	Mexico	Tanzania
Colombia	India	Pakistan	Turkey

Finally, Guatemala required workers to self-insure against unemployment under a law mandating individual saving for that purpose.

A major development during the 1990s has been the adoption of UC systems by countries that had state-controlled economies in the 1980s. Compulsory social insurance UC systems has been established in these former communist states, except for Bulgaria, Serbia, and Slovenia, which have means-tested programs.

The remainder of this section describes three UC systems that differ from those of the G-7 nations. These include a voluntary social insurance program (Sweden), a solely means-tested program (Australia), and a severance pay law (Mexico).

Voluntary Social Insurance: Sweden

Sweden is the largest of the three Scandinavian countries that had voluntary UI systems in 1993. There are two aspects of voluntarism in this system. First, unemployment funds for UI are established voluntarily by trade unions. Second, although union members generally must participate in their union's fund, nonunion workers in the industry may voluntarily accept coverage by the union fund. Workers over age 64 are excluded. About two-thirds of all employees are covered by this system. Workers ineligible for UI and new labor force entrants if over age

20 are covered by a means-tested UA plan called the "labor market support program." UI is administered by the National Labor Market Board, and UA is administered by county labor boards and local employment offices.

The UI system is funded by employee, employer, and government. Employees pay from K32 ($3.87) to K100 ($12.10) a month, the exact amount varying by fund. These employee contributions cover 5 percent of UI costs. Employers are taxed at a rate of 2.14 percent of payroll, which covers about 60 percent of UI costs and two-thirds of UA costs. Government funds pay for the balance of UI and UA costs.

Eligibility for UI requires twelve months of membership in a union fund, including at least four of the last twelve months before unemployment. Eligibles must be registered at an employment office and be capable of work. Individuals whose unemployment is a result of voluntary quitting, misconduct, or refusal of suitable work are usually disqualified for four weeks. Eligibility rules for UA are basically the same, except for the work history requirement. A person can meet the requirement either by working for at least four of the past twelve months or by meeting an education or training criterion.

The UI benefit amount varies by fund and wage level, ranging from K210 ($25.41) to K598 ($72.36) a day. It is pegged to 80 percent of the average wage in each covered trade. Benefits are payable for up to 300 days and are considered taxable income.

The UA benefit amount is K210 ($25.41) a day and is payable for up to 150 days. For those ages 55 to 59, the maximum benefit duration is 300 days. For those ages 60 to 64, or for dislocated workers ages 55 to 59, the maximum benefit duration is 450 days.

Unemployment Assistance: Australia

Australia was the most industrialized nation offering unemployment benefits solely on the basis of a means test in 1993. First enacted in 1944, this UA program covers all employed persons and is funded from general government revenue. Benefits are administered by the Department of Social Security. Local offices of the Department of Employment, Education, and Training receive claims and apply a work test.

To be eligible, an unemployed worker must be at least 16 years old and be under pensionable age (65 for men, 60 for women). Eligibles must be capable of and available for work and actively looking for jobs. Jobless individuals whose unemployment is a result of voluntary quitting, misconduct, or refusal of suitable work are subject to disqualification for up to 12 weeks. Those unemployed because of a labor dispute are disqualified for the duration of the dispute.

Benefits are paid after a one-week waiting period for as long as an individual is qualified. Benefit amounts depend on income, marital status, age, number of children, amount of rent, and location of residence. The means test has been liberalized numerous times to allow the disregarding of more income in computing the benefit.

Severance Pay: Mexico

In Mexico, the only form of unemployment benefit is a government requirement that employers pay departing employees a severance benefit under prescribed circumstances. Mexico has two forms of severance pay: the *cesantia*, payable when separation occurs without just cause, and the *antiquedad*, payable based on tenure without regard to the reason for termination.

The *cesantia* equals three months of pay plus 20 days of pay per year of service. Pay is defined to include bonuses, commissions, and benefit payments except profit sharing. A worker must have been employed for at least a year to be entitled to this benefit upon job loss without just cause. Examples of just cause are a worker's engaging in dishonest, negligent, immoral, or violent acts, or coming to work in an intoxicated state. The reason for dismissal of an employee must be communicated in writing to be considered justified.

The *antiquedad*, adopted in 1970, equals 12 days of pay per year of service but cannot exceed twice the minimum-wage salary. It is payable upon retirement, death, disability, or termination of employment. To qualify for this benefit upon voluntary termination, the individual must have worked for at least fifteen years with the firm. No minimum service period is required for involuntary termination, death, or disability, but service is counted only back to 1970 for involuntary termination. For jobless workers near retirement ages 60 to 64, the Mexican Social Security system also pays reduced pension benefits. The reduction is 5 percentage points per year for each year under age 65.

Appendix 14.A
Program Descriptions for the G-7 Nations

Canada

Objectives

When the UI system was established in 1940, the central objective was to provide workers with economic security during short-term unemployment by paying benefits related to past contributions but not to exceed wages. Emphasis was given to adherence to insurance principles in the system design. A major reform of the system in 1971 added a second objective: aiding the reentry of jobless workers into the labor market.

Administration

A national agency, the Canada Employment and Immigration Commission, administers UC through regional and local offices. The nation is divided into sixty-two regions for the purpose of administering UC. Most of these regions represent urban labor markets, with rural areas of provinces making up the balance. Payroll taxes that fund the system are collected by the national revenue agency.

Financing

Revenue is raised from a payroll tax on both employer and employee. In 1993, the employer paid 4.2 percent and the employee 3.0 percent on the first $C745 ($580) of each covered worker's weekly wage. No general government revenue is used to support the program.

Coverage

All wage and salary jobs are covered except those providing less than 15 hours of work per week and paying less than $C149 ($116) a week. Self-employed fishermen are covered under special rules. Provincial government jobs are covered at the option of those governments.

Eligibility

To qualify for UI benefits, an unemployed person must have worked for a minimum number of weeks during the prior 52-week period. The qualifying period can be longer than 52 weeks for those who were ill, injured, pregnant, or in training. An insurable week is one in which the person worked at least 15 hours or earned at least $C149 ($116). The minimum number of weeks required varies by unemployment in the region, from 10 weeks where the unemployment rate is over 15 percent to 20 weeks where the rate is 6 percent or less. A new entrant or reentrant to the labor force needs 20 weeks to qualify.

Persons who refuse suitable jobs or refuse required training are disqualified for periods ranging from 7 to 12 weeks. Individuals jobless because of labor disputes are disqualified for the duration of the dispute. Those who quit jobs or were fired for misconduct are disqualified until they requalify from subsequent employment.

Benefits

Benefits are equal to 57 percent of average insured gross earnings over the prior 52 weeks, subject to a weekly maximum of $C425 ($331). For those who refuse jobs or training, the benefit is only 50 percent of average earnings, however. Benefits are fully taxable as income. Benefit payments begin after a two-week waiting period.

The duration of benefits varies with the number of insurable weeks of work and the regional unemployment rate. The maximum duration is at least 17 weeks for persons with 20 weeks of work in regions with unemployment of 6 percent or less. The maximum duration for those who worked every week of the qualifying period is at least 35 weeks. Durations reach as long as 50 weeks for some combinations of work history and regional unemployment, as shown in appendix table 14A.1.

Appendix Table 14A.1 Maximum Duration of UI Benefits, Canada, 1993

Regional unemployment rate	Weeks worked in past year			
	13	26	39	52
6.1 % or less	NE	22	29	35
6.1% - 7.0%	NE	25	32	38
7.1% - 8.0%	NE	28	35	41
8.1% - 9.0%	NE	32	39	45
9.1% - 10.0%	NE	36	43	49
10.1% - 11.0%	NE	40	47	50
11.1% - 12.0%	NE	44	50	50
12.1% - 13.0%	34	46	50	50
13.1% - 14.0%	36	48	50	50
14.1% - 15.0%	38	50	50	50
15.1% - 16.0%	40	50	50	50
Over 16.0%	42	50	50	50

NOTE: NE means not eligible.

Benefits are limited to 15 weeks if unemployment is because of sickness or maternity and to 10 weeks if because of parental care.

Employment Services

The Employment Commission maintains lists of available jobs and provides counseling on job search and retraining programs. The agency offers job training and work experience programs for the long-term unemployed. The use of UI funds for training has expanded rapidly since 1990.

France

Objectives

Since 1984 legislation, the UC system has consisted of two distinct parts. For workers who have lost their jobs involuntarily, UI provides benefits that are mainly wage-related but that decline as the period of unemployment lengthens. The "solidarity" UA program provides a need-based benefit to UI exhaustees and to certain categories of new labor force entrants and reentrants.

Administration

The system is supervised by a national agency, the Ministry of Health and Social Security. Funds are managed by ASSEDICs, an acronym for associations of employers. Payments are administered by UNEDIC, an employee organization. Municipalities distribute payments in places where these organizations have no offices.

Financing

Employers and employees are required to contribute to the ASSEDICs. Employers pay 4.18 percent of all wages. Employees pay 2.42 percent of earnings up to F12,610 ($2,106) a month, plus an extra 0.55 percent on monthly earnings between F12,610 ($2,106) and F55,440 ($9,258). The government pays for the solidarity program that benefits certain persons ineligible for UI.

Coverage

Workers under age 60 (or under 65 and not covered for a social security old-age pension) are covered by UI, except for domestic employees and seasonal workers. There are special rules covering construction and longshore workers, the merchant marine, and aviators. Certain new entrants are covered by the solidarity program, including new labor force entrants ages 18-25, apprentices, freed prisoners, recently discharged military veterans, newly widowed or divorced women, single women with children, and unemployed workers who have exhausted their UI benefits.

Eligibility

To be immediately eligible for UI, the jobless worker must be involuntarily unemployed and have worked for at least 91 days or 520 hours during the twelve months preceding job loss. Unemployment cannot be due to misconduct or to refusal of suitable job offers. Those who leave jobs voluntarily are disqualified from benefits, but they may gain eligibility after 121 days if they meet a job search requirement. A claimant must be able to work and be registered at a job exchange.

Eligibility for a solidarity benefit for those who have exhausted their UI benefits necessitates employment in at least five of the past ten years, but this requirement can be reduced by one year per child for childrearing for as many as three children. Eligibility is also income-tested, with the limits set at F5,104.40 ($852) a month for a single person, F10,208.80 ($1,705) for a couple.

Benefits

The UI benefit is 57.4 percent of wages over the prior twelve months. Benefits range from a minimum of F133.76 ($22.34) per day to a maximum of F314.63 ($52.54). Benefits are paid after an eight-day waiting period and are taxed the same as earnings.

Extension periods are granted beyond the original benefit period at the discretion of the ASSEDICs. The lengths of these periods depend on employment history and age. Benefits in an extension period are reduced by 8 percent to 17 percent of the original amount. Maximum benefit durations and reduction rates for benefit extensions are shown in appendix table 14A.2.

The solidarity benefit is F72.92 ($12.18) a day. A higher rate of F104.73 ($17.49) is paid to those ages 55 to 58 1/2and employed at least twenty years and those age 58 1/2 and older and employed at least ten years. Benefits are payable for periods of six months but may be renewed. Eligibility terminates at age 60 for those with old-age pension coverage.

**Table 14A.2 Maximum UI Benefit Durations and Reduction Rates for
Benefit Extensions, France, 1994**

Work history and age	Maximum duration 1st period (days)	Maximum duration 2nd period (days)	Benefit cut 2nd period (percent)
122 days in last 8 months	122	0	N/A
182 days in last year	122	91	15
243 days in last year and			
under age 50	122	334	17
age 50 or older	214	425	15
426 days in last 2 years and			
under age 25	214	699	17
age 25 to 49	275	637	17
age 50 or older	457	913	15
821 days in last 3 years and			
age 50 to 54	610	759	15
age 55 or older	822	1,003	8

NOTE: N/A means not applicable.

Employment Services

UI beneficiaries are required to register with an employment exchange where information on available jobs is maintained. The government can use UI funds for skills development activities and to pay allowances to persons in training. The long- term unemployed have access to subsidized public or private jobs. UI benefits may be continued for claimants who are starting businesses.

Germany

Objectives

The Employment Promotion Act of 1969, which established the present German UC system, states the intention that the program contribute to the prevention of unemployment and underemployment as well as assist unemployed workers with income replacement.

Administration

The UC system is supervised nationally by the Federal Ministry of Labor and Social Affairs. Contributions for this system and for other parts of the social security system are collected by sickness funds operated by various localities, enterprises, and occupational groups. Unemployment benefit payments are administered by the Federal Institute for Labor through its regional and local offices.

Financing

Funds for UI are raised from the compulsory social security tax on employers and employees. The UI share of these contributions comes from a payroll tax of 6.5 percent on the first DM86,400 ($49,680) of annual earnings, split equally between employee and employer.[14]

Coverage

All employees with earnings subject to the social security tax are covered by UC. Individuals exempted are those working less than 15 hours a week. Those employed less than two months or fifty working days in a year are also exempt.

Eligibility

To be eligible for UI benefits, unemployed workers must be under age 65, capable of and available for work, and registered with a local employment office. Eligibility also requires the person to have worked in insured employment for at least 360 days during the past three years (180 days for seasonal workers). Otherwise qualified individuals are disqualified for up to 12 weeks for voluntary leaving, misconduct, participation in a strike, participation in training, or refusal of a suitable job offer.

A means-tested UA program covers those who fail to qualify for UI benefits if they had insured employment for at least 150 days during the past year. Persons exhausting their UI benefits may also be eligible. In addition, assistance is available for jobless workers in retraining programs.

Benefits

The UI benefit amount is 68 percent of after-tax income for persons with children and 63 percent for others. It is payable without a waiting period. Benefits are not subject to the income tax.

The maximum duration of UI benefit payments differs according to length of work history and age. For those under age 42, maximum benefit durations vary proportionately from 35 weeks with sixteen months of covered work up to 52 weeks with two years of covered work. For those 42 or older, benefits can be paid for up to 78 weeks with thirty-six months of covered work. For those 44 or older, benefits can be paid for up to 95 weeks with forty-four months of covered work. For those 49 or older, benefits can last up to 113 weeks with fifty-two months of covered work. For those 54 or older, benefits can continue up to 139 weeks with sixty-four months of covered work.

The means-tested UA benefit is 58 percent of after-tax income for persons with children and 56 percent for others. Benefits are available for one year but may be extended for one-year periods indefinitely.

Employment Services

Beneficiaries must register with an employment office. The administering agency can use payroll tax funds to provide job counseling and training. Income maintenance grants are available for persons in training. Claimants starting businesses can receive benefits for up to six months.

Italy

Objectives

The UI system provides a small basic benefit. This amount may be augmented with supplementary benefits to replace wages more adequately and to provide job continuity in firms experiencing downturns or operational disruptions.

Administration

Benefit payments are administered by the Ministry of Labor and Social Welfare through the National Social Insurance Institute. Payroll taxes that support the program are collected by the Treasury.

Financing

Employer payroll taxes fund UI benefit costs. The tax is assessed on wages in excess of L54,886 ($34) a day. The tax rate is 1.61 percent for industrial managers and 1.91 percent for others. Industrial employers pay an additional 0.3 percent (0.8 percent in the construction industry) for special benefits and 2.2 percent for the wage supplement fund (1.9 percent for firms with fewer than fifty workers). General government revenue pays for administration and for part of the cost of wage supplements.

Coverage

All workers in private employment are covered except occasional and seasonal workers and part-time employees.

Eligibility

To be eligible for basic UI benefits, a jobless worker must have at least two years of insured employment, at least 52 weeks (43 weeks in the construction industry) of which occurred in the past two years. Special UI benefits, available to industrial and construction workers, require at least 13 weeks of continuous covered employment as well.

Eligibility further requires that the jobless worker be registered at an employment office and be capable of and available for work. Claimants may be disqualified for thirty days if unemployment results from voluntary leaving or misconduct or if a suitable job or prescribed training is refused.

Benefits

The basic UI benefit is 20 percent of wages and is payable for up to 180 days after a 1-week waiting period. This benefit is not available to business executives. Construction workers are limited to 90 days of benefits. Agricultural workers are limited to 270 days minus the number of days actually worked, not to exceed 180 days. All benefits are subject to the income tax

Special benefits are available to employees in industrial firms with more than fifteen employees and commercial firms with more than two hundred employees. This benefit fully replaces past wages for up to one year. Any subsequent benefits are reduced to 80 percent of wages. Again, executive-level personnel are not eligible. Special benefits, which do not include any dependents' allowances, are reduced for any basic benefits received.

The special UI benefit is available for up to twelve months. This duration is longer for older workers (24 months for those ages 40-49, thirty-six months for those age 50 or older). Durational limits also apply to the use of these benefits by a particular company for its workers. The normal term is twelve months, but a company undergoing reorganization can use this program for up to twenty-four months, with two twelve-month extensions allowed. An operational unit within an eligible firm can use these benefits for no longer than thirty-six months in a five-year period.

Employees of firms covered by special benefits who are partially unemployed may be eligible for wage supplementation. However, wage supplementation cannot be paid to persons receiving special UI benefits. The supplements are in amounts sufficient to replace 80 percent of lost wages and are paid for three-month periods. Wage supplements cannot be received for more than twelve months in a two-year period.

Employment Services

Claimants must register with a local placement office where information on available jobs is maintained.

Japan

Objectives

The UC system was revised in 1992 to emphasize its role as "employment insurance," which reflects its multiple objectives: to help maintain the incomes of workers during unemployment, to stabilize employment, and to strengthen the employment security of workers through skills development.

Administration

The system is administered by a national agency, the Employment Security Bureau under the Ministry of Labor.

Financing

Most of the cost of the system is borne by employer and employee payroll taxes. Both employees and employers pay 0.55 percent of wages for a total of 1.10 percent. (Employees who are seasonal or construction workers pay 0.65 percent, as do employers.) In addition, employers pay 0.35 percent of wages to support employment services (0.45 percent for construction employers). These payroll taxes apply to total wages. General government revenue is used to pay one- fourth of benefit costs.

Coverage

All workers are covered except those age 65 or older, certain day laborers and seasonal workers, part-time workers employed less than 22 hours a week, and government pensioners. Jobs with small firms (fewer than five employees) in the agriculture, forestry, and fishing industries are covered on a voluntary basis.

Eligibility

To be eligible, a worker must have been in insured employment for at least six of the last twelve months. The reference period can be extended to up to forty-eight months for those out of the labor force because of illness, injury, pregnancy, or for hard-to-employ cases.

Eligibility requires registration with an employment security office. An eligible must be capable of and available for work and report to the local office every four weeks. A claimant may be disqualified for up to three months if unemployment resulted from voluntary leaving, misconduct, refusal of a suitable job offer, or failure to attend recommended training.

Benefits

The basic benefit applicable for most workers varies by wage level. The benefit is 80 percent of past wages at lower wage levels and 60 percent at higher levels.[15] The minimum basic benefit is ¥2,390 ($22.56) a day; the maximum is ¥9,040 ($85.34). A separate benefit schedule for insured day laborers ranges from ¥1,770 ($16.71) a day for laborers with the lowest wages to ¥6,200

($58.53) for those with the highest wages. Benefits are paid after a one-week waiting period and are not subject to taxation.

Unemployed workers age 65 or older receive a lump-sum benefit that ranges in value from 50 days of the basic benefit for those in insured employment less than one year to 150 days for those in insured employment ten years or more. Unemployed insured seasonal workers receive a lump-sum benefit worth 50 days of basic benefits.

The maximum duration of UI benefit eligibility depends on age and work history as shown in appendix A table 14A.3

Table 14A.3 Maximum Duration of UI Benefits, Japan, 1993

Age	Period of insured employment			
	Under 1 year	1-4 years	5-9 years	Over 9 years
Under 30	90 days	90 days	90 days	180 days
30-44	90 days	90 days	180 days	210 days
45-54	90 days	180 days	210 days	240 days
55-64	90 days	210 days	240 days	300 days
Difficult-to-employ and				
under 55	90 days	240 days	240 days	240 days
55-64	90 days	300 days	300 days	300 days

If a worker obtains a steady job before half of the applicable maximum benefit period has expired, a reemployment allowance is paid that is worth from 30 to 120 days of the basic benefit amount.

Benefit durations are briefer for "short-time" workers (those employed between 22 and 33 hours a week) age 30 and older. Those ages 30 to 54 must have worked at least five years to receive benefits for 180 days. Those over 54 have a maximum duration of 210 days with ten or more years of service. Difficult-to-employ individuals are also limited to 210 days (180 days if under age 55). The benefit amount for short-time workers is 60 percent of lost wages.

Benefit durations can be extended for up to ninety days for workers forced into retirement by the bankruptcy of a firm or by an industrial recession, for workers awaiting placement in a training program, and for those seeking job placement in "remote areas." A national ninety-day extension is triggered when the number of insured unemployed exceeds 4 percent of the workforce covered by UI.

Employment Services

Employment services aimed at combating structural unemployment and labor market problems associated with factors such as age and region are an integral part of the Japanese UI system. These services include skills development training and support activities such as job vacancy listings, relocation assistance, and job search assistance. Firms can receive employment stabilization subsidies to allow them to retain employees during short-term downturns. These funds can be used to support production activities or on- the-job training. Employers who hire dislocated workers age 45 and older may also receive subsidies.

United Kingdom

Objectives

Under 1992 legislation, the UC system provides a fixed amount of income support for those with substantial work histories who lose their jobs involuntarily. However, brief disqualification periods and a broad program of need-related aid result in significant income support for the unemployed generally.

Administration

The UC system is administered by two national agencies. The Department of Social Security is responsible for tax collection and the awarding of income-tested UA benefits. The Department of Employment administers UI benefits through 9 regional and 1,759 local offices.

Financing

UI benefits are funded by part of the payroll tax that finances the overall Social Security system. For the year ending March 31, 1992, UI benefits comprised 4.1 percent of all benefits financed by the payroll tax. Income-tested UA is funded from general government revenue.

The social security system employer tax applies to total earnings, while the employee share of the tax applies only to the first £420 ($622) of weekly wages. Revenue is allocated among all the insurance programs (pension, sickness, maternity, unemployment, and work injury benefits), the National Health Service, which is mostly government funded, and redundancy payments (severance benefits).

Social security tax rates are graduated according to wage level. The employee pays 2 percent on the first £56 ($83) per week and 9 percent on additional wages up to the overall ceiling. Employees over pension age (65 for men, 60 for women) do not pay the employee tax. Employers pay from 4.6 percent to 10.4 percent of wages, the rate rising with the wage level.

Coverage

All workers who earn at least £56 ($83) a week are covered. The self-employed are excluded.

Eligibility

All jobless workers who had earnings in the prior tax year of at least 50 times the minimum threshold of taxable earnings, i.e., £56 ($83) a week, are eligible for full UI benefits. Reduced benefits can be paid to those with earnings of at least twenty-five times the earnings threshold. To remain eligible, beneficiaries must register with a job exchange and be physically capable of and available for work.

Those workers who left jobs voluntarily or engaged in misconduct can be disqualified for 26 weeks. This disqualification period also applies to those who refuse a suitable job or fail to accept job training. Those who are jobless because of a labor dispute are disqualified for the duration of the dispute. After UI benefits are exhausted, a person can regain eligibility only after returning to work for at least 8 weeks. There is no work history requirement for UA eligibility.

Benefits

A flat-rate benefit of £44.65 ($66.13) is paid weekly to the jobless worker, plus another £27.55 ($40.80) for a spouse or dependent adult. Those over pension age receive higher benefits: £56.10 ($83.08) for the worker, £33.70 ($49.91) for the spouse/dependent adult, £9.80 ($14.51) for the first dependent child, and £10.95 ($16.22) for each additional dependent child. Benefits are payable, after a three-day waiting period, for up to 52 weeks. UI benefits are taxed the same as earned income.

Redundancy benefits are paid by an employer in a lump sum to employees under pension age who are dismissed after at least 104 weeks of continuous employment by the employer. The benefit equals years of service times £205 ($304) times a factor for weeks of pay per year of service. This factor is 0.5 for those ages 18 to 21, 1.0 for those 22 to 40, and 1.5 for those 41 to 64.

The social security system includes need-based UA, for which the unemployed who meet a needs test are eligible indefinitely. This benefit for those age 18 or over with no other income is £44.00 ($65.16) a week, £69.00 ($102.19) for couples.[16] Additional benefits are available for children.

Employment Services

Beneficiaries must register with a labor exchange operated by the Department of Employment. This agency maintains information on available jobs. Intensive job counseling and job search assistance are provided. Training allowances are available to persons in job training, and some travel expenses for job search may be reimbursed. UI benefits may be continued for claimants who are starting new businesses.

United States

Objectives

Before establishment of the UI system in the Social Security Act of 1935, principles were set forth by the Committee on Economic Security that have since guided the program without major change. The system was intended to compensate jobless workers for short periods of unemployment with payments proportionate to wages and not subject to any means test. Establishment of UI was left to the states, but state action was induced through a federal tax on employers that is reduced substantially if a state has a UI program in compliance with federal law. Specific provisions of eligibility and benefits were left to the states, and the states administer benefit payments and revenue collection; however, financial control over program administration was placed with the federal government to assure an adequate quality of state administration. Financing was to rely on employer taxes, and possibly on employee taxes as well, but no subsidy from general government revenue was included. Finally, it was intended that the system be designed to promote stabilization of employment. Problems of long-term unemployment were to be met by creation of public jobs rather than by long-term UI benefits, an objective that has not been pursued.

Administration

Fifty-three state employment security agencies administer UI through local offices in each of the fifty states, the District of Columbia, Puerto Rico, and the Virgin Islands. The U.S. Department of Labor oversees state compliance with federal law, provides grants to state agencies for administrative expenses, and provides research and statistical services. The U.S. Treasury Department receives state and federal unemployment tax revenue, maintains a set of trust fund accounts for the system, and reimburses state agencies for their benefit expenditures.

Financing

Benefits are financed through the Unemployment Trust Fund by payroll taxes levied by the states. These taxes are applied solely to employers in all but three states, where employees are also taxed. In 1993, state taxes averaged 2.3 percent of taxable wages and 0.9 percent of total wages in covered jobs. Tax rates are experience rated by individual firm to some degree in all states. The 1993 ceilings on taxable yearly wages ranged from $7,000 in thirteen states up to $23,200 in Alaska. Each state program has a federal trust fund account that is credited with its tax receipts.

A federal payroll tax of 0.8 percent on the first $7,000 of each covered worker's annual wages is levied on employers as authorized by the Federal Unemployment Tax Act (FUTA). The FUTA tax pays for the federal share of the permanent extended benefits (EB) program, federal and state administration of UI, and loans to states that experience insolvency in their trust fund accounts.

Coverage

Federal law indirectly compels state UI programs to cover most jobs. Nonfarm jobs are covered for employers with at least one worker in 20 or more weeks or with a quarterly payroll of at least $1,500. Farm jobs are covered for agricultural employers that have at least ten employees in 20 weeks or pay at least $20,000 in quarterly cash wages. Domestic employment is covered for employers that pay cash wages of at least $1,000 quarterly. Federal law directly requires coverage for jobs in state and local governments and most nonprofit organizations. The largest uncovered worker category is the self-employed. UI covers 98 percent of all wage and salary workers.

Eligibility

States determine UI eligibility requirements. Most states require that a worker have covered wages above a minimum level during the first four of the past five calendar quarters to be eligible. The median minimum earnings required in 1993 was $1,390. Nine states require employment by the worker for at least a minimum number of weeks (15 to 20) during the base period. In addition, thirty-four states stipulate that a substantial part of the required minimum earnings fall within one quarter as a criterion of serious attachment to the labor force.

States disqualify workers who leave jobs voluntarily, with all but six states extending the disqualification for the duration of the unemployment spell. Jobless workers are also disqualified for willful misconduct on a job (for the entire spell in fifty jurisdictions), refusal of suitable employment (for the entire spell in forty jurisdictions), a labor dispute (for its duration in fifty-two jurisdictions), fraud, or receipt of disqualifying income. This last disqualification usually results in an offset of UI benefits by some or all of the disqualifying income. Federal law requires that states reduce UI benefits for pension benefits received from a base-period employer and for social security benefits received.

Benefits

UI benefit levels and durations are set in state law. Most states peg benefits to 50 percent of the prior gross wage level, but all states set benefit caps that result in lower wage replacement for those who earn more than the average wage. Benefit maximums in 1993 ranged from $133 a week in Puerto Rico to

$468 a week in Massachusetts (for a worker with dependents). Fourteen states provide supplemental benefits for workers with dependents. All UI benefits are fully taxable as income. A waiting period of one week is applicable in forty-two states; there is no wait in the others.

The UI system was designed to compensate for job loss because of normal business cycles. Thus, regular benefit durations are limited to no more than 26 weeks in all but Massachusetts and Washington, where benefits can last for 30 weeks.

The federal-state EB program, funded 50-50 from federal and state payroll taxes, is automatically triggered in an individual state when its *insured* unemployment rate over 13 weeks exceeds 5% percent and is at least 120 percent of the rate during the same 13-week period of each of the past two years. At state option, a rate above 6 percent will trigger EB regardless of the relationship to the rates of preceding years. EB provides an additional 13 weeks of benefits. Since March 1993, states can elect to trigger EB when their *total* unemployment rate exceeds 6.5 percent and is at least 110 percent of the rate in either of the past two years; 20 weeks of benefits are available if the total rate exceeds 8.0 percent. As of July 1995, only seven states had this provision in force as an option. Only Alaska, Puerto Rico, and Rhode Island were paying EB that month.

Since UI was not designed to help displaced workers faced with long-term unemployment and with the need to make career transitions, Congress acted in 1962 to provide special help to workers dislocated by U.S. trade policies. Under the TAA program, workers who are certified as eligible may receive cash benefits and training, and firms may receive technical or financial assistance to cope with import competition. TAA cash benefits are at the same dollar level as UI benefits in the state where the recipient is paid. TAA benefits are paid only after UI benefits expire and are, thus, an extension of the regular UI program. The combined duration of TAA and UI benefits, including any EB or emergency benefits, is limited to 52 weeks (78 weeks in the case of workers engaged in approved training that lasts beyond 52 weeks). To be eligible, a worker must have been employed with a single trade-affected firm during at least 26 of the 52 weeks preceding layoff, must have received wages of at least $30 per week, and must meet the state requirements for UI eligibility.

There is no need-tested benefit integrated with UI. U.S. assistance programs apply differently to different categories of needy people, and benefits in some programs vary widely by state. The assistance program most closely related to UC is the unemployed parent component of the federal-state Aid to Families with Dependent Children (AFDC-U).[17] To qualify for AFDC-U, the unemployed parent must have a minimum work history, meet a test of unemployment in addition to a need test, and accept work or training as required by the state. Time spent in school can substitute for part of the required work history.

Employment Services

UI beneficiaries are eligible for assistance from the U.S. Employment Service, which maintains listings of available jobs. States are required to identify UI claimants most likely to have long spells of unemployment and to refer them to job search assistance services. Federally funded job training is available from a separate program for dislocated workers under the Job Training Partnership Act. UI can be received while in training only if the state approves the training course for the individual. States can allow UI claimants to start new businesses in lieu of job search.

Workers who receive TAA cash benefits must participate in job training unless exempted by the Secretary of Labor. (Those eligible under special provisions enacted with NAFTA cannot be exempted.) Cash benefits are extended for up to 26 additional weeks when training lasts beyond the normal TAA eligibility period. Special allowances of up to $800 are available to TAA beneficiaries for job search expenses and for relocation expenses.

Appendix 14.B
Major Events in the Development
of Unemployment Compensation

Appendix Table 14B.1 Major Events in the Development of Unemployment Compensation

Decade	Canada	France	Germany	Italy	Japan	United Kingdom	United States
Early 1900s		Private contributory unemployment benefit funds organized by trade unions or mutual benefit societies and subsidized by government contributions	Help for members who became unemployed provided by trade unions and voluntary communal insurance funds			Cash benefit plans for unemployed organized by trade unions and workmen's associations	
1910–1919		national UA scheme established. Benefits provided through funds created and operated locally. subsidized by government revenue		Decree issued in 1919 making UI compulsory for most manual workers		First country to legislate a national compulsory UI program with passage of the National Insurance Act of 1911	
1920–1929			Compulsory national UI program established in 1927 for all wage earners and lower-paid salaried employees			UI extended to most workers in industry and commerce in 1920	

(continued)

654

Appendix Table 14B.1 (continued)

Decade	Canada	France	Germany	Italy	Japan	United Kingdom	United States
1930–1939	Employment and Social Insurance Act passed in 1935. UI program funded by tax revenue from employers, employees, and government. Law found unconstitutional and never implemented			Decree issued in 1939 extending UI, financed through employer taxes and general government revenue, administered by the National Social Insurance Institute (INPS)		UI benefits limited following financial strain on government in the mid-1930s. Means-tested UA program initiated	UI established by the Social Security Act of 1935 as a federal-state program to provide temporary financial aid and maintain consumer spending in recessions
1940–1949	Unemployment Insurance Act of 1940 established compulsory UI program and National Employment Service to operate in conjunction. Program administered by Unemployment Insurance Commission	Social security established. Unemployment not regarded as insurable risk		The Fund for Supplemental Earnings (CIG) instituted in 1941 to guarantee part of the pay of workers and salaried staff whose pay was threatened by reduced work under certain circumstances. Fund financed through employer taxes to the INPS	Unemployment Insurance Law enacted in 1947 established first compulsory UI scheme in country	Enactment of unified system of social insurance contained in the comprehensive National Insurance and Industrial Injuries Scheme of 1946	

1950-1959	1940 UI Act repealed and replaced by Unemployment Insurance Act of 1955. Designed to make UI more effective; expanded coverage, eased qualifying conditions, increased benefit rates, lengthened duration, and increased allowable earnings	Private contributory plans nearly extinct. Legislation enacted in 1951 to improve existing programs and provide work projects for the unemployed Following a national labor-management agreement in 1958, UI scheme established to provide coverage to all firms belonging to trade associations or interoccupational organizations affiliated with the National Council of French Employers (CNPF)	Federal Institution for Placement and Unemployment Insurance established in 1952 to administer UI			Temporary Unemployment Compensation program enacted in 1958 providing one-half of regular benefit entitlement up to 13 weeks, financed through federal loans to states.

(continued)

Appendix Table 14B.1 (continued)

Decade	Canada	France	Germany	Italy	Japan	United Kingdom	United States
1960-1969		UI made compulsory in 1967, extending to all workers in industrial and commercial sectors. Administered by joint labor-management bodies at the national and regional levels (the UNEDIC and the ASSEDIC), scheme was private contributory insurance program receiving no government funds. Public means-tested UA extended to cover unemployed in all regions	1927 Act replaced by Employment Promotion Act (AFG) in 1969, providing UI benefits financed by earnings-based payroll taxes and means-tested UA for those ineligible for UI or who have exhausted UI, financed by government funds. Act provides job training and other benefits. Complemented by the Federal Social Assistance Act to aid those not entitled to UI or UA	Special UI established in 1968 to aid those made redundant by sectoral or local economic cirses. Additive to basic UI, financed with government funds, and administered by INPS		UA merged into a general supplementary benefit system in 1966. Earnings Related Supplement (ERS) also introduced, based on prior-year earnings; supplemented flat-rate UI benefits for up to 6 months	Temporary Extended Unemployment Compensation passed in 1961, providing one-half of regular benefit up to 13 weeks, financed by a temporary increase in FUTA tax TAA authorized to compensate workers displaced by import competition

1970-1979	Unemployment Insurance Act of 1971 enacted. Intended to make UI compatible with other social security programs; included universal coverage, eased eligibility, and offered new benefits in case of sickness, maternity, and retirement. Distinguished between claimants with major labor force attachment eligible for regular benefits and those with minor attachment eligible for special benefits (sickness, maternity, job training)	Government established unified UI system in 1979, financed by earnings-based taxes and government funds	As of 1977, an unemployed person who cannot find a job comparable to the one from which terminated must accept another job after 4 months if pay is at least 80% of former wage	New rules established for basic benefits paid by the Earnings Supplemental Fund	Old law replaced by employment insurance system in 1975. Program designed to provide income security for unemployed persons and contribute to a national workforce policy. Emphasizes continuous skill development for all workers	UC restructured in 1975. New scheme based on earnings-related payroll tax paid by both employers and employees, but benefit still a flat-rate award	Permanent extended benefits program established in 1970, providing up to 13 weeks of benefits, financed equally by FUTA tax and state taxes. Emergency Unemployment Compensation Act in 1971 temporarily extended benefits for up to an additional 13 weeks, financed by FUTA tax. Temporary supplemental benefits passed in 1974 provided up to 26 weeks of benefits, financed through FUTA tax and federal general funds. TAA eligibility rules eased and benefits liberalized in 1974

(continued)

Appendix Table 14B.1 (continued)

Decade	Canada	France	Germany	Italy	Japan	United Kingdom	United States
1980-1989		Dual UI-UA system restored in 1984 following failure of unified scheme; consists of UI, financed by payroll taxes on employees and employers and administered jointly by UNEDIC-ASSEDIC, and a revamped UA "solidarity" scheme, financed by general government funds				ERS abolished in 1982, leaving only basic flat-rate benefit and supplementary benefit system	Eligibility for EB and TAA tightened in 1981 Federal Supplementary Compensation passed in 1982, extended benefits temporarily, durations varying by state unemployment. Benefits financed by federal general funds UI benefits made fully subject to income tax in 1986. TAA claimants required by 1988 act to undergo job retraining unless waived

1990-1993	Bill C-21 passed in 1990. Intended to increase private-sector training and make UI more responsive to needs of jobless; reduced the maximum benefit period in most regions, extended coverage to workers over 65, provided for a multi-tier special benefit structure, and encouraged greater use of program funds for experiments. Government no longer contributes general funds to UI	Benefits and financing restructured; disqualification period for voluntary quits lengthened	UC system established temporarily for former GDR; consisted of flat-rate benefit plus redundancy allowance UI payroll tax rate raised, benefit duration increased	1991 law imposed new restrictions on special UI benefits to avoid overuse by employers with surplus workers	UI payroll tax rate increased for employers, reduced for employees	Disqualification period lengthened for those jobless voluntarily or due to misconduct	Temporary Emergency Unemployment Compensation (EUC) passed in 1991 to provide additional benefits to those who exhausted UI and EB, financed by FUTA taxes More liberal trigger for EB permitted at state option in 1992 law Job search assistance required by 1992 law for UC claimants likely to be long-term unemployed

Appendix 14.C
Backup Tables for Charts

Table 14C.1 Public Expenditures for UC Programs in the G-7 Nations, Fiscal Years Beginning in 1970-1993

Nation	\	\	\	\	\	Fiscal year beginning in	\	\	\	\	\	\
	1970	1975	1980	1985	1986	1987	1988	1989	1990	1991	1992	1993
Public expenditures for UC as percent of GDP												
Canada	1.67	2.76	2.32	1.87	1.86	1.64	1.57	1.57	1.91	2.28	2.25	2.00
France	0.32	0.78	1.46	1.20	1.24	1.31	1.31	1.27	1.31	1.47	1.61	NA
Germany[a]	0.40	1.49	1.12	1.41	1.31	1.34	1.34	1.20	1.09	1.51	1.51	2.02
Italy	0.18	0.45	0.47	0.75	0.57	0.49	0.40	NA	0.55	0.60	0.64	NA
Japan	0.27	0.48	0.40	NA	NA	0.40	0.43	0.34	0.22	0.23	0.26	NA
United Kingdom	0.47	0.70	0.94	2.01	1.93	1.56	1.10	0.84	0.95	1.38	1.28	1.23
United States	0.42	1.18	0.62	0.61	0.56	0.51	0.44	0.47	0.49	0.68	0.61	0.45
Public expenditures for UC as percentage of GDP per percentage point of unemployment												
Canada	0.29	0.40	0.31	0.17	0.20	0.19	0.20	0.21	0.24	0.22	0.20	0.18
France	0.13	0.19	0.23	0.12	0.12	0.12	0.13	0.13	0.14	0.15	0.15	NA
Germany[a]	0.80	0.44	0.40	0.20	0.20	0.21	0.21	0.21	0.22	0.34	0.32	0.35
Italy	0.06	0.13	0.11	0.12	0.08	0.06	0.05	NA	0.08	0.09	0.09	NA
Japan	0.22	0.25	0.20	NA	NA	0.14	0.17	0.15	0.10	0.11	0.12	NA
United Kingdom	0.15	0.15	0.13	0.18	0.17	0.15	0.13	0.12	0.14	0.16	0.13	0.12
United States	0.09	0.14	0.09	0.08	0.08	0.08	0.08	0.09	0.09	0.10	0.08	0.07

SOURCE: OECD (1994). The unemployment rates used to adjust the OECD data are from the *Economic Report of the President*, February 1994.

NOTE: NA means not available.

a. Data before 1991 for Germany exclude the eastern states. For 1991 and later, data are for the unified Germany.

662

Table 14C.2 Unemployment Rates Used to Adjust Statistics in Appendix Table 14C.1

Year	Canada	France	Germany	Italy	Japan	U.K.	U.S.
			Unemployment rates for				
1970	5.7	2.5	0.5	3.2	1.2	3.1	4.9
1971	6.2	2.8	0.6	3.3	1.3	3.9	5.9
1972	6.2	2.9	0.7	3.8	1.4	4.2	5.6
1973	5.5	2.8	0.7	3.7	1.3	3.2	4.9
1974	5.3	2.9	1.6	3.1	1.4	3.1	5.6
1975	6.9	4.2	3.4	3.4	1.9	4.6	8.5
1976	7.1	4.6	3.4	3.9	2.0	5.9	7.7
1977	8.1	5.2	3.4	4.1	2.0	6.4	7.1
1978	8.3	5.4	3.3	4.1	2.3	6.3	6.1
1979	7.4	6.1	2.9	4.4	2.1	5.4	5.8
1980	7.5	6.5	2.8	4.4	2.0	7.0	7.1
1981	7.5	7.6	4.0	4.9	2.2	10.5	7.6
1982	11.0	8.3	5.6	5.4	2.4	11.3	9.7
1983	11.8	8.6	6.9	5.9	2.7	11.8	9.6
1984	11.2	10.0	7.1	5.9	2.8	11.8	7.5
1985	10.5	10.5	7.2	6.0	2.6	11.2	7.2
1986	9.5	10.6	6.6	7.5	2.8	11.2	7.0
1987	8.8	10.8	6.3	7.9	2.9	10.3	6.2
1988	7.8	10.3	6.3	7.9	2.5	8.6	5.5
1989	7.5	9.6	5.7	7.8	2.3	7.3	5.3
1990	8.1	9.1	5.0	7.0	2.1	6.9	5.5
1991	10.3	9.6	4.4	6.9	2.1	8.8	6.7
1992	11.3	10.4	4.7	7.3	2.2	10.0	7.4
1993	11.2	11.2[a]	5.8[a]	10.3[a]	2.4[a]	10.4	6.8

SOURCE: *Economic Report of the President*, February 1994.
a. Based on data for first three quarters.

NOTES

This is an update of an earlier report (CRS Report for Congress No. 92-622-EPW) originally prepared at the request of the Senate Committee on Finance and the House Committee on Ways and Means. It was first published as a Joint Committee Print (S. Prt. 102-88, WMCP 102-41) in April 1992. With the permission of the Committees, the report was made available for general congressional use.

1. Abbreviations of currency names used in this chapter are as follows: £-British pounds; $C-Canadian dollars: F-French francs; DM-German marks; L-Italian lira; Y-Japanese yen; K-Swedish kronor; $-U.S. dollars.

2. These exchange rates were as follows: 1 British pound = $1.481; 1 Canada dollar = $-.779; 1 French franc - $0.167; 1 German mark = $0.575; 1 Italian lira = $0.000619; 1 Japanese yen = $0.00944; 1 Swedish kronor = $0.121. In some charts, the following abbreviations are used: Canada = CAN; France-FRA; Germany-GER; Italy-ITA; Japan-JPN; United Kingdom-GBR; United States-USA; Massachusetts-MA; Mississippi-MS.

3. See appendix 14.B for a chronological listing of major developments in each G-7 country.

4. The U.S. system operates in each of the fifty states plus the District of Columbia, Puerto Rico, and the Virgin Islands.

5. This discussion refers to the nominal tax rates applied to employee paychecks. The actual incidence of employer and employee taxes is not addressed. Many economists believe that payroll taxes on employers ultimately are borne by employees in the form of lower wages.

6. The share of the U.K. program paid from employee taxes could not be determined.

7. The international literature classifies the United States as a nation without a UA program. However, in 1990 federal legislation mandated that all state welfare systems provide Aid to Families with Dependent Children (AFDC) to families with an unemployed parent. In the states affected by this mandate, such aid may be denied for families that have received benefits in at least 6 of the preceding 12 months. The program is administered by welfare agencies and is financed by state funds and federal formula matching grants.

8. No comparable figures were obtained for Japan.

9. A few state programs in the United States use higher wage replacement rates at lower wage levels in computing benefits.

10. The program in Puerto Rico has a lower UI benefit maximum than does any state program.

11. The insured unemployment rate is the proportion of workers claiming UI benefits of total workers covered by UI.

12. The total unemployment rate is the proportion of the total civilian labor force that is unemployed and seeking work.

13. In 1993, South Africa was still under its apartheid system, which excluded lower-paid black workers from UI coverage.

14. The taxable wage ceiling is DM63,600 ($36,570) in the former GDR.

15. It should be noted that wage figures used by the Japanese program for benefit computation exclude overtime pay and bonuses, which together constitute nearly one-third of total cash compensation in Japan.

16. The benefit for individuals ages 18-24 with no children is £34.80 ($51.54).

17. In March 1995, the House of Representatives passed legislation to repeal AFDC and provide grants to states for welfare programs of their own design. Similar legislation was under consideration by the Senate for action during the 104th Congress.

References

Blaustein, Saul J., and Isabel Craig. 1977. *An International Review of Unemployment Insurance Schemes.* Kalamazoo, MI: W.E. Upjohn Institute.

Brodsky, Melvin M. 1994. "Labor Market Flexibility: A Changing International Perspective," *Monthly labor Review (November):* 53–60.

Burtless, Gary. 1984. "Jobless Pay and High European Unemployment." In *Barriers to European Growth: a Transatlantic View,* Robert Z. Lawrence and Charles L. Schultze, eds. Washington, DC: Brookings Institution.

Calcoen, Francis, Louis Eeckhoudt, and Dominique Greiner. 1988. *Indemnization du chômage: une comparaison internationale.* Commissariat Général du Plan. Paris: La Documentation Française.

Commercial Laws of the World: Mexico Labor Laws. Part II. 1988. Ormond Beach, FL: Foreign Tax Law Publishers, December.

De Luca, Loretta, and Michele Bruni. 1993. *Unemployment and Labour Market Flexibility: Italy.* Geneva: International Labour Office.

Dingledine, Gary. 1981. "A Chronology of Response: the Evolution of Unemployment insurance from 1940 to 1980." Prepared for Employment and Immigration Canada, Ottawa, Minister of Supply and Services Canada, Ottawa.

Disney, R. 1981. "Unemployment Insurance in Britain." In *The Economics of Unemployment in Britain,* John Creedy, ed. London: Butterworth.

García de Blas, Antonio. "Unemployment Benefits in Spain and other European OECD countries. *International Labour Review* 124, 2 (March-April: 147-161.

Gustafsson, B.A., and N.A. Klevmarken, eds. 1989. *The Political Economy of Social Security.* Amsterdan: North-Holland.

International Labour Office. 1976. *Social Security for the Unemployed.* Geneva: ILO.

_____. 1987. *Employment Promotion and Social Security.* Report IV (1), Ch. III. International Labour Conference, 73rd session. Geneva.

"International Unemployment Benefits in 12 Countries." 1982. *European Industrial Relations Review* 105 (October): 12-19.

Kane, Matt, and Paula Duggan. 1991. *Dislocated Workers: Coping with Competition and Conversion.* Northeast Midwest Institute.

Kerschen, Nicole, and Francis Kessler. 1990. "Unemployment Benefit in France and the Federal Republic of Germany: Social Protection or Employment Market Regulation? Some Legal Aspects," *International Social Security Review* 43, 3: 270-286.

Library of Parliament [Canada]. Research Branch. 1990. *Bill C-21: Amendments to the Unemployment Insurance Act and the empLoyment and Immigration Department and Commission Act.* Legislative summary by Jean–Daniel Bélanger and Kevin B. Kerr. Ottawa.

Moorthy, Vivek. 1989-1990. "Unemployment in Canada and the United States: the Role of Unemployment Insurance Benefits," *Federal Reserve Bank of New York Quarterly Review* (Winter): 48-61.

Muñoz, Carlos Rosado. "Report from Mexico." *Benefits and Compensation International*, January/February, p. 2-10.

Organization for Economic Cooperation and Development. 1979. *Unemployment Compensation and Related Employment Policy Measures: General Report and Country Studies.* Paris: OECD.

_____. 1984. *High Unemployment: A Challenge for Income Support Policies.* Paris: OECD.

_____. 1988. *Employment Outlook: September 1988.* Paros: OECD.

_____. 1989. *Employment Outlook: July 1989.* Paris: OECD.

_____. 1991. *Employment Outlook: July 1991.* Paris: OECD.

_____. 1993. *The Public Employment Service in Japan, Norway, Spain and the United Kingdom.* Paris: OECD.

_____. 1994. *Employment Outlook: July 1994.* Paris: OECD.

Organization of American States. General Secretariat. 1970. "A Statement of the Laws of Mexico in Matters Affecting Business."

Parliament of the Commonwealth of Australia. Legislative Research Service. 1986. "Commonwealth Social Security Cash Benefits since Federation: a Chronology of Major Events to September 1986." Basic Paper No. 1, 1986-87, Department of the Parliamentary Library

Reubens, Beatrice G. 1989. "Unemployment Insurance in the United States and Europe, 1973-83," *Monthly Labor Review* 112 (April): 22-31.

Shreve, David L., and Scott A. Liddell. 1991. "Made in Japan: Employment Insurance." *State Legislatures* 17 (August): 27-29.

Unemployment Insurance: Regular Benefits. 1991. Canada, Employment and Immigration.

U.S. Department of Health and Human Services. 1994. "Social Security Programs Throughout the World—1993." Research report 63, SSA publication No. 13-11805, Social Security Administration, Office of International Policy, May..

U.S. Library of Congress. 1994a. "How the Unemployment Compensation System Works." Congressional Research Service Report for Congress No. 94-11 EPW, by James R. Storey. Washington.

————. 1994b. "Trade Adjustment Assistance: the Program for Workers." Congressional Research Service Report for Congress No. 94-801 EPW, by James R. Storey.

————. 1994c. "Unemployment Compensation: a History of Extended Benefits for the Long-Term Unemployed." Congressional Research Service Report for Congress No. 94-458 EPW, by James R. Storey and Gene Falk.

Wandner, Stephen A., and Jon C. Messenger. 1990. "U.S. Perspective on the Potential Use of Self-Employment Programs." Prepared for Association of Public Policy Analysis and Management, 12th Annual Research Conference, San Francisco, October 20.

CHAPTER 15

Summing Up
Achievements, Problems and Prospects

Christopher J. O'Leary
W.E. Upjohn Institute for Employment Research
Stephen A. Wandner
Urban Institute and UI Service, U.S. Department of Labor

The unemployment insurance (UI) program began modestly. Initial coverage and eligibility provisions reflected a depression-era concern about the ability to finance new unemployment benefits. Based on federal law, coverage was originally restricted to firms having eight or more employees, each working at least 20 weeks in a year. No agricultural, household, nonprofit, or government employees were covered.

The benefit replacement rate most state laws set—50 percent up to a maximum weekly benefit amount of $15—was quite generous. However, benefits were usually not payable until after a 3-or-4-week waiting period had elapsed, and maximum benefit durations ranged between 12 and 20 weeks, being 16 weeks in most states. Payment was only made to involuntarily unemployed persons who were able and available for work. Eligibility and disqualification rules were tight. Unemployed workers who quit their previous job, refused suitable work, or were discharged for misconduct were generally disqualified for the duration of their unemployment (Blaustein 1993, pp. 159-169).

As World War II began, unemployment plummeted and the outlook for the UI program became more optimistic. The program entered a period of expansion, which continued into the 1960s and 1970s. It was felt that more benefits via higher benefit maximums, longer benefit durations, and decreased waiting periods could be financed. States also expanded coverage, while at the same time reducing taxes and increasing the use of experience rating.

Today, there is powerful pressure to reduce the size of government and to decrease or eliminate some government programs, especially domestic ones. Despite this situation, the UI program today is respected as a fundamental part of the foundation for a competitive labor market. There are political pressures to transfer at least some of the federal responsibilities under the program to the states. The main target of *devolution* advocates is the administrative funding of the program. Nonetheless, it appears likely that UI will survive as a model federal-state program, even if there is a tilt toward more state control.

Benefit liberality reached its high point in the 1970s; since then, the generosity of both the regular and extended benefit programs has been in decline. Both state and federal UI policy has become increasingly restrictive. The permanent Extended Benefit program has been especially affected.

Federal UI policy is highly cyclical. In periods of prosperity, the program has largely been ignored; during recessions, pressures build to extend benefit durations. Because of the prior weakening of the permanent Extended Benefit program, during the past two recessions temporary emergency programs have been the primary vehicle for extending durations. These issues are examined in the following section of this chapter.

The chapter then presents summary comments on UI taxation. The discussion of benefit financing reviews trends in financing, proposals to increase the taxable wage base, and experience rating in relation to temporary and permanent layoffs. Administrative funding is considered in terms of distributional issues between states and the adequacy of annual federal budget appropriations.

Although ideas for reforms have come from many sources, there has been no comprehensive revision of the UI program since the enactment of the Unemployment Compensation Amendments of 1976. Two advisory bodies have been established by Congress to review the UI program and to make policy recommendations: the National Commission on Unemployment Compensation in 1976 and the Advisory Council on Unemployment Compensation in 1991. The fourth section of this concluding chapter reviews the recommendations of these two bodies, followed by a discussion of the important concept of preserving the insurance principle in section five.

During the past decade, various innovative ideas to change the UI system have been proposed and investigated. The integration of the UI system into a broader reemployment system has also begun as part of the response to the growth in permanent job loss and worker dislocation. Ideas for new approaches to the UI program, particularly for reemploying UI recipients, have emerged from a series of state and federal field experiments in UI conducted over the past ten years. Some of the findings from these experiments have resulted in federal legislation that improves the reemployment incentives in UI. This experience is discussed, along with the response of the UI system to new technologies for administration of benefits and the system's potential to adjust to fundamental changes in the labor force behavior of American workers. The concluding section considers the likely future of the UI program.

Benefit Trends in the Unemployment Insurance System

The total benefits paid by the UI system can be expressed as the product of the number of benefit recipients, the average benefit level, and the average duration of benefits. The information needed to compute the total can be gathered as the answers to three simple questions: who, how much, and how long? More specifically:

Who?	Persons with recent labor market experience unemployed through no fault of their own
How much?	Partial wage replacement
How long?	Temporary wage replacement

Trends in benefit payments from the system depend on answers to one or more of these and related questions. This is the approach of our brief review of coverage and eligibility in this section.

Who Receives Benefits? Coverage, Eligibility, and Disqualifications

Coverage under UI is generally defined by the industry or other characteristics of the employer. UI coverage has gradually expanded over the past sixty years as it became clear that covering all experienced wage and salary workers was feasible. The 1976 amendments left experienced wage and salary workers uncovered in only a very few industries and types of firms.

Given the nature of UI as an insurance system, the reason for job separation is crucial to determining eligibility, and thus how many of the UI-covered ultimately receive benefits. The UI program generally only compensates experienced wage and salary workers who have lost their jobs through no fault of their own.

In the Current Population Survey (CPS), the household survey from which total employment and unemployment are estimated, one may enter unemployment for any one of four reasons. One may have *lost a job*, *left a job*, be a *new entrant to the labor force*, or be a *reentrant* returning to the labor force after some hiatus. Under the various current state laws, as shown in table 15.1, UI only has the potential to compensate 40 to 60 percent of all the unemployed who are job losers. Since UI typically provides only 26 weeks of benefits, its true potential is the even smaller fraction of job losers who are unemployed up to 26 weeks. A sizable proportion of this population actually receives UI benefits.

The relationship between the number of job losers and the number of workers claiming UI—the average weekly insured unemployment (AWIU)—in the regular UI program has fluctuated over time. Throughout the 1970s, the number of regular program UI claimants approximated the number of job losers. Since the early 1980s that fraction has been at a much lower level, although there are signs of rebound since 1984. Actual benefit receipt reflects demographic and economic factors as well as state UI laws. Chapters 2, 3 and 4 of this book reviewed the issues of coverage and of initial and continuing eligibility that influence who collects UI benefits.

Coverage

As noted, since the 1976 amendments, most wage and salary workers are in jobs covered by UI. Agricultural and household workers are

Table 15.1 Job Losers and Other Unemployed Workers, by Reason for Unemployment, 1967-1994

Calendar year	Job losers Level (thousands)	Job losers Percent of total	Job leavers Level (thousands)	Job leavers Percent of total	Reentrants Level (thousands)	Reentrants Percent of total	New entrants Level (thousands)	New entrants Percent of total	Total unemployment (thousands)
1967	1,229	41.3	438	14.7	945	31.8	396	13.3	2,975
1968	1,070	38.0	431	15.3	909	32.3	407	14.4	2,817
1969	1,017	35.9	436	15.4	965	34.1	413	14.6	2,832
1970	1,811	44.2	550	13.4	1,228	30.0	5.4	12.3	4,093
1971	2,323	46.3	590	11.8	1,472	29.3	630	12.6	5,016
1972	2,108	43.2	641	13.1	1,456	29.8	677	13.9	4,882
1973	1,694	38.8	683	15.6	1,340	30.7	649	14.9	4,365
1974	2,242	43.5	768	14.9	1,463	28.4	681	13.2	5,156
1975	4,386	55.3	827	10.4	1,892	23.9	623	10.4	7,929
1976	3,679	49.7	903	12.2	1,928	26.0	895	12.1	7,406
1977	3,166	45.3	909	13.0	1,963	28.1	953	13.6	6,991
1978	2,585	41.7	874	14.1	1,857	29.9	885	14.3	6,202
1979	2,635	42.9	880	14.3	1,806	29.4	817	13.3	6,137
1980	3,947	51.7	891	11.7	1,927	25.2	872	11.4	7,637
1981	4,267	51.6	923	11.2	2,102	25.4	981	11.9	8,273
1982	6,268	58.7	840	7.9	2,384	22.3	1,185	11.1	10,678
1983	6,258	58.4	830	7.7	2,412	22.5	1,216	11.3	10,717
1984	4,421	51.8	823	9.6	2,184	25.6	1,110	13.0	8,539
1985	4,139	49.8	877	10.6	2,256	27.1	1,039	12.5	8,312

(continued)

674

Table 15.1 (continued)

Calendar year	Job losers Level (thousands)	Job losers Percent of total	Job leavers Level (thousands)	Job leavers Percent of total	Reentrants Level (thousands)	Reentrants Percent of total	New entrants Level (thousands)	New entrants Percent of total	Total unemployment (thousands)
1986	4,033	49.0	1,015	12.3	2,160	26.2	1,029	12.5	8,237
1987	3,566	48.0	965	13.0	1,974	26.6	920	12.4	7,425
1988	3,092	46.1	983	14.7	1,809	27.0	816	12.2	6,701
1989	2,983	45.7	1,024	15.7	1,843	28.2	677	10.4	6,528
1990	3,322	48.3	1,014	14.8	1,883	27.4	654	9.5	6,874
1991	4,608	54.7	979	11.6	2,087	24.8	753	8.9	8,426
1992	5,291	56.4	975	10.4	2,228	23.7	890	9.5	9,384
1993	4,769	54.6	946	10.8	2,145	24.6	874	10.0	8,734
1994	3,815	47.7	791	9.9	2,786	34.8	604	7.6	7,996
1967–1994 average		49.5		11.9		26.9		11.7	

the main groups outside UI coverage. A much larger group that could be covered consists of the self-employed. Reducing or eliminating requirements for substantial work experience to embrace new labor force entrants and reentrants could also greatly increase the number of workers covered by UI, although coverage of these last two groups is hard to justify on insurance grounds.

Self-employment has grown rapidly in the United States. According to the U.S. Small Business Administration, the number of self-employed workers in the United States rose from 5.99 million individuals in 1981 to 6.46 million in 1985. In 1985, 9.1 percent of all nonagricultural workers were engaged in self-employment (U.S. Small Business Administration 1989). This sharp growth has removed an increasing portion of the U.S. labor force from potential UI coverage. There are considerable conceptual and practical barriers to covering the self-employed within the current UI framework. These include difficulties in distinguishing periods of employment from periods of unemployment, determining the level of wages and salaries during periods of employment, and ascertaining reasons for separation.

Making coverage available to workers without recent labor market experience would allow some new entrants and reentrants to be beneficiaries under the UI program. Such coverage opens up another series of problems. First, UI in the United States is an insurance program that provides protection against the risk of involuntary unemployment. Covering those with no recent labor market experience would violate the insurance principle by allowing benefits to be paid to those who choose to leave the status of nonemployment for that of unemployment. This would make the UI program a form of unemployment compensation or unemployment assistance that exists in some other industrial countries. Second, there is the issue of setting the level and duration of benefits. Clearly there would be no wage or employment history on which to base benefits; they would have to be uniform or be based on need.

Covering new entrants and reentrants to the labor force would result in UI becoming a dual system. Benefits for experienced workers would be based on labor market experience—an insurance principle—while benefits for everyone else would be based on need—a welfare principle. Both parts would have to be administered, simultaneously and side-by-side. Other developed industrial nations have shown little enthusiasm for such coverage.

Eligibility and Disqualification

Over the past five decades, states have gradually tightened UI eligibility criteria. This tightening has involved both initial eligibility and continuing eligibility for UI benefits. To retain the insurance character of UI, states have tended to exclude most claimants who voluntarily leave a job from initial UI eligibility. Over the years, the states have wrestled with whether to make these unemployed workers eligible after some fixed, limited period of time or to disqualify them for the entire period of their unemployment. The logic of a limited disqualification is that, while an unemployed worker may have originally left a job voluntarily, after a certain period of time the unemployment effectively becomes involuntary, as a result of labor market conditions and not because of the personal choice to quit the prior job. At first, most states disqualified claimants for the whole benefit year. As can be seen in table 15.2, by 1952, most states had adopted limited-duration disqualifications. The pendulum has swung back sharply since 1970.

Table 15.2 Number of States with Disqualifications for the Duration of Unemployment, by Reason for Disqualification

	Voluntary leaving	Discharge for misconduct	Refusal of suitable work
1952	12	6	13
1960	18	11	15
1970	27	25	23
1980	43	33	30
1990	50	42	41
1995	50	41	41

SOURCE: U.S. Department of Labor (various years, 1952-1995).

A trend toward tightening eligibility was completed by 1990. While from the 1940s through much of the 1960s the UI program served both job losers and, with a delay, job leavers, the tide then turned. Today, nearly all states serve job losers only. As can be seen from table 15.1, the result has been a cut in the portion of unemployed workers who could potentially receive UI from about three-fifths to about one-half. It does not seem likely that the current state restrictions on eligibility for voluntarily leaving a job—or for other reasons, such as discharge for misconduct or refusal of suitable work—will change substantially in the near future.

How Long Are Benefits Provided?

The duration of benefits is related to two different policy consider-ations: the maximum potential duration of benefits under the regular program and the availability and potential duration of extended bene-fits. For the first two decades of the UI program, there were no extended benefit programs. The question to be answered was the fol-lowing: How long a period of temporary unemployment should be compensated?

In 1958, Congress began a lengthy, fitful debate over the issue of long-term unemployment compensation. The discussion concerned whether there was a federal responsibility to deal with unemployment that states decided endured beyond the "temporary" period they could afford to insure, and whether this should be addressed from the stand-point of the affected individual or of whole geographic areas.

Regular Unemployment Insurance Duration

The appropriate maximum potential duration of benefits under the regular UI program seems to have been settled by consensus. A maxi-mum potential duration of 26 weeks of regular benefits is now the norm. Only two states, Washington and Massachusetts, offer a different maximum duration of 30 weeks.

At the inception of the federal-state UI program, there was a lack of uniformity among states on the maximum potential duration of bene-fits. Because of early actuarial studies that expected far greater demands on the UI system than in fact occurred, six months of benefits seemed financially out of reach. In 1940, with all state UI programs operational, the most popular maximum potential duration of benefits was 16 weeks. As seen in table 15.3, twenty-seven states offered up to 16 weeks, fourteen had shorter potential durations, and nine had longer potential durations: only two states ventured to the current norm of 26 weeks.

Table 15.3 Maximum Duration of the Regular Unemployment Insurance Program (in weeks)

	12-15	16	17-19	20	21-25	26	27-39
1940	14	27	4	3	0	2	0
1945	2	12	4	20	7	5	0
1950	7	4	2	22	9	13	0
1955	0	3	1	10	9	27	1
1960	0	0	0	2	7	33	9
1965	1	0	0	0	2	40	9
1970	1	0	0	0	2	41	10
1975	0	0	0	1	0	42	9
1980	0	0	0	0	0	42	9
1985	0	0	0	1	0	48	3
1990	0	0	0	1	0	50	2
1995	0	0	0	0	0	51	2

SOURCE: U.S. Department of Labor, *Significant Provisions of Unemployment Laws*, various issues, 1940-1995.

State attitudes about the maximum potential duration of UI changed rapidly after World War II. The war years had been a period of low unemployment, and an expected postwar recession never materialized. As a result, maximum durations expanded rapidly. In the late 1940s, a large plurality of states selected 20 weeks as their maximum. In the 1950s, however, a consensus began to emerge that 26 weeks was the right figure for the UI program. By 1960, thirty-three states had legislated 26-week maximums, and by 1980, forty-two. Interestingly, between 1960 and 1980 about nine states flirted with longer (27- to-39-week) durations. Since 1990, seven of them have dropped back to the consensus 26-week limit.

Today, a maximum of six months of regular UI benefits is viewed as standard. It is the base from which extended benefits have been considered and implemented. The 26-week maximum duration is likely to continue to be a fixed feature for the near future of the regular UI program. The determination of states not to pay more than 26 weeks of benefits pointed to the need for extended support during a period of high unemployment. When the permanent Extended Benefit program was created in 1970, it took for granted the emerging norm of 26 weeks of regular UI benefits and built an extension upon that base.

Extended Duration of Unemployment Insurance Benefits

Debate on extended UI benefits centers on two main issues. The first has been a concern since the 1950s: How to deal with long-term cyclical unemployment? The other issue dates mainly from the early 1980s and concerns long-term unemployment due to structural change rather than to fluctuations in the business cycle.

Despite concerns about the importance of long-term cyclical unemployment and the problem of workers who are permanently separated from their previous employment, most unemployed persons are only temporarily disconnected from their jobs. As a result, the UI program mainly provides short-term income support to workers who return to the same or similar jobs. In fact, since 1971, the average duration for an insured spell of unemployment has varied between a low of 5.4 weeks in 1974 and a high of 8.1 weeks in 1993. The duration per spell of unemployment remained at a high level of 7.9 weeks in 1994, despite the improved economy. Nonetheless, only 27- 40 percent of regular program beneficiaries exhausted their entitlement to UI benefits in each of the past twenty-five years.

The policy history of extended UI benefits reflects the view of the federal government that most recessions are national in scope and require a federal policy response. The programs also reflect the political reaction of Congress to the needs of constituents when recessions increase both the numbers of job losers and their durations of unemployment. High rates of regular benefit exhaustion have frequently prompted a congressional response.

As discussed in chapter 6, long-term unemployment during recessionary periods has generated a congressional response in the form of both the permanent Extended Benefit (EB) program and a series of temporary (generally third-tier) emergency programs. The first temporary emergency program was enacted during the 1958 recession. The permanent EB program, enacted in 1970, was designed to eliminate the need for such ad hoc congressional responses to each recession. That intent has not been realized. Regardless of the strength of the permanent EB program, since its enactment, Congress has felt a need to intervene with additional programs in each recession.

Table 15.4 Extended Benefits and Emergency Program Benefits as a Percentage of Regular Program Benefits

Payment period		Extended benefits as a percentage of regular benefits	Emergency benefits as a percentage of regular benefits
Recession	Examined		
1974-1975	1974-1977	17.7	14.9
1980-1982	1980-1985	7.4	9.9
1990-1991	1990-1994	0.5	24.9

SOURCE: U.S. Department of Labor, UI Database.

Table 15.4 summarizes the relative importance of the permanent and temporary extended benefit programs over the past two-and-a-half decades by listing the percentage of regular benefits paid by each during recession periods. The table shows that the permanent EB program as originally enacted was a true second-tier program. During the 1974-1975 recession, EB payments exceeded the temporary Federal Supplemental Benefits despite the high level of payments by this third-tier program. EB payments declined in the early 1980s after the legislative tightening of the program in 1981. Finally, in the most recent recession, EB payments became negligible, and Emergency Unemployment Compensation bore the full weight of providing benefits for regular program exhaustees.

How Much Is Paid in Weekly Benefits?

A central standard of UI since program inception has been replacement of 50 percent of lost wages and salaries for the great majority of claimants. Most state UI formulas do replace about half of lost wages and salaries up to a maximum benefit. However, despite fifty years of exhortation and unsuccessful federal legislative efforts, the goal of replacing half of prior wages for the great majority of UI recipients has not been approached. The main impediment is usually the fixed state maximum benefit level, which constrains the replacement rate for high-wage individuals (see Haber and Murray 1966, pp. 441-444; O'Leary 1996).

In general, during the past half century, the rule advocated to achieve the goal of 50 percent wage replacement for most workers has been to set the maximum benefit amount at two-thirds of the average weekly wage in the state. While nine states had provisions in 1996 to set the maximum weekly benefit amount at or above two-thirds of the state average weekly wage (see table 5.2 in chapter 5), as table 15.5 shows, in 1993, on the basis of aggregate average data, only one state had a maximum weekly benefit that high. In most states, in fact, the maximum was less than 50 percent of their average weekly wage.

Table 15.5 Maximum Weekly Benefit Amount as a Percentage of the Average Weekly Wage, Calendar Year 1993

	Number of states
Less than 40%	8
40 - 49%	23
50 - 59%	15
60 - 65%	6
66 2/3% or more	1

SOURCE: U.S. Department of Labor, UI Database.

As a result, the U.S. gross replacement rate—the average weekly benefit amount divided by the average weekly wage— has been considerably below the targeted 50 percent. Throughout the post-World War II period, UI benefits have generally replaced about one third of lost income. As shown in table 5.1, since 1947 the gross replacement rate has only varied between 0.32 and 0.37.

Individual state replacement rates reflect specific legislative provisions, and the national replacement rate masks big differences between states. At the high end, Hawaii replaces 51 percent, and Kansas and Rhode Island replace 44 percent. At the low end, California and Alaska replace 28 percent.

The Gap Between Insured and Total Unemployment

Since the early 1980s, there has been growing interest in the proportion of unemployed workers who receive UI benefits. The U.S. Department of Labor has funded four studies to better understand this issue (see Burtless and Saks 1984; Corson and Nicholson 1988; Vroman 1991). This research has provided insight into the reasons for the *gap* between total unemployment, as measured by the CPS, and insured unemployment. Another formulation of this concept is the *recipiency rate,* which is the proportion of all unemployed who receive UI benefits.

As discussed in chapter 2, the gap has also become an important policy issue because of the belief that closing much of it is within the control of state and federal governments. However, research funded by the Department of Labor has shown that much of the gap is due to factors not directly influenced by policy action. The causal factors identified by research include the changing industrial mix of employment in the United States and the way that unemployment is measured.

The gap has been a target of critics who argue that the UI system is inadequate, both with respect to the regular UI program at all times and to extended benefit programs during recessionary periods. The size of the gap is related to nearly all of the benefit payment provisions of the program. Eligibility and disqualification provisions directly determine who receives benefits, and duration provisions determine how long benefits are paid. Furthermore, the level of UI benefits may affect whether unemployed workers apply for benefits and how long they draw benefits.

Another major concern about the gap, measured as the ratio of insured unemployment to total unemployment, is the fact that UI benefit provisions keep the ratio low for the regular UI program as compared to that of other developed industrial nations. The gap also varies with the business cycle and falls during periods of economic expansion. As a result, advocates for wider availability of regular benefits frequently criticize the program because of the low percentage of the total unemployed drawing UI benefits during peaks in the business cycle (see Baldwin and McHugh 1992).

As shown in table 15.6, the annual average recipiency rate for the regular program has varied between 29 and 50 percent since 1967. The

Table 15.6 Percentage of Unemployed Receiving UI, National Averages, 1967-1994

Year	Regular state UI (percent)	All programs (percent)
1967	41	43
1968	39	42
1969	39	41
1970	44	48
1971	43	52
1972	38	45
1973	37	41
1974	44	50
1975	50	75
1976	40	67
1977	38	56
1978	38	43
1979	40	42
1980	44	50
1981	37	41
1982	38	45
1983	32	44
1984	29	34
1985	31	34
1986	32	33
1987	31	32
1988	31	32
1989	33	33
1990	36	37
1991	40	42
1992	34	52
1993	32	48
1994	34	37

NOTE: The category "all programs": includes regular state UI, and UI benefits for former civilian federal employees (UCEF), former armed services personnel (UCX), railroad employees (RR), extended benefits (EB), federal supplemental benefits (FSB), special unemployment assistance (SUA), federal supplemental compensation (FSC), and extended unemployment compensation (EUC).

size of the gap reflects the nature of the UI program as a system to partially compensate for job loss. While job losers make up about half of all unemployed persons, as can be seen in table 15.1, their share of the total grows during periods of recession. Policy actions that could reduce the gap include broadening coverage, extending program duration, and easing initial and continuing eligibility provisions.

While small potential increases in coverage among agricultural employees, domestic workers, and nonprofit employees can be made, expanding coverage can reduce the gap for the regular UI program only by expanding beyond the traditional areas and diminishing its insurance character. Examining the situation for all UI programs, including extended benefit programs, reveals another possible way to close the gap. During recessions, extended benefit programs have greatly raised the ratio of the insured to total unemployed. The ratio reached as high as 75 percent in 1975. Thus, although generous extended benefit programs would do little to reduce the large gap in times of low unemployment, extended benefits could cut the gap considerably during recessionary periods when job losers become a much larger share of all unemployed.

Finally, table 2.1 shows the wide differences in the gap among states. In 1993, the proportion of the unemployed claiming UI ranged from 64 percent in Alaska to 15 percent in South Dakota. The gap also varies systematically by region of the country. It tends to be smallest in New England and on the West Coast, and largest in the South, the Southwest and in the Rocky Mountain states. The wide disparity in the gap by state is evidence that differences in state policy and state administration with regard to regular UI program parameters are the principal policy determinant. Thus, to a considerable extent, closing the gap is an issue of the tightness or looseness of state UI law and policy.

Although one may speak of closing the gap, in reality, eliminating it is an illusion—if we compare UI claimants to the total population of total unemployed persons. The gap exists partly because of the exclusion of new entrants and reentrants, whose coverage is beyond the scope of an insurance program.

By the 1980s, the UI program had evolved into a system that pays benefits to job losers only for a period of up to 26 weeks, except in times of recession. As a result, a reasonable baseline for analyzing UI recipiency can be directed at unemployed workers who have lost their job and who are unemployed for under 27 weeks. This approach would suggest comparing actual recipiency to the level of recipiency if all job losers unemployed less than 27 weeks claimed UI benefits. For this group, it can be seen in figure 15.1 that the UI program serves the great majority of short-term job losers. While the proportion has declined somewhat in recent years, since the early 1980s the UI program has still served about four-fifths of this segment of the unemployed population. State and federal policy changes could have opened up benefit receipt to a wider number of unemployed workers which would have raised the recipiency rate further. For example, eligibility could be extended to a small portion of unemployed workers who had low base-period earnings or had worked part-time.

Trends in Unemployment Insurance Financing

Benefit Financing

Overly pessimistic economic assumptions used during the design of the federal-state UI system in the 1930s resulted in lower-than-expected benefit charges and higher-than-needed revenues. There was a substantial buildup of reserves prior to initial benefit payments in the late 1930s. On top of this, the virtual full employment during the years of World War II resulted in the excessive accumulation of reserves. As a result, as shown in figure 8.2, UI taxes were reduced sharply at the end of the war, largely through the state-by-state spread of experience rating.

Despite initial overfunding, the UI system began moving toward long-term financial problems. The process started with the imposition of a maximum UI taxable wage base, set at $3,000 in 1939. It continued with the failure of state and federal legislators to follow the example set by the social security system of gradually increasing the taxable wage base to more or less keep up with inflation. The result of the diverging taxable wage bases for the two programs is summarized in figure 8.4.

While the taxable wage base has remained relatively constant in nominal terms, it has steadily declined both in real terms and relative to

Figure 15.1 Regular Program Insured Unemployed as a Percenage of Job Losers Unemployed Less Than 27 Weeks

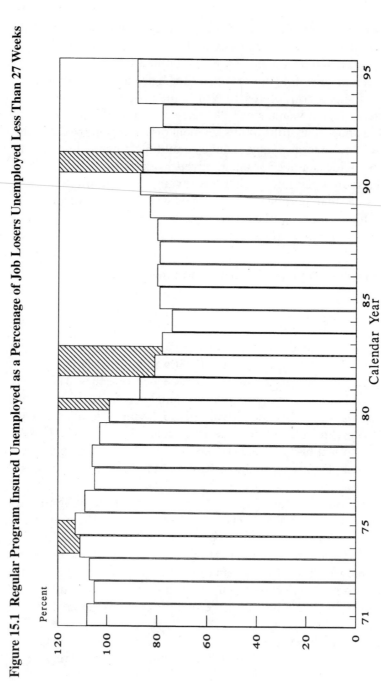

SOURCE: U.S. Department of Labor, Employment and Training Administration, Unemployment Insurance Service and U.S. Department of Labor, Bureau of Labor Statistics..

NOTE: Recessions are indicated from peak (P) to trough (T) by shaded bands.

average wages. The small increases in the taxable wage base have proved to be only modest and temporary exceptions to the trend. Although the UI average tax rate on taxable wages has been on an upward trend since World War II, as shown in figure 8.3, the UI system has not achieved a sound financial footing in large part because of the shrinking taxable wage base. Benefit levels, on the other hand, have increased with wages and prices and have remained relatively constant in real terms.

Chapter 9 points óut that, although the period from 1979 to the present has seen some rebuilding of the UI trust fund, reserves have not reached the level attained just before the 1974-1975 recession. The rebuilding was spurred in part by the decision of the federal government to begin charging interest on state trust fund borrowing in 1982. Although this provided a strong incentive for states to maintain a solvent trust fund, the recovery of adequate state trust fund reserves has been modest. As chapter 9 discusses, part of the explanation for this limited growth in reserves may be the increased reliance by states on a responsive financing system rather than on a system that makes extensive and substantial use of forward funding. State legislatures have felt political pressure to reduce UI tax rates, even when state trust fund accounts have been below the level considered sufficient on an actuarial basis to weather the next recession.

One policy conclusion from this analysis that economists widely accept is a need to increase the UI taxable wage base and then to index the wage base to keep up with inflation. This is a conclusion of Levine in chapter 8. It has also been a recommendation of the National Commission on Unemployment Compensation in 1980 and of the Advisory Council on Unemployment Compensation in 1995. Despite this widespread policy consensus, strong opposition in the business community has meant little movement in the UI taxable wage base throughout six decades of the program, and no increase in the base in well over a decade. The result is an enormous difference between the taxable wage bases of the two programs which started at the same time. While the indexed wage base for social security stands at $65,400 in 1997, the UI program continues with a federal taxable wage base of $7,000 and little prospect for change.

Another concern of economists in their study of the UI system since at least the 1970s has been the impact of imperfect experience rating.

Analysis has demonstrated how less-than-perfect experience rating offers incentives to employers to initiate temporary layoffs. For example, Levine concludes in chapter 8 that layoffs would be 20 to 50 percent lower in a perfectly experience-rated system.

While perfect experience rating has never been a goal of the state or federal policy makers, the degree of experience rating differs widely among states. Analysts have tried to draw attention to this variation by developing empirical measures of experience rating. These indexes have been analyzed and measured over the past decade and a half (see Wandner and Crosslin 1980; Topel 1984; Hunt and O'Leary 1989; Vroman 1989). The Department of Labor has published an experience-rating index for each state since 1988. There is not yet any indication that its publication has resulted in any measurable change in overall experience rating or even in a narrowing of variation among states in their degree of experience rating.

Although most economists believe that the degree of experience rating should be increased, policy makers cannot necessarily agree on whether or how this should be done. For example, in its final report released in January 1996, the Advisory Council on Unemployment Compensation did not offer a majority recommendation on this matter.

Most analysis of the experience rating of UI taxes has been directed at its role in financing temporary periods of unemployment. Brechling and Laurence (1995) have investigated how experience rating might operate in response to permanent layoffs. As mentioned throughout this book, permanent job separations resulting from business restructuring and plant closings have increased tremendously since the 1980s. New UI financing strategies must address this issue.

Brechling and Laurence (1995) conclude in their book that increasing the extent of experience rating is as appropriate in the case of permanent layoffs as in the case of temporary layoffs, but caution that it is more difficult to accomplish. They argue that, just as for temporary layoffs, experience rating for permanent layoffs can be improved by raising maximum tax rates and lowering minimum tax rates. However, Brechling and Laurence assert that these actions alone are not sufficient. They advocate additional steps to require that firms with declining employment internalize a greater share of the costs that result from their layoffs.

Brechling and Laurence (1995) recommend two additional changes: (1) shortening the time lag when determining the UI tax rate for an employer; and (2) uniform adoption of the reserve ratio method of experience rating, with several modifications. To minimize the time lag in setting employer tax rates, they propose that the UI tax rate for the current year be determined by the employer's reserve ratio at the end of the prior year.

They favor the reserve ratio system of experience rating for two main reasons. First, a positive trust fund balance could easily be incorporated as an asset on the firm's balance sheet, while a negative balance could be entered as a liability. Requiring these entries on the balance sheet may induce firms to more fully consider the UI tax consequences of layoff actions. Second, if a firm goes into bankruptcy, its positive balance would be refunded, while any negative balance would make the state UI trust fund a creditor in legal proceedings. These recommendations directly address the problem the UI program faces in financing benefit payments for *inactive* employers. Finally, Brechling and Laurence recommend that firms be paid interest on their positive trust fund balances and be charged interest on their negative balances. Interest owed by negative balance employers would be collected in cash, while interest payable would be added to the firm's positive balance. By penalizing negative balances and rewarding positive balances, these policy recommendations are intended to encourage firms to build up UI trust funds.

The analysis of the financing of both temporary and permanent layoffs assumes that raising experience-rated charges to employers will result in greater internalizing of UI costs by employers imposing layoffs. Employers, however, are not charged for layoffs until determinations are made by the state UI agency that they are responsible for the given layoffs. As a result, firms have an incentive to challenge the attribution of layoffs to them. The growth of challenges related to benefits and separation issues and the growth of private *service bureaus,* which manage UI accounts for both private and public employers, are indications that employers are choosing to dispute potential charges to their UI account, either themselves or through their agents. To date, there has been no study of the effect of UI service bureaus on the personnel policies of employers or on the operation of UI. Such a study would enlighten policy on experience rating and benefit eligibility; however, proper data to investigate this issue would be very difficult to obtain.

Administrative Financing

Administrative financing is discussed at length in chapter 13 as a federal-state relations issue. In one sense, UI administrative financing should be very simple and straightforward. The UI program is very efficiently administered, it is highly automated, and its costs are low. Administration costs about six cents per dollar of benefits paid and about three cents per dollar of tax collections. Nonetheless, there are a number of controversial questions in UI administrative financing. Who should collect FUTA tax money that is used for administrative financing and other purposes? How should the administrative funds be distributed among the states? Also, how much money should be distributed each year?

In chapter 13, West and Hildebrand discuss the issue in the context of the search for balance between the federal and state partners in the system. Contention between the partners is probably greatest over the question of how big the total administrative financing level should be, as opposed to the question of how money should be allocated among states.

Just as subsidies flow from employers with low layoffs to employers with high layoffs due to imperfectly experience-rated financing of benefit charges, cross subsidies between the states have long existed in administrative financing. These cross-subsidies have been measured by the U.S. Department of Labor for nearly two decades, and the results have been published and made available to the states and other interested parties (see Van Erden and Wandner 1979). Unlike the undesirable subsidies in benefit financing, the subsidies in administrative financing are intentional and closely managed. The principal reason for administrative cross-subsidies is to accommodate the differences in UI workloads, which result mainly during recessionary periods that do not impact all regions of the country equally. These cross-subsidies accommodate regional downturns such as the "Oil Patch" recession of the mid-1980s. Persistent cross-subsidies also result from the higher cost of administering UI programs in low-density, low-population regions.

While many cross-subsidies tend to be intermittent and to move from one portion of the country to the other, historically there have been some persistent "winners" and "losers" among the states. Not surprisingly, the persistent losers have tended to spearhead the demand for devolution of UI administrative funding. The call for an end to cross-subsidies in UI administrative financing and more limited calls for the end of federal extended benefits seem to represent a retreat from the national public policy focus of UI.

Of great public policy concern is the developing problem of inadequate total resources for UI administrative financing. UI is an entitlement program and, as such, it is treated as a "mandatory" item in the federal budget. The funds needed to pay UI benefits are thus automatically appropriated. Administrative financing, however, is treated as "discretionary" under the federal budget. This means that UI administrative financing must compete with other items for funding within the single, limited federal budget appropriation for the U.S. Departments of Labor, Education, and Health and Human Services. As a result, there is no guarantee that the funding needed to administer UI workloads and to cover state salary increases will be made available. There is a basic contradiction in recognizing that UI benefits payments are driven by state unemployment, while ignoring the fact that claims loads affect administrative costs as well. Concern over administrative financing is heightened by the unique nature of the UI program: no other federally funded program expands and contracts so much over the business cycle.

If UI administrative financing remains a discretionary item in the federal budget, the long-term survival of the UI system as a national unemployment program will be in jeopardy. Unfortunately, efforts by the states and the executive branch to work with Congress toward making UI administrative financing "mandatory" under the federal budget, or to adopt some other similar rule, have not been successful.

Ideas for Reform and Change: Recommendations from Two National Commissions

There has been no comprehensive reform of the UI system since 1976. The Congress that enacted the Unemployment Compensation Amendments of 1976 did not expect that a two-decade hiatus in reform legislation would follow. Indeed, the 1976 legislation established the National Commission on Unemployment Compensation (NCUC). The final report of the NCUC was issued in 1980 and has languished since then. In 1991, Congress established the Advisory Council on Unemployment Compensation (ACUC) to take a fresh look at UI policy issues.

The reports and recommendations of these two commissions reflect their mandates to make major policy recommendations about the future direction of the UI program. Both were given the task of conducting a thorough review of the entire program. They each provided a different view of the potential scope and nature of major UI reform. This section briefly reviews both sets of recommendations to identify the similarities and differences in their findings.

The scope and nature of the recommendations from these two panels differ greatly. The recommendations reflect the many changes that have occurred over the past two decades. The relevant changes affected the structure of the U.S. economy, the political environment at the state and federal levels, and state and federal government budgetary situations.

Nonetheless, there are some similarities between the two sets of recommendations. First, a shared principle is the ideal of insulating the UI program from federal budget considerations and from the influence of federal agencies other than the U.S. Department of Labor. This is reflected in the common recommendations to remove the UI trust fund from the federal unified budget, exempt UI benefits from federal income taxation, and let the states—instead of the Internal Revenue Service—collect the FUTA tax. The ACUC goes a step further in this regard and offers a recommendation to remove federal impediments to the collection of UI taxes for independent contractors. Second, there is agreement on a number of minor issues, such as

• extending agricultural coverage

- making nonprofit organizations pay the FUTA tax

- strengthening the appeals process

However, the particulars of the NCUC and the ACUC recommendations on these and other matters differ significantly.

Increasing Federal Controls: National Commission on Unemployment Compensation

The Unemployment Compensation Amendments of 1976 included the reforms upon which there was agreement. Congress left an agenda of further issues to be considered and created the NCUC to investigate the alternatives (see NCUC 1980).

The NCUC saw its role as completing the work begun by the Social Security Act of 1935: building a comprehensive, soundly financed income maintenance program for unemployed workers. Its members also wanted to insulate the program from federal budgetary disputes that might interfere with the operation of the UI system.

On the benefit side, the NCUC approved an ambitious set of recommendations. For the regular UI program, it proposed a wide variety of federal standards that would raise benefit payments by increasing the maximum benefit level, raise replacement rates for benefit paid below the maximum level, and reduce the earnings required to qualify for the maximum duration of benefits. It also recommended federal requirements increasing coverage, easing eligibility requirements, and limiting the reasons for disqualifications.

The NCUC further proposed a greatly enhanced extended benefits program, recommending lower thresholds for states to "trigger on" the existing permanent EB program during periods of high unemployment. In addition, it recommended a permanent emergency third-tier program, over and above EB, which would also be triggered on by severe unemployment.

Moreover, the NCUC saw its role as the creator of a number of new federal programs. These included significant new UI plans such as reinsurance, which would buffer the states from unusually heavy benefit costs, allowing them to maintain state solvency by pooling their independent state UI trust fund accounts. It also included major initiatives that went beyond the scope of the UI program, such as means-tested unemployment assistance for UI program exhaustees, an income maintenance program for displaced homemakers, and a lifetime reserve benefit program for workers 60 years of age and over.

At the same time, the NCUC recommended that the funding capacity of the program be raised. It suggested that this be accomplished by expanding federal requirements for the states. The primary emphasis, however, was on federal legislative initiatives. The NCUC proposed that the federal taxable wage base be increased substantially and indexed for future adjustments. States were also asked to expand the tax capacity of their UI systems, largely by improving their state experience-rating provisions.

If enacted, the NCUC recommendations would have greatly increased UI system costs. A substantial portion of the additional program cost would have been accommodated by a rise in state and federal UI payroll taxes. The NCUC also recommended more federal control of the system and more uniformity among individual state UI programs.

The composition and views of the NCUC membership reflected the Democratic Congress and President of the late 1970s. The final report of the Commission was completed on Labor Day, 1980. Shortly afterward, Ronald Reagan was elected president. As a result, the final report was put aside. Today, as in the 1980s, it seems that the economic, political, and social environment gives little chance for adoption of most of the NCUC recommendations.

Exhorting States to Reform: Advisory Council on Unemployment Compensation

The Emergency Unemployment Compensation Amendments of 1991 (Public Law [P.L.] 102-164), which initiated Emergency Unemployment Compensation as a temporary third-tier extended benefit program during the 1990-1991 recession, also established the ACUC. The legislation gave the Council a broad mandate to review the UI program, instructing the council "to evaluate the unemployment compensation program, including the purpose, goals, countercyclical effectiveness, coverage, benefit adequacy, trust fund solvency, funding of State administrative cost, administrative efficiency, and other aspects of the program and make recommendations for improvement."

The final report of the Council was submitted in February 1996. The Council also released two annual reports, in February 1994 and February 1995.

The Council found "a pressing need to reform the Extended Benefit program," and its 1994 report concentrated on the permanent EB program (ACUC February 1994). It proposed that extended benefits trigger on in all states when the seasonally adjusted total unemployment rate (TUR) in the state exceeds 6.5 percent.[1] The ACUC recommended that the EB trigger continue to be based on statewide data and not on local or regional measures. To finance the increase in the cost of EB, the Council advocated that the federal UI taxable wage base be increased from $7,000 to $8,500.

The Council also recommended eliminating the federal requirement that individuals receiving EB must accept any job offered that pays at least the minimum wage or forfeit eligibility for EB. The Council advocated a policy of allowing states to set their own work tests for EB, just as they do for the regular UI program.

By congressional mandate, the Council also considered the UI system's treatment of alien agricultural workers. Until January 1, 1995, wages paid to legal, temporary alien agricultural workers were exempt from the Federal Unemployment Tax Act (FUTA). The Council found that earnings of alien agricultural workers should be subject to the FUTA tax for two reasons. First, this levy would eliminate the cost advantage these workers offer to employers over domestic workers on whose earnings the tax must be paid. Second, the UI trust fund already bears the cost of certifying alien workers before their admittance to the United States, by funding the operation of the certifying agency, the U.S. Employment Service.

In its February 1995 report, the Council made recommendations on a broad range of issues, mostly dealing with the regular UI program and its financing. On the benefit side, the ACUC did not call for any federal standards. Instead, it urged the states to adopt a series of new approaches to UI eligibility, with the principal goal of improving benefit eligibility and adequacy for low-wage, part-time, intermittent, and seasonal workers. Because the changes would be targeted to a small portion of the potentially eligible population of unemployed workers, there would be only a limited impact on the overall UI program. A small number of additional workers—mostly, but not exclusively, low-wage workers—would be able to collect UI benefits.

With respect to financing, the ACUC placed its emphasis on increasing the "forward funding" of the UI program, to ensure sufficient balances in the individual state trust funds to finance benefits in future recessions. The ACUC offered only recommendations to states regarding financing. It proposed that the program develop a new measure of adequacy of funding: the average of benefits paid by a state in its three highest-cost years during the previous twenty years. States were urged to maintain sufficient reserves to pay at least one year of benefits at that level. To encourage states to maintain adequate funding, the ACUC proposed giving them an additional percentage point of interest on all their UI reserve balances in excess of one "high-cost" year of reserves. To assure no additional cost to the federal budget, the interest rate premium would be funded by reducing—by two-tenths of a percentage point or whatever the balancing percentage is—the rate paid on a portion of the reserves of a state, the amount by which such reserves fall short of the new target trust fund balance.

Proposals for federal legislative requirements were limited to providing incentives to states to forward-fund their programs. The incentives recommended would be conditional interest-free loans or loan premiums and discounts for states that strive for forward funding of UI benefits.

With few exceptions, the final report of the ACUC (1996) concentrated on issues dealing with benefit payment and benefit financing provisions. In a vote divided along business and organized-labor lines, the ACUC recommended raising the taxable wage base to $9,000 and then indexing it to the annual increases in national average total wages in covered employment. As part of the same recommendations, the 0.2 percent FUTA surcharge would be removed.

Proposed changes on the benefit side of the program dealt with the repeal of selected federal standards regarding denial of benefits to professional athletes, reduction of benefits by the amount of pension payment, denial of benefits between school terms, and certain restrictions on EB receipt. The ACUC also recommended that federal guarantees strengthen the right to representation during appeals.

The main thrust of the final report, however, dealt with four other issues: federal-state relations, certain administrative matters, data and reporting, and administrative financing. With respect to the federal-state relationship, the ACUC proposed a new, narrow concept of federal responsibilities. The federal government should concentrate on two national objectives: assuring that states provide benefits without interstate competition and assuring forward funding of the UI tax system.

The ACUC also developed a novel approach to federal administration and oversight. It asserted that the federal partner should no longer mandate a broad and comprehensive scheme of performance measures and should only require measures affecting those national interests that conflicted with the interests of the states. Such conflicts were not found to exist with day-to-day operations of the program, for example, in the traditional areas of program administration dealing with the timeliness, quality, and accuracy of the benefit payment and tax collection processes. Thus, designing those measures should be left to the states. In particular, the ACUC recommended eliminating federal indicators of tax revenue and benefit payment accuracy, quality, and timeliness. It proposed that states be encouraged to develop their own wage replacement measures. As a result, these indicators would not necessarily be subject to interstate comparison or to national aggregation.

According to the ACUC, existing federal performance measures should be replaced with "measures of access to the UI system." These indicators would deal with issues such as access to information about UI, ease of applying for benefits, and access to the system by seasonal, low-wage, and part-time workers. Thus, the existing federally mandated measures of day-to-day program performance would be replaced with indexes assessing how state policy and administration affect access to UI benefits.

The ACUC placed considerable emphasis on the data needs and reporting requirements of the UI system. Its recommendations included creating state-by-state UI data bases of comparable program data, implementing a new biennial supplement to the CPS dealing with UI issues, improving the state employment and wage (ES-202) reports, and developing a national longitudinal wage record data base.

Finally, the ACUC recommended improvements to UI administrative financing. Congress was urged to provide adequate administrative funding on a regular basis. Grants to support innovation for cost effective administration were also advocated.

Summary

Recommendations of the ACUC made in the mid-1990s were far more modest than those offered by the NCUC in 1980. The ACUC recommendations also appear to be more sensitive to the contemporary policy context in the states and Congress than were the recommendations of the NCUC. The current mood is dominated by a political aversion to raising taxes and increasing expenditures. Despite the focused and measured advice of the ACUC, in this environment, federal UI legislative reform is likely to be limited and incremental.

Retaining the Insurance Concept

As an insurance program, UI has to deal with the moral hazard of paying benefits to workers who may be purposely avoiding employment. This risk is addressed by the UI work test, which checks labor force attachment through Employment Service (ES) registration and provision of employment exchange and reemployment services. Many states also impose a weekly work search requirement.

The stringency of work search requirements varies considerably among states. Some states stipulate that unemployed workers who are not job attached make and document three job contacts per week. Other states have no specific requirements about job contacts or documentation. In all states, verification of reported work search contacts is limited or nonexistent.

There has been a strong tendency for states to reduce their work search requirements over time. By 1990, only 33 states required that individuals report their work search contacts. This trend is partly the result of the widely held belief that the work search requirement is not necessary or effective in promoting return to work. These changes also appear to be related to the introduction of the Benefits Quality Control program, which measures benefit payment accuracy and finds a high level of errors with regard to the work search process. Elimination of the work search requirement reduces the potential for erroneous payments based on its improper application.

It is important for the states to have accurate information about the impact of the work test on the cost of the UI program and on the ability to assist individuals in returning to work. There has been little research on evaluating alternative approaches to the work search requirement. One demonstration project has been conducted, the Washington Alternative Work Search Experiment. The project tested four different work search approaches, ranging from a streamlined one that did not require claimants to report employer contacts, to a customized version that tailored claimants' work search to their labor market characteristics and included intensive reemployment services early in the spell of unemployment. The demonstration showed that, relative to the usual Washington work search requirement of three employer contacts per week, the streamlined approach significantly increased UI duration and UI payments, while the customized version with mandatory reemployment services significantly reduced UI payments (Johnson and Klepinger 1991, 1994).

Responding to concerns relevant to the findings of the Washington Alternative Work Search Experiment that work search requirements can affect UI durations and UI payments, the Department of Labor initiated the Maryland Work Search Demonstration in 1991. Its primary objective was to determine whether the stringency of the work search requirement affects UI durations, UI payments, and wages in subsequent employment. The demonstration was designed to provide data for policy initiatives for the states and the Labor Department to increase the effectiveness of the UI work search process. It both tested the benefits of the work search requirement and attempted to measure the effectiveness of the enforcement aspect compared to the reemployment services aspect.

The Maryland demonstration involved four treatment groups, each with a work search requirement differing with respect to stringency, verification of claimant contacts, and the provision of reemployment assistance. In the experimental design, claimants were randomly assigned to one of the four treatment groups or to a control group. Claimants in the control were given the current search requirements and services. Enrollment into the experiment began in 1993 and concluded in early 1995.

The evaluation of the demonstration found that each of the four treatments had their expected effects. Additional work search contacts and verifications were each effective in reducing the duration of UI spells. Participation in a job search workshop—which was not targeted to those most in need as in worker profiling—was somewhat less effective in reducing UI spells. Finally, removing the requirement to report job search contacts was found to increase the UI spell, but the increase was relatively small, expecially compared to the similar Washington Alternative Work Search Experiment treatment, given the requirement to maintain regular contact with the UI local office (Klepinger et al. 1997).

Adapting to a Changing World

Dislocation and the Need for Reemployment Services

In response to the growing importance of dislocated workers among the insured unemployed, the UI program has become more involved in promoting reemployment. Although dislocated workers represent only 10 to 20 percent of UI claimants, they are the group of unemployed individuals in greatest need of reemployment assistance. The UI system has a natural role in helping them because nearly all dislocated workers who remain jobless for long periods claim UI benefits. Since most dislocated workers apply for UI benefits when they first become unemployed, the UI program has the potential to direct claimants to reemployment services early in their spell of unemployment.

The Problem of Worker Dislocation

Worker dislocation as a policy issue in the United States can be traced back at least to the early 1960s. In 1961, unemployment climbed to 6.7 percent, a figure considered very high at the time. There were widespread fears that an acceleration in technological change—termed "automation"—would displace large numbers of workers in autos, steel, textiles, and other basic industries (Davidson 1972). In response, the Kennedy administration proposed and enacted the Manpower Development and Training Act (MDTA), the first national program designed to retrain experienced workers for new jobs.

However, by 1964, unemployment had dropped back below 5 percent, and the nation entered a long period of economic expansion. Most experienced workers were again employed in their former jobs, and it had become clear that the threat of widespread technological unemployment had been greatly exaggerated. In this environment, the focus of MDTA and other government-sponsored programs shifted to the needs of the economically disadvantaged in response to the newly-declared "War on Poverty."

After a twenty-year hiatus, worker dislocation reemerged as a major national issue in the early 1980s. During the 1981-1982 recession, the national unemployment rate climbed to a post-World War II record high of 10.7 percent. Plant closings and permanent mass layoffs in steel, autos, footwear, textiles, and other industries dislocated millions of experienced workers, and the worst fears of the early sixties became a reality in the eighties. Unlike the 1960s, many of the laid-off workers continued to be unemployed despite a strong economic recovery, as manufacturing employment declined sharply. By the end of 1984, with the economy nearly two years into recovery, unemployment remained well above 7 percent. The new economic reality of structural unemployment had become painfully clear.

In 1984, the Bureau of Labor Statistics (BLS) at the U.S. Department of Labor began conducting surveys to determine the size and characteristics of the dislocated worker population. While there are no universally accepted definitions of who is or is not a "dislocated worker," the BLS definition is a commonly used one. BLS defines dislocated workers as individuals who had at least three years of tenure with their last employer and lost their job for reasons other than temporary layoff, for example, a plant closing or relocation, or the elimination of the job or shift.

These BLS dislocated worker surveys are special supplements to the CPS, a monthly survey of about 60,000 households carried out by the Bureau of the Census for BLS. They are conducted every two years and solicit retrospective information about the previous five years. For example, the 1984 survey asked about experience from January 1979 to January 1984. The BLS survey covering the period from January 1989 to January 1994 indicated that the problem of worker dislocation is substantial and growing. Based on this survey, there were 2.8 million workers in 1991 and 1992 who had at least three years of tenure with their employer and who were permanently displaced from their jobs, up from 2.2 million such workers in 1989 and 1990. The 1991 and 1992 figures represent a rate of displacement of 3.8 percent for long-tenured workers, up from 3.1 percent in the prior two years. If all workers (regardless of tenure) who were displaced from their jobs are included in the count, the total number of dislocated workers in the BLS count rises to 5.4 million individuals for the years 1991 and 1992 (Gardner 1995).

A recent study by the Congressional Budget Office looked at trends in worker dislocation throughout the decade of the 1980s. It used data from the BLS displaced worker surveys conducted in 1984, 1986, 1988, 1990, and 1992. The study points out that the number of dislocated workers during the 1980s varied substantially with the business cycle, ranging from a high of 2.7 million during the recession in 1982 to a low of 1.5 million in 1988, five years into the economic recovery (Ross and Smith 1993, p. 7). However, during most of those years, the total number of dislocations ranged between 1.5 and 2 million workers annually.

While not all of these dislocated workers would have difficulty becoming reemployed, a large proportion of them, especially those with long job tenure, could benefit from some type of reemployment assistance. For example, workers with three or more years of tenure with their previous employer had longer spells of unemployment and were more likely to experience a reduction in earnings of 20 percent or more than were workers with less than three years of tenure (Ross and Smith 1993, pp. 20-25).

Reemploying Dislocated Workers: The Role of Unemployment Insurance

The traditional role of the UI program is to provide temporary partial wage replacement to unemployed workers. In the process, the UI program tests whether unemployed workers are able, available, and actively seeking work. In most states, emphasis has been more on checking continuing attachment to the labor force than on attempting to promote reemployment.

In the 1980s and early 1990s, the problem of worker dislocation had become a prominent concern for insured unemployed workers. One indication of this recognition is that when the Unemployment Insurance Service developed its first "Mission, Vision, Values, Goals" statement in 1992, it adopted the following: "The program's mission is to provide unemployed workers with temporary income support and to facilitate re-employment" (Wandner 1992). This statement made clear the emphasis placed on reemployment by the federal partner in the UI system.

Recently the UI program has been serving between 8 and 10 million unemployed workers each year. About one to two million of these individuals are dislocated workers, or about 10 to 20 percent of all workers served. These people, however, have needs beyond income support, and they frequently will have great difficulty in returning to work without the assistance of reemployment service providers, generally either the ES or the Economic Dislocation and Worker Adjustment Assistance (EDWAA) program.

Even though dislocated workers represent a reasonably small portion of all beneficiaries of the UI system, they have received increasing attention in recent years. As seen in figure 15.2 for 1993, overall the UI program serves about half of all dislocated workers. Many dislocated workers return to work quickly, even though they have been permanently separated, and apparently never file for UI benefits. In a recent dislocated worker study summarized in figure 15.3, UI was found to serve less than one-third of the dislocated workers unemployed less than five weeks, but 80 to 90 percent of those unemployed 15 weeks or longer. This is the great majority of all long-term unemployed dislocated workers who are likely to need reemployment services.

Encouraging New Ideas and Experimentation

Finding Out What Works

For many years, the U.S. Department of Labor has used demonstrations and evaluations to determine the effectiveness of existing programs. Its willingness to evaluate current programs and to test the potential of new initiatives using field experiments represents a desire to learn what works and what does not work. These efforts have generally been an attempt to develop the most effective and efficient programs possible to help employ and reemploy America's labor force. The Department has also periodically reviewed the research it has con-

Figure 15.2 Total Unemployment, UI Beneficiaries, and Dislocated Workers, Calendar   Year 1993

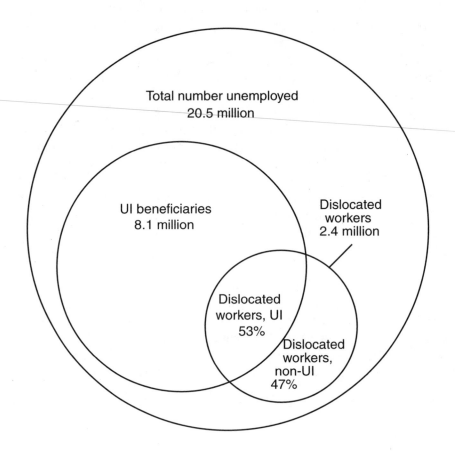

Total number unemployed
20.5 million

UI beneficiaries
8.1 million

Dislocated
workers
2.4 million

Dislocated
workers, UI
53%

Dislocated
workers,
non-UI
47%

705

Figure 15.3 Displaced Workers Who Receive UI, by Duration of Unemployment

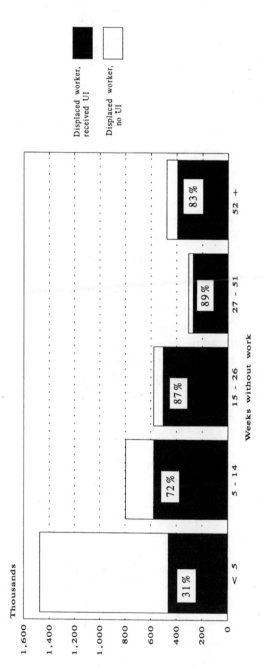

Displaced worker, received UI

Displaced worker, no UI

SOURCE: U.S. Department of Labor, Bureau of Labor Statistics, Displaced Worker study, 1988.

ducted to help determine what works and to develop and select from policy options (U.S. Department of Labor 1995).

Most of the initial Labor Department experiments were not related to the UI program. Beginning in the early 1980s, however, a demonstration dealing with the UI work search requirement was done in Charleston, South Carolina (Corson, Long, and Nicholson 1985). In the mid-1980s, the Unemployment Insurance Service became active in operating a series of experiments that tested and evaluated new approaches to return claimants to work, particularly if they were permanently separated from their previous employer and appeared to be in need of reemployment assistance.

The impetus for the UI demonstrations and their reliance on the field experiment approach came from a number of different places. First, the dislocated worker problem was becoming more important in the U.S. economy, and recognition of it as a public policy concern was increasing. In 1985, awareness of this issue within the Department of Labor became greater when William Brock became Secretary of Labor, having worked on international aspects of worker dislocation as the Special Trade Representative. Second, in a period of extreme federal budget stringency, it was difficult to expect adoption of new policy initiatives that recommended extra or expanded programs. The exception to this situation would rest on an analysis of cost effectiveness that demonstrated that the new program would be beneficial to society as a whole and, if possible, to the government sector, such that the program might actually save money for the federal government. Third, with frequent political divisions between Congress and the executive branch of the federal government, agreement about which economic policies work and which do not work is promoted by an evaluation method that is simple and direct.

Field experiments involve random assignment of large numbers of claimants to treatment and control groups, with the response to a new program change estimated as the difference in the average behavior of the two groups. With field experiments, there is no need to make questionable modeling assumptions or to use sophisticated statistical analysis to yield meaningful results. Evidence from classically designed field experiments involving random assignment makes forging policy agreements easier.

Just as the U.S. Department of Labor has done, some states have undertaken their own tests of what works to promote reemployment. Several states have committed resources to undertake studies and have initiated programs based on the results. Some of the state studies have involved experimental designs. In the 1970s and 1980s, Nevada tested two Claimant Employment Projects that were found successful in reducing UI durations by having a UI and ES team provide more intensive reemployment services to UI claimants. The Reemploy Minnesota project duplicated the treatment of intensive job search assistance from the New Jersey experiment. The Washington Alternative Work Search Experiment evaluated alternative UI work search requirements and the provision of job search assistance (see U.S. Department of Labor 1990; Johnson and Klepinger 1991, 1994). In addition, in 1984, Illinois independently initiated the nation's first experimental test of the reemployment bonus (Woodbury and Spiegelman 1987).

The Unemployment Insurance Experiments

Since the reemergence of worker dislocation as a national policy issue in the early 1980s, the Department of Labor has conducted eight experiments designed to test different reemployment service strategies to assist dislocated workers in making the transition to new employment. The following is a chronological list of the field experiments undertaken.

Experiment	**States involved**
Multitreatment: job search assistance, training grants, relocation grants, and reemployment bonuses	New Jersey
Reemployment bonus	Washington and Pennsylvania
Self-employment assistance	Massachusetts and Washington
Work search	Maryland
Job search assistance	District of Columbia and Florida

The goal of these studies has been to determine what works for dislocated workers, what doesn't work, and why. More specifically, these field experiments were designed to determine the impacts of various reemployment services, or combinations of services, on the subsequent labor market experience of dislocated workers. They examined outcomes such as employment, earnings, and receipt of UI benefits and other income transfer payments. These studies have also attempted to estimate the cost-effectiveness of various services and to measure the return on investment of each service from the perspectives of participants, the government, and society as a whole (see Corson et al. 1992; Decker and O'Leary 1995; O'Leary, Spiegelman, and Kline 1995; Benus et al. 1995).

Conclusions about the Experiments

To date, analysis of the UI demonstrations has yielded three strong conclusions:

- Worker profiling and reemployment services: It is possible to develop a service delivery system such that the state UI and reemployment service providers can identify dislocated workers early in their unemployment spell, determine the unique needs of individuals, and then promptly match each worker with appropriate and effective reemployment assistance.

- Job search assistance: Comprehensive job search assistance is a highly cost-effective strategy for accelerating the reemployment of dislocated workers. The experiments suggest that more suitable jobs are available than are yielded by casual, undirected job search. This reemployment service provided net benefits to participants, the government, and society as a whole. Job search assistance is an option that can be effective and efficient when made widely available for dislocated workers.

- Self-employment assistance: Self employment is of interest to only a small portion of dislocated workers, but half of those who participated in experimental trials succeeded at starting their own microenterprises. The final evaluation of the Massachusetts demonstration provides impact and benefit-cost analyses indicating that self-employment has promise as a labor market intervention for a small share of unemployed workers.

The conclusions about the effectiveness of job search assistance are widely held, based on a number of state and federal experiments. For example, Meyer (1995) finds that

> The job search experiments... try several different combinations of services to improve job search and increase the enforcement of work search rules. Nearly all combinations reduce UI receipt and... increase earnings. . . . The main treatments have benefits to the UI system that exceed cost in all cases, and societal-level cost-benefit analyses are favorable . . . (p. 128).

He recommends that "On the services side we should consider making job search assistance universal. The exact combination of services we should include is not completely clear, but jobs search workshops and individual attention by the same personnel seem promising" (p. 125. See also Ross and Smith 1993; *The Economist* 1996).

Implementation of Unemployment Insurance Reemployment Promotion Options

In March and October 1993, Congress enacted worker profiling legislation as sections of two extensions of the Emergency Unemployment Compensation Act. The October legislation required states to implement worker profiling provisions and to have their UI programs refer likely dislocated workers to reemployment services provided by existing state and federal programs. Under the Worker Profiling and Reemployment Services (WPRS) system, the UI role ends with the identification and referral of likely dislocated workers to reemployment services. The UI system cannot provide reemployment services and federal law does not allow UI trust fund money to pay for services. Traditional reemployment service providers must make the services available. With dislocated workers representing one to two million UI beneficiaries per year, the UI program is dependent on the ES and the EDWAA programs to devote substantial resources to providing these services.

To help with the implementation of this legislation, the Department of Labor provided states with technical assistance and over $20 million in funding to establish worker profiling mechanisms. The EDWAA program also provided states with nearly $20 million to build the capacity to provide reemployment services. By mid-1996, the WPRS initiative was operational in all states. Nearly 400,000 unemployed workers had been profiled and referred to reemployment services during the early six-month operational period from October 1995 through March 1996.

As a result, implementation of the WPRS initiative generally has resulted in a cooperative and interdependent relationship between UI, the ES and the dislocated worker (EDWAA) portion of Job Training Partnership Act (JTPA) programs at the state level. This relationship has helped to create a kind of *one-stop shopping* for reemployment services that has been gradually introduced by the states and promoted by the federal government. The UI system has become a "gateway" through which dislocated workers pass to receive reemployment services from ES and EDWAA.

The primary emphasis of WPRS has been on the early identification of dislocated workers and referring them to reemployment services— primarily job search assistance. However, as both the New Jersey experiment and the early implementation of WPRS have shown, a small but significant portion of the dislocated workers cannot find employment through basic reemployment services alone. Many of these hard-to-place clients are referred to retraining, even though participation in training is voluntary under WPRS. About one-fifth of the unemployed workers referred to reemployment services under the WPRS initiative were referred to retraining during the early phase of implementation (Wandner 1996, 1997).

In another reemployment promotion option, the early evaluations of the self-employment demonstration projects had shown both substantial positive economic impacts and net savings to the federal budget by 1992. These findings were widely disseminated, and they made possible and encouraged two policy initiatives to enact enabling federal legislation. The first was inclusion of a budget-neutral, self-employment initiative in the comprehensive workforce development plan of the Clinton administration, which was first made public in August 1993 and later was introduced as the proposed Reemployment Act of 1994 (see Wandner 1992; U.S. Department of Labor 1994a, 1994b).

For the UI program the proposed Reemployment Act placed equal emphasis on income replacement and reemployment. This initiative was named "Unemployment Insurance Flexibility," and it had three components. The first was a self-employment allowance, to be given in the form of periodic payments, which states would be authorized to adopt permanently. Secondly, states were authorized to adopt reemployment bonuses to be paid to permanently separated workers who speed their return to employment. Finally, the short-time compensation program to promote work sharing, which already existed in eighteen states, was encouraged and reauthorized.

A separate legislative effort was developed in mid-1993 by a group of legislators including Representative Ronald Wyden and Senators Edward Kennedy and Harris Wofford. They proposed a freestanding bill that would also authorize state self-employment programs involving periodic payments. The sponsors requested and received support from the Clinton administration for this bill which became an amendment to the North American Free Trade Agreement (NAFTA) implementation legislation (P.L. 103-182). As passed, the provisions expire five years after enactment, in December 1998.

Title V of the NAFTA Implementation Act provides that states may establish self-employment assistance (SEA) programs for unemployed workers as part of their UI programs. To establish such plans, participating states must enact legislation conforming to the federal legislation. The states of California, Connecticut, Delaware, Maine, Maryland, Minnesota, New Jersey, New York, Oregon, and Rhode Island have enacted legislation. Other states are considering similar legislative proposals. Self-employment programs can be initiated only after a state implementation plan is approved by the Department of Labor. On April 17, 1995, New York became the first state to implement a self-employment program. As of 1997, programs were operational in California, Delaware, Maine, Maryland, New Jersey, New York, and Oregon.

In states that operate SEA programs, UI claimants identified through worker profiling are eligible to participate. State SEA programs provide participants with periodic (weekly or biweekly) self-employment allowances during start-up of the self-employment activity. These support payments are the same weekly amounts that the UI claimant would otherwise receive in benefits, but participants can work full-time on starting their business enterprise instead of searching for wage and salary jobs. They can also fully retain any after-tax earnings from self-employment without any impact on their weekly self-employment stipend. The traditional UI work search provisions are waived and do not act as a barrier to self-employment for UI recipients.

Technology and the Decline of Unemployment Insurance Local Offices

Background

State UI program staff serve a large population of beneficiaries whose number varies inversely with the business cycle. In recent years, between 8 and 10 million claimants annually have received benefits. Funding for administration of the UI program, including staff salaries, also varies with the business cycle. The total of personnel staffing UI offices has fluctuated in recent years between 38,200 in 1990 (before the last recession) and 48,200 in 1993. This variation has been largely handled through the use of temporary employees. Among these workers, about two-thirds are front-line staff who deal directly with benefit payments, while the others work in the UI tax revenue function.

Since UI administrative costs are paid for with funds held in the U.S. Treasury, they must be appropriated by Congress. Of late, administrative funding of UI has come under increasing scrutiny. As the information economy expands, Congress expects more administrative efficiency. At the same time, there has been increased concern that the UI system serve its customers—beneficiaries and employers—with close personal attention that improves over time.

The result is a UI program under pressure to enhance administrative performance while constrained by ever-dwindling financial resources. Additionally, the UI program and all other federal programs have begun to operate in accordance with the Government Performance and Results Act of 1993, which requires the management of programs to achieve measurable and objective performance outcomes. The centerpiece of improved UI operational efficiency has been a steady process of automation. Simultaneously, there has been an effort to bring all states up to an acceptable level of overall performance, while supporting continuous improvement in all states.

The Decline of In-Person Claims Taking

The local UI office still has the public image of a place with long lines and lengthy waits to file for UI benefits. This image is perpetuated by the repeated use of television news library film clips from the 1982 recession showing long lines in large, urban UI offices. Such clips are frequently shown when the latest UI initial claims figures are announced. The present reality is much different. States have actively pursued alternatives to in-person claims filing, which can improve customer service and reduce administrative costs. Swarms of claimants rarely clog local UI offices today. Instead of coming to the local UI office, individuals increasingly file claims by mail or telephone, or employers file the claims for laid-off workers; alternatively, mass applications for benefits are taken by local UI office staff at the site of large layoffs. Claimants still filing in person find lines reduced by having their in-take interview scheduled in advance to reduce peak-load problems, and by redesigned local offices and operational procedures. As telephone initial claims spread, local office lines will disappear altogether, and in many states there will be no physical local UI offices, only "virtual" offices accessed by telephones and computers.

Originally, UI program operations were largely manual. Both initial and continued claims were filed in person. The move away from in-person claims began in the 1960s and 1970s, with the acceptance of continued claims by mail. Unemployed workers still initially filed for benefits in local UI offices, but states began giving them continued claims forms, which they could then mail in on a weekly or biweekly basis. In the 1990s, interactive voice response units combined the power of telephones and computers to allow individuals to call in their continued UI claims. With touch-tone phones, claimants could now dial up the UI system and enter the data requested.

Today, in all but two states, fewer than 25 percent of continued claims are filed in person. All states allow at least some of their claimants to file continued claims by mail, and, as a result, nearly four-fifths of claimants nationwide file continued claims that way. In addition, filing by telephone has rapidly begun to replace both claims by mail and in person. Continued claims filed by telephone went from zero in 1991 to 11 percent by 1994. Meanwhile, in-person claims filing has steadily declined, reaching 9 percent in 1994.

While in-person continued claims taking has gradually declined over the past three decades with the spread of mail and telephone procedures, the taking of initial claims remained almost exclusively in person until the 1990s. States began to take some initial claims over the telephone in the 1980s, but this was largely a low-volume, manual process, introduced in rural areas where geographically fixed local offices could not cost-effectively serve the small number of widely dispersed claimants. The taking of initial claims by telephone has recently gained in popularity because of new communication technologies, budget constraints on UI administrative funding, and new approaches to customer service. Colorado led the way by eliminating all of its local UI offices in 1992, leaving ES offices open, but without any UI counterpart. Since then, other states are following suit. California, Massachusetts, and Wisconsin are operating or implementing telephone initial claim systems. Many other states are now actively involved in planning or implementing remote initial claims taking.

The Changing Labor Force and Unemployment Insurance

For some time, permanent, full-time attachment to the labor force among U.S. workers has been declining. There has been a corresponding increase in looser and more intermittent attachment. This has meant a rise in the number of workers categorized as part-time, seasonal, intermittent, and low wage.

The UI program, at both the federal and state levels, has maintained its traditional focus on providing strict insurance benefits for strongly attached workers and has not adapted to these changes. This fact has been discussed for decades. It was raised by the NCUC. More recently it has been raised by the ACUC. The following are some potential policy options for adapting the UI system to the current labor market environment. Taken together, these proposals might help to adapt the UI program to the changing nature of the labor force in the United States.

1. Low-wage worker eligibility for UI: At present, all states, except Washington State, determine UI eligibility using quarterly wages during a one-year base period. This means that workers with higher hourly earnings are eligible for UI with fewer hours worked than are low-wage workers. A remedy for this situation could be to base eligibility on quarterly or annual hours worked instead of on quarterly earnings. The ACUC has recommended that the annual amount worked be set at 800 hours—the equivalent of about two full days of work a week throughout a year.

   To put this idea in perspective, one should note that the Canadian government has adopted a similar proposal involving hours worked. The Canadian plan ties the hours-of-work requirement to the unemployment rate in the area. A claimant could be eligible with as few as 420 hours of work in the base year if the regional unemployment rate were 13.5 percent or more, or need at least 700 hours if the unemployment rate were below 5.5 percent.[2]

2. Part-time worker eligibility: In most states, part-time workers who are unemployed and seeking part-time work cannot receive UI unless they are searching for full-time work. Thus, individuals who chose to work part time are not eligible for UI. The ongoing and continued part-time status of these workers could be recognized and encouraged by allowing previously part-time workers to collect UI while they are again seeking part-time work.

3. Seasonal worker eligibility: In many states, the ability of seasonal workers to receive UI benefits is limited. Fifteen states permit workers in seasonal industries to collect UI only during the season in which the industry work is normally conducted. In addition, thirteen of these states do not allow earnings in seasonal employment to count toward the monetary eligibility requirement, even if the worker subsequently works in a nonseasonal job. The purpose of these provisions is to prevent workers with only seasonal labor force attachment from collecting UI benefits during the off-seasons.

   Eligibility could be broadened by allowing the use of seasonal wages for establishing eligibility, as long as workers also have nonseasonal employment. The Wisconsin approach might be followed. Wisconsin allows workers to use seasonal wages if they earned at least $200 in nonseasonal employment during the year preceding the date of filing a UI claim.

4. Relatively recent labor force entrants: The standard base period, geared to the cycle of wage record systems, is the first four of the last five completed calendar quarters. With frequent movement into and out of the labor force, labor force attachment may be too recent to establish monetary eligibility using the standard base period. Six states—Maine, Massachusetts, Ohio, Rhode Island, Vermont and Washington—have responded to this situation by allowing workers who are not able to qualify for benefits using

the normal base period to use an alternate, and more recent, one. It could be the last four completed calendar quarters or the most recent 52 weeks. Use of these more recent base periods generally requires requesting recent wage and employment data from the prior employer(s), rather than relying on previously reported quarterly wage records.

The ACUC has recommended that such an alternative base period be adopted nationwide. Recent estimates indicate that this approach would increase UI beneficiaries by 6 to 8 percent and raise total costs by 4 to 6 percent (Vroman 1995).

Another method for incorporating more recent wages would be to accelerate the use of the lag quarter as part of the base period. This approach would require employers to report employment and wage data more rapidly. The state would process and use these data for benefit eligibility determinations as soon as they became available. This technique would have two advantages. It would allow states to use the most recent four quarters of data within one to two months after the end of a quarter. It would also obviate the need for states to return to any wage request reporting by employers. Employer wage requests result in added employer and state agency administrative costs and in decreased data accuracy.

5. Expanding agricultural coverage: The UI system covers almost all wage and salary workers except agricultural workers on small farms. Eight states, including the major farm states of California, Florida, and Texas, provide broader UI coverage of agricultural work. While a percentage of American agricultural workers are covered because they work on large farms or in states that already provide small-farm coverage, the remaining workers on small farms in other states are still left without the protection of UI benefits. The steps taken in the eight states might be used as models for all states.

Looking Ahead

Looking ahead to the future of the UI program, there seem to be at least four major themes. First, given the national political environment, the prospect for and likely scope of UI reform appear to be only modest in the near term. While the program is not likely to disappear or shrink precipitously, it is also not likely to expand greatly.

Arguing for its continued existence is the widespread belief that the UI program, like social security, is a social insurance critical to the well-being of the American workforce and the U.S. economy. The UI program is also likely to benefit from its highly decentralized form of administration. Its cooperative federal-state partnership has frequently been cited as a model working relationship between the states and the federal government.

Yet, the program that survives is not likely to have much in the way of enhancements in its benefit structure or increased revenues to fund these benefits or program administration. The UI program grew for the first three decades of its existence, but, in the 1970s to early 1980s, it reached a peak from which little further development can be expected in the near term.

The most uncertain area is extended benefits. It is not likely that there will be reform of the permanent EB program prior to a recession, if at all. It generally takes an economic downturn to draw congressional attention to the needs of constituents back home who experience prolonged periods of unemployment. As noted, Congress has shown its preference for creating temporary emergency unemployment benefit programs in times of recession, and that may be its response to future downturns. Nonetheless, the permanent EB program is moribund and needs to be revived. It is good public policy to have an automatically triggered, second-tier UI program available, such that Congress only needs to add emergency extended programs during particularly severe recessions.

Second, public policies regarding the tax system and administrative financing are deficient and need repair. The taxable wage base has been inadequate for many years and puts an undue burden on tax rates for the system to remain solvent. Experience rating is limited and calls out for improvements. Administrative financing is proving inadequate to process the benefit and tax function of the program. The federal budget process needs to be modified to recognize that both the benefit and administrative portions of the UI program should be treated as "mandatory" under federal budget law. Instead of being treated as a discretionary part of the UI program, administration should be treated as an entitlement.

Third, the public and its elected officials are intent on getting "value for money" in all government programs, including UI. The pressure of budget deficits has heightened the emphasis for a solid return on investment. For UI, this has meant increased concern about customer service, meeting a set of outcome goals, and continuous improvements in effectiveness and efficiency. As we have seen, the UI program has been working to enhance efficiency for many years. It has been automating its processes for decades and is increasingly making use of remote claims taking. Always relatively goal-oriented, it is becoming more so. This trend is likely to continue.

At the same time, the UI system is likely to retain its emphasis on program performance and on continuous improvement of that performance. Whereas, in the past, UI has tended to rely largely on objective measures of customer service, in the future, it will also incorporate measures of customer satisfaction, which will be used for program assessment and policy development.

Finally, the issue of worker dislocation is likely to remain a major concern to the UI program, as well as to the rest of the employment and training system. The fact that the UI program sees most dislocated workers when they first become unemployed is likely to keep the program at the focal point of the reemployment system. It is not anticipated that the UI program itself will provide or fund reemployment services, but UI will probably continue to be a referral agency, identifying and sending dislocated workers to reemployment service providers.

NOTES

1. A redesigned CPS was implemented in January 1994 and appears to have increased the measured TUR somewhat; the ACUC recommendation was based on the old CPS methodology.

2. See Government of Canada 1995. This provision was implemented on January 5, 1997. It also includes a higher hours requirement of 900 hours for reentrants and new entrants to the labor force.

References

Advisory Council on Unemployment Compensation. 1994. "Report and Recommendations." ACUC, February.

_____. 1995. "Unemployment Insurance in the United States: Benefits, Financing, Coverage." ACUC, February.

_____. 1996. "Defining Federal and State Roles in Unemployment Insurance." ACUC, January.

Anderson, Patricia, Walter Corson, and Paul Decker. 1991. "The New Jersey Unemployment Insurance Reemployment Demonstration Project: Follow-Up Report." Unemployment Insurance Occasional Paper 91-1, U.S. Department of Labor, Employment and Training Administration.

Baldwin, Marc, and Richard McHugh. 1992. *Unprepared for the Recession: The Erosion of State Unemployment Insurance Coverage Fostered by Public Policy in the 1980s.* Washington, DC: Economic Policy Institute.

Benus, Jacob M., Terry R. Johnson, Michelle Wood, Neelima Grover, and Theodore Shen. 1995. "Self-Employment Programs: A New Reemployment Strategy. Final Report on the UI Self-Employment Demonstration." Unemployment Insurance Occasional Paper 95-4, U.S. Department of Labor, Employment and Training Administration.

Blaustein, Saul. 1993. *Unemployment Insurance in the United States: The First Half Century.* Kalamazoo, MI: W.E. Upjohn Institute.

Brechling, Frank, and Louise Laurence. 1995. *Permanent Job Loss and the U.S. System of Financing Unemployment Insurance.* Kalamazoo, MI W.E. Upjohn Institute.

Burtless, Gary, and Daniel Saks. 1984. "The Decline in Insured Unemployment During the 1980s." Working paper, Brookings Institution.

Canada, Government of. 1995. *A 21st Century Employment System for Canada: Guide to the Employment Insurance Legislation.* Ottawa, December.

Corson, Walter, Paul Decker, Shari Dunstan, and Stuart Kerachsky. 1992. "Pennsylvania Reemployment Bonus Demonstration Final Report." Unemployment Insurance Occasional Paper 92-1, U.S. Department of Labor, Employment and Training Administration.

Corson, Walter, David Long, and Walter Nicholson. "Evaluation of the Charleston Claimant Placement and Work Test Demonstration." Unemployment Insurance Occasional Paper 85-2, U.S. Department of Labor, Employment and Training Administration.

Corson, Walter, and Walter Nicholson. 1988. "An Examination of Declining UI Claims During the 1980s." Unemployment Insurance Occasional Paper

88-3, U.S. Department of Labor, Employment and Training Administration.

Davidson, Roger H. 1972. *The Politics of Comprehensive Manpower Legislation.* Baltimore: Johns Hopkins University Press.

Decker, Paul T., and Christopher J. O'Leary. 1995. "Evaluation Pooled Evidence from the Reemployment Bonus Experiments," *Journal of Human Resources* 30, 3 (Summer): 534-550.

The Economist Staff Writer. 1996. "Training and Jobs: What Works?" *Economist*, April 6-12: 19-21.

Gardner, Jennifer M. 1995. "Worker Displacement: A Decade of Change," *Monthly Labor Review* 119, 4 (April): 45-57.

Haber, William, and Merrill G. Murray. 1966. *Unemployment Insurance in the American Economy: An Historical Review and Analysis.* Homewood, IL: Richard D. Irwin.

Hunt, Timothy L., and Christopher J. O'Leary. 1989. "Experience Rating of Unemployment Insurance in Michigan and Other States: A Microeconomic Comparison for 1988." Report to the Michigan Employment Security Commission and Michigan Department of Commerce. W.E. Upjohn Institute, August.

International Labour Office. 1990. *The Promotion of Self-Employment.* Geneva: ILO.

Johnson, Terry R., and Daniel Klepinger. 1991. "Evaluation of the Impacts of the Washington Alternative Work Search Experiment." Unemployment Insurance Occasional Paper 91-4, U.S. Department of Labor, Employment and Training Administration.

_____. 1994. "Experimental evidence on Unemployment Insurance Work-Search Policies," *Journal of Human Resources* 29, 3 (Summer): 695-717.

Klepinger, Daniel H., Terry R. Johnson, Jutta M. Joesch, and Jacob M. Benus. 1997. "Evaluation of the Maryland Unemployment Insurance Work Search Demonstration." Unemployment Insurance Occasional Paper, forthcoming. U.S. Department of Labor, Employment and Training Administration.

Meyer, Bruce D. 1995. "Lessons Learned from the U.S. Unemployment Insurance Experiments," *Journal of Economic Literature* 33 (March): 91-131.

National Commission on Unemployment Compensation. 1980. "Unemployment Compensation: Final Report." July.

O'Leary, Christopher J. 1996. "The Adequacy of Unemployment Insurance Benefits." In *Advisory Council on Unemployment Compensation: Background Papers*, Vol. 3. Washington, DC: ACUC, January.

O'Leary, Christopher J., Robert G. Spiegelman, and Kenneth J. Kline. 1995. "Do Bonus Offers Shorten Unemployment Insurance Spells? Results from the Washington Experiment," *Journal of Policy Analysis and Management* 14, 2 (Spring): 245-269.

Ross, Murray N., and Ralph E. Smith. 1993. *Displaced Workers: Trends in the 1980s and Implications for the Future.* Washington, DC: Congressional Budget Office.

Spiegelman, Robert G., Christopher J. O'Leary, and Kenneth J. Kline. 1992. "The Washington Reemployment Bonus Experiment Final Report." Unemployment Insurance Occasional Paper 92-6, U.S. Department of Labor, Employment and Training Administration.

Topel, Robert H. 1984. "Experience Rating of Unemployment Insurance and the Incidence of Unemployment," *Journal of Law and Economics* 27 (April): 61-90.

U.S. Department of Labor. Various years. "Comparison of State UI Laws." Employment and Training Administration, Unemployment Insurance Service.

_____. 1990. "Reemployment Services to Unemployed Workers Having Difficulty Becoming Reemployed." Unemployment Insurance Occasional Paper 90-2, U.S. Department of Labor, Employment and Training Administration.

_____. 1994a. "Self-Employment as a Reemployment Option: Demonstration Results and National Legislation." Unemployment Insurance Occasional Paper 94-3, U.S. Department of Labor, Employment and Training Administration.

_____. 1994b. "The Workforce Security Act of 1994." Consultation Paper, January 19.

_____. 1995. "Unemployment Insurance Quality Appraisal Results FY 1994." Employment and Training Administration.

U.S. Department of Labor. Office of the Chief Economist. 1995. *What's Working (and what's not): A Summary of Research on the Economic Impacts of Employment and Training Programs.* Washington, DC, January.

U.S. Small Business Administration. 1989. *The State of Small Business: A Report of the President.* Washington, DC: Government Printing Office.

Van Erden, James D., and Stephen A. Wandner. 1979. "Interstate Cross-Subsidization in the Financing of the Unemployment Insurance System." Unpublished paper, June.

Vroman, Wayne. 1989. "Experience Rating in Unemployment Insurance." Unemployment Insurance Occasional Paper 89-6, U.S. Department of Labor, Employment and Training Administration.

_____. 1991. "The Decline in Unemployment Insurance Claims Activity in the 1980s." Unemployment Insurance Occasional Paper 91-2, U.S. Department of Labor, Employment and Training Administration.

_____. 1995. "The Alternative Base Period in Unemployment Insurance." Unemployment Insurance Occasional Paper 95-3, U.S. Department of Labor, Employment and Training Administration.

Wandner, Stephen A. 1997. "Early Reemployment for Dislocated Workers in the United States," *International Social Security Review*, forthcoming.

_____. 1996. "Implementing the Worker Profiling and Reemployment Services Initiative," *Workforce* 5, 2 (Fall): 39-47.

_____. Editor. 1992. "Self-Employment Programs for the Unemployed." Unemployment Insurance Occasional Paper 92-2, U.S. Department of Labor, Employment and Training Administration.

Wandner, Stephen A., and Robert L. Crosslin. 1980. "Measuring Experience Rating." In *Unemployment Compensation: Studies and Research*, Vol. 2. Washington, DC: National Commission on Unemployment Compensation.

Wandner, Stephen A., and Thomas Stengle. 1997. "Unemployment Insurance: Measuring Who Receives It," *Monthly Labor Review* 120, 7 (July): 15-24.

Woodbury, Stephen A., and Robert G. Spiegelman. 1987. "Bonuses to Workers and Employers to Reduce Unemployment: Randomized Trials in Illinois," *American Economic Review* 77 (September): 514-530.

Appendix A
Significant Benefit Provisions
of State Unemployment Insurance Laws
January 1, 1996

Unemployment insurance programs, which operate in the fifty states, Washington, D.C., Puerto Rico, and the Virgin Islands, encompass tremendous variety in benefit provisions. This appendix offers a summary of the differences in a way that is limited but suggestive of the wide range of benefit provisions in effect across the country.

Table A.1 State Minimum and Maximum Weekly Benefit Amount (WBA) and State Minimum and Maximum Potential Duration of Benefits for Total Unemployment on January 1, 1996

State	Minimum WBA[a]	Maximum WBA[b]	Minimum Duration[c]	Maximum Duration
Alabama	$22	180	15	26
Alaska	44-68	212-284	16	26
Arizona	40	185	12	26
Arkansas	47	264	9	26
California	40	230	14	26
Colorado	25	272	13	26
Connecticut	15-25	350-400	26	26
Delaware	20	300	24	26
DC	50	359	20	26
Florida	10	250	10	26
Georgia	37	205	9	26
Hawaii	5	347	26	26
Idaho	44	248	10	26
Illinois	51	251-322	26	26
Indiana	87	217	8	26
Iowa	33-40	224-274	11	26
Kansas	65	260	10	26
Kentucky	22	238	15	26
Louisiana	10	181	26	26
Maine	35-52	202-303	21	26
Maryland	25-33	250	26	26
Massachusetts	14-21	347-521	10	30
Michigan	42	293	15	26
Minnesota	38	303	10	26
Mississippi	30	180	13	26
Missouri	45	175	11	26
Montana	57	228	8	26
Nebraska	20	184	20	26
Nevada	16	237	12	26
New Hampshire	32	216	26	26
New Jersey	60	362	15	26
New Mexico	42	212	19	26
New York	40	300	26	26
North Carolina	25	297	13	26
North Dakota	43	243	12	26
Ohio	66	253-339	20	26

State	Minimum WBA[a]	Maximum WBA[b]	Minimum Duration[c]	Maximum Duration
Oklahoma	16	247	20	26
Oregon	70	301	4	26
Pennsylvania	35-40	352-360	16	26
Puerto Rico	7	133	26	26
Rhode Island	41-51	324-404	15	26
South Carolina	20	213	15	26
South Dakota	28	180	15	26
Tennessee	30	200	12	26
Texas	42	252	9	26
Utah	17	263	10	26
Vermont	25	212	26	26
Virginia	65	208	12	26
Virgin Islands	32	214	13	26
Washington	75	350	16	30
West Virginia	24	290	26	26
Wisconsin	52	274	12	26
Wyoming	16	233	12	26

SOURCE: U.S. Department of Labor, "Comparison of State Unemployment Insurance Laws," Employment and Training Administration, Unemployment Insurance Service, 1995.

a. When two amounts are given, the higher figure includes dependents' allowances. Augmented amount for the minimum weekly benefit amount (WBA) includes allowances for one dependent child.

b. Augmented amount for the maximum WBA includes allowances for maximum number of dependents. In the District of Columbia, Maryland, and New Jersey the maximum is not affected by dependents.

c. Potential duration of benefits for claimants who qualify for minimum WBA with minimum qualifying wages.

Appendix B
Selected Unemployment Insurance Financial Data

The tables below are intended to summarize state unemployment insurance transactions. Table B.1 lists data for each state in 1995, the most recent year for which data are available, and table B.2 lists similar data for the nation as a whole in each year dating back to the beginning of the federal-state unemployment insurance (UI) system. The tables show the total amount collected in tax contributions, the amount distributed in benefits, the reserves at year end, and the percentages of total covered payrolls represented by each.

Beginning in 1972, some employers, mainly nonprofit firms, could opt to provide UI on a reimbursable basis, rather than facing the regular state UI tax schedule. Reimbursing employers are essentially fully experience rated and have no net effect on trust funds. Therefore, figures in the summary tables of this appendix include only taxable employers and exclude reimbursable employers.

727

Table B.1 Selected Unemployment Insurance Financial Data by State, Calendar Year 1995

State	Contributions collected[a] amount (thousands of dollars)	Estimated average employer tax rate (percent of total wages)	Benefits paid Amount (thousands of dollars)	Benefits paid Percent of total wages	Reserves as of January 31 Amount (thousands of dollars)	Reserves as of January 31 Percent of total wages
United States	$21,972,163	.86	$20,119,898	.80	$35,403,296	1.40
Alabama	129,795	.37	177,607	.53	534,470	1.61
Alaska	91,354	1.71	114,124	2.02	201,017	3.56
Arizona	216,013	.61	149,997	.42	534,640	1.48
Arkansas	163,094	.88	155,585	.87	200,866	1.12
California	2,825,654	.96	2,963,739	.96	2,104,220	0.68
Colorado	185,487	.47	179,307	.46	480,582	1.22
Connecticut	544,012	1.26	435,310	1.00	116,692	0.27
Delaware	70,336	.86	60,232	.72	271,807	3.24
District of Columbia	123,936	.92	94,750	.78	68,636	0.57
Florida	694,134	.58	634,534	.54	1,806,432	1.53
Georgia	352,260	.48	270,382	.38	1,453,118	2.03
Hawaii	150,249	1.60	180,435	1.75	213,496	2.07
Idaho	74,621	.92	91,741	1.09	243,090	2.88
Illinois	1,367,931	1.01	1,075,674	.80	1,629,210	1.22
Indiana	232,239	.41	223,869	.39	1,228,070	2.16
Iowa	122,109	.51	152,972	.65	725,149	3.10
Kansas	54,852	.16	137,144	.56	704,008	2.88

Kentucky	222,643	.75	211,389	.72	470,826	1.61
Louisiana	205,428	.64	138,302	.43	1,003,378	3.15
Maine	116,393	1.27	101,506	1.13	95,289	1.06
Maryland	493,048	1.08	331,332	.75	605,415	1.36
Massachusetts	1,074,938	1.43	731,615	.97	527,273	0.70
Michigan	1,389,706	1.34	843,181	.82	1,497,688	1.45
Minnesota	398,020	.79	328,442	.67	459,621	0.94
Mississippi	135,159	.77	111,931	.65	551,318	3.19
Missouri	362,615	.70	271,915	.55	196,933	0.40
Montana	56,651	.95	53,472	.91	122,242	2.08
Nebraska	37,881	.27	44,288	.33	194,283	1.45
Nevada	153,172	.89	143,123	.81	297,866	1.69
New Hampshire	58,232	.48	34,984	.31	250,884	2.25
New Jersey	1,115,631	.87	1,253,780	1.30	1,987,790	2.06
New Mexico	81,067	.73	65,176	.60	354,874	3.25
New York	2,045,217	1.02	1,988,026	.99	248,978	0.12
North Carolina	196,848	.28	315,503	.47	1,531,117	2.27
North Dakota	25,174	.61	30,354	.75	57,415	1.41
Ohio	982,877	.91	647,673	.59	1,600,533	1.46
Oklahoma	112,889	.49	100,069	.44	521,683	2.32
Oregon	188,726	.85	339,991	1.20	905,985	3.21
Pennsylvania	1,747,964	1.57	1,475,508	1.37	1,914,777	1.78
Puerto Rico	146,470	1.52	220,954	2.34	634,291	6.71

(continued)

Table B.1 (continued)

State	Contributions collected[a] amount (thousands of dollars)	Estimated average employer tax rate (percent of total wages)	Benefits paid Amount (thousands of dollars)	Benefits paid Percent of total wages	Reserves as of January 31 Amount (thousands of dollars)	Reserves as of January 31 Percent of total wages
Rhode Island	170,562	2.07	182,083	2.20	110,086	1.33
South Carolina	189,268	.63	170,827	.57	556,650	1.84
South Dakota	9,873	.21	13,029	.27	51,622	1.09
Tennessee	275,087	.55	256,409	.52	822,821	1.66
Texas	997,812	.60	930,927	.54	584,866	0.34
Utah	86,228	.55	58,684	.37	468,030	2.93
Vermont	44,037	.95	46,725	1.02	206,720	4.51
Virginia	281,661	.45	201,491	.32	788,787	1.27
Virgin Islands	6,558	1.44	7,821	1.34	40,064	6.86
Washington	600,024	1.16	793,643	1.64	1,417,701	2.93
West Virginia	122,117	1.08	133,056	1.16	164,036	1.44
Wisconsin	419,376	.84	416,647	.85	1,503,641	3.06
Wyoming	24,735	.73	28,640	.85	142,310	4.22

SOURCE: U.S. Department of Labor, Employment and Training Administration, Unemployment Insurance Service.

a. Contributions collected include contributions and penalties from employers and employee contributions in states that tax workers. In 1996, employee contributions were only collected in Alaska, New Jersey, and Pennsylvania. In years prior to 1996, employee contributions were collected at times in Alabama, California, Indiana, Kentucky, Louisiana, Massachusetts, New Hampshire, and Rhode Island.

Table B.2 Selected Unemployment Insurance Financial Data for the United States, 1938–95

Year	Contributions collected[a] amount (thousands of dollars)	Estimated average employer tax rate (percent of total wages)	Benefits paid Amount (thousands of dollars)	Benefits paid Percent of total wages	Reserves as of January 31 Amount (thousands of dollars)	Reserves as of January 31 Percent of total wages
1938	818,501	2.69	393,783	1.50	1,110,625	4.22
1939	824,876	2.66	429,298	1.47	1,537,797	5.28
1940	853,780	2.50	518,700	1.60	1,817,110	5.60
1941	1,006,328	2.37	344,324	.82	2,524,463	5.99
1942	1,139,333	1.98	344,083	.63	3,387,888	6.19
1943	1,325,423	1.86	79,644	.12	4,715,510	7.13
1944	1,317,049	1.67	62,384	.09	6,071,925	8.78
1945	1,161,883	1.50	445,867	.67	6,914,010	10.38
1946	911,836	1.24	1,094,845	1.49	6,860,044	9.35
1947	1,095,522	1.19	755,142	.90	7,303,287	8.44
1948	999,635	1.01	789,931	.82	7,602,964	7.91
1949	986,906	1.07	1,735,991	1.85	7,009,585	7.47
1950	1,191,435	1.18	1,373,113	1.33	6,972,181	6.76
1951	1,492,506	1.20	840,411	.71	7,781,930	6.56
1952	1,367,676	1.08	998,238	.78	8,327,427	6.52
1953	1,347,632	.93	962,219	.69	8,912,680	6.41
1954	1,136,151	.79	2,026,868	1.48	8,218,954	6.00
1955	1,208,788	.81	1,350,264	.91	8,260,724	5.56

(continued)

Table B.2 (continued)

Year	Contributions collected[a] amount (thousands of dollars)	Estimated average employer tax rate (percent of total wages)	Benefits paid Amount (thousands of dollars)	Benefits paid Percent of total wages	Reserves as of January 31 Amount (thousands of dollars)	Reserves as of January 31 Percent of total wages
1956	1,463,261	.88	1,380,728	.84	8,573,431	5.21
1957	1,544,233	.85	1,733,876	1.00	8,659,312	4.99
1958	1,470,841	.84	3,512,732	2.05	6,831,292	3.99
1959	1,955,664	10.60	2,279,018	1.22	6,674,297	3.57
1960	2,288,440	1.15	2,726,849	1.40	6,418,822	3.29
1961	2,449,942	1.24	3,422,558	1.72	5,567,780	2.80
1962	2,951,841	1.39	2,675,565	1.26	6,038,626	2.84
1963	3,018,817	1.34	2,775,222	1.24	6,421,119	2.88
1964	3,047,288	1.26	2,521,575	1.05	7,090,270	2.96
1965	3,053,646	1.18	2,166,011	.84	8,172,316	3.17
1966	3,030,126	1.05	1,771,292	.62	9,664,712	3.40
1967	2,678,119	.86	2,092,364	.69	10,705,198	3.54
1968	2,551,573	.76	2,029,957	.61	11,715,954	3.54
1969	2,545,161	.69	2,125,809	.58	12,636,017	3.46
1970	2,505,814	.64	3,847,312	1.01	11,902,575	3.11
1971	2,636,599	.64	4,951,507	1.23	9,725,314	2.41
1972	3,896,620	.88	4,481,854	.98	9,402,983	2.06
1973	4,995,166	.99	4,005,191	.79	10,882,144	2.13
1974	5,218,967	.92	5,977,411	1.06	10,520,181	1.87

Year						
1975	5,210,855	.88	11,753,643	2.01	3,070,231	0.52
1976	7,532,078	1.20	8,972,637	1.38	871,380	0.13
1977	9,170,529	1.28	8,345,948	1.16	950,381	0.13
1978	11,193,446	1.41	7,722,347	.93	4,554,185	0.55
1979	12,095,041	1.26	8,556,908	.91	8,582,608	0.91
1980	11,414,649	1.06	13,768,135	1.34	6,591,827	0.64
1981	11,624,545	1.02	13,221,592	1.17	5,644,584	0.50
1982	12,206,070	1.03	20,649,840	1.76	(2,644,584)	(0.23)
1983	14,548,669	0.20	17,755,392	1.44	(5,803,331)	(0.47)
1984	18,111,266	1.39	12,598,229	.92	2,204,797	0.16
1985	19,296,983	1.30	14,124,342	.96	10,069,416	0.68
1986	18,111,266	1.14	15,402,735	.99	15,402,260	0.99
1987	17,576,976	1.04	13,617,007	.81	23,174,690	1.38
1988	17,720,628	.96	12,579,703	.69	31,103,671	1.71
1989	16,451,876	.84	13,641,569	.71	36,870,882	1.92
1990	15,221,274	.73	17,320,777	.86	37,937,017	1.88
1991	14,510,670	.71	24,582,501	1.20	30,488,785	1.49
1992	16,972,655	.79	23,956,510	1.10	25,846,579	1.19
1993	19,831,045	.90	20,687,678	.92	28,001,956	1.25
1994	21,802,096	.92	20,438,509	.86	31,343,551	1.32
1995	21,972,163	.86	20,119,898	.80	35,403,296	1.40

SOURCE: U.S. Department of Labor, Employment and Training Administration, Unemployment Insurance Service.

a. Contributions collected include contributions and penalties from employers and employee contributions in states that tax workers. In 1996, employee contributions were only collected in Alaska, New Jersey, and Pennsylvania. In years prior to 1996, employee contributions were collected at times in Alabama, California, Indiana, Kentucky, Louisiana, Massachusetts, New Hampshire, and Rhode Island.

Index

Federal Unemployment Tax Act (FUTA, 1935), 355

Federal Unemployment Account (FUA), 358, 370, 379

minimum federal requirements for state employer tax credits, 593-95

revenues to Extended Unemployment Compensation, 266

state standards for suitable work, 136-37

tax credit for states under, 131

tax offset scheme, 35

tax revenues in UTF, 575

taxes paid (1994), 447

UI benefits for certain excluded unemployed, 56

UI federal-state tax system, 547-48

underreported taxes, 447

Feldstein, Martin, 26, 176, 347, 533

Ferris, J. S., 110

Fictitious Employer Detection System (FEDS), 432

Fineshriber, Phyllis H., 165, 200

Flemming, J. S., 179-80, 248

Florida

Job Search Assistance Demonstration, 491

Tampa Employment Service Center, 489-90

France

administration of UC system, 603-4, 638

coverage under UC system, 609-12, 638

eligibility and benefits under UC system, 612-26, 638-40

financing of UC system, 604-9, 638

major events in UC development, 653-59

objectives of UC system, 603, 638

UC employment services, 625, 627-28, 640

Fraud

UI system, 28-37, 423 ff.

FSB. *See* Federal Supplemental Benefits (FSB).

FUA. *See* Federal Unemployment Tax Act (FUTA, 1935).

FUTA. *See* Federal Unemployment Tax Act (FUTA, 1935).

Gardner, Jennifer M., 521, 522, 702

Garfinkel, Irwin, 176

General Accounting Office (GAO), 69, 70, 470, 569, 579, 584

Germany

administration of UC system, 603-4, 640-41

coverage under UC system, 609-12, 641

eligibility and benefits under UC system, 612-26, 641-42

financing of UC system, 604-9, 641

major events in UC development, 653-59

objectives of UC system, 603, 640

UC employment services, 625, 627-28, 642

Gilder, George, 25

Gordon, Chrisopher J., 16

Gottschalk, Peter, 138

Government, federal

payment of extended benefits, 69-70, 256-57, 264-67, 549

required state conformity and compliance, 550-73

See also Department of Labor; Employment Service (ES); Extended Benefits (EB) program; Federal Unemployment Tax Act (FUTA, 1935)

Government, state

autonomy over basic UI program, 187

conformity and compliance with federal law, 550-73

determining potential benefit duration, 213-20

744

750

The Authors

Patricia M. Anderson is currently assistant professor of economics at Dartmouth College, a position she has held since receiving her Ph.D. from Princeton University in 1991. Since 1994, she has also been affiliated with the National Bureau of Economic Research as a faculty research fellow. She has written extensively in areas relating to the UI system, including such topics as experience rating and labor demand, benefit take-up propensities, the incidence of the UI payroll tax, and cross-subsidization in the UI system. Other research interests include job turnover and mobility. Her authored or co-authored papers have appeared in such journals as the *Quarterly Journal of Economics, Journal of Labor Economics, Journal of Public Economics, Brookings Papers on Economic Activity,* and *Tax Policy and the Economy.*

David E. Balducchi is chief of Planning and Review, U.S. Employment Service. He received a B.A. in political science from St. Ambrose University and an M.P.A. from Drake University. He began his employment security career in 1971 working for the Iowa Department of Employment Services in a local office. Since 1976, Mr. Balducchi has worked for the U.S. Department of Labor in unemployment insurance and employment service programs with assignments to the Office of Management and Budget and the U.S. Congress. During a 1992 Congressional Fellowship, he worked on the staff of U.S. Senator Harris Wofford (D-Penn.) with responsibility for unemployment insurance, historic preservation, and national service and helped draft legislation creating the National Civilian Community Corps. Mr. Balducchi has worked on the Labor Department's proposed Reemployment Act, One-Stop and Worker Profiling and Reemployment Services (WPRS) initiatives.

Laurie J. Bassi is vice-president for research at the American Society for Training and Development, where she joined the staff in 1996. She holds a B.A. in economics and mathematics from Illinois State University, an M.S. in industrial relations from Cornell University, and a Ph.D. in economics from Princeton University. Dr. Bassi's research has covered a broad range of topics, including: a variety of aspects of the U.S. unemployment insurance program, the effects of training both from a micro- and macroeconomic perspective, and the extent and effect of work reorganization. Prior to joining ASTD, Dr. Bassi was a professor in both the Economics Department and the Graduate Public Policy Program at Georgetown University. From 1993-1996, she served as the executive director of the Advisory Council on Unemployment Compensation and from 1988-1989 was the deputy director of the Commission on Workforce Quality and Labor Market Efficiency. She has published widely, including articles in the *Journal of Human Resources, American Economic Review,*

Monthly Labor Review, Review of Economics and Statistics, and *Journal of Policy Analysis and Management*.

Saul J. Blaustein has been engaged in research and evaluation of problems in unemployment, unemployment insurance (UI), income maintenance, and employment programs with special emphasis on legislative policy issues since 1955. He was awarded a B.S. in social science by the City College of New York and did graduate studies in economics at UCLA and George Washington University. He is currently a member of the National Academy of Social Insurance. From 1967 to his retirement in 1986, he was a senior economist at the W.E. Upjohn Institute for Employment Research. During the previous 16 years he worked for the U.S. Department of Labor in Washington, D.C., including 12 years (1955-1967) as a research analyst and research director in the Bureau of Employment Security. While at the Upjohn Institute, he commissioned and edited a series of 15 research monographs, which provided a comprehensive review of the UI system in the United States. He is author or co-author of 15 articles and 3 books on UI. The books are entitled *Unemployment Insurance in the United States: The First Fifty Years* (1993), *Job and Income Security for Unemployed Workers* (1981), and *An International Review of Unemployment Insurance Schemes* with Isabel Craig (1977).

Walter S. Corson is a vice-president at Mathematica Policy Research. He earned a B.A. in mathematics from Williams College and subsequently undertook graduate work in economics at the Massachusetts Institute of Technology. He has conducted research on labor policy issues and conducted numerous studies for the U.S. Department of Labor, focusing primarily on the unemployment insurance system and dislocated worker programs. He has written and co-authored policy reports in these areas, including reports on unemployment insurance extended benefits and nonmonetary eligibility policy, which were published as books by the W. E. Upjohn Institute for Employment Research: *The Federal Supplemental Benefits Program* with Walter Nicholson (1982), and *Nonmonetary Eligibility in State Unemployment Insurance Programs: Law and Practice* with Alan Hershey and Stuart Kerachsky (1986).

Paul T. Decker is a senior economist at Mathematica Policy Research, Inc. Prior to joining Mathematica in 1988, he earned an A.B. in economics from the College of William and Mary and a Ph.D. in economics from the Johns Hopkins University. He is currently conducting several studies of the effectiveness of training and other employment services for displaced workers. These studies include nationwide evaluations of the Economic Dislocation and Worker Adjustment Assistance program and the Worker Profiling and Reemployment Services systems. Dr. Decker is also conducting the evaluation of the Job Search Assistance Demonstration, which was operated in Florida and the District of Columbia between 1994 and 1996. His previous research on unemployment insurance claimants and dislocated workers has been published in the *Journal of Human Resources* and the *Industrial and Labor Relations Review.*

R. Mark Gritz is a senior economist for a component of Battelle Memorial Institute that conducts social science research focused on health and welfare issues. He received a B.S. in economics from Colorado State University in 1981 and a Ph.D. in economics from Stanford University in 1987. Prior to joining Battelle in 1992, he was an assistant professor in the Department of Economics at the University of Washington. His unemployment insurance-related research includes analyses of UI benefit take-up rates, the effects of UI policies on unemployment, and the dynamics of UI benefit receipt. His other research interests include evaluation of education and training programs, participation in low-wage labor markets, school-to-work transitions, participation in welfare programs, economic mobility, and survey research. He has authored or co-authored papers that have appeared in the *Journal of Econometrics, Journal of Human Resources, Journal of Business and Economic Statistics,* and *Empirical Economics.*

Gerard (Jerry) Hildebrand is chief of the Conformity and Compliance unit of the Unemployment Insurance Service in the United States Department of Labor. He has been employed in the unemployment insurance field for the Department of Labor since 1978, working in benefits, tax, quality control, and legislation. He holds a B.A. in English from the University of Wisconsin-Madison. His article on the interpretation and application of federal unemployment insurance law was published in the Fall 1995 & Winter 1996 issue of the *University of Michigan Journal of Law Reform.*

Terry R. Johnson is a senior economist and director of Research Operations for a component of Battelle Memorial Institute that conducts social science research focused on health and welfare issues. He received his Ph.D. in economics from the University of Washington in 1975 and, from 1975 to 1984, he was an economist, senior economist and director of the Employment and Training Research Program at SRI International. While at SRI, he directed the only national evaluation of the effectiveness of the U.S. Employment Service, as well as evaluations of other employment and training programs and demonstrations for unemployed workers. Since joining Battelle in 1984, he directed numerous experimental and quasi-experimental evaluations of ongoing federal and state education and job training programs, as well as demonstration programs, to better understand the effectiveness of alternative reemployment strategies, including job search assistance, training, and self-employment assistance, and of alternative UI work search requirements on employment outcomes. He is currently serving as co-principal investigator of the National Job Corps Impact Evaluation, the Job Search Assistance Demonstration, and the Maryland Unemployment Insurance Work Search Demonstration. He authored or co-authored articles on program evaluation studies and other topics that have been published in the *Journal of Political Economy, Journal of Human Resources, Econometrica, Evaluation Review, Industrial Labor Relations Review, Review of Economic Studies,* and *Economic Inquiry.*

Phillip B. Levine is an assistant professor of economics at Wellesley College and a faculty research fellow at the National Bureau of Economic Research. He holds a B.S. in industrial and labor relations, an M.S. in labor economics from Cornell University, and a Ph.D. in economics from Princeton University. His research has been devoted to empirical examinations of public policy questions, including the unemployment insurance system, abortion policy, welfare policy, and education policy. He is currently serving a one-year term as senior economist on the Council of Economic Advisers (the work for his chapter in this book was completed before his appointment).

Daniel P. McMurrer is a research associate at the Urban Institute in Washington, D.C. He received a B.A. in politics from Princeton University in 1990 and a M.P.P. in public policy from Georgetown University in 1993. From 1993 to 1996, he was a research analyst for the Advisory Council on Unemployment Compensation, where he conducted empirical research with Laurie Bassi on topics including unemployment insurance replacement rates and competition among the states in setting unemployment insurance tax rates. For the Urban Institute, he has written on the subject of job stability, and is currently working with Isabel Sawhill on a series of papers on economic opportunity in the United States.

Michael J. Miller is leader of the Actuarial Team in the Unemployment Insurance Service of the U.S. Department of Labor. The Actuarial Team is responsible for making all UI cost and revenue estimates related to the federal budget and federal legislation; analyzing trust fund adequacy and experience rating issues; providing technical assistance to states in trust fund forecasting, tax system design, and building statistical profiling models; and developing and monitoring research projects in the areas of UI actuarial techniques, fund adequacy, experience rating, and the economic effects of UI taxation. He has been with the Division of Actuarial Services since 1976. He received a B.S. in economics from the University of Wisconsin in 1975 and an M.A. in economics from George Washington University in 1983. He has co-authored and presented papers on UI workload forecasting at meetings of the American Statistical Association and the International Time Series Association.

Jennifer A. Neisner was awarded a B.A. in political philosophy from Haverford College in 1990. She joined the Congressional Research Service (CRS) in 1991, where she worked on a variety of legislative policy issues related to income maintenance through 1995, including social security, welfare reform, and unemployment insurance. She is currently a health policy analyst at CRS in the areas of medicaid, substance abuse, and mental health.

Walter Nicholson is the Ward H. Patton Professor of Economics at Amherst College and a senior fellow at Mathematica Policy Research. He received his Ph.D. in economics from the Massachusetts Institute of Technology. His research focuses on the analysis of labor market policies including unemployment compensation, welfare, and trade adjustment assistance. Most recently, Professor Nicholson has been involved in a project examining short-time compensation programs in the United States and in an evaluation of emergency unemployment benefits during the 1991-92 recession. He is author of *The Federal Supplemental Benefits Program* with Walter Corson (W.E. Upjohn Institute, 1982) and of two widely used texts in microeconomic theory.

Christopher J. O'Leary is a senior economist at the W.E. Upjohn Institute for Employment Research where he joined the staff in 1987. He holds a B.A. in economics from the University of Massachusetts at Amherst and a Ph.D. in economics from the University of Arizona. In unemployment insurance research, he has worked on evaluating the potential response to reemployment bonuses for the Washington State Employment Security Department, measuring experience rating of taxes across states and estimating the effects of profiling for the Michigan Employment Security Commission, and evaluating benefit adequacy for the Advisory Council on Unemployment Compensation in the U.S. Department of Labor. For the World Bank he has designed performance management systems for active labor programs in Hungary and Poland, for the International Labor Office he has evaluated active labor programs in Hungary, and for the National Academy of Science he has reported on employment policy in transition economies. He has authored or co-authored papers that have appeared in the *Journal of Human Resources, International Labour Review, Applied Economics,* and the *Journal of Policy Analysis and Management.*

Robert Pavosevich has worked as an actuary in the Fiscal and Actuarial Services Division of the Unemployment Insurance (UI) Service of the U.S. Department of Labor since 1988. He is responsible for assisting states with actuarial studies of their benefit financing systems and forecasting UI trust funds. In this position, he also works to develop econometric models, which simulate the benefit and tax structures of state UI systems. He also worked on an evaluation of experience rating for the Advisory Council on Unemployment Compensation in the U.S. Department of Labor. Mr. Pavosevich earned an M.S. degree in economics at the American University in 1986. He also has done graduate studies at the University of Zagreb, Croatia, and holds a Bachelor of Science degree in economics from the University of California, Riverside.

Murray A. Rubin obtained B.A. and M.A. degrees at Rutgers University and later pursued graduate studies in political science at Ohio State University. In 1960, he joined the staff of the Unemployment Insurance Service of the Labor Department's former Bureau of Employment Security, where he specialized in state and federal UI legislation. As chief of the Division of Program Policy and Legislation, he was responsible for review of state UI legislation for conformity with federal law, preparation of draft legislation to assist states, negotiation with state officials on issues of nonconformity, and development of federal UI legislative programs. He retired from the Department after 29 years of government service. In 1979, he was appointed Consultant for Legislative Studies for the National Commission on Unemployment Compensation, where he prepared reports on a number of major UI issues. His book *Federal-State Relations in Unemployment Insurance: A Balance of Power* was published by the Upjohn Institute in 1983. Until his death in 1990, he served both governmental and private organizations as a consultant on unemployment insurance.

Burman H. Skrable is currently an operations research analyst with the Unemployment Insurance Service of the U.S. Department of Labor in Washington, D.C. He holds a B.A. in economics from University of Santa Clara and an M.A. and Ph.D. in economics from Cornell University. He has taught at SUNY Cortland, University of Santa Clara, and George Mason University. He has been with the Department of Labor since 1972 and with the UI Service since 1983. There he has worked mostly with the design, implementation, and operation of UI Quality Control programs. In this capacity, he has designed or directed a number of quality control research and evaluation projects. These have included an evaluation of the Benefits Quality Control program and pilot projects testing the accuracy of denied claims, the efficacy of telephone verifications, the accuracy of benefit charging, and the validation of tax report data. He is currently overseeing a second pilot test of measuring denials accuracy.

James R. Storey has been a specialist in Social Legislation at the Congressional Research Service (CRS) since 1987. His legislative responsibilities include unemployment benefits, retirement savings plans, and the earned income tax credit. Before CRS, he spent 10 years in research and consulting on retirement policy as a research director at the Urban Institute and as a vice-president of Chambers Associates, Inc. He also worked for two congressional committees, the Joint Economic Committee and the Senate Budget Committee, and three federal agencies, the National Institutes of Health, the Office of Management and Budget, and the Office of the Secretary of Health and Human Services. He holds an M.S. degree in industrial administration from Carnegie-Mellon University. He has had many articles published by CRS, the Urban Institute, and several professional journals.

Wayne Vroman is an economist at the Urban Institute. He holds a Ph.D. in economics from the University of Michigan and has authored many articles, papers, and monographs on various aspects of unemployment insurance including taxes, trust funds and benefits. He has written two books on unemployment insurance financing which have been published by the W.E. Upjohn Institute: *The Funding Crisis in State Unemployment Insurance* (1986) and *Unemployment Insurance Trust Fund Adequacy in the 1990s* (1990).

Stephen A. Wandner received his Ph.D. in economics from Indiana University. He has been an economist, policy analyst, and actuary with the U.S. Departments of Labor and Commerce. From 1978 to 1995, he was deputy director of the Office of Legislation and Actuarial Services in the Unemployment Insurance Service; recently he served as acting director. At present, he is a visiting senior research associate at the Urban Institute. At Labor, he directed unemployment insurance research, evaluation, and demonstration projects. Beginning in 1985, he initiated a series of eight field experiments that tested job search assistance, training, relocation allowances, reemployment bonuses, and self-employment assistance as early reemployment services for UI claimants who are dislocated workers. Since 1993, he has worked on implementation and evaluation of two federally legislated programs: Worker Profiling and Reemployment Services and the Self-Employment Assistance. Most recently, he has directed a Lifelong Learning Demonstration cosponsored by the Departments of Labor and Education, which encourages incumbent workers to invest in their own education and training.

Thomas West is currently serving the Michigan Employment Security Commission as director of its governmental relations activities. He is responsible for the coordination of his agency's program and policy issues with business and labor organizations. He also has had extensive experience with the legislative process at both the federal and state levels involving all aspects of unemployment insurance. While with the Michigan agency over the last 26 years, he has served as interim chair of the Michigan UI Advisory council, has represented the State of Michigan on a number of federal work groups studying administrative financing issues, and has headed Michigan's unemployment insurance research activities. He holds a B.A. in economics from Michigan State University and an M.B.A. from Wayne State University. In 1993 he worked with Chris O'Leary on *Suggested Rules for an Unemployment Insurance Law for Poland* prepared for the Polish Ministry of Labor and Social Policy.

Stephen A. Woodbury is a professor of economics at Michigan State University, where he has taught since 1982, and a senior economist at the W.E. Upjohn Institute for Employment Research. He has also held appointments at Pennsylvania State University and the University of Stirling. During 1993-94, he was deputy director of the Advisory Council on Unemployment Compensation in Washington, D.C. He received a B.A. in economics from Middlebury College in 1975 and a Ph.D. in economics from the University of Wisconsin-Madison in 1981. His research has focused on topics in employee benefits, nonwage labor costs, and unemployment insurance, and includes *The Tax Treatment of Fringe Benefits* with Wei-Jang Huang (Upjohn Institute, 1991), "The Displacement Effect of Reemployment Bonus Programs" with Carl Davidson (*Journal of Labor Economics*, 1993), and "Optimal Unemployment Insurance" with Carl Davidson (*Journal of Public Economics*, 1997).

About the Institute

The W.E. Upjohn Institute for Employment Research is a nonprofit research organization devoted to finding and promoting solutions to employment-related problems at the national, state, and local level. It is an activity of the W.E. Upjohn Unemployment Trustee Corporation, which was established in 1932 to administer a fund set aside by the late Dr. W.E. Upjohn, founder of The Upjohn Company, to seek ways to counteract the loss of employment income during economic downturns.

The Institute is funded largely by income from the W.E. Upjohn Unemployment Trust, supplemented by outside grants, contracts, and sales of publications. Activities of the Institute comprise the following elements: (1) a research program conducted by a resident staff of professional social scientists; (2) a competitive grant program, which expands and complements the internal research program by providing financial support to researchers outside the Institute; (3) a publications program, which provides the major vehicle for the dissemination of research by staff and grantees, as well as for other selected work in the field; and (4) an Employment Management Services division, which manages most of the publicly funded employment and training programs in the local area.

The broad objectives of the Institute's research, grant, and publication programs are to (1) promote scholarship and experimentation on issues of public and private employment and unemployment policy; and (2) make knowledge and scholarship relevant and useful to policymakers in their pursuit of solutions to employment and unemployment problems.

Current areas of concentration for these programs include causes, consequences, and measures to alleviate unemployment; social insurance and income maintenance programs; compensation; workforce quality; work arrangements; family labor issues; labor-management relations; and regional economic development and local labor markets.